D0574468

# THEATRE

## *Art in Action*

## Consultants

**Dr. Robert D. Taylor** (Senior Consultant) Associate Professor of Interdisciplinary Arts and Performance, Arizona State University West; First Vice President, American Alliance for Theatre & Education; Executive Board Member, Arizona Theatre Alliance. **Dr. Robert D. Strickland** (Senior Consultant) District Supervisor, Theatre Arts, Miami–Dade County Public Schools; Past President, Florida Association for Theatre Education; member, Florida Department of Education Writing Teams for Teacher Certification Examination for Theatre, Curriculum Frameworks/Standards, and Course Descriptions. **Dr. Lorenzo García** Assistant Professor, Department of Dance and Theatre Arts, University of North Texas; member, American Alliance for Theatre & Education; editor, *Stage of the Art.* **Mary Morris** Theatre teacher, Nimitz High School, Houston, Texas; acting instructor, North Harris Community College; participant, theatre exchange program in conjunction with Checkpoint Charlie Foundation, Berlin, Germany. **William Peery** Theatre teacher, Pomona High School, Arvada, Colorado; recipient, Secondary Theatre Teacher of the Year Award, Alliance for Colorado Theatre; co-author, drama curriculum for Jefferson County Schools. **Dr. Nefretete Rasheed** Creative Arts Therapist, Interfaith Medical Center, Brooklyn, New York; Director, Aspirations, Inc., organization promoting teaching and healing through the arts.

## Reviewers

**Frank Chuter** Speech teacher, Nimitz High School, Houston, Texas. **Dr. David Downs** Associate Professor of Theatre, School of Speech, Northwestern University, Evanston, Illinois; author, *The Actor's Eye: Seeing and Being Seen.* **Leslie Holland** Director of Programming, Arts Exchange, Steppenwolf Theatre, Chicago; Guest Instructor, Humanities Department, University of Chicago. **John Ogden** English and drama teacher, coordinator of Humanitas Program, Los Angeles High School, Los Angeles. **Phillip Moss** Chair, Creative and Performing Arts Department, University Liggett High School, Grosse Pointe Woods, Michigan; Michigan State Advocate for Theatre Education. **Richard Pettengill** Director of Arts in Education, Goodman Theatre, Chicago; Adjunct Professor of Dramaturgy, Theatre School, DePaul University, Chicago; dramaturg, Goodman and Court Theatres, Chicago. **Jay Seller** Theatre Director, Horizon High School, Thorton, Colorado; recipient, National Outstanding High School Theatre Program Award, Educational Theatre Association; member, Colorado State Board of the International Thespian Society. **Bruce Siewerth** Director of Theatre Services, theatre and stagecraft teacher, Evanston Township High School, Evanston, Illinois.

The editors of *Theatre—Art in Action* would like to thank Dennis and Karen Christilles, Donald Abramson, Mary K. Hawley, Michael McGhee, Laura Blobaum Knoerr, Karen Kuehner, Mark Stansfield, and William H. Wallace for their contributions to the development of this program.

# THEATRE

## *Art in Action*

**National Textbook Company**

*a division of* NTC/Contemporary Publishing Group • Lincolnwood, Illinois USA

**Project Editor:** Lisa Abel
**Cover Design:** Vita Jay
**Cover Photo:** T. Charles Erikson/Theatre Pix

ISBN: 0–8442–5307–3

Acknowledgments begin on page 593, which is to be considered an extension of this copyright page.

Published by National Textbook Company,
a division of NTC/Contemporary Publishing Group, Inc.
4255 West Touhy Avenue
Lincolnwood (Chicago), Illinois 60646-1975 U.S.A.

Manufactured in the United States of America.

8 9 0 VH 0 9 8 7 6 5 4 3 2 1

# Preface

Theatre is a creative idea expressed in performance—*art in action*. Theatre is also a highly collaborative art that requires effort by an ensemble, a group whose individuals function together to create a whole. In theatre, this ensemble includes actors, directors, producers, designers, stage crews, publicity people, and others. The process by which theatre people create a performance is always challenging. It involves hard work, but it is also a lot of fun. The path to a live performance is an exciting journey for everyone involved.

## An Active Approach

A short time ago, a group of people met with the goal of creating a new theatre program for high school students. We were animated by a love of theatre and collectively we represented a wide range of experience, both in theatre education and in professional theatre. From the first we decided that this new program would emphasize a hands-on approach to learning about theatre. It would be practical and performance-based. This decision grew out of a shared recognition that existing materials in theatre education seemed more concerned with *reading about* theatre than with *doing* theatre.

Our basic goal in developing *Theatre—Art in Action* was to assist you in learning about theatre by offering a variety of interesting and stimulating activities and performance projects. At every stage, what you are reading is reinforced and extended with engaging things to do. These range from Exercises in which you can immediately apply the skills you are learning; through more complex Activities at the end of each chapter to help you and your teacher assess your progress; to 40 large-scale Projects that will provide creative challenges for you and your fellow classmates.

## How the Book Is Organized

The structure of the book is also a departure from the structure of existing texts. Three major strands deal with Acting, Directing & Producing, and Technical Theatre. These strands are organized into four sections: Exploration, in which you will learn about basic tools and techniques; Preparation, in which you begin to get ready for a production; Performance, in which you move through the rehearsal process to opening night, and Specialization, in which you can discover more about various types of specialized theatre activities.

## The Importance of Writing

Writing is an essential element in theatre. Without playwrights we would have little to perform. Critics and theorists have helped give direction to the evolution of performance. Actors have long written about their craft, as have directors, designers—even producers. Writing will be important to you both in your performance work and as a way of recording your growth and your discoveries as you learn about the art of theatre.

Writing is integral to *Theatre—Art in Action*. An article following this Preface will introduce you to the value of using a Theatre Notebook and suggest some ways of getting your own notebook started; throughout the text you will encounter reminders to include writing products and other materials in your notebook; finally, a section on Writing & Theatre (pp. 530–569) provides guidelines and models for basic types of theatre writing, from a script analysis to a press release.

## Learning about Theatre History

With its roots in such basic human activities as ritual, dance, and storytelling, theatre has a very long history. Theatre almost certainly extends back to the unrecorded beginnings of human culture, but even theatre's recorded history can be traced for thousands of years.

A historical perspective is important to understanding theatre. Knowing the way theatre arts have been practiced in earlier times and in different cultures can enrich your understanding of the possibilities of performance.

Theatre is not history, however; theatre is creativity in action. A unanimous decision was made by the development team that *Theatre—Art in Action* would not be a history textbook. No attempt has been made to cover the history of world theatre in a comprehensive or systematic way—which would require an entire book by itself. Nevertheless, this text will provide you with a variety of opportunities to sharpen your historical perspective.

First, you will be invited to glimpse the broad sweep of theatre history in a 15-page illustrated Outline of Theatre History (pp. 1–15). Take a few minutes to explore this timeline; many of the individuals, dramatic forms, and theatre traditions you encounter here will be addressed in greater depth elsewhere. Second, you will find a Historical Profile following each Acting and Directing & Producing chapter. These profiles serve two purposes: they provide important background on major playwrights and theatre traditions; and they include a scene from a play offering opportunities for acting or directing practice.

## Careers in Theatre

One of the most important issues involved in any area of study is its links to the world of work. What kind of jobs might you do with a background in theatre? *Theatre—Art in Action* helps you explore answers to that question. When you encounter an activity in the book that is labeled "Job Shadow," it will suggest how you might get a look at a variety of careers for which theatre education could provide useful background. The program is also linked to the work world with a Careers & Theatre section (pp. 570–579), a series of profiles in which various theatre professionals talk about their jobs and how they got them.

## Get Started!

Theatre is art in action; theatre is collaborative art; theatre is hard work; theatre is fun. *It is fun*—but it is serious fun. You must be prepared to invest yourself fully in the process of doing theatre. If you do, you can have a wonderful time. Enjoy the work!

***Rob Taylor***
***Bob Strickland***

# Contents


**Preface** v

**Using a Theatre Notebook** xx

**An Outline of Theatre History** 1

## Section 1. Exploration 16

### Chapter 1. Acting 18

Self-Awareness 19

The Ensemble Ethic 20

Movement 20

Pantomime 28

Voice 30

Improvisation 36

Storytelling 38

### Activities 40

### Historical Profile: The Storytelling Tradition 44

from *Sundiata, an Epic of Old Mali,* recorded by D. T. Niane 48

## Chapter 2. Directing & Producing 50

The Roles of Director and Producer 51

The Production Team 54

The Performance Space 56

## Activities 64

## Historical Profile: Sophocles 66

from *Antigone,* translated by Robert Fagles 69

## Chapter 3. Technical Theatre 74

The Stage Crew 75

Set Construction and Prop Crews 76

Lighting and Sound Crews 82

Costume and Makeup Crews 90

## Activities 98

## Exploration Projects 100

1: Telling a Story 100
2: Animal Pantomime 103
3: Improvisation and Tableau 105
4: Soundscapes 107
5: Perspectives on Theatre Spaces 110
6: Analyzing Theatre Spaces 112
7: Building a Model Stage 115
8: Shop Inventory 118
9: Sewing Demonstration Board 120
10: Makeup Scrapbook 123


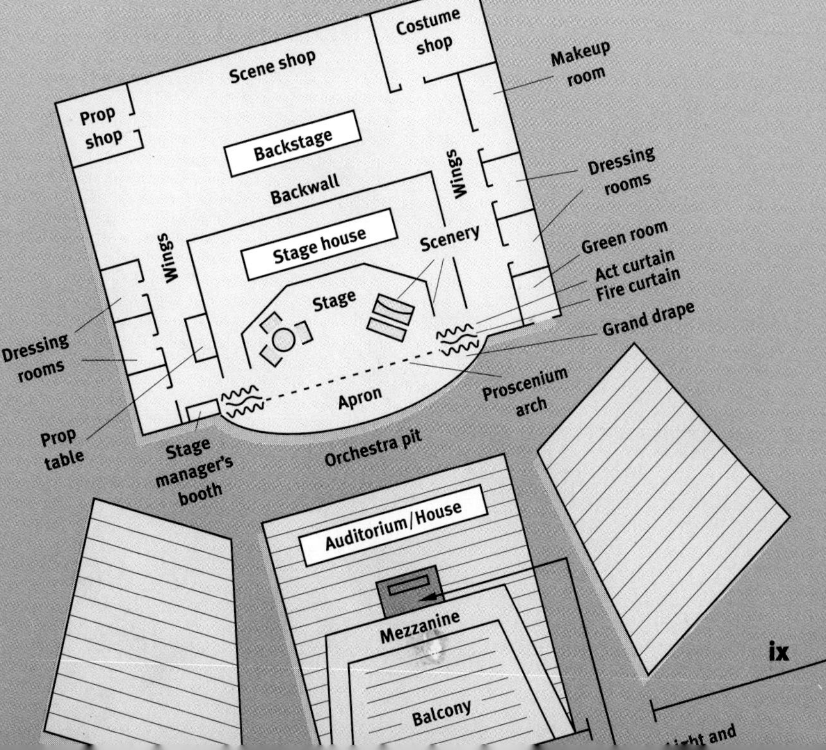

# Section 2. Preparation 126


## Chapter 4. Acting 128

The Characterization Process 129

Motivation and Behavior 134

Creating Specific Characters 136

Stage Movement Basics 140

Auditions 146

**Activities 150**

**Historical Profile: Shakespeare 154**

from *A Midsummer Night's Dream* 158

## Chapter 5. Directing & Producing 162

Choosing a Play 163

Genre 164

Working with the Script 166

Style 174

The Director's Role in Design 176

Stage Composition 177

Blocking 182

The Director's Promptbook 183

The Business of the Play 185

The Stage Manager 187

**Activities 188**

**Historical Profile: Molière 192**

from *Tartuffe*, translated by Richard Wilbur 196

## Chapter 6. Technical Theatre 202

Emergence of the Design Team 203
Elements of Production Design 204
Set Design 206
Set Construction 210
Joining, Bracing, and Stiffening Scenery 218
Scene Painting 223
Prop Design and Construction 226
Lighting Design 228
Sound Design and Production 232
Costume Design and Production 234
Makeup Design 238

## Activities 240

## Preparation Projects 244

11: Open Dialogue with Stage Movement 244
12: Building Characters 247
13: Delivering a Monologue 249
14: Entrances and Exits 252
15: Creating Stage Pictures 255
16: Developing a Director's Promptbook 257
17: Producing a Play 260
18: Designing a Set 263
19: Reupholstering a Set Prop 266
20: Grid Transfer 268

## Section 3. Performance 270

### Chapter 7. Acting 272

Working with the Script 273

Acting Styles 278

The Rehearsal Process 282

The Performance 291

### Activities 294

### Historical Profile: Kabuki 296

from *The Zen Substitute* by Okamuka Shiko 299

### Chapter 8. Directing & Producing 306

Desire and Dedication 307

A Young Director's Journal 308

### Activities 324

### Historical Profile: Chekhov 326

from *Uncle Vanya,* adapted by David Mamet 330


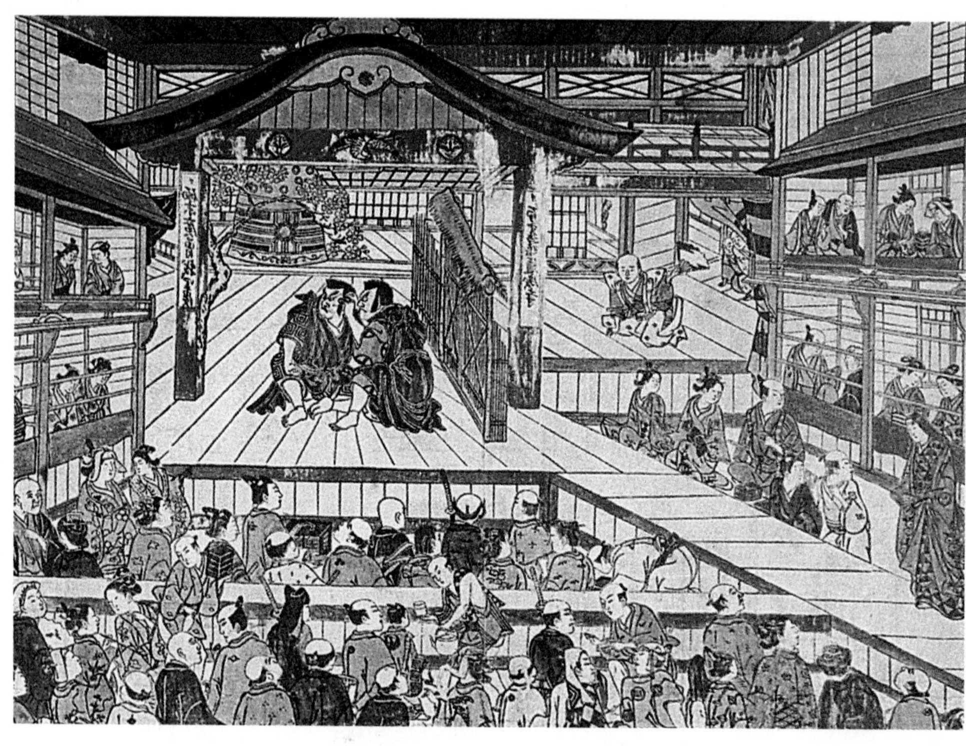

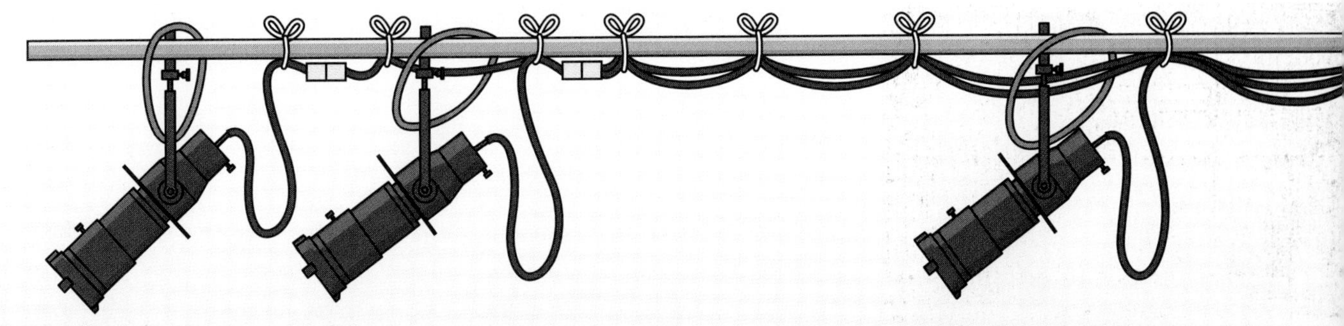


## Chapter 9. Technical Theatre 334

Shifting Scenery 335
Organizing Props 337
Hanging, Focusing, and Running Lights 339
Setting Up Sound 345
Completing Costumes 346
Applying Makeup 349
Final Rehearsals 352
Tech Rehearsal 353
Dress Rehearsal 355
Run of the Show 357
Postproduction 360

## Activities 362

## Performance Projects 366

21: Duet Performance 366
22: Characterization Using Animal Traits 369
23: Commedia dell'Arte Performance 371
24: Stage Composition and Emphasis 374
25: Dealing with a Difficult Actor 377
26: Directing a One-Act Play 379
27: Creating a Gobo 382
28: Making a Show Tape 384
29: Analyzing Scene Changes 387
30: Old-Age Makeup 390

## Section 4. Specialization 394

### Chapter 10. Acting 396

Reader's Theatre 397

Movement Specialties 399

Voice Specialties 410

Masks 412

Musical Theatre 415

Film and TV 418

Multimedia and Performance Art 420

### Activities 422

### **Historical Profile: Beckett** 426

from *Waiting for Godot* 430

### Chapter 11. Directing and Producing 436

Reader's Theatre 437

Musical Theatre 440

Film and TV 446

Multimedia and Performance Art 453

### Activities 454

### **Historical Profile: Wilson** 456

from *Seven Guitars* 460

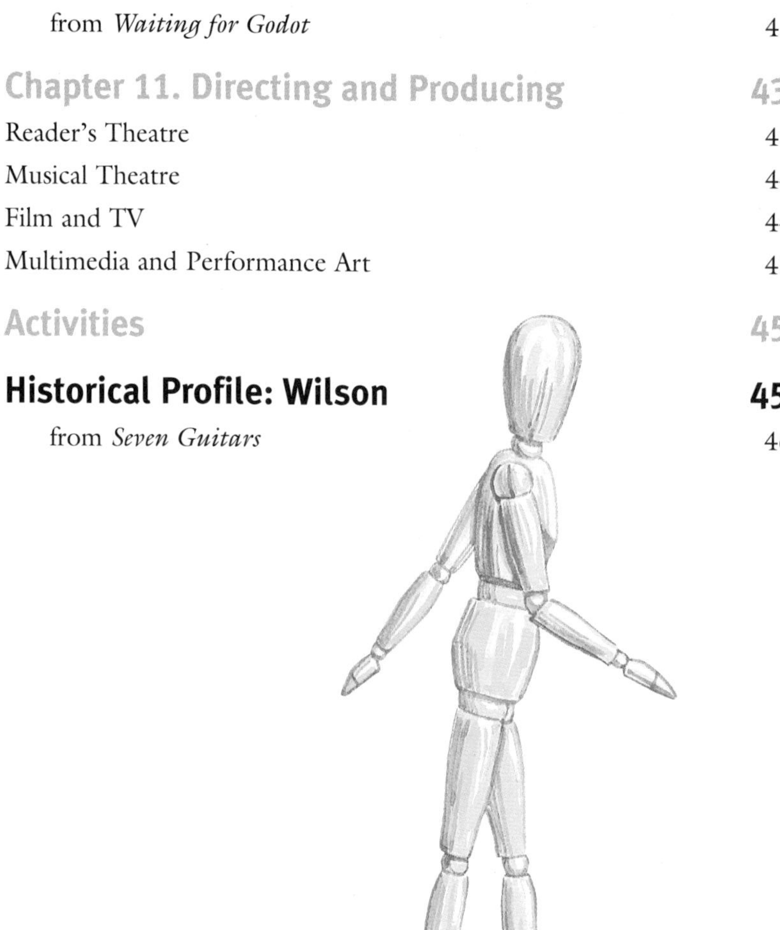

## Chapter 12. Technical Theatre 464

Scenery Techniques 465
Prop Techniques 470
Lighting Techniques 478
Sound Techniques 483
Costume Techniques 485
Makeup Techniques 491

## Activities 496

## Specialization Projects 500

31: Using an Accent 500
32: Performing a Song 503
33: Staging a Fight 506
34: Acting On-Camera 509
35: Directing a Reader's Theatre Piece 512
36: Developing a Musical 515
37: Three-Dimensional Scenery 518
38: Projecting a Background 520
39: Creating Jewelry 523
40: Making a Mask 525

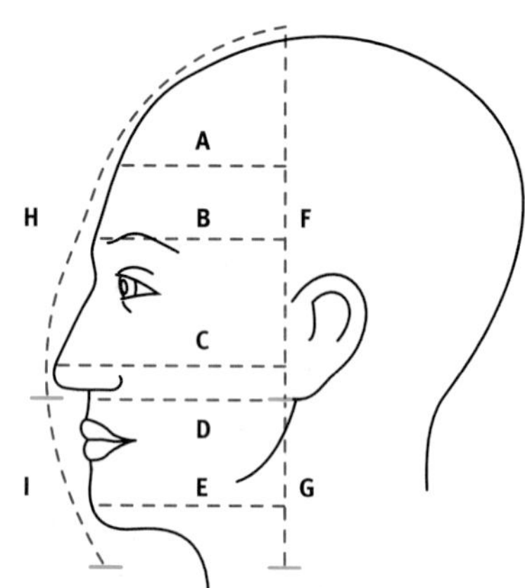


## Resources 529


**Writing & Theatre** **530**

Analyzing Drama 530
Writing a Play 534
Writing a Review 540
Promoting a Show 544
Writing a Screenplay 551
Adapting Reader's Theatre 558
Writing a Research Paper 562

**Activities** **566**

Analysis of *The Tempest*
Determining the Spine
Found Dialogue
Stage Directions
Rating the Reviewers
A Perfect Production
Feature Story
Promotional Gimmicks
Scripting a Commercial
Conflict Chart
Short Short Adaptations
Literary Collage
Developing a Thesis Statement
Personal Research

## Careers & Theatre 570

The Producer 570
The Director 571
The Stage Manager 572
The Actor 573
The Set Designer 574
The Lighting Designer 575
The Costume Designer 576
The Choreographer 577
The Playwright 578
The Critic 579

## Glossary 580

## Acknowledgments 593

## Index 597


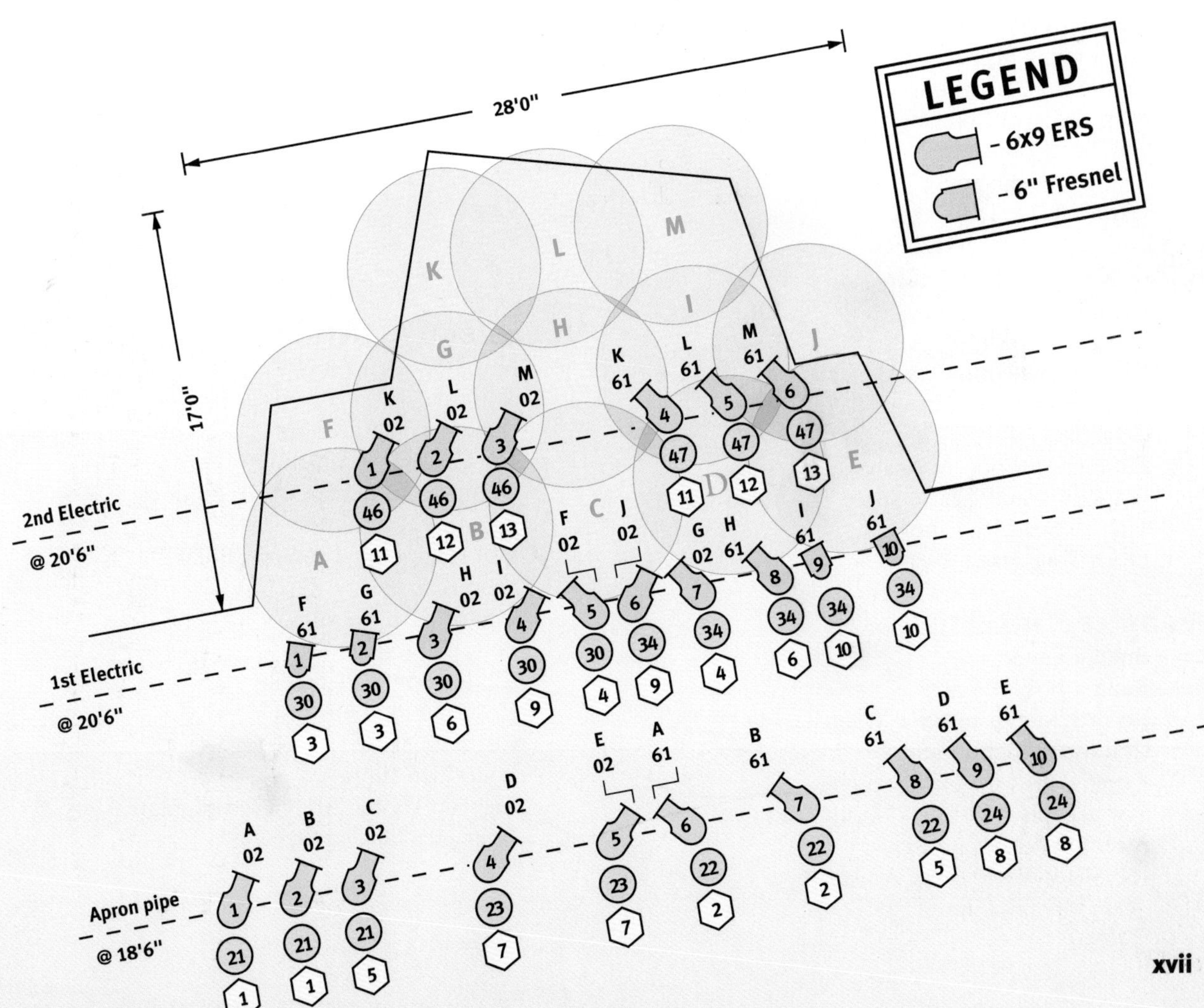

# Activities

**Chapter 1 Activities** 40
Video Observation
Photograph Analysis
Personal Physical Warm-up Routine
Relaxation Through Storytelling
Group Pantomime
Attic Trunk Pantomime
Story Pantomime
Personal Voice Warm-up Routine
Improvising Scenes
Place & Character Improvisations
Prop-Prompts Improvisation
Tall Tale Contest
Around the Campfire
Warped Fairy Tales

**Chapter 2 Activities** 64
Stage Picture Scrapbook
Form a Play Club
Job Shadow—Business Manager
Past Productions Survey
Go to See a Play
Production Concept Analysis
Diagram Your Theatre Space
Theatre Space Inventory
Learn Your Stage Areas

**Chapter 3 Activities** 98
Build a Frame
Build a Box
Record Sounds to Set a Mood
Conduct a Lighting Survey
Experiment with Hand-Stitches
Sew a Tunic
Assemble a Makeup Kit
Job Shadow—Makeup Artist

**Chapter 4 Activities** 150
Characters in a Crowd
Express Your New Experiences
Senses & Emotions Improvisations
Create a Country
Round Table Discussion
Analyzing Behavior
Self-Analysis
Using Models
Wearing Many Hats
Subtext
Opening on a Arena Stage
Cold Readings
Stealing the Scene
Beats and Transitions

**Chapter 6 Activities** 188
Top Ten Plays
Script Evaluation Form
Classifying by Genre
First Impressions
Script Analysis
Dramaturg
Realistic Stage Direction
Nonrealistic Style
Draw a Ground Plan
Picture Analysis
Stage Composition Observation
Blocking a Scene
Check the Royalties
Play Program
Job Shadow—Graphic Artist

**Chapter 6 Activities** 240
Assessing Elements
Thumbnails
Build a Miniature Flat
Job Shadow—Carpenter
Compare and Contrast Techniques
Painting Techniques
Pull/Rent/Buy/Borrow/Build
Prop List
Lighting Analysis
Found Sounds
Job Shadow—Electrician
Costume Plotsand List
Costume Sketch
Found Costumes
Makeup Design from a Photograph
Character Makeup Sketch

Chapter 7 Activities 294
Character Biography
Researching Background
Formal Situations
Tragic Hero/Heroine
Incorporating Stage Business
What-If Character Building
Hot Seat
Group Warm-ups

Chapter 8 Activities 324
Choosing a Play
Community Resources
Theatre Company Logo
Rehearsal Schedule
Theatre Promotion
Mock Audition
Casting a Play
Blocking Rehearsal
Coaching Actors

Chapter 9 Activities 362
Running and Floating
Prop Table
Rig a Batten
Experiment with Colored Light
Sound Cues Practice
Supplement Your Pattern Stock
Job Shadow—Tailor
Special Effects
Reshape Your Face
From Rehearsal Space to Stage
Mock Dress Parade
Quick Costume Changes
Front-of-House Staff
Strike Checklist

Chapter 10 Activities 422
Read a Scene
Read a Duet
Dramatic Dance
Miming a Sequence of Emotions
The Lonely Road
Slow-Motion Fight
Martial Arts Expert
Job Shadow—Radio Announcer
Understanding Dialect
Masked Monologue
Creating a Dance Number
Stage and Film Acting
Maintaining Continuity
Performance Piece

Chapter 11 Activities 454
Visualizing Reader's Theatre
Adapting Scripts
Optioning Unfamiliar Musicals
Production Concept for a Musical
Plays into Film
Job Shadow—TV Director or Producer
Direct a Multimedia Performance

Chapter 12 Activities 496
Designing Three-Dimensional Scenery
Build a Profile
Build a Papier Mâché Object
Choosing Fabrics
Portrait Painting
Fake Feast
Silhouette Projections
Projected Captions
Mixing Sound
Life Masks
Making Jewelry
False Face
Blood Pack

## Using a Theatre Notebook

Everyone involved in theatre has a need and an opportunity to do some type of writing at one time or another. Dramatists write plays and theatre reviewers write criticism. Publicity people write promotional copy for ads, posters, and programs. Actors jot notes about their observations and characters they play. Directors, producers, and those who work in the areas of technical theatre (such as sets, props, lighting, sound, costumes, and makeup) do a wide range of preliminary work on paper. This preliminary work may include sketches or drawings as well as writing. Using a Theatre Notebook is a good way to organize the different kinds of information you will record as you learn and do theatre.

## Getting Started

The best structure for a Theatre Notebook is a three-ring binder into which you can insert blank or lined paper. Reserve this notebook for theatre topics; make it a record and a resource for everything that you learn and experience in theatre. If you like, decorate the cover. Inside, create the following four divisions (you may decide to create others later):

- Playgoing Log
- Acting Notes
- Directing & Producing Notes
- Technical Theatre Notes

The material you include in each of these divisions should be casual notes to yourself in whatever form is most useful for you. You may choose to develop some of these notes later into more finished forms of writing to share with other actors, directors, producers, technical people, or—in the case of plays or promotional writing—with theatregoers. You may eventually develop some of this material into a portfolio of your best writing about theatre.

In addition to your Theatre Notebook, you may find it useful to create a file (a large envelope or a box will do) in which you can keep odd-sized, loose items, such as theatre programs, ticket stubs, magazine illustrations, newspaper clippings, sketches, and so on. These materials can be used later for reference, as sources of ideas, or to form a collage.

## Playgoing Log

Performance is the essence of theatre. To fully understand your theatre experience, you should attend as many performances of theatrical events as you can. In addition to plays, all kinds of performances, including dance, music, film, TV—even sporting events—can teach you something about audience response and the nature of the theatre experience.

Keep a record of plays you attend and your reactions to them in the section of your notebook labeled Playgoing Log. Your log may be an informal collage of drawings, pictures, and comments; or your impressions may be formal and organized. You might develop your own format or use one of the methods below for keeping your Playgoing Log. Whatever your approach, you will find the following guidelines helpful:

- Save your theatre program. It includes names and details you may need for reference later.
- Write notes during the performance or soon afterwards to record your immediate reactions and thoughts.
- Allow yourself time to think about a performance before you fill out your log.

Remember, your purpose in completing a Playgoing Log is to communicate with yourself. You may find years later that you need to remember details from a play you have seen. Capturing those details in writing now will make them available to you then.

## Ledger Format

A ledger format like the one below prompts you to write about various aspects of a play and organizes your comments under topic headings. Draw up a blank chart with headings such as those shown here. After you have seen a play, just fill in the blanks, including examples from the performance to support your assessments. Be sure to leave a large space for general comments.

| **Date** | March 3 |
|---|---|
| **Theatre** | Carlson Theatre |
| **Play & Author** | Joseph and the Amazing Technicolor Dreamcoat by Andrew Lloyd Webber and Tim Rice |
| **Plot** | This show is a musical based on a Bible story. Joseph is spoiled by his father, and so his brothers hate him and sell him as a slave. He ends up in Egypt, and because he can tell what dreams mean, he gets rich and famous. |
| **Character** | Joseph, his father and brothers, Pharaoh, a businessman and his wife, and many others |
| **Setting** | The settings are Israel and Egypt. |
| **Theme** | Even though Joseph was kind of a jerk, he ended up rich and took care of his family. |
| **Style** | It's all music and singing—not realistic. |
| **Language** | The dialogue is generally humorous. |
| **Production** | The costumes were cool—especially the colored dreamcoat. Also, the pyramid looked good. |
| **Music/Dance** (if relevant) | Most of the songs and dancing are funny—like the brothers doing a square dance even though this was in Biblical times. |
| **General Comments** | The best part for me was the person who played Pharaoh. He dressed and sang like Elvis. This surprised everyone and was really funny. I think both kids and adults would like this show because it's funny and fast-paced, so you don't get bored. Also, it's brief. |

### The ABC Format

The ABC format challenges you to write brief statements about the Action, the Basic Human Situation, and the Main Character of a play. You can also add a section for general comments.

> ***Date:*** *March 22*
>
> ***Theatre:*** *Lincolnshire High School*
>
> ***Play:*** *The Night Thoreau Spent in Jail by Jerome Lawrence and Robert E. Lee*
>
> ***Action Statement:*** *Thoreau protests the Mexican War by not paying his taxes and is jailed for one night.*
>
> ***Basic Human Situation:*** *An idealist fights social evils by practicing civil disobedience.*
>
> ***Main Character:*** *Henry David Thoreau*
>
> ***General Comments:*** *I thought this junior-class production was a real winner. The cast and crew used the simple stage settings very effectively to dramatize the life of Thoreau. I didn't know much about Thoreau, but this play covers a lot of incidents in his life. I especially liked Peter Orth in the title role. He was inspiring as the courageous individualist who dared to walk to the beat of a different drummer.*

## Acting Notes

Acting Notes is a section in which you can record your experiences as an actor. Your acting notes can provide you with extra memory. They can remind you of the first time you attempted an exercise, the first time you read or saw a particular play, the first time you struggled with or excelled in an activity or a role. They can take you back to the freshness of your first opinions—and the reasons you thought and felt the way you did. These notes may also serve to chart your personal growth and help you monitor your physical, mental, and emotional progress. They can help you evaluate your performances by providing a place to record your self-assessment and feedback from others, such as directors, other actors, and the audience. Your acting notes will be a repository for thoughts and ideas that might enrich the roles you play. Some actors make it a habit to jot down observations about characters in plays and people on the street. Later, they use those observations to help them create specific characters. Because these are your notes, it doesn't matter what form they take, but here are some formats you might find useful:

### Three-Column Format

Divide a page into three columns, headed Activity, Objectives, and Response. In the first column, name the activity and give a short description of it. In the second column, list the objective or objectives for the activity. In the third column, record your response to the activity, including your personal evaluation of your performance.

| *Activity* | *Objectives* | *Response* |
|---|---|---|
| *Stand onstage and choose a point on the back wall. Try to project your voice to that point. Start with the vowels of your name, then your whole name. Lift your arms over your head and try again.* | *(1) To develop the ability to control your voice and project it in the theatre (2) to develop the habit of diaphragmatic breathing* | *This is going to be one of my greatest challenges this year. My voice seems naturally weak. Diaphragmatic breathing is easy to do, but it's hard to remember to do it.* |

### Collage Format

Some people have an eye for design, a flair for art, or a visual memory. If you tend to be visual rather than verbal, you might create visual records of the work you do by using pictures or drawings that form a collage of ideas and impressions about your acting. The collage format doesn't necessarily do away with words; you will probably still need to label activities, objectives, and your own responses. You may even want to include sentences or paragraphs about your work, yet visual media might take a more prominent place. You might, for example, find it easier to sketch stick figures to record the movements in a scene than to describe the movements in writing. A picture in *Fitness* magazine might show the muscle group you want to isolate.

## Directing & Producing Notes

You can record your experiences as a director or producer in this section. A director must be a communicator. Much of the communication takes place orally, face to face, but some of it is in writing. Your directing notes can help you understand scripts, plan a play's design and actions, and develop an awareness of the subtle changes in meaning brought about by changes in stage lighting, vocal variation, and so on.

At the beginning of your theatre education, your directing notes might include jottings about theatre space and the ways it can be used; or they might focus on people and places you have observed or plays you have read. They might include drawings of movement patterns or architectural elements. They might be organized or random. Later, when you analyze a script and work with a cast of actors and a crew of technical people for that script, your notes will get tighter and more specific; but for now, simply jot down the things that interest you in an informal manner, such as the entries that follow here:

- I'm imagining a group of actors packed tightly together, jostled as if riding in a subway car. What other situations create the same kind of boundaries as that physical confinement?
- Grossinger's Drug Store has some terrific 1890s architectural elements. Have designer take some photos for future reference.
- Can't get it out of my mind, that scream that begins like a strangled growl in the throat and builds in pitch and intensity to become a shriek of pain and horror. What actor did this in what play?

Like the director, the producer must be a skilled communicator, both orally and in writing. Your producing notes can help you record ideas and information in such areas of theatre business as fundraising, promotional methods, media contacts, and designs for programs and advertising. Producing notes might look like the following:

- Interesting idea for a poster advertising *The Miracle Worker*—have the title of the play written both in braille and ordinary English.
- Fundraiser for this year's theatre season—traveling skits, from city park to city park, all in one day.

## Technical Theatre Notes

A tech person's preliminary notes might be essentially the same as those of a director, actor, or playwright. Once you start working with a specific play, you might sketch a setting or describe a mood you hope to create. You might photocopy or include photographs showing effects you hope to achieve. You might list props needed or costumes to be made.

For now, think of your Theatre Notebook as a reference library for yourself. If you are particularly interested in an area of technical theatre, start collecting materials that refer to that area. Look for both common and uncommon examples. Photographs, magazine and newspaper articles, essays you have downloaded from the Internet, your own notes on fantastic ideas as well as practical solutions—all might serve to stimulate your creative approach to some future production. Notes on using certain tools and pertinent safety reminders might help you put these tools to use. Remember to add captions or descriptions that identify the time, place, and other details of the source of your ideas that might be useful.

Following are examples of the types of entries that might be of use to you:

- Architectural elements found on public buildings

- Patterns of light and shade made by the sun on a single building over the course of a single day
- Effects of a variety of lighting fixtures in one room
- Costumes of a certain time period, such as the 1920s
- Descriptions of how pioneers used to make soap, weave cloth, shoe horses, and so on
- Inventory of items found in reproduced period rooms
- Faces of all ages, showing hair treatments and aging of skin
- Different makeup effects, including "makeovers"
- Descriptions of the sounds heard in a factory, at the seashore, during an auto accident

Throughout this book, you will often be reminded that the writing you are doing in many of the exercises, activities, and projects should be included in your Theatre Notebook. In this way, it is hoped you will develop the valuable habit of using such a notebook as a way of enriching your experience of theatre.

2500 B.C. 600 B.C.

# An Outline of Theatre History

**Shamanism** Common to all traditional cultures, the shaman is a priestly figure who communicates directly with the gods through ritual for the benefit of the community. Employing elements of performance such as characterization, dialogue, music, song, dance, illusion, clowning, ventriloquism, and hypnotism, shamanism may be linked to the origins of Western theatre through its connection with the worship of the Greek god Dionysus. This painting shows an American Indian shaman.

**Dance** Expressing the rhythms of life and common to all humanity, dance is another probable origin of theatre. Animal imitation, pantomime, gymnastics, and rhythmic movement entertained all early humans, who presumably elaborated simple dance forms, increasing their dramatic quality. The addition of masks and costume (as with these Dogon dancers) and sound to these performances would have been obvious ways to heighten their impact.

**Ritual** Through the repeated, unvarying, and symbolic actions of ritual, early humans sought to achieve success in battle and hunting; to ensure adequate rain and sun; and to express their duty to the community and the gods. The art and artifacts of preliterate peoples around the world all attest to this universal human habit of ritual that appears to have been the original theatre. Perhaps as early as 2500 B.C., a ritual depicting the myth of the god Osiris (shown here) in dramatic form began to be performed annually in Egypt.

**Storytelling** Closely related to ritual is myth. Myths and stories have certainly entertained and educated human beings since the beginnings of language. Oral storytelling traditions led to India's great epic cycles of the *Mahabharata* and *Ramayana* and to the *Iliad* and the *Odyssey,* the epics of the Greek poet Homer (shown here). With the human tendency to imitate and elaborate, these tales provided a great storehouse of plots for subsequent dramatists.

600 B.C.

1 A.D.

**Origin of Greek Theatre** The Greek philosopher Aristotle, who observed the basic human tendency to imitate, recognized the origins of Greek theatre in the dithyramb, a hymn sung and danced to honor the god Dionysus. This had evolved from earlier ecstatic dances by female celebrants of shamanism (shown here). The dithyramb was performed at annual festivals of Dionysus by a chorus of 50 men and related episodes from the god's life.

**Golden Age of Greece**
The Greeks of Athens invented Western drama. Athenian playwrights used myths and heroic legends drawn from Homer and other sources, but shaped them to reflect contemporary issues. Theatre was a civic responsibility: writer and actor helped the people confront current political or religious problems. Greek drama was at its height between 500 and 400 B.C., when three Athenian tragedians, Aeschylus, Sophocles, and Euripides, and the comic playwright Aristophanes were creating their works. This statuette depicts a tragic actor.

**Roman Theatre** Although based on Greek forms, Roman theatre differed in being largely for entertainment. The farces of Plautus were based on stock characters, such as the braggart soldier and the scheming slave. Terence included less buffoonery in his comedies and had a more realistic treatment of character and dialogue. Seneca wrote violent, blood-and-thunder tragedies that were intended to be recited rather than performed. This wall painting shows a scene from Plautus.

**Decline of Western Theatre**
Before the Byzantine Emperor Justinian married her, the Empress Theodora (shown here) was an actress. While secular authority wavered, the Church firmly opposed the theatre. In 692 A.D. a Church council passed a resolution intended to forbid theatrical performances of all kinds, an event often used to mark the end of classical theatre in the West.

**Sanskrit Drama** Theatre in India is ancient. Dated to around 200 A.D., the *Natyasastra* (The Science of Dramaturgy) was the first guide to acting, makeup, costume, and dance. Plays in India's classical language, Sanskrit, appeared as early as 100 A.D., but the best date from after 320. Based on episodes from the Indian epics, the *Mahabharata* and *Ramayana,* Sanskrit plays were never tragedies; good always triumphed over evil. The greatest Sanskrit dramatist, Kalidasa, lived from around 375 to 415 A.D. This actor is costumed as Ravana, a demon king from the *Ramayana.*

550 A.D. 1000 1500

## Theatre in China

Sometime after the beginning of the Tang Dynasty (618–906) in China, the various elements of story, dance, song, and comic pantomime came together in a single performance. Unlike the permanent theatre space typical of Greek drama, the performance area in Chinese theatre was established by the simple method of drawing a chalk circle on the ground. This statuette shows a Tang Dynasty dancing girl.

## Hroswitha and Hildegard

In the late 900s, a German nun named Hroswitha became the first person to write plays for over a thousand years. She took as her model the Roman dramatist Terence, but adapted the comic form to tell the lives of saintly women and teach lessons about virtue. Her example was followed in the 1100s by another German nun, Hildegard of Bingen, who wrote a musical play in which personified virtues aid the human soul in its struggle to get to heaven. This self-portrait by Hildegard shows her spiritual awakening.

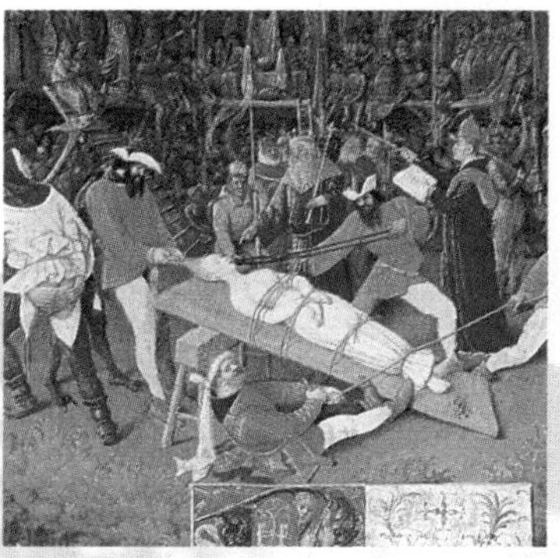

## Types of Medieval Drama

The three main types of medieval European drama were the mystery play, the miracle play, and the morality play. Mystery plays depicted episodes from the Bible. Miracle (or saint) plays dealt with the lives of saints and martyrs. Morality plays presented personified virtues and vices in dramas depicting the moral struggle of the soul. This manuscript illumination shows a saint play of the martyrdom of St. Apollonia.

## Origin of Medieval Theatre

As with Greek theatre, medieval theatre grew out of religious ritual; in this case the Easter liturgy of the Church. Around 925 the singing of the hymns telling the story of Christ's Resurrection was transformed into a dramatic dialogue delivered by priests, one impersonating an angel and others the three women visiting Christ's tomb (the scene shown in this medieval illumination). This brief drama was the source of the mystery play, one of the characteristic forms of medieval theatre.

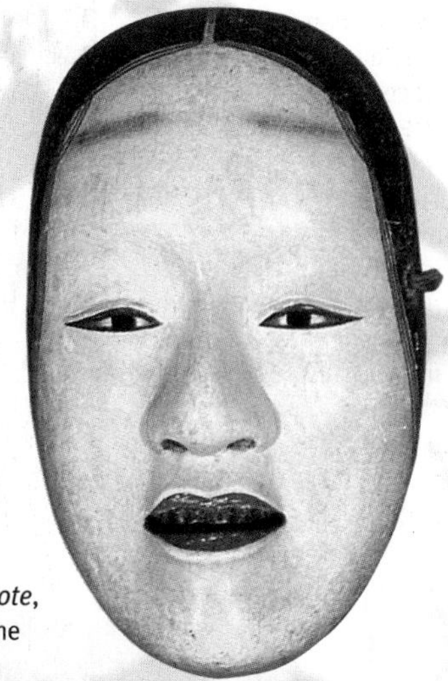

## Noh Drama

In the 1300s in Japan, two actors, Kanami Kiyotsugu and his son Zeami Motokiyo, developed Noh drama, one of the great traditional forms of Japanese theatre. In Noh plays, masked male actors employ highly stylized dance and poetry to tell stories of ghosts, doomed love, and revenge. This Noh mask is referred to as *Ko-omote*, "little face," a mask suitable for the roles of innocent young girls.

1500

**Renaissance Set Design** Rediscovered in the 1400s, the influential treatise *De Architectura,* by the Roman writer Vitruvius, enabled Renaissance builders to reconstruct classical scenic designs. Sebastiano Serlio's *Architettura* (1545) followed this classical tradition, but was greatly influenced by the Renaissance innovation of linear perspective. Serlio's three basic scenes—for comedy (shown here), tragedy, and pastoral—could be used for any play produced at the time.

**Rise of English Drama** Renaissance ideas came late to England, where medieval influences were felt well into the 1500s—when Elizabeth I banned all religious plays. The resulting secularization of theatre, combined with classical ideas from Italian humanism, led university students and graduates to write for London theatre companies. Notable among these "university wits" was Christopher Marlowe, whose *Dr. Faustus* (shown here) is a transitional work, showing elements of the medieval morality play, but also anticipating Shakespeare in its use of blank verse.

**Commedia dell'arte** Its origins shrouded in mystery, *commedia dell'arte,* a professional form of theatrical improvisation with stock characters (shown here) and standard comic routines, or *lazzi,* became very popular in Italy in the 1500s and flourished for more than 200 years. These comic scenarios of young lovers and disapproving fathers, of gullible masters and tricky servants, influenced many dramatists and performers, from Molière to the Italian actor and playwright Dario Fo, winner of the 1997 Nobel Prize for Literature.

**Shakespeare**

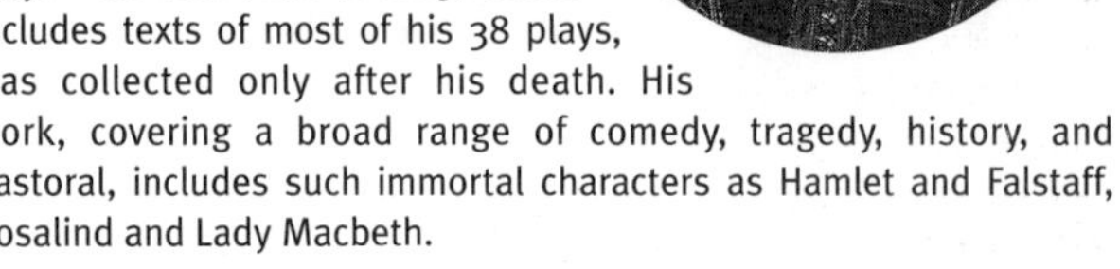

The greatest playwright in the English language, Shakespeare was also an actor-manager of a professional company. He wrote to be performed; the script was only important until the actors knew their lines. Shakespeare never bothered to publish his plays—the First Folio of 1623, which includes texts of most of his 38 plays, was collected only after his death. His work, covering a broad range of comedy, tragedy, history, and pastoral, includes such immortal characters as Hamlet and Falstaff, Rosalind and Lady Macbeth.

**Kabuki** One of the principal forms of Japanese theatre, Kabuki came into existence around 1600 when a female dancer named Okuni created performances combining traditional Buddhist dances with more popular contemporary forms. Kabuki performances by women were soon banned by the government, inaugurating the tradition of female impersonation by male actors, who were rigorously trained from an early age in specialized voice and movement. Elaborate makeup and costume are also essential to Kabuki performances, such as shown here.

1650

1700

## French Neoclassical Theatre

Based on the critical theories of the Greek thinker Aristotle and the Roman poet Horace, the neoclassical ideal was influential throughout Europe in the mid-1600s. Dramatic unities of time, place, and action; division of plays into five acts; purity of genre; and the concepts of decorum and verisimilitude were taken as rules of playwriting, particularly by French dramatists. Asked to evaluate Corneille's *Le Cid* (shown here), the French Academy based its judgment *entirely* on how closely the play adhered to neoclassical principles.

## Molière

Molière tried to follow the neoclassical rules in his comedies, which were inspired by the *commedia dell'arte*. A theatrical innovator in introducing indoor settings into his works, he directed and performed in most of his plays—finally dying onstage during a performance of *The Imaginary Invalid!* Always a controversial writer, Molière was forced by the Church to twice rewrite *Tartuffe,* a study of religious hypocrisy. This painting shows Molière (far left) and other actors of his time.

## Spain's Golden Age

Lasting from 1580 to 1680, and coinciding with the height of Spain's wealth and power, this period saw the work of such playwrights as Lope de Vega and Pedro Calderón de la Barca. The poster above shows a scene from Calderón's play *Life is a Dream.* The typical performance space in Spain in this period was the *corral,* or courtyard theatre, similar to the English innyards upon which the design of Elizabethan playhouses was ultimately based.

## Masques

Popular from the early 1600s, English court masques were expensive, lavish spectacles that combined huge casts, gorgeous costumes (such as the Inigo Jones design here), beautiful scenery, lots of music, and elaborate stagecraft—even flying machines! The entire court took part in productions that cost as much as $30,000, an enormous sum at the time. With scripts by playwrights such as Ben Jonson and designed by architect Inigo Jones, masques were often performed to celebrate such observances as Twelfth Night and Mardi Gras.

## Restoration Drama

During the Puritan Commonwealth, professional theatre was banned in England, but after the Restoration of the monarchy in 1660, the London stage flourished. Especially popular was the Restoration comedy of manners (shown here), with its ribald wit and fashionable characters, as practiced by such playwrights as Sir George Etherege, William Wycherley, and William Congreve. Another successful dramatist was Aphra Behn, the first English woman to earn her living as a professional writer. The Restoration stage also saw the arrival of the first women to act professionally.

1700

1735

**Theatre in America** The first playhouse in the American colonies was built in Williamsburg, Virginia, in 1716. Given a temporary check by the religious revivalism of the Great Awakening in the late 1730s and '40s, colonial theatre got a new start with the arrival in 1752 of an English acting troupe headed by William Hallam, which marks the beginning of professional theatre in America.

**The Middle-Class Audience** In the early 1700s, the middle class emerged as the dominant element among British theatregoers. The moralistic taste of this new audience established the popularity of two new dramatic forms—sentimental comedy and domestic tragedy. In comedies such as Sir Richard Steele's *The Funeral* (shown here), the emphasis was not on laughter but on virtue triumphant. The complementary form was domestic tragedy, like George Lillo's *The London Merchant* (1731), which shows the destruction of a good man who yields to temptation.

**David Garrick** The greatest British actor of the 1700s, Garrick dominated the stage from his sensational debut in 1741 as Shakespeare's Richard III (shown here) until his retirement in 1776. Equally good in comic and tragic roles, he introduced a new, natural style of speech and movement into English theatre. Garrick was also the manager of the Drury Lane Theatre, where he introduced a number of innovations to the English stage, including closely supervised rehearsals, three-dimensional stage settings, and concealed stage lighting.

**Ballad Opera** The popularity of Italian opera in England in the early 1700s produced a burlesque form, the ballad opera, which combined spoken dialogue and songs set to popular tunes. The first and most successful ballad opera was John Gay's *The Beggar's Opera,* first performed in 1728, in which the chief characters are beggars and thieves. This painting by William Hogarth shows a performance of *The Beggar's Opera.*

**Goldoni versus Gozzi** Italian theatre in the mid-1700s was dominated by the rivalry between Carlo Goldoni and Carlo Gozzi, two playwrights who used the *commedia dell'arte* tradition in markedly different ways. Beginning his career crafting scenarios for *commedia* troupes, Goldoni later wrote plays in which the stock characters and situations of the *commedia* were made more realistic. By contrast, Gozzi used *commedia* characters to create satiric fairy tales, such as his *Love for Three Oranges* (shown here), emphasizing the fantastic elements that Goldoni avoided.

1810

1850

**"Laughing Comedy"** In 1773 British playwright Oliver Goldsmith attacked the currently popular sentimental comedy and proposed a "laughing comedy," which was more realistic and more humorous. In his skillfully plotted and swiftly paced comedy *She Stoops to Conquer* (shown here), Goldsmith offered masterly support of his arguments. Other departures from sentimental comedy in the 1770s were the plays of Richard Brinsley Sheridan, such as *The Rivals* and *The School for Scandal,* whose fashionable characters and witty dialogue recalled Restoration comedy.

**Melodrama** Characterized by cliff-hanging plots and heart-tugging emotional appeals, melodrama became highly popular in America during the first half of the 1800s. Related to both sentimental comedy and domestic tragedy in its strongly moralistic character, melodrama celebrated virtue above all else and insisted that vice would ultimately be punished. This poster advertises a melodrama based on Harriet Beecher Stowe's antislavery novel *Uncle Tom's Cabin.*

**Georg Büchner** During his brief lifetime, the German playwright Georg Büchner reacted against the Romanticism that had come to dominate theatre in Germany. Before he died from typhoid fever at the age of 23, Büchner created both *Danton's Death* and *Woyzeck* (shown here). In *Woyzeck,* Büchner's sympathetic treatment of a lower-class character destroyed by factors of heredity and environment anticipated naturalism.

**German Romantic Drama** In the late 1700s, German theatre was changed radically by the Romantic movement known as *Sturm und Drang* ("Storm and Stress"), which idolized Shakespeare and dismissed the neoclassical dramatic unities. In the masterpiece of German Romantic drama, *Faust* (shown here), Johann Wolfgang von Goethe adapted the old legend of a bargain with the devil into a Romantic tribute to the aspirations of the human spirit.

**Peking Opera** During the 1800s, acting companies based in the Chinese capital of Peking assumed a dominant role in theatre in China, establishing the tradition of Peking Opera. While it has a huge repertoire of plays, the major emphasis in Peking Opera is on the performance of the actors. All parts are played by males who undergo rigorous training from an early age. Sets and props are minimal, but costuming (shown here) is very elaborate. The stylized movement and song are accompanied by string and percussion instruments.

1850

1860

## Henrik Ibsen

"Father of modern drama," Norwegian playwright Ibsen ranged in style from the folk tale quality of *Peer Gynt* (1867); through the realism of *A Doll's House* (1879); to the symbolism of *When We Dead Awaken* (1899), late in his career. The impact of many of his works, particularly *A Doll's House* (shown here), in which a middle-class woman deserts husband and family to start a new life, was shocking. The famous concluding stage direction ("From below, the sound of a door slamming shut") seemed to mark the end of an era.

## Sarah Bernhardt

An attractive French actress with a beautiful voice, whose style would be considered flamboyant and exaggerated today, Sarah Bernhardt enjoyed a long career performing in most of the major works of her day. She became a world-renowned star, rewarded with roles ranging from Shakespeare to the formulaic "well-made" plays of Victorien Sardou, France's most popular playwright, who wrote parts especially for her. In the latter part of her career, Bernhardt toured the United States a number of times.

**Émile Zola** The French writer Zola and his fellow naturalists wished to go a step further than Ibsen's realism. Basing their views on contemporary scientific theory and believing that everything in life was dictated by heredity and environment, the naturalists saw their works as scientific "case studies." Zola championed naturalism with dramatizations of novels such as *L'Assommoir* (shown here). While some playwrights, such as Henri Becque, followed Zola's example, naturalism was not influential until André Antoine opened the Théatre Libre in Paris in 1887, beginning the Independent Theatre Movement, later copied in many countries.

**The Meiningen Troupe** During the last quarter of the 1800s, a German nobleman, the Duke of Saxe-Meiningen, (shown in the center here) made his court theatre the most highly respected touring company of the period and became the first true theatre director. Emphasizing long rehearsal periods and experimenting with recent technical advances in stagecraft and actor preparation, the Meiningen troupe influenced theatrical innovators such as Stanislavski and Antoine.

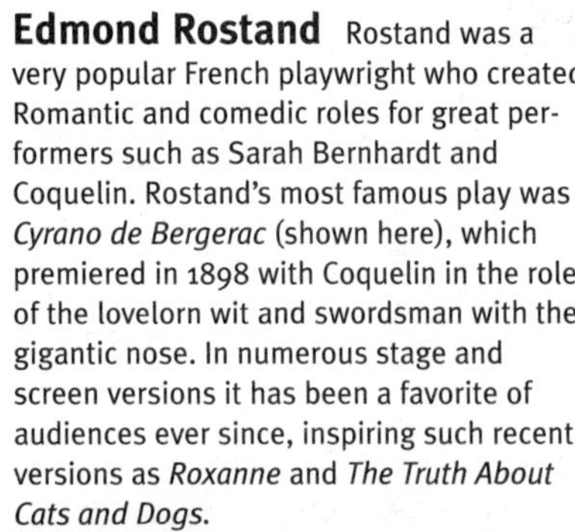

**Edmond Rostand** Rostand was a very popular French playwright who created Romantic and comedic roles for great performers such as Sarah Bernhardt and Coquelin. Rostand's most famous play was *Cyrano de Bergerac* (shown here), which premiered in 1898 with Coquelin in the role of the lovelorn wit and swordsman with the gigantic nose. In numerous stage and screen versions it has been a favorite of audiences ever since, inspiring such recent versions as *Roxanne* and *The Truth About Cats and Dogs*.

1875 | 1885 | 1900

**Bernard Shaw** Born in Ireland, Shaw began his theatrical career as a theatre critic in London, attacking the formulaic "well-made" plays that were fashionable in the late 1800s. Influenced by Ibsen, Shaw wanted the theatre to explore controversial issues. His first play, *Widowers' Houses* (1892) was about slum landlords; *Mrs. Warren's Profession* (1893) explored prostitution. Once established as a successful playwright, Shaw became deeply involved in the production of his works, choosing leading actors, superintending rehearsals, and dictating the length of runs. This scene is from Shaw's play *Candida* (1897).

**Anton Chekhov** Initially a medical student who wrote short stories to pay for his studies, Anton Chekhov had matured by the turn of the century into Russia's greatest dramatist. In his masterpieces—*The Seagull, Uncle Vanya* (shown here), *The Three Sisters, The Cherry Orchard* —he evokes the atmosphere of a society on the edge of change, where individuals feel such uncertainty that they attempt to distract themselves with routine and daydreams. Going beyond simple realism, Chekhov's work has inspired modern playwrights in all styles of theatre.

**Special Effects** In the 1800s, technology was introduced to create stage effects such as the ghost illusion shown here. American producer David Belasco was a notable innovator in theatre technology, especially in stage lighting. Applying European ideas of naturalistic staging to traditional American melodrama and musical theatre, he achieved an extraordinary degree of scenic realism in his production.

**Moscow Art Theatre** Perhaps the most influential company in theatre history, the Moscow Art Theatre was founded by Konstantin Stanislavski and Vladimir Nemirovich-Danchenko in 1898. Emphasizing Stanislavski's inner "artistic truth" in acting rather than external effect and influenced by movements in naturalism and realism, the theatre found success in performing plays by Russian playwrights such as Anton Chekhov (shown here reading) and Maxim Gorky. Subsequent tours brought the Stanislavski system to the United States, where adaptations eventually led to the American "Method" style of acting.

**The Arrival of Cinema** From its invention in the late 1880s by Thomas Edison and George Eastman as an experimental toy, the motion picture developed rapidly. From the first, the stage provided stars and stories for the movies. This scene is from a film featuring Sarah Bernhardt as Queen Elizabeth.

1900

## Constructivism

Constructivism was an antirealist artistic movement developed in Russia shortly before World War I. Following the Russian Revolution in 1917, a number of constructivists became important figures in the art world of the new Soviet Union. Influenced by constructivist aesthetics, Russian directors such as V. E. Meyerhold created productions in which the stage designs (as shown here) were frankly artificial, employing machine-like, or abstract forms.

**Expressionism** An artistic movement that developed in Europe around the time of World War I, expressionism directly influenced playwrights, particularly in Germany. Initially optimistic, German expressionism later focused on tragic issues as a result of the horrors of the war. Ernst Toller's *Man and the Masses* (1921), an outstanding example of expressionist drama, still influences playwrights today with its fragmented and distorted view of reality centered on the individual perception of the main character. The scene shown here is from an expressionist staging of Franz Kafka's story *The Metamorphosis*.

## Rabindranath Tagore

Indian poet and playwright Tagore was influenced by the traditions of classical Sanskrit drama, Bengali folk drama, and Western theatre. His plays generally include dance, mime, and song; and the later works are often strongly symbolic. He was the first modern Indian dramatist to achieve a worldwide reputation, receiving the Nobel Prize for Literature in 1913.

## The Abbey Theatre

In 1904 Irish poet and playwright W. B. Yeats and his friend, playwright and folklorist Lady Augusta Gregory, co-founded the Abbey Theatre in Dublin to present works by Irish playwrights on Irish subjects. In the years that followed, the Abbey premiered works by Yeats, Lady Gregory, J. M. Synge, Sean O'Casey, and many others, creating a new Irish drama that had strong influences on both modern theatre and Irish politics. This image of the legendary Queen Maeve has been the Abbey's emblem since its founding.

**Gordon Craig** British scenic designer and director Gordon Craig sought to capture the feeling of a dramatic work rather than present a realistic setting. During his career he designed productions for the Abbey Theatre and the Moscow Art Theatre. Craig's impact on modern direction and stage design has largely resulted from the influence of his theoretical writings. This design was done by Craig for a 1909 production of *Macbeth*.

1920 | 1930 | 1940

**Eugene O'Neill** While almost unvaryingly tragic, O'Neill's plays reveal a variety of specific influences. Expressionism is reflected in *The Hairy Ape* and *The Great God Brown.* The American playwright's interest in theatrical experiment and innovation produced *Strange Interlude*, where he applied stream of consciousness technique to the stage. His central fascination with ancient Greek drama resulted in his trilogy *Mourning Becomes Electra,* which translates the action of the *Oresteia* of Aeschylus to an American setting.

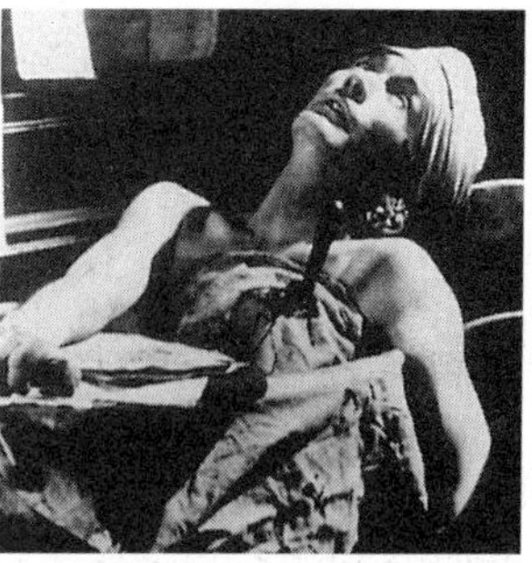

**Antonin Artaud**
An outstanding figure in French avant-garde theatre in the 1920s and '30s, Artaud (shown here in the role of Jean Paul Marat) was a playwright, actor, and director. Believing that conventional verbal communication had become meaningless, Artaud located examples of effective nonverbal communication in sources as diverse as Balinese dance and the Marx Brothers. His idea of a nonverbal "theatre of cruelty" were ignored in his lifetime but had a great influence decades later on experimental directors such as Jerzy Grotowski and Peter Brook.

**Lillian Hellman** A number of talented women wrote for the American stage in the 1920s and '30s, including Susan Glaspell, Edna Ferber, and Edna St. Vincent Millay. The most significant female playwright of the period was Lillian Hellman, whose best-known dramatic works include *The Children's Hour* and *The Little Foxes* (shown here). Marked by skillful plotting and characterization, Hellman's plays often dealt with controversial issues and showed a concern for social justice.

**Laurence Olivier** Olivier was an extraordinarily creative and versatile man of the theatre. The British actor was equally brilliant in classical, Shakespearean, and modern plays, in both comic and tragic roles. He was also active as a director and theatrical administrator. Olivier also had a distinguished movie career, notable for his own film versions of *Henry V, Hamlet* (shown here), and *Richard III.*

**Epic Theatre** In the 1920s and '30s, reacting against what they saw as over-emphasis on artistic illusion and aesthetic emotion in theatre, two Germans, director Erwin Piscator and playwright Bertolt Brecht, sought to create a new style, called "epic theatre" or "theatre of alienation," that would serve a Marxist social purpose of educating audiences. Abandoning traditional techniques of stagecraft in their productions, Piscator and Brecht employed frankly artificial devices such as posters, cartoons, and film sequences in order to distance the audience from theatrical illusion and allow them to concentrate on a play's message. This scene is from Brecht's *The Life of Galileo.*

1940

**Samuel Beckett** Little understood when first produced in 1953, the tragicomic play *Waiting for Godot* (shown here), by Irish-born playwright Samuel Beckett, depicts derelict characters repeating senseless phrases in an unending round of pointless activity. Included by critic Martin Esslin in his influential category "theatre of the absurd," Beckett's play is farce at its core, best acted by gifted comedians.

**Tennessee Williams**
In the decade following World War II, American playwright Tennessee Williams crafted *The Glass Menagerie, A Streetcar Named Desire* (shown here), and *Cat on a Hot Tin Roof*, achieving an international reputation. In his characters, who tenaciously cling to fragile, transparent illusions, only to see them brutally shattered, Williams showed a genius for creating fully developed individuals that challenged the best contemporary actors to display their greatest talents.

**Arthur Miller** Perhaps the most intelligent of 20th century American playwrights, Miller is best known for his *Death of a Salesman* (shown here). First performed in 1949, and since produced to great acclaim worldwide, the play successfully combines realism and symbolic expressionism in a study of personal wealth versus personal value.

**Broadway Musicals** Mainly a comic form before World War II, American musical theatre achieved a new maturity in 1943 with *Oklahoma!* by Richard Rogers and Oscar Hammerstein II. This production (shown here) began the Golden Age of the Broadway musical, typified by shows with simple plots, memorable songs, large casts and choruses, and lavish multiple sets.

**Thornton Wilder** Best known for *Our Town* and *The Skin of Our Teeth* (shown here), Wilder was the finest American playwright of the period immediately before World War II. His great ability was to apply contemporary theatricality to simple parables on the nature of life.

1950 1960 1970

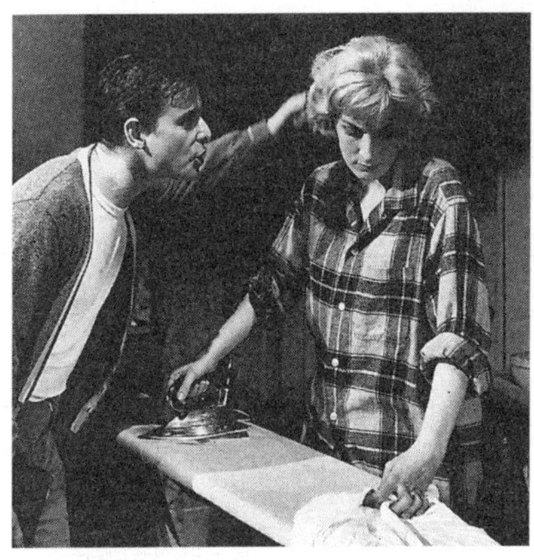

**John Osborne** In 1956 Osborne's play *Look Back in Anger* (shown here) attacked the settled smugness of the British class system and in its main character, Jimmy Porter, provided a symbol of the "angry young men" who felt they had no place in postwar Britain.

**Edward Bond** When challenged by the government for unlawful performances in the mid-1960s, Bond's savagely realist plays *Saved* (shown here) and *Early Morning* created a debate that ultimately led to the end of censorship, which had plagued British theatres since Shakespeare's day. Ranging from opera to Greek epic to kitchen-sink realism, Bond's plays always challenge the political status quo in Britain.

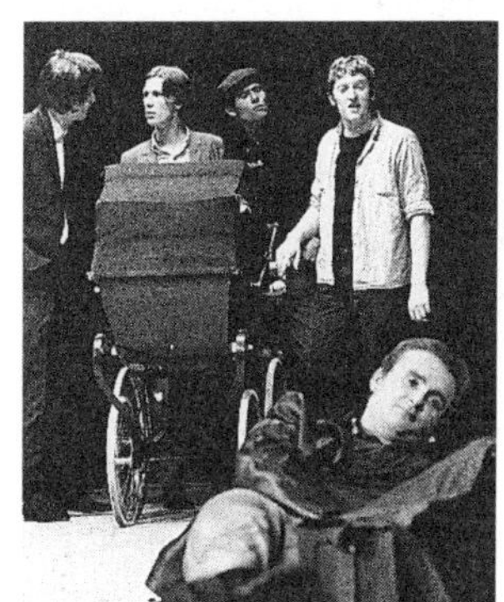

**Lorraine Hansberry** Although she completed only two plays, *A Raisin in the Sun* (shown here) and *The Sign in Sidney Brustein's Window,* before her early death, Hansberry's contribution to theatre history is noteworthy. Her creation of believable black characters inspired many subsequent African American dramatists working in the realistic vein.

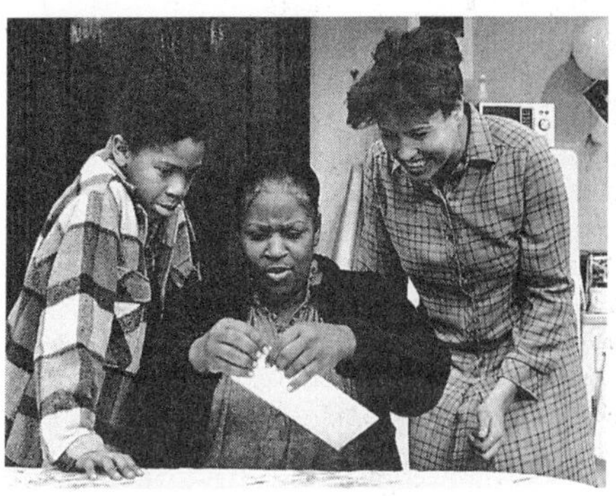

**Edward Albee** Creator of inspiring plays such as *Who's Afraid of Virginia Woolf* (shown here) and *Three Tall Women,* Albee is a widely read dramatist with a knowledge of theatre history. An artist who is not afraid to experiment in a variety of styles, from absurdist through allegory and symbolism to naturalism, the American playwright forms a link between the modern classics of Miller and Williams and contemporary theatre.

**Neil Simon** Perhaps the most representative American playwright of the era of the sitcom, Simon established his reputation in the 1960s with his comedies *Barefoot in the Park* and *The Odd Couple* (shown here) and has continued with a long string of successes through the years, delivering to theatre (and movie) audiences what they want.

1970

**Peter Brook** A major force in experimental theatre since the early 1960s, British director Peter Brook spent several years researching Antonin Artaud's "theatre of cruelty." Brook's productions, such as *Marat/Sade, A Midsummer Night's Dream,* and *The Mahabharata* (shown here), are marked by an emphasis on ritualistic elements and a strong visual quality.

**Hispanic American Theatre** Contemporary Hispanic-American theatre began with the Teatro Campesino (Farmworker's Theatre), founded in 1965 by Mexican American Luis Valdez to further the cause of striking farmworkers. Valdez later reached Broadway with his play *Zoot Suit* (shown here), dealing with ethnic prejudice and violence in Los Angeles during World War II. Other successful Latino dramatists include Cuban American Maria Irene Fornés, who received critical acclaim for her 1977 play *Fefu and Her Friends.*

**August Wilson** August Wilson's commitment to portraying African Americans realistically and sensitively and to "raise consciousness through theatre," has produced some of the finest plays of the contemporary theatre, including *Ma Rainey's Black Bottom, Fences* (shown here), *Joe Turner's Come and Gone, The Piano Lesson, Two Trains Running,* and *Seven Guitars.* Each of these plays is set in a different decade, and taken together, form a cycle presenting African American life in the 20th century.

**Sam Shepard** American dramatist Sam Shepard began his career in the 1960s, writing plays for New York's Off-Broadway theatre. Shepard's work, including *Buried Child* (shown here) and *Fool for Love,* is marked by a combination of lyricism and violence.

**Ntozake Shange** *for colored girls who have considered suicide/when the rainbow is enuf* by African American playwright Ntozake Shange was a groundbreaking work when it appeared in the mid-1970s. Combining poetry, music, dance, and drama, Shange's play (shown here) powerfully depicted the brutal oppression of black women by black men.

1980 | 1990 | 2000

**Caryl Churchill** Creating political theatre in the tradition of Bertolt Brecht, British playwright Caryl Churchill writes plays with feminist and socialist themes, such as *Top Girls* (shown here), which features famous women from the past who defied conventions.

**Tony Kushner** A turning point in the treatment of homosexual themes in the American theatre occurred in 1993 with Tony Kushner's two-part *Angels in America* (shown here), a drama about the gay community and public policy in the age of AIDS.

**Kenneth Branagh** The most ambitious film versions of Shakespeare in the 1990s have come from British actor/director Kenneth Branagh, who has directed and starred in *Henry V* (shown here), *Much Ado About Nothing,* and *Hamlet.*

**Julie Taymor** Taymor's designs for productions such as *Juan Darien* (shown here) and *The Lion King* reflect her extensive study of world theatre and commitment to a multicultural theatre.

**Wendy Wasserstein** Women have produced some of the most significant American plays of the recent past, including Beth Henley's *Crimes of the Heart,* Marsha Norman's *'night, Mother,* and Wendy Wasserstein's *The Heidi Chronicles.* Wasserstein's play (shown here) portrays the women's movement of the 1970s and '80s in a series of episodes from the life of its main character.

# Exploration

## Acting

19 Self-Awareness
20 The Ensemble Ethic
20 Movement
28 Pantomime
30 Voice
36 Improvisation
38 Storytelling
40 Activities

44 **Historical Profile:** The Storytelling Tradition


## Directing & Producing

51 The Roles of Director and Producer
54 The Production Team
56 The Performance Space
64 Activities

66 **Historical Profile:** Sophocles


## Technical Theatre

75 The Stage Crew
76 Set Construction and Prop Crews
82 Lighting and Sound Crews
90 Costume and Makeup Crews
98 Activities


## Projects

100 1: Telling a Story
103 2: Animal Pantomime
105 3: Improvisation and Tableau
107 4: Soundscapes
110 5: Perspectives on Theatre Spaces
112 6: Analyzing Theatre Spaces
115 7: Building a Model Stage
118 8: Shop Inventory
120 9: Sewing Demonstration Board
123 10: Makeup Scrapbook

# Acting exploration

**An artist may work with paint or clay. A musician may play a piano or a drum. As an actor, your instrument of expression is yourself—your body and your voice. A playwright gives a character a situation and words to speak, but you give life to the character with movement and speech. To play a variety of characters different from yourself, you need to explore your instrument and train it to be as versatile as possible.**

## THE LANGUAGE OF THEATRE

**articulation** the clear and precise pronunciation of words
**articulators** the parts of the body that create consonant sounds
**gesture** an expressive movement of the body or limbs
**improvise** to speak or to act without a script
**inflection** variety in speech
**pantomime** acting without words through facial expression and gesture
**project** to make your voice fill the performance space
**resonance** a quality caused by vibration that enriches vocal tone
**resonators** the parts of the body that create vowel sounds
**script** the text of a play

# Self-Awareness



Because acting is about creating characters who live through you, it is important that you know yourself well. When you understand the similarities and differences between you and the characters you portray, those similarities and differences can be accentuated by your body and your voice.

To develop your self-awareness, you will need to observe yourself from the outside—how you speak and act—and reflect upon yourself from the inside—how you think and feel. The exercises below can help you get started.

## EXERCISE Partner Observation

With a partner, take turns observing each other. Make notes, draw sketches, and talk about your observations. Begin by making general observations about your partner's body type: height, shape, and special features (short legs, long fingers, broad shoulders, and so on). Be frank, but sensitive.

Next, look at the way your partner stands and sits. Observe the position of the head, shoulders, arms, hands, torso, legs, and feet. Note any tension in the body.

Now look at your partner's walk: the pace (fast, slow, or medium), stride (long, short, or medium), footfall (heavy or light), swing of the arms, movement of the head and shoulders, and angle of the torso.

Then observe and describe the shape of your partner's face and its features. Also note your partner's hair and hairstyle.

Finally, have your partner talk to you about the following: a happy event, a boring chore, something surprising, and something aggravating. Observe and describe your partner's facial expressions and any other expressive body movements. Also listen to and describe your partner's voice while discussing each topic.

## EXERCISE Personal Reflection

JOURNAL ENTRY #2

Make the following observations about yourself in your Theatre Notebook: What are my most interesting qualities? What things am I best at? What things am I worst at? What situations upset me? What situations rarely upset me that often upset others? What do people say about me that I agree with? What do people say about me that I disagree with? Why do I want to be involved in theatre? Which well-known actor seems to be most like me? Why? Which well-known actor do I admire most? Why?

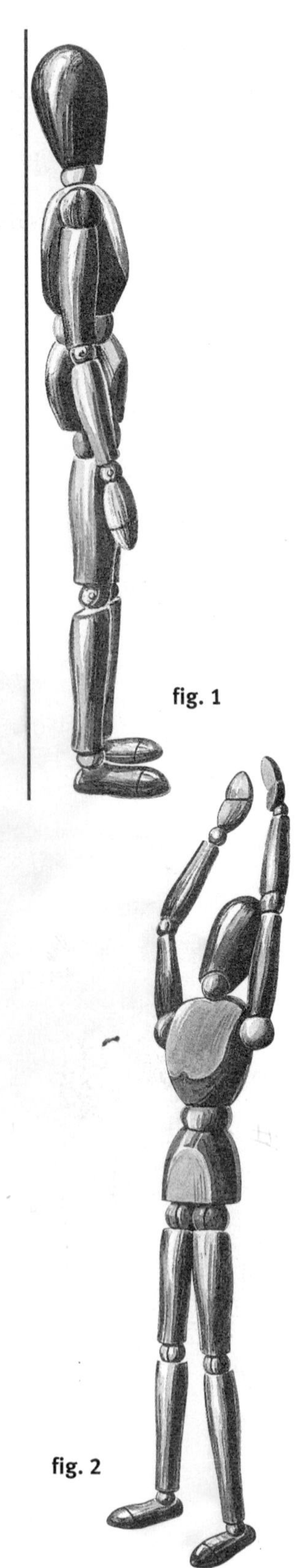
fig. 1

fig. 2

# The Ensemble Ethic

Awareness of self is only part of what it takes to be a successful actor. Awareness of others is essential. This book presents many opportunities to interact with other students who are interested in acting as well as those who are interested in directing, producing, and technical theatre. Through your interactions, you will begin to develop working, trusting relationships and to learn what it takes to be part of an ensemble, a group whose individuals function together to create a whole.

# Movement

As you explore how your body moves, you will discover its capabilities and its limitations. The exercises and activities in this chapter will provide you with ways to work on extending those limitations to ready you for the physical demands of acting.

## Posture

Your posture is your customary way of holding your body. A good posture not only allows you to relax while standing, it provides you the necessary balance for instantaneous movement in any direction. What is good posture? Stand with your feet a little apart, aligned under your shoulders. Imagine yourself suspended by a string from the top of your head. If you were to stand against a wall, your heels, buttocks, and shoulder blades would touch the wall, with your head balanced comfortably on top of the column formed by your body. (fig. 1)

## Physical Warm-Ups

Physical warm-ups prepare and energize your body for rehearsal and performance. Warm-ups loosen and limber up your muscles, leaving your body responsive and alert and thereby reducing your risk of injury, especially in vigorous movement situations. Warm-ups also help you remove mental and physical distractions and focus your full attention on the task at hand.

The next few pages present warm-up exercises you can do as an individual as well as exercises you can do as part of a group. To perform the exercises, you need a large open space free of obstacles. Wear clothing that stretches and is easy to move in; workout gear is ideal. Wear tennis shoes—or go barefoot, which will enhance your balance. If possible, do the warm-ups before meals or two to three hours after to avoid disrupting your digestion. Music may be used to maintain a steady rhythm. While performing the exercises, be attentive to the physical safety of yourself and others and respect everyone's feelings and ideas.

You may wish to have someone read the exercises while you perform them until you are familiar with the sequence of actions in each. Practice the exercises regularly to master them.

## EXERCISE Breathing

Stand erect with your feet shoulder-width apart. Inhale deeply through your nose as you count slowly to 4. Feel your chest expand as the air fills your lungs. Now exhale through your mouth as you count slowly to 4. Feel your chest relax as the air is expelled from your lungs. Don't let your shoulders move up and down. Repeat several times.

Next, lift your arms as you inhale to form an arch overhead where your fingertips touch. As you exhale, lower your arms back to your sides. Repeat 4 times.

Finally, inhale and form an arch again, but this time tilt your head back, stretching your chin up (fig. 2). As you exhale, bring your head forward to look at the floor. Repeat 4 times.

fig. 3

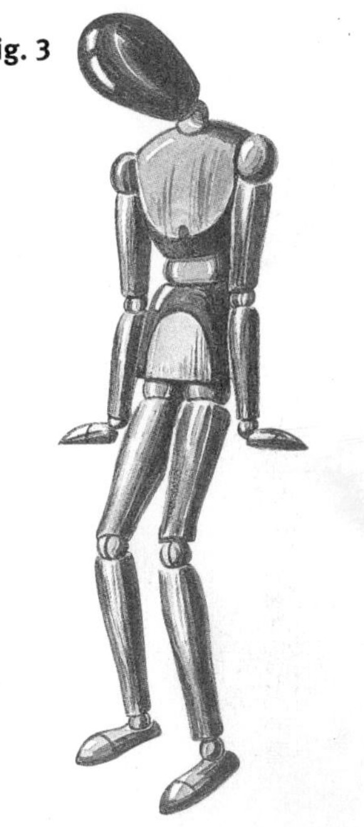

## EXERCISE Breathing with Resistance

Repeat the breathing pattern of the previous exercise, but this time when you exhale and tilt your head forward, open your hands as wide as possible with your palms facing out.

Pressing your palms out, bring your arms down to your sides. With your palms parallel to the floor, press down as if you were trying to push something through the floor. At the same time, bend your knees slightly. Your arms should be rigid as if some force is pushing them up as you are pushing them down (fig. 3).

Notice how this movement affects your air flow. You may need to exhale in short bursts instead of the 4-count steady flow. Repeat 4 times.

fig. 4

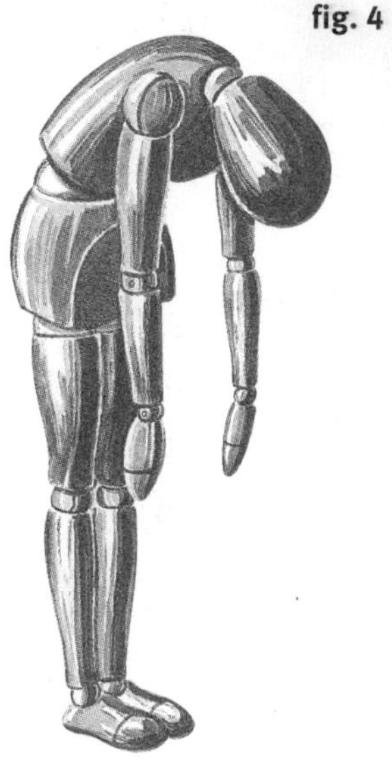

## EXERCISE Standing Alignment

Stand erect with your feet shoulder-width apart. Breathe normally, but deeply. Imagine a heavy weight is attached by a string to the top of your head, gradually pulling your head forward and down. Allow the rest of your body to follow your head and curve over, as if the vertebrae that form your spine were spilling over one by one.

Keep your legs straight and your arms relaxed and dangling (fig. 4). When you can't go any further, bend your knees slightly. Try to go a little further whenever you exhale. Shake your head lightly from side to side to release any tension.

After a minute or so, begin reversing the movement. Start from the base of your spine, feeling each vertebrae, one by one, return to its place. Keep your knees slightly bent until you are in an upright position. Bring your head up slowly. Repeat 2 times. Afterward lightly shake out your body.

## EXERCISE Lying Alignment

Lie on your back on the floor, legs together. Then slowly peel yourself up from the floor—head first, then shoulders, then torso—and fold yourself over the top of your legs as far as you can go.

fig. 5

Hold the position for a few moments, breathing evenly in through your nose and out through your mouth. You may gently grip your ankles or calves, but don't pull. Keep your head bowed against your legs (fig. 5). Recover by slowly rolling back down along your spine to your head. Repeat 2 times.

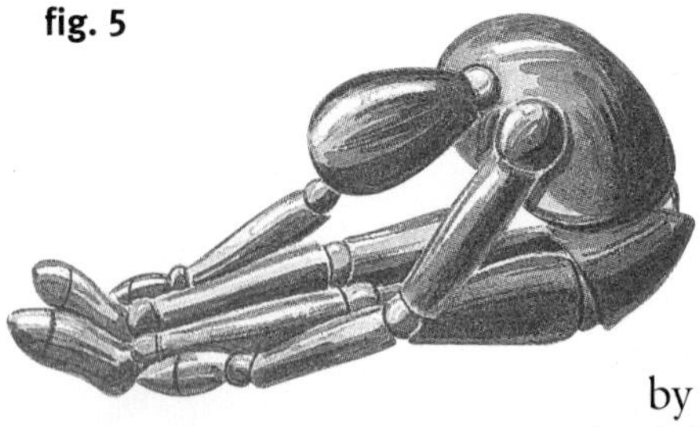

Next, turn over onto your stomach, placing your palms under your shoulders with your elbows close to your ribs. Rest your forehead on the floor.

Lift your head, followed by your body, away from the floor by straightening your arms. Press your shoulders down. Your back is now in an arch.

Tip your head back and look up, breathing evenly in through your nose and out through your mouth. Don't drop your head back. Tilt it back slowly, stretching your chin up (fig. 6).

Finally, bring your head back and lower your body, beginning with your pelvis and continuing until your chin rests on your hands again. Repeat 2 times.

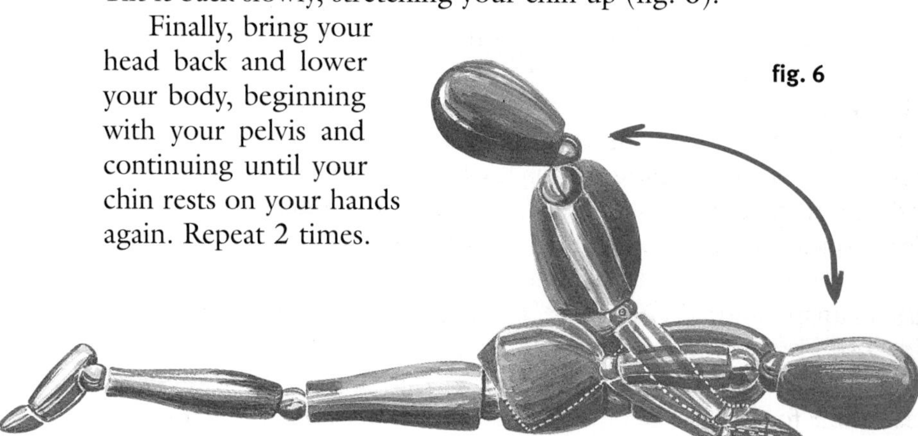

fig. 6

## EXERCISE Isolation

To isolate means to set apart or detach. In isolation exercises you move an individual part of your body without moving the rest of your body. This teaches you to control all parts of your body.

These exercises should be done slowly and smoothly. They should not hurt; if you feel pain, don't force the movement any further.

Music with a steady beat will be helpful for these exercises. Each movement takes 1 count.

**HEAD** Tilt your head forward and back for 8 counts. Be careful to tilt your head back slowly, stretching your chin up. Turn right and left for 8 counts. Tilt from side to side for 8 counts, keeping your shoulders level (fig. 7). Slowly circle to the right all the way around for 8 counts. Then circle to the left all the way around for 8 counts.

fig. 7

**NECK** With your arms overhead and your palms together framing your face, move your head from side to side for 4 counts and then circle it around for 4 counts, like an "Egyptian head" (fig. 8). Thrust your chin out and up and then return to normal (the "chicken neck") for 4 counts.

**SHOULDERS** With your arms relaxed at your sides, lift both shoulders up towards your ears and then press them down for 16 counts. Push your shoulders forward and then pull them back for 16 counts. Roll your shoulders back and around for 16 counts. Then roll them forward and around for 16 counts. Bounce your shoulders for 8 counts. Finally, shimmy for 16 counts (quickly alternate right and left shoulders forward as you bend up and down at the waist). Begin slowly and build in speed.

fig. 8

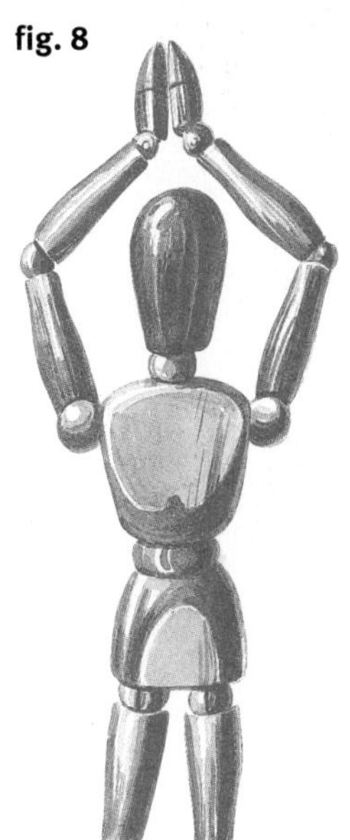

**ARMS** With your right arm, draw a big circle in the air to your right for 8 counts. Now do the same with your left arm to your left side. Then bend your knees as you swing both arms forward and around for 8 counts, straightening your legs when your arms return to your sides. Do the same, swinging your arms backward.

**RIBS** Keeping your shoulders in place, move your rib cage from side to side for 16 counts and forward and back for 16 counts (fig. 9). Move your rib cage in a square formation, forward to right to back to left for 4 times for 16 counts. Do the same in the opposite direction.

fig. 9

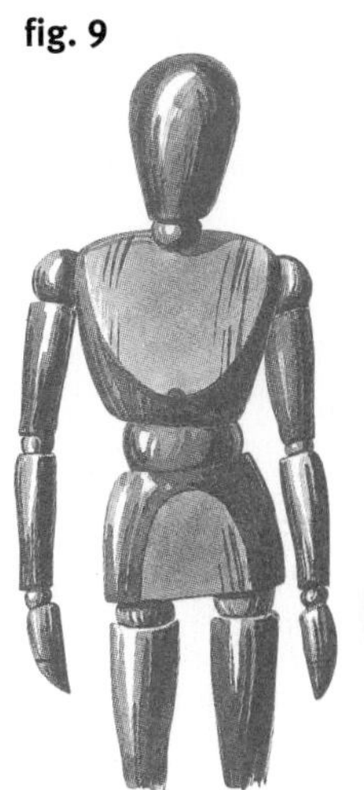

**OTHER BODY PARTS** Pretend you are working a hula-hoop with your hips. Circle your ankles and your wrists. Wiggle each of your fingers alone and in combinations. Make these movements slowly to a steady beat.

## EXERCISE Basic Stretching

fig. 10

Stand with your feet wide apart and slightly pointed out. Reach your right hand toward the ceiling. At the same time, bend your right knee so that your body weight shifts to the right side. Increase the resistance by reaching with your left hand for the floor (fig. 10). Shift your weight to the left side, straightening your right leg and bending your left knee. At the same time, switch arms, reaching up with your left arm and down with your right. Repeat rhythmically for 16 to 32 counts.

Do the exercise again, stretching your arms straight out to the side rather than up. Repeat for 16 counts.

Vary the exercise once more. This time, reach your right hand across your body toward your left foot. Then reach your left hand across your body toward your right foot. Repeat for 16 counts.

Finally, lightly shake out your body.

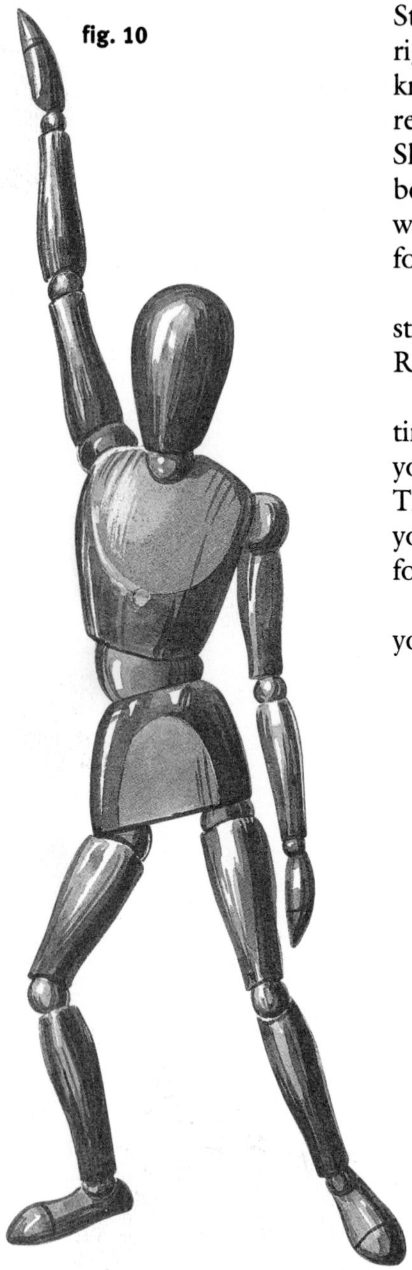

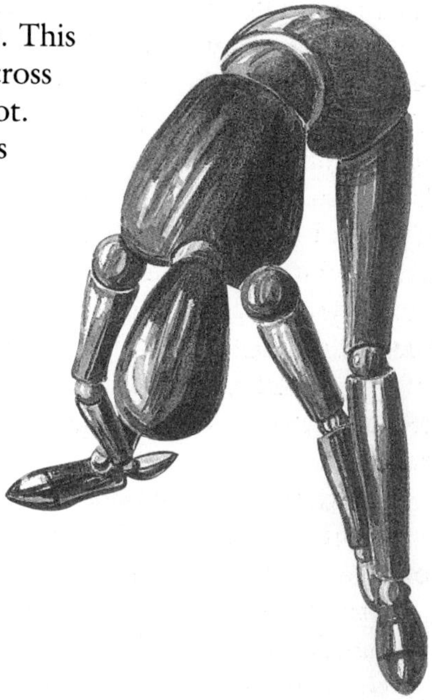

fig. 11

fig. 12

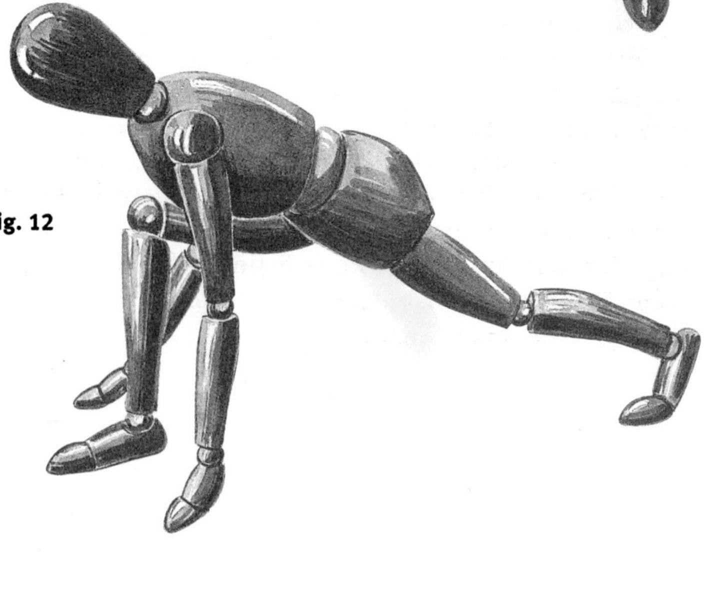

## EXERCISE Fold-and-Lunge Stretching

Stand with your feet wide apart and slightly pointed out. Bend over to grab your ankles or calves, or place your hands on the floor (fig. 11). Remain folded over, breathing evenly in through your nose and out through your mouth. Bend your knees and then straighten your legs. Repeat. Now spread your legs apart a little wider but stay folded over. Shift your weight from right to left in your hips. You will feel the stretch in the backs of your legs. Repeat for 16 to 24 counts.

Next, turn to your right and take a lunging position with your right knee bent and your weight on your right foot. Make sure your right knee is behind your toes, not over or in front of them. Put your hands on the floor on either side of your right foot. Your left foot is extended behind you, toes flexed under, with your left knee off the floor (fig. 12). Feel the stretch.

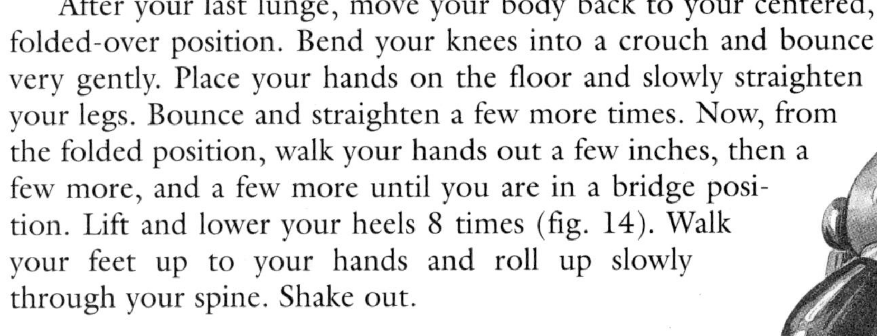
fig. 13

Now rest your left knee on the floor and stretch by straightening your back. Place your hands on top of your right thigh and push your weight forward. Return your hands to the floor and straighten both of your legs, keeping your body centered over your right leg. Remain facing right, but shift your weight back so that it's distributed between both your legs (fig. 13). Feel the stretch.

Finally, try to flatten your spine by pressing your chest lengthwise along your right leg. You may lift your head to increase the stretch. Repeat 2 to 4 times. Reverse the exercise by lunging forward on your left leg and stretching your right leg back. Repeat 2 to 4 times.

After your last lunge, move your body back to your centered, folded-over position. Bend your knees into a crouch and bounce very gently. Place your hands on the floor and slowly straighten your legs. Bounce and straighten a few more times. Now, from the folded position, walk your hands out a few inches, then a few more, and a few more until you are in a bridge position. Lift and lower your heels 8 times (fig. 14). Walk your feet up to your hands and roll up slowly through your spine. Shake out.

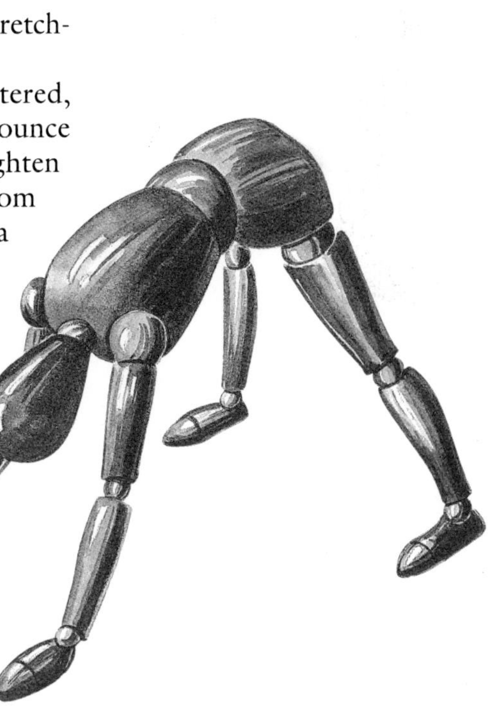
fig. 14

## EXERCISE Space Exploration

Working with a small ensemble of five to seven people, walk around in the space, using the entire area. Periodically, change your direction and pace; avoid colliding with each other. Take big or little steps, but keep up your energy and keep moving. Breathe evenly, in through your nose and out through your mouth.

Think about where you might be going—to catch a bus, cash a check, visit a friend, get to a class.

Now become aware of the other people in the room. Where might they be going? Follow someone. Be aware of who is behind you or beside you. Move faster. Weave in and out.

On a cue from a leader or teacher, freeze your movement. Observe the still photograph your ensemble has become. Then on another cue, start to move backward. Without looking, sense who is near or behind you.

Next try moving in slow motion. Notice how this changes your energy. Try to move in a crouch and on tip-toe. Can you stay balanced? Can you leap in slow motion?

Finally, try moving in fast-forward. Leap, collapse, roll on the floor. Freeze in some dramatic pose. Move and relate to others in the space. See if you can interact with them using only movement. Become someone's mirror or someone's shadow.

## EXERCISE Partners

Choose a partner. Facing your partner, move in any way you choose. Really tune into each other so that when one of you stops moving, the other does as well. Start again. Take brief or long pauses. There is no leader and no follower; it's a movement conversation with no talking allowed.

At some point, one of you should stop moving—yet remain involved—while the other continues to move. When the moving person stops, the still one should respond and start moving. Move in opposition to one another. Make your movement conversation interesting. Try to pass on information and energy to each other. Have a serious movement conversation; have a hilarious one.

## EXERCISE Rhythm

Rhythm is the pattern and spacing of repetitious sound or action or movement. It's the beat of the music or the quickness of your stride as you walk or run. Rhythm is important to an actor because it affects speed and timing and energy.

With the ensemble sitting in chairs in a circle, begin stomping out a steady rhythm with your feet. Use one foot, then the other, then both. Try different patterns and then find a new steady rhythm. One at a time, introduce your rhythm to the circle. Everyone will add a different pattern to the previous rhythm. Concentrate and maintain your rhythm as new patterns are introduced.

Now add your hands. Don't lose the beat. Make sure you find a rhythm you can hold on to before getting into complicated patterns. See if you can create different sounds by slapping your calves, thighs, chest, or other body parts.

Create an orchestra with your different sounds. Choose someone to be the conductor. Do a variety of performances—big and loud, very quiet, very fast, very slow, and so on.

## EXERCISE Cool-Down

Stand with your eyes closed, breathing regularly. On an exhale, squat down and allow yourself to roll through your spine until you are lying on your back on the floor.

Now inhale and curl up, bringing your chin to your chest. At the same time, bring your knees up and lock your fingers around them. Your spine should be rounded. As you exhale, slowly rock backward along your spine onto your shoulders and neck. Do this several times to relieve any tension, breathing in as you roll up and out as you roll back (fig. 15).

Now roll out and lie flat on your back again. Relax and feel your body growing heavy as if it were sinking into the floor. Slowly lift your right arm. Feel how heavy it is. Let it relax even more as you return it to the floor. In this way, individually lift and lower your arms, legs, hips, shoulders, and head. Now tense your right leg as tightly as you can. Then release it gently. Rock it back and forth. Repeat the process with your other leg, arms, torso, shoulders, and head.

Close your eyes and let your thoughts drift as if you were watching a movie. Don't dwell on any one image, just let the images come and go. After a period of time take a few deep breaths. Tense and release your whole body again. Open your eyes and wake up feeling refreshed and alert.

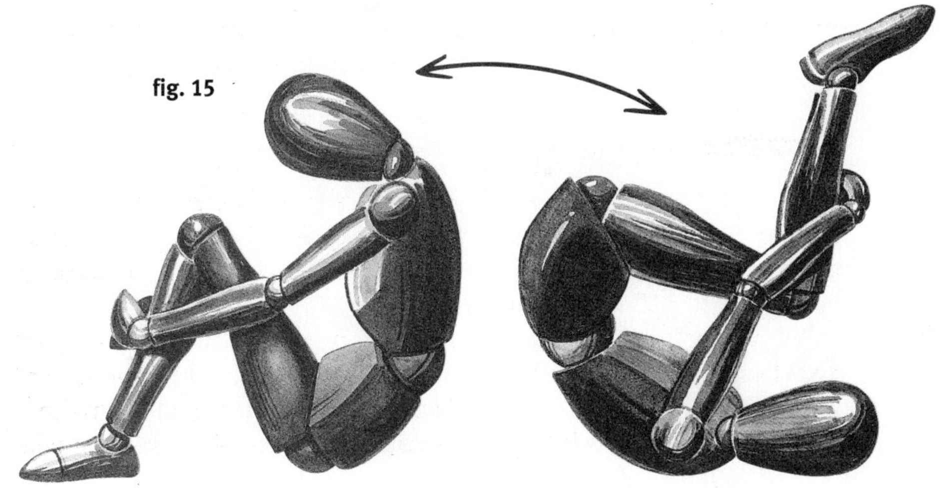
fig. 15

# Pantomime

Pantomime is acting without words by using facial expressions and gestures, expressive movements of the body or limbs. The term is used to cover several different types of movement:

- any movement that tells the audience something significant or meaningful about a character
- movement that tells a story through silent action alone
- movement that portrays an activity without using the actual objects involved in the activity

For successful stage pantomime, you need to use your facial expressions and body movements to communicate your reactions—physical and emotional—to characters, events, objects, and environments.

In his play *Our Town,* Thornton Wilder specified that actors pantomime scenes of daily life. What activity do these actors appear to be pantomiming?

To create the illusion of using imaginary objects, you need to portray their specific physical characteristics. Pay special attention to consistency—in spatial relationships and the shape of objects.

Strive to give your pantomimed actions and stories a beginning, middle, and end.

Used onstage, pantomime creates varied theatrical effects. In the final scene of Rodger's and Hammerstein's *The Sound of Music* the Von Trapp family escapes the Nazis by walking across the mountains from Austria to Switzerland. Creating realistic mountains onstage would be bulky and too expensive for a scene that lasts a few minutes; a backdrop and pantomime can do the trick. Thornton Wilder's *Our Town,* set in turn-of-the-century small-town America, includes many pantomimed scenes of daily life—cooking, sharing a soda, pumping water, delivering newspapers, and so on. Actual items could easily be used for these scenes, but Wilder specified pantomime. The effect achieved is an appropriate quality of universality and fluid transitions between scenes that shift quickly across time and space.

### EXERCISE Floating Ball

Take a tiny ball out of your pocket. It's a magic ball that floats in space. Place it in the palm of your hand and raise it to shoulder-height in front of you. Remove your palm from below it, leaving it floating in space just where you left it. Circle around it, admiring it from every angle. Take it out of the air and put it back into your pocket.

### EXERCISE Moving a TV

Imagine you are in your own room. You just got a new TV. Open the box and take it out, lifting with your body. Show expression of effort on your face. Place it in a spot in your room and plug it in. Step back and look at it. Fiddle with the reception. Change channels. Decide to move it. Unplug it and pick it up. Repeat the moving process several times before you finally decide on a spot and watch TV. Be careful to keep the shape of the TV and plug constant. Watch the cord and the antennae! Make the story—and each action—have a beginning, middle, and end.

# Voice

As an actor, your voice is a crucial element in your performance. First, it must be heard by everyone in the audience; not only because some of your lines contain information necessary to their understanding of the plot, but because audiences justifiably become annoyed when they have to strain to hear any actor. Second, it must convey the kind of character you are playing. Third, it must convey what your character thinks and feels about the events that are taking place. Just as you train your body to gain strength, flexibility, and endurance, you can train your voice to gain these same qualities.

## Diaphragmatic Breathing

Proper breathing is as essential for a stage voice as proper posture is for stage movement. For effective use of your voice as an actor, you need to learn **diaphragmatic breathing.** Your diaphragm is the connective muscle and tissue between your abdominal and chest cavities. In diaphragmatic breathing, your diaphragm contracts when you inhale, causing your abdomen to expand. This forces your rib cage to expand as well, enlarging the chest cavity. Air rushes in through your mouth or nose, down your windpipe, or trachea, and into your

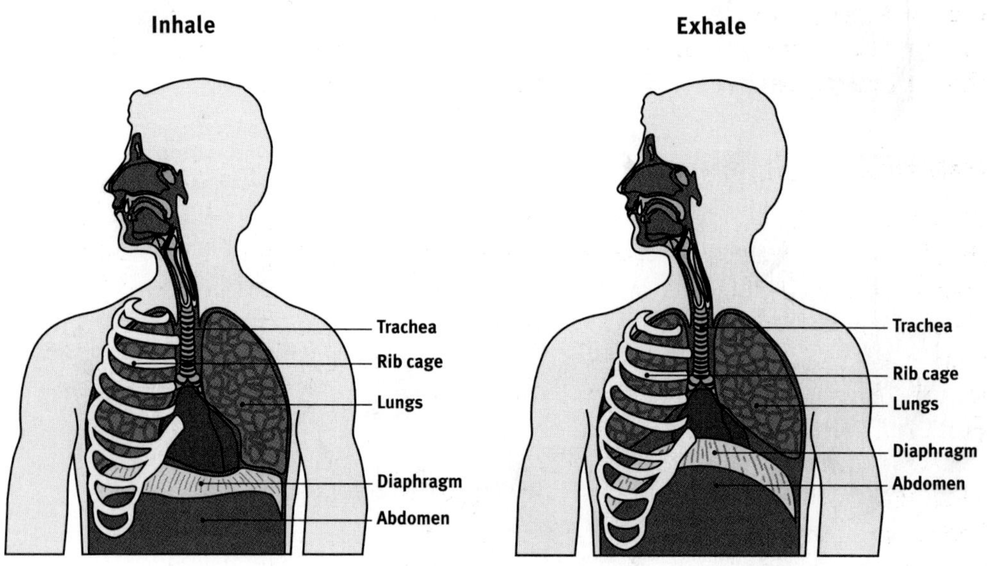

lungs. When you exhale, the process is reversed: your diaphragm expands and your abdomen and rib cage contract, forcing air out of your lungs.

Diaphragmatic breathing makes full use of the power of your diaphragm in the breathing process. It increases your air capacity and improves your breath control. Such control is vital for exhaling slowly and steadily, which allows you to sustain your breath longer and use your voice more efficiently.

### EXERCISE Diaphragmatic Breathing

Lie on the floor. Place a book on your stomach. Let your back widen as you relax in this position. Breathe deeply. The book should rise and fall as your abodomen moves in and out with the movement of your diaphragm.

Now repeat the exercise first sitting and then standing, putting your hands on your stomach instead of a book. You should be able to feel your hands move in and out if you are breathing from your diaphragm. Be sure to keep your shoulders level.

## Voice Warm-Ups

You can gain more control over your voice by doing some of the exercises on the following pages. Before doing any of them, however, you need to warm up your face and upper-body. Do some of the physical warm-up exercises described on previous pages or run through your personal physical warm-up routine if you have one.

### EXERCISE Facial Stretch

Pinch your face in toward the center: your eyes should be squeezed shut, your lips puckered, and your eyebrows pushed down. Hold for 3 counts. Then open up your face: lift your eyebrows, open your eyes wide, drop your jaw and open your mouth. You'll look like a *very* surprised person. Hold for 3 counts. Repeat several times.

Now stick your tongue out as far as you can. Roll it. Then flick it. Vocalize the syllable *la*. Find as many variations on that sound as you can make with your tongue. For instance, you can make trills or rolls. Next, repeat the vocalizing, but change your face. Try twisting it to one side or opening your mouth really wide. How do these expressions affect your sound?

If you feel any stress or tension in your face, lightly massage your jaws, cheeks, and temples.

## Making and Shaping Sounds

The air that supplies you with essential oxygen as you breathe also carries the sound of your voice. You inhale air through your nose or mouth, down your windpipe, or trachea, and into your lungs. When you exhale, air moves up your trachea to your voicebox, or larynx, which contains your vocal folds. When air moves through your vocal folds, they vibrate. Those vibrations are heard as sound. When you speak or sing you affect the sound by making constant adjustments to the shape of your vocal folds and the speed of the exhaled air.

The sound is further shaped in your mouth and throat. Vowels are open, sustained sounds. They make your voice audible, able to be heard. They are formed by the resonators—the hard and soft palates, throat, and sinuses. The openness and flexibility of your resonators affect your voice's resonance, a quality caused by vibration. Resonance enriches vocal tone.

Consonants are stopped or shaped sounds. They are formed by the **articulators**—your jaw, lips, tongue, teeth, and soft palate. Your skill at using both consonants and vowels affects your **articulation,** the clear and precise pronunciation of words.

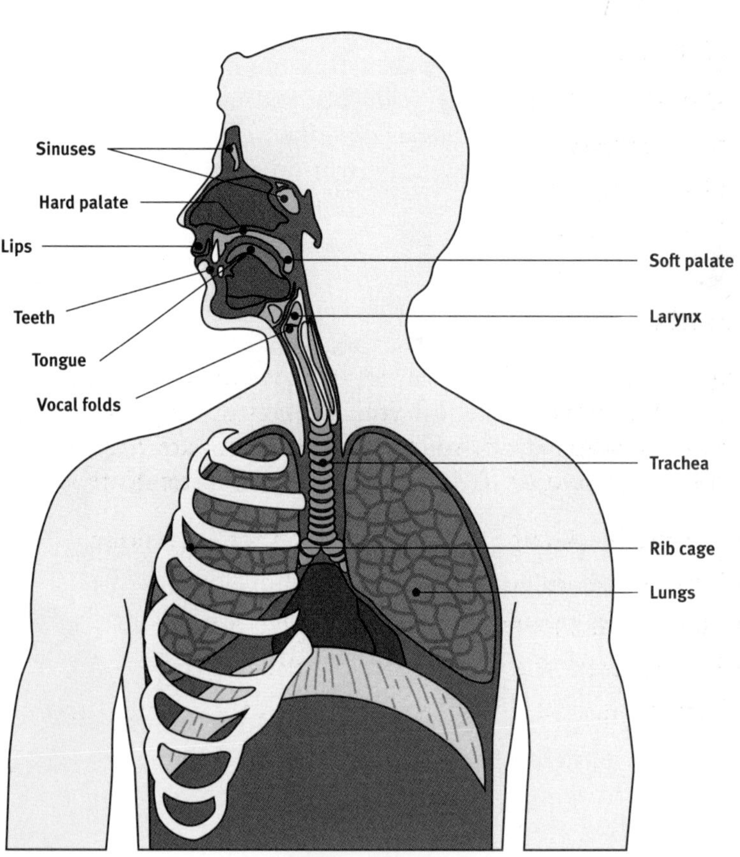

## EXERCISE Vowels

Stand or sit upright, with proper posture. Inhale and drop your jaw as far as you can. As you exhale, vocalize a prolonged *aaahh.* The sound should be placed low and in the back of your throat, and you should feel vibrations from the sound. Place one hand on your throat and the other on your chest to feel the resonance there.

Repeat this exercise using the vowel sounds in *make, deep, go, room,* and *join*. The sounds in *make* and *deep* are placed toward the front of your mouth; you may feel the vibration in your teeth and face. The sounds in *go* and *room* are placed midway between the front of your mouth and the back of your throat.

The vowel sound in *join* is called a diphthong, which means it's made up of two vowel sounds. It begins with an *oh* and ends with an *ee.* The back of your throat and the front of your mouth are both used to make this sound.

Vocalize the following syllables. Do the first group with a bouncing, laughing pattern. For each group, hold the last sound of each set until you run out of air.

1. He he he he
   Ho ho ho ho
   Ha ha ha ha
   Hi hi hi hi
   Hoo hoo hoo hoo
2. Me me me me
   Mo mo mo mo
   Moo moo moo moo

## EXERCISE Consonants

Tongue twisters can help you master consonant sounds. Practice reading these aloud in a firm voice. Then try reading them faster and faster, still articulating them clearly. You can create your own for all the consonant sounds. Write them in your Theatre Notebook.

- The big black bug bled bad blood on the barn floor.
- Burnt toast, toy boats.
- Aluminum, linoleum, chrysanthemum, geranium.
- The sick sixth sheik's sixth sheep's sick.
- I can think of six thin things and of six thick things, too.

## Projection

If you use your normal conversational level of speaking onstage, no one will be able to hear you except your fellow actors. Actors need to project their voices. To **project** your voice is to use it in such a way that it fills the performing space so that every member of the audience can hear and understand you. Merely increasing the volume of your speaking voice may not be sufficient. Shouting is not projecting. You need to focus your voice to a particular spot and to speak clearly with sustained control. Diaphragmatic breathing (p. 30) is important for projection.

Sometimes your character must speak in a very low voice or even a whisper. In the stage whisper, you use a lot of air but little volume, and your consonants come through more clearly than your vowels. If you are practiced in projection, the audience will still be able to understand you, even though you are whispering.

### *EXERCISE* Projecting to the Back Wall

Standing in a large room or theatre space, visually choose a spot on the back wall. Get into a comfortable position, take a deep breath, and project just the vowels of your name to that spot on the wall. Then project your whole name.

Lift your arms over your head and try the exercise again. You should notice that your sound is louder because you have more air power. The increase comes when your ribs are expanded, making more room for air in your lungs. Your objective is to achieve this increase from a normal position through diaphragmatic breathing.

### *EXERCISE* Long-Distance Poetry

Standing in a large room or theatre space, choose a point midway between you and the back of the room. Using diaphragmatic breathing, project your voice to that point. Speak nursery rhymes, lines of poetry, or song lyrics that you may know. After practicing several times, ask a partner to sit in that spot and give you an evaluation of how well you are projecting.

## Expression

You need to speak loudly and clearly onstage, but you also need to speak with expression. This means using variety in your voice to express your changing thoughts and emotions. This variety in speech is called **inflection,** and it can come through changes in these elements:

- **pitch** how high or low your voice is
- **volume** how loud or soft your voice is

- **tempo** how fast or slowly you speak
- **phrasing** how you divide your speeches into smaller parts, adding pauses to create emphasis and a rhythmic pattern of sounds and silences
- **quality** whether your voice is shrill, nasal, raspy, breathy, booming, and so on

Inflection can go far toward changing meaning or emotional content in a speech. Consider, for example, the far different meanings conveyed by the same speech with different words emphasized:

> ***I*** can't tell you not to go.
>
> I ***can't*** tell you not to go.
>
> I can't ***tell*** you not to go.
>
> I can't tell ***you*** not to go.
>
> I can't tell you ***not*** to go.
>
> I can't tell you not to ***go.***

## EXERCISE Changing Inflection

Practice saying a few simple sentences or a brief speech from a play using variety in pitch, volume, tempo, phrasing, and vocal quality. Try emphasizing different words. How does the meaning or emotional content change with each change of inflection?

## EXERCISE Nonsense Conversation

With a partner, have a gibberish conversation. Use the inflection of your nonsense words to express and convey your meaning to each other. If you can't think of words to use, simply repeat a syllable, such as *la*.

## EXERCISE Character Voices

Find a short poem or nursery rhyme. Read or speak it using various voices, such as that of a young child, a very old person, a whiny person, a laughing person, a whispering person, a raspy-voiced person, a nervous person, and so on.

# Improvisation

In theatre, to **improvise** means to speak or to act without a **script,** of the text of a play. In improvisation, or improv, you must create speeches and actions immediately and without preparation. This requires spontaneity, imagination, and the ability to use past personal experiences. When you are working with a partner or a group, it also requires that you pay close attention to what your fellow actors are saying and doing and respond accordingly; cooperative flexibility is vital for improvisation.

## Improvising a Sketch

Actors use theatrical improvisation in several ways. One is to work with others to create a sketch, skit, or short play. Often the particulars of the sketch—the characters, place, conflict, and theme—will be chosen at random or assigned to you just before you begin. You must make decisions about your character within seconds: Who are you? Why are you here? How do you feel? Do you have any special physical characteristics or gestures? What does your voice sound like? What do you want? You may not know who the other characters are until they begin speaking. Whatever your character does or says next should be in direct response to the other characters. Never deny what they present; work with them, not against them.

Some theatre companies, such as Chicago's Second City, have become famous for their improvisational comedy sketches.

Even though you have no script, it's still possible to give form to an improvised sketch. You can work together to determine a beginning, middle, and end. Try to establish the place and the characters' relationships as soon as possible. Then steer your character toward your goal or toward the end of the sketch. At the same time, the other characters will steer toward their goals or toward potential endings that you may know nothing about. Of course, your character can influence the other characters as much as they influence you.

### EXERCISE Liar, Liar

Work with a partner in the following improvisation game: Begin an action, for example, stomping your foot. Your partner asks you, "What are you doing?" You lie, saying, for example, "I'm swimming upstream." Your partner must then pretend to do this. Now it's your turn to ask, "What are you doing?" Your partner must lie, saying, for example, "I'm talking on the phone," which you must then do, and the game goes on. . . .

### EXERCISE Police and Suspect

Work with a partner to present the following improvisation: One of you is a police officer asking questions to a burglary suspect. The suspect was caught inside the mayor's house with a bag of valuables. The suspect must answer the officer's questions without admitting to the crime. The police officer must ask clever questions to trip up the suspect. Both of you must listen carefully and work with each other.

### EXERCISE Customer Service

Working with a group of five to seven people, improvise a busy customer service desk at a large department store five minutes before closing time. Appoint one person as store manager, one as a clerk, and the rest as customers. Each customer should determine the product they are returning or inquiring about. Work toward the goal to get out of the store with what you need before closing time. You have five minutes!

## Improvising a Character

Another way to use improvisation is in character development. While studying a script or in the early stages of rehearsal, you can imagine your character in different situations and improvise speeches and actions that are consistent with your character. This helps you get to know your character better and may give you ideas for vocal inflections or gestures that you can use in the scripted scenes. Skill in improvising can also come to your rescue when you are onstage with an actor who has forgotten his or her lines. In such situations, you need to ad-lib, another term for improvising conversation or action.

## Storytelling

Storytelling, in which one or more people tell stories to others, is often accompanied with dramatic movement and voice; thus, it can be considered the earliest form of acting. It has been around since the days of the cave dwellers whose wall paintings may have helped illustrate their stories. Myths, folktales, and legends probably evolved from those ancient stories. In some cultures storytelling is still used to transmit news and information to the whole village or to impart values from one generation to the next.

Storytelling isn't just for kids, as is evident from the enjoyment on the faces of the adults listening to a master storyteller at the National Storytelling Festival.

Modern storytelling and theatre have much in common. Both grew out of the impetus to share human experiences. To achieve that goal, both imitate those experiences in the dramatic presentation of a story to an audience. Like the storyteller, the playwright and screenwriter may use traditional or novel themes and characters to reinforce or challenge accepted ideas.

One major difference between the traditions of storytelling and theatre is that storytellers generally *tell* a story, punctuating it with the imitation of character voices and gestures, while actors generally *show* a story, supplying explanation when necessary.

Storytelling is characterized by the following elements:

- Storytellers acknowledge the presence of their listeners and interact with them, even changing their stories during the telling to get a desired response.
- Storytellers may take on many characters but usually don't stay in one character throughout the telling of a story.
- Stories told may involve many interwoven plots, span many years, and take more than one session to finish.

While some forms of theatre do contain these elements, the difference is a matter of degree.

The storytelling tradition is alive and well today. Professional storytellers perform at schools, community gatherings, and national storytelling festivals. Storytelling is a skill that most successful comedians, salespeople, motivational speakers, and religious leaders share, and its techniques can be seen daily in plays, movies, and television.

## EXERCISE Family Stories

Family gatherings are common places for telling stories. Think of a story about someone in your family that is often told at such gatherings. As a class, share these stories. Listen to the way your classmates explain the background of the story, describe the characters and the actions, and conclude the story. Which stories were the most interesting? Why?

# Activities

**Self-Awareness**

**VIDEO OBSERVATION** Using a videocamera, have a partner record your movements for about five minutes, making sure that your whole body is visible in the viewfinder. Stand, walk, sit, and talk naturally during this time. Pick a topic for discussion, such as family vacations, to make it easier. When you are through, videotape your partner's movements for five minutes. Play back the videotape. Write a short summary of your partner's outward appearance and characteristic physical movement and voice. Do the same with the videotape of yourself; compare it to what your partner wrote. Put the summaries about yourself in your Theatre Notebook.

**Self-Awareness**

**PHOTOGRAPH ANALYSIS** Collect as many informal, unposed photographs of yourself as you can. For each photo, make objective notes about your posture and movement, how you are interacting with any other people or animals in the photo, and what your facial expressions convey. Compare your objective observations with what you remember feeling at the time the photo was taken. Think about how you present yourself to others. Put the photos and your comments in your Theatre Notebook.

**Movement**

**PERSONAL PHYSICAL WARM-UP ROUTINE** Use the warm-up exercises described in the previous pages or others that your teacher gives you to put together a personal physical warm-up routine of about 15 minutes. Consider your body's strengths and limitations, what makes you feel good and what you feel you need to work on. List and describe the exercises that make up your routine in your Theatre Notebook. Run through your routine before every rehearsal or theatre class, or when you just need to get yourself energized.

**Movement**

**RELAXATION THROUGH STORYTELLING**
Work with a partner in this relaxation activity. Lie on your back on the floor, breathing normally, eyes closed. Remain still while your partner improvises a simple story for you, one that takes you through a peaceful environment; for example, "You're lying down on a soft hearth rug. A fire of sweet-smelling logs is burning low. Outside the window the snow falls softly. . . ." Allow yourself to relax deeply by visualizing the tranquil scene. When the narrative is finished, lie still for a minute or two. Then, switch roles and guide your partner through a relaxing experience.

PANTOMIME

**GROUP PANTOMIME** Begin by yourself with a tiny, imaginary ball that you casually toss and catch. Find a partner and throw the little ball back and forth. Have fun playing together. Gradually, the ball increases in size and weight, and it gets harder to throw and catch. Eventually it's too heavy for just two people to throw. Call in other people to help. Eventually your group gets the ball to move, but then you can't stop it! The ball becomes dangerous—like a truck rolling toward you!

PANTOMIME

**ATTIC TRUNK PANTOMIME** Use pantomime to create this situation: You discover a heavy trunk in a dusty attic and pull it out to the center of the floor. It's an old trunk with a rusty lock, and it's difficult to open. (Do you need to break the lock open?) When you get it open, pull out an old piece of clothing—a jacket, a skirt, a hat, a shawl—and try it on. (Is it musty? Is it soft or rough?) Find a jar with a wide mouth and screw the cap off. (Are the contents sweet, sour, or smelly?) Find an old watch, an expensive ring, or another piece of jewelry. Find an old photo album. What else can you find? When you have thoroughly investigated everything in the trunk, put it all back inside, close the lid, and push the trunk away.

PANTOMIME W/HMWK - PTS

**STORY PANTOMIME** Work by yourself or with others to tell a story without using words. It should have a beginning, middle, and end with specific characters and actions. Rehearse together, then perform your story pantomime for the class. Here are some situations that you might develop into stories:

- searching for something lost in a messy bedroom
- going for a ride with a reckless driver on a winding mountain road
- making a bungee jump from a bridge over a raging river
- checking out at a grocery store and realizing you have lost your money
- recognizing a childhood friend on a subway train
- trying on clothing you can't afford in a high-priced boutique
- getting annoyed with people in front of you in a movie theatre

# Activities

### VOICE

**PERSONAL VOICE WARM-UP ROUTINE** Use the warm-up exercises described in the previous pages or others that your teacher gives you to put together a personal voice warm-up routine of about 15 minutes. Consider your vocal strengths and limitations and what you feel you need to work on. You might want to combine it in some way with your physical warm-up routine. List and describe the exercises that make up your routine in your Theatre Notebook. Run through your routine before every rehearsal or theatre class.

### IMPROVISATION

**IMPROVISING SCENES** Work with a partner to improvise a scene based on one of the following situations or on a situation of your own creation. Try to include a beginning, middle, and end.

- You were taking care of your friend's cat at your house, but it has disappeared. Your friend comes to pick it up.
- Your mom reluctantly lets you borrow her car to celebrate getting your license. You break the side mirror pulling the car into the garage. Your mother discovers the damage.
- You confront a classmate in the library who has been spreading nasty rumors about you. You must do it quietly without getting thrown out of the library.

### IMPROVISATION

**PLACE & CHARACTER IMPROVISATIONS** As a class write a variety of places on one set of cards (for example, "a zoo") and a variety of people on another set of cards (for example, "a car salesman"). With a partner, draw one place card and two character cards and improvise a scene based on your choices.

*IMPROVISATION*

**PROP-PROMPTS IMPROVISATION** Gather together a variety of everyday objects—a hammer, a hubcap, panty hose, a mop, a fork, and so on. With a partner, choose an object as your prop and perform a quick improvisation with it—no more than 30 seconds. Use the object in the way it was intended or use it for another purpose entirely, essentially making it another object. Keep choosing until you have used all the objects, or let other pairs do a prop improvisation. Strive to give each improvisation a beginning, middle, and end.

*STORYTELLING*

**TALL TALE CONTEST**

A tall tale is a humorous story that uses realistic detail and a literal, straight-faced manner to tell about extravagantly impossible happenings. Create a tall tale to explain why you were once late for class or to explain some other event. Make it as outrageous and detailed as you can. Join your classmates in a tall tale contest, with the audience determining whose tale was the tallest.

*STORYTELLING*

**AROUND THE CAMPFIRE** Have everyone sit in a circle around an imaginary campfire in the center. If possible, dim the lights. Take turns telling scary stories. Tell your story as if it happened to you. Use a different voice for each character and feel free to gesture or to move around to illustrate a point. Include vocal sound effects for added interest. Work for an emotional response—fright—from your listeners.

*STORYTELLING*

**WARPED FAIRY TALES**

Choose a traditional folk tale or fairy tale and think of ways to "warp" it, like reversing the gender of the characters, changing the ending, or making the good guys bad and the bad guys good. For example, you might begin your story like this: "Once upon a time there was a beautiful little troll . . ." or "This is the story of the three little wolves . . ." Practice telling your story out loud, using a different voice for each character. Tell your story to the class and watch their reactions.

# *The* Storytelling Tradition

"The teller of stories," observes the great folklorist Stith Thompson, "has everywhere and always found eager listeners. Whether his tale is the mere report of a recent happening, a legend of long ago, or an elaborately contrived fiction, men and women have hung upon his words and satisfied their yearnings for information or amusement, for incitement to heroic deeds, for religious edification, or for release from the overpowering monotony of their lives." As Thompson points out, the storytelling tradition encompasses a great variety of forms, including myths, heroic legends, saints' lives, animal fables, family sagas, jokes and nonsense stories, and many, many others.

What is common to all these forms is the art of the storyteller. The best storytellers can captivate their audiences and hold them spellbound with what are essentially acting techniques, such as character voices and expressive gestures. Often they make use of repetition and rhythm—even music. A well-told story may hold the audience in suspense even when the listeners know how events will turn out—as is often the case with storytelling in oral cultures.

Every written literary tradition has been built on a foundation of storytelling and oral performance, for the art of words appears long before the art of writing. For example, centuries after a Greek expeditionary force destroyed the city of Troy, oral poets told and retold stories of the heroic deeds of the warriors on both sides. It was not until over four hundred years had passed that the Greek poet Homer gathered these stories together into the epics known as the *Iliad* and the *Odyssey.* Homer may have composed his poems orally, as his predecessors had; or he may have written them down, employing what was then a new invention—the Greek alphabet. The great mass of stories later collected as *The Thousand and One Nights* circulated orally for centuries in the Muslim world before they became associated with perhaps the most famous of all fictional storytellers, Scheherazade (shown here). The case of Scheherazade, though fictional, suggests the prominent role woman have always taken in the storytelling tradition.

Historically, the oral tradition of a culture has tended to be eroded by the arrival of print media such as books and newspapers. This process is being accelerated today by the worldwide influence of electronic media such as movies and television; however, the art of the storyteller continues to be practiced. Modern storytellers can be found today performing in schools and storytelling festivals and any other situations in which an audience is gathered to listen with imagination and appreciation. The stories told may be old—hundreds, even thousands of years old—but by the dramatic art of the storyteller they are rendered fresh and new.

## The Role of the Griot

One of the oldest and most distinguished storytelling traditions in the world is that of the West African oral historian known as a **griot** (grē′ō). Griots were once employed by kings and the wealthy to serve as living repositories of the histories of their dynasties and ancestors. As the scholar D. T. Niane observes, "each princely family had its griot appointed to preserve tradition; it was from among the griots that kings used to choose the tutors of young princes." In the 1950s, Niane recorded centuries-old traditions preserved by a griot from a village in the West African country of Guinea. These

A griot named Rafiki is a character in the new musical production of *The Lion King.*

stories recounted the deeds of Sundiata (sün jä´tä), who founded the Mali Empire in the mid-1200s. As the griot himself observes, "without us the names of kings would vanish into oblivion, we are the memory of mankind; . . . the world is old, but the future springs from the past. . . ."

The storytelling tradition was kept alive in Africa longer than in other regions, partially because written forms of many African languages were not introduced until comparatively recently, and partially because the African griot was so much more than just an entertainer. The griot—also known as *gewel, jaly,* or *ayan*—is the guardian and transmitter of a people's culture. The griot transmits from generation to generation the myths, legends, laws, history, and codes of behavior of a particular culture. The position of griot is highly respected, and it is often inherited. Some families in West Africa have claimed this honor for many generations. The griot recorded by Niane claims that his family has held the position "since time immemorial." The griot must therefore have an exacting memory to keep straight a vast amount of genealogical information, successions of royalty, and precise wordings of important decrees. The historical and spiritual life of the citizens of the community—past, present, and future—rest with the art of the griot.

In his 1974 book *Roots,* American author Alex Haley tells how he was able to use information transmitted through family storytelling to trace his ancestry back to "the African," Kunta Kinte, kidnapped into slavery in 1767 from his village of Juffure in The Gambia, West Africa, and of how he met the present-day griot of Juffure, who not only recited Kunta Kinte's lineage but told the story of his disappearance. Thus, names and details kept alive for 200 years were confirmed, as yet another generation made connection with its long-ago past. Comments Haley, "It is rightly said that when a griot dies, it is as if a library has burned to the ground."

## The Art of the Griot

A griot's storytelling is an event. It is frequently the focal point of a festival that the entire community attends. Drums and percussion instruments such as gourds or rattles may be used to set an insistent, hypnotic rhythm. The griot tells his or her story with skilled expression, changing voices for characters and adding gestures, movements, and vocal sound effects. Music is very important; the songs are an integral part of the storytelling. The audience is encouraged—and expected—to participate in the story as well by chanting repeated, formulaic responses or sometimes by taking up some of the songs.

The tradition of the griot had nearly died out by the middle of the 20th century. This was partly due to the impact of European colonization on traditional African societies. Added to this was a lack of any notation system that could supplement the written word in preserving melodies and percussive rhythms that are so much a part of the griot experience. Today, however, many dedicated people are using technology and developing new approaches to salvage what remains of this ancient and proud tradition.

(top) The roles of this griot of the Dogon people of Mali extend beyond storytelling; here he performs a ritual to foretell the future from animal tracks. (bottom) TAIFA, a modern African American storytelling troupe, performs at the National Storytelling Festival.

## Try It Out

Retell the following story in the words used here or in your own words. What different voices can you use to suggest the characters of the hero and his foe? Should you actually move into a different position to play each character, or simply turn from side to side? What expressive gestures can you make to dramatize their terrible threats to each other? Might some of this dialogue be effectively sung or chanted or accompanied by percussion instruments?

*from*

# Sundiata, *an* Epic *of* Old Mali

*Recorded by* **D. T. Niane**

The following excerpt is from an oral history of Sundiata, the founder of the empire of Mali in West Africa, who reigned from 1230 to 1255. The hero Sundiata and his evil opponent, the sorcerer king Soumaoro (sü mä ō´rō), taunt each other on the eve of the climactic battle that will decide who rules Mali.

Sundiata went and pitched camp at Dayala in the valley of the Niger [River]. Now it was he who was blocking Soumaoro's road to the south. Up till that time, Sundiata and Soumaoro had fought each other without a declaration of war. One does not wage war without saying why it is being waged.[1] Those fighting should make a declaration of their grievances to begin with. Just as a sorcerer ought not to attack someone without taking him to task for some evil deed, so a king should not wage war without saying why he is taking up arms.[2]

Soumaoro advanced as far as Krina, near the village of Dayala on the Niger and decided to assert his rights before joining battle. Soumaoro knew that Sundiata also was a sorcerer,[3] so, instead of sending an embassy, he committed his words to one of his owls. The night bird came and perched on the roof of [Sundiata's] tent and spoke. [Sundiata] in his turn sent his owl[4] to Soumaoro. Here is the dialogue of the sorcerer kings:[5]

**SOUMAORO.** Stop, young man. Henceforth I am the king of Mali. If you want peace, return to where you came from.[6]

**SUNDIATA.** I am coming back, Soumaoro, to recapture my kingdom. If you want peace you will make amends to my allies and return to Sosso[7] where you are the king.

**SOUMAORO.** I am king of Mali by force of arms. My rights have been established by conquest.

1. There is a transition here from narration to explanation and then back to narration. How might you show vocally what is going on?
2. This sounds like an important lesson for kings and villagers alike. How might you emphasize it?
3. Should the word *sorcerer* be stated matter-of-factly, or with mystery and dread so as to impress the audience?
4. How might you use movement and/or gesture to suggest the flying of the owls? How might you use posture to suggest the appearance of the perched owls?
5. Should the owls speak in owl-like voices or—magically—with the voices of the sorcerer kings?
6. Who is the hero and who is the enemy? How might you differentiate your character voices to suggest these opposing roles?
7. **Sosso** Soumaoro's capital

**SUNDIATA.** Then I will take Mali from you by force of arms and chase you from my kingdom.[8]

**SOUMAORO.** Know, then, that I am the wild yam[9] of the rocks; nothing will make me leave Mali.

**SUNDIATA.** Know, also, that I have in my camp seven master smiths who will shatter the rocks. Then, yam, I will eat you.

**SOUMAORO.** I am the poisonous mushroom that makes the fearless vomit.

**SUNDIATA.** As for me, I am the ravenous cock, the poison does not matter to me.

**SOUMAORO.** Behave yourself, little boy, or you will burn your foot, for I am the red-hot cinder.[10]

**SUNDIATA.** But me, I am the rain that extinguishes the cinder; I am the boisterous torrent that will carry you off.

**SOUMAORO.** I am the mighty silk-cotton tree that looks from on high on the tops of other trees.

**SUNDIATA.** And I, I am the strangling creeper that climbs to the top of the forest giant.[11]

**SOUMAORO.** Enough of this argument. You shall not have Mali.

**SUNDIATA.** Know that there is not room for two kings on the same skin, Soumaoro; you will let me have your place.

**SOUMAORO.** Very well, since you want war, I will wage war against you, but I would have you know that I have killed nine kings whose heads adorn my room. What a pity, indeed, that your head should take its place beside those of your fellow madcaps.[12]

**SUNDIATA.** Prepare yourself, Soumaoro, for it will be long before the calamity that is going to crash down upon you and yours comes to an end.[13]

Thus Sundiata and Soumaoro spoke together.[14] After the war of mouths, swords had to decide the issue.[15]

## Extension

Choose a folk tale or short story you know and create a speech for a narrator to set up the characters and situation. You might even write a ballad—or adapt an existing one—to perform this function.

8. In what tone of voice might such a boast be spoken?
9. **yam** a root vegetable like a sweet potato

10. Such boasting and name-calling survives today in the African American game of "playing the dozens." How might you expect an audience to respond to these lines? If you were to encourage the audience to respond orally, how and when would you do so?
11. The argument is escalating. At what point does it build to a climax?

12. How might Sundiata's "evil opponent" phrase such a terrible threat?
13. The hero Sundiata has the last word here. In what heroic, ringing tones can you conclude this argument?
14. What sort of transition might you make from dialogue back to narration?
15. If you are using a drum or percussion accompaniment, how can you use it to build this part of the story to a climax?

**". . . there is not room** for two kings on the same skin, . . ."

# Directing & Producing

**What happens onstage during a play is achieved through careful analysis, detailed planning, and exacting rehearsal—always in the service of an artistic vision of what the whole ought to be. This vision comes from the director and producer. They are the ones responsible for exploring each facet of a production and seeing it brought to life.**

## THE LANGUAGE OF THEATRE

**apron** the acting area of the stage that extends beyond the proscenium

**arena stage** a performance space in which the audience sits all around the stage; sometimes called **in-the-round**

**downstage** the stage area toward the audience

**house** the auditorium, or the area where the audience sits

**production concept** how the play should look and feel

**proscenium stage** a performance space in which the audience views the action as if through a picture frame

**scenery** onstage decoration to help establish the time and place of a play

**stage manager** the director's technical liaison backstage during rehearsals and performance

**thrust stage** a combination of the proscenium and the arena stages, with the audience sitting on two or three sides of the acting area

**upstage** the stage area away from the audience

# The Roles of Director and Producer

The **director** oversees the entire process of staging a production, coordinating everything that actually happens onstage. As a director, you read and re-read the script, interpreting its meaning and forming a vision of how the production should look and how the action should unfold. You then conduct auditions, choose the cast, divide the play into rehearsal units, and schedule the rehearsals. Through such techniques as placing or moving the actors onstage, you help them establish relationships between their characters, express emotions, and tell the story effectively. At each stage of rehearsal you evaluate both the total performance and the work of each actor. At the same time, you consult with the designers and technicians who construct and light the scenery, and provide sound, costumes, and makeup, as well as with those who will be in charge of a production during its run.

In the professional theatre, all these people—director included—work for the **producer,** who handles the business end of a production. As a producer, you secure rights to present a play, raise the money, hire the actors and the staff, arrange for the rental of the theatre, and supervise publicity and ticket sales. In school theatre, however, the director often also functions as producer.

## Emergence of the Director

In the acting companies of the late 1500s and the 1600s, there was no individual who fulfilled all the functions of a director in the modern theatre. An actor-manager was responsible for hiring and coaching the actors and acquiring the scenery. Although many different plays were performed, stage movements and the look of each production remained basically the same.

In the second half of the 1800s, theatre started changing. With an emphasis on theatrical realism and advancements in technology, sets and lighting became more elaborate, requiring more than the traditional actor-manager to unify and coordinate the efforts of all the individuals now involved in the production of a play.

George II, Duke of Saxe-Meiningen (1826–1914), is generally considered to be the first modern director, the first person to operate as a controlling force and guiding imagination behind a theatrical production. The Duke formed a private resident company of actors (called the Meiningen Troupe) at his small court theatre in Germany, designing all the costumes, scenery, and props. He was innovative in many ways, such as the use of platforms to provide more levels on which actors could perform, and presenting crowds as small groups that included main actors rather than the traditional line-up of people drawn from the audience.

## The Director's Skills

A director must have a visionary bent, a knack for seeing beyond the daily trials of the production process to the final, polished performance. A director must inspire, motivate, and focus people of varying talents and personalities toward the fulfillment of that common mission. Concentration, patience, communication, and imagination are therefore vital skills for a director.

A director must also have a strong visual sense to create clear, meaningful stage pictures. Balance and proportion in the arrangement of actors on a set is essential. Young directors often study art to attune themselves to the principles of size and shape, line and mass, color and pattern.

Since the theatre is a place of action, a director must develop skill at handling movement—its rhythm, pacing, and style. A director must be able to explain to an actor how and why a particular movement is necessary for a scene, to motivate the actor to perform the movement, and if necessary, to demonstrate it for the actor.

A broad knowledge of the technical areas of theatre and experience as an actor will make communicating your ideas easier and more productive.

Most importantly, a director must be able to analyze a play and present an interpretation of it through each stage picture, each movement, each word. One way to develop skills at play script analysis is to read as many plays as you can, sorting out characters' intentions, the significance of certain phrases, and the overall impact of the play. A knowledge of theatre history and history in general is also helpful for applying theatrical conventions and understanding the context of a play.

## The Director's Staff

In school and college theatre, a teacher is usually the director, but students generally fill the roles of those who might be considered the director's staff: the assistant director, stage manager, and prompter.

The **assistant director** helps keep the rehearsal process organized and running smoothly, taking on duties that range from coordinating rehearsal schedules and rehearsing movement with actors to making sure that actors are speaking the correct lines and that all the director's instructions are written down. In some theatres, the duties of the assistant director are handled by the stage manager.

The **stage manager** is the director's technical liaison backstage during rehearsals and performance, giving directions, solving problems, and ensuring smooth transitions between scenes. A sharp stage manager is key to a well-run show.

The **prompter**'s primary duty is to feed lines to actors when they forget them. The prompter must follow every line in rehearsal and

This scene from Joseph L. Mankiewicz's *All About Eve,* a famous 1950 movie about the theatre, shows an exchange between a producer and director during the casting of a show.

performance, knowing just when the line should be delivered, and providing assistance when it's not.

## The Producer's Skills

Because a producer is ultimately responsible for the financial success or failure of a show, financial management skills are crucial. A producer should not only understand the costs of running a typical production but be able to project and manage expenses for productions with special requirements.

A producer must also be able to predict an audience's reception of a particular play; this requires marketing savvy. Producers keep close tabs on successful plays and look for ways to deliver what the people want, while making a profit for the theatre company.

Like a director, a producer must be able to analyze a play, but with a slightly different intent: When a playwright or a director approaches a producer with a play, the producer must be able to assess both its artistic merit and commercial potential.

## The Producer's Staff

The wide range of responsibilities of the producer are often divided between the business manager and the artistic director. The **business manager** is responsible for fundraising, publicity, programs, ticket sales, and paying bills. In your school, a student or administrative staff member may perform the duties of the business manager. The **artistic director** handles hiring the director, cast, and designers. This role may be filled by a production committee in some theatres.

# The Production Team

From the beginning of the production process, the director and producer and their staffs work closely with the **design team,** those who will design and coordinate the production's set, props, lighting, sound, costumes, and makeup. Together these people form the **production team.**

The first production meeting takes place soon after a script has been chosen. In most cases, the choice of the play is made as early as possible to allow ample time for planning and if necessary, fundraising. Scripts are generally chosen by the director or producer. In school theatre, the theatre teacher or department may decide which plays to produce. In community and professional theatre, a board of artistic directors or a production committee may make such decisions.

## The Production Concept

The first production meeting addresses the script and the **production concept**—how the play should look and feel. The production concept is initially roughed out by the director, often in consultation with the producer, after a close reading of the script. The production team helps to refine the concept.

The illustrations on pages 54-55 reflect very different production concepts. The production of Shakespeare's *The Temptest* (below) uses glowing colors and striking textures to express the magical quality of the play.

Sophocles' *Antigone* uses the minimal sets and everyday costuming of ancient Greek theatre in muted contemporary forms. Can you see any similarities between this production concept and that for *The Tempest,* described on the opposite page?

In this first meeting, the producer may contribute ideas about how the play should be promoted to the community. The producer will certainly have budget issues to present. As a member of the production team, what you would like to do must be weighed against what you can afford to do. Some plays will appear to require more money to produce than others; however, there is almost always a way to produce a play without going over the budget if the production design team works together, pooling resources of experience and creativity. In school theatre, parents and community organizations are often willing to volunteer time and skills, contribute funds, and loan costumes or props; these efforts can considerably affect a production's budget as well as its quality.

Based on discussions in the initial meeting, the designers begin formulating ideas that will meet the needs of the production concept. Further meetings follow, some formal, some informal. Once decisions about the set design are made, rehearsals can begin. Changing needs discovered during rehearsals may necessitate adjustments to the set design, but eventually decisions about the set are finalized. Decisions about other aspects of the production design (props, lighting, sound, costumes, and makeup) are made throughout the rehearsal process. Sometimes the decisions are reached by consensus of the production team; sometimes they are reached between the director and another member of the team. Decisions involving additional expenses not foreseen in the production's budget usually must be approved by the producer. By opening night, all decisions have been made. The production concept has been brought to life.

# The Performance Space

One of the first and most important steps in your training as a director or producer—or as an actor, designer, technician, or writer for the theatre—is understanding the nature of the performance space.

Theatre is defined by three things: a story to tell, performers to tell it, and an audience to respond to it. That means theatre can happen any time or any place those three things come together. In fact, the times and places where theatre happens vary widely, as illustrated here.

DIRECTING
PRODUCING

## Types of Stages

The performance space influences practically all decisions made in the production of a play, including the selection of the play to be produced. As a director or producer, you must be aware of the performance space that you have to work with, of its potentials and limitations. You must know, in addition, something about performance spaces in general. Ordinarily, they are classified according to where the audience sits in relation to the performers.

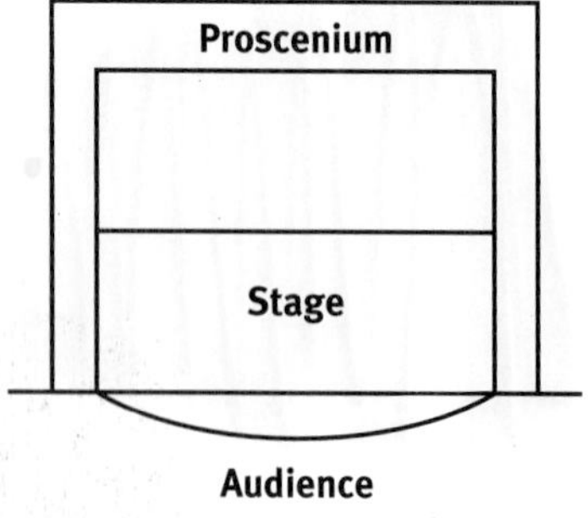

A **proscenium stage** is like a picture frame. The audience sits on one side to watch the action through the frame. Often, curtains hide the scenery until the play begins.

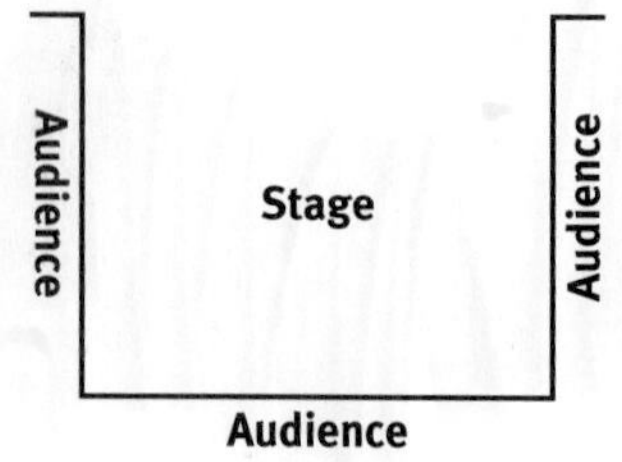

A **thrust stage** is a combination of the proscenium and the arena stages. The audience sits on two or three sides of the acting area, which projects, or thrusts, into the audience area from a rear wall, which has some kind of scenery. The actors enter and exit through the audience as in an arena stage and also through doors in the rear-wall scenery.

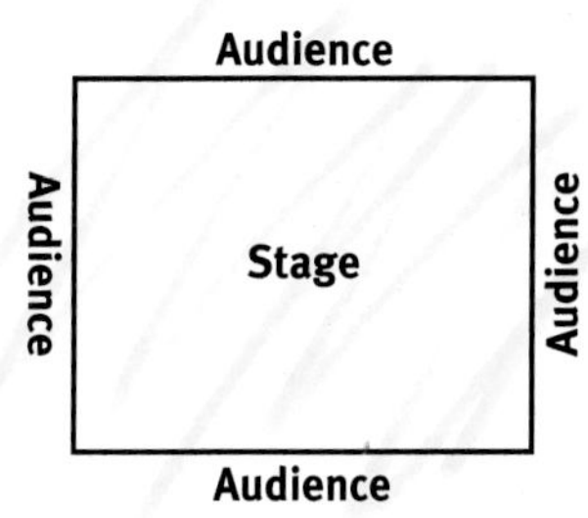


An **arena stage** is sometimes called **in-the-round** because the audience sits all around it. The actors enter and exit from the aisles or sometimes from tunnels under the audience.

## Theatre Space Layout and Terms

No matter what the type of stage, most of the terms used for the stage and audience areas are the same. To be able to communicate effectively and efficiently as a director or producer, you must understand the general layout of the entire theatre space and the terms that describe it.

### The Lobby

This is the area where the audience gathers before and after performances and during breaks. The **box office,** where playgoers can buy tickets, is usually located in the lobby. Theatre business personnel often have their offices attached to this part of the theatre.

### The Auditorium/House

The auditorium, or the area where the audience sits—no matter how it is arranged—is called the **house.** In many theatres, the down-front seats nearest the stage are called the **orchestra.** The **orchestra pit** is the area for musicians; it may extend underneath the stage. In some theatres, there are one or more **balconies,** projecting upper floors, with more audience seating. A lower balcony is often called a **mezzanine.**

At the rear of the house or the top of the balcony may be located a **light booth** or **sound booth,** or both, to house the technicians who control the lights, music, or special sound effects. In many theatres, these controls are in the backstage area.

## The Stage House

The **stage house** is the area including the **stage,** where the actors perform, and the **fly space** above, where lights and scenery may be flown, or suspended on ropes. In a proscenium stage theatre, the area begins just behind the **proscenium arch,** the picture frame through which the scenery and action are viewed. The **scenery** consists of onstage decoration to help establish the time and place of a play. Several layers of curtains can close off the stage from the audience's view: a **fire curtain,** consisting of metal or fireproof fabric to prevent fire from spreading; an **act curtain,** for between scenes, which is of lighter fabric and is decorated in keeping with the mood or theme of the play; and the **grand drape,** the front curtain, which is typically made of luxurious fabric in deep colors. Proscenium stages often include an **apron,** an acting area that extends forward beyond the arch. In proscenium and thrust stages, the **back wall** of the stage house separates it from the backstage area. Doors in the back wall allow large pieces of scenery to be brought onstage.

## Backstage

The **backstage** area defines all areas other than the acting space. It includes the **wings,** the area immediately outside the scenery, unseen by the audience. In the wings is the **stage manager's booth,** the place from which the stage manager calls the actors to the stage, gives the order to raise or lower the curtain, gives cues to both the lighting and sound crews, and supervises changes of scenery. Also in the wings is the **prop table,** where all items carried onstage by the actors are placed. Depending on the building that houses the theatre, the backstage area may also include a **call board,** a bulletin board on which are posted rehearsal times, performance changes, and special notices; **dressing rooms,** private or semiprivate areas where actors put on makeup, change clothes, and store their costumes for a show; a **makeup room,** separate from the dressing room and devoted to makeup; and a **green room,** a lounge area in which actors may wait while not onstage or greet audience members after the performance. Many theatres also have a backstage **stage door,** a private door for actors and theatre personnel, not accessible to the audience.

In addition, the backstage area of most theatres includes storage for lights, permanent scenery pieces, and furniture; a **scene shop,** where scenery is built; perhaps a separate **paint shop,** where scenery is painted; a **costume shop,** where costumes can be made, maintained, and stored; and a **prop shop,** where props are constructed or stored.

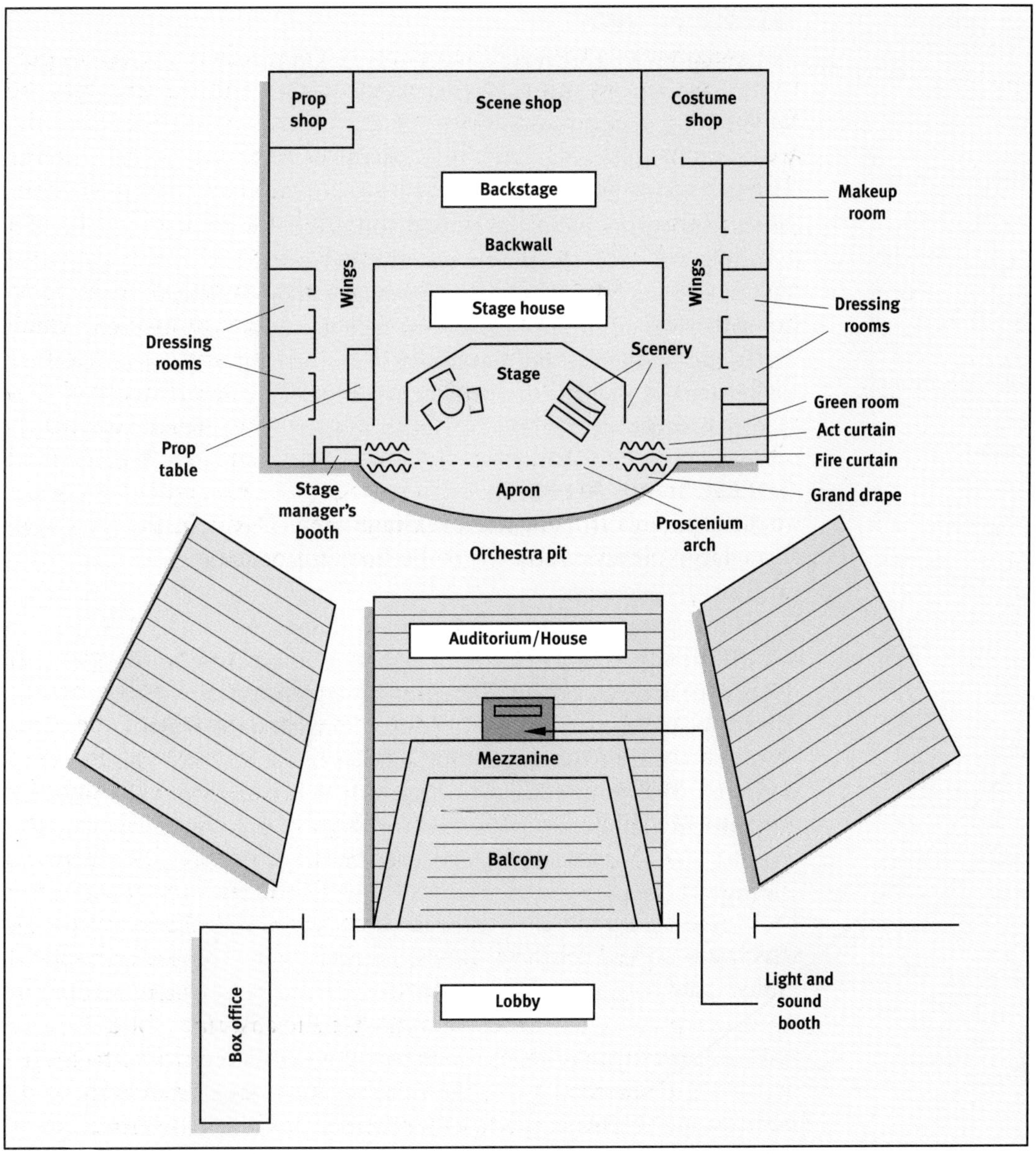
Prop shop
Scene shop
Costume shop
Backstage
Makeup room
Backwall
Wings
Wings
Stage house
Dressing rooms
Dressing rooms
Scenery
Stage
Green room
Act curtain
Prop table
Fire curtain
Stage manager's booth
Apron
Grand drape
Proscenium arch
Orchestra pit
Auditorium/House
Mezzanine
Balcony
Light and sound booth
Lobby
Box office

Theatre space layout

DIRECTING
PRODUCING

# Stage Areas

In addition to the terms used for different areas of the theatre, actors, directors, and technical crews have a kind of shorthand to identify areas of the stage.

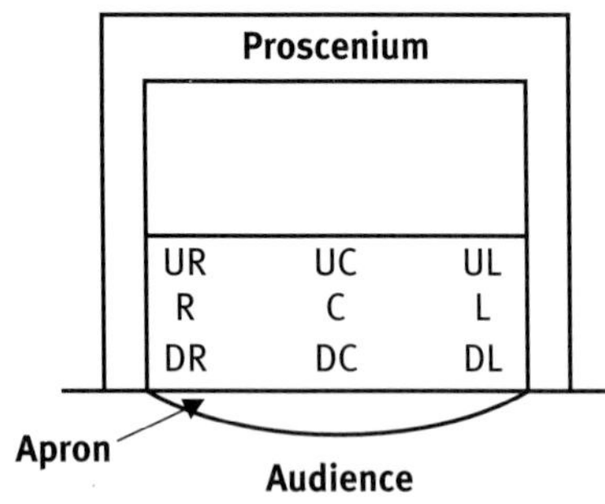


## Proscenium Stage Areas

Since the terms were developed long ago by actors and directors working on proscenium stages, the perspective is that of an actor facing the audience from such a stage. **Right** and **left,** for example, refer to your right and left as you face the audience. **Upstage** is away from the audience, and **downstage** is toward the audience. **Center,** or **centerstage,** is the center of the acting area. To these nine stage areas, some directors prefer to add right- and left-of-center designations.

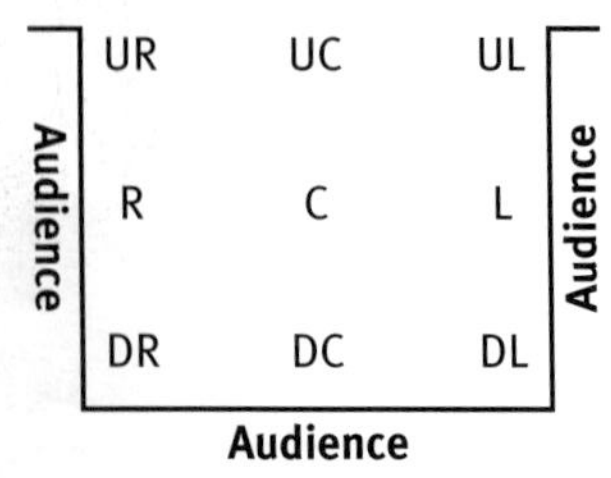


## Thrust Stage Areas

A thrust stage can be labeled in the same way as a proscenium stage. Upstage is always away from the audience, in the direction of the wall or the scenery.

Thrust stages come in a variety of shapes. Modified thrust stages are theatres with a proscenium opening and a large apron that projects into the audience. The performance area of the thrust stage that appears on p. 58 has a herringbone shape. Shakespeare's Globe Theatre was a thrust stage. One scholar has speculated that the playwright's frequent resort to lines that break into three parts—"Tomorrow and tomorrow and tomorrow" and "Friends, Romans, countrymen"—reflects the need to address the three sides of the acting area.

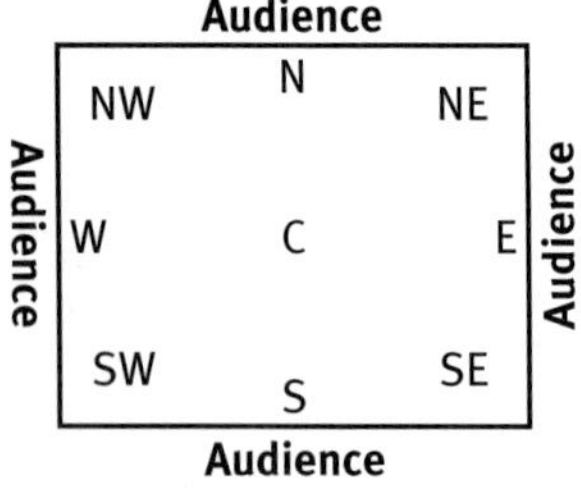


## Arena Stage Areas

Since arena stages have audiences on all sides, every direction is toward the audience, and up and down are irrelevant. Instead, actors may use the compass method. One area, probably a main entrance, is called north; the outer edge of the stage is labeled with the other points of the compass. Another method is the clock method, in which the main entrance is called 12 o'clock; the outer edge of the stage is labeled with the other hours of the clock. As with the proscenium stage, the center of the acting area is labeled **C** for **center.**

**Key**

| | |
|---|---|
| R = right | N = north |
| L = left | S = south |
| U = upstage | E = east |
| D = downstage | W = west |
| C = center | |

## Upstage/Downstage

The terms *upstage* and *downstage* have their origin in an innovation in stage design that was introduced during the Renaissance. In the playhouses of the time, audiences were seated (or stood) on a level space in front of the stage. In order to give them a better view (and to heighten the illusion of depth created by the perspective employed in Renaissance scenic design), the stage floor was actually slanted upward, or **raked,** toward the back of the stage. An example of a mobile raked stage can be seen in this illustration, which depicts a travelling company of actors in the mid-1600s.

# Activities

*The Roles of Director and Producer*

**STAGE PICTURE SCRAPBOOK** Begin a collection of striking images to serve as a visual resource in developing production concepts. Look for pictures that evoke a particular feeling and those that have interesting compositions of people and settings. Collect images representing a variety of visual styles and historic periods. Note how color is used and the way your eye moves across the images to a focal point. Write your responses to these pictures in your Theatre Notebook.

*The Roles of Director and Producer*

**FORM A PLAY CLUB** Gather together a small group of students and form a Play Club in which you read and periodically meet to discuss plays. You can start with a list of suggested plays provided by your teacher or librarian. Explore area bookstores and the libraries for additional interesting titles. Record ideas discussed at your Play Club in your Theatre Notebook.

*The Roles of Director and Producer*

**JOB SHADOW—BUSINESS MANAGER** Arrange with an area theatre or other business to observe a business manager at work for a day or a few hours; if you are especially interested in theatre or the arts, but cannot coordinate job shadowing at a theatre, consider inquiring at other arts organizations, such as art councils, cultural centers, and museums. Explain that you are interested in witnessing the day-to-day operations of a business manager. Professionals are busy, but if you are polite as well as interested, they are usually willing to let you observe them at work and to answer questions about their training and background. Be sure to first get permission from your parents, teacher, and the supervisor of the business or organization where you will job shadow.

*The Production Team*

**PAST PRODUCTIONS SURVEY** If your school has files on past productions, get permission to review them. Look at the choices made—type of play, casting, performance space. Can you find out who made the choices—the director, producer, or a production team? What can you find out about the production concept for the shows? How much did the shows cost and how much money did they make? What conclusions can you draw about the success of the productions? Can you make any judgments about the type of play audiences prefer to see at your school? Use this information to evaluate play scripts in your school and community library. See if you can make a choice about an appropriate production for your community. Write about your survey and your choice in your Theatre Notebook.

### The Production Design Team

**GO TO SEE A PLAY** As a group, with your family, or as an individual go see a play. Observe the audience and the performance space. Study the program, which usually identifies all the personnel involved in the production. Think about what problems, limitations, or budget issues the production design team may have dealt with. Predict what their concept may have been. Did they achieve it? What was your overall impression? Discuss your observations with the class or write them down in your Theatre Notebook.

### The Production Design Team

**PRODUCTION CONCEPT ANALYSIS** Think about a film or TV program that you enjoy—*Clueless, Titanic, The X-Files, The Simpsons*—and analyze the production concept it reflects. What kind of images come to your mind when you think about this production? What forms and colors predominate? What prevailing mood does the production convey? When you have analyzed the different elements that contribute to the overall production concept, then summarize them and include your analysis and summary in your Theatre Notebook.

### The Performance Space

**DIAGRAM YOUR THEATRE SPACE** Working by yourself or with a partner, construct a diagram of your school's stage and backstage areas. Measure the areas carefully so that you can draw your diagram to scale, or in direct ratio to the size of the actual space; for example, 1 inch on your diagram equals 4 feet in the actual space.

### The Performance Space

**THEATRE SPACE INVENTORY** Working by yourself or with a partner, take inventory of your school's stage and backstage areas. Make a chart that lists all the theatre space terms in the descriptions or the diagram. Create columns labeled Have and Lack. If your school's theatre has a sound booth in the house, for example, put a check in the Have column; if it has no stage manager's booth, check the Lack column.

### The Performance Space

**LEARN YOUR STAGE AREAS** Working with a partner, use masking tape to divide your school's stage or other large floor space into the areas shown in diagrams for the proscenium stage. (If your school has an arena or thrust stage, use the appropriate diagram.) Have the first person give directions, such as "up right center, up left, down left," while the second person moves to those areas as quickly as possible. Then switch roles. Continue until you both have memorized the stage areas.

HISTORICAL PROFILE

# Sophocles

Sophocles (sof´ə klēz), one of the three greatest writers of Greek tragedy, lived from about 496 to 406 B.C. The son of a wealthy manufacturer, he lived his entire life in Athens, at the height of that city's political and cultural success. The young Sophocles studied what we would now call theatre arts. He entered the annual theatrical competitions sacred to the god Dionysus, both as actor and playwright. In 468 his play won first prize; but soon, because of his relatively weak voice, he gave up performing. During his long career Sophocles wrote 123 plays; 24 of them won first prize, and the rest second.

Sophocles was a conscious innovator in the theatre. He was the first playwright to have three actors onstage at the same time, which allowed for the development of more dramatically complex scenes. He increased the number of singers in the **chorus,** a group of performers in Greek theatre who functioned as a commentary on and as an accompaniment to the action of a play. Breaking with the past, he turned from the tradition of writing three interconnnected plays featuring a diversity of characters to writing single dramas of concentrated action that focus upon a dominant individual. Sophocles wrote about a partly-mythical heroic era of Greek history; yet he did not evade contemporary problems, but used the ancient tales to comment on the Greece of his own time. Today only seven of Sophocles' tragedies survive. They include *Oedipus the King, Oedipus at Colonus, Antigone,* and *Electra. Oedipus the King* has been called the most perfect example of Greek tragedy that we have today.

## The Theatre Space

Greek drama was not simply entertainment; it had links with sacred ritual and with the Athenian social and political system. All plays were written for the annual spring festival of Dionysus, held in a large open-air theatre built into the natural slope of a hill. (The illustration on the right shows the Theatre of Dionysus at Athens.) The theatre held 14,000 to 15,000 spectators seated on bleachers. Performances took place during daylight hours on the **orchestra,** a semicircular stone pavement with an altar in the center. This area was backed by a permanent building called the **skene,** (skē´nē) which served as a setting for all plays. In front of the skene was a framework called the **proskenion** (prō skē´nē on) that supported a wide, shallow stage. (Skene and proskenion survive in our modern words *scene* and *proscenium.*)

## The Conventions of Greek Drama

Because the Greek outdoor theatre was so large, actors could not depend on facial expressions or vocal inflections to convey their characters. Presumably, they had to rely on large, simple physical gestures and on their ability to declaim the poetry of the script. They were helped by donning stylized character masks (like the one being held by an actor in the fragment of a Greek vase painting shown on page 68). Such masks could easily be seen from the top rows of the audience; some researchers believe that these masks also acted as megaphones to help project the voice. These masks also helped just three actors to play all the roles in a play, including the female characters—there were no actresses.

In addition to the leading actors, there was a chorus of perhaps 15 actors who represented townspeople or other groups. The chorus undoubtedly remained in the orchestra where they sang, danced in ritualistic, formal patterns, and commented on the action. Because the original texts of Greek dramas rarely have stage directions, we don't know whether the main characters moved among the chorus at times or confined themselves to the raised stage.

## Style of Costumes

Theatrical costumes were essentially the same as the Greeks' daily wear, with perhaps some exaggeration for effect. Both men and women draped themselves in robes of finely woven wool or linen. Although much variety was possible through draping, pleating, tucking, and layering, there was little tailoring—the basic dress remained the simple rectangular shape in which cloth had been woven on the loom (see illustration, p. 72). A variety of colors was available through dyeing, however, and elaborate patterns were embroidered or woven into the cloth. These robes were held in place with pins, laces, or belts. Both men and women wore sandals, but men—especially soldiers—sometimes wore calf-high boots. With the addition of a top robe and the switch of a mask, an actor could complete a costume change within minutes and be ready to portray a different character. Chorus members probably dressed alike, or in variations on a basic pattern, and wore similar masks.

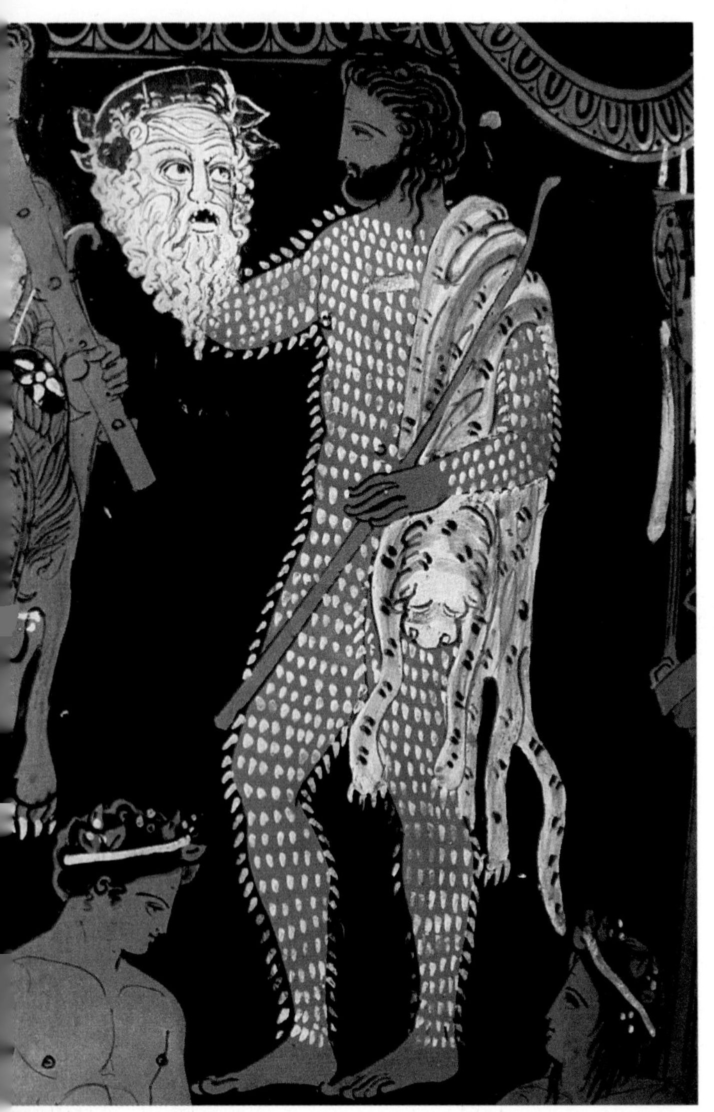

## Try It Out

Work with your actors to plan and stage the following scene from Sophocles' play *Antigone*. Depending on your resources, you may want to try one or more of the following approaches.

1. Make simple masks—flat cardboard ones will do—for the actors to perform in. Be sure that holes for eyes and mouth are large enough so the actors can see and speak clearly.
2. Stage the scene in a large space, such as a gymnasium or football field, to see what effect this has on voice and movement.
3. Stage the scene with two males wearing female masks, as the Greeks did.

*from*

# Antigone

*Translated by* **Robert Fagles**

**A**ntigone (an tig´ ə nē) and Ismene (is mē´nē) are daughters of Oedipus (ed´ ə pəs), once king of Thebes, an ancient Greek city. But their brothers Eteocles (e tē´ ə klēz) and Polynices (pôl ə nī´sēz) have just killed each other in a bloody civil war over who would become king, and their uncle, Creon (krē´on), has taken the crown himself. Creon, calling Polynices a traitor, has forbidden anyone to bury him, which according to Greek religion means that he will be denied access to the land of the dead.

**ANTIGONE.** My own flesh and blood—dear sister, dear Ismene,[1]
how many griefs our father Oedipus handed down!
Do you know one, I ask you, one grief
that Zeus[2] will not perfect for the two of us
while we still live and breathe? There's nothing,
no pain—our lives are pain—no private shame,
no public disgrace, nothing I haven't seen
in your griefs and mine. And now this:
an emergency decree, they say, the Commander[3]
has just now declared for all of Thebes.
What, haven't you heard?[4] Don't you see?
The doom reserved for enemies
marches on the ones we love the most.

**ISMENE.** Not I, I haven't heard a word, Antigone.
Nothing of loved ones,
no joy or pain has come my way, not since
the two of us were robbed of our two brothers,
both gone in a day, a double blow[5]—

1. Since there is no curtain, the actors must enter in view of the audience. Should they enter together or come from different entrances? If so, who enters first?

2. **Zeus** (züs) the chief god of the Greeks, ruler of gods and human beings

3. **Commander** Creon

4. What action does Ismene do to make Antigone ask this?

5. There are many speeches of pain, disgrace, and doom in this scene. How might you pace it so that it builds to a climax?

6. **Argos** town in southern Greece, enemy of Thebes, in the recent war.

7. What actions are suggested by Antigone's words about bringing Ismene to a private place?

8. How might Ismene react physically here?

9. How might Antigone show her outrage both vocally and physically?

10. How does Antigone regard Creon? How might she say his name?

11. How might Antigone demonstrate her own sense of "breeding" through her posture?

not since the armies of Argos[6] vanished,
just this very night. I know nothing more,
whether our luck's improved or ruin's still to come.

**ANTIGONE.** I thought so. That's why I brought you out here,
past the gates, so you could hear in private.[7]

**ISMENE.** What's the matter? Trouble, clearly . . .
you sound so dark, so grim.[8]

**ANTIGONE.** Why not? Our own brothers' burial!
Hasn't Creon graced one with all the rites,
disgraced the other? Eteocles, they say,
has been given full military honors,
rightly so—Creon has laid him in the earth
and he goes with glory down among the dead.
But the body of Polynices, who died miserably—
why, a city-wide proclamation, rumor has it,
forbids anyone to bury him, even mourn him.[9]
He's to be left unwept, unburied, a lovely treasure
for birds that scan the field and feast to their heart's content.

Such, I hear, is the martial law our good Creon[10]
lays down for you and me—yes, me, I tell you—
and he's coming here to alert the uninformed
in no uncertain terms,
and he won't treat the matter lightly. Whoever
disobeys in the least will die, his doom is sealed:
stoning to death inside the city walls!

There you have it. You'll soon show what you are,
worth your breeding,[11] Ismene, or a coward—
for all your royal blood.

**"He's to be left unwept, unburied, a lovely treasure for birds that scan the field and feast to their heart's content."**

unwept

UNBURIED

**ISMENE.** My poor sister, if things have come to this,
who am I to make or mend them, tell me,
what good am I to you?

**ANTIGONE.** Decide.
Will you share the labor, share the work?

**ISMENE.** What work, what's the risk? What do you mean?

**ANTIGONE.** *(raising her hands).*[12] Will you lift up his body with these bare hands
and lower it with me?

12. How large a gesture would be effective here?

**ISMENE.** What? You'd bury him—
when a law forbids the city?[13]

13. How should Ismene react at hearing Antigone's words?

**ANTIGONE.** Yes!
He is my brother and—deny it as you will—
your brother too.
No one will ever convict me for a traitor.

**ISMENE.** So desperate, and Creon has expressly—

**ANTIGONE.** No,
he has no right to keep me from my own.

**ISMENE.** Oh my sister, think[14]—
think how our own father died, hated,
his reputation in ruins, driven on
by the crimes he brought to light himself
to gouge out his eyes with his own hands—
then mother . . . his mother and wife, both in one,
mutilating her life in the twisted noose[15]—
and last, our two brothers dead in a single day,
both shedding their own blood, poor suffering boys,
battling out their common destiny hand-to-hand.

14. Antigone has all but accused Ismene of being a coward. Does cowardice seem to be Ismene's controlling emotion in this scene? If not, what is it? What does Antigone's controlling emotion seem to be?

15. Ismene might indicate these terrible actions through pantomime. Would it be in her character to do so?

Now look at the two of us, left so alone . . .
think what a death we'll die, the worst of all
if we violate the laws and override
the fixed decree of the throne, its power—
we must be sensible. Remember we are women,
we're not born to contend with men. Then too,
we're underlings,[16] ruled by much stronger hands,
so we must submit in this, and things still worse.

16. How might Ismene use physical gestures to emphasize her attitude toward being "women" and "underlings"?

I, for one, I'll beg the dead to forgive me—
I'm forced, I have no choice—I must obey
the ones who stand in power.[17] Why rush to extremes?
It's madness, madness.

17. Does Ismene have a valid argument here? Should she be speaking with certainty or uncertainty?

18. Is Antigone disappointed with Ismene, or did she expect her sister to act as she does? How harshly should she speak to her here?

19. Why does Antigone believe this? How does that belief influence her actions?

20. Should Antigone actually start to move away on this line?

21. How might Ismene react physically?

22. Would Ismene lower her voice here—even though they are in private?

23. How should Antigone interpret this line vocally?

24. How has Antigone been acting to prompt Ismene's word "fiery"?

**ANTIGONE.** I won't insist,
no, even if you should have a change of heart,
I'd never welcome you in the labor, not with me.
So, do as you like, whatever suits you best[18]—
I will bury him myself.
And even if I die in the act, that death will be a glory.[19]
I will lie with the one I love and loved by him—
an outrage sacred to the gods! I have longer
to please the dead than please the living here:
in the kingdom down below I'll lie forever.
Do as you like, dishonor the laws
the gods hold in honor.

**ISMENE.** I'd do them no dishonor . . .
but defy the city? I have no strength for that.

**ANTIGONE.** You have your excuses. I am on my way,[20]
I will raise a mound for him, for my dear brother.

**ISMENE.** Oh Antigone, you're so rash—I'm so afraid for you![21]

**ANTIGONE** Don't fear for me. Set your own life in order.

**ISMENE.** Then don't, at least, blurt this out to
anyone.
Keep it a secret. I'll join you in that,
I promise.[22]

**ANTIGONE.** Dear god, shout it from the rooftops.[23]
I'll hate you
all the more for silence—tell the world!

**ISMENE.** So fiery—and it ought to chill
your heart.[24]

**ANTIGONE.** I know I please where I
must please the most.

**ISMENE** Yes, if you can, but you're in love with impossibility.

**ANTIGONE** Very well then, once my strength gives out
I will be done at last.

**ISMENE.** You're wrong from the start, you're off on a hopeless quest.

**ANTIGONE.** If you say so, you will make me hate you,[25]
and the hatred of the dead, by all rights,
will haunt you night and day.
But leave me to my own absurdity, leave me
to suffer this—this dreadful thing. I will suffer
nothing as great as death without glory.
*(Exit to the side.)*[26]

**ISMENE.** Then go if you must, but rest assured,[27]
wild, irrational as you are, my sister,
you are truly dear to the ones who love you.
*(Withdrawing to the palace.)*

25. Should this speech be said with hatred?

26. How fast or slowly should Antigone exit? How should she hold her body?

27. Does Ismene speak as Antigone is leaving? Does Antigone hear this speech?

## Extension

The most important influence of Greek drama probably lies in the thousands of references and reinterpretations of themes and characters by playwrights, poets, composers, and other artists over the centuries. In addition, some modern experimental playwrights and designers have used masks in various ways, for various purposes.

1. Create a three-dimensional mask or buy a commercial one that has simple features and little expression. Study the mask from different angles, under different lighting, or as the wearer takes different positions. Even a simple mask can seem to take on an amazing variety of expressions under different conditions. How can you plan to make use of this quality in performance?
2. Design masks for at least two main characters in a play you're familiar with. Include details of age, physical type, and characteristic emotion.
3. With the help of your teacher or librarian, research a modern play or production that uses masks. Ask yourself: Why did the playwright or designer decide to use masks? What effect do these masks create?

# Technical Theatre

exploration

**Theatre is a collaborative art form; it depends upon people working together. For every actor that you see onstage, there may be a dozen people working behind the scenes to create the environment and effects that support and enhance the performance. These people work in the technical areas of theatre—usually called tech.**

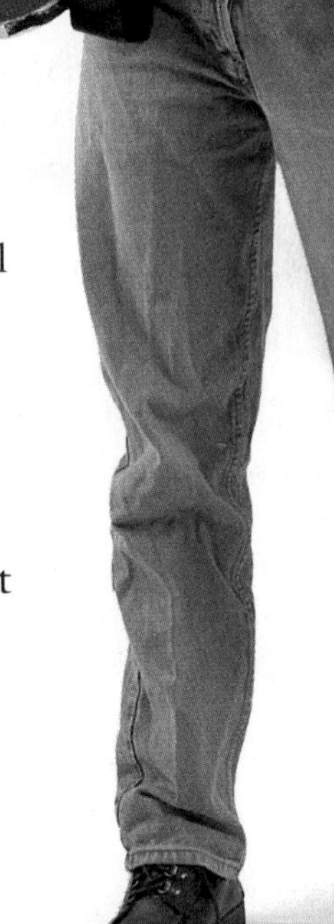

## THE LANGUAGE OF THEATRE

**batten** a wood or metal pipe from which stage lights, drops, and scenery are hung

**cue** a signal for something to happen

**drop** or **backdrop** a large canvas or muslin curtain that hangs at the back of the stage setting

**flat** a set piece consisting of a light-weight frame covered with canvas, muslin, or wood

**platform** a set piece with a solid top and braced legs, made to support the weight of actors, furniture, and props

**property** or **prop** anything that an actor handles onstage as well as furniture and other items used to enhance the set

**set** the onstage physical space and its structures in which the actors perform

**stage crew** the group of people working on set construction, props, lighting, sound, costumes, and makeup

**throw** the distance light can be cast from a lighting instrument

# The Stage Crew

The tech crews are the groups of people working on set construction, props, lighting, sound, costumes, and makeup. Generally, a technical director or shop foreman supervises these people, collectively known as the **stage crew**.

The set construction crew creates the **set,** the onstage physical space and its structures in which the actors perform. The set is conceived by a **set designer,** then built and painted by the set construction crew, which may later become the **shifting crew**—those responsible for changing the set from scene to scene.

The properties, or prop, crew is in charge of gathering and organizing **props**—anything actors handle onstage as well as furniture and other items used to enhance the set. Props may be rented, borrowed, bought, or built. In the professional theatre, a **prop master** manages the prop crew.

**Lighting** is any illumination of the set and actors during a performance. It is needed to make them visible, but it can also establish a play's time, place, and mood. The **lighting designer** decides what kinds of lights are needed, where to focus them, and when to turn them on. The lighting crew places the lights and runs them during the show.

The **sound designer** decides what kinds of music and sound effects are needed and whether they should be live or recorded. The sound crew is responsible for collecting, preparing, and running the sound for a performance. The **sound,** or audio, component of a production may include amplification of actors' voices in addition to music and sound effects.

Any clothing an actor wears onstage for a performance is called a **costume.** Costumes are designed or chosen by the **costume designer.** They may be rented, bought, or borrowed. Or, they may be sewn by the costume crew, who is also responsible for keeping costumes repaired and clean from one performance to the next.

In the theatre **makeup** refers to cosmetics and hairstyling, including false hairpieces and false features. Actors use makeup to emphasize facial features so that they stand out onstage or to add age or special qualities called for by the characters. Actors usually put on their own makeup, but when there are many actors or the makeup is complicated or specialized, as in horror makeup, the job may be done by a makeup crew, or makeup artists, supervised by a **makeup designer.**

Although you may be interested in one area of tech work—or in acting directing, or producing—you should familiarize yourself with the work done by all members of the stage crew. The following pages will introduce you to the working spaces and tools of each tech crew, demonstrate some basics in each technical area, and acquaint you with vital safety issues.

# Set Construction and Prop Crews

The **scene shop** is the stage crew's center of operations; it's the primary workspace for the set construction crew and usually for the prop crew as well, although some large theatres have a separate prop shop. It's the place where drawings become models and models become full-sized sets.

No single shop has every tool and useful feature, but every shop has a basic collection of tools. Most shops have high ceilings and large doors (for moving large pieces of scenery from shop to stage) and a variety of work areas, plus cabinets and storage areas where tools, supplies, and stock sets and props are kept. A scene shop has to be well organized, because it is often bursting with activity.

# Set Construction and Props: Equipment and Supplies

## Hand Tools

### MEASURING TOOLS

**tape measure** for measuring long distances
**combination square** for marking 45° and 90° angles
**framing square** for checking 90° joints for accuracy
**carpenter's level** for determining true horizontal and vertical

### MARKING TOOLS

**chalk line** coated with chalk dust to leave a line when stretched between two points and snapped lightly
**compass** for marking circles

### HAMMERS

**claw hammer** for driving or removing nails
**tack hammer** for setting and driving tacks
**mallet** for pounding things without leaving hammer marks

### CUTTING TOOLS

**crosscut saw** for cutting wood
**hack saw** for cutting metal
**backsaw** and **miter box** for making accurate crosscuts or angle cuts
**plane** for smoothing wood edges
**file** (wood rasps or metal) for shaping and smoothing
**utility knife** for light cutting

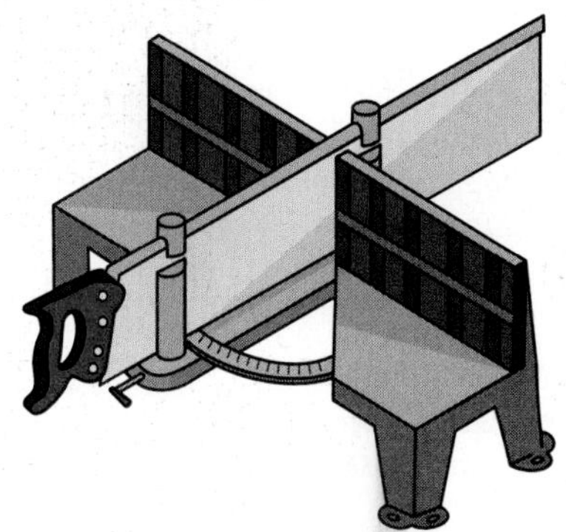

**Backsaw and miter box**

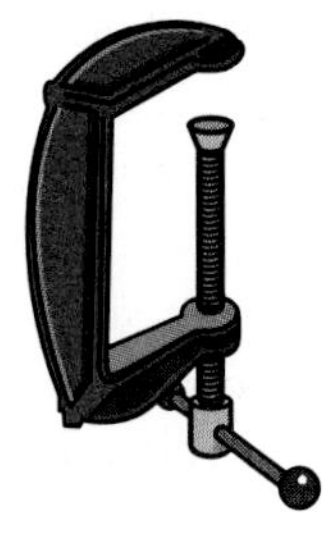

**C-clamp**

### DRILLING TOOLS

**hand drill** for drilling into wood
**push drill** for making starter holes
**brace** for holding the drill bit
**interchangeable bit** for drilling holes in wood, plastic, or metal

### PLIERS

**slip-joint pliers** for clamping, gripping, or bending materials
**needle-nose pliers** for reaching into small places and gripping tiny objects
**locking pliers** for grasping and locking on various objects

### SCREWDRIVERS

**standard slotted screwdriver** for driving standard screws
**Phillips screwdriver** for the crossed slot in a Phillips screw

### WRENCHES

**adjustable-end (Crescent) wrench** for loosening or tightening a variety of nuts, especially in lighting instruments
**pipe wrench** for loosening or tightening large nuts or pipe fittings
**combination wrenches** (open- and closed-end, or box-end) for loosening and tightening of specific-sized nuts in hard-to-get-at places

**Wood clamp**

### ASSORTED HAND TOOLS

**c-clamps, wood clamps,** and **furniture clamps** for eliminating warping, and for holding work together during assembly
**table vise** for holding wood and other objects in place while working on them
**wrecking bar** for prying apart nailed boards
**staple gun** or **tacker** for attaching fabric to wood
**putty knife** for applying and smoothing wood putty

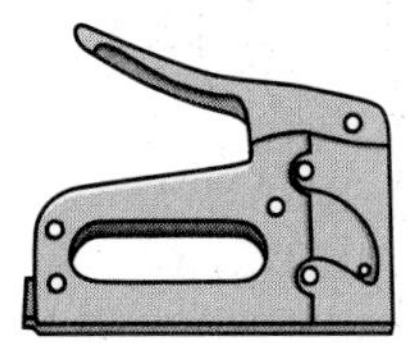

**Staple gun**

### PAINTING TOOLS

**brushes** (assorted sizes, including small artist brushes for detail work) and **sponges** for painting scenery
**rollers** for rolling paint onto a surface
**roller-** and **brush-handle extenders** for painting tall scenery
**spray gun** for painting very large surface areas
**10-quart buckets** and **paint paddles** for mixing paint
**drop cloth** for catching spilled paint

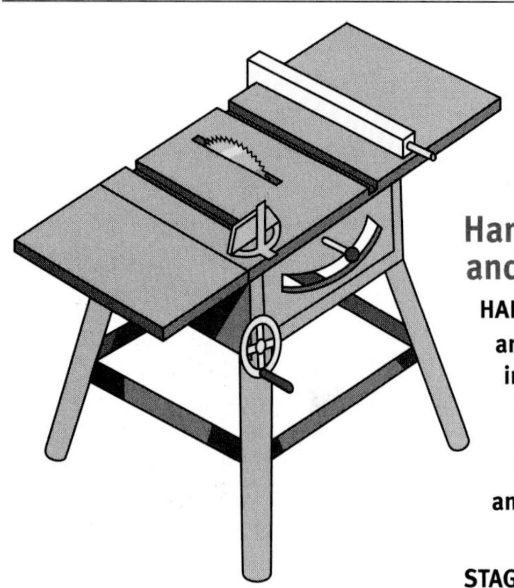

Circular table saw

## Power Tools

**STATIONARY CUTTING TOOLS**

**circular table saw** for ripping lumber
**radial-arm** or **pull-over saw** for cross-cuts and angle cuts as well as ripping lumber
**band saw** for making curved cuts
**belt** or **disk sander** for sanding wood or metal

**PORTABLE CUTTING TOOL**

**sabre saw** with interchangeable blades for making curved cuts in plywood, composition board, lumber, metal, and plastic

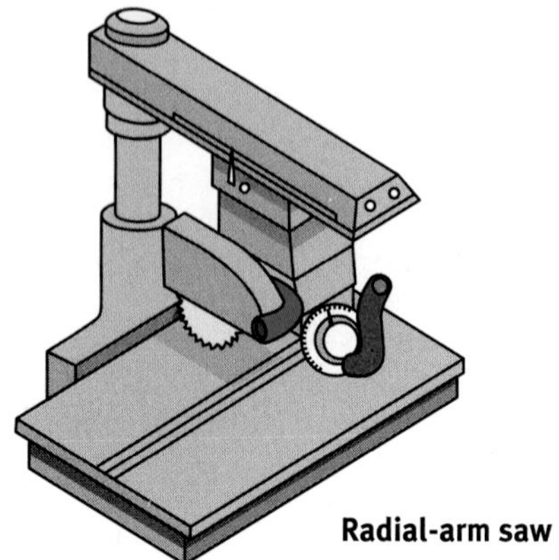

Radial-arm saw

**PORTABLE DRILLING TOOL**

**electric hand drill** with variable speed and reverse action, for driving or removing screws

## Hardware, Materials, and Supplies

**HARDWARE**

**angle irons, corner plates, mending, plates, hinges** (butt, strap, t-strap, loose-pin, tight-pin, spring), **double clips, turnbuckles, cable clamps, screw hooks and eyes, grommets**

**STAGE HARDWARE**

**stage brace, brace cleat, foot iron, stage screw, floor plate, lash-line eye, lash-line cleat, lash-line hook, tie-off cleat, stop cleat, stop block**

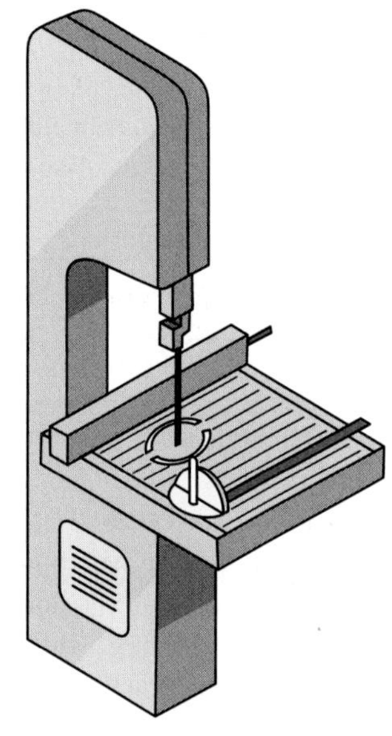

Band saw

**FASTENERS**

**nails** (common, box, finishing, double-headed, screw, clout), **screws** (standard slotted, Phillips drywall, assorted), **nuts, bolts, corrugated fasteners, brads**

**MATERIALS**

**sandpaper** in various weights, or roughnesses, for smoothing wood, plastic, or metal surfaces
**fireproof muslin** or **canvas** for stretching over wooden frames to make scenery pieces

**ADHESIVES**

**white glue, wheat paste, contact cement, cyanoacrylate cement (Krazy Glue, Super Glue)**

**TAPE**

**duct, masking, electrical, fluorescent, gaffer's, dutchman**

**ROPE, CABLE, AND WIRE**

**manila rope** for raising and suspending loads
**clothesline** for lashing flats together
**nylon rope** for general use
**fishing line** for fastening or suspending things invisibly
**stovepipe wire** and **baling wire** for fastening but not for supporting a load
**piano wire** for carrying moderate loads

**PAINTING SUPPLIES**

**paint** (casein or latex) for painting scenery
**wood stain** for staining picture frames and other prop pieces
**spray paint** for painting props
**cleaning solvents** for cleaning painting tools

**SAFETY SUPPLIES**

**goggles** to protect eyes
**respirator masks** (disposable) for protecting the respiratory tract

# Set Construction Basics

Despite the endless variations among theatres and the plays they produce, all theatres have certain **stock units,** standard set pieces that can be adapted and used for various purposes. Those pieces include flats, platforms, drops, and props (including furniture). All of these stock units are designed to be easily constructed, moved, and stored.

A **flat** is a light-weight frame covered with canvas, muslin, or wood. Most flats are 2–4 feet wide and 8–12 feet tall. They are usually painted and positioned vertically next to each other to form walls. A **platform** is a set piece with a solid top and braced legs made to support the weight of actors, furniture, and props. A **drop,** or **backdrop,** is a large canvas or muslin curtain that hangs at the back of the stage setting; it can be lighted or painted for special effects.

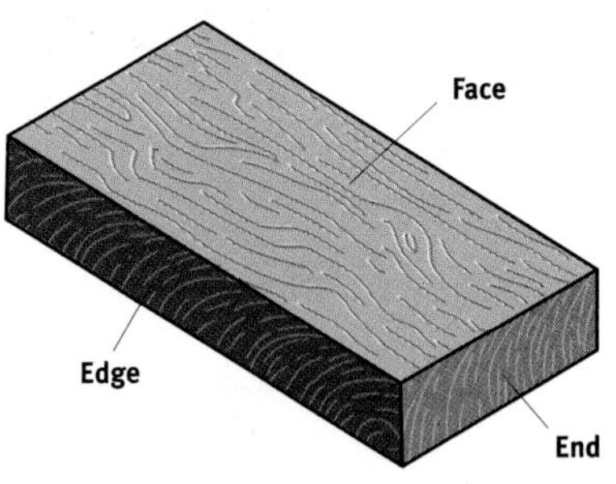


Flat and platform frames, as well as many props, are often constructed from wood—either stock lumber, such as pine and fir, or sheet goods, such as plywood. Wood is cut and joined in various ways to construct scenery. Before cutting any wood, however, you should measure carefully. An old carpenter's motto says, "Measure twice and cut once."

## Measuring Wood

Lumber used for construction is referenced by its thickness and width, but the stock size of lumber refers to the rough mill cut and not to the finished dimension of the wood. Thus, a 2×4 piece of lumber really measures about 1½ inches high by 3½ inches wide; these dimensions may also vary slightly from board to board.

The dimensions of stock lumber and sheet goods correspond to the wood surfaces, referred to by the terms *end, edge,* and *face.* The edge and end are of the same thickness, while the face is the surface defining the width.

## Saw Cuts and Joints

You can cut wood across the grain, which is a **cross cut;** with the grain, which is a **rip cut;** or at an angle, which is a **miter** or **bevel cut.** You can cut all the way through the wood, or part way, depending on how you will join the wood.

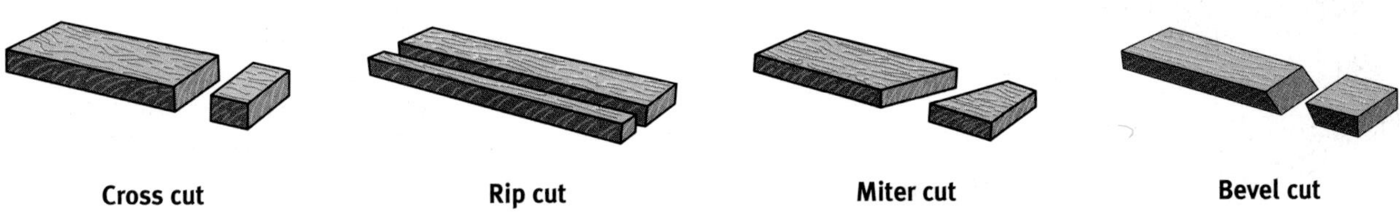

Lap joint

**LAP JOINT** In a **lap,** or **overlap,** joint, the face of one board is fastened to the face of another board. Use nails or glue and screws to fasten the boards.

**BUTT JOINT** A **butt joint** is made when two boards are cut square and joined in one of four ways: end-to-face, end-to-edge, edge-to-edge, or end-to-end. Use nails or glue and screws to join the boards. This is not a very strong joint; it needs some type of reinforcement.

**MITER JOINT** A **miter joint** is a kind of butt joint in which two boards are cut at an angle and joined. You can use glue and corrugated fasteners, but to make a strong joint, use glue and nails or screws. This joint is often used to make frames that show a nice 90° corner finish or to form corners wider or narrower than 90.°

**TECH TIPS: CUTTING AND JOINING**

- When measuring wood to be joined, it may be necessary to subtract the thickness of the wood from the finished dimension before cutting.
- Draw a pencil line to mark the place where you want to make a cut. Then make sure you save, or cut on the outside of, the line. If you cut on the line you drew, you will lose up to ⅛ inch of your board.
- To guide a hand saw while cutting, keep it vertical. Keep your index finger outside the handhold and pointed at your line. Use light pressure only; using heavy pressure may cause the saw to bind, or catch, and spring out of the cut.
- Circular saws cut upward, so they may splinter the top of your board. Always put the good side face down before using a circular saw.
- A common way to join boards is to **toenail.** When you do this, you drive the nail on a 60° angle from the first board down into the second board.
- Avoid placing nails in a row along the edge of a board; that can create a split in the wood. Use two nails on the end of a board.
- Unless you are using a power hand drill to drive your screws, use a hand drill to make a starter hole into materials you plan to screw together. The starter hole should be about the diameter of the shaft of the screw without its flanges (spiral ribs).

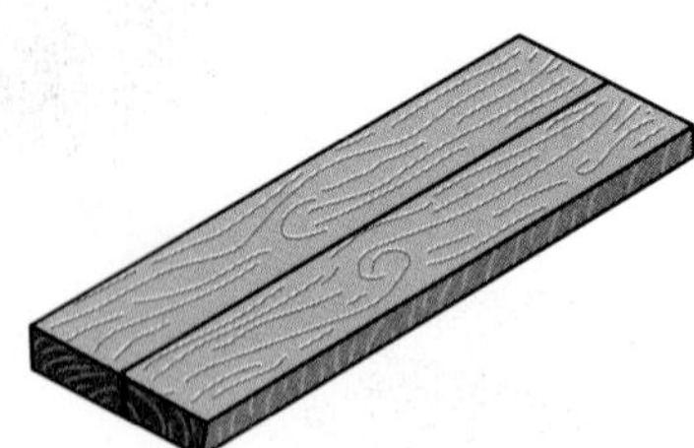

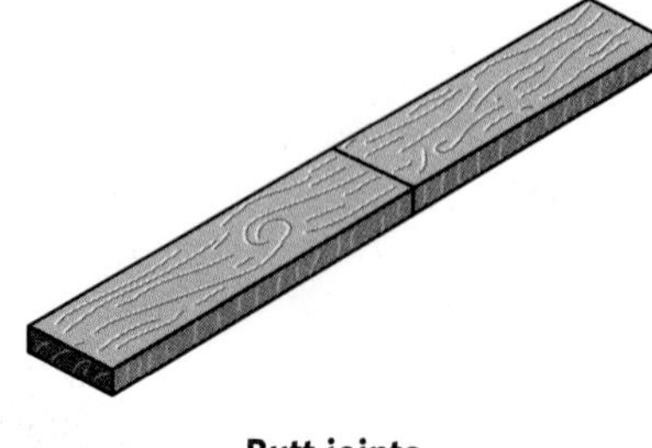

Butt joints

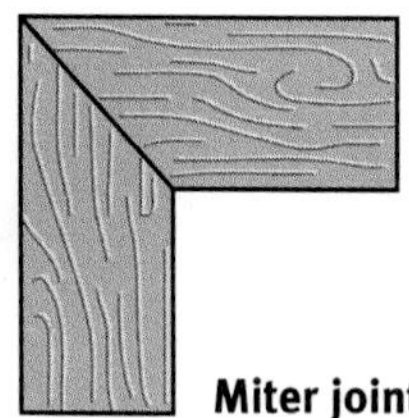

Miter joint

## SAFETY TIPS The Scene Shop

- Keep the shop clean and safe. At the end of each work session, replace tools, vacuum or wet-mop floors, empty trash, and make sure exits are free from obstructions.
- Get help when lifting heavy objects. Lift objects by bending your knees, not your back.
- Never climb a ladder unless someone on the ground is holding it steady. Never stand on the top step of a ladder, no matter how secure it seems.
- Stay aware of work going on around, above, or underneath you.
- Wear safety glasses or goggles to protect your eyes from splinters and dust.
- Use a dust mask to protect your lungs from sawdust and other debris.
- Wear steel-toed shoes or shoe caps whenever you are working with heavy tools or supplies.
- Wear protective headgear whenever anyone in the space is working overhead.
- Use a claw hammer on nails only. It may splinter or chip harder metals.
- Before using a plane on any lumber, make sure the lumber is clamped to the workbench or firmly anchored in a vise.
- Make sure electrical cords are clear of saw blades, water, and damp objects.
- Never wear baggy clothes, jewelry, ties, or scarves while operating a power tool; they can get caught.
- Wear a face shield when using power tools to protect yourself from chips and splinters.
- Make sure power saws are equipped with blade guards. Never remove a blade guard from a stationary saw.
- Make sure your blade is sharp, so wood does not bind, or catch, in the saw. Avoid twisting or forcing wood against the saw blade.
- Keep your hands away from the blades of power saws. Use a push stick to feed small pieces.
- Unplug any power tool before changing the blade or bit or when it's not in use.
- Wear ear plugs while working with noisy tools.
- Always use cable clamps in pairs.
- Wheat paste is often laced with poison so rodents and insects won't eat it in storage. Don't leave it on your skin or get it in your mouth.
- Never touch cyanoacrylate cement (Krazy Glue or Super Glue). It can bond skin to skin or to other materials.
- Paint in well-ventilated areas.
- Oil-, alcohol-, and lacquer-base (and some synthetic-base) paints, stains, and finishes are extremely flammable. Work well away from any open flame.
- Wear a respirator mask when using a paint sprayer or when working around fumes from glues, paint, and other substances.
- Always wash out brushes and other painting tools, including sponges and rags, with appropriate cleaning solvents. Hang them to dry away from direct heat.
- Inspect all ropes before use; immediately notify your teacher or technical director of any cuts, gouges, worn fibers, discoloration, kinks, or twists; these are signs of reduced strength.

## Lighting and Sound Crews

The lighting and sound crews stay busy in a variety of workspaces: they can be found in the scene shop, where lighting instruments, electrical cable, and other equipment are often stored and maintained; on the stage, where lights and microphones are hung and positioned; backstage, where speakers, projectors, and other equipment may be placed; and in the light and sound booths, usually located in the house. From their booths in the house during a show, the light board and sound board operators can see and hear what the audience hears and make any necessary adjustments.

# Lighting: Equipment and Supplies

## Lighting Equipment

### LIGHTING CONTROL EQUIPMENT

**lighting control board** and **system** for controlling the operation and intensity of lighting instruments; computerized lighting systems operate lights based on information input and stored electronically on disk or CD

**headset** for communicating between the light board operator and the stage crew; may be a complex system or radio- or battery-operated

### LIGHTING INSTRUMENTS

**ellipsoidal reflector spotlight (ERS)** for throwing a strong, focused beam from a distance; sometimes called a **Leko**

**Fresnel spotlight** for shorter throws covering a large area with soft, diffuse light

**followspot** for throwing bright, focused light on a moving performer

**ellipsoidal reflector floodlight,** or **scoop** for illuminating large areas of the stage

**strip lights,** or **border lights** for washing light over a large area of the stage or onto scenery

Ellipsoidal reflector spotlight

Fresnel spotlight

## Lighting Supplies

### LAMPS

**incandescent** (standard lamps with medium, mogul/bipost, or candelabra/prefocus screw bases) for use in strip lights, floodlights, and wall sources; wattage varies according to use

**halogen lamps** (energy-efficient, high-intensity lamps with medium and candelabra/prefocus bases) for use in spotlights; wattage varies according to type and use

### LIGHTING INSTRUMENT ACCESSORIES

**gelatins,** or **gels** (color filters) for casting colored light from a spotlight

**gel frames** for holding gels

**gobos,** or **cookies** (metallic disks with cut patterns) for casting light patterns from a spotlight

**top hats** for narrowing the beam of a spotlight

**barn doors** (folding flaps on a metal frame) for shaping the beam of a light

**plano-convex, step,** and **Fresnel lenses** for spotlights

### ELECTRICAL AND RIGGING SUPPLIES

**male/female connectors** (twist-lock, locking grounded-pin, Edison), **twofers, triples, electrical cable, wire strippers, wire crimpers, 9-volt batteries** (for headsets), **electrical tape, duct tape, safety chains**

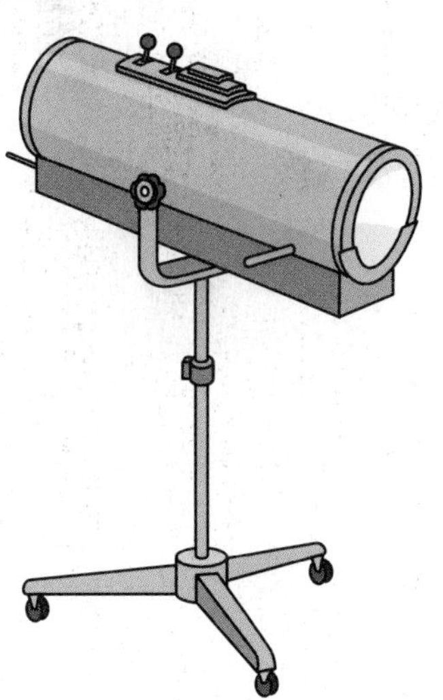

Followspot

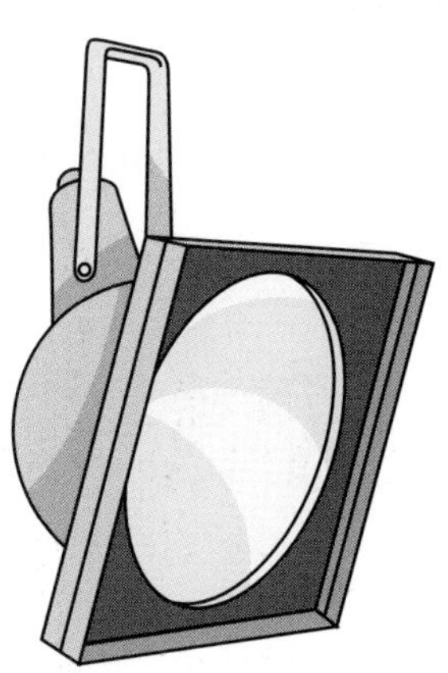

Floodlight

Strip lights

## Lighting Basics

Four basic types of lighting instruments are used for stage lighting: spotlights, floodlights (scoops), followspots, and strip lights. Their uses reflect differences in the **throw,** or distance, the light can be cast and the nature of the circular beam cast—a hard- or soft-edged light.

A lighting instrument is composed of four basic parts: the **lamp,** which is the source of light; the **reflector,** which reflects the light; the **lens,** which shapes the light; and the metal **housing,** which encloses the system. The housing includes features that allow color filters, or **gels,** and other devices to be attached to the instrument for enhancement and control of the light beam. The housing also has a handle from which to **hang,** or attach and position, the light. Most lights are hung above the stage on a wood or metal pipe called a **batten.** Followspots are usually mounted on a wheeled light stand and positioned in a balcony or the light booth.

The lights are controlled from the lighting control board, which houses or is connected to a dimmer. A **dimmer** is an electrical device that controls the brightness of the lighting instruments. One dimmer switch may control more than one instrument.

Each stage light is connected to the system by an electrical cable running from the instrument to a stage outlet. A standard electrical cable on a lighting instrument is two feet long. When the light is more than two feet from an outlet, or when several instruments need to be plugged into the same outlet, you need to make an extension cable.

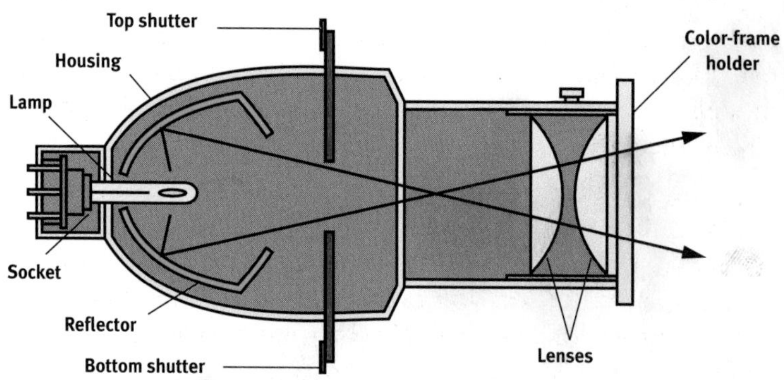


**Cutaway of an ellipsoidal reflector spotlight**

## Extension Cables

Extension cables should be standard lengths, rather than the exact length needed for a particular show, since they will be reused many times and are easier to store and identify in standard lengths, such as 5 feet, 10 feet, 25 feet, and so on. To indicate the different lengths, you can label each cable with different colored tape.

Electrical cable consists of a thick rubber insulation that covers three copper-strand wires. Each of the three copper wires has its own color-coded coating: the white wire is the neutral wire, the green wire is the ground wire, and the black wire is the hot wire.

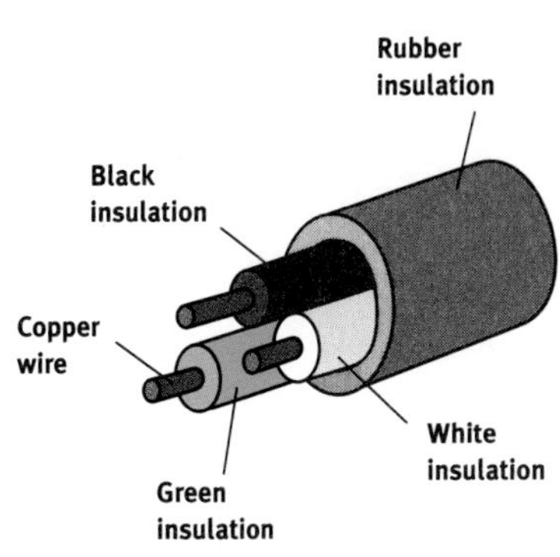


Electrical cable cutaway

### MAKING AN EXTENSION CABLE

1. With a utility knife or the blade part of a large wire stripper, carefully cut and strip away the rubber insulation about 1 ½ inches below both ends of the length of cable you have chosen.
2. Carefully strip ½ inch of colored insulation off each wire, without cutting into the copper strands. Use a wire stripper at the proper gauge opening for your cable.
3. Choose a male twist-lock or locking grounded-pin connector. The male connectors are plugs; the female connectors are receptacles. Make sure to choose one with an electrical rating that corresponds to your cable rating. Electrical ratings are stated on the cables and connectors in amperes; an ampere is the unit of measurement for electrical current. Attach the connector using the built-in cable clamps.
4. Open the male connector. Inside are three screw terminals, colored silver, gold, and green. Attach the white (neutral) wire to the silver terminal, the green (ground) wire to the green terminal, and the black (hot) wire to the gold terminal. In newer models, the terminals are marked white, green, and black. Crimp the wires, using a wire crimper, for easier hook-up.
5. Repeat the procedure for the other end of the cable, using a female connector. You can now connect the male end of another cable length to the female connector. By using a twofer (Y) or multiple connector, you can connect more than one lighting instrument to your original; a twofer has two female connectors at the top and a male at the bottom.
6. When completed, test the extension cable with any lighting instrument on a non-dimmer outlet to make sure your connections are correct and solid. Be careful not to overload the outlet.

Male and female connectors

Twofer

# Sound: Equipment and Supplies

## Sound Equipment

### SOUND CONTROL EQUIPMENT

**sound control board** for controlling the operation and volume of speakers and microphones; inputs and controls music, voice-overs, or effects from tapes, records, and CDs
**headphones** for listening to and fine-tuning the sound track
**headset** for communicating between the sound board operator and the stage crew; may be a complex system or radio- or battery-operated

### RECORDING AND PLAYBACK EQUIPMENT

**amplifiers** for providing a power supply to speakers and other audio equipment
**equalizers** for evening out sound production during multiple-microphone usage
**mixer** for mixing input sounds from microphones, turntables, tape decks, or other input devices
**speakers** for projecting sound into the house
**compact disk player, turntable, cassette deck,** and **reel-to-reel deck** for recording and playing music, voice-overs, or effects
**microphones (floor mic, standing mic, hanging mic, wireless mic)** for recording and amplifying music and voices
**transmitter** and **body pack** for operating wireless microphones

## Sound Supplies

### ASSORTED RECORDING SUPPLIES

**cassette tapes, reel-to-reel tapes, microcassette tapes, splicing tape, nonrecording cue tape, grease pencils, 9-volt batteries** (for wireless microphones and headsets)

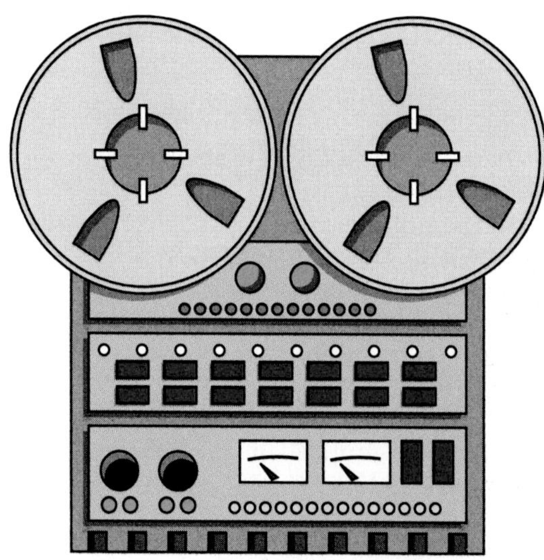

**Reel-to-reel tape deck**

## Sound Basics

In a sound system, sound is transmitted as electrical signals from a device such as a microphone or turntable and recorded onto magnetic tape—or, in a computerized system, onto a computer file. The signals are blended in a **mixer** and sent to **equalizers,** which even out their tone. The manipulated signals are then boosted by **amplifiers** to drive **speakers,** from which they are broadcast as audible sound.

Most sound used for theatrical production is recorded on reel-to-reel tape decks; the ¼-inch tape is easy to edit and mark with exact cues. A cue is a signal for something to happen; in this case, a cue is a point on the tape at which recorded sound should begin to play. In computerized systems, all editing is done on the computer; no tape is required.

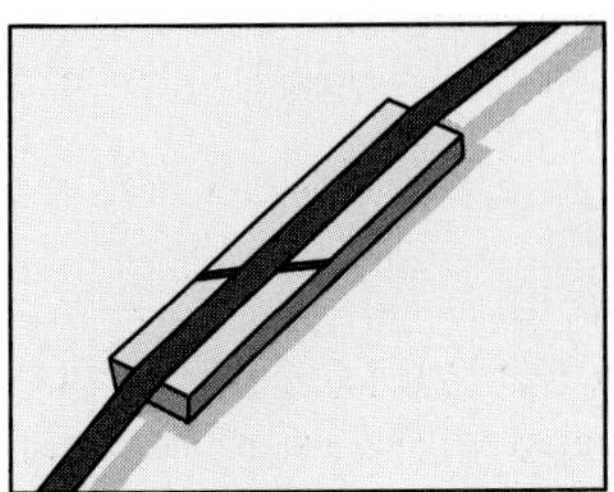
fig. 1

### Editing Audiotape

Editing audiotape involves **splicing,** the cutting and rejoining of pieces of magnetic tape containing recorded sound. It takes practice, but you can splice together sounds from various sources to create a seamless and continuous series of sounds. More often, however, you will edit to create a **show tape,** a tape of distinct sound segments that will be played at particular points in a performance.

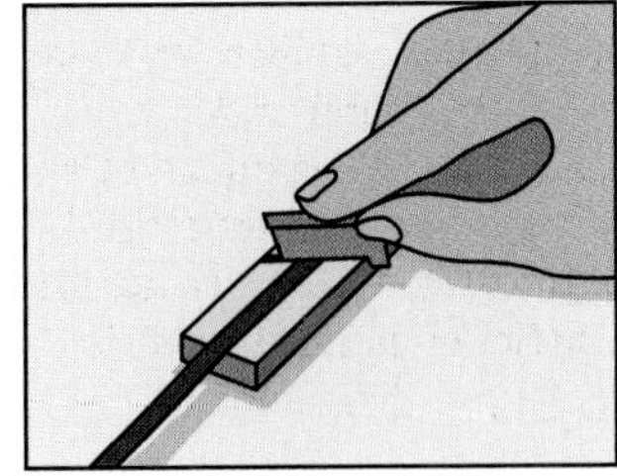
fig. 2

On a show tape, the nonrecording leader tape, or **cue tape,** runs between segments of tape with recorded sound. The cue tape segments are labeled using a grease pencil. It's best to leave at least ½ inch of magnetic tape between the splice and the beginning of a cue and about 1 foot of magnetic tape after the sound ends. Insert about 2 feet of leader tape between cues.

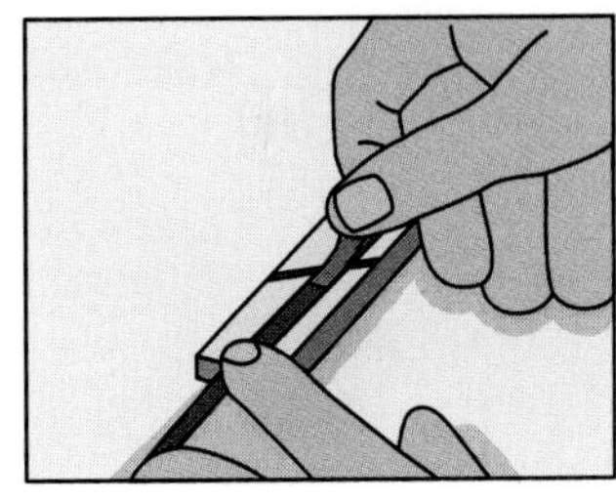
fig. 3

#### SPLICING AUDIOTAPE

1. Place the uncut audiotape, magnetic (shiny) side down, in the groove of a splicing block and cut it with a nonmagnetic single-edge razor blade (fig. 1). If no splicing block is available, cut the tape with a scissors at a 45° angle; a 90° splice tends to create a gap in the sound production at the point of the splice (fig. 2).
2. Do the same with the end of the second tape to be joined to the first—whether recorded audiotape or cue tape.
3. Lay both ends in the splicing block next to each other and firmly apply a short (1-inch) piece of splicing tape to join the two tapes (fig. 3).
4. Trim away any edges (fig. 4).

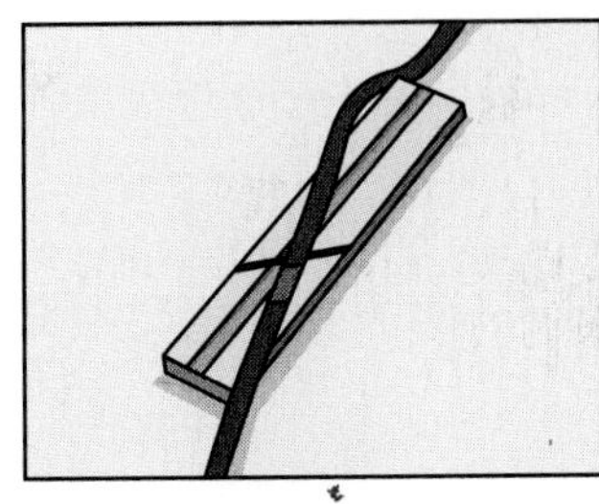
fig. 4

### TECH TIPS: RECORDING AND EDITING SOUND

- Record sounds at a high enough volume to avoid unwanted "noise" but not so high that you have distortion; it's easier to decrease the volume on the playback and maintain quality than to increase the volume, which can also increase the noise level.
- When you are finished recording a sound, use the pause lever before pressing the stop button to avoid a popping sound.
- Instead of marking your sound cues on leader tape, you can record them orally onto the recording tape. This means you have to use a headset when you are cueing sound. Leave 2 feet of recording tape between the sounds, with volume set at 0.
- Use reel-to-reel tape recorders instead of cassette tape recorders for sound that needs editing. Standard cassette recorders travel at a slow speed, which means the sound takes up a very small space on the tape. This makes the sound difficult to locate and edit.

## Tape Loops

Because recorded sounds must often be cued up in overlapping patterns, it's a good idea to have more than one tape deck. When a sound or sound effect must continue in the background of a scene for an extended period of time (for example, rainfall, crickets, or wind), you need to make a **tape loop.** A tape loop requires the use of a reel-to-reel tape deck, and no other use can be made of that particular deck while the loop is running during the scene. Other sounds, effects, music, and so on, can be run through the system at the same time, but not from the deck being used for the loop.

### MAKING A TAPE LOOP

1. Locate (or create) the desired sound or effect. Record it on high-quality magnetic recording tape repeatedly for at least 2 feet of tape. Be careful that the sounds do not overlap, but are smoothly consistent throughout the tape.
2. Carefully place the tape around both reels, but do not attach it. If possible, use small reels. Run one end through the tension rolls and heads of the machine. Bring the two ends of the tape together, leaving no slack in the loop. On the dull side of the tape, mark with a grease pencil the spot where they come together.
3. Carefully remove the tape from the tape deck and splice the two ends together at the grease-pencil mark.
4. Replace the loop carefully around the empty reels, holding back the tension rollers while slipping the tape past the heads. If the tension seems tight enough, play the tape.
5. If the tension is not tight enough, resplice the loop to make it smaller. If there is a jump or glitch in the sound at the splice, you may have to resplice a small amount to eliminate it.

## SAFETY TIPS Working with Electricity

- Know where the master switch and circuit breakers are located. A **circuit breaker** protects a circuit from overloading.
- Wear rubber-soled shoes when working around electricity.
- Use tools with plastic or rubber insulation.
- Use a wooden or fiberglass ladder to avoid conducting electricity; wood and fiberglass are insulators. If you must use a metal ladder, make sure it has rubber casters and foot pads.
- Don't touch bare wires, even if you are sure they are disconnected.
- Disconnect tools and equipment from electrical circuits before working with them.
- Unplug lights before changing bulbs; a socket contains live wires.
- Don't work in damp locations or put a drink where it could spill on wiring or equipment. Most liquids are conductors.
- Don't overload circuits by trying to bypass fuses or get around circuit boards. Like circuit breakers, fuses protect circuits from overloading.
- Don't clip off the **grounding plug** (the third prong) from ground circuits; use a ground plug adapter instead.
- Always disconnect electrical devices by pulling the plug, not the cord.
- To avoid sparks and shocks, check cords, cables, and connectors periodically; immediately notify your teacher or technical director if any are cracked, worn, or frayed.
- Keep cords, cables, and connectors clean and free of debris.
- Be sure all elements of a cable connection carry the same electrical rating.
- Coil cables and hang them on the wall when not in use. Keep them in coil by plugging the connectors together and/or tying them with rope or twine.
- If electrical shock should occur, shut off the power immediately.
- Report any shock, no matter how minor, to your teacher or director.
- If you are not sure what you are doing, stop! Ask your teacher or technical director for help or advice.
- Keep halogen lamps free of dust, grease, and fingerprints. Marks on the surface cause uneven heat distribution, which can cause them to explode.
- Don't overload the electrical circuit when using a twofer or other multiple connector.

# Costume and Makeup Crews

The costume shop is the workshop of the costume crew, the place where costumes are designed, cut, fitted, and sewn; rented or found costumes are altered; and used costumes are cleaned and repaired. The costume shop may also contain a storage area for keeping a variety of costumes from production to production. In many schools and small theatres, costumes are constructed by the costume crew—and often by the actors themselves—wherever equipment and supplies are available.

The makeup crew is unique in theatre because it includes the actors themselves. Makeup artists or makeup designers may assist them as they prepare themselves for the stage, usually in front of a well-lit dressing room mirror.

In some theatres, a makeup room or cabinet is stocked with makeup for actors to use, although most actors have their own makeup kit.

# Costumes: Equipment and Supplies

## Basic Equipment

**MEASURING TOOLS**

**plastic tape measure** for taking measurements and general measuring
**sewing gauge** for accurate measuring of hems and seam allowances

**MARKING TOOLS**

**tracing paper** and **tracing wheel** for transferring markings from pattern to fabric
**chalk- or wax-based tailor's chalk** for marking fabric during fittings

Pinking shears

**CUTTING TOOLS**

**shears,** or **scissors** for cutting fabric with a straight cut
**pinking shears** for cutting fabric with a zigzag that won't ravel
**seam ripper** for taking stitches out of fabric
**long, wide cutting table** (about 6 feet by 4 feet) for spreading out fabric for cutting

**FITTING EQUIPMENT**

**dress form,** or **dressmaker's dummy** in adjustable size for fitting and sizing costumes
**full-length mirror** for actors and crew members to see the costume from all angles

**SEWING EQUIPMENT**

**straight-stitch sewing machine** for sewing together cut pieces of fabric

**CLEANING AND PRESSING EQUIPMENT**

**washer and dryer** for laundering costumes
**steam iron** and **ironing board** for pressing fabric
**portable steamer** for taking minor wrinkles out of clothing and for shaping felt

**STORAGE**

**bins or drawers** for storing fabrics, scraps, jewelry, accessories, patterns, and sewing supplies
**moveable clothes rack** for hanging costumes during construction and throughout the production

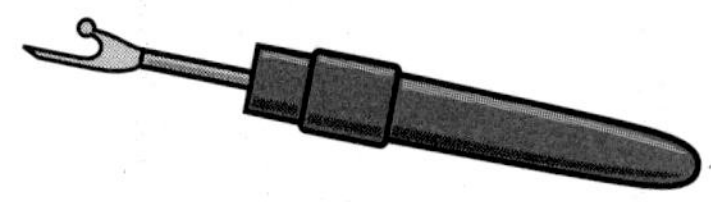

Seam ripper

## Materials and Supplies

**GENERAL**

**fabric, thread, pin cushion, thimble, pins (straight, glass-headed, safety)**

**SEWING NEEDLES**

**general hand-sewing needles, darning needles, upholstery needles, sewing machine needles**

**FASTENERS**

**straight pins, safety pins, grommet set, seam-binding tape, hot-glue gun, staple gun, glue sticks, snaps, hooks and eyes, Velcro, assorted buttons**

TECHNICAL THEATRE

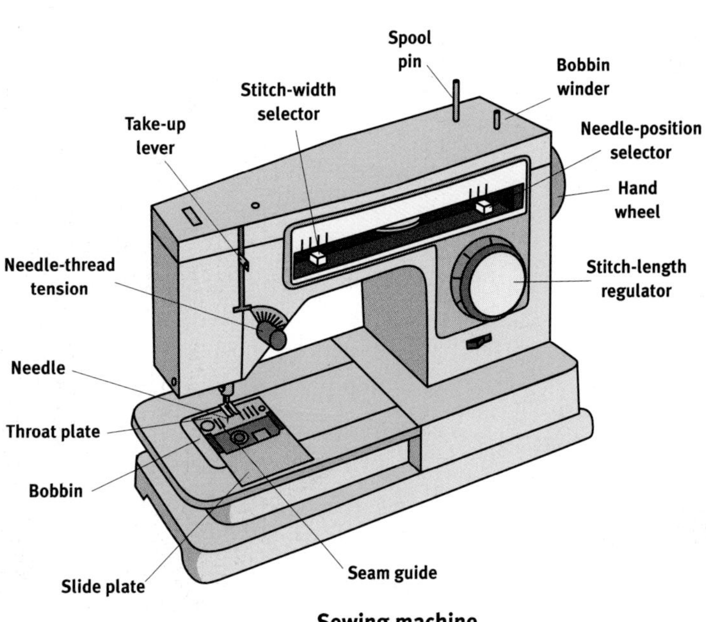


Sewing machine

## Sewing Basics

Clothing is put together by sewing seams. A **seam** is a line of stitches that joins two or more pieces of fabric. The **seam allowance** is the distance between the edge of the fabric and the seam; the standard seam allowance is ⅝ inch wide.

Machine sewing is the most efficient way to sew costumes, but hand-stitching may be required for hemming and adding details.

Whether sewing by hand or machine, the plain seam is the most common seam.

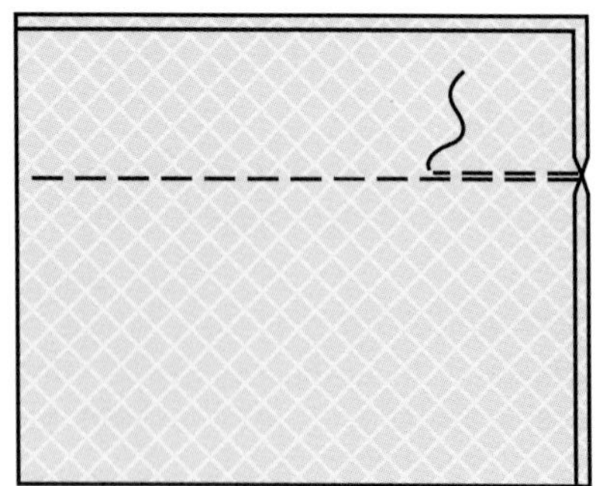

Plain seam

#### SEWING A PLAIN SEAM

1. Place the right sides of the fabric together. Insert pins to hold the fabric together. Place your pins at right angles to the seam, across the seam allowance, with the pin heads at the outer edge.
2. Stitch along the seam line using a standard seam allowance.
3. Press the seam allowances flat, then open.

### Basic Hand Stitches

- **running** Make a running stitch by pulling the needle in and out of material in a straight line.
- **basting** To baste a hem or seam, use long running stitches and space them widely apart. This will hold the fabric until you are ready to do final stitching.
- **backstitch** For a strong, permanent seam, use a backstitch. Take one forward stitch; then begin a short stitch from the back of it. Repeat the process to form overlapping stitches.
- **slipstitch** Use a slipstitch for hems. Loop a small stitch from the outside of the fabric, under the folded edge of the hem, and up. Pull it through, and begin again. Keep the stitches loose.

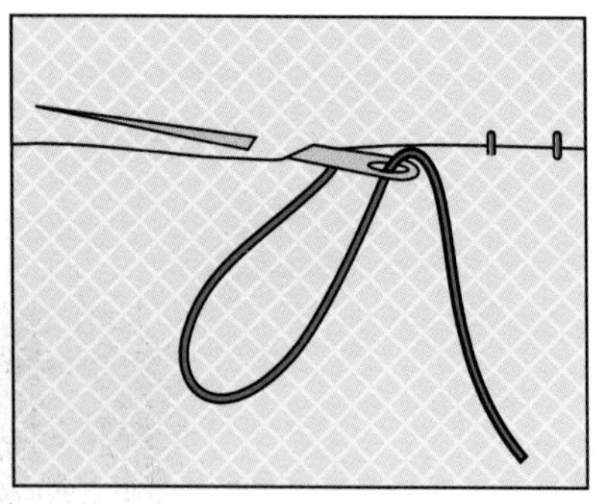

Slipstitch

#### TECH TIPS: HAND STITCHING

- To make needle threading easy, use a needle threader. Insert the wire of the needle threader through the needle's eye. Then insert the thread through the wire and pull the threader back through the needle, drawing the thread through the eye.
- For durability, double your thread when hand stitching. Don't cut the thread any longer than 18 inches doubled, however, or it will tangle easily. When you run out of thread, rethread and begin where you left off.
- When you start a row of hand stitches, take a stitch in the same place twice before moving ahead.
- For a strong knot at the end of a row of hand stitches, take a backstitch. Then take one more stitch in the same place and leave a small loop. Pass the needle through the loop. Pull tight to tie the knot; then trim the thread.

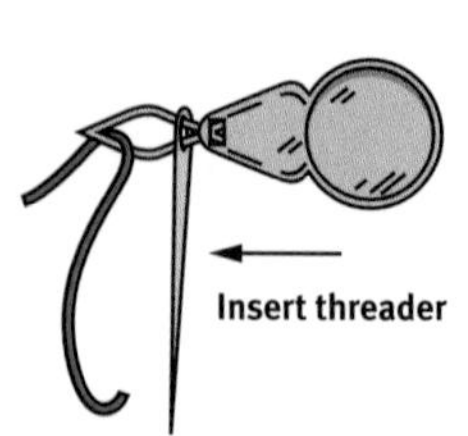


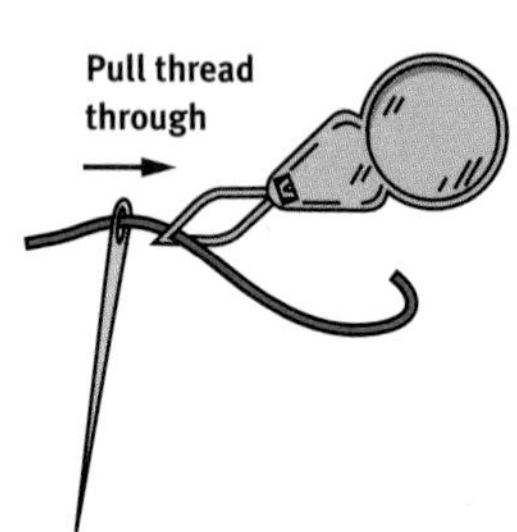

## Machine Sewing

Each brand of sewing machine differs slightly from the next; follow the manual's instructions for threading and operating the sewing machine available to you.

Sewing straight seams on a machine is fairly simple once you learn to guide the fabric evenly and keep a steady force on the foot pedal, but turning a corner can be tricky.

**TURNING A CORNER**

1. Make a mark on the fabric with chalk at the point where the seam lines intersect at the corner.
2. Stop the machine just before the mark and use the hand wheel to make the next few stitches.
3. With the needle in the fabric, lift the presser foot and pivot the fabric into position for stitching the other side of the corner.
4. Lower the presser foot and continue stitching.

**TECH TIPS: MACHINE SEWING**

- Learn to stitch in a straight line by stitching without thread over lined paper. The needle will punch holes in the paper, which you can check to see if the stitching is straight.
- Keep a steady, medium speed while machine sewing to avoid fabric bunching up.
- Use a seam guide to help you sew straight along the seam allowance.
- As in hand stitching, to prevent seams from pulling out, stitch backward for a few stitches at the beginning and end of each seam.

## Seam Finishes

Most seams require some type of finish to prevent the edges of the seam allowances from unraveling. Press your seams before and after doing a finish.

**STITCH AND PINK** Stitch ¼ inch from each edge of the seam allowances. Use a pinking shears to trim the edges. Pinking shears make a zigzag cut, which prevents raveling in most fabrics.

**ZIGZAG** Zigzag stitch along the raw edges of each seam allowance. Use wider stitches for heavier fabrics.

# Makeup: Equipment and Supplies

## Basic Equipment

### FACILITIES

**large, well-lit mirrors** with a counter for actors to use when applying makeup

**sink with liquid antibacterial soap dispenser** for dampening sponges or cotton swabs when putting on makeup and for cleaning brushes and sponges after finishing

### STORAGE

**bins or drawers** for storing makeup supplies, capes, and towels

## Supplies

### COSMETICS

**foundation** (colors from clown white to dark brown) to provide a base of color for the skin; may be greasepaint or creme, which are oil-based; or pancake, which is water-based

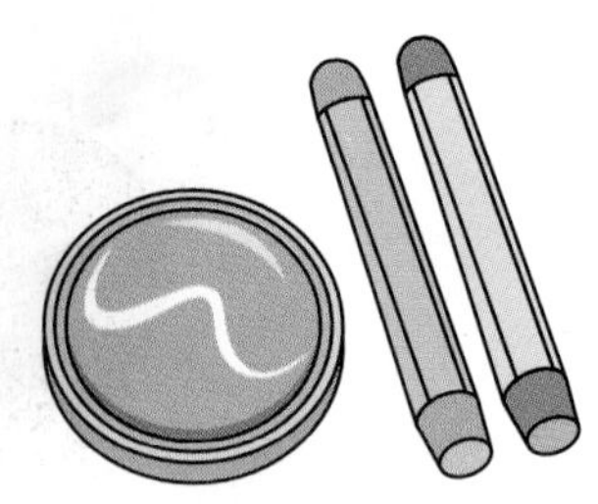

Greasepaint

Pancake

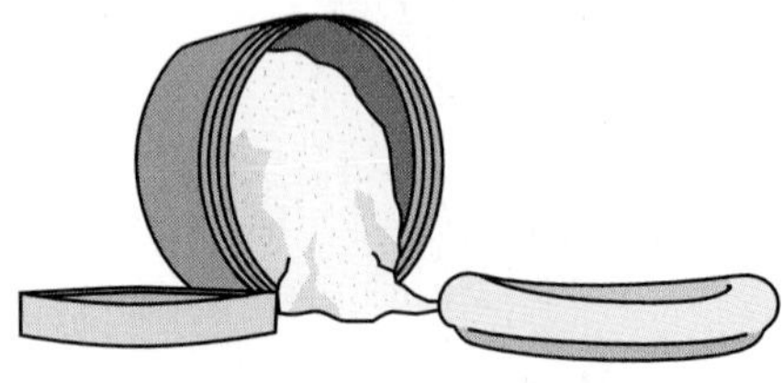

Loose powder and puff

**translucent powders** (colors similar to foundation shades) for setting greasepaint makeup and for reducing shine

**rouge powder** or **creme color** (various red and brown shades) for cheeks and lips

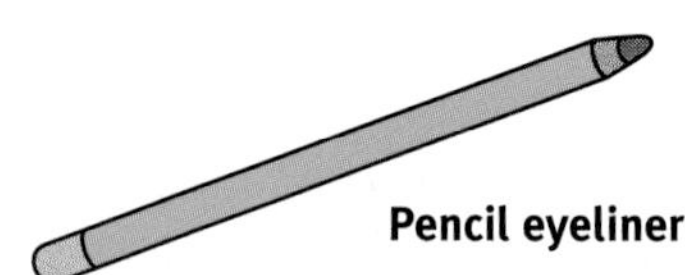

Pencil eyeliner

**shadow colors** or **liners** (various colors) for eyeshadow or for special effects

**eyeliner** (pencil or creme; black and brown) for lining eyes

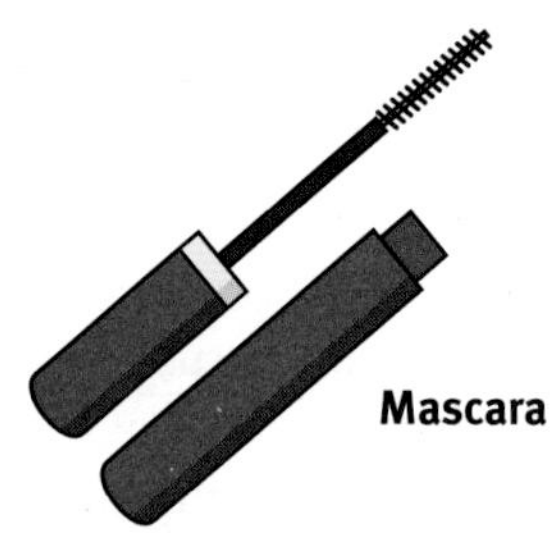

Mascara

**mascara** (brown, black, and white) for coloring and thickening eyelashes and eyebrows

**lipsticks** (various colors) for coloring lips; use only those made for stage

**cold cream, makeup remover, mineral oil, rubbing alcohol** for removing makeup

**tissues, cotton balls, pads,** and **swabs** for blotting, blending, and cleaning up

**powder puffs** for applying translucent powder

**powder brush** for removing excess powder

**makeup brushes** (various sizes) for highlighting, lining eyes, and shading

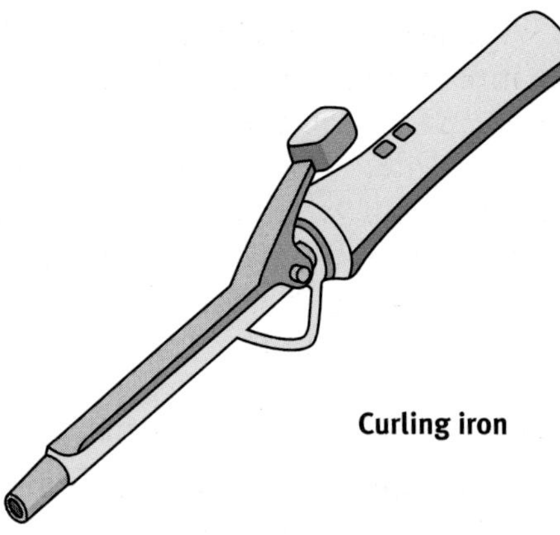

Curling iron

### HAIRSTYLING SUPPLIES

**curling iron, electric rollers, hand-held hair dryer** for styling hair

**wig forms** for storing and styling wigs

**colored hairspray** for temporary hair color change (white, gray, and black)

**hair gel, spray,** and **mousse** for arranging hair

**hair pins** and **bobby pins** for holding hair and wigs in place

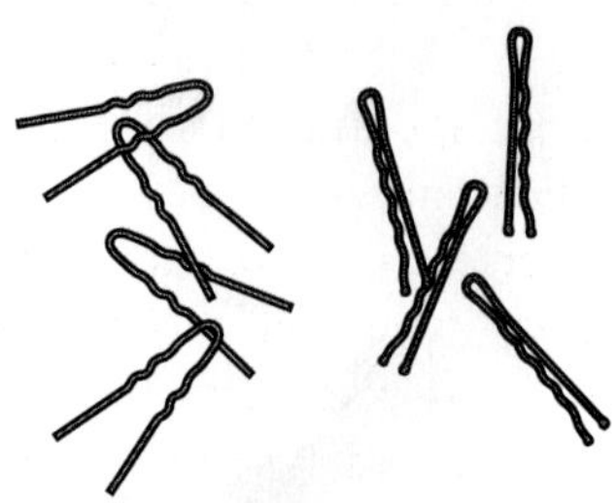

Hair pins and bobby pins

**hairbrushes** and **combs** for styling hair (various sizes)

**crepe hair** for creating facial hair (gray, black, brown, and light brown)

### SPECIAL EFFECTS SUPPLIES

**false eyelashes** and **lash curler**

**liquid latex** and **spirit gum** for attaching facial hair pieces and three dimensional makeup to the skin

**spirit gum remover** for removing spirit gum from the skin

**nose putty** and **derma wax** for altering facial features

**collodian** for special effects makeup

## Makeup Basics

Stage makeup usually consists of **foundation,** makeup applied to the entire face to provide a base of uniform color; color to emphasize eyes and lips; and any contouring color to model the features to create an effect. Hairstyling is an integral part of makeup and may involve wigs, beards, and other hairpieces. Stage makeup that is not intended for dramatic reshaping of the face or features is known as **straight makeup.** Makeup that is used to create a specific character is called **character makeup.**

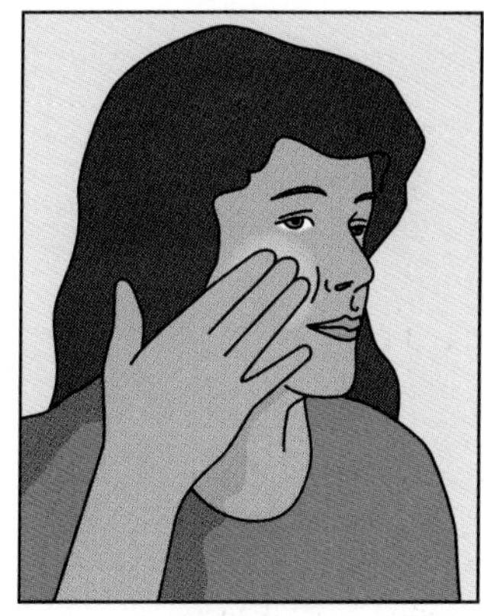

**Foundation**

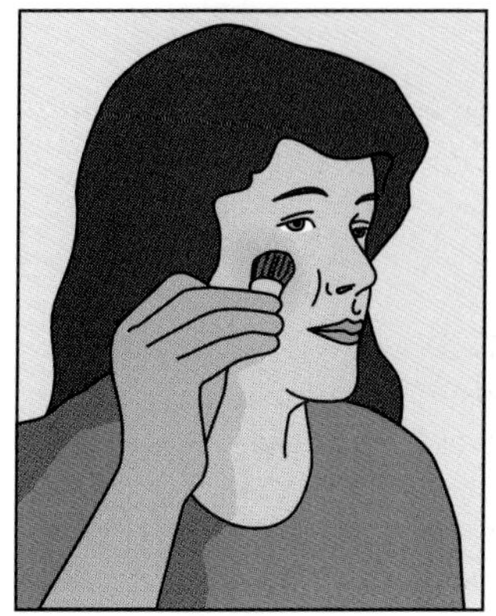

**Rouge**

### APPLYING STRAIGHT MAKEUP

1. Prepare your skin by first removing any previous makeup. Make sure your face is cool, clean, and dry. With oily skin use an astringent. For dry skin or for a more uniform foundation texture, apply a nongreasy moisturizer. If you shave, do so at least a half hour before applying makeup. If your hair tends to fall into your face, tie it or pin it back.
2. Choose either greasepaint, creme, or pancake foundation in a color that is close to your own skin tone. Because they stay moist, greasepaint and creme are easier for beginners to use. All of your other makeup should be of the same base (oil-based or water-based) as your foundation.
3. Use your fingertips or a sponge to dab on the foundation; then lightly blend it. If you are using pancake, use a lightly moistened sponge and stroke on the foundation; too much moisture in your sponge will result in streaking. Smooth the foundation over your entire face, into your hairline, under your chin, and down your neck to just below where your costume neckline rests. If your ears show, apply foundation to them also. You should end up with an even-looking surface of color.
4. Next, apply rouge. If it is moist, stroke it on and blend the edges with your fingers or a sponge. If it is dry, brush it on and blend the edges with the brush. The rouge should highlight the part of your cheeks that look round when you smile.
5. Using your own lip brush, outline the edges of your lips with rouge or lipstick. Then fill in the rest of your lips.
6. Line your eyes with a small eyeliner pencil or brush. The line should not be heavy, and should begin on the upper lid about one-third of the distance from the inside corner of your eye. Continue the line to just beyond the outer end of your upper lid. On your lower lid, draw the line from the center to the outer edge of your eye. Blend to soften the ends of each line.

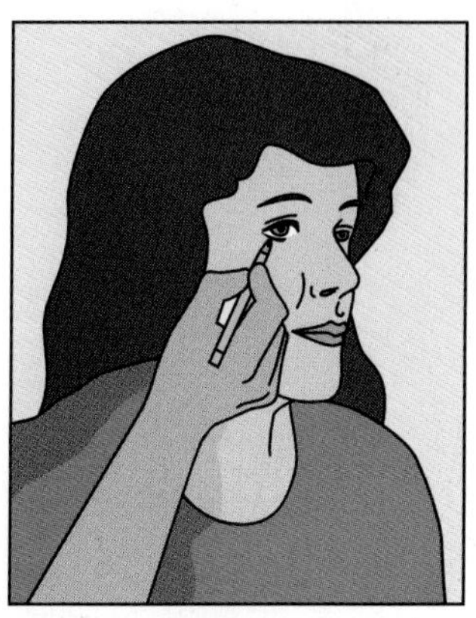

**Eyeliner**

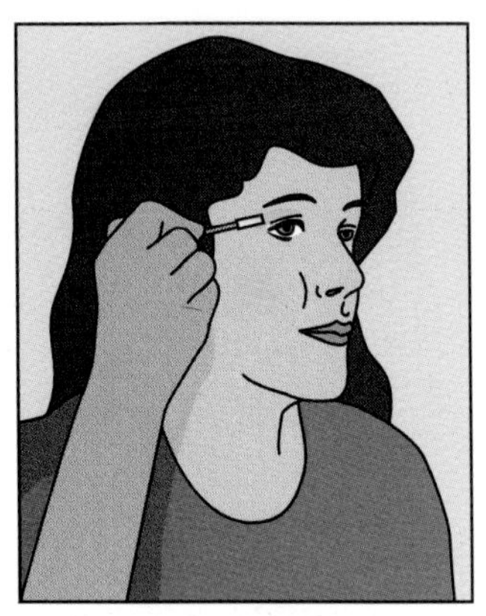

Eye shadow

7. For the remainder of your eye, use a shade lighter than your foundation on the area just below your eyebrow. Powder your lids lightly before applying creme shadow to prevent creasing. In the crease of your eye and on your upper eyelid, use a color slightly darker than your foundation. Brown is most natural. You may also choose a color that coordinates with your costume color.
8. If you are using greasepaint or creme, it's time to powder. Dip the puff into the powder. Gently shake off the excess. Carefully pat the powder onto your face and neck. Don't drag the puff across your face. Lift it directly up between pats so that you don't streak the makeup underneath. When your face is covered with powder, use a powder brush to lightly dust off the excess. Afterwards, if your rouge appears too washed out, reapply it.

   Pancake foundation does not require powdering, although if you sweat, you may want to absorb any shine with a compact powder.
9. Finally, using your own mascara brush, apply mascara to all your upper eyelashes and the outer half of your lower lashes. If your eyebrows are too light, you may also use mascara or an eyebrow pencil to darken them slightly.

## Makeup Kit

In many cases, actors are required to buy their own stage makeup. In any case, it is a good idea for actors to have their own stage makeup kit. You can add to it as the need arises. Start off with foundation, powder, a few shadow colors, a lighter foundation, a couple of rouges, eyeliner, mascara, powder puffs, a powder brush, a lipstick brush, a few small brushes, some cosmetic sponges, cotton balls and swabs, makeup remover or baby oil, bobby pins and a ponytail holder, a comb and brush, and astringent or rubbing alcohol. A fishing tackle box or small carrying case are good for storing and carrying your kit.

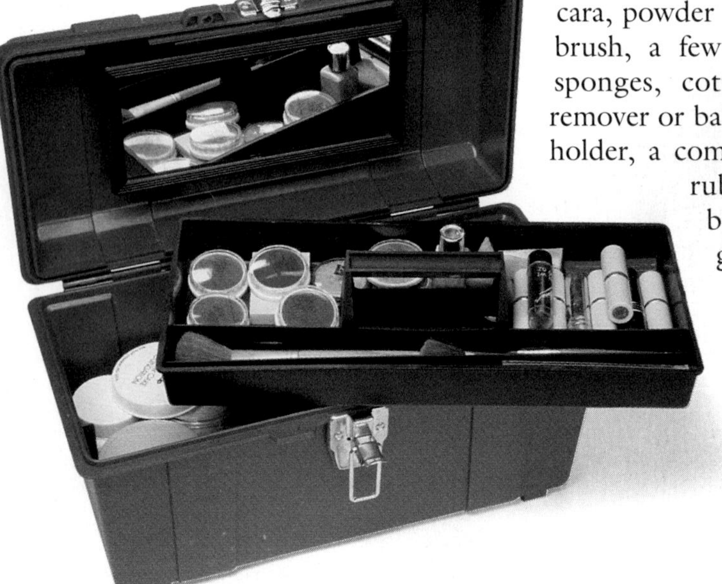

## SAFETY TIPS Costumes and Makeup

### SAFETY TIPS: COSTUMES

- When carrying or handing off scissors, hold them by clasping your fist around the closed blades, not the handles.
- Put pins and needles away after use.
- Never hold pins or needles in your mouth.
- Never test an iron by touching it.
- Place a hot iron on a metal iron rest when not in use.
- Work outdoors or in a well-ventilated area when using sprays of any kind.
- Avoid using razor blades to rip seams. They are sloppy and dangerous.
- Use a thimble to protect your finger from puncture when you push needles through fabric.

### SAFETY TIPS: MAKEUP

- Hair spray and acetone are highly flammable; When using them, there should be no open flames or smoking cigarettes in the room.
- Warn the people you are hairspraying before you begin so they can shield their faces.
- For health reasons, do not use sponges, eyeliner, mascara, lipstick, or lipstick brushes on more than one actor. Do not share these with other actors.
- Make sure there is adequate ventilation in the makeup room.
- If you are allergy prone, do a skin test with the makeup or hair products you will be using well in advance of the performance.
- Remove wigs, facial hairpieces, and makeup promptly after performances. Be especially careful around your eyes.
- When applying eye makeup to other people, check to see if they wear contact lenses. If they do, be even more careful and gentle, and check with them frequently to see that their lenses are still in place.
- If applying liquid latex to your skin, be sure to shave beforehand. When you pull off the latex, hair will come with it.

# Activities

*Set Construction and Prop Crews*

**BUILD A FRAME** Under supervision from your teacher, work with a partner to build an open frame 2 feet square out of 2 x 4 lumber. Use overlap, butt, or miter joints and common nails. Have the frame checked for accuracy; then take it apart without bending the nails.

*Set Construction and Prop Crews*

**BUILD A BOX** Plan and build a multiuse box for actors. The box should be strong enough to function as a table, chair, platform, or container. First, make a drawing or cardboard model of the box, including the dimensions. Plan for a cube of about 18 inches square. List the materials and tools you will need. Then with proper supervision from your instructor, use the materials to build the box.

*Light and Sound Crews*

**RECORD SOUNDS TO SET A MOOD** Use a tape recorder to create a soundtrack that will set a mood—spooky, serene, joyous, sorrowful. Use music, sound effects, vocalizations (though not words). Play the recording in class and see if listeners can identify the sounds and if they feel you have achieved a mood.

*Light and Sound Crews*

**CONDUCT A LIGHTING SURVEY** Observe the lighting effects in various places around school, home, and your community. How does the lighting in places affect your mood? What mood is it trying to establish, if any? Observe colors, intensity (brightness), and angle of lights, as well as various light sources—the sun, lamps, candles, fluorescent lights. Record your observations in your Theatre Notebook.

*Costume and Makeup Crews*

**EXPERIMENT WITH HAND-STITCHES** Practice threading a needle and making and finishing a row of the various hand stitches explained in this chapter. Experiment with different sized needles, weights of thread, and weights of fabric. Use large needles with heavier thread for thicker fabric and smaller needles with finer thread for thinner and more delicate fabric.

*Costume and Makeup Crews*

**SEW A TUNIC** Use a large piece of paper to draw the outline of a tunic, which is a wide, long top with a scoop neck and bell sleeves. Make sure you give enough space so you can get the tunic over your head. Cut out the pattern. Then use tailor's chalk to trace the outline of the pattern on fabric. Cut the fabric and sew it together along the seam lines; cut the edges of the neck, sleeves, and bottom with pinking shears to prevent unraveling, or hem them. Use your tunic for costumes in your classroom performances. You can make long ones to serve as dresses or belt them with cord for another style.

*Costume and Makeup Crews*

**ASSEMBLE A MAKEUP KIT** Using the information provided, assemble your own makeup kit. Label all your supplies with your name so that, for safety reasons, others will not use your products. Using your makeup kit, apply straight makeup on your face.

*Costume and Makeup Crews*

**JOB SHADOW—MAKEUP ARTIST** Arrange with an area theatre or TV station to observe a makeup artist at work for a day, or a few hours. You may be able to attend a dress rehearsal at a theatre or observe a TV anchor getting made up for a news broadcast. Explain that you are interested in witnessing the day-to-day operations of a makeup artist. Professionals are busy, but if you are polite as well as interested, they are usually willing to let you observe them at work and to answer questions about their training and background. Be sure to first get permission from your parents, teacher, and the supervisor of the business or organization where you will job shadow. Record your observations in your Theatre Notebook.

# Projects

exploration

PROJECT 1

## Telling a Story

**ASSIGNMENT** In a small group, perform a story using movement and narration.

| Project Planner | |
|---|---|
| Product | Performance that tells a story |
| Purpose | To communicate effectively through narration, body position, and movement |
| Specs | To accomplish this project, you will<br>• develop cooperation skills within your group<br>• choose a story suited to your audience<br>• determine the story events you need to perform<br>• discover unique ways of using position and movement<br>• help develop a narration<br>• perform your story in a way that is understandable and enjoyable to your audience |

### Creating

**DEVELOP YOUR STORY** As an ensemble, choose a story. It may be a short story from a literature anthology, a fairy tale, a movie, a television show, or a story compiled from shared experiences. A good story should have a sequence of events: a beginning, a middle, and an end.

**ANALYZE YOUR STORY** Work together to do the following:

1. Identify the characters in the story.
2. Establish where the story takes place.
3. Itemize what events take place.
4. Determine the order in which the events take place.

**PLAN THE NARRATION** Decide who is telling the story. You have several choices here: You can use an unnamed narrator. You can share the narration among several narrators. You can have one of the characters in the story tell about the events, or several characters in the story can take turns telling about events.

The storyteller or tellers may work from notes, but don't write out the whole story for someone to read. Rather, rehearse the story enough times so that the storytellers know it by heart. The idea is for each storyteller to use his or her own words, not words from a book or words that have been otherwise written down.

**CREATE THE MOVEMENT** While the storytellers are talking to the audience, the rest of the ensemble will pantomime the action. You can have one person act the main character, or you can share the main character among several actors. Experiment with actors playing nonhuman characters and scenery; for example, what could you do with your bodies to suggest trees, a mountain, a fence, a river, an automobile? What characteristics do you need to play a dog, a bear, a snake, a bird? What about using actors to play fear, greed, happiness?

At the same time, experiment with your voices to create sound effects like wind, rain, forest animals, a city street. You could use a familiar song as background music by humming or singing it with one syllable, such as *ah* or *la*.

**REHEARSE THE STORY** Your ensemble should rehearse the story with all its elements—narration, movement, and sound and lighting effects—until everyone is comfortable with his or her part and with the overall effect. Try to use your entire performance space imaginatively, creating different levels and shapes. Think about movement variations such as stops or freezes, fast-forward, slow motion, changes in direction, and changes in focus (in which one or more actors move while the others stay frozen). You might consider beginning and ending your story with actors frozen in movement as if in a picture (tableau).

## Performing

When you are ready, perform your story in front of the class or another small group. Plan in advance how you will take your places to begin your performance. If you are not working on a proscenium stage with a curtain to draw or lights that you can black out, you should consider that you are onstage from the minute you leave your seat—while taking your place onstage, throughout your performance, and while returning to your seat. Keep your focus on the story to be told, whether you are playing a narrator, a main character, or a tree.

## Responding

How well you have fulfilled the Specs in the Project Planner will help assess your project. You may also ask yourself, your ensemble, or your audience these questions to help you improve:

- Could you understand the story that was told?
- Did the narrators speak loudly and clearly enough?
- Were the separate characters clear?
- Did your group use a variety of movements?
- Was there any movement that seemed out of place or didn't help to tell the story?
- Did your group use the space well?
- Did everyone stay focused on the story being told?
- What other ways might you expand or polish your ensemble performance?

Include responses to these questions in your Theatre Notebook.

## Adapting the Project

1. Work with several other groups to tell a longer, more complex story. Each group can take a part of the story—one or more events—to dramatize in their own fashion. This means that certain characters may be played by several different actors during the course of the whole story. Or, one or more central characters can interact with different groups in particular settings during the course of the story. Put your parts together in order to tell the whole story for your audience.
2. Create a book for the story that was developed. Someone could take a series of photographs of your performance. Or you might cut out pictures from magazines or newspapers to illustrate the events of the story. Mount your pictures in a notebook in the order in which the actions were performed. Have the narrators write captions for the pictures to help tell the story.
3. Have someone videotape your performance and add the tape to a video library. You might create a series of stories: choose other stories to perform that are connected to your story by a character type, such as a young daredevil; a setting, such as the desert; a theme, such as honesty; or a genre, such as horror. You might elaborate on the production aspects by using music, scenery, artwork, or costumes. The videos may be shown to other classes or for assemblies.

# Animal Pantomime

PROJECT 2

**ASSIGNMENT** Create a pantomime story based on the exploration of animal movement.

## Project Planner

| | |
|---|---|
| Product | Performance of a pantomime story featuring an animal character |
| Purpose | To expand movement capabilities, increase observation skills, and use them to develop an animal character |
| Specs | To accomplish this project, you will<br>• imagine the animal's behavior in different situations<br>• develop a story about the animal with a beginning, middle, and end<br>• use pantomime to perform your story for the class<br>• identify and imitate the animal's movements |

## Creating

**CHOOSE AN ANIMAL** Think of a specific animal that you like or that particularly interests you. Ask yourself questions about the animal, such as the following:

- What species or animal family does it belong to?
- What is its anatomical structure?
- How does it move?
- Where does it live?
- What does it like to eat?
- How does it get its food?
- How does it protect itself?
- What are its predators?
- What kinds of sounds does it make?
- What reactions does it display that seem like human emotions?
- How does it stay clean?
- Does it travel in a group or alone?

**DEVELOP YOUR MOVEMENTS** Find a space on the floor, and from a relaxed position, begin to assume the characteristics of the animal you have chosen. Think about how old your animal is. Are you just learning to walk or fly? Are you near the end of your life? Do you have a family? Then find an activity for your animal. Are you hunting for food? Performing a mating ritual? Protecting your young? Taking a swim or bath? Relaxing after a meal? Define your animal in this way through its traits and movements.

If you have the opportunty, observe your animal in some of its daily routines. You may study a household pet, a zoo animal, an animal in the wild, or a film of wildlife in its native habitat. Watch your animal walk, stretch, lie down, and eat. As you watch, try to copy its movements.

Once you have defined your animal and its activity, introduce a conflict. Are you being chased? Is there a fire? Is the weather bad or food scarce? Are you lost or in danger? Is there another animal threatening you? Are you ill or wounded? Find a way to end or escape your conflict.

## Performing

Refine and develop your story to make it interesting and believable. Give it a title. Think about how you want your audience to feel as they watch your story. Rehearse your pantomime until you are comfortable with it and confident that you have thoroughly explored your animal and its movements. Finally, perform your pantomime for the class. You might use recorded music or sounds to accompany your performance.

## Responding

How well you have fulfilled the Specs in the Project Planner will help assess your project. You may also ask yourself or your classmates these questions to help you improve:

- How complex and detailed were my movements and story?
- Did my story have a beginning, middle, and end?
- Did the audience understand the story?
- Did I achieve a similarity in movement to my animal?
- Could the audience identify the humanlike emotions I portrayed?

Include responses to these questions in your Theatre Notebook.

## Adapting the Project

1. With a partner or a small group, portray the same or different animals in a family or community or in an encounter with another rival animal. Improvise your interactions. Even though you are improvising, try to tell a story with a beginning, middle, and end.
2. Humans are often described as having animal characteristics. Develop a human character with some of the movements you used for your animal. Put your character into a situation with other animal-like human characters and develop some actions or dialogue for your character.

# Improvisation and Tableau



**ASSIGNMENT** In a small group, create a tableau to represent a picture and develop an improvisation based on the situation depicted in the picture.

## Project Planner

| | |
|---|---|
| **Product** | **Performance of a tableau with improvisation** |
| **Purpose** | **To develop insight about how body positions and movement demonstrate character** |
| **Specs** | **To accomplish this project, you will**<br>• **work cooperatively within a small group**<br>• **analyze the situation in a picture**<br>• **develop and portray a character based on the picture**<br>• **create a relationship with other characters**<br>• **improvise words and actions suggested by the situation** |

## Creating

**CHOOSE A PICTURE** A technique sometimes used on stage is the **tableau,** a silent and motionless depiction of a scene, often from a picture. Playwright James Lapine and composer Stephen Sondheim based their musical *Sunday in the Park with George* on the life and work of the French painter Georges Seurat (1859–1891). In one scene from the musical the characters form a tableau that mirrors Seurat's painting, *A Sunday Afternoon on the Island of La Grande Jatte* (p. 444). What Lapine and Sondheim did was to start with the painting and imagine characters and the situations that could bring them all together at the same time and place, in certain positions.

Work with your group to choose a picture. It may be a famous work of art, a photograph from a magazine or newspaper, a scene from a movie, or a family photograph. The picture you choose must have people in it—at least as many people as are in your group. Choose a picture that has strong visual appeal, will be easy to perform, and will yield an interesting situation for developing an improvisation. As you make your choice, ask questions about the picture and discuss relationships and situations suggested by it.

**PLAN YOUR TABLEAU** Cast members of your group as characters in the picture. If there are more characters in the picture than you have members, make choices about which ones to include. Determine the furniture, costumes, and props you need; keep it as simple as possible so you can set up and take down quickly.

Arrange your bodies in exactly the same positions as those of the characters in your picture. Have someone step out of the tableau to check your positions against the picture or ask someone outside your group to do the same. You might also ask someone to take a Polaroid photograph of your group, or if possible, work in front of a large mirror, such as one found in a dance studio.

**DEVELOP YOUR IMPROVISATION** Your improvisation will start from the tableau. While you are finding your positions in the tableau, begin to develop your improvisation by providing the dramatic details to questions the picture has raised, including the following:

- Who are these characters, and what is their relationship to each other?
- Why did they come together at this time?
- What will happen to these characters from this moment on?

Put your details together to develop a story with a beginning, middle, and end—even though your improvisation may not show the entire story. As an alternate approach, discover the answers to these questions through a preliminary improvisation based on your tableau. Throughout the development of the improv, work on establishing a personality for the character you will portray and keep your character's goal in mind.

Decide next how long you will hold the tableau before beginning the improv and which character will speak first to lead it off. Do your improvisation two or three times. Each time will be somewhat different—that is the nature of improvisation. Your group may discover, however, one line of development or one ending that you prefer over the others. Agree to preserve that for your performance.

## Performing

Display your tableau to the audience. Take your places quickly and efficiently. As you perform, play close attention to what others are saying and doing, and let your speeches and actions be a response to theirs.

Knowing when to end an improvisation can be tricky. If you have decided on an ending, everyone will be working toward it; otherwise, you may need to designate one member of your group to make a decision and to signal the others somehow when to stop.

## Responding

How well you have fulfilled the Specs in the Project Planner will help assess your project. You may also ask yourself, your ensemble, or your audience these questions to help you improve:

- Did the ensemble convincingly reproduce the original picture?
- Did the story that developed make sense?
- Were the separate characters clear?
- Were there any lines or movements that seemed out of place or didn't help tell the story?
- Did everyone stay focused on the story being told?
- Did the improvisation end in a reasonable or appropriate place?

Include responses to these questions in your Theatre Notebook.

## Adapting the Project

1. Develop a second improvisation to explore what happened to the characters prior to the picture; that is, how did these characters end up in these positions?
2. With your group, choose two pictures. Use one picture as the basis for a starting tableau. Use the second picture as the basis for a final tableau. You will probably need to discuss your characters in advance. Use improvisation to develop the situation and actions that take you from your starting positions to your final positions.

# Soundscapes

PROJECT 4

**ASSIGNMENT** Work with a partner or small group to create a performance combining movement with sound.

## Project Planner

| | |
|---|---|
| **Product** | A performance combining sound and movement |
| **Purpose** | To explore different kinds of sound and understand their effects in a performance |
| **Specs** | To accomplish this project, you will<br>• work creatively with a partner or small group<br>• listen attentively and critically<br>• choose sounds that are dramatic or appropriate to an environment<br>• experiment to create a variety of sounds using your body, sound effects, and instruments<br>• perform a movement with sound |

## Creating

**EXPLORE ENVIRONMENTS** Sit quietly and listen to the sounds around you. As you identify the sounds, write them down. Now imagine the sounds you might hear in different environments such as a subway, airport, playground, forest preserve, grocery store, video game arcade, beach, mall, and so on. Next, choose one of these environments to explore further.

Individually, write down people and objects you would see, actions that might occur, and sounds you would hear in your chosen environment. For example, if you choose the environment of a beach, you might see people in swimsuits, lifeguards, towels, large umbrellas, beach chairs, flotation devices, coolers, a volleyball net and ball, and beach toys. You might see people walking along the sand, reading, splashing in the waves, surfing, and playing games. You would hear the sound of the surf, the laughter of children, people calling out to each other, seagulls squawking, and a lifeguard's whistle.

Now pantomime some of the actions and experiment with movements that suggest some of the sounds on your list.

**CHOOSE AN ENVIRONMENT** With your partner or group, compare notes and demonstrate some of the movements you have developed. Work together to choose an environment that offers rich creative possibilities. Then create a group list of objects, actions, and sounds.

Prepare the sounds of the environment you have chosen. Collect sounds using at least three of the following methods:

- Visit the actual environment and tape-record the sounds there.
- Create the sounds with your body and voice.
- Simulate the sounds with instruments or with objects that, when shaken, scraped, or clapped together, create sound effects. For example, an old standby sound effect for thunder in the theatre is to rattle a large, flexible sheet of metal. You can record these individual sounds or keep the objects on hand during your performance.
- Use your body movements to suggest sounds. For example, jumping up into the air and spreading your arms wide while wiggling your fingers might suggest the sound of a splash.
- Purchase commercial sound effects tapes or disks with the environmental sounds you want. Sometimes these are available at music stores. (Pay attention to copyright restrictions on use of recorded sounds.)

**DEVELOP YOUR SOUNDSCAPE** Combine your sounds to create a soundscape. This will be, in effect, a modern dance with sound effects, except that the dance part will be movements that suggest sounds. Experiment with different combinations and different layerings until you achieve an interesting effect. If you are using sound recordings, you may need to re-record some sounds, editing as necessary to get the effect you want (p. 87).

## Performing

Rehearse your soundscape until you are comfortable with the presentation and timing of all sounds and confident that you can reproduce them in performance. Perform your soundscape for your classmates or other small groups.

## Responding

How well you have fulfilled the Specs in the Project Planner will help assess your project. You may also ask yourself, your partners, or your classmates these questions to help you improve:

- Did the sounds my group chose create an overall impression of our chosen environment?
- Did my group rehearse enough to ensure a smooth performance?
- Did the audience understand the connection between our movements and sounds?
- Which sounds, if any, were unclear and how could they have been better presented?

Include responses to these questions in your Theatre Notebook.

## Adapting the Project

1. Create another soundscape with the addition of instrumental music. Listen to a variety of instrumental music to find selections appropriate to the environment you choose. Stay away from the obvious; for example, using rock music for the environment of a rock music concert or teen event. To layer all your sounds, you may need two tape recorders—one for music and the other for sounds.
2. Create another soundscape with added visual elements, such as costumes, posters, slides, photos, postcards, original art, and so on—all of which suggest a particular environment. You might, for example, have images from slides projected onto your bodies during your performance, or wear sheets with paintings of your environment.

PROJECT 5

# Perspectives on Theatre Spaces

**ASSIGNMENT** Work with a group of four actors to explore theatre spaces from an audience's point of view and document your conclusions.

## Project Planner

| | |
|---|---|
| Product | An annotated series of diagrams showing actors onstage viewed from different audience perspectives |
| Purpose | To explore the three major kinds of stages and the effect that audience position has on the audience's perception of actors onstage |
| Specs | To accomplish this project, you will<br>• develop a cooperative director/actor relationship with classmates<br>• create a theatre space in an open area<br>• position actors in various stage areas<br>• study the actors from various perspectives and draw conclusions about their positions relative to you<br>• draw diagrams showing all the positions<br>• annotate the diagrams with your conclusions |

## Creating

**ESTABLISH YOUR THEATRE SPACE** On a large area of open floor, use masking tape to recreate the diagram of the proscenium stage areas as shown on page 62. The stage area should be at least 15 feet wide by 10 feet deep. Label the areas by taping down paper signs marked "up left," "down center," and so on.

Position Your Ensemble Enlist four of your classmates to be actors. Position them in the four stage areas that you have chosen beforehand; for example, Actor A: down right, Actor B: up center, Actor C: down center, and Actor D: up left.

**EXAMINE THE RESULTS** Sit on a chair in what would be the audience area, at least 10 feet away from the stage area. Study the actors carefully. You are seeing them from the viewpoint of an audience member sitting slightly above stage level. Draw a diagram to indicate what you see. You can use simple figures for the actors and arrows to indicate which way they are facing. Then have the actors change positions as indicated here. Draw a diagram for each change.

1. All actors face you.
2. Actors B, C, and D face Actor A.
3. Actors A, C, and D face Actor B.
4. Actors A, B, and D face Actor C.
5. Actors A, B, and C face Actor D.

For each change of direction, ask yourself these questions. Take notes on your answers.

- Which actor is nearest to me?
- Which actor appears the tallest?
- Which actor draws my attention the most?

Work quickly so that your actors don't become tired and bored. You might find it easier to prepare a partial diagram of the stage areas in advance, leaving room for notes, and then photocopy it as many times as you need.

**EXPLORE OTHER PERSPECTIVES** You have now looked at your actors as if they were performing on a proscenium stage. Now position yourself stage left and study the actors from this new perspective. Have them face the same five directions as you take notes on your answers to the same three questions. Repeat the activity from a stage right perspective. So far, you have viewed the actors from three different sides of a stage, as if they were performing on a thrust stage.

Next position yourself upstage and repeat the activity. You have now viewed the actors from four sides, as if viewing them on an arena stage. Thank your actors and dismiss them.

## Presenting

You should have 20 diagrams. They may be hastily drawn, with scribbled notes. You may wish to redraw them in neater fashion, or to revise your notes somewhat for presentation. When your revisions are complete, gather your diagrams together in a binder and add a title. Finally, add a paragraph stating what you have learned from your study. You might want to include this assessment paragraph in your Theatre Notebook.

## Responding

How well you have fulfilled the Specs in the Project Planner will assess your project. You may also ask yourself these questions to help you improve:

- Did I seriously study the different effects created by viewing the actors from different angles?
- Did I come to a conclusion regarding changes in effects arising from changes in audience perspectives and actor positions?
- Did I treat my actors with respect?

Include responses to these questions in your Theatre Notebook.

## Adapting the Project

1. Repeat the activity from a position sitting on the floor so that the actors are slightly above you. Then use a stepladder to get a perspective of looking down at the actors as if from a higher seat in the audience. (Enlist someone to hold the ladder while you do your sketches.) Add the sketches from these different perspectives to your binder and add another summarizing paragraph to account for these new perspectives.
2. Repeat the activity without the sketches, allowing the actors to take turns stepping down to see the stage pictures while you take their place. This lets them have a sense of what the audience sees.

PROJECT 6

# Analyzing Theatre Spaces

**ASSIGNMENT** Present an illustrated analysis of various kinds of theatre spaces.

### Project Planner

| | |
|---|---|
| Product | Illustrated analysis of theatre spaces |
| Purpose | To become aware of various theatre spaces and present an analysis of their pros and cons for staging productions |
| Specs | To accomplish this project, you will<br>• research various kinds of theatre spaces in your school or community<br>• assemble a number of illustrations<br>• organize the illustrations into groups based on type, location, purpose, and so on<br>• write captions for the illustrations describing the spaces and the pros and cons of each<br>• assemble and present the illustrations on paper with captions or as a videotape with narration |

## Creating

**DO THE RESEARCH** Brainstorm a list of theatre spaces in your school and community. Don't confine yourself to obvious proscenium stages, such as local community theatre groups or movie theatres might have. Consider possible performance areas such as a park, stadium, forest preserve, lecture hall, dance studio, warehouse, or church.

Find out who is in charge of each theatre space and contact that person by letter or phone asking permission to visit the space and photograph or videotape it.

**TAKE PICTURES AND GATHER INFORMATION** Getting pictures of these theatre spaces can be as simple or as sophisticated as your equipment and your experience allow. You could use a Polaroid, instant, or 35-mm camera to shoot still photos. You could use a video camera/recorder. You might also find it helpful to draw detailed diagrams of some spaces.

Start with a theatre space in your school. Photograph the general space and as many details as you can, such as proscenium arch, orchestra pit, stage house, light and sound booth, and so on. Taking pictures in a theatre can be tricky, because you seldom have natural light to work with. Be sure you understand the capabilities of your camera and the film you are using, so that your pictures come out clear.

Now go on to photograph theatre spaces in your community. If you live in a small town or rural area, there may be few formal spaces, but look for alternative spaces. If you live in a city, theatre spaces may be so numerous that you will have to limit your project to a number that you can handle successfully.

Be sure to take notes at the same time that you are getting your pictures so that you will have accurate information on which to base the captions you will write. Consider where and how a performance would be staged in the space and where an audience would sit. Also consider the acoustics, the sound-transmission characteristics of the space. Look for the pros and the cons from the perspectives of the audience, actors, director, and tech crews.

**ORGANIZE YOUR MATERIALS** Once you have gathered the pictures of the theatre spaces you will use and the information about them, you will need to organize them in some fashion. You could, for example, group all the pictures you have taken of an old, restored opera house in one section and all the pictures of an amphitheatre in the zoo in another section. Or, you could group details such as entrances, stage areas, lighting systems, and so on. The variety and nature of your pictures may suggest other methods of organization.

**WRITE YOUR CAPTIONS** What you write about the pictures will depend to some extent on the pictures themselves and on your method of organization and presentation. If you will present photographs with written captions, a simple, informative paragraph of one or two sentences will be best. If you are planning to narrate a videotape presentation, you may only need prompting notes. Be sure to include your speculations about the potential of each space for theatre productions—the problems and the promise of each space.

## Presenting

Assemble your pictures and captions into the illustrated essay you have planned and present it for review by your classmates. A photo album or posterboard series would be appropriate for a collection of still photographs. A narrated videotape presentation will work best for video images.

## Responding

How well you have fulfilled the Specs in the Project Planner will help assess your project. You may also ask yourself or your classmates these questions to help you improve:

- Was I imaginative in listing various kinds of theatre spaces to research and resourceful in contacting the appropriate people for permission?
- Was I practiced enough in the technology used so that all the illustrations came out clear?
- Did I assemble and organize enough illustrations to make a worthwhile picture essay?
- Did I write clear and informative captions for all the illustrations?
- Does the medium I used make the illustrations completely accessible to readers?

Include responses to these questions in your Theatre Notebook.

## Adapting the Project

Work with a partner or with a group to compile this analysis. In this case, you could brainstorm possible research sites together to come up with a more comprehensive list. Clearly establish who will do what. Consider sending two people to each space for a more balanced point of view.

# Building a Model Stage

**ASSIGNMENT** Using cardboard or another lightweight material, build a scale model of your school's theatre space.

## Project Planner

| | |
|---|---|
| **Product** | Model theatre |
| **Purpose** | To practice accurate measuring and to develop manipulative skills |
| **Specs** | To accomplish this project, you will<br>• accurately measure your school's theatre space, noting the measurements on a rough sketch<br>• plan how to translate those measurements into a scale model<br>• select the tools needed and the most appropriate medium<br>• construct a model theatre<br>• work neatly and with careful attention to detail<br>• follow the appropriate safety guidelines |

## Creating

**MEASURE YOUR THEATRE SPACE** First draw a rough sketch of your school's theatre space. If your school has a proscenium stage, you will have to decide how much of the top part of the proscenium to include. Next, use a tape measure to measure every distance and note the dimensions on your sketch. You may need to enlist a classmate to help you with the tape measure, and possibly, with the use of a ladder. Measure accurately; an error at this time may be magnified in your finished product.

**DETERMINE YOUR SCALE** Your first step before working with any materials is to decide on a scale. In model building, **scale** refers to the size of the model compared to the size of what it represents. For example, a ¼-inch scale would mean that ¼ inch in the model equals 1 foot in the original, and 1 inch in the model equals 4 feet in the original. If your stage floor is 30 feet by 20 feet, therefore, your model floor will be 7½ inches by 5 inches.

**DECIDE ON A MEDIUM** In this context, medium means the material with which you work. Cardboard is lightweight and easy to cut with scissors or a utility knife, but it may be flimsy and easily crushed. Foamcore is also lightweight and easy to cut with a knife, but it's harder to glue neatly and the cut edges are hard to disguise. Balsa wood is lightweight and easy to cut, but you need a little practice to cut it neatly. Balsa can be painted more successfully than cardboard or foamboard. Another option is matte board, which is available at art supply or hobby stores. It is easy to work with, and the rougher side holds paint well. Use cardboard and matte board as thick as you can work with successfully; foamcore and balsa that are ⅜-inch thick will give you a substantial model.

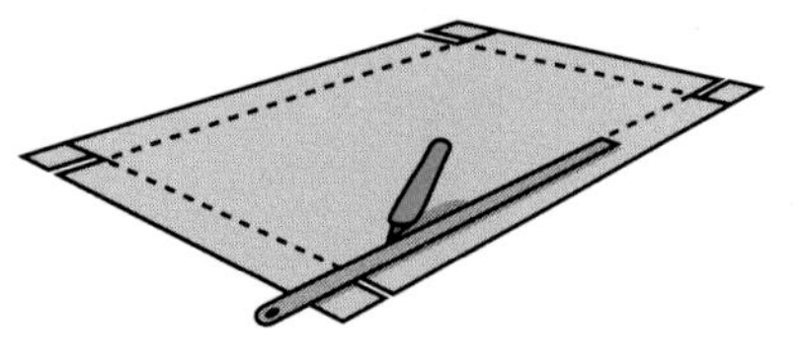

**Proscenium pattern**

Regardless of which material you choose, it's wise to make a preliminary rough model with poster board and tape to avoid wasting time and materials and to check your measurements.

**PREPARE A PATTERN** If you are using cardboard or matte board, you may want to prepare a pattern on a large sheet of paper before transferring it to the material and cutting it out. Draw the dimensions (in scale) of your stage floor in the middle of your paper. Next add rectangles on all sides that are the height of the stage; the height is figured from the floor of the house where it meets the stage to the stage floor level. You may want to add a tab on one end of each of these to allow for gluing.

Transfer this pattern to the board and cut it out carefully. Use a sharp knife such as a utility knife and a metal straight-edge ruler to cut straight lines. Be sure to have some material underneath, like an extra sheet of cardboard, so that you don't ruin the table surface. You are going to fold your pattern into a shallow box, something like a shoebox lid. Before you fold, score (make a shallow cut) along the fold lines to make the folds neater. Be careful not to cut all the way through. When you score, make the folds bend *away* from the cutting line.

Fold the tabs under the sides and glue them with white glue or household cement. Be careful not to get glue on the outside of your model.

**USING BALSA WOOD OR FOAMCORE** You don't need to prepare a pattern for either of these materials because you won't fold them; the floor and sides are separate pieces. Measure carefully and draw your lines with pencil; then cut out the pieces with a sharp knife.

Use household cement to glue balsa wood and a white glue or a special hobby glue for the foamcore. On a foamcore model, add a narrow strip of paper along each corner to strengthen the joints and disguise the cut edge.

If your school's stage is an arena stage, you may be finished with your model. If like many arena stages, however, yours has stepped levels around it, make a model floor as described above for each level and stack them, gluing the pieces together with tabs on the inside.

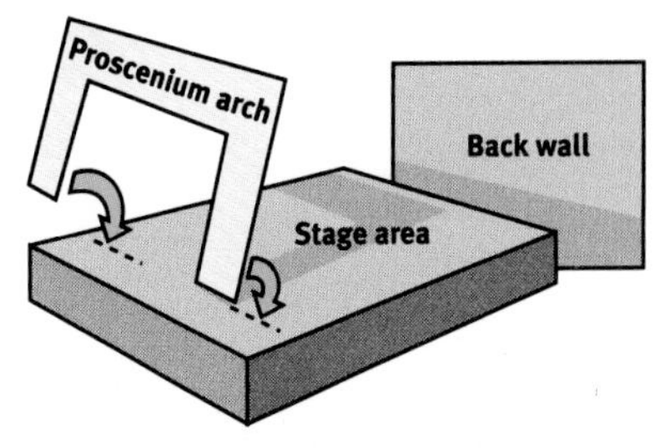


**ADD THE BACK WALL AND PROSCENIUM** If your stage is a thrust stage, you will now need to add a back wall. If it's a proscenium stage, you need to add a back wall and proscenium. Measure and cut the back wall from your material—cardboard, matte board, balsa, or foam-core—adding at the bottom a band that is equal to the height of the stage. In this way you can simply fasten the back wall to one wall of the boxlid that is your stage.

If there is a proscenium, measure and cut it, including the opening. Again, add at the bottom the height of the stage so that when you insert the proscenium into the stage floor, it will be the correct height. Mark the placement of the proscenium on the stage. Cut slots in the stage floor in which to fit the sides of the proscenium. Make sure the slots are the exact width of the proscenium arch sides or slightly smaller. Then insert the proscenium. On the underside, reinforce the sides of the proscenium with tabs of material taped on each side of the slots. You can add strips of material between the top of the proscenium and the top of the back wall to strengthen your model.

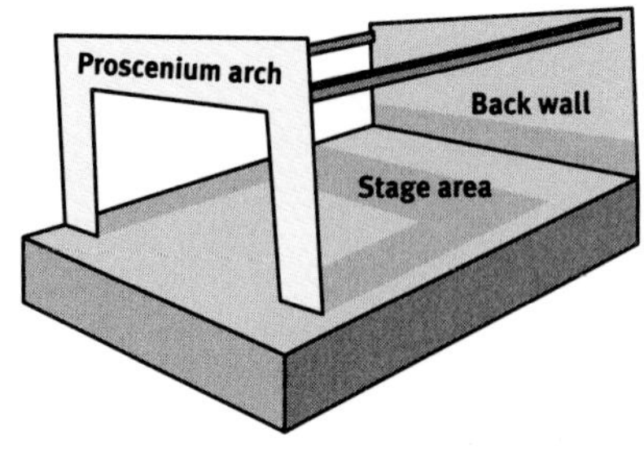


**FINISHING TOUCHES** Depending on the design of your school stage and on your skill as a model builder, you may add finishing touches, such as curtains. If you wish, spray paint your model in a neutral color such as gray or tan. Be sure to wear a mask and spray in a well-ventilated area over newspaper.

## Presenting

Display your model theatre in the classroom or theatre area. You may find use for it later when you design sets for your school theatre. Keep your measurements; they may also come in handy for later designs.

## Responding

How well you have fulfilled the Specs in the Project Planner will help assess your project. You may also ask yourself these questions to help you improve:

- Is the model truly to scale; that is, is it an accurate miniature representation of the school theatre?
- Did I work carefully, so that lines are straight, corners are sharp, and there are no visible smears of extra glue?

Include responses to these questions in your Theatre Notebook.

## Adapting the Project

1. Make another model of the same theatre space in a larger scale, such as 1/2 inch, or in a more permanent medium, such as wood. Add more detail, such as flies, a stage-manager's desk, or lighting grids.
2. Make a model of a stage that is a different type from your school's stage. !f you don't have one available to measure, use your old measurements and imagine what a different stage about the same size would be like.

PROJECT 8

# Shop Inventory

**ASSIGNMENT** Inventory the equipment and supplies in the workspaces of a technical area: set construction and props, costumes, or lighting.

## Project Planner

| | |
|---|---|
| Product | Written inventory of equipment and supplies |
| Purpose | To become familiar with the tools of a technical area and how and where they are stored |
| Specs | To accomplish this project, you will<br>• choose one of three technical areas: set construction and props, costumes, or lighting<br>• develop a method for ensuring that all equipment and supplies are included<br>• inspect the equipment and supplies in the workspaces of that technical area and list each one<br>• provide a written inventory that can be your personal reference or an official reference for the technical area |

## Creating

**DEVELOP YOUR PLAN** Choose one of these technical areas that interests you: set construction and props, costumes, or lighting. If your school has a separate sound booth or makeup room, these may have enough equipment and supplies to make an inventory worthwhile.

With your teacher, arrange for access to the technical workspaces and the equipment and supplies. Then plan your method of approach to ensure that you list all equipment and supplies. You can do this by looking in every work area, cupboard, and storage area in turn, listing the equipment and supplies you find there. Or, you could start with a checklist compiled from the lists that appear between pages 77–94, adding any items that are not on the list for your technical area. You will probably need to ask your teacher or consult a technical handbook to identify equipment and supplies that are unfamiliar to you. Get your teacher's advice, too, about how detailed to make your inventory. You will not want to count every nail, but it will be useful to know which kinds of drill bits are on hand and how many spools of thread in particular colors are in stock. You may need to make decisions about inventorying stock scenery items or scrap lumber, and if your costume shop is extensive, it may have dozens of costumes or costume pieces in storage.

**TAKE INVENTORY** As you look at the various equipment and supplies, mentally review their uses. Handle them, if you can—observing the standard safety precautions. As part of your inventory, you might include a description of their particular uses, as well as where they are stored. Some shops rely on a rigid system of organization and storage, so after you have finished with the equipment and supplies, put them back exactly where you found them. Close and lock each cupboard or secure each area when you are done there.

| No. | Item | Use | Location |
|---|---|---|---|
| 3 | slip-joint pliers | clamping, gripping, or bending materials | tool rack in cupboard C |
| 3 | needle-nose pliers | reaching into small places; gripping tiny objects | tool rack in cupboard C |

Inventory Chart

## Presenting

If you are going to keep your inventory for your own study and review, your annotated checklist may be all you need to do. If your inventory will be available to others, however, you should type it to make it easy to read. If your inventory is to become the official shop inventory, laminate it to protect it from getting dirty and put it on a clipboard to hang up in the shop area, or put it in a three-ring notebook.

## Responding

How well you have fulfilled the Specs in the Project Planner will help assess your project. You may also ask yourself these questions to help you improve:

- Did the method I developed for ensuring that all equipment and supplies are included work as it was supposed to?
- Did I inspect each piece of equipment and list it, including its use and location?
- Did I provide a written inventory in a form that is most appropriate for study and review or that can be kept in the technical area as a reference?

Include responses to these questions in your Theatre Notebook.

## Adapting the Project

1. If your shop is extensive, work with a partner to do the inventory as outlined. Decide how to split the work so that you both do your fair share and benefit from the knowledge gained. For inventorying an extensive costume collection, work with a small group, listing the following for each costume on index cards or as entries in a searchable computer database: type/use, size, color, period or style, condition, and plays used in.
2. Take photographs of equipment and supplies that are stored in certain areas. For clear pictures, arrange a few items on a white sheet on the floor and stand over it to take your photos, making sure not to cast a shadow; you may need to add extra lights if the workspace is dark. Mount the photographs along one side of a large piece of poster board. Then code the equipment and supplies in the photos by number using small circular stick-on labels that you can write on. On the other side of the poster board, write the number, name of the equipment or supply item, and a description of its use. Hang the poster next to the location where the pictured equipment and supplies are stored. You may need two or more posters for storage locations with many items of equipment and supplies.

PROJECT 9

# Sewing Demonstration Board

**ASSIGNMENT** Practice and present basic seams and research their uses.

### Project Planner

| | |
|---|---|
| Product | **Demonstration board of basic seams and summaries of their uses** |
| Purpose | **To become familiar with basic seams used in sewing** |
| Specs | **To accomplish this project, you will**<br>• **cut and sew swatches of cloth using various stitches**<br>• **describe the uses of each seam**<br>• **create a demonstration board of your finished seams**<br>• **follow the appropriate safety guidelines** |

## Creating

**CUT THE FABRIC** You can use any kind of scrap fabric to make these samples, but knits and heavier fabrics take more experience to handle. Cotton or cotton and polyester blends would work well.

Cut your fabric into pieces, roughly 5 ½ inches × 8 ½ inches (half the size of a piece of typing paper). If you cut the swatches with pinking shears (which make zigzag cuts), the edges won't ravel. You need two pieces of fabric for each seam. You can sew the seams by hand or by machine. Have your teacher or shop foreman demonstrate the basics of machine sewing, including winding the bobbin and threading the needle. If you use a sewing machine, begin and end all stitches by running the machine backward about ¼ inch along the seamline to lock the seam, then trim the threads. For hand-sewing, tie a knot at each end with the loose threads.

Prepare a hot iron for pressing finished seams.

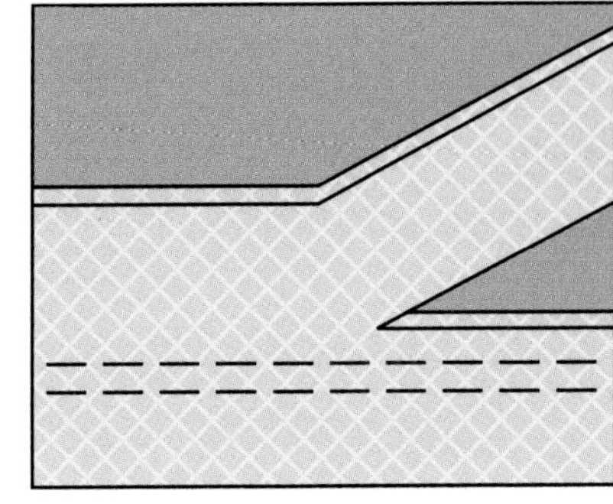

Double-stitched

## SEW THE SEAMS

### Double-Stitched Seam

1. Stitch a plain seam (p. 92).
2. Stitch again, 1/8 inch into the seam allowance, using a straight or zigzag stitch.
3. Trim the fabric close to the second row of stitches.
4. Press the seam allowances flat, then to one side.

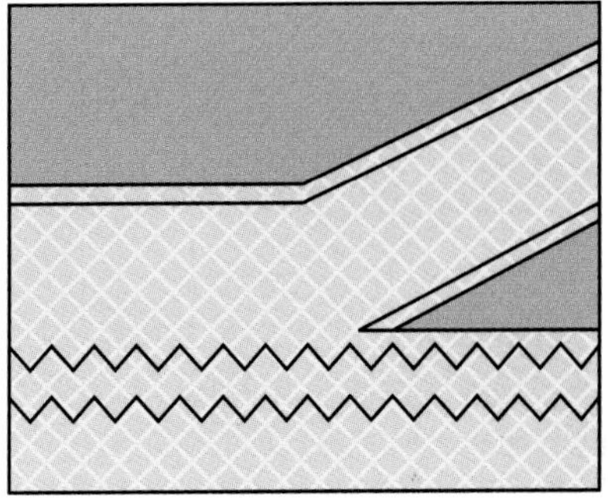

Stretch-knit

### Stretch-Knit Seam

1. Zigzag stitch along the seamline.
2. Zigzag stitch again, 1/4 inch into the seam allowance.
3. Trim the fabric close to the second row of stitches.
4. Press the seam allowances flat, then to one side.

For stretch knit seams at the neck, shoulders, and waist, apply seam binding or twill tape to the fabric in the place where you will stitch the seam and stitch a double-stitched seam, stretching the fabric slightly as you stitch.

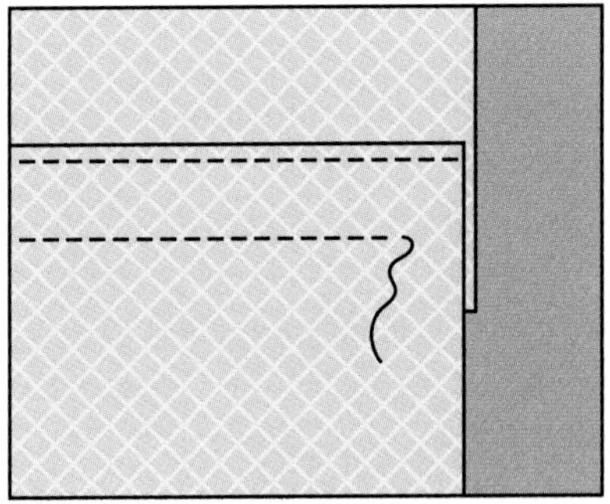

Lapped seam

### Lapped Seam

1. Trim away the seam allowance on one piece of fabric.
2. Use a pencil or tailor's chalk to draw a 5/8 inch seamline on the right side of the second piece of fabric.
3. Place the wrong side of the first piece of fabric on the right side of the second piece of fabric so that it overlaps and the trimmed seamline runs along the marked seamline. Secure the overlap with glue stick or double-sided basting tape.
4. Stitch closely along the trimmed edge. Topstitch on the overlap, about 1/4 inch from the first stitch.

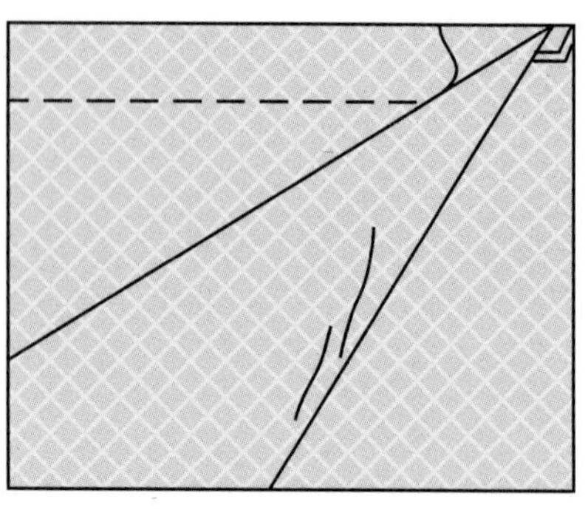
French seam

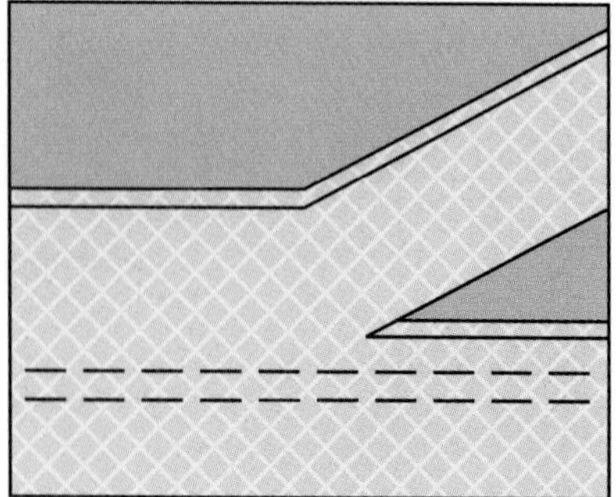
Topstitched seam

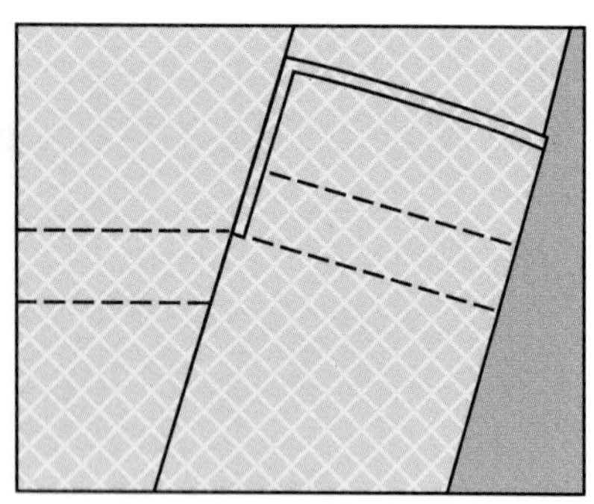
Welt seam

**French Seam**

1. Stitch a seam with the *wrong* sides of the fabric together, leaving a seam allowance of 3/8 inch.
2. Trim the seam allowances to 1/8 inch and press them open.
3. Fold the fabric with right sides together along the seam and press it again.
4. Stitch the fabric together 1/4 inch from the folded seam.
5. Press the seam allowances flat, then to one side.

**Topstitched Seam**

1. Stitch a plain seam and press the seam allowances open.
2. On the right side of the fabric, topstitch on both sides of the seam, 1/8 inch from the seamline.

**Welt Seam**

1. Stitch a plain seam and press the seam allowances to one side.
2. Trim the underneath seam allowance to 1/4 inch.
3. Topstitch through both seam allowances, 1/4 inch from the seam.

## Presenting

Use a fabric marking pen or a stick-on label to label each of the seams you have made. Research the uses of each, and then write a caption summarizing the use and the advantages and disadvantages of each seam. Include tips for making the seam as strong as possible. Using pins or strips of Velcro, attach the seam samples to a bulletin board, large piece of cardboard, or foamboard to make a demonstration board of your finished seams. Under each sample, attach its caption. Refer to the demonstration board as you sew costumes for a play. As an alternative, mount the samples on heavy paper and keep the samples in a three-ring notebook.

## Responding

How well you have fulfilled the Specs in the Project Planner will help assess your project. You may also ask yourself these questions to help you improve:

- Did I cut the fabric and sew the seams neatly?
- Do I understand the uses of each seam I made?
- Are my captions clear enough that others could use the demonstration board to learn about seams?
- Did I follow the appropriate safety guidelines?

Include responses to these questions in your Theatre Notebook.

## Adapting the Project

1. Add samples of a plain seam and hand-sewn and finishing stitches described on pages 92–93 to your demonstration board.
2. Research the uses of various types of fabrics. Collect swatches from a fabric shop and add these to your sewing demonstration board. Include captions that explain which fabrics are best suited to which types of clothing.

# Makeup Scrapbook

PROJECT 10

**ASSIGNMENT** Create a scrapbook showing a variety of facial types and hairstyles and organize them according to a system.

### Project Planner

| | |
|---|---|
| **Product** | An illustrated resource of makeup and hairstyles for a makeup artist |
| **Purpose** | To become familiar with facial types and hairstyles |
| **Specs** | To accomplish this project, you will<br>• locate illustrations of facial shapes, skin tones, and features, and hair colors and styles for men and women from various ethnic and racial groups and time periods<br>• label the time and place associated with each image<br>• collect and mount the illustrations in a scrapbook, organized by a system you devise |

## Creating

**LOCATE THE ILLUSTRATIONS** Using magazines, newspapers, the Internet, photographs, and photocopies from books, collect examples of various facial types and features for men and women. Make a point to locate images of prominent and unusual facial characteristics. For example, you might collect a variety of noses, mouths, eyes, chins, foreheads, and teeth.

Find faces showing people of different time periods and ethnic and racial groups. Also collect examples of different hair colors and styles for men and women. Include beards, mustaches, and wigs in this collection.

Choose images that are large and clear whenever possible. Where you cannot get a copy of the image, make a sketch. Try to determine the period and place of the person in each image; for example, contemporary Spain, medieval Europe, 1800s America, and so on.

**ORGANIZE AND MOUNT YOUR COLLECTION** Decide on a logical system of organization for your collection. You could begin by showing various facial shapes, then present particular features, then skin tones. You might have a separate section for hairstyles, perhaps organized by period styles.

Mount your images in a scrapbook or photo album. Another alternative is to mount them on paper and insert them into plastic jackets in a three-ring binder. If you do that, you can easily reorganize and add new images in appropriate categories. Make sure you label your images neatly and clearly.

## Presenting

Present your scrapbook as a resource for the class or keep it for yourself. Invite your classmates to suggest character types for some of the images you have collected. Or, call for volunteers who might let you try out some hairstyles on them. Study the images in your scrapbook and keep it on hand when it comes time to do makeup for a production. See if you can reconstruct some of the facial types and hairstyles.

## Responding

How well you have fulfilled the Specs in the Project Planner will help assess your project. You may also ask yourself these questions to help you improve:

- Did I prepare and mount the images neatly?
- Are my labels clear enough that others could use the makeup scrapbook as a resource?
- Is my system of organization a logical and flexible one?
- Do I understand how the images will be used in the future for doing theatre makeup?

Include responses to these questions in your Theatre Notebook.

## Adapting the Project

1. Using examples from your makeup scrapbook, plan the makeup for a character in a play. Choose a play you have read or read a new one. Think about how the character looks. Mark the pages in your scrapbook that have images reflecting that character. Using those images, draw a composite sketch of the character. Make general notes in your Theatre Notebook about how you might apply makeup to yourself or a friend to create the appearance of the character.
2. Add costumes, including shoes and hats, to your collection to make it a makeup and costume resource.

theatre—art in action

# Preparation

## Acting

129 The Characterization Process
134 Motivation and Behavior
136 Creating Specific Characters
140 Stage Movement Basics
146 Auditions
150 Activities
154 **Historical Profile:** Shakespeare


## Directing & Producing

163 Choosing a Play
164 Genre
166 Working with the Script
174 Style
176 The Director's Role in Design
177 Stage Composition
182 Blocking
183 The Director's Promptbook
185 The Business of the Play
187 The Stage Manager
188 Activities
192 **Historical Profile:** Molière


## Technical Theatre

203 Emergence of the Design Team
204 Elements of Production Design
206 Set Design
210 Set Construction
218 Joining, Bracing, and Stiffening Scenery
223 Scene Painting
226 Prop Design and Construction
228 Lighting Design
232 Sound Design and Production
234 Costume Design and Production
238 Makeup Design
240 Activities


## Projects

244 11: Open Dialogue with Stage Movement
247 12: Building Characters
249 13: Delivering a Monologue
252 14: Entrances and Exits
255 15: Creating Stage Pictures
257 16: Developing a Director's Promptbook
260 17: Producing a Play
263 18: Designing a Set
266 19: Reupholstering a Set Prop
268 20: Grid Transfer

# Acting

preparation

**If you are new to theatre, acting may appear easy, but creating a believable character is hard work. You need to tap into the best of your physical, intellectual, and emotional resources. The payoff for your preparation comes when you and the audience connect in a performance.**

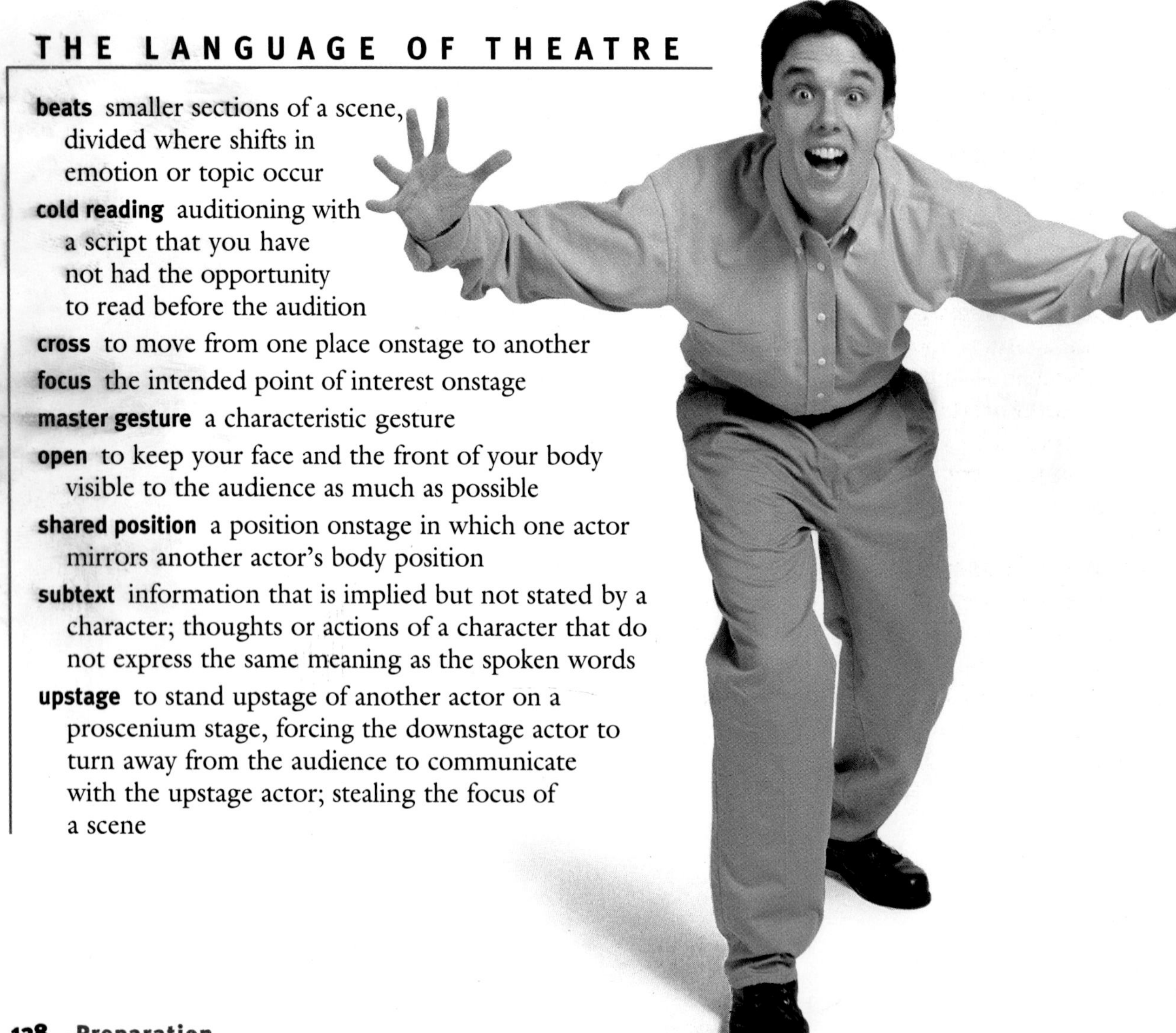

## THE LANGUAGE OF THEATRE

**beats** smaller sections of a scene, divided where shifts in emotion or topic occur

**cold reading** auditioning with a script that you have not had the opportunity to read before the audition

**cross** to move from one place onstage to another

**focus** the intended point of interest onstage

**master gesture** a characteristic gesture

**open** to keep your face and the front of your body visible to the audience as much as possible

**shared position** a position onstage in which one actor mirrors another actor's body position

**subtext** information that is implied but not stated by a character; thoughts or actions of a character that do not express the same meaning as the spoken words

**upstage** to stand upstage of another actor on a proscenium stage, forcing the downstage actor to turn away from the audience to communicate with the upstage actor; stealing the focus of a scene

# The Characterization Process

Whether you are creating a wholly new character or portraying a scripted character in a play, the characterization process is essentially the same. That process is a combination of making observations, drawing upon your experience, and tapping into your imagination. Through these actions you come to understand a character and seek to express that character through the use of your body and your voice.

## Observation

Observing other people and the world around you provides an endless source of inspiration for characterization. Become a sponge, absorbing all you encounter. Take notes and make sketches in your Theatre Notebook. Store your impressions in your memory too, where you can call upon them for future reference.

### Use All Your Senses

To be a thorough, effective observer, you must use all your senses and notice the details as well as the big picture: the still silhouette of a bird perched on a wire over a busy intersection; the persistent hissing of an old radiator in a corner of your grandmother's cozy house; the warm, buttery crunch of popcorn in the dark and the magical atmosphere of the movie theatre.

### Take Another Look

Look at new things and re-examine what is familiar. Go window-shopping at stores that carry items you have never really looked at before. Sketch or describe in detail items that you use every day, such as your toothbrush or your pillow. Look at things differently by altering your normal routines and habits—take a new route, start at a different time, try walking instead of riding, go outside in all kinds of weather.

### Become a People Watcher

Wherever you go, listen to the way people talk, watch how they move and interact with others, and reflect upon what they might be thinking. Study their faces and facial expressions. Note the way they wear their hair and the manner in which they dress. Speculate on where they live, what they do for a living, and what their attitudes are on various subjects.

### EXERCISE Character Resources in Nature

Using your observations of nature, create a character that embodies one of the four elements: earth, air, fire, or water. Work with other actors to create a series of interactions among the element characters; for example, fire falls in love with water. Try the same thing with different types of weather, ecosystems, and seasons.

### EXERCISE Object Characterization

Study a chair. Look at its texture and color. Is it old or new? Sit in it. Is it comfortable? Imagine the chair as a character. Now try to be like the chair, taking on characteristics such as "old and wooden" or "soft and welcoming." Then do the same with other common objects. Be a basketball, round and bouncy. Be a stapler, quick and efficient. Use the characteristics you discover in the objects to create new characters.

### EXERCISE Expressive Faces

Find a photo of an expressive face, or use one of the faces on this page if you like. In front of a mirror, work on mimicking the expression of that face. What sort of character or characters do you see developing? Try this exercise with various faces. See how many characters you can begin to create, starting from a facial expression alone.

## Experience

As an actor, you should collect a variety of life experiences. You can then use these experiences as a resource to create interesting characters. To broaden your scope of experience, challenge yourself with the activities outlined here.

#### BROADENING YOUR EXPERIENCE

- Go to events that you ordinarily wouldn't attend.
- Talk to people you have never talked to before.
- Get to know people who are very different from you in age, background, or outlook.
- Leave your neighborhood and see how other people live.
- Do something alone and away from your normal group of friends at least once a week.
- Spend 20 minutes a day reading a newspaper.
- Watch television shows about foreign countries or historical figures.
- Watch a wide variety of movies, including those you wouldn't normally watch.

- Read as many plays as you can.
- Read novels with interesting, detailed characterizations.

What you learn from broadening your scope of experience can also be used to interpret characters that live within the framework of plays. For example, if you are cast as a character in *The Music Man* by Meredith Wilson, you will better understand the desires and frustrations of the characters in that musical if you have played an instrument or seen a marching band. Awareness of the challenges faced by those with sight and hearing impairments will help you understand the struggles and triumphs of Helen Keller and Annie Sullivan in William Gibson's *The Miracle Worker.*

## Sense Memory

The way a character reacts to an object or setting reveals something about the character. As an actor, you will frequently need to ask yourself, "What can my character see, hear, taste, smell, or touch in this situation? How should my character react to what I sense?" A script provides some of this information, but you may have to determine if the object or setting is familiar or unfamiliar to your character, pleasant or unpleasant, and so on. You may also need to fill in the gaps that the set does not provide; that is, although you may be able to interact with props and scenery and react to lighting and sound, you will have to rely on your sense memory to supply any missing sensory stimuli that can't be reproduced onstage.

Your **sense memory** is your memory of sights, sounds, smells, tastes, and textures. Using sense memory, you can mentally transport yourself to a different situation so that you can act as though you were genuinely there. It's a tool that helps you define a character in a certain situation.

To access and apply your sense memory, ask yourself questions such as those posed here.

A day at an area Renaissance fair will give you a feeling for Shakespeare's Elizabethan characters and settings, which you can draw upon when you play Shakespearean roles.

### USING SENSE MEMORY

- Have I ever been in a situation like this or one similar to it?
- What did I see, hear, smell, taste, and touch during that experience?
- How did I react to what I sensed and what specific actions did I take?
- How can I recall those reactions, and which of those actions can I use to portray my character effectively in this situation?

## Emotional Memory

Emotions are basic building blocks for characterization. Through empathy (emotional identification) with your character, you gain understanding of that character. You can do this by using **emotional memory,** the technique of calling upon memories of your own emotions to understand the emotions of a character. Remember, however, that you can't stop at understanding your character's emotions; you must be able to express them clearly with your body and your voice. Only by expressing your character's emotions can you also gain the empathy of the audience, which makes your character more interesting to them.

To generate and express the emotions of your character in a situation, ask yourself questions such as those posed here.

### USING EMOTIONAL MEMORY

- Have I ever experienced emotions like those my character is experiencing?
- What was my circumstance?
- What did I feel?
- What specific actions did I take?
- How can I recall those emotions in this situation, and which of those actions can I use to portray my character effectively in this situation?

## Action-Generated Emotion

The technique of emotional memory is an "inside-out" approach to expressing emotions. You can also employ an "outside-in" approach to generate emotions in yourself that will help you express your character's emotions. By performing actions associated with particular emotions, you can sometimes generate those emotions in yourself. The approach is most effective when you can apply actions you have actually observed in people experiencing the target emotion.

To apply the technique of using action to generate emotion, ask yourself questions such as those posed here.

### USING ACTION TO GENERATE EMOTION

- Have I ever seen a person acting as if he or she were experiencing the emotions my character is experiencing?
- What was that person's circumstance?
- What specific actions did that person take?
- Which of those actions can I use to portray my character effectively in this situation?

Then perform the actions and ask yourself the following question:

- Did performing these actions make me experience the emotions my character is experiencing?

### EXERCISE Sense, Empathize, and Express

Imagine that you are acting in a scene in which you are lost in the woods. You are supposed to feel fear of dying and sadness at the thought of never again seeing those you love. Employ the techniques of sense memory and emotional memory to express the situation and emotions of your character. If you have no similar experiences to draw upon for the emotional memory technique, or if you are having difficulty feeling the emotions, try using actions to generate them.

## Imagination

Onstage your imagination helps you create another reality for yourself. You are speaking the words and performing the actions of someone you have never met, someone who lives in a place that may or may not exist. Your mind must often fill in the details to make the scene genuine to you and your audience.

Your imagination is like a muscle; the more you exercise it, the more effective it becomes. Try the following exercises; then tap into your imagination and come up with some of your own.

### EXERCISE The Letter

Work with a partner for this exercise. Each of you should write a brief letter and put it in a sealed envelope with your partner's name on the outside. It could be a love letter, a "Dear John" letter, an announcement of a birth or death, a threat, and so on. Next, create a set with a table and chair. Place your letter on the table. Have your partner enter, approach the table, pick up the letter, and read it, reacting to the contents both mentally and physically as fully as possible. Assess your partner's reaction and performance. Now switch roles and read your partner's letter.

### EXERCISE Famous People in Common Situations

Imagine how a famous person from the past would act in a common situation of today: Cleopatra unable to find her favorite ice cream at the supermarket, Shakespeare stuck in a traffic jam. Perform an improvisation showing how the known characteristics of these famous people would be revealed in these new situations. Then reverse the exercise, transplanting a famous person of today into a common situation of the past: Jackie Chan trying to put on a suit of armor in medieval Europe, Madonna herding unruly cattle on a ranch in the Old West.

# Motivation and Behavior

The behavior of an actor onstage should never be arbitrary. Whether you are a character in an improvisation or a scripted play, your character needs a **motivation,** or clear reason, to do or say anything. Your motivation determines your **objectives,** your goals or intentions. A character generally has an overall objective as well as objectives for each scene. These objectives may be outlined in a script, may be supplied by a director, or may come from your understanding of your character.

In many situations, there is something that stands between you and the achievement of your goal, something that is preventing you from meeting your objective. This is known as an **obstacle.** Obstacles create the conflict in a story. Characters generally develop a strategy to overcome an obstacle. The **outcome** of a conflict is the result of action taken by the characters to overcome their obstacles and achieve their objectives. The consequences of the outcome are known as the **stakes.**

Imagine that you are portraying the character of Odysseus in an adaptation of the *Odyssey.* You play the scene in which Odysseus and his men are trapped in the cave of the Cyclops Polyphemus. A large stone that only the Cyclops can move blocks the entrance. Odysseus offers very strong wine to the Cyclops as the one-eyed monster feasts on one after another of Odysseus's men.

**MOTIVATION**
Why am I doing what I am doing?

**OBJECTIVE**
What do I want to do?

**OBSTACLE**
Who or what is preventing me from doing it?

**STRATEGY**
What am I going to do about it?

**ACTION**
How am I going to do this?

**OUTCOME**
What is the result of my actions?

**STAKES**
What do I stand to gain or lose?

**ODYSSEUS** *(offering a goatskin full of wine to the Cyclops).* Cyclops, would you like something to wash down your food?

**CYCLOPS** *(takes the wineskin and drinks from it).* Mmmm! I like you, Greek! I'm going to do you a favor. What's your name?

**ODYSSEUS.** My name is Nobody.

**CYCLOPS** *(takes another huge gulp from the wineskin, then laughs).* Nobody, because you shared this delicious drink with me, I'm going to eat you last! *(continues drinking and laughing; laughter dies out, and he falls asleep, snoring)*

**ODYSSEUS** *(whispering to his men).* Quick! Have you heated up the stake in the fire? Bring it here. *(stabs the Cyclops in his eye with the stake)*

**CYCLOPS** *(wakes screaming in pain).* Aaaaaaah! *(tears the stake from his eye and gropes wildly about the cave)* Help! I'm blinded! Help!

**OTHER CYCLOPSES** *(offstage; on the other side of the boulder blocking the cave entrance).* What is wrong, Polyphemus? Who is hurting you?

**CYCLOPS** *(yelling).* It's Nobody!

**OTHER CYCLOPSES.** Well then, quiet down, in the name of Zeus!

Here is how you might break down the scene:

**Motivation** We are in danger of being eaten alive.

**Objective** Escape from the cave

**Obstacles** The Cyclops; the stone blocking the cave entrance

**Strategy** Disable the Cyclops

**Action** Drug and blind the Cyclops

**Stakes** Freedom or horrible death

**Outcome** Successfully crippled the Cyclops, improving our chances of escape

# Creating Specific Characters

You are now ready to begin working with specific characters in a script. You will need to develop your character from this script using the skills you have just learned, plus some new ones.

## Background and Status Quo

Your background influences what you do, what you think about things, and how you express your emotions. Very often, present behavior is determined by events of the past. Determining your character's background and **status quo** (present circumstances) will affect how you develop your character onstage. Some information is provided in your script; for example, what the playwright says about you, what you say about yourself, and what other characters say about you. Some information must be contributed by you from your observations, experience, and imagination. Imagine that you are your character and answer questions such as those posed here.

**BACKGROUND**

- What kind of family did I come from?
- How did I interact with my family while I was growing up?
- Was it a well-adjusted home life, or were there many conflicts?
- Of what social status and how much wealth did my family have?
- How have health issues influenced my life?
- How intelligent am I and how much education do I have?
- What do I do for a living?
- How old am I?
- What are my religious or spiritual beliefs?
- What kind of clothes do I prefer?
- Am I an emotionally expressive person?
- In what ways do I express my emotions?
- How would I describe myself—am I temperamental? moody? explosive? calm? passive? quiet? withdrawn?
- What is my sense of humor like?
- What is my best trait? my worst trait?
- What is my relationship to the other characters in the play?
- How do I treat other characters?

**STATUS QUO**

- Where am I today?
- Who is with me?
- What am I doing?

- What is happening to upset my world?
- How does that make me feel?
- What do I want to do?
- Who or what is preventing me from doing it?
- What am I going to do about it?
- How am I going to do this?
- What do I stand to gain or lose?



## Character Movement

The manner in which your character moves is one of the most important aspects of characterization. Entire characters have been built around a characteristic gesture, or **master gesture.** Most characters lead with the parts of their bodies that reflect their nature. This is known as a **leading center.** A sensual character might lead with her hips or shoulders; a nosy character might lead with his nose. Before determining a master gesture or leading center, however, consult the script. Find out what the playwright says about your character's body and the way you move as well as what your character and other characters say about your character's body. Then ask yourself questions such those posed here.

**CHARACTER MOVEMENT**

- What is my posture like?
- How do I walk?
- How do I use my hands?
- What are my distinctive facial expressions?
- Are my gestures large and wide, or small and contained?
- Do I have a master gesture?
- How subtle are my gestures?
- What are the rhythm and tempo of my movements?
- Do I have a clear leading center?
- Do I enjoy moving?
- Do I have any difficulty moving?
- How does emotion affect my movements?
- How do my movements reveal what I am thinking or feeling, even if my words say something else?

Groucho Marx established his scheming wise-guy character with a combination of master gestures—a low, long-striding walk, and a wiggling of his eyebrows while smoking his cigar.

## Character Voice

Approach developing your character's voice using the same methods you have used for developing the rest of the role. First look in the script for answers to questions such as "What does the playwright say about my voice?" and "What do I or other characters say about it?" Then ask yourself questions such as those posed here.

**CHARACTER VOICE**

- What are the pitch, rhythm, and tempo of my words and sentences?
- Do I enjoy talking?
- Do I have any speech problems?
- How does emotion affect my speech?
- What qualities does my voice have?
- How does my voice reveal what I'm thinking or feeling, even if my words say something else?
- What words do I emphasize?
- Do I speak with an accent?

## Motivation and Behavior

You may have noticed that several of the questions posed for determining your status quo (p. 136) are the same questions you can use to determine your motivation and behavior. This is because your status quo—and your background—will influence your motivation and behavior throughout a play. You will need to determine your objectives, obstacles, strategies, actions, stakes, and outcome for each scene in which your character appears (p. 134). Write them in the margins of your script or in your Theatre Notebook so you can refer to them in rehearsal.

## Subtext

People do not always say what they mean. Information that is implied but not stated by a character is the **subtext.** The subtext may be thoughts or actions of a character that do not express the same meaning as the spoken words. The subtext may also reveal how a character's background influences that character's thoughts and actions.

You can use what you have concluded to be your character's subtext to help determine your actions and emotional responses to what other characters say. Sometimes your character's reaction to another character's line is set up to reveal the subtext of that line. The playwright knows that at times the audience needs a clear indication of the subtext to understand the meaning of the play.

Thus, by "reading between the lines" you can discover the subtext that impacts the action of a scene. Make notes in your script about subtext—especially when it differs dramatically from what is written in the script.

Recall this scene from the adaptation of the *Odyssey.* You analyzed Odysseus's motivation and behavior in this scene earlier (p. 135). This time, look at the possible subtext for Odysseus and the Cyclops (underlined) and how an actor's actions and inflection can reveal a character's subtext (bracketed in blue).

**ODYSSEUS** [forces smile over pained expression] *(offering a goatskin full of wine to the Cyclops)*. Cyclops, would you like something to wash down your food? You man-eating beast! I'm only giving you this wine to pretend that I'm your friend. The wine is very strong and we hope it will put you to sleep so we can blind you. [looks away from Cyclops eating; upset, but tries to maintain composure]

**CYCLOPS** *(takes the wineskin and drinks from it)*. Mmmm! [smacks lips, wet with blood and wine, very loudly] Look at me enjoying my feast of your men. I like you, Greek! You silly fool! Do you think you can win me over? [nods at Odysseus with approval] I'm going to do you a favor. I'm only pretending to like you so I can humiliate you with my "favor." [grins broadly] What's your name? I'm pretending to care about you so I can find out more about you.

**ODYSSEUS.** [bows low as if grateful] My name is Nobody. I use a false and silly name that I know you are too stupid to question, and which may come in handy for my plan.

**CYCLOPS** *(takes another huge gulp from the wineskin, then laughs)*. Nobody, because you shared this delicious drink with me, I'm going to eat you last! Oh, I'm so clever! I never had any intention of sparing your life. My cruel joke amuses me. [laughs hideously; ignores Odysseus; absorbed in drinking] *(continues drinking and laughing; laughter dies out, and he falls asleep, snoring)* I'm not worried about the Greeks escaping.

**ODYSSEUS** *(whispering to his men)*. Quick! Have you heated up the stake in the fire? Bring it here. Our lives depend on moving quickly and quietly. [takes stake and climbs carefully to the Cyclops] *(stabs the Cyclops in his eye with the stake)* Take that, you monstrous drunk! Our trick worked, and now we have an advantage over you! [backs up to join men against cave wall] We're not out of danger yet.

**CYCLOPS** *(wakes screaming in pain)*. Aaaaaaah! *(tears the stake from his eye and gropes wildly about the cave)* Help! I'm blinded! Help! If I get my hands on those Greeks, I'll rip them limb from limb and gobble them all up at once!

**OTHER CYCLOPSES** *(offstage; on the other side of the boulder blocking the cave entrance)*. [yelling with panic and concern in their voices] What is wrong, Polyphemus? Who is hurting you? Why is he making such a racket? He must be in deep trouble.

**CYCLOPS** *(yelling)*. [unable to find cave opening; stumbling about in pain and panic] It's Nobody! Come here and kill Nobody! I can't find him!

**OTHER CYCLOPSES.** [disgusted] Well then, quiet down, in the name of Zeus! What an idiot! I hope he doesn't disturb us again.

# Stage Movement Basics

Once you have developed a character, you need to be able to move your character effectively around the performance space. Movement onstage consists of a few basic actions: entering, exiting, standing, sitting, reclining, gesturing, turning, stopping, and **crossing**—or moving from one place to another.

To master the craft of acting and, ultimately, to connect with the audience, you need to learn some guidelines for stage movement. Keep in mind that these are only guidelines; your director or the needs of your character may require you to ignore them.

## Body Positions

As you prepare for work onstage, you will come to realize the importance of how your body is positioned in relation to the audience. This is especially challenging on a proscenium stage, where a specific terminology is used to identify conventional body positions.

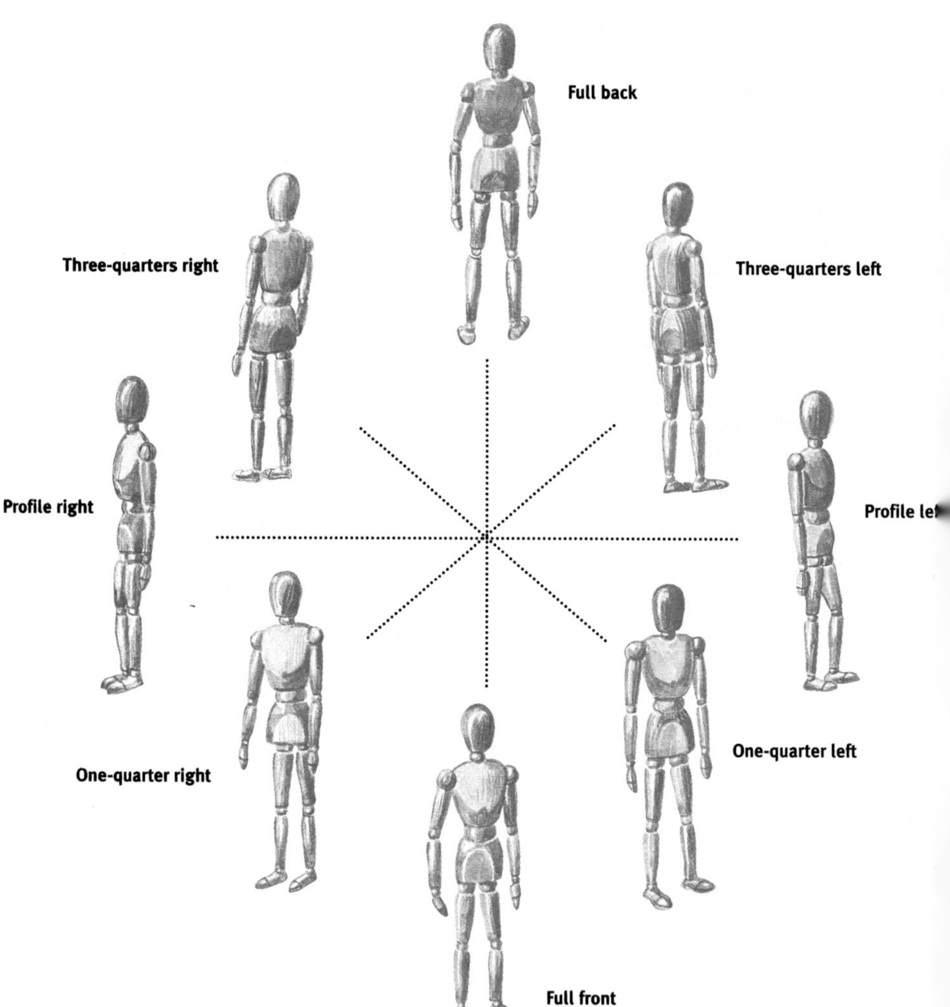

## Opening to an Audience

In any performance space, you should try to keep your face and the front of your body visible to the audience as much as possible. This is called **opening** to the audience. On arena and thrust stages, the challenge is to shift your position frequently so that you are occasionally open to everyone in the audience. To keep open on a proscenium stage, you can follow the conventions described here.

### KEEPING OPEN ON A PROSCENIUM STAGE

- **Sitting** If you are sitting in profile, keep open by using the one-quarter position, especially if you are delivering lines.
- **Standing** Use the full front, one-quarter right, or one-quarter left positions.
- **Gesturing** or **handling a prop** While gesturing or handling a prop, use your upstage hand.
- **Turning** Turn in the direction of your downstage hand.
- **Moving right or left** Move right by leading with your right foot. Move left by leading with your left foot.
- **Crossing** Make crosses upstage in an upstage arc. Make crosses downstage in a downstage arc. Make crosses directly across the stage in a slight upstage arc.
- **Entering** Enter the stage leading with your upstage foot.
- **Entering** or **exiting through doorways** Open a door with your upstage hand. As you go through the doorway, pull the door behind you and switch hands, closing it with your other hand.

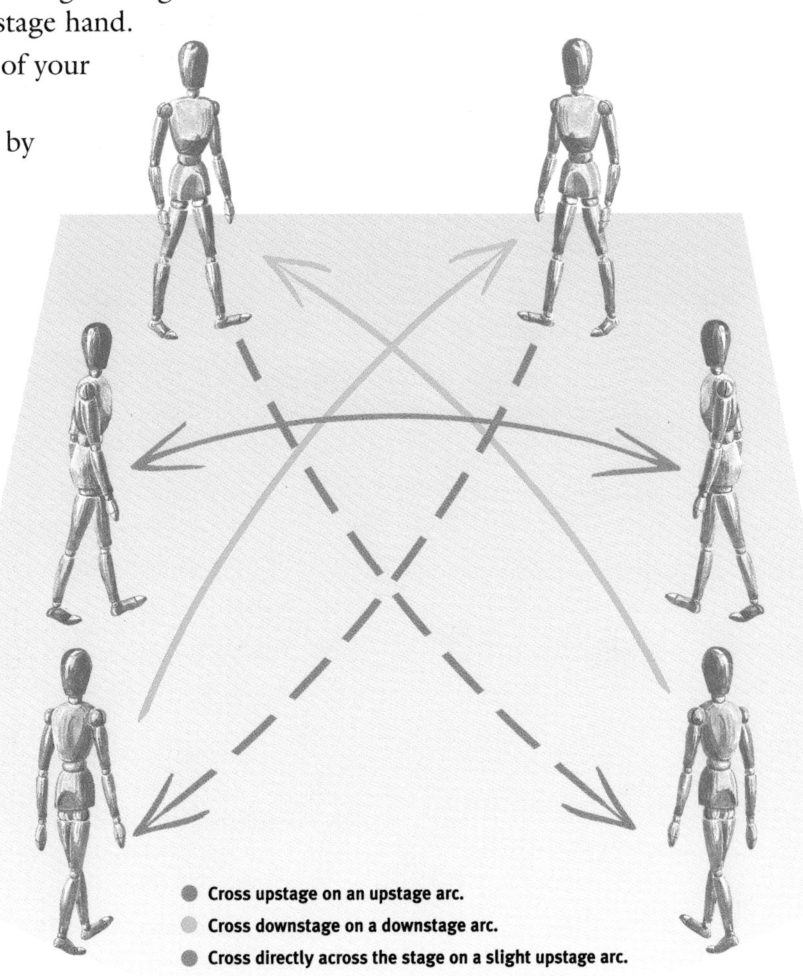


**Crossing on a proscenium stage**

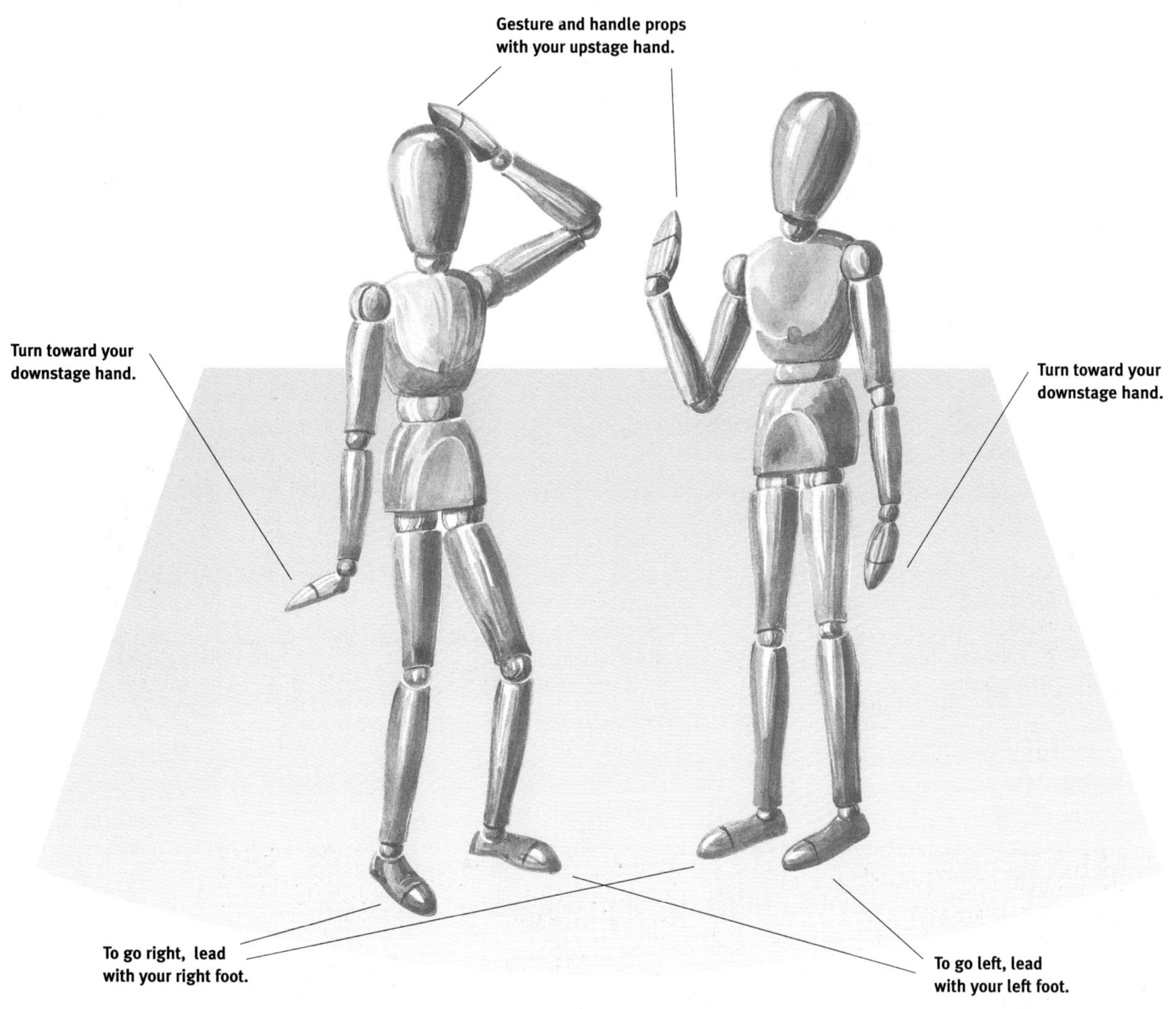


**Keeping open on a proscenium stage**

## EXERCISE Keeping Open

On a proscenium stage or a space set up as a proscenium stage, work with a partner to practice keeping open while moving onstage. Your partner should sit in the audience and give directions for stage movement, such as "enter stage right; cross downstage center while shaking your fist; stop in one-quarter left position; turn right; cross upstage right." You should respond to the directions by applying the guidelines for keeping open. Take turns giving and responding to directions. Work through various combinations of movements until you thoroughly understand the conventions and their importance for the proscenium stage.

## Dominant Stage Areas and Positions

Awareness of your position relative to other actors onstage is just as important as awareness of your position relative to the audience. The most dominant positions onstage are usually those that are the most open, such as full front. Certain stage areas also have dominance: center and downstage positions are strongest. A character framed by a doorway, window, or archway is also in a dominant position, as are those who are positioned at a higher level than others. When you are playing a scene, be conscious of what your position implies about your importance in the scene and about your relationship with the other actors.

## Sharing the Stage

One position commonly used for brief scenes between two actors onstage is the **shared position** in which one actor mirrors another actor's body position—usually at a one-quarter position. Both actors should be about the same distance from the audience, not one upstage of the other. When one actor is upstage of another on a proscenium stage, it is called **upstaging.** Upstaging forces the downstage actor to turn away from the audience to communicate with the upstage actor.

George Farquhar's *The Beaux' Strategem* (above), and Neil Simon's *Proposals* (left) each demonstrate use of the shared position.

## Focus

In terms of stage movement, the **focus** is the intended point of interest onstage. Directors coach actors in their line delivery and movement based in part on the knowledge that the audience takes its cues for focus from the actors. An actor in a dominant position or one who is moving or talking is generally the focus. By following the conventions described here, you can avoid stealing the focus of a scene, which is also called upstaging.

#### MAINTAINING THE FOCUS

- **Upstaging** Unless directed to do so, don't upstage yourself or another actor.
- **Talking and moving** Give your concentrated attention to actors who are talking or moving. Don't move when important lines, especially punchlines, are being spoken—whether by you or by other actors.
- **Sitting** When you go to a sitting position from a standing position, don't look directly at the chair before you sit down; feel for it with the back of your leg, then sit. If you look at the chair, so will the audience.
- **Crossing** On a proscenium stage, cross upstage of seated actors; cross downstage of standing actors.
- **Eye Contact** Avoid making eye contact with the audience unless you are directed to by the script or the director. This draws attention to the audience. Keep your head up and your eyes focused on a plane just above the audience's heads (usually about your eye level). Don't focus on the ceiling or floor.

## Posture and Poise

You should already be making an effort to sit, stand, and move with good posture (p. 20). If you have a tendency to slouch or to stand too stiffly, work on changing that habit. Unless such a posture is required to create a specific character, keep your posture straight, but natural, with your weight evenly distributed over both feet.

Naturalness is also important as you move. You should strive to appear natural in the movement of your character while maintaining an easy control of your balance. This quality of control, or poise, can be achieved by learning how to shift your weight smoothly and easily as you move. The guidelines described here can help you achieve poise in two common stage movements.

**MAINTAINING POISE**

- **Rising** To rise from a seated position, place one foot slightly ahead of the other and push off with your back foot, keeping your weight on that foot as you rise. Lead with your chest, inhaling as you rise. This will put you in a steady, balanced position and will also ready you for movement or speaking.
- **Stopping and turning back on a cross** Count the steps you need to make the cross, arranging it so your last step on the cross is on your upstage foot. Pivot on the ball of your upstage foot and turn back, keeping your weight on that foot.



## EXERCISE Focus and Poise

Practice focus and poise by performing this scene as if you were on a proscenium stage. Get help for the sound effects from two classmates. Begin by sitting in a chair, reading a book; focus on the book. You hear a knocking on the door across the room; focus on the door as you set aside your book. Rise and cross to answer the door. Before reaching the door, you hear the phone ring in another room. Stop and turn, focusing on the ringing phone. Should you answer the door or the phone? Suddenly, both the knocking and the ringing stop. Return to your chair, sit down, and take up your book to read again.

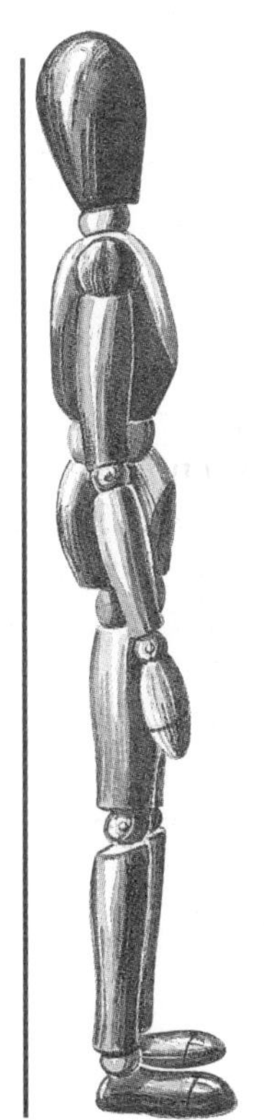

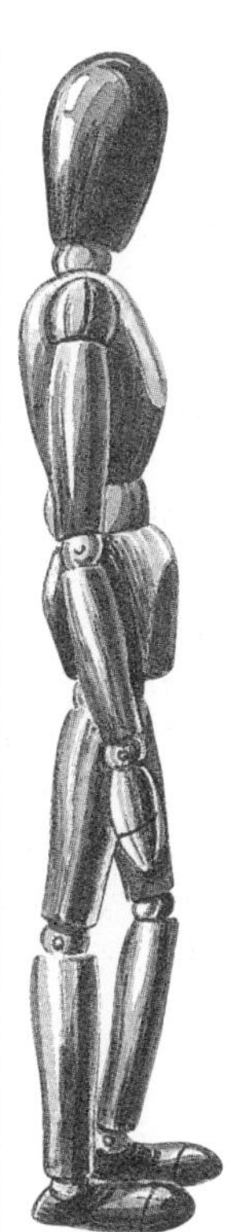

Good posture

Bad posture

# Auditions

Now that you understand the basics of creating a character and are familiar with basic stage movements, you are ready to audition for a **role,** or part, in a play. To be **cast,** or chosen, for a role, you need to audition to demonstrate your talents. An **audition** is like an interview; it gives you a chance to meet the person doing the hiring, leave an impression of yourself, and show a sample of your work. A good audition is extremely important. You can't give a great performance if you don't get a role.

## Audition Preparation

Make sure you know the time and location of the audition. Sometimes it's necessary to arrange in advance for a specific date and time with the **auditors,** those conducting the auditions. Usually, the director, and perhaps the assistant director, are conducting the auditions. For musical auditions, the musical director is one of the auditors.

If you can find out what play you are auditioning for, read it in advance. You should bring a resumé of your theatre experience and a photograph of yourself to the audition; get these items ready and put them where you will remember them.

Plan to wear shoes in which you can move comfortably (no high heels, platforms, or floppy sandals), clothing that is comfortable (but not sloppy), and a style and color that is flattering to you (but not outrageous or distracting). If you are called back for a second or third audition, make sure to wear the same clothing so that the auditors can remember you more easily.

Go through your warm-up ritual before you audition.

## Monologues

There are generally two ways an audition is handled. The actor performs two contrasting monologues or the actor reads from the actual script.

A **monologue** is a story, speech, or scene performed by one actor alone. The purpose of performing two monologues at an audition is to show the range of your acting abilities. You may therefore want to choose one comedic and one tragic role. Or, you may want to show contrast in other ways, through a difference in the characters' social status, time period, age, or personality. Some audition notices specify the types or time periods for characters.

In choosing material for your monologues, your sources may include plays, novels, or short stories. Choose monologues that work for you. The suggestions outlined here may help you make your selections.

**CHOOSING YOUR MONOLOGUE**

- Find a character that interests or intrigues you.
- Try to find a character that is within your age range—2 or 3 years younger than you and no more than 10 years older.
- It's easier to choose a segment where there is only one character speaking in addition to your character.
- Choose a segment that can stand alone.
- Find a segment that presents a variety of emotions and a climactic moment to grab the auditor's attention.
- Look for an unusual monologue that has not been done very often. You may ask your teacher for advice.

Whether you use a play or other fictional work, you will likely have to rearrange the scene you have chosen to contain only the lines of your character. Leave out the lines of others, but make a note of where their replies would be. You will need to imagine that they respond to you nonverbally.

## Analyzing Your Monologue

Before learning and rehearsing your monologue, it's helpful to read the entire play or work from which it's taken. Then apply the movement, voice, improvisation, and character development techniques you have learned to analyze and rehearse your monologue.

It might be helpful to break down your monologue into **beats,** the smaller sections of a scene that usually come at points where a character shifts moods or emotions or changes the topic. Think about how you should orchestrate these beats to build your scene to an effective climax.

You will also need to consider what movements, gestures, or words make up the bridges, or **transitions,** between your beats; careful attention to smooth transitions between beats is necessary to prevent a choppy performance; your aim should be a seamless scene with appropriate rhythm and pacing and an apparent, logical sequence of ideas. The use of beats and transitions is not for monologues alone. Breaking down entire scenes with multiple characters in dialogue is often helpful to better understand and express the distinct parts of a scene

## Performing Your Monologue

When performing your monologue, don't spend a lot of time looking at the imaginary character. Use the techniques of pantomime to place the character in a specific spot and imagine him or her to be a certain height or moving in a certain way. Be consistent: when you look at that character, look at that same spot.

Imagine the total environment of the situation. Use the entire space allotted to you; don't remain rooted in one spot. Remember that this is a dynamic exchange between two characters, even if one of them is not speaking.

## Reading from the Script

As noted earlier, read the entire play if the script is available to you before the audition. You may be auditioning for one part, but the auditors may ask you to read for others; therefore, you have to know the plot and the relationships of the characters.

If the script is unavailable to you before the audition, you will be auditioning with what is called a **cold reading.** When you arrive and the script is handed to you, always ask permission to read the material to yourself first before reading it aloud. Try to determine the objectives (p. 134) of your character in the scene. If other characters are involved, determine their relationship to your character and plan how to interact with them.

When reading for the auditors, concentrate on your character's objectives and interact with other characters in the scene. Don't bury your face in the script. The auditors would rather see your face, your interpretation, and your relationship with other characters than have a perfect word-for-word reading. Remember to communicate and project.

### Audition Etiquette

- Make sure you are better than on time: try to arrive 15 minutes early.
- Bring a pen or pencil to fill out the audition forms.
- Remember that you are being evaluated from the moment you enter the audition area. Be confident, courteous, relaxed, and pleasant.
- Say your name clearly and positively for the auditors.
- Listen carefully to any instructions the auditors may give. This is important information, which you should try your best to incorporate.
- If there is only one light source, ask the auditors if they can see you. If not, move into the light according to their instruction.
- Don't make apologies for yourself and don't ask inappropriate questions after an audition, such as "Did you like me?" or "When do you think you'll make a decision about the casting?"
- Don't limit your thinking and precast yourself for any one particular role. Be willing to accept any role offered you.

## Callbacks

If the auditors liked your audition, you may be asked to return. This is called a **callback.** Sometimes casting requires more than one callback. You will generally either receive notice of a callback by phone or as a posting at a central posting spot in the theatre.

At a callback, you may be asked to read various parts from the script or to engage in creative exercises that tell the auditors more about your talents. You may have a brief personal interview with the director, so be prepared to speak about yourself and elaborate upon your theatre experience.

If you don't receive notice for a callback, you can assume you didn't get the part. This is one of the most frustrating aspects of being an actor. Everyone—from professional to beginner—wants to know why he or she wasn't cast. Usually, you will never find out. Casting is a very subjective job and highly dependent on the chemistry of the entire production. If you have behaved professionally and given an audition to the best of your abilities, the auditors were simply looking for someone of a different type than you. Keep trying. Eventually they will want someone just like you!

# Activities

### The Characterization Process

HMWK 9/17

**CHARACTERS IN A CROWD** Go to a place where a large number of people are gathered, such as an airport, shopping mall, or park. Choose one person to observe for at least two minutes. Record information about that person in your Theatre Notebook. Do the same for at least two other people. Concentrate on details such as posture, walk, facial features, and gestures. Work on recreating each person as a character. Try combining elements from different people you observed to create a new character. Improvise a scene between your character and a character created by another actor.

### The Characterization Process

HMWK 10/1

**EXPRESS YOUR NEW EXPERIENCES** Follow one of the suggestions for broadening your experience (p. 130-131). In your Theatre Notebook, write about this new experience. Use that information to perform a short scene that presents the difficulties and enjoyments of trying something new. Use props and enlist the assistance of your classmates, if necessary, or pantomime your interactions with objects, settings, and people. Give your scene a beginning, middle, and end.

### The Characterization Process

10/1

**SENSES & EMOTIONS IMPROVISATIONS** As a class, write on one set of cards a variety of settings that have a range of sensory stimuli (for example, a rainforest) and on another set a variety of emotions (for example, elation). With a partner, select one setting card and two emotion cards and improvise a scene based on your choices. Discuss why your characters may be feeling the emotions you have drawn and try to create a simple story to guide your improvisation. Use sense memory and emotional memory to help you express the emotions of your characters in your situation.

### *The Characterization Process*

**CREATE A COUNTRY** Work with a small group to create an imaginary country. Give it a name and list its characteristics—government, economic power, natural resources, terrain, climate, social classes, cultural pastimes, and customs. Think about the inhabitants of this imaginary nation and develop several characters from various levels of society. Perform a few improvisations with these characters, working through scenes that present various aspects of the country you created. Work with another group to create interactions among characters from different countries.

### *The Characterization Process*

**ROUND TABLE DISCUSSION** Working with a small group, select various characters from history or literature. Try to include as wide a variety of types and periods as possible; for example, Amelia Earhart, Bart Simpson, Henry David Thoreau, Robin Hood, Madam Curie, and Scarlett O'Hara. Have each member of your group choose one character. Imagine how that character might relate to the others. What might each have in common with another? What questions might they ask each other? What topics would they discuss? Then improvise a round-table discussion in which all partake.

### *Motivation and Behavior*

**ANALYZING BEHAVIOR** Work with a small group to choose a familiar scene from a fairy tale, favorite movie, or novel. Assign characters. Analyze your character's behavior in the scene, breaking it down into motivation, objective, obstacle, strategy, action, stakes, and outcome. Perform your scene keeping these analysis in mind. How do they affect the way you present your characters?

### *Motivation and Behavior*

**SELF-ANALYSIS** Why do you do what you do? Why do you say what you say? Spend five minutes noting your behavior in your Theatre Notebook. Then analyze each major movement and statement in terms of motivation, objectives, obstacles, strategies, actions, stakes, and outcome. Can you isolate a few major objectives in your behavior? How might you make these objectives clear onstage?

# Activities

### *Creating Specific Characters*

**USING MODELS** Use a familiar person, such as one of your parents or siblings, or a famous person, such as a politician or actor, to create a character. Build from what you know of that person's background, movement, and voice. Work on perfecting your character's physical characteristics. Avoid exaggerating unless you are trying to create a caricature of that person. Then, working with another actor, invent a situation involving your character and a character created by your partner. Establish your character's status quo in that situation and do a short improvisation between the two characters.

### *Creating Specific Characters*

**WEARING MANY HATS** A costume piece can often inspire the creation of a character. Hats are great for this. Gather together a collection of hats. Look carefully at each hat. Think about the person who would wear this hat. Where does this person live? What is his or her occupation? How would you describe this person? How does he or she walk? talk? gesture? If you were to play this character, how would he or she be different from you? Now, try on each hat, one at a time. See if you can become the person who wears the hat.

### *Creating Specific Characters*

HMWK 11/6

**SUBTEXT** Read a play and choose a character to analyze. Find a scene in which your character is interacting with one or more characters. Transcribe your portion of the scripted dialogue in that scene to your Theatre Notebook on one side of a page. Then, using what you know about your character from your analysis, write the subtext for your dialogue opposite the written script. Underline the subtext of your thoughts and bracket the subtext you might reveal by your actions, as shown in the example for Odysseus and the Cyclops (p. 139). If necessary, use lines to connect the script with the corresponding subtext.

*Stage Movement Basics*

**OPENING ON AN ARENA STAGE** Experiment with basic stage movements on an arena stage or in a space simulating an arena stage. Get a feel for having an audience at your back and turning toward them, for crossing toward an audience, for entering and exiting out through aisles next to the audience, for making gestures that can be seen by a large portion of the audience. Working with another actor, perform a short improvisation to get a sense of moving with purpose around the arena space. How often can you open yourself to the audience on each side of the stage without your movements seeming unnatural or unmotivated?

*[Au]ditions*

**[CO]LD READINGS** To prevent panic at an audition, [pr]actice doing cold readings. Gather together a vari[et]y of plays. Find monologues in them. Don't use [th]e same criteria you use to choose your own mono[lo]gues; just find one for a character that is your [s]ame gender and about your age. Take 10 minutes [t]o prepare. Look at the cast of characters to get a [q]uick indication of relationships. Then perform the [c]old reading of the monologue to a member of your [f]amily or another classmate. You might also practice reading a variety of parts from plays you know and plays you don't know to prepare for cold readings for various roles from one play.

*Stage Movement Basics*

**STEALING THE SCENE** With one or two other actors, perform a scene for your classmates in which you intentionally violate all of the guidelines for maintaining the focus of a scene (p. 144). You can make it subtle or obvious, but don't tell your audience what you are doing. Then ask for their response to your scene and see how distracted they were by the lack of appropriate focus.

*Auditions*

**BEATS AND TRANSITIONS** Choose a scene from a play to break into beats and transitions. It can be a monologue or dialogue between one or more characters. If you choose a scene with multiple actors, work with other actors, each of you taking a part. Determine the beats and transitions for the entire scene. You might transcribe the scene and mark it, using brackets to enclose each beat and an arc to indicate transitions. When you have done this, act out the scene, employing your understanding of the beats and transitions within it. Then, in your Theatre Notebook, respond to the value of this method for analyzing and expressing the dynamic shifts of a scene.

Historical Profile

# Shakespeare

William Shakespeare was born in Stratford-on-Avon, England, in 1564. His father, John Shakespeare, was a successful glove-maker and merchant who rose through various administrative offices to become high bailiff (mayor) of Stratford. Shakespeare's mother, Mary Arden, came from a well-to-do landowning family. He attended the Stratford Grammar School, which was noted for the excellent education it provided. In 1582 Shakespeare married Anne Hathaway; the couple had three children, one of whom died at the age of 11.

By 1594 Shakespeare was established in London, where he became a shareholder in the acting company known as the Lord Chamberlain's Men, later the King's Men. In 1599 his company built a new theatre called the Globe. When the company purchased Blackfriars Theatre in 1608, Shakespeare was also a shareholder. He did do some acting—even appearing before Queen Elizabeth I—but his major contribution was as playwright. He is credited with 37 plays. In addition, he wrote some nondramatic poetry, notably a sequence of 154 sonnets.

During the theatrical season he lived in London while his family remained in Stratford. His connection with the stage was a profitable one: by 1597 he was wealthy enough to purchase New Place, the second largest house in Stratford. Around 1610 he retired to Stratford, journeying to London as necessary to take care of theatrical business. Shakespeare died in 1616 and was buried in Trinity Church, Stratford, where he had been baptized 52 years earlier.

It was not the custom of the time to publish plays; generally they were the property of the acting company for which they had been written. Elizabethan printing was often of poor quality, and it seems unlikely that Shakespeare supervised the printing of any of his plays. This accounts for the many misprints and differences from one printing to another that are found in his works. After his death, two friends and members of his acting company collected 36 of his plays together in the First Folio, published in 1623.

This view of the newly reconstructed Globe theatre in London shows the stage, the Tiring House, and a section of the galleries surrounding the Pit.

Popular and admired in his time, Shakespeare was less esteemed by the neoclassical writers of the late 1600s and 1700s. He was rediscovered in the 1800s and has been revered ever since—sometimes excessively, an attitude referred to as "bardolatry," after the nickname bestowed upon him, "the bard," an antiquated term for a writer. Today he is generally acknowledged as the greatest playwright in the English language. His characters in such plays as *Romeo and Juliet, Hamlet, Macbeth, Othello, A Midsummer Night's Dream,* and *The Tempest* are some of the most vital and fascinating fictional people ever created.

## The Theatre Space

Shakespeare wrote most of his plays for his acting company's own theatre, the Globe. There was not one Globe, but two: when the first burned down in 1613 a new theatre was promptly erected on the same spot. The new Globe was torn down in 1644, after the Puritan government closed all the theatres, and no contemporary pictures of either theatre are known to exist.

What is known is that it was open to the sky, apparently having evolved from temporary stages set up in the courtyards of inns earlier in the century. It was a many-sided structure, with an outside diameter of perhaps 84 feet. Inside, three galleries surrounded an open area called the Pit, which provided standing room for theatregoers who couldn't afford gallery seats—and were therefore called

"groundlings." One estimate is that the Globe could accommodate an audience of about 2,000.

Plays were held in the afternoon because no artificial lights were used. There was no scenery; one permanent structure called the Tiring House served as a background for all scenes. The main acting area was a thrust stage that jutted out into the Pit. This platform contained trapdoors that might be used for special appearances and disappearances. The main stage entrances were large doors at either side. At the back was a curtained recess known as the Study that might be used for interior scenes. A balcony called the Tarras (terrace) provided another acting area, and this may have been flanked by windows at which actors could also appear. The stage was covered by a large canopy supported by architectural pillars.

After much planning and research, a reconstruction of the Globe opened in London in 1997 to continue the tradition of performing Shakespeare's plays for new generations of theatregoers.

## Styles of Costumes

In Shakespeare's day both male and female roles were played by men; most actors performed in contemporary costumes, with little attempt at period authenticity. For the wealthy, Elizabethan dress meant luxurious materials in a wide range of colors and textures, trimmed with jewels, embroidery, fur, or lace.

Male costumes featured doublets—short jackets that ordinarily opened up the front, with a standing neckband, and often a short shaped skirt. The waistband came just above the hips and was pointed in front. Shirts worn underneath were revealed only by their collars and cuffs. A striking and characteristic feature was the ruff, which stood out from the top of the high neckband and was pleated or supported by wire or cardboard to extend from four to nine inches. Under their doublets men wore breeches, short trousers puffed out or padded and reaching mid-thigh or just above the knees. Long stockings and shoes with thick soles but no heels completed the picture. Later these shoes might be decorated with large puffs of ribbon. Hair was worn generally short, and even young men wore beards, often neatly trimmed to a point.

The most notable element of female costumes was the farthingale, a hoop that extended the hips greatly—sometimes as much as three or four feet. From this fell a voluminous skirt, sometimes draped or cut in front to reveal an underskirt in a different color or fabric. In contrast, tops were tight, flat across the chest, and long-waisted, with a point in front. Underneath, corsets with stays of bone or wood helped create the waspish waists and flat chests thought fashionable. Women, like men, wore ruffs at the neck or sometimes wired to rise behind the head.

Women's hats were copies of men's. Fashionable women affected a small hat perched jauntily on their stiffly dressed hair. Women's shoes were like men's but made of rich materials. When they had heels, they were wide, clumsy, and not particularly high. Chains, earrings, brooches, and finger rings were worn in great profusion by both men and women.

## Acting Styles

Experiments in the newly reconstructed Globe theatre demonstrate that an actor standing in the middle of the thrust stage can be seen and heard everywhere in the house without shouting lines or exaggerating gestures; but Shakespeare wrote famous lines of advice for Hamlet to give a troop of actors, warning them not to "mouth" their speeches nor "saw the air" with their hands, but to "use all gently," so it's probable that acting styles of the day contained some of these excesses. Even so, Shakespeare's plays were never acted in his lifetime with the naturalness that was to come centuries later. For one thing, many of Shakespeare's plays were written in verse, either rhymed or unrhymed (blank verse). Actors trained in classical methods learned to declaim the verse in a way to emphasize its poetry, but it's not necessary to read Shakespeare's verse as verse in order for the beauty of his language to come through.

## Try It Out

Stage the following scene of a comic misunderstanding between young lovers. Since it is set in ancient Greece you might wear robes or simple stylized costumes, or you might add a few costume pieces such as ruffs for an Elizabethan flavor. The challenge here will be in movement: there are many attacks and retreats that you will need to work out carefully. Although this scene is written in unrhymed verse, don't let that bother you. Let the punctuation guide you to interpret each line for its sense. Use the sidenotes and a dictionary, if necessary, to be sure you understand every word in your own lines.

*from*

# A Midsummer Night's Dream

In a rather complicated series of events, four young people find themselves lost in the woods outside Athens, in ancient Greece. Both Demetrius (di mē´trē əs) and Lysander (lī san´dər) start out in love with Hermia (hėr´mē ə). Hermia elopes with Lysander, and Demetrius follows them. Helena is in love with Demetrius, and she follows him. During the night, fairies mistakenly give both Demetrius and Lysander magic potions that make them fall in love with the first person they see—which happens to be Helena. Both Demetrius and Lysander desert Hermia and chase after Helena. Hermia cannot understand Lysander's change of heart, and Helena believes the young men are making fun of her.

**LYSANDER** (*to* HERMIA). Hang off, thou cat, thou burr! Vile
thing, let loose,
Or I will shake thee from me like a serpent![1]

**HERMIA.** Why are you grown so rude? What change is this,
Sweet love?[2]

**LYSANDER.** Thy love? Out, tawny Tartar,[3] out!
Out, loathèd med'cine! O hated potion, hence!

**HERMIA.** Do you not jest?

**HELENA.** Yes, sooth,[4] and so do you.

**LYSANDER.** Demetrius, I will keep my word with thee.[5]

**DEMETRIUS.** I would I had your bond, for I perceive
A weak bond[6] holds you. I'll not trust your word.

1. What action and facial expressions might accompany Lysander's words?
2. How might Hermia react to these stinging insults from her former lover?
3. **tawny Tartar** referring to Hermia's relatively dark hair and complexion
4. **sooth** truly
5. The men had agreed to fight a duel over Helena.
6. **weak bond** that is, Hermia's arm (with a pun on *bond*, "oath," in the previous line). If Hermia is clinging to Lysander, what are the others doing?

**LYSANDER.** What, should I hurt her, strike her, kill her dead?
Although I hate her, I'll not harm her so.

**HERMIA.** What, can you do me greater harm than hate?
Hate me? Wherefore? O me, what news, my love?
Am not I Hermia? Are not you Lysander?
I am as fair now as I was erewhile.[7]
Since night you loved me; yet since night you left me.
Why, then you left me—O, the gods forbid!—
In earnest, shall I say?

7. **erewhile** just now

**LYSANDER.** Ay, by my life!
And never did desire to see thee more.
Therefore be out of hope, of question, of doubt;
Be certain, nothing truer. 'Tis no jest
That I do hate thee and love Helena.

**HERMIA** (*to* HELENA). O me! You juggler! You cankerblossom![8]
You thief of love! What, have you come by night
And stol'n my love's heart from him?

8. **cankerblossom** worm that destroys the flower bud, or wild rose

**HELENA.** Fine, i' faith!
Have you no modesty, no maiden shame,
No touch of bashfulness? What, will you tear
Impatient answers from my gentle tongue?
Fie, fie! You counterfeit, you puppet,[9] you!

9. **puppet** dwarfish woman (in reference to Hermia's smaller size)

**HERMIA.** "Puppet"? Why, so! Ay, that way goes the game.
Now I perceive that she hath made compare
Between our statures;[10] she hath urged her height,
And with her personage, her tall personage,
Her height, forsooth, she hath prevailed with him.
And are you grown so high in his esteem
Because I am so dwarfish and so low?
How low am I, thou painted maypole? Speak!
How low am I? I am not yet so low
But that my nails can reach unto thine eyes.[11]
(*She flails at* HELENA *but is restrained.*)[12]

10. Helena is taller than Hermia; how might Hermia use this to scorn Helena?

11. What action does this line suggest? How should the men respond?

12. What comic business can you devise for Hermia being restrained?

"**Why** are you grown so **rude?**
What **change** is this,
Sweet love?

13. **curst** viciously bad-tempered

14. What is Helena saying here? What action might accompany these lines?

15. Is Helena sincere in her attempt to pacify Hermia?

16. **stealth** stealing away

17. **chid me hence** driven me away with his scolding

18. **so** if only

19. **fond** foolish

20. How might the men indicate their willingness to shield Helena?

21. **keen and shrewd** fierce and vicious

22. How might Hermia renew her attack yet make it somehow new and different?

23. **minimus** tiny creature

24. **knotgrass** a weed, a brew of which was thought to stunt the growth.

25. What might Demetrius do to prevent Lysander from taking Helena's part?

26. **intend** give sign of

**HELENA.** I pray you, though you mock me, gentlemen,
Let her not hurt me. I was never curst;[13]
I have no gift at all in shrewishness;
I am a right maid for my cowardice.
Let her not strike me. You perhaps may think,
Because she is something lower than myself,
That I can match her.[14]

**HERMIA.** Lower? Hark, again!

**HELENA.** Good Hermia, do not be so bitter with me.
I evermore did love you, Hermia,[15]
Did ever keep your counsels, never wronged you,
Save that, in love unto Demetrius,
I told him of your stealth[16] unto this wood.
He followed you; for love I followed him.
But he hath chid me hence[17] and threatened me
To strike me, spurn me, nay, to kill me too.
And now, so[18] you will let me quiet go,
To Athens will I bear my folly back
And follow you no further. Let me go.
You see how simple and how fond[19] I am.

**HERMIA.** Why, get you gone. Who is 't that hinders you?

**HELENA.** A foolish heart, that I leave here behind.

**HERMIA.** What, with Lysander?

**HELENA.** With Demetrius.

**LYSANDER.** Be not afraid; she shall not harm thee, Helena.[20]

**DEMETRIUS.** No, sir, she shall not, though you take her part.

**HELENA.** O, when she is angry, she is keen and shrewd.[21]
She was a vixen when she went to school;
And though she be but little, she is fierce.

**HERMIA.** "Little" again? Nothing but "low" and "little"?
Why will you suffer her to flout me thus?
Let me come to her.[22]

**LYSANDER.** Get you gone, you dwarf!
You minimus,[23] of hindering knotgrass[24] made!
You bead, you acorn!

**DEMETRIUS.** You are too officious
In her behalf that scorns your services.
Let her alone. Speak not of Helena;[25]
Take not her part. For, if thou dost intend[26]

Never so little show of love to her,
Thou shalt aby[27] it.

**LYSANDER.** Now she holds me not.
Now follow, if thou dar'st, to try whose right,
Of thine or mine, is most in Helena. (*Exit.*)[28]

**DEMETRIUS.** Follow! Nay, I'll go with thee, cheek by jowl.
(*Exit, following* LYSANDER.)

**HERMIA.** You, mistress, all this coil is 'long of you.[29]
Nay, go not back.[30]

**HELENA.** I will not trust you, I,
Nor longer stay in your curst company.
Your hands than mine are quicker for a fray;
My legs are longer, though, to run away. (*Exit.*)[31]

**HERMIA.** I am amazed and know not what to say. (*Exit.*)

27. **aby** pay for

28. Here the men renew their offer to fight a duel. What movements and gestures by Lysander and Demetrius might indicate their intent?

29. **coil is 'long of you** trouble is because of you

30. **go not back** that is, don't retreat (Hermia is again proposing a fight.)

31. If Helena is running away from Hermia, does she exit in the same direction as the men?

## Extension

Shakespeare's plays continue to be popular, with new movies and stage versions of his works almost every year, such as this recent production of *The Taming of the Shrew,* with Morgan Freeman and Tracey Ullman, set in the American Old West.

1. With the help of your teacher or librarian, choose a movie adaptation of one of Shakespeare's plays, such as *West Side Story* (based on *Romeo and Juliet*) or *Forbidden Planet* (based on *The Tempest*). Examine how the filmmakers made use of Shakespearean materials in their new work.

2. Choose a **soliloquy** (monologue) from a Shakespeare play or create a monologue by combining several long speeches by one character. As you rehearse it, plan what sort of modern setting or costuming you could use to cast new light on the material, the play, or the character. Perform your soliloquy for the class.

# Directing & Producing

Preparation

**Preparation for a performance begins long before opening night and continues right up until the curtain rises. Even before rehearsals start, the director has chosen, analyzed, and interpreted the play, cast the actors and planned their movements, and provided the overall design concept to the design team. The producer has been busy making sure that the curtain will rise to a full house.**

## THE LANGUAGE OF THEATRE

**blocking** coordination of actors' movements onstage

**dénouement** the final resolution of the conflict in a plot

**exposition** the beginning part of a plot that provides important background information

**farce** comedy with exaggerated characterizations, abundant physical or visual humor, and often an improbable plot

**ground plan** a top-view drawing of the floor plan of a set, usually in scale

**inciting incident** the event that sets into motion the action of a plot

**level** height of an actor's head onstage

**plane** the depth of an actor's position onstage

**royalty** a fee paid to produce a play

**stage** (verb) bring to life on stage

# Choosing a Play

One of the most exciting moments in theatre is deciding which play to **stage,** or bring to life on the stage. Visions fill your head as you recall plays you have seen, heard about, or read: young lovers divided by their feuding families, a tense jury room, a magician on an enchanted island, a community paralyzed by fear of witchcraft, a young girl hiding from the Nazis. Wouldn't it be great to be able to direct or produce one of those plays?

At this point in the theatre process, anything seems possible. Of course, you need to be aware of the limitations on time and money available to produce a play in your school, but every production works within such restraints. Remember that theatre can happen any time and any place you have a story to tell, performers to tell it, and an audience to respond to it. You can create theatre even under the most limited conditions, provided you work with an attitude of positive, cooperative, and creative resourcefulness.

The choice of a play may be a cooperative process between the director and producer, or the producer may choose a script for a director to stage. Often, a director is free to choose a play to direct. If you have that choice as a director, take the opportunity to review a number of scripts before making your final decision. Choose a play that moves you personally, will communicate effectively with your intended audience, and has an important message to convey. As you make your choice, consider the features or limitations of your performance space, whether you have actors to cast the play and technicians to meet the specific challenges of the play, as well as the availability of other resources required to produce the play. During your selection process, consult with your producer on these issues.

There are many places to find scripts. Your school or community library may have play collections and catalogs for companies that publish scripts. You may research via the Internet for these catalogs or for unpublished plays. Students in your class or your school may have written good plays. You may even write one yourself. Another possibility is to adapt a script from a published story or poem. There may be copyright issues involved in adapting published literature, so check with your teacher before you take on that challenge.

Your first directorial efforts don't need to be full-length plays; you will probably learn more about directing by first working with a small cast on a variety of short and simple pieces before moving on to large-scale productions. You can also learn about directing—and producing—by acting or doing tech work in plays and observing the methods of directors and producers for those plays.

# Genre

Plays can be generally categorized according to type, or **genre.** As you search for scripts, you may find them classified by the following types:

## Comedy

Comedy is usually light and amusing and typically has a happy ending. *The Odd Couple* by Neil Simon is an example of a comedy that was a popular stage play, movie, and TV series.

## Farce

Farce is comedy with exaggerated characterizations, abundant physical or visual humor, and often an improbable plot. The musical *A Funny Thing Happened on the Way to the Forum* by Burt Shevelove, Larry Gelbart, and Stephen Sondheim includes stock characters typical of farce.

## Tragedy

Tragedy is a serious drama typically describing a conflict between the main character and a superior force (such as destiny) and having a sorrowful or disastrous conclusion. Shakespeare wrote many tragedies, including the now-classic *Romeo and Juliet,* the story of family rivalry and forbidden love ending in the death of two young lovers.

## Drama

The word **drama** is often used to describe a play with serious subject matter, but not necessarily a disastrous ending. Arthur Miller's *Death of a Salesman* is a modern drama that explores the last days of a failing salesman's life, revealing that his quest for success has isolated him from his family.

## Working with the Script

Once the script has been chosen, you will proceed with a detailed script analysis. This involves reading the script many times to accomplish several different goals. One of your earliest goals should be to understand thoroughly the playwright's intent and to develop a vision for your own production. As a director, your job is to communicate your understanding and vision to your actors, to the design team and their crews, and, ultimately, to the audience.

During the play selection process, you probably read or skimmed several plays. Your first thorough reading of the play you choose should be done in one sitting so that you can experience the emotional impact of the play. After this reading, record your reactions in your Theatre Notebook. Your notes will come in handy as you begin your analysis in earnest and proceed to formulate the production concept. By way of example, imagine that you have chosen *The Glass Menagerie* by Tennessee Williams. After reading the script the first time, ask yourself, "What does this play make me think and feel?"

***The Glass Menagerie* by Tennessee Williams**

***First Reactions: What does this play make me think and feel?***

*I feel immense sadness after reading this play. I feel sorry for these people who are disappointed in themselves and their lives. They feel their dreams are never going to come true. Tom has tried to run away from it all, but he's still looking over his shoulder, still trapped by love and guilt. I also feel angry at Amanda for pushing her children and trying to make them perfect.*

*It makes me think that we expect too much out of life. It also makes me think about how difficult it is to balance what I want with my responsibility to other people, especially my family.*

After your first reading you should also have a rough idea of the playwright's message; that is, what the playwright is saying to you. Write a few statements in your Theatre Notebook, answering the question, "What is the playwright saying to me?"

***Playwright's Message: What is the playwright saying to me?***

- *You can't always make people's dreams come true for them.*
- *Adversity doesn't make everyone stronger; some people are crushed by it.*
- *Your family remains a part of you all your life.*

## Elements of a Play

Now that you have a sense of the emotional impact of the play and the playwright's message, you are ready to consider how the playwright communicates those feelings and ideas. You can begin by looking at the basic elements of the play's story: plot, character, setting, and theme. The theme is expressed through the words and actions of the characters in a series of situations that make up the plot. Each situation takes place in a setting.

You will need to do a detailed analysis of each element. In preparation for your analysis, summarize each element in your Theatre Notebook. You have already addressed the element of theme, which may be considered the playwright's message, by answering the question, "What is the playwright saying to me?" Now address the other elements by answering these questions: What happens? (plot) Who does it happen to? (characters) When and where does it happen? (setting) A sample of these summaries for *The Glass Menagerie* follows.

***Plot Summary: What happens?***

*Tom Wingfield works in a factory but wants to live a life of adventure and leave his family; his father left years ago. Laura, his sister, is so embarrassed about a limp she has that she can't handle society. Amanda, his mother, makes a deal with Tom: he must bring home an eligible man to meet Laura before he can leave; Amanda believes that marriage is Laura's only hope for a future. The friend Tom brings home, Jim O'Connor, is someone Laura knew and liked in high school, although her mother and brother don't know this. Jim encourages Laura to come out of her shell and even gives her a kiss. Jim doesn't want to mislead Laura so he explains that he's in love with another girl. He leaves, Amanda and Laura are broken-hearted, and Amanda blames Tom. Shortly afterward, Tom loses his job and leaves home. The story is told from the perspective of Tom, years later, still living with his memories, guilt, and sadness about his family.*

***Character Summary: Who does it happen to?***

*The mother, Amanda, is a former southern belle who speaks, thinks, and acts like the gentility of the old South, making her appear foolish. Her children, Tom and Laura, are in their twenties. Laura is very shy. She speaks and moves very hesitantly. Tom is a poet. He is full of anger and frustration, especially around his family. As the narrator, he is pensive and wistful. Jim O'Connor, also in his twenties, works with Tom. He is an optimistic, ambitious man who speaks like a salesman and corporate climber.*

### *Setting Summary: When and where does it happen?*

*The time period for the play is the 1930s, but the prologue and epilogue take place later, when Tom has left home and joined the merchant marines. The action takes place in a tenement in St. Louis, Missouri. The living room, dining room, and part of the outside alley with a fire escape can be seen. Laura's bed folds out from the sofa in the living room. Also in the living room is a knickknack shelf stacked with many glass animals. According to the stage directions, the walls are transparent so that with lighting changes, one stage area can dissolve into another.*

## Plot Analysis

Now you are ready to begin analyzing the play. Begin with the plot. **Plot** is the structure of the play. Playwrights continually experiment with plots, striving to tell their story uniquely. As a beginning director, you need to understand some of the common structural components. Answering the questions posed for each component will help you get started. Write your responses in your Theatre Notebook. A sample of how to analyze plot is included here, again using *The Glass Menagerie*.

### Exposition

The **exposition** is the part of a play that provides important background information to the audience. It occurs in the beginning of a play. Ask yourself: How are the characters and story introduced? What are the basic relationships? What is the atmosphere, mood, time, and locale? What is the situation? What has happened before the first scene of the play?

***Exposition***

*In the prologue, Tom tells the audience a number of facts: Before the events that he is about to narrate occurred, the father has left the household. Within the first part of the first act, dialogue between the characters reveals that Laura has dropped out of business college. Amanda, who had a wonderful youth with many admirers, now lives a disappointing life she never could have imagined. Tom hates his job and doesn't get along with his mother. The family has been living in a tenement as a result of poverty—partly because of the father's desertion and partly because of the circumstances of the Great Depression. Tom provides the main source of income for the family. Laura is incapable of taking care of herself; she dropped out of school and is paralyzed with shyness in society. Amanda wants the best for her children and tries to remain optimistic, although she constantly compares her life now to the happy one she led as a teenager.*

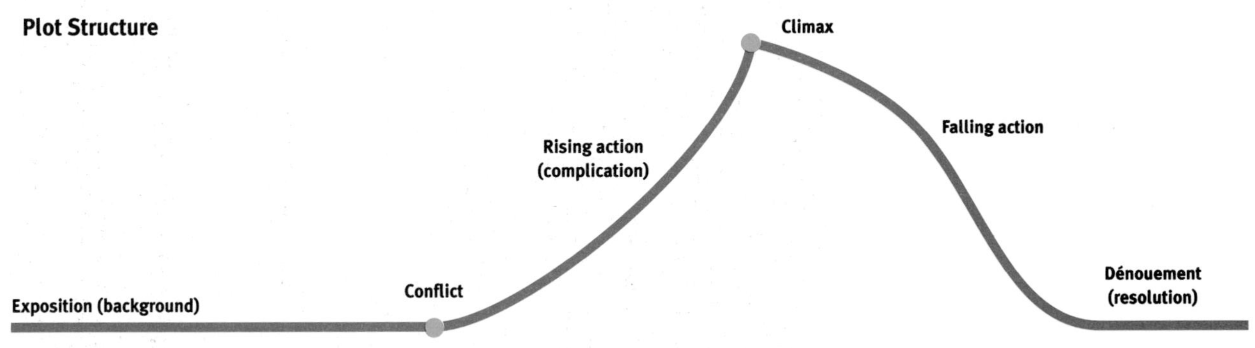

## Inciting Incident

The **inciting incident** is the catalyst for the play's action. It may take the form of an idea or action on the part of the main character, or it may occur through some external force imposed upon a character. Ask yourself: What is the event that sets into motion the action of the play? What incident is the source of conflict that upsets the balance and leads to changes in character relationships?

### *Inciting Incident*

*The inciting incident is Amanda's discovery that Laura has dropped out of business college and her realization that Laura will never be capable of surviving on her own. This leads to Amanda's decision that Laura must have a boyfriend and get married.*

## Rising Action

The **rising action** of a play consists of complications and discoveries, which create conflict. It makes up the middle portion of a play. Ask yourself: What are the factors leading to changes in character relationships? What are the complications that develop? Are there new characters introduced and what effect do they have on the established characters? What happens when new information is revealed to the characters? What are each character's objectives? What obstacles stand in the way of accomplishing those objectives? How are each character's objectives in opposition to other characters' objectives?

### *Rising Action*

*Amanda discovers that Tom is planning to leave and join the merchant marines; Tom discovers that his mother suspects his plans. This leads to an urgency and sense of desperation in both characters, which adds more tension to their relationship. Amanda feels that if Tom leaves, the family will fall apart. Tom feels that if he stays, he will go crazy.*

*One of Tom's objectives is to escape from his unhappy life. At first he does this by leaving the house nightly to go to the movies or pursue other forms of entertainment. His mother worries about his absences, fearing he will become an alcoholic like his father. Tom's behavior is in opposition to her objective, which is to see her children successful. She confronts Tom about his habits and urges him to advance at his existing job.*

*When a new character, Jim, is introduced, hopes rise as everyone looks forward to the possibility that Jim and Laura will fall for each other. This creates a temporary harmony between Amanda and Tom. It causes Amanda to lapse into the behavior of her youth as she prepares for a "gentleman caller." It also creates a nearly unbearable nervous state in Laura, who has admired Jim since high school. She is both hopeful that he will be kind to her as he once was and fearful that he will reject her because of her handicap.*

## Climax

The **climax** is the turning point in the plot when everything comes to an emotional crest and the rising action becomes the falling action. It usually occurs close to the end of the play. Ask yourself: What is the play's peak of emotional intensity? What is the final turning point?

### *Climax*

*The climax comes during Jim's visit. Laura's nerves cause her to fall ill during dinner. After dinner, Jim goes to talk to her. With his charm and because of her admiration of him, he breaks through her shyness barrier and becomes momentarily enchanted with her. He even gets her to dance with him and gives her a kiss. One of her glass animals, a unicorn, is broken in the process. Jim almost immediately recognizes that he has made a mistake and reveals that he is engaged to another girl. There is no hope for a relationship between them. Laura is completely crushed with his announcement. He apologizes for the misunderstanding. She gives him the broken unicorn.*

## Falling Action

The **falling action** is the series of events following the climax. Ask yourself: What events occur to resolve the conflict?

### *Falling Action*

*Jim explains to Amanda that he is engaged and he leaves. Amanda blames Tom for bringing home an ineligible man. This event not only crushes Laura but also her mother, causing Tom to feel angry and guilty for failing to solve his family's problems. The broken dreams of his mother and sister compound his desperation, making it more difficult for him to concentrate on his dreams of leaving and having a life of his own.*

### Dénouement

The **dénouement** (dā nü maN′), meaning "unknotting," is the resolution of the conflicts that made up the rising action. Ask yourself: What conflicts are resolved? What inner conflicts do the characters continue to experience even though the outcome of a situation appears to be determined?

#### *Dénouement*

*Tom has a final fight with Amanda and leaves to join the merchant marines. He continues to live with the pain of being unable to help his sister.*

## Character Analysis

A play is a story about characters in conflict. The character with whom the audience identifies most strongly is the **protagonist,** or main character. The person, situation, or inner conflict in opposition to the main character's goals is the **antagonist.** Characters other than the protagonist and antagonist are known as **secondary characters.**

You will need to discover each character's purpose in the play, and his or her motives and desires. As a director, you may want to write an analysis for each character in the play as a way to focus your thoughts and to help your actors achieve fully realized characters. Ask yourself the following questions, writing your analysis for each character in your Theatre Notebook: What does the play say about this character? What does this character say about himself or herself? What do other characters say about this character? What motivates this character's words or actions? What is his or her subtext? What is the emotional makeup of this character? How does this character change or develop through the course of the play? How does this character use language? Does this character have a regional dialect?

## Setting Analysis

Even though you know when and where the play takes place, you still need to analyze the details of the setting. Ask yourself these questions as you consider how the setting in a play is evoked: What are the viewable elements? What are common sights and sounds in the time and place of the play? What sound effects and/or music specified in the script contribute to the setting? What is the time of day for each scene?

## Theme Analysis

When you have finished your in-depth analysis of the play's other elements, reconsider what you think is the playwright's message, analyzing how it is emphasized in the script. Complicated plots include both the central theme and secondary ideas; look for these and note them. To uncover further meaning, search for recurring ideas that are interwoven in the plot. Find out more about the playwright to gain further insight about his or her viewpoint and background. Write all these ideas in your Theatre Notebook to refer to as you develop your production concept. Ask yourself questions such as these: Are there any specific statements or actions by the characters that explicitly or implicitly announce the theme? Are there symbols in the play that represent the theme? At what points does the theme emerge most distinctly in the play? Is the theme subtle or obvious?

Keep this analysis in the forefront of your mind during rehearsals and share it with your actors. Consider the value of creating a formal statement of the theme for yourself and everyone involved in the production. It can be direct or poetic.

## Symbolism

In working with your script, you should determine if the playwright has employed symbolism. A **symbol** is a concrete image used to represent something abstract, such as a concept or an idea. In *The Glass Menagerie,* Laura's collection of glass animals, and the unicorn in particular, function as symbols. When the unicorn is broken, what is being conveyed symbolically?

A dead seagull symbolizes lost hope in Anton Chekhov's *The Seagull.* What might the torch symbolize in this scene from the play?

## The Dramaturg

A **dramaturg** is a special consultant who provides specific in-depth knowledge and literary resources to the director, producer, or the entire theatre company. A dramaturg's responsibilities fall into three areas: reading and evaluating plays being considered for production; researching literary, historical, or sociological questions relating to a play that is being produced; and providing feedback to the director about a production from a literary standpoint.

Dramaturgs have been around since the 1800s, but it's only in the last 25 years that they have become really important. In the complex environment of contemporary theatre, a dramaturg provides directors and producers with a more efficient way to sort through and evaluate the great mass of literature and background information available.

## Style

In addition to classification of plays by genre, many plays can be classified according to the style in which they are written. From your analysis of the play, you should be able to determine the style of the production. Today, the dominant stylistic approach to playwriting is **realism.** In realistic plays, playwrights try to represent life situations accurately. If the action takes place in a kitchen, the set will likely have appliances found in a modern kitchen and may even have running water. Events and actions are reproduced to give the illusion of real life.

*Born Yesterday* by Garson Kanin is written in a realistic style, reflected through the use of a realistic set and dialogue that tells a slice-of-life story.

*Blood Wedding* by Federico García Lorca, on the other hand, is a nonrealistic play, which is reflected in the nonrealistic set and poetic language of the play.

The Keystone Cops, popular in the silent films of the early 1900s, use stylized movements originating in the theatrical conventions of melodrama and vaudeville during the 1800s.

Some plays are written in a theatrical or nonrealistic style. Plays of this type present an abstract or conventionalized view of human activity. They don't attempt to disguise that the situation isn't real and may even expose the artificial world of the stage. Nonrealistic plays don't necessarily reflect how people actually behave or talk. The settings may merely suggest a real place instead of re-creating it.

In general, style reflects the time period during which a play was written and its prevailing culture and conventions—including manners and costume, as well as the available technology for producing plays. Often the style of a play reflects current philosophies and approaches in the fine arts and literature.

The style of a play is usually evident in the language of the play. Shakespeare and Molière, for example, wrote in verse, according to conventions of their times. Most modern plays use naturalistic-sounding speech for the dialogue.

It's important to study the theatrical style of the play you choose to direct. If you've selected a play by anyone other than a realistic modern playwright, you will need to study and observe other productions of work by the same playwright or from the same time period. Learn about the theatrical conventions of the period. Study stylized movement that is used, such as use of a fan or bowing in the comedy of Molière's time or the gymnastics and slapstick of the Keystone Cops.

# The Director's Role in Design

As a director you must develop a production concept to describe to the designers and technicians (p. 54). At the same time, you must create a ground plan for each setting of your play, which you will use for staging scenes during rehearsals, and which the set designer will use to design the set, or sets, for the play. A **ground plan** looks something like the floor plan of a house; it's usually done to scale.

You need to accomplish the following with your ground plans:

- Establish the boundaries of the set.
- Define the acting areas.
- Determine entrances and exits for the acting areas.
- Specify the characteristics of each acting area.
- Place scenery, furniture, and props where actors can move around them in interesting paths and still be seen, and where they will not interfere with exits and entrances.

A published play may contain an illustration of the ground plan from the first professional production, which you can adapt to your performance space. Shown here is the ground plan for Arthur Miller's *Death of a Salesman*.

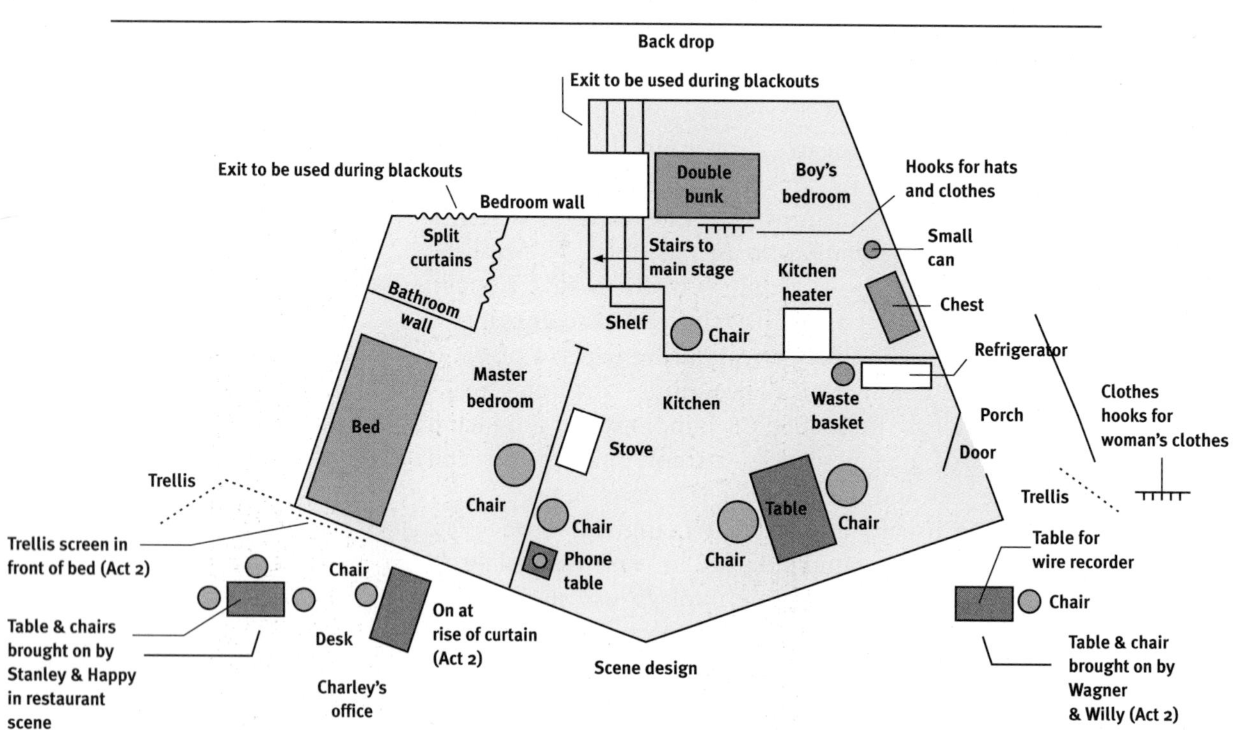

# Stage Composition

You are now ready to begin staging your show. Using what you have learned through your analysis, you will need to visualize every scene and action of the play, including where the actors are placed and how they enter and move around the set you have in mind. Make sketches of your general ideas in your Theatre Notebook shortly after completing your analysis.

In essence, you will be creating a series of pictures that tell the story. Each picture should emphasize the characters or action that is most important at that moment to tell the story; that is, the focus (p. 144). Four composition elements help establish focus: body positions (p. 140), stage areas (p. 62), levels, and planes.

## Focus and Body Positions

A strong body position can be used to instantly draw the audience's attention to a particular character. Full front is the most dominant stage position because the audience can see the actor's face. Three-quarters back is a weaker position since the audience sees little of the actor's face. In creating a stage picture remember how the actors' body positions influence audience focus.

Also remember that there are no absolutes in creating a stage picture. Many factors, including your experience and intuition, may influence your decisions about what is most effective. A play's style, for example, affects actors' body positions. Because realistic plays emphasize portraying an illusion of truth, they demand a more natural approach to stage pictures. In a realistic play a character at the center of action who maintains a full-front position may seem artificial or fake to the audience. In a less realistic play, such as those by Shakespeare, or a musical comedy, audiences don't expect to see real life. Because of such demands as singing or talking directly to the audience, more nonrealistic positions are acceptable.

The full-front position here in Molière's *Illusions* is accepted as a convention of plays written at the time.

## Focus and Stage Areas

Areas of the stage are strong or weak in focus depending on how close the area is to the audience. Centerstage is very strong because it's the center of focus. On a proscenium stage, upstage left or right is a weak position because it's difficult for the audience to see the action as clearly. Downstage areas are the strongest because the actors are closest and most visible to the audience.

## Arrangements for Emphasis

Arrangement of body positions onstage, in combination with spoken lines, helps determines the focus of a scene. Lighting, sound, costumes, and makeup can also be implemented to establish focus. Focus is not always on one actor. There are several distinct types of arrangements for emphasis that reflect the desired focus of a stage picture. In **direct emphasis,** the focus of the stage picture is on one actor. Two different, but equal focuses in a stage picture create **duoemphasis.** Arrangements with a **secondary emphasis** are less focused than in a direct or duoemphasis arrangement. Secondary emphasis is most often used for a character or group of characters who are reacting to the main character. If the main character is standing full front, downstage center, a secondary focus might place a reacting character upstage right in profile. Secondary emphasis may also be used for an inanimate object like a ring, legal papers, a piece of furniture, or even a corpse. **Diversified emphasis** results in scenes in which there is a frequent change of focus among five or more characters of equal importance to the plot or in an ensemble scene. In these situations, as dialogue dictates, the speaking character can achieve temporary emphasis by simple shifts of body position.

When planning your emphasis in a stage picture, try to achieve visual balance; it's generally more pleasing to the eye. Try not to concentrate too much activity or set decoration in one specific area of the stage, which will throw off the balance.

## Levels

In directing, a **level** refers to the height of an actor's head onstage. An actor who is higher or taller than the other actors onstage generally will attract attention. When you direct actors to change to different levels you change the focus of the scene. Different levels may be utilized through actors positioned on step units and platforms, actors lying or sitting on the stage floor, or actors seated or standing on furniture or set pieces.

In this production of Shakespeare's *Twelfth Night,* variation in levels is achieved though actors positioned vertically on an inventive construction of grates and circular stairs.

## Planes

The use of **planes** to achieve focus refers to the positioning of actors at different depths onstage. The farther downstage an actor is, the larger he or she will appear in relation to other actors who are upstage; the larger an actor appears, the more the audience focuses on that actor.

### Diagonals

A **diagonal** is a composition of two actors who are not on the same plane or in a shared position. In a diagonal, one actor is upstage of the other, often creating a feeling of tension.

### Triangles

When there are three or more actors onstage, a **triangle** composition is used. Triangles utilize diagonals on each leg of the triangle. Triangles may vary in the length of the legs or in the size of the angles. Using flat triangles (those that have little depth) is not much more effective than using a line.

Use of a diagonal composition creates tension between the downstage group and the upstage figure in this scene from Anton Chekhov's *The Three Sisters.*

Dramatic depth is achieved in this triangle composition for Athol Fugard's *Master Harold and the Boys.*

## Stage Composition for Arena and Thrust Stages

Since the audience is seated on three or four sides of the action, actors performing on arena and thrust stages are required to move more frequently than on a proscenium stage. By doing so, no segment of the audience misses out on too much of the action. On an arena stage, at any given point in the performance some part of the audience will be viewing only the back of an actor; therefore, a scene that might normally only require two or three stage pictures for a proscenium stage might require six or seven stage pictures for arena and thrust stages. On an arena or thrust stage set, the director should watch rehearsals from different areas of the house to be sure that the view is reasonably good for all audience members.

Voltaire's *Candide* is performed here in the round; that is, in an arena-type performance space.

# Blocking

The coordination of all the actors' movements onstage is called **blocking.** After you have visualized and established the stage composition of scenes, you will need to guide the actors into position for their entrances for a scene and explain what you have interpreted as their movement throughout the action of the scene.

The reason you plan and write down the blocking is to bring to life your interpretation of the play script. Blocking physicalizes the characters. Through the process of blocking, you will give actors the opportunity to show what their characters want and to utilize body language to communicate their relationships to other characters. The blocking process also helps you visualize the dramatic action and conflicts of the play.

To make choices about blocking, you will need to answer questions such as these for each scene:

- What are the characters' objectives?
- What action do they take to accomplish their objectives?
- What obstacles stand between them and accomplishing their objectives?
- Does any character have a hidden motive or feeling regarding another character?
- How do the characters interact?

## Interactive Onstage Movement

Three types of interactive character movement occur onstage: one character moving toward another stationary character, one character moving away from another stationary character, and one character moving toward another character who is moving away (a chase).

Moving toward another character implies that the moving character wants confrontation or emotional contact with the other character. Moving away from another character says that the moving character is avoiding contact or confrontation. A chase means that one character wants to avoid contact, while the other wants contact.

Usually you will direct actors to move as they begin or finish speaking their lines; movement draws the audience's focus. The character speaking is generally the one who should have focus because his or her lines move forward the action of the play. Sometimes, because of the playwright's intent, you may choose to have the speaking character remain still while another character moves.

Don't use movement just because you want to keep the audience interested. Movement should always be motivated by the play script or the objectives of the characters (p. 134).

# The Director's Promptbook

Some blocking is included by the playwright in the script. Your additional blocking comments may be written in the margin of the script or in a promptbook. A **promptbook** consists of the script pasted onto larger pages, thereby allowing space for notes and other material related to understanding, visualizing, and communicating your ideas about the script and the production.

### MAKING A PROMPTBOOK

1. Take apart two copies of the script and tape or glue each page to a larger, blank piece of paper. (You need two copies because one side of the printed page will be affixed to your notebook page.)
2. Insert a blank page between each script page to allow extra space for notes.
3. Include a rehearsal schedule and a contact sheet listing the name, position or character, and phone number of everyone in the cast and crew.
4. Include pages for your ideas and analysis.
5. Insert all pages into a three-ring binder. This allows you to easily add or replace pages.

You may choose to paste a photocopy of your ground plan on the blank pages between the script pages of your promptbook. You can mark blocking on it using the abbreviations for the stage areas (p. 62) and other shorthand blocking symbols, such as those shown here.

**Blocking Symbols**

|  |  |  |  |  |  |  |  |
|---|---|---|---|---|---|---|---|
| Ⓑ | = Bill (circled letter of character's name) | P→ | = push | // | = lean | bz | = business |
| | | T→ | = take | < | = speak | pu | = pick up |
| | | G→ | = give | • • • | = pause | st | = step |
| ent | = enter | R↑ | = rise | ∽↗ | = path of cross | h | = chair |
| X | = cross | L↓ | = lie down | w/ | = with | π | = table |
| 2 | = to | L→ | = look | @ | = at | ⊓ | = bed |
| $↑ | = stand | L→← | = look at each other | bf | = before | sofa symbol | = sofa |
| $↓ | = sit | ⊣ | = stop | fr | = from | ↗ | = door |
| K↓ | = kneel | ∞ | = turn | O | = around | ⊟ | = window |

U = upstage D = downstage C = centerstage L = left R = right

**Promptbook pages for *The Importance of Being Earnest* by Oscar Wilde**

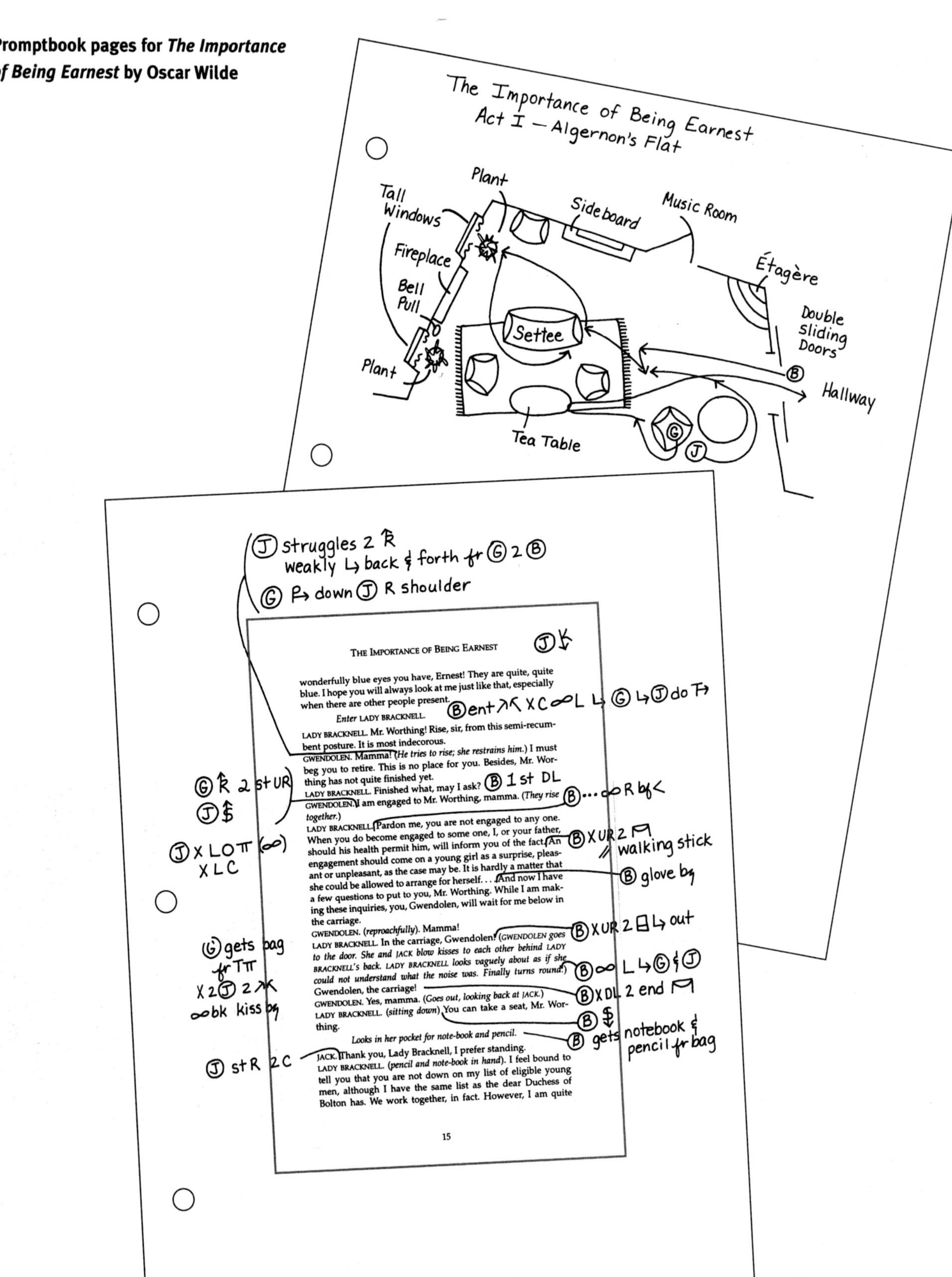


THE IMPORTANCE OF BEING EARNEST

wonderfully blue eyes you have, Ernest! They are quite, quite blue. I hope you will always look at me just like that, especially when there are other people present.

*Enter* LADY BRACKNELL.

LADY BRACKNELL. Mr. Worthing! Rise, sir, from this semi-recumbent posture. It is most indecorous.

GWENDOLEN. Mamma! (*He tries to rise; she restrains him.*) I must beg you to retire. This is no place for you. Besides, Mr. Worthing has not quite finished yet.

LADY BRACKNELL. Finished what, may I ask?

GWENDOLEN. I am engaged to Mr. Worthing, mamma. (*They rise together.*)

LADY BRACKNELL. Pardon me, you are not engaged to any one. When you do become engaged to some one, I, or your father, should his health permit him, will inform you of the fact. An engagement should come on a young girl as a surprise, pleasant or unpleasant, as the case may be. It is hardly a matter that she could be allowed to arrange for herself. . . . And now I have a few questions to put to you, Mr. Worthing. While I am making these inquiries, you, Gwendolen, will wait for me below in the carriage.

GWENDOLEN. (*reproachfully*). Mamma!

LADY BRACKNELL. In the carriage, Gwendolen! (GWENDOLEN *goes to the door. She and* JACK *blow kisses to each other behind* LADY BRACKNELL'S *back.* LADY BRACKNELL *looks vaguely about as if she could not understand what the noise was. Finally turns round.*) Gwendolen, the carriage!

GWENDOLEN. Yes, mamma. (*Goes out, looking back at* JACK.)

LADY BRACKNELL. (*sitting down*) You can take a seat, Mr. Worthing.

*Looks in her pocket for note-book and pencil.*

JACK. Thank you, Lady Bracknell, I prefer standing.

LADY BRACKNELL. (*pencil and note-book in hand*). I feel bound to tell you that you are not down on my list of eligible young men, although I have the same list as the dear Duchess of Bolton has. We work together, in fact. However, I am quite

15

# The Business of the Play

While the director is busy analyzing the script, preparing a ground plan, visualizing the stage pictures, and working out the blocking, the producer and the producer's staff are busy with the business of the play.

## Permissions

Before you can produce a play, you need to make arrangements for permissions. All published plays still protected by copyright require permission to be produced. Permission is granted by the publisher in the name of the copyright holder, who may be the publisher or more often, the playwright. Permission usually involves payment of a **royalty,** a flat fee that can range widely. Unless the producer has an established track record with a publishing company, fees and deposits are usually due before permission is granted and scripts are sent.

To request permission, fax or write the publisher with the following information (a phone call is not sufficient):

- dates of production
- number of seats in the house
- ticket price
- type of producing organization (professional or nonprofessional)

## Promotion

Advertising and public relations are the most effective ways to get an audience. Public relations involves keeping the media informed of important or newsworthy occurrences in your production. This builds interest in the community and gets people talking. If you have a public relations or promotions writer (p. 544) on the production staff, you should send out three or four news releases to area newspapers and radio/TV stations including photos as indicated in the production schedule.(See Promoting a Show in Writing & Theater.) Posters need to be created and distributed at least two to three weeks in advance of an opening, but start developing ideas earlier and get them approved by the production team (p. 54). A phone number or location for ticket orders and sales should be made available as soon as possible; make sure you have your box office staffed at the hours posted. Ads need to be run in local papers and on local radio for the two weeks in advance of opening night. Double-check them to ensure you have all the pertinent information and that it is correct.

## Programs

If programs are used, their design should be coordinated with the posters and ads. Proper credit must be given to the playwright and publisher; guidelines for doing so are provided in the production contract with the publisher. Cast and crew members should be recognized by their parts or positions, the director should be named, and recognition and thanks should be given to people outside the cast and crew who have contributed in any way to the production. Identification of the scenes and setting of the play, ad space purchased by local businesses, and if budget allows, pictures and short biographies of cast and crew members may also be included in the program.

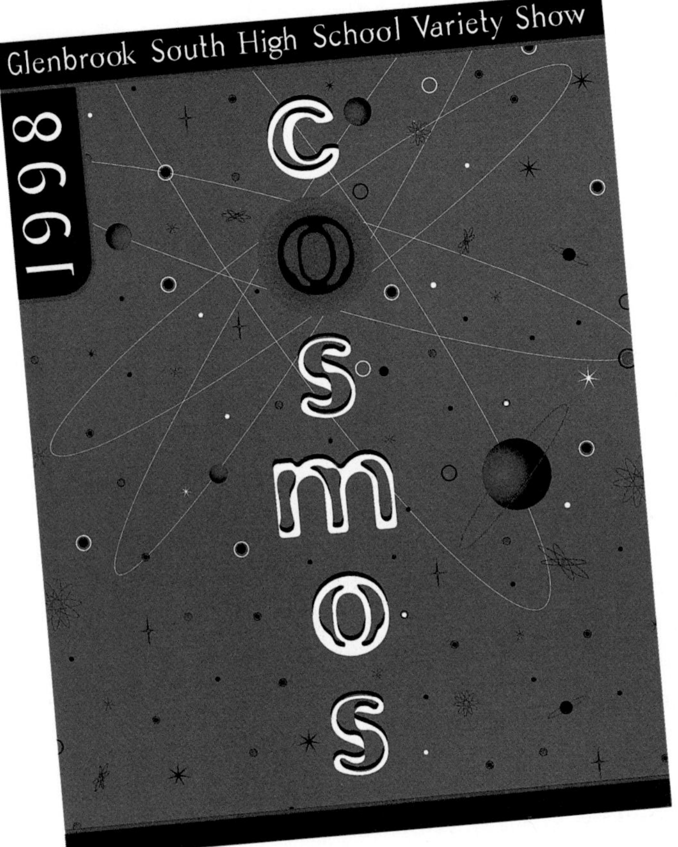

# The Stage Manager

If there is no assistant director, the stage manager helps the director with the casting and rehearsals. Following is a list of the wide range of duties and responsibilities of the stage manager during preparation for the performance:

## Duties Prior to Rehearsal Period

- Participate in production team meetings (p. 54).
- Post audition and callback notices.
- Prepare the audition space and materials, which include pencils, scripts, and forms.
- Assist the director during auditions.
- Prepare a list of alternates for each role.
- Post the cast list.
- Assist in selecting crew members.
- Prepare cast and crew contact sheets, which include addresses and phone numbers.
- Assist the director and technical director in planning the rehearsal schedule.

## Duties During Rehearsals

- Post a rehearsal schedule and distribute schedules to cast and crew; update the schedule when necessary.
- Distribute scripts to cast and crew.
- Prepare the rehearsal space. Arrive one hour early to lay out the ground plan (marked with tape on the floor) and to work with the tech crew to acquire rehearsal furniture and properties.
- Take roll call at the beginning of each rehearsal; contact those who are missing. Inform the director regarding any illnesses or emergencies that would delay or cancel rehearsals. Keep accurate account of absences or tardiness.
- Communicate throughout rehearsal with cast and crew and notify the director of any important concerns.
- Keep track of where cast and crew are during rehearsals and be responsible for dismissing them from the rehearsal space.
- Arrange appointments for costume fittings.
- Coordinate all technical rehearsals with the director and the technical director.
- Create your own promptbook (p. 183) to note all blocking and director's instructions to cast and crew.

# Activities

*Choosing a Play*

**TOP TEN PLAYS** Conduct a survey of your classmates, asking them to list their favorite plays. Based on the survey, compile a top ten list of plays and distribute the list. Students can use this list when considering plays they would like to read, see, or take part in. Expand your survey to include parents and the rest of your community.

*Choosing a Play*

**SCRIPT EVALUATION FORM** Using the criteria mentioned on p. 163, create a script evaluation form. Use it to evaluate one or two plays. Revise it as necessary. Then use it to evaluate five more plays. Include these in your Theatre Notebook. Contribute your form and your evaluations to your theatre program.

*Genre*

**CLASSIFYING BY GENRE** Work together with a small group. Each of you should write a list of plays you have read or seen and a list of movies you have seen over the last year. Compare and discuss the lists. Classify them according to genre. Are there plays and movies you found it impossible to classify? Under what categories might you classify them? Create a chart in which you list these plays and movies by genre. Include the chart in your Theatre Notebooks, updating it now and then.

*Working with the Script*

**FIRST IMPRESSIONS** Read a play in one sitting. Write your immediate response to the play in your Theatre Notebook. Then try to determine the playwright's message. Do this for several plays. How do your responses change as you become more experienced at expressing your response and interpeting the theme? Now ask a friend to read some of the same plays. Compare your interpretations of the themes for these plays. If you like, add your friend's first impressions to your Theatre Notebook.

### *Working with the Script*

**SCRIPT ANALYSIS** Select a play and analyze it's plot, characterization, setting, and theme. Begin with summaries of each. When you have finished your analysis, formulate a statement about the theme that you would use if you were directing the play, one that would guide your production concept and your actors.

### *Working with the Script*

**DRAMATURG** Select a play and perform a dramaturg's function, researching the play's background and developing recommendations about how it should be staged. Write your ideas for the production concept, scenery, costumes, and so on in a report. Present this report as you would to a director considering a production of this play. Include illustrations that would serve as useful reference images for the director or design team.

### *Style*

**REALISTIC STAGE DIRECTION** Imagine setting a play in a room that you know very well. Write the opening stage directions in which the room is described. Try to depict it so exactly that someone reading the play would be able to picture the setting clearly. Refer to published plays for a model on this type of description. How might your stage directions differ if you wanted to describe the room in a nonrealistic play?

### *The Director's Role in Design*

**DRAW A GROUND PLAN** Read a one-act play. Imagine that you have the opportunity to direct this play. Pick out a performance space and draw a ground plan for your set, including the set props you need. Then read the play again and make sure that it will work for all the action required. Revise as necessary.

### *Style*

**NONREALISTIC STYLE** Read several plays by playwrights who write plays with a nonrealistic style, such as Eugene Ionesco, William Saroyan, Jean Anouilh, Luigi Pirandello, Caryl Churchill, and Ntozake Shange. What are the settings of these plays like? Does the language differ from naturalistic speech you hear every day? How? What is the relationship of the actors to the audience? What special challenges would face you doing a nonrealistic play? Write your answers to these questions in your Theatre Notebook.

# Activities

*Stage Composition*

**PICTURE ANALYSIS** Working with several other students, study a painting or photograph of a group of people. Look at the arrangement of the people in the picture and determine how levels and planes are used. Note which methods of emphasis are used to create the focus.

*Stage Composition*

**STAGE COMPOSITION OBSERVATION** Gather together a group of three to five students of varying heights to serve as actors. As director, do the following: (1) have the actors line up on the same plane; (2) on that plane, direct each actor individually to move so that all body positions are represented by the group; (3) direct the actors to maintain these positions and have each move to a different stage area; (4) have one or more of the actors sit , crouch, or stand on a chair. Study the composition you have created, noting how it creates interest and focus. Do the activity again. How many stage compositions can you create by combining body positions, levels, and planes?

*Blocking*

**BLOCKING A SCENE** Find and analyze a short scene from a familiar play with a small number of characters. Create a ground plan and determine the blocking for the scene. Then find a space where you can tape the boundaries of the ground plan on the floor. Gather together any simple set pieces you might need. Ask actors to go through your blocking for the scene. How does it work? Write your response to the effectiveness of your blocking in your Theatre Notebook, including suggestions for how it might have been improved.

*The Business of the Play*

**CHECK THE ROYALTIES** Choose a couple of plays and inquire about the royalties for producing them. Include information required by publishers in your letters, as noted on page 185; use sample information representative of what you would specify if you produced the play in your school. Present the results of your survey to the class.

*The Business of the Play*

**PLAY PROGRAM** Create a program for a play you would like to produce. Some programs simply state the play's title, author, dates of production, publisher's copyright information, and the names of the director, cast, and technical crew. Others are more elaborate, featuring pictures of the show, as well as biographies and head shots of the actors, director, and designers. Be as creative as you can. You might want to include your finished program in your Theatre Notebook.

*The Business of the Play*

**JOB SHADOW—GRAPHIC ARTIST** If you are interested in the process by which such theatre promotional pieces as posters and programs are created, you might want to observe a graphic artist at work for several hours. Professionals are busy, but if you are polite as well as interested, they are usually willing to let you observe them as they work and to answer questions about their training and background. Be sure to first get permission from your parents, teacher, and the supervisor of the business or organization where you will job shadow.

HISTORICAL PROFILE

# Molière

The works of France's greatest playwright were banned in his hometown, and he died while performing in one of his own plays. Born Jean Baptiste Poquelin in 1622, Molière (mōl yâr′) was the son of a successful Paris interior decorator who had achieved the office of upholsterer to the king. Both his mother and stepmother died by the time he was 14, and Molière's father saw to his education in the classics, philosophy, and the law. (One of Molière's fellow students was Cyrano de Bergerac, the long-nosed wit and swordsman immortalized in Edmond Rostand's play.) Everyone expected the young man to follow his father in the family business, but at 21 he chose the theatre as his profession and adopted Molière as his pen name. Perhaps he did so to protect his family: theatre people of the day had no social standing and were, in fact, often in trouble with the Church.

Joining nine young men and women to found an acting troupe, Molière toured the country for 12 years. Though he was twice arrested for debt during those early years, Molière remained with the company and eventually began to write plays as well as perform. In 1658 his company successfully performed one of his comedies, *The Love-Sick Doctor,* before the French court, and from then on his fortunes improved. Molière's comedies were satirical in nature, and nothing was sacred. While the court was delighted with each new play, middle-class theatregoers were less gratified as they recognized their customs and behaviors ridiculed on Molière's stage. As he continued to write, direct, and perform in over 30 plays, he made many enemies.

In Molière's France, theatre often took place in found spaces, such as this performance at the palace of Louis XIV at Versailles.

His late marriage to a much younger woman was largely an unhappy one. Two of his three children died in infancy, and his estrangement from his father over his chosen profession was never resolved. An ultimate irony of his life was that he would suffer a fatal hemorrhage in 1673 while performing the title role of the hypochondriac in his own play, *The Imaginary Invalid.* Priests refused to hear the actor/playwright's final confession, and only the intercession of King Louis XIV allowed his body to be buried in a churchyard four days later.

## The Theatre Space

Most theatres of Molière's day were converted ballrooms or indoor tennis courts: long, narrow rooms with shallow stages at one end and grandstands and galleries arranged around the remaining three walls. Sight lines and acoustics were left to chance. The only seats that directly faced the stage were at the far end of the room, and the best view from that vantage point was that of the patrons who purchased cheap standing-room-only tickets for the area directly in front of the stage. Sometimes seats directly on the stage itself were sold to aristocratic young men who wanted to show off their fine clothes. There was no stage curtain, and scenery was comparatively simple, showing a single room or a street corner. Lighting was provided by hundreds of wax candles and small oil lanterns, which must have contributed to a rather smoky atmosphere by the end of the evening.

The elaborate theatrical costumes of Molière's day, which reflected the fashions of the time, are displayed in this production of his comedy *The School for Wives.*

## Style of Costumes

If the scenery was comparatively plain, the costumes were not, displaying an exuberance of colors, curls, ribbons, laces, puffs, flounces, and feathers on both men and women. Actors appeared in the latest elegant fashions of the day, with no concern for historical accuracy. Fashions changed from year to year, as they do today, and players had to provide their own costumes.

For the men, such a costume might include a shirt cut very full, so that it bloused over the breeches and puffed at the sleeves, worn with a kind of necktie fashioned from yards of lace or fine cloth, arranged in a variety of decorative folds. A very short, short-sleeved coat showed off this shirt to advantage. Breeches were very full—so full sometimes that they looked like a petticoat—and fastened above the knee. They were worn with long stockings and square-toed shoes with high heels. Men of fashion wore wigs in natural colors but elaborate styles. As accessories they might carry long decorative walking sticks, delicate handkerchieves, or broad-brimmed hats decorated with ostrich feathers.

Women might wear a full skirt, long enough to trail behind; sometimes an overgown was open in front and turned back or draped to show its own lining and to reveal an undergown. Necklines were low, square-cut or in a wide V, and sleeves were long or elbow-length and quite full, sometimes folded back in a cuff. Often necklines and sleeves were designed to reveal the lace or fine linen of the underclothes. The waistline was low and came to a point, and the bodice laced up the front. Built into these gowns were strips of bone to help cinch in the waist and to control posture. Shoes were similar to men's, but with higher heels and in delicate fabrics such as satin, brocade, or embroidered silk. Women often carried fans or sometimes little hand-warming muffs. They did not wear wigs to the extent that men did but had their hair dressed in ringlets, sometimes wired to stand away from the face.

## Acting Styles

The kind of costumes worn by Molière's men and women do not allow natural movement. Instead, they encourage posing to show off rich fabrics or elegant tailoring. The accessories actors carried invited graceful gestures—broad or fluttery—with their hands. It was not possible for anyone to flop back in an easy chair; instead, men and women perched rather stiffly on the edges of straight-backed chairs after carefully arranging their costumes to show off to the best advantage.

The stage always requires some degree of exaggeration, so that even those audience members farthest away can see and hear the play. Actors and actresses of Molière's theatre were faced with the challenge of projecting his cleverly rhymed verse throughout a difficult, poorly lit theatre space filled with a noisy audience. To project effectively, they adapted an exaggerated, declamatory style of acting that made use of a convention of larger-than-life stylized gestures that were thought appropriate to show certain emotions.

## Try It Out

Work with your actors to stage the following scene from Molière's *Tartuffe*. Your greatest challenge here will probably be the blocking of the quarreling young lovers and of the maid Dorine, who is in and out of the action. Encourage your actors to interpret their characters truthfully but to make use of what they understand of the acting styles of the period.

*from*

# Tartuffe

*Translated by* **Richard Wilbur**

**V**alère (vä lâr) and Mariane are in love, although Mariane's father wants her to marry the older Tartuffe (tär tüf´), a religious hypocrite. Dorine is the maid, and she is present observing the scene from the beginning.

1. Speaking rhymed verse so that it sounds like natural conversation is always a challenge to actors. Instruct your cast to read for the sense—punctuation will help—rather than the rhymes.
2. With what tone of voice might Valère make this accusation?
3. With what tone of voice might Mariane admit to Valère's accusation?

**VALÈRE.** Madam, I've just received some wondrous news
Regarding which I'd like to hear your views.[1]

**MARIANE.** What news?

**VALÈRE.** You're marrying Tartuffe.[2]

**MARIANE.** I find
That Father does have such a match in mind.[3]

**VALÈRE.** Your father, Madam . . .

**MARIANE.** . . . has just this minute said
That it's Tartuffe he wishes me to wed.

**VALÈRE.** Can he be serious?

**MARIANE.** Oh, indeed he can;
He's clearly set his heart upon the plan.

**VALÈRE.** And what position do you propose to take, Madam?

4. Why does Mariane say she doesn't know what position she should take on the question?

**MARIANE.** Why—I don't know.[4]

**VALÈRE.** For heaven's sake—
You don't know?

**MARIANE.** No.

**VALÈRE.** Well, well!

**MARIANE.** Advise me, do.

**VALÈRE.** Marry the man. That's my advice to you.[5]

**MARIANE.** That's your advice?

**VALÈRE.** Yes.

**MARIANE.** Truly?

**VALÈRE.** Oh, absolutely.
You couldn't choose more wisely, more astutely.

**MARIANE.** Thanks for this counsel; I'll follow it, of course.[6]

**VALÈRE.** Do, do; I'm sure 'twill cost you no remorse.

**MARIANE.** To give it didn't cause your heart to break.

**VALÈRE.** I gave it, Madam, only for your sake.

**MARIANE** And it's for your sake that I take it, Sir.

**DORINE** *(withdrawing to the rear of the stage)*.[7] Let's see
which fool will prove the stubborner.[8]

**VALÈRE.** So! I am nothing to you, and it was flat
Deception when you . . .

**MARIANE.** Please, enough of that.
You've told me plainly that I should agree
To wed the man my father's chosen for me,
And since you've deigned to counsel me so wisely,
I promise, Sir, to do as you advise me.[9]

5. If Valère and Mariane consider themselves in love, why does he tell her to marry Tartuffe? With what emotions might he deliver this line?

6. How can Mariane make it clear to the audience that Valère's advice is *not* what she expected him to say?

7. Dorine has to be out of the main action for a while, but still in a position to hear what's going on. How can you block her movements to indicate this?

8. Dorine's line is an example of an **aside**, a statement spoken half to herself, half to the audience. What might her tone of voice be? her facial expression?

9. What feelings is Mariane experiencing at this point? Should she show them to Valère? How might she reveal them to the audience?

"Let's see which **fool** will prove to be the **stubborner.**"

**VALÈRE.** Ah, no, 'twas not by me that you were swayed.
No, your decision was already made;
Though now, to save appearances, you protest
That you're betraying me at my behest.

**MARIANE.** Just as you say.

**VALÈRE.** Quite so. And I now see
That you were never truly in love with me.[10]

10. Does Valère really believe what he's accusing Marianne of? Why does he do it?

**MARIANE.** Alas, you're free to think so if you choose.

**VALÈRE.** I choose to think so, and here's a bit of news:
You've spurned my hand, but I know where to turn
For kinder treatment, as you shall quickly learn.

**MARIANE.** I'm sure you do. Your noble qualities
Inspire affection . . .

**VALÈRE.** Forget my qualities, please.
They don't inspire you overmuch, I find.
But there's another lady I have in mind
Whose sweet and generous nature will not scorn
To compensate me for the loss I've borne.

**MARIANE.** I'm no great loss, and I'm sure that you'll transfer
Your heart quite painlessly from me to her.[11]

11. This quarrel goes on for quite a number of lines. How might you pace the scene so that the actors don't arrive at the peak of their emotional expression too soon?

**VALÈRE.** I'll do my best to take it in my stride.
The pain I feel at being cast aside
Time and forgetfulness may put an end to.
Or if I can't forget, I shall pretend to.
No self-respecting person is expected
To go on loving once he's been rejected.

**MARIANE.** Now, that's a fine, high-minded sentiment.

**VALÈRE.** One to which any sane man would assent.
Would you prefer it if I pined away
In hopeless passion till my dying day?
Am I to yield you to a rival's arms
And not console myself with other charms?

**MARIANE.** Go then: console yourself; don't hesitate.
I wish you to; indeed, I cannot wait.[12]

12. Why does Marianne say she "cannot wait" for Valère to find another lover?

**VALÈRE.** You wish me to?

**MARIANE.** Yes.

**VALÈRE.** That's the final straw.
Madam, farewell. Your wish shall be my law.
*(He starts to leave, and then returns: this repeatedly.)*[13]

13. Valère's repeated attempts to leave may seem comical, but remember—to him they are absolutely serious. How can you block his movements so that the repetition itself doesn't get boring?

**MARIANE.** Splendid.

**VALÈRE** *(coming back again).* This breach, remember, is of your making;
It's you who've driven me to the step I'm taking.

**MARIANE.** Of course.

**VALÈRE** *(coming back again).* Remember, too, that I am merely
Following your example.

**MARIANE.** I see that clearly.

**VALÈRE.** Enough. I'll go and do your bidding, then.

**MARIANE.** Good.

**VALÈRE** *(coming back again).* You shall never see my face again.

**MARIANE.** Excellent.[14]

14. Where is the moment of peak emotional expression in this quarrel?

**VALÈRE** *(walking to the door, then turning about).*
Yes?

**MARIANE.** What?

**VALÈRE.** What's that? What did you say?[15]

15. Valère knows that Mariane said nothing. What's he doing here?

**MARIANE.** Nothing. You're dreaming.

**VALÈRE.** Ah. Well, I'm on my way.
Farewell, *Madam.* *(He moves slowly away.)*

**MARIANE.** Farewell.

**DORINE** *(to* MARIANE*).* If you ask me,
Both of you are as mad as mad can be.[16]
Do stop this nonsense, now. I've only let you
Squabble so long to see where it would get you.
Whoa there, Monsieur Valère!
*(She goes and seizes* VALÈRE *by the arm; he makes a great show of resistance.)*

16. Dorine now reenters to take the scene in hand. Where and how should she move? How should she speak to assert her authority over these people who are, after all, of the social class of her employer?

**VALÈRE.** What's this, Dorine?

**DORINE.** Come here.

**VALÈRE.** No, no, my heart's too full of spleen.
Don't hold me back; her wish must be obeyed.

**DORINE.** Stop!

**VALÈRE.** It's too late now; my decision's made.

**DORINE.** Oh, pooh!

**MARIANE** *(aside).* He hates the sight of me, that's plain.
I'll go, and so deliver him from pain.

17. Both Valère and Mariane could easily escape from Dorine as she rushes back and forth between them. How can you avoid their actually reaching the exits? How would you block this so that they never actually reach the exits?

**DORINE** *(leaving* VALÈRE, *running after* mariane*).*[17]
And now you run away! Come back.

**MARIANE.** No, no.
Nothing you say will keep me here. Let go!

**VALÈRE** *(aside).* She cannot bear my presence, I perceive.
To spare her further torment, I shall leave.

**DORINE** *(leaving* MARIANE, *running after* VALÈRE*).*
Again! You'll not escape, Sir; don't you try it.
Come here, you two. Stop fussing and be quiet.
*(She takes* VALÈRE *by the hand, then* MARIANE, *and draws them together.)*

**VALÈRE** *(to* DORINE*).* What do you want of me?

**MARIANE** *(to* DORINE*).* What is the point of this?

**DORINE.** We're going to have a little armistice. *(To* VALÈRE.*)*
Now, weren't you silly to get so overheated?

18. How might both Mariane and Valère show that they are cooling down from the heat of their quarrel?

**VALÈRE.** Didn't you see how badly I was treated?[18]

**DORINE** *(to* MARIANE*).* Aren't you a simpleton, to have lost your head?

**MARIANE.** Didn't you hear the hateful things he said?

19. What might Dorine's tone of voice be when she tells the lovers that they are "great fools"? What expression might she show them?

**DORINE** *(to* VALÈRE*).* You're both great fools.[19] Her sole desire, Valère,
Is to be yours in marriage. To that I'll swear.
*(To* MARIANE.*)* He loves you only, and he wants no wife
But you, Mariane. On that I'll stake my life.

**MARIANE** *(to* VALÈRE*).* Then why you advised me so, I cannot see.

**VALÈRE** *(to* MARIANE*).* On such a question, why ask advice of *me?*

20. What is the most logical—and symbolic—position for Dorine to be in as she attempts to join the lovers' hands?

**DORINE.** Oh, you're impossible. Give me your hands, you two.[20]
*(To* VALÈRE.*)* Yours first.

**VALÈRE** *(giving* DORINE *his hand).* But why?

**DORINE** *(to* MARIANE*).* And now a hand from you.

**MARIANE** *(also giving* DORINE *her hand).* What are you doing?

**DORINE.** There: a perfect fit.
You suit each other better than you'll admit.
*(*VALÈRE *and* MARIANE *hold hands for some time*[21] *without looking at each other.)*

**VALÈRE.** *(turning toward* MARIANE*).* Ah, come, don't be so haughty. Give a man
A look of kindness, won't you, Mariane?
*(*MARIANE *turns toward* VALÈRE *and smiles.)*[22]

**DORINE.** I tell you, lovers are completely mad![23]

21. How long should this last?

22. How quickly should Mariane turn toward Valère? What kind of smile should she give him?

23. It wouldn't be out of style to have Dorine address this line to the audience, as a kind of punchline for the scene.

## Extension

Look for the same kind of rapid-fire exchange of dialogue and misunderstandings that get blown up all out of proportion when you watch movies—particularly the "screwball" comedies of the 1940s (such as Howard Hawks's *His Girl Friday,* shown here) and your favorite television sitcoms.

1. Describe a situation in a comedy you have seen in which lovers quarrel. How do they resolve the situation?
2. As a director, work with four actors to develop a pantomime of a quarrel in which two people don't want to back down and the other two try to make peace.

# Technical Theatre

Everyone who participates in theatre expresses or illuminates the action onstage in some way. Designers and tech crews create the appropriate environment for the action, which may involve weeks of preparation to design and produce.

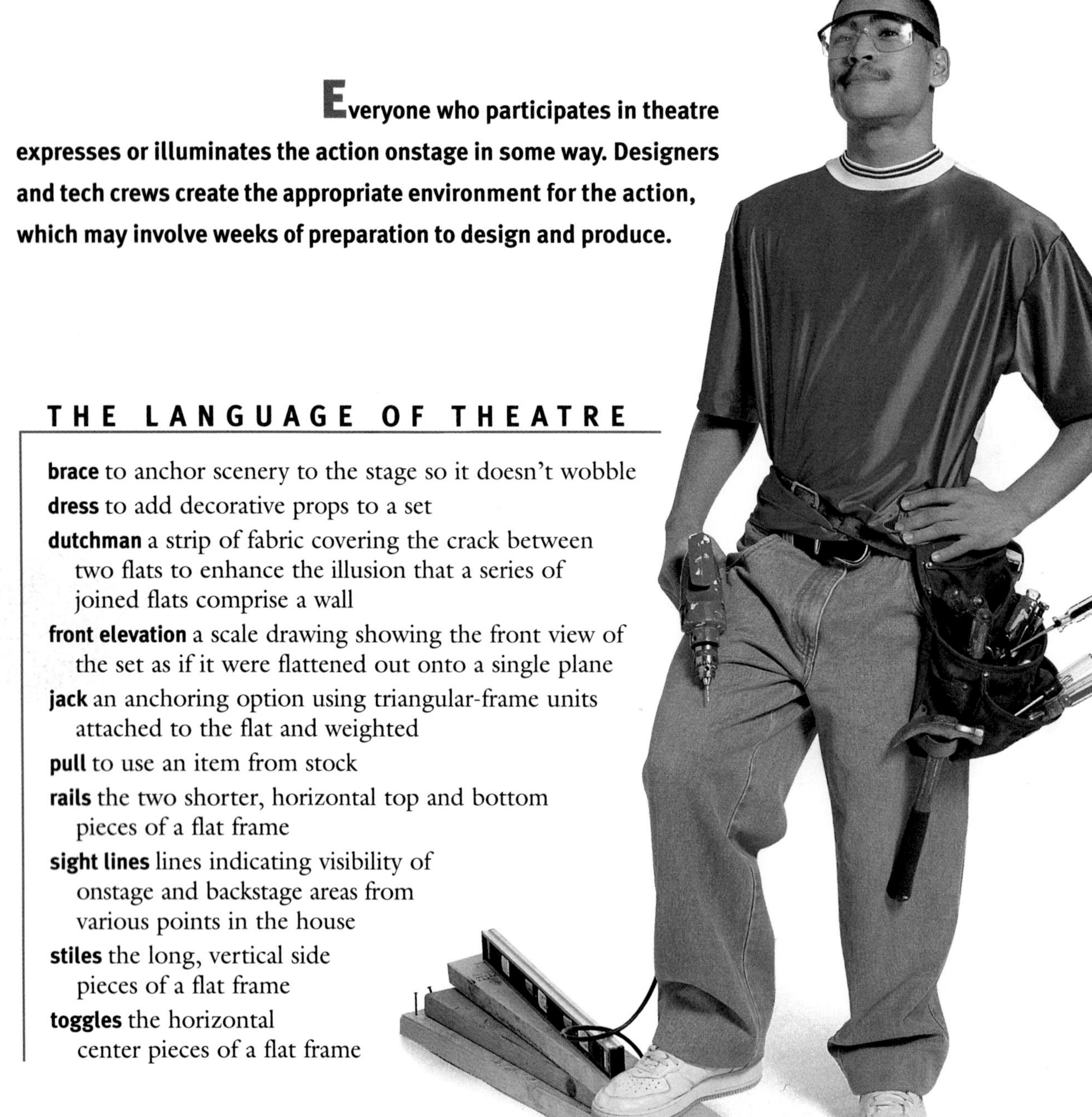

## THE LANGUAGE OF THEATRE

**brace** to anchor scenery to the stage so it doesn't wobble

**dress** to add decorative props to a set

**dutchman** a strip of fabric covering the crack between two flats to enhance the illusion that a series of joined flats comprise a wall

**front elevation** a scale drawing showing the front view of the set as if it were flattened out onto a single plane

**jack** an anchoring option using triangular-frame units attached to the flat and weighted

**pull** to use an item from stock

**rails** the two shorter, horizontal top and bottom pieces of a flat frame

**sight lines** lines indicating visibility of onstage and backstage areas from various points in the house

**stiles** the long, vertical side pieces of a flat frame

**toggles** the horizontal center pieces of a flat frame

# Emergence of the Design Team

As a member of the design team (p. 54), you should have broad working knowledge of each technical theatre specialty. Some of these specialties have been present in essence from the beginnings of theatre, while others have developed relatively recently.

## Set and Prop Design

Modern theatrical design originated in two movements of the late 1800s. The first aimed at realism in stage sets and props, such as those of producers André Antoine and David Belasco. (Antoine once hung beef carcasses onstage to make a butcher shop scene more realistic.) The second was a reaction against realism led by designers Adolphe Appia and Gordon Craig who believed that a play's environment should convey a dramatic feeling, not merely present a historically or geographically accurate setting.

## Lighting Design

Most early theatre was performed in daylight. Later, indoor theatres used candles or gaslights. When electric lighting came into use in the 1800s, it was seen simply as a way of enabling the audience to better see the performance. Eventually, lighting came to be viewed as a vital component in the total visual impact of the production.

## Sound Design

Music has always been an important component of theatre, and sound effects are often essential to convey certain action in a play. Sound design has become increasingly important with the development of new audiotechnologies, such as computerized electronic mixing and miniaturized microphones and transmitters.

## Costume Design

Historically accurate costume is a relatively recent phenomenon. In Shakespeare and Molière's theatre companies, most actors performed in the clothes of the time. Costume design today provides various information about the characters, such as historical period, social class, personality, and so on; but the costume designer also contributes to the total production concept.

## Makeup

Makeup is one of the oldest theatrical arts, having origins in the masks and face-painting of ancient ritual and dance. In the mid-1900s, typecasting in the American theatre de-emphasized the importance of theatrical makeup. In recent years, with an upsurge of theatre at all levels, offering a wider variety of parts to actors, the makeup artist has assumed new importance.

# Elements of Production Design

An effective production design should be informative, expressive, appropriate, and usable, although one element may dominate.

## Informative Design

To be informative, a production design must communicate the time and place of the play. Sam Shepard's *Buried Child* is set on a contemporary Illinois farm.

## Expressive Design

For a design to be expressive, it must evoke the theme and mood of the play. This dramatic adaptation of Amy Tan's *The Joy Luck Club* expresses the theme that your heritage influences your life.

## Appropriate Design

To be appropriate, a design must be suitable for the play's action and the performance space. In this production of Henrik Ibsen's *A Doll's House,* the set is suitable for the action, which takes place in the confines of a well-ordered home, as well as for the performance space, which is a shallow proscenium stage, perfect for a play about a stifled wife.

## Usable Design

Most importantly, an effective design must be a usable design. This modern set for Shakespeare's *Hamlet* is at once flexible, workable, and dramatically dynamic.

# Set Design

The set design is the hub around which all other aspects of the production design revolve. As a set designer, your work will be integrated with the other technical designers. Together you may brainstorm creative possibilities and tackle problems, but for them as well as for you, the production design must be grounded in the play. Your first step, therefore, in developing any set design is to analyze the play.

## Script Analysis for the Set Designer

Read the script as soon as possible. Discuss it with the director and other members of the design team (p. 54). Work from the production concept if one has been defined by the team; otherwise, find out on your own all that you can about the time, place, and style of the play. Think about its meaning and overall mood.

You might want to make some sketches or collect pictures representing the time, place, climate, mood, and type of people the play will present. You will certainly want to explore the technical demands of the play in light of the space in which the play will be performed. If you are unfamiliar with the space, take time to evaluate the possibilities and problems it presents.

## Sketches and Renderings

Once you know the play and its requirements, make several **thumbnail sketches,** or rough drawings, of your first ideas about the set. In some cases, the director may already have presented an idea about the set, perhaps at the first production design meeting. If so, you can work from that to create your thumbnails; out of those you make, choose the one that seems most promising.

A thumbnail sketch fulfills several functions. It provides a working concept for a set, offers a plan that is easy to build upon and change, and serves as a jumping-off point from which the director and the rest of the production design team can brainstorm and refine the set.

After the sketch has been made, presented, discussed, and modified, you can use it as the basis for creating a color **rendering.** A rendering is a finished representation of the set. Renderings can be produced with colored pencil, paint, pastels, marking pens, or a computer graphics program. A rendering is drawn to **scale,** which means drawn at a fixed ratio to the full size of that item. If your drawing of the set is at a scale of ½ inch to 1 foot, ½ inch on your drawing will equal 1 foot on the set. Most theatrical design plans are done on a ½-inch or ¼-inch scale.

Thumbnail sketch (top) and color rendering (above) of a set for John Osborne's *Look Back in Anger*

## Set Design Plans

Sketches and renderings help you focus your production concept. They also assist the director in developing the action for a play. To build and position the set pieces, however, you will need to create design plans, which consist primarily of a ground plan and a front elevation.

### Ground Plan

The set designer's ground plan is a scale mechanical drawing of the set, based on the director's general ground plan (p. 176). It's the major reference drawing for the designer and the set and prop construction crews. The ground plan offers a top view of the set in its position on the stage area. Its purpose is to show the location, position, and measurements of set pieces on the stage. It may include the position of **backing,** which consists of flats, draperies, or drops placed backstage of openings to the stage. Backing is necessary to **mask,** or hide, the backstage areas from the audience's view.

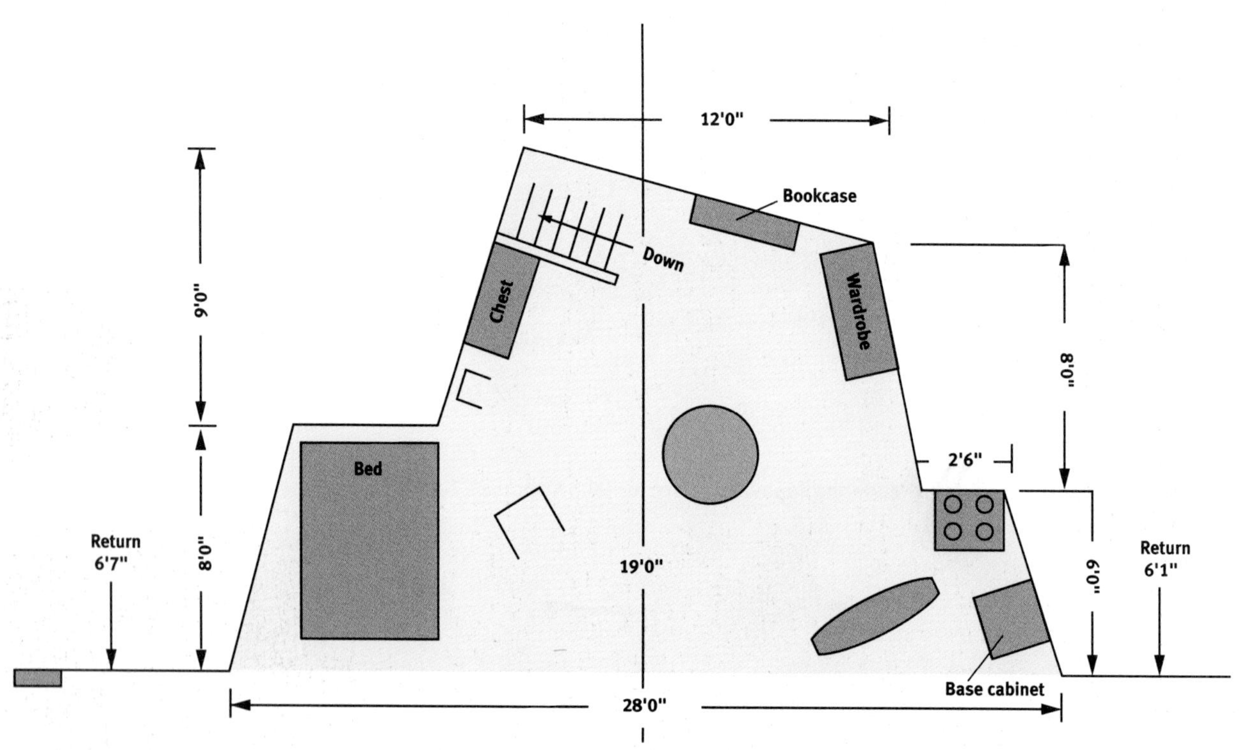


**Ground plan for the set of *Look Back in Anger,* based on the thumbnail and rendering (p. 207)**

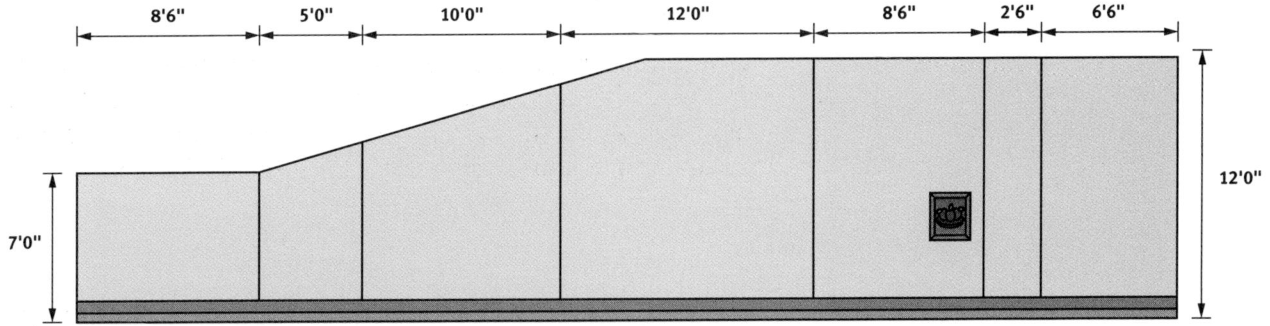


**Front elevation for the *Look Back in Anger* set (pp. 207–208)**

## Front Elevation

A **front elevation** offers a front view of the set as if it were flattened out onto a single plane, and drawn to scale. Its purpose is to show the vertical dimensions and proportions of the set that can't be shown on the ground plan. It may also show the style and decorative features of walls, doors, windows, and fireplaces, as well as the placement and style of baseboards, cornices, and paintings.

## Supplementary Design Plans

Many designers supplement these basic drawings and models with **sectionals,** which present vertical and horizontal "slices" of the set, and drawings showing **sight lines,** lines indicating visibility of onstage and backstage areas from various points in the house. Designers may also develop detailed drawings of three-dimensional objects that are part of the set.

# Models

Some set designers, particularly in professional theatre, prefer to work with three-dimensional models of the sets they design. For brainstorming, you can build a simple, scale model, (p. 115), or you can build a **production model,** a complete scale model of the set with all its set pieces.

# Set Construction

Once the set design has been confirmed, construction begins. You may have stock units that can be readily adapted for each production, or you may build new flats and platforms for each show.

## Flats

Flats form the basic units of scenery in most productions. They are aligned and joined vertically to form walls, which are painted. Because they are lightweight, sets composed of flats can be moved easily to accommodate scene changes.

Flats are made with 1 × 3 stock lumber and covered with fabric or wood. The standard dimensions of a flat are 2 to 4 feet wide and 8 to 12 feet tall. The frame consists of two long, vertical side pieces, called **stiles;** two shorter, horizontal top and bottom pieces, called **rails;** and, depending on the height of the flat, from one to three horizontal center pieces, called **toggles.** The rule-of-thumb is to place a toggle approximately every 3 to 4 feet. If the flat is wider than 4 feet or exceptionally tall (12 feet or more), two diagonal braces made of 1 × 2 stock lumber placed in opposite corners may be required for stability. To provide extra support, a small piece of plywood known as a **keystone** bridges each joint where the toggles butt against the stiles. A triangular piece of plywood called a **cornerblock** bridges the corner joints where stiles and rails butt.

#### CONSTRUCTING A FLAT

1. Measure, cut, and lay out the pieces of 1 × 3 stock lumber, face-side down (p. 79), in the shape of the flat, with the stiles butting up against the top and bottom rails and the toggles evenly spaced between the stiles.
2. Make four cornerblocks of ¼-inch plywood (10-inch squares, cut diagonally) and two keystones for each toggle (2½ inches × 8 inches). A traditional keystone is slightly larger at one end than the other, but it is easier and less expensive to cut the ends straight, with no loss in effectiveness. If diagonal braces are used, they should be 2 feet long, cut at each end at a 45° angle.
3. Use a carpenter's square to make sure corners are square. Then place your cornerblocks ¾ inch from the edges of the corners and prepare to nail them in. The ¾-inch margin is crucial since other flats may butt up against the flat at a corner, and cornerblocks and keystones must not interfere with the alignment.
4. Place lath or clout nails (1⅛ inch long) into the cornerblocks and keystones, in the pattern shown, but don't nail them in all the way. (Place clout nails so the flat side is at a right angle to the wood grain to avoid splitting the wood.)

5. After checking the accuracy of the flat size, place a ¼-inch × 12-inch steel plate (clinch plate) under each corner. Now drive the nails into the cornerblocks. When the tips hit the steel plate they will turn up into the wood, or clinch, which anchors the cornerblocks in place. Do the same with the keystones.

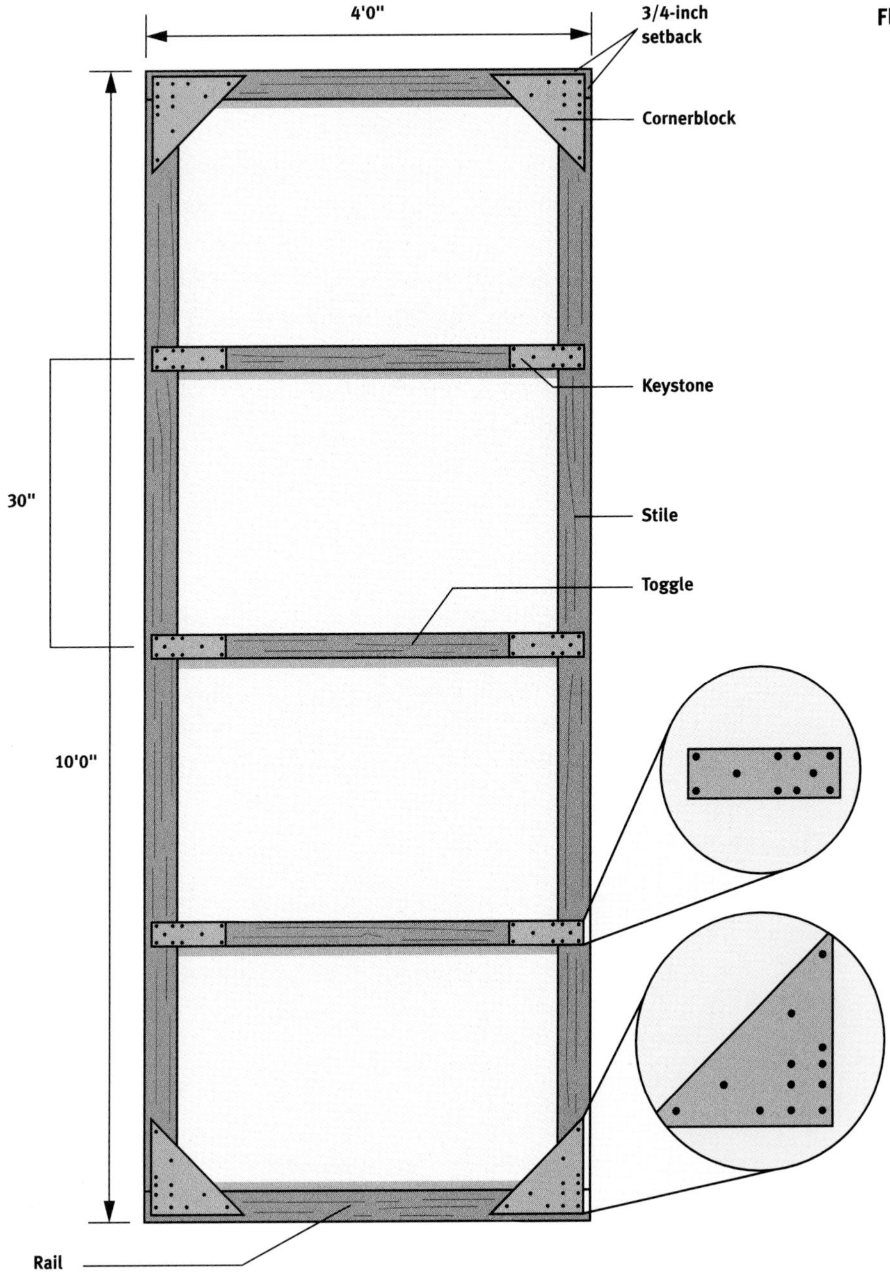

4'0"
3/4-inch setback
Cornerblock
Keystone
30"
Stile
Toggle
10'0"
Rail

**Flat construction**

fig. 1

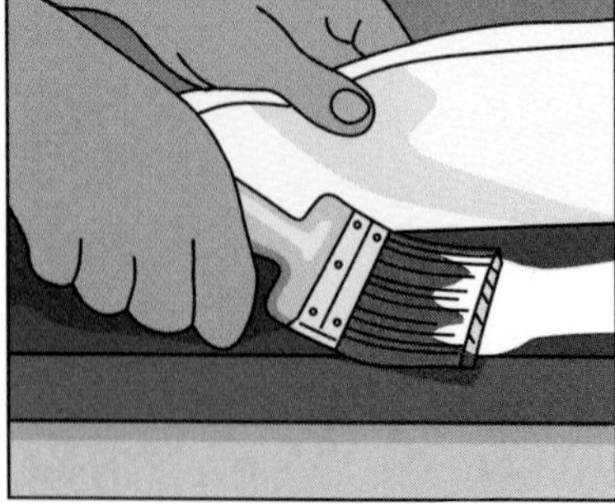

fig. 2

fig. 3

### COVERING A FLAT

1. Turn the frame over so it is resting on the corner blocks and keystones.
2. Measure and cut a piece of fabric 4 inches longer and wider than the frame.
3. Starting at the center of one stile, tack or staple the fabric to the inside edges of the frame. Place your staples 1 foot apart. (fig. 1)
4. Pull the fabric tight (but not so tight that it puckers around the staples) and staple the opposite stile, also starting in the center. Then do the top and bottom rails.
5. Pull back the fabric from the outside edges and apply a coating of glue to the faces of the stiles and rails. (fig. 2) Don't apply glue to the toggle.
6. Replace the fabric, smoothing out any wrinkles with your hand. If wrinkles persist, sprinkle warm water over the top of the fabric and ease the wrinkles out. Don't leave the wrinkles to dry or they will be a permanent feature of the flat.
7. After the glue dries (several hours or overnight), use a utility knife to trim excess fabric from the outside edges of the flat. Trim into the edges about ⅛ inch to avoid loose threads hanging over. (fig. 3)
8. Remove the staples.

You may want to consider using hard-cover flats for stock units, particularly if your flats sustain heavy usage. Hard-cover flats are simpler to make than fabric-covered units, though slightly more expensive. The cover material, typically a sheet of wood such as lauan, is simply glued and stapled to the frame.

## Doors

Most onstage doors open backstage and upstage, which means the hinges are on the upstage side. This helps mask backstage area and keeps the actors open to the audience during entrances and exits.

### CONSTRUCTING A DOOR FLAT

1. Measure, cut, and lay out the pieces for a flat in the manner described previously.
2. Allow for an opening in the frame of at least 30¼ inches × 81 inches. (A standard door is 30 inches × 80 inches, and you need room for it to swing open and for hinges and hardware.) Make the entire flat at least 1 foot or more larger than the door opening; anything less will be too little support for the door.

3. The bottom rail should go across the entire length of the flat, including the door opening. This will keep the flat from twisting out of alignment before it is covered and dry.
4. Place the cornerblocks as shown.
5. Cover the entire flat, and be sure to place glue (but not staples) on the faces of the interior door frame.
6. When dry, trim the excess fabric from the outside edges of the flat. Then cut the fabric from the door opening and trim the edges there as well.
7. Cut off the bottom rail in the area of the door opening and replace it with a sill iron, which is a ¼-inch steel strap. The sill iron should extend at least 1 foot on either side of the opening. The bottom edge of the rail on which the sill iron is placed should be cut (trimmed) ¼ inch to accommodate it.

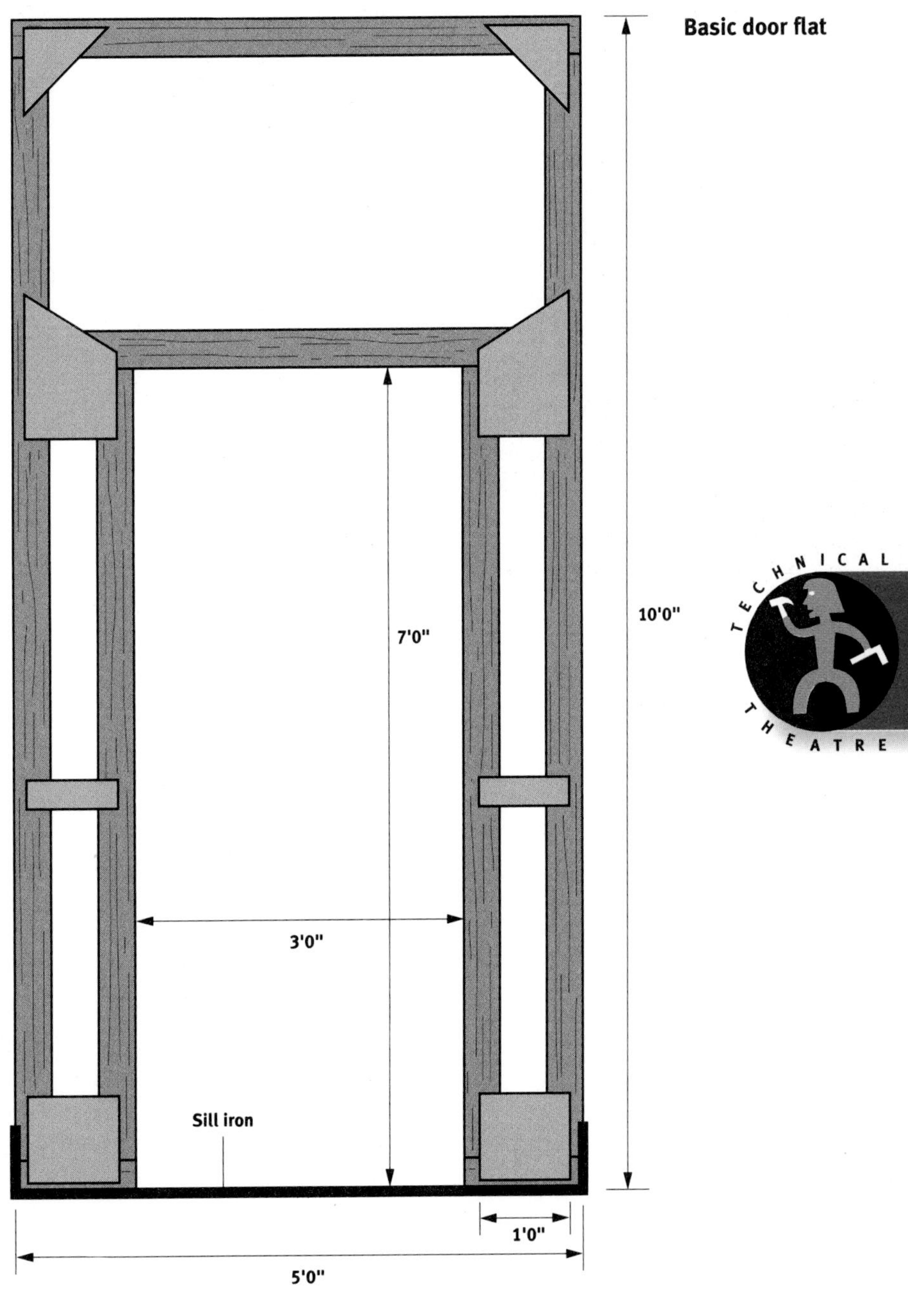


Basic door flat

## Platforms

Platforms are used to create multiple levels on a stage. They must be strong enough to support the weight of actors, furniture, and props. The easiest and most economical platform to build is the rigid wooden platform.

Rigid wooden platforms are formed of three parts: the top, or **deck,** the supporting frame, and the legs. The frame, a ladder-like construction of rungs, or **joists,** is constructed something like a flat frame but stronger. Most platform frames are built to standard sizes such as 4 feet by 8 feet, 4 feet by 4 feet, or 2 feet by 2 feet. The deck, made of ¾-inch plywood, is screwed to the frame.

You can attach legs of any length to each of the four corners, although legs taller than 18 inches need to be reinforced with diagonal braces on each side placed at a 45° angle.

Some set construction crews prefer to use pipe or other metal framing for platforms. Because of its strength, metal is especially useful for making tall platforms.

Another type of platform is the parallel, which has a removable deck and a hinged base that can be folded up and stored flat.

## CONSTRUCTING A RIGID WOODEN PLATFORM

1. Measure, cut, and lay out the pieces of 2 × 4 stock lumber, edge-side down (p. 79), in the shape of the platform frame, with the stiles butting up against the top and bottom rails and the joists spaced no more than 2 feet apart between the stiles.
2. Check the accuracy of your joints with a carpenter's square. Then screw the frame together.
3. Measure and cut the plywood deck (¾ inch or thicker). Attach the deck to the frame with screws placed at 6 to 8 inch intervals.
4. Measure and cut the legs. Attach the legs with bolts from the outside. If necessary, add diagonal braces on all sides.

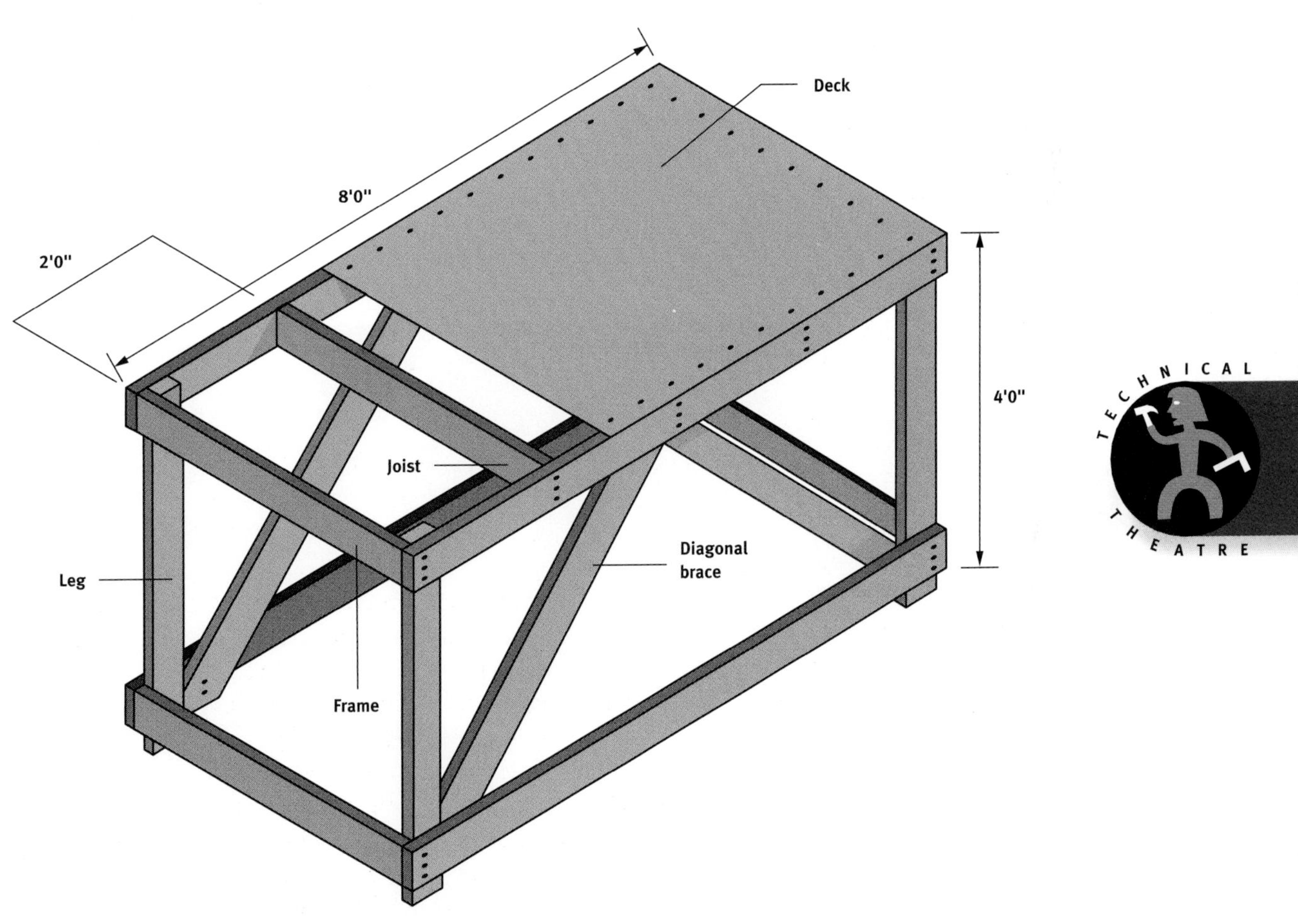


**Rigid wooden platform**

## Drops

Most drops are made of heavyweight muslin attached to battens. They are frequently used to create a background for outdoor or city settings or are painted to create the illusion of the sky. They are raised and lowered in the **fly space,** the area above the stage, by means of a **counterweight system** of ropes, steel cables, pulleys, and weights.

**Scrim** drops are made of sharkstooth scrim or theatrical gauze, dyed or lightly painted with thinned paint. Scrims are so lightweight that they are transparent when lit from behind. They are useful in creating surprise changes or special effects during a scene.

The most common way of suspending a drop from a batten is to tie it onto the batten. Batten clamps are also used; they grip two lengths of lumber that sandwich the top of the drop.

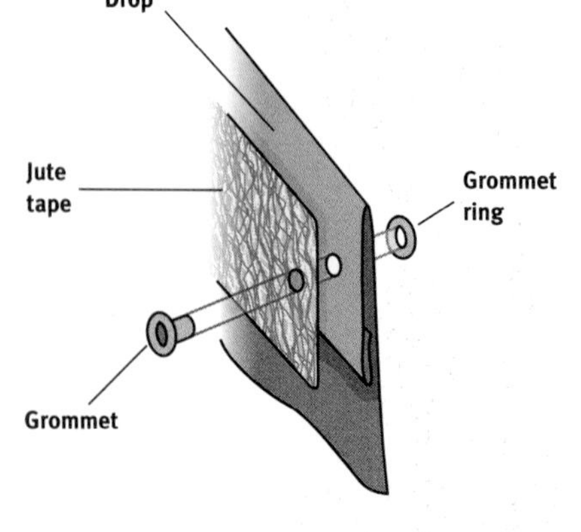


**HANGING A TIE-SUPPORTED DROP**

1. Make holes 1 inch down and 1 foot apart in the jute tape along the top of the drop.
2. Reinforce the holes with grommets.
3. Make ties using 36-inch shoelaces or strips of scrap muslin. Loop the ties through the grommets and tie them to the batten.

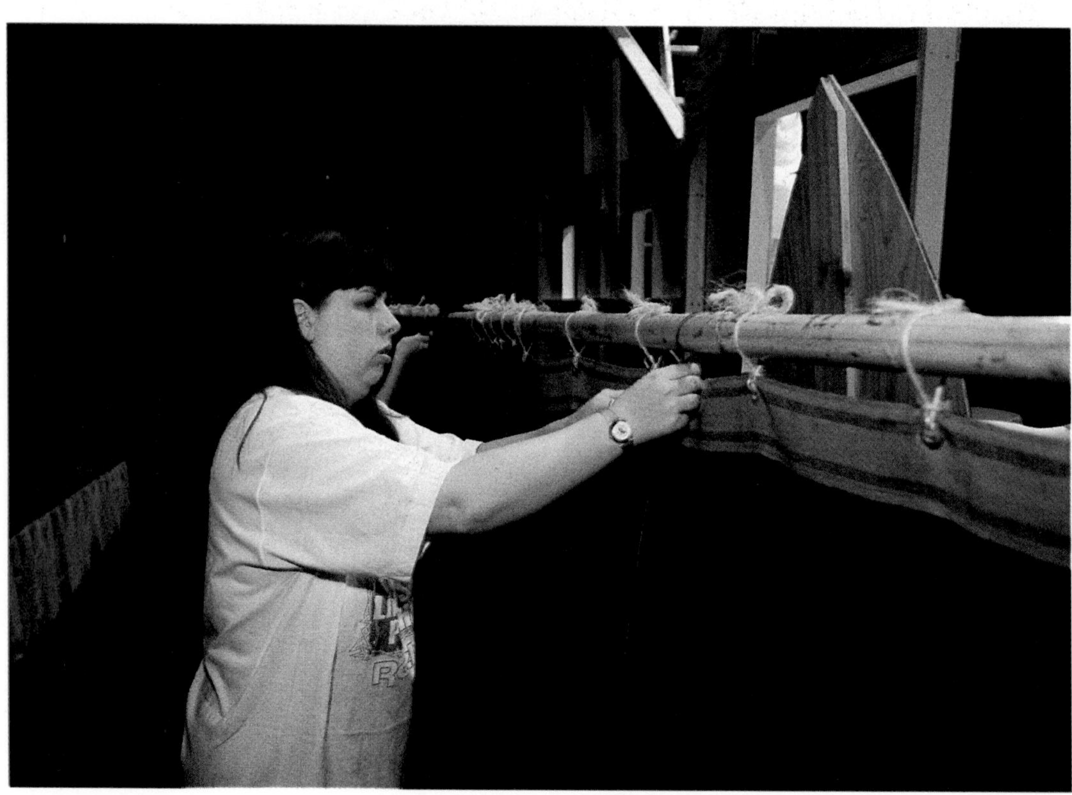

## HANGING A BATTEN-CLAMP DROP

1. Sandwich the top of the drop between two 1 × 3 boards. Depending on the length of the drop, the boards on each side of the drop may need to be joined in end-to-end butts to create a continuous length.
2. Using the batten clamp, clamp the boards together with the drop between them. You may need several people to hold the boards in place while you secure the batten clamps around them.

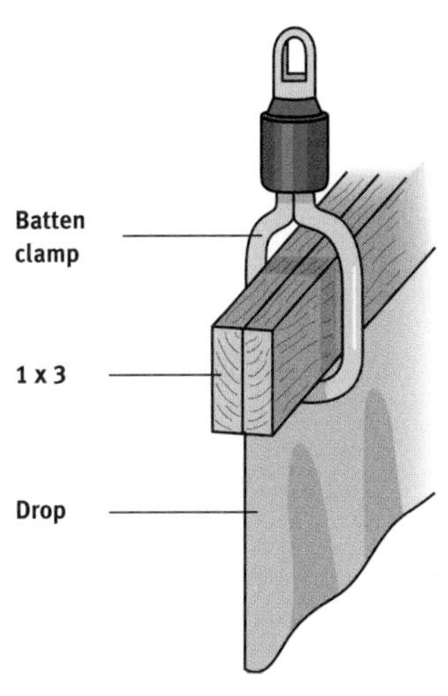

Many theatres use a counterweight system to raise and lower battens from which drops are suspended. Use a counterweight system under your teacher's supervision.

# Joining, Bracing, and Stiffening Scenery

Scenery units can be joined in many ways, depending on how sturdy and transportable you need them to be. You can join platforms and flats permanently using nails, bolts, and screws. Or, you can make smaller, transportable units and anchor, or **brace,** them temporarily to the set.

## Joining Flats

**Lashing** flats is the traditional method of temporarily joining flats. Rope is laced through specialized hardware attached to the flats and tied off. Lashing can be used to join flats either end-to-end to form a wall, or where flats butt together at corners.

**Lashed flat**

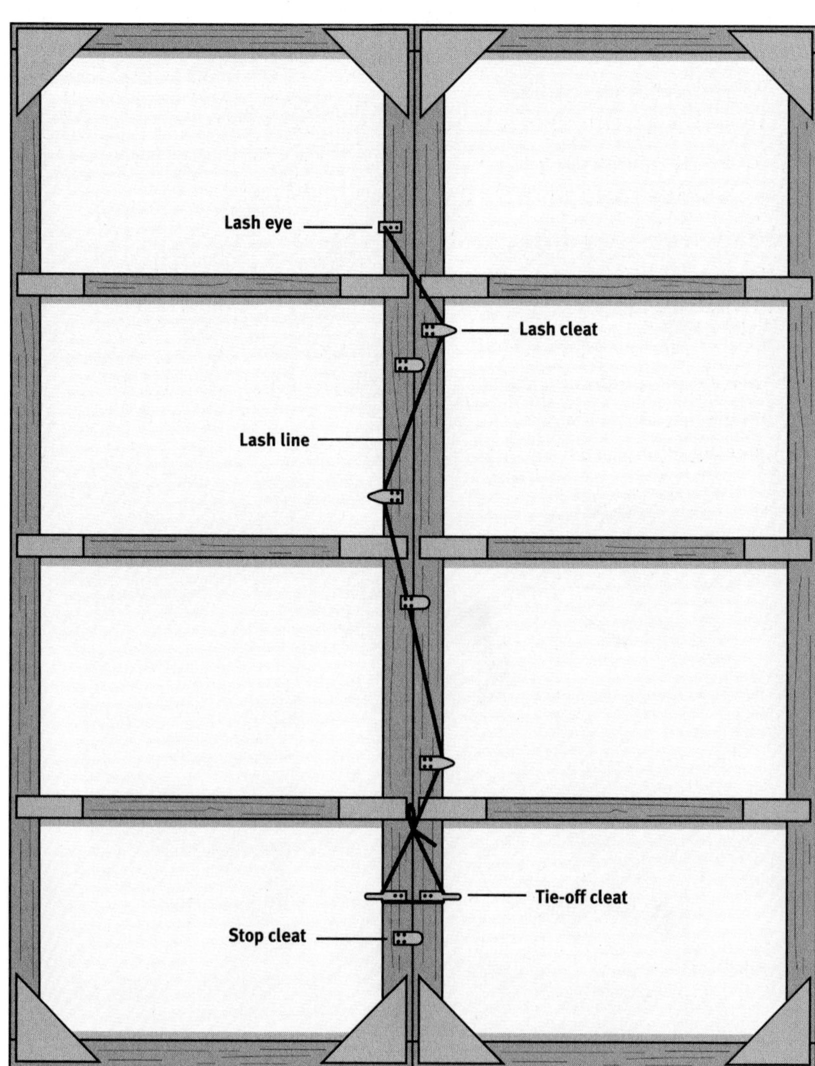

Flats can also be joined temporarily using hinges. Loose-pin hinges placed every four feet are commonly used for this method. When the units need to be taken apart and moved, the pin is removed and the flats can be separated.

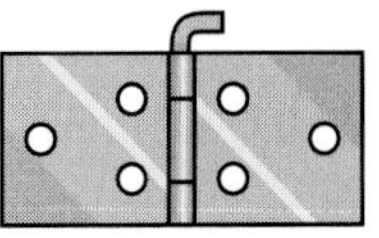

Loose-pin hinge

To enhance the illusion that a series of joined flats comprise a wall, you can cover the crack between two flats with a strip of fabric known as a **dutchman.**

**APPLYING A DUTCHMAN**

1. Cut or tear a strip of heavyweight muslin or canvas about 4 inches wide and as tall as your flat.
2. Feather the edges (pull threads off) to about ⅜ inch.
3. Apply glue to the front of the flats along the edges to be joined in a strip at least as wide as the dutchman strip.
4. Place the dutchman strip carefully over the crack, making sure the feathered front don't bunch up. Spread glue over the dutchman with a brush by stroking the feathered edges out toward the center of the flat. Avoid letting the dutchman sag into the crack.
5. When the glue is thoroughly dry, paint over the dutchman and any excess glue with a base coat of paint. Don't attempt to paint a final coat over an unprimed dutchman.
6. Once the final coat of paint is on the flats, the feathered edge will disappear and the surface will in effect be seamless.

A dutchman tape is now available (although it's expensive), which replaces muslin and glue for hiding the seams of joined flats. Feathered dutchman strips (small pieces) are also good for patching small holes in flats. Whenever possible, patch the flat from the back. Two people are necessary for this process.

## Connecting Platforms

When you are using more than one platform to create a surface, you will need to connect the platforms securely together. If you have built wooden platforms, you can bolt them together using 4-inch bolts through the framing of each unit. Use two or three bolts per side, with at least one at each end. If you need to move the platforms during the course of a show, use C-clamps wherever you might have placed bolts.

## Bracing Scenery

Some theatres brace flats and platforms by using hinges, foot irons, or specialized bracing hardware to attach scenery to the stage floor with screws. Many theatres don't allow holes in the stage floor, and in nontraditional performance spaces it's often impossible anyway. A workable alternative is to attach the stage brace to a rubber-based floor plate that is weighted for stability.

Another anchoring option is to use **jacks,** triangular-frame units hinged to a flat that are stabilized with counterweights or sandbags laid over the base of the frame.

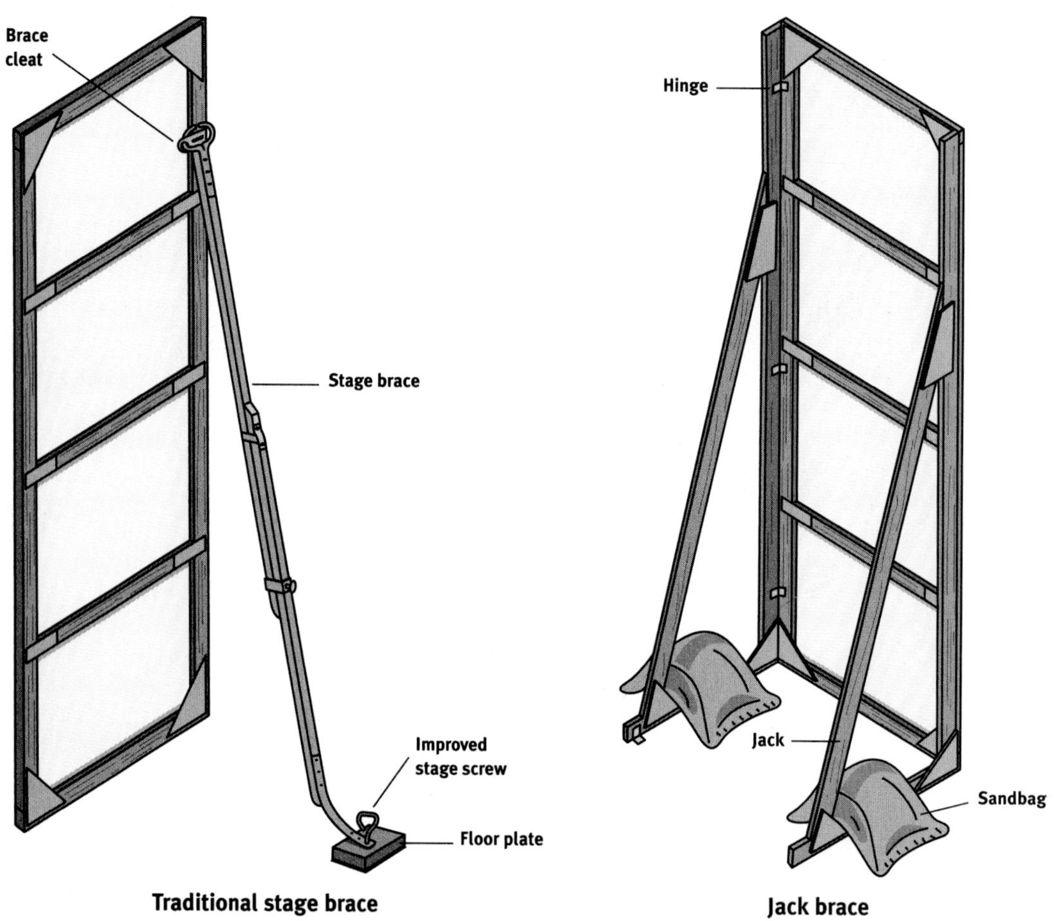


Traditional stage brace

Jack brace

## Stiffening Scenery

A wall of flats is a fragile piece of scenery. Even if you lash the flats together, they can shift and move. Or, they may be slightly warped, creating an uneven plane. The use of a 1 × 3 piece of lumber serving as a **stiffening batten** across the back of two or three adjacent flats can correct these problems. Using an L-shaped configuration, with the edge of one board butted against the face of another, provides the greatest support. Stiffening battens may be permanent or semipermanent to accommodate quick scene changes.

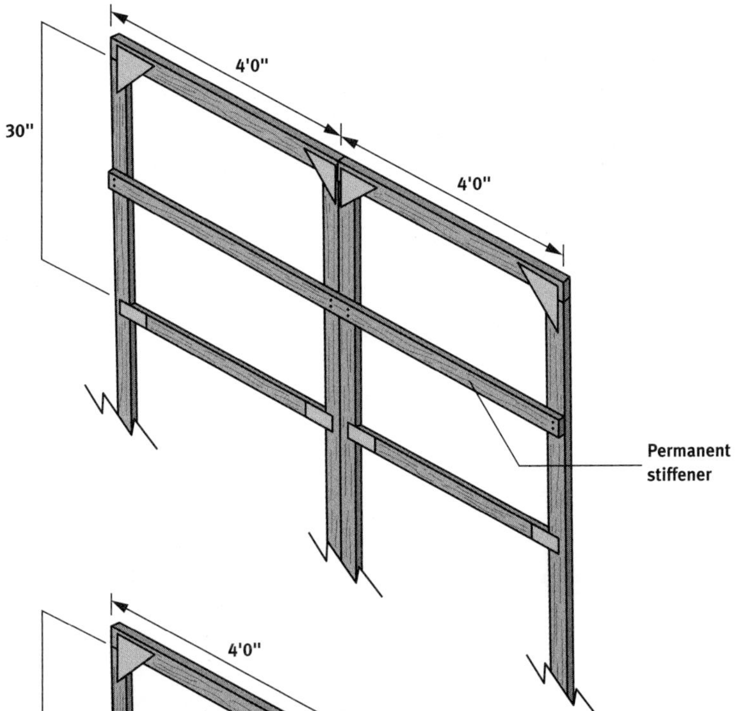

4'0"
4'0"
30"
Permanent stiffener

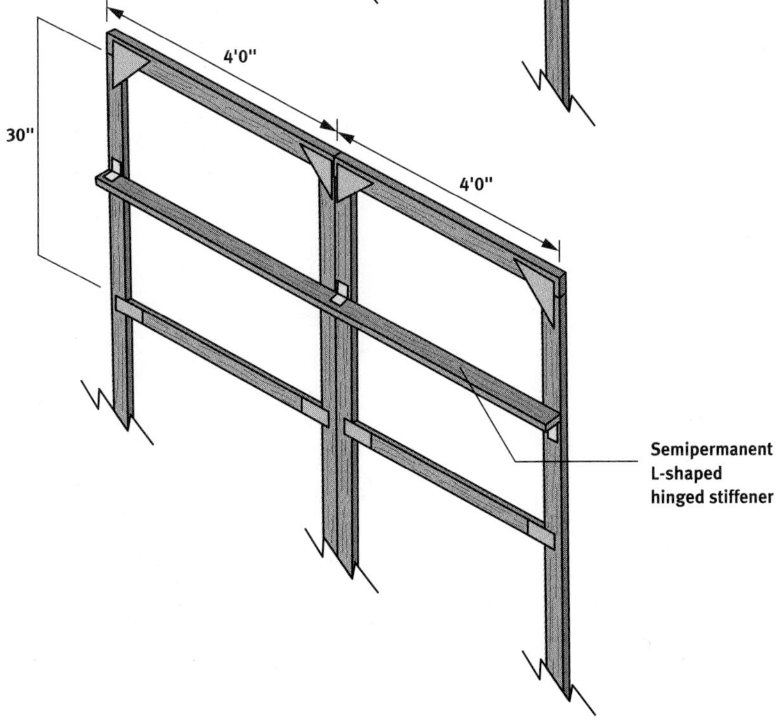

4'0"
4'0"
30"
Semipermanent L-shaped hinged stiffener

# Scene Painting

The painting techniques you use backstage can transform simple platforms into sidewalks or hardwood floors and flats into foliage or marble. These transformations make scene painting one of the most rewarding jobs in technical theatre. In the past, many scene painters mixed their own paints to achieve the color and texture they desired. Today, many theatres buy premixed color paints and concentrate on creating special effects.

## Preliminary Coats

You will need to apply one or two base coats to most scenery before you paint the effects you want to achieve.

### Sizing

If you are using fabric-covered flats, you will need to **size** them with a preliminary coat of paint if they have not been painted before. A size coat will shrink the fabric slightly and tighten it on the frame. It will also fill the holes in the fabric and smooth it for painting. For a sizing coat, use white interior latex paint and water (at a 2:1 ratio) or water and hot glue (at a 16:1 ratio). By applying a small amount of pigment with your sizing coat, you can see where you have painted.

Painted foliage and lighting create startling effects for this set of Bertolt Brecht's *The Caucasian Chalk Circle.*

## Prime Coat

All scenery requires a **prime coat** of paint to supply a uniform base for the final layer. Some scene painters mix leftover paint from old productions to make a "garbage" paint they can use as a prime coat. Others prefer to use white or black paint.

## Base Coat

The next layer, the **base coat,** is the foundation layer on which you will paint effects. Paint large surfaces from the top down, so you can catch any drips on the way down the surface. Paint doors, windows, and ledges by starting at one end and working your way across. Label or tape off areas with wet paint so other people don't accidently mar your work before its dry.

**TECH TIPS: PAINTING**

- Dip your brush no more than about ¾ of the way into the paint.
- Use cross-hatch strokes to achieve a flat, finished surface.
- To avoid seams in the painted surface, keep a wet edge.
- If you must stop painting before you have finished a surface, feather the edge. Come back to the paint job from the opposite end and work toward the feathered edge.

# Painting Techniques

Various painting techniques may be applied to add texture and visual interest to a painted surface. Some of the resulting textures can be modeled with detail brushwork to create the outlines of stone, moldings, and so on.

## Scumbling

Varying effects can be achieved with the technique known as **scumbling,** which results from the wet blending of several hues in patterns created with any combination of curved or straight brush strokes. Use separate brushes for each color and apply at once or in quick succession. The paint must be wet for the blending, so you must work quickly. Brush across the pattern again with a dryer brush if you want a soft blend

## Stenciling

Create wallpaper effects or borders by designing or purchasing a stencil pattern, then painting that pattern onto the surface. To ensure accurate placement, mark a chalk line on the surface using the stencil before applying paint. Be sure to pat the stencil with your brush; brushing can force paint under the stencil.

**Stenciling**

## Spattering

In **spattering,** you use quick jerks of a paint brush to fling drops of paint onto a painted surface. You should use at least two colors that are different from your base coat. The first color should be a full shade lighter or darker than the base coat, but of the same hue: if the base coat is light, use a darker shade; if the base coat is dark, use a lighter shade. Your second spatter color should be a color opposite the base color on the color wheel. To make flats look old, spatter with black or gray.

The technique requires you to dip your brush lightly into your first spatter color. Then, standing 3 to 5 feet away from the surface you want to spatter, hold your brush with the bristles up and tilted toward the surface. Slap the brush handle against the heel of your empty hand or a board. Small droplets will fly onto the surface. (For larger drops, use more paint and move closer.) After the first spatter color has dried (usually three or four hours), you can apply your second spatter color.

**Stippling**

## Stippling

**Stippling** techniques and effects vary widely. Experiment. Obtain a sea sponge (available at art supply stores) and dip it into the paint. Dab it lightly onto the surface. You apply additional colors in the same manner to accent the pattern. Or, wad up a rag and dip it in the paint. Sweep it gently across the surface in a pattern of small arcs. Using a featherduster for stippling creates interesting foliage patterns. Layer shades and tones of green, brown, and yellow.

**Marbling**

## Marbling

You can simulate marble using a combination of spattering and scumbling. Scumble using a lot of paint in a loose line, then spatter with large drops of paint in the same colors.

## Brickwork

To create the illusion of bricks, you can use a combination of stenciling and spattering, with added detail. Stencil bricks onto a surface painted the color of mortar. Then spatter the entire surface at close range to give it a rough look. Paint a slight shadow under each brick.

In this version of *Don Juan* by Molière, the simple set is enhanced by painted flats evoking the heavens. What painting techniques do you think were used to create the effect?

## Dry Brush

The **dry brush** technique is commonly used to create wood grain effects. To dry brush, dip your brush into the paint, and then scrape most of the paint off. Use the nearly dry brush to streak dark paint onto the surface. Different hues of brown paint streaked over a wood-color base creates a standard effect. Paint a darker hue over the base, then a lighter hue over that. Be sure to make all your brush strokes in the same direction to simulate the wood grain. Knot holes and paneling lines can be added to complete the effect.

**Dry brush**

# Prop Design and Construction

The set you create communicates the time, place, and mood of a production. The props offer specific clues about the characters in a play and the world they inhabit. **Set props,** such as furniture, appliances, lamps, and rugs, help establish the play's era and the financial status of the main characters. **Decorative props,** such as curtains, pictures, linens, knickknacks, and magazines, offer clues about lifestyle. They also convey both the period and the personalities of the characters who own them. The addition of such items to the set is known as **dressing** the set. **Hand props** are props used by the characters during the performance. Depending on the play, they may include items such as a book, telephone, letter, fan, fireplace poker, gavel, and bottle. They should be usable and in most cases, should suggest the personality traits and lifestyle of the characters that use them.

## Script Analysis for the Prop Master

The prop master must research the period in which the play is set, the society the play is about, and the conditions under which the action will take place. This information will be important once the prop crew sets out to create or acquire the props. The prop crew must understand the use of the prop in the play and other requirements, such as color, time period, and style. You can't simply request an alarm clock if the play calls for an old-fashioned wind-up alarm clock or you might get a modern electric clock-radio. Getting the right props requires careful analysis and a well-prepared, specific prop list.

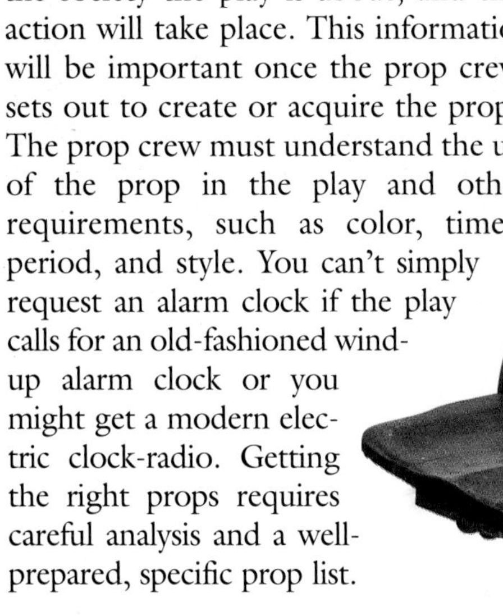

## Prop Plot

Often a play script includes a prop list citing all the necessary props as defined by the playwright. Consult this list and the script to create a **prop plot,** a list of props needed for each scene. Using your prop plot, you can begin gathering and organizing the props the play requires. Denote items that can be **pulled,** or taken from stock, and whether they need to be modified, as well as those that need to be rented, bought, borrowed, or built. Specific requirements for the prop should be noted on your plot. Members of the prop crew should have specific assignments for acquiring or fabricating props to ensure that all are accounted for.

Note that because props suffer heavy, repeated use, borrowing is risky business. Never borrow an item your theatre can't afford to pay for if something should happen to it.

## Prop Construction

Large set props, such as thrones or beds, are often constructed by the set construction crew. Smaller set props may be pulled from stock or acquired from thrift stores or garage sales. Tables and wooden chairs can get a new look with the simple application of paint. Sofas and chairs can be reupholstered. A lamp can get a new shade.

For curtains and draperies, you can use inexpensive fabrics such as corduroy and velveteen to simulate lush fabrics like velvet and silk. Chiffon or netting can serve to make sheers. Choose ties and valances that suggest the period you want to depict.

The simplest way to obtain hand props is to buy them and adapt them for your particular production. Those that are difficult to find may be fabricated with papier mâché, plaster, or other materials.

# Lighting Design

Set designers may envision lighting effects they hope to see and may even sketch in ideas on a ground plan, but they don't usually determine the location of lights or the way in which the lights are hung. Decisions about the way to hang the lights are left to the lighting designer and crew.

## Script Analysis for the Lighting Designer

As a lighting designer, your decisions about lighting can dramatically affect the production. To make informed decisions about lighting design, read the script with the ground plan in hand and make notes in your Theatre Notebook about changes in location, mood, and time of day. Discuss the style and mood of the play with the director and set designer. As you develop a design that fits the production concept, make sketches or collect pictures showing the moods and effects you would like to achieve.

Side lighting is used to create the effect of a painting in this production of *A Game of Love and Chance* by Pierre Carlet de Chamblain de Marivaux. What mood is suggested by the lighting? What time of day is suggested?

The fluorescent lighting effect for this production of David Mamet's *Oleanna* helps to create the harsh, uncomfortable atmosphere of a threatening office environment.

## Acting and Lighting Areas

To achieve the lighting effects you have decided upon, you will need to manipulate the distribution of light over the stage area; the intensity, or brightness, of light that strikes the stage; the movement of light in followspots; and the color of individual lamps.

The stage is usually broken up into **acting areas,** spaces onstage defined by the blocking patterns of actors in a scene. Each acting area must be lit at some point in the performance. Often, more than one acting area is lit at once; therefore, to create a smooth wash of light, you will need to overlap the light beams shining on each acting area by about one-third. These light beams, which are approximately 8 to 12 feet in diameter where they strike the stage floor, can be referred to as **lighting areas.**

Generally, each lighting area should be lit by at least two lighting instruments at 90° angles toward each other. One is the **key light,** which is the brightest of the two. The other is the **fill light,** which fills in shadows created by the key light. Often one of these two instruments will have a warmer-colored gel and one will have a cooler-colored gel.

## The Lighting Key

The angle and color for each lighting area can be shown in a simple diagram called a **lighting key.** Keeping the principle light source in mind (sunlight, lamplight, firelight) will help you decide which colors to use with which instruments. The colors of the set and costumes will be affected by the colors of your lights, so you can't really test the effectiveness of your lighting key until the set is mostly dressed and costumes are designed.

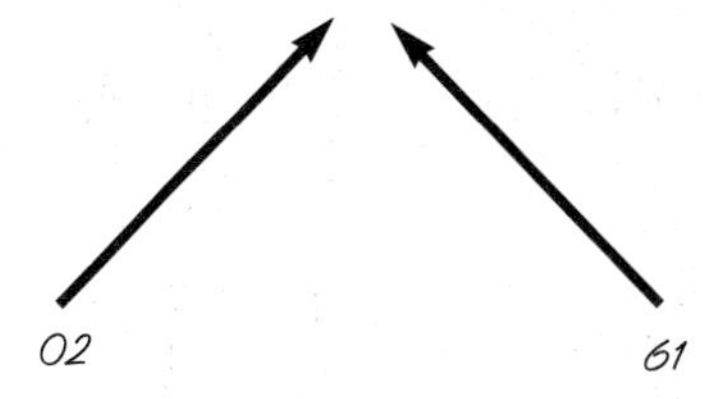


**Two-source lighting key for John Osborne's *Look Back in Anger***

To help you keep track of the lighting configuration you have designed, draw a **lighting plot,** which shows where you intend to place various lights and prepare an **instrument schedule,** which puts this information into a chart format for reference.

## The Lighting Plot

The simplest way to create a lighting plot is to use a copy of the set designer's ground plan (p. 208), which should show the set within the theatre space. Identify the acting areas on the stage so you can angle lights into those areas. Add information regarding the location of electrical circuits and existing lights. Then add the lighting instruments and information about each according to your design. After completing your plot, record the information on an instrument schedule.

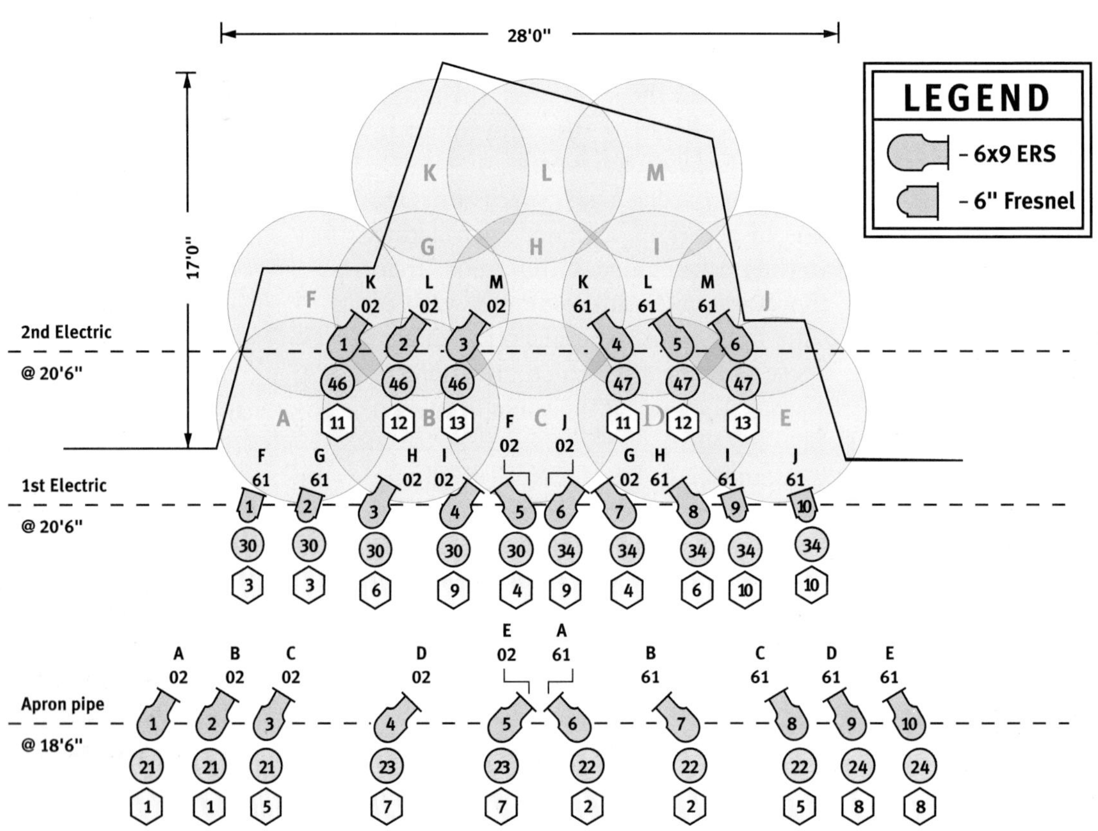


Lighting plot for John Osborne's *Look Back in Anger*

## The Instrument Schedule

Provide the following information on your instrument schedule:

- **Instrument number:** Number each instrument according to the batten from which the light hangs and the order in which it hangs on the batten.
- **Focus area:** Use a letter to identify the lighting area of each instrument.
- **Gel color:** Use a number or letter to identify the color gel you will be using.
- **Wattage:** Note the lamp wattage of each instrument.
- **Circuit number:** Note the circuit number where you will plug in each instrument.
- **Dimmer:** Identify the dimmer that will control each instrument.

**Instrument Schedule**

Show: *Look Back in Anger* Crew: *Daria*

| Instrument Number | Unit Type | Focus Area | Gel Color | Wattage | Circuit Number | Dimmer (Channel) |
|---|---|---|---|---|---|---|
| AP1 | 6x9 ERS | A | 02 | 750 | 21 | 1 |
| AP2 | 6x9 ERS | B | 02 | 750 | 21 | 1 |
| AP3 | 6x9 ERS | C | 02 | 750 | 21 | 5 |
| AP4 | 6x9 ERS | D | 02 | 750 | 23 | 7 |
| AP5 | 6x9 ERS | E | 02 | 750 | 23 | 7 |
| AP6 | 6x9 ERS | A | 61 | 750 | 22 | 2 |
| AP7 | 6x9 ERS | B | 61 | 750 | 22 | 2 |
| AP8 | 6x9 ERS | C | 61 | 750 | 22 | 5 |
| AP9 | 6x9 ERS | D | 61 | 750 | 24 | 8 |
| AP10 | 6x9 ERS | E | 61 | 750 | 24 | 8 |
| 1E1 | 6"Fresnel | F | 61 | 500 | 30 | 3 |
| 1E2 | 6"Fresnel | G | 61 | 500 | 30 | 3 |
| 1E3 | 6x9 ERS | H | 02 | 500 | 30 | 6 |
| 1E4 | 6x9 ERS | I | 02 | 500 | 30 | 9 |
| 1E5 | 6x9 ERS | F | 02 | 500 | 30 | 4 |
| 1E6 | 6x9 ERS | J | 02 | 500 | 34 | 9 |
| 1E7 | 6x9 ERS | G | 02 | 500 | 34 | 4 |
| 1E8 | 6x9 ERS | H | 61 | 500 | 34 | 6 |
| 1E9 | 6"Fresnel | I | 61 | 500 | 34 | 10 |
| 1E10 | 6"Fresnel | J | 61 | 500 | 34 | 10 |
| 2E1 | 6x9 ERS | K | 02 | 500 | 46 | 11 |
| 2E2 | 6x9 ERS | L | 02 | 500 | 46 | 12 |
| 2E3 | 6x9 ERS | M | 02 | 500 | 46 | 13 |
| 2E4 | 6x9 ERS | K | 61 | 500 | 47 | 11 |
| 2E5 | 6x9 ERS | L | 61 | 500 | 47 | 12 |
| 2E6 | 6x9 ERS | M | 61 | 500 | 47 | 13 |

# Sound Design and Production

Sound fulfills three distinct functions in the theatre: it amplifies speech, provides special effects, and supplies music to enhance the mood and meaning of a play. You can manipulate the sounds you produce by changing the tone, intensity, or balance of sound through the speakers.

## Script Analysis for the Sound Designer

Like the other designers, the sound designer must read the script to understand its needs. Read once for meaning, and then a second time to imagine the sound effects. In your Theatre Notebook write a list of what you hear as you read. You can refine the list later.

Some scripts will require nothing more than music and a few doorbells; others have more unusual and challenging demands. For Eugene Ionesco's *Rhinoceros,* sound technicians had to recreate the sound of stampeding rhinos. They produced the sound simply by thumping gently on a live microphone, then playing the tape at reduced speed.

## Collecting Sounds

Before you reach for your favorite song, remember that recordings, like books, are copyrighted. If you wish to record sounds from television, radio, or prerecorded sources, you must make sure the sound is in the public domain or get written permission from the copyright holder.

Nevertheless, you can use recordings to get ideas for sounds you will need. You also can experiment with sounds to create effects of your own. For example, you might tape a sound and alter the speed on the playback. You can change the settings on your equalizer to boost the treble or bass. You can add reverberation, or cause feedback to mix with the sound. You might also put the sound through a synthesizer or add other sounds to the mix.

### Sources of Sound

You can categorize the sounds you collect for a production into three general categories:

- **recorded sounds** recorded music and sound effects available on records, tapes, and CDs
- **created sounds** music played live and sounds created by you
- **found sounds** sounds heard in locations such as zoos, construction sites, and playgrounds

Adaptations of L. Frank Baum's *The Wizard of Oz* demand special sound effects for such events as the tornado and the booming voice of the great and powerful Oz.

## Making Show Tapes

Once you have collected all the sounds you need for a show, you need to arrange them on show tapes so they will be easy to use during the performance.

The simplest way to run sound for a show is to record all the sounds onto a single tape. One cue follows the other, with cue tape spliced in between (p. 87). If a sound is needed more than once, you record it separately for each cue.

Sometimes, you may need to run more than one sound at a time. For example, you may need to play ballroom music for the duration of a scene, then supply a shotgun blast on cue. To handle the two sounds smoothly, you will need to record the sound on two separate tapes and play them back using two tape players, one running a tape loop (p. 88).

# Costume Design and Production

Like the set designer, the costume designer works closely with the director to create a plan for costumes. By necessity, the costume designer also works with the actors, assessing how their body types and characters will affect the costuming. To prepare for these consultations, the costume designer should analyze the script first.

## Script Analysis for the Costume Designer

Many scripts reflect specific costume needs. Think about how to express the character's style and personality in the costume. Also consider the effect of costume color on the mood of a scene. You may find value in matching or color-coding characters' costumes to denote relationships among characters; for example, workers in a dreary office might all wear gray, or one couple might wear blue. Make your comments in your Theatre Notebook as you read the play, including sketches in pencil or color.

After the production design concept is firm, research the era and create sketches and color renderings from which the costume crew can make, or **build,** individual costumes. These sketches are also important to guide you in modifying stock costumes.

These color renderings for characters from Shakespeare's *King Lear* include sample swatches of the cloth that will be used to build individual pieces of each costume.

## Costume Management

Because each costume has several pieces and each character wears at least one costume, the costume crew must be extremely organized. Most professional costumers become adept at drawing up and keeping detailed lists and forms.

### Costume Plot

To keep track of the costume items for each character, develop a **costume plot.** List each character and each scene in the play in which the character appears. Then itemize each costume piece the character wears for each appearance. If the character changes costumes within a scene, note that as well.

| Costume Plot | | | | | |
|---|---|---|---|---|---|
| Show: *This Piece of Land* | | | | | |
| Act & Scene | Character | Actor | Costume | Accessories | Notes |
| *One-act, no scene breaks* | *The Singer* | *Wade* | *Faded jeans*<br>*Checkered shirt* | *Black or brown boots* | *1930s style; very worn* |
| *One-act, no scene breaks* | *Rosa* | *Tara* | *House Dress* | *Apron*<br>*Black or brown shoes*<br>*Kerchief*<br>*Wedding ring* | *1930s style; very worn* |

### Costume List

The costume plot will help you organize your thoughts and develop a **costume list,** which should list every character and all of his or her clothing and accessories. When you are ready to obtain or build the costumes, you can transform your costume list into a pull/rent/buy/borrow/build/list.

| Costume List | | Pull | Rent | Buy | Borrow | Build | Size |
|---|---|---|---|---|---|---|---|
| Show: *This Piece of Land* | Sketch #: *2* | | | | | | |
| Character: *Rosa* | Actor: *Tara* | | | | | | |
| Item | Notes | | | | | | |
| *House dress* | *cotton; blue; worn* | *x* | | | | | *12* |
| *Apron* | *white; cotton; worn* | | | | | *x* | |
| *Black or brown shoes* | *thrift store; lace-up; distress* | | | *x* | | | *8* |
| *Kerchief* | *blue; worn (fade with bleach)* | | | *x* | | | |
| *Wedding ring* | *cheap; paint gold* | | | *x* | | | *7* |

## Pull/Rent/Buy/Borrow/Build List

To organize the sewing or acquisition of each costume, make a **pull/rent/buy/borrow/build list.** The list should identify the actor, character, and pieces required, as well as size information. Copy the list five times, so that you have a pull list, a rent list, a buy list, a borrow list, and a build list. On each list, check off the items that apply to that list. Assign members of the costume crew to take on the tasks.

| ☑ **Pull** | ☐ **Rent** | ☐ **Buy** | ☐ **Borrow** | ☐ **Build** | |
|---|---|---|---|---|---|
| Show: *This Piece of Land* | | Crew: *Maria* | | Era: *early 1930s* | |
| Done | Character | Actor | Item | Description | Size |
| *X* | *The Singer* | *Wade* | *shirt* | *checkered* | *M* |
| | *Rosa* | *Tara* | *dress* | *cotton; blue; very worn* | *12* |
| *X* | *Perry* | *Dareesh* | *shirt* | *blue; very worn; plaid* | *L* |
| *X* | *Sister Waters* | *Nina* | *dress* | *collar; conservative* | *14* |
| *X* | *Sister Waters* | *Nina* | *handbag* | *white; simple* | |
| *X* | *Sister Waters* | *Nina* | *hat* | *to match dress; simple* | *fit* |
| *X* | *Miss Nancy* | *Janelle* | *dress* | *pastel; summer; youthful* | *10* |

August Strindberg's *A Dream Play* offers a costume designer the opportunity to play with dressing real characters in surreal costumes.

## Costume Measurement Cards

Have each actor fill out a costume measurement card. You will need to know the measurements and standard clothing size of an actor when you pull, rent, buy, or borrow clothing and to purchase a pattern if you need to build the costume. These same cards (updated if necessary) may be used again for other productions with the same actors.

## Costume Production Calendar

Most costume designers establish a production calendar. To create your own production calendar, count backward from opening night to identify final dates when costumes must be ready for performance and rehearsals; dates for **fittings,** in which actors try on costumes to assess necessary adjustments; and dates for sewing, shopping, measuring, and design approval. Remember to keep receipts and careful records of purchases in order to make exchanges, return items, and get reimbursed.

Many Kabuki productions call for actors to wear large, colorful wigs and highly stylized makeup.

# Makeup Design

More than any other technical element, makeup determines the way in which the audience perceives characters. It can turn teenagers into old people, pleasant-looking people into grotesques, and humans into animals, goblins, and other fantasy creatures.

## Script Analysis for the Makeup Designer

Makeup for a production is designed and planned much like other technical elements, beginning with script analysis. The makeup designer—or, in a small production, the actor—must research the characters or types presented in the production.

## Character Makeup Sketches

For character makeup, begin by creating a character sketch unrelated to the actor. A character sketch allows you and the director and designer to clarify your thoughts and plan the look of the character. To get material for your sketch, look at the description of your character in the script and whatever other sources you are using. For example, if you were designing makeup for the character of the Scarecrow in the adaptation of L. Frank Baum's *The Wizard of Oz,* you might begin by looking at the original source, the description of the Scarecrow in Baum's book: "It's head was a small sack stuffed with straw, with eyes, nose, and mouth painted on it to represent a face. An old, pointed blue hat, that had belonged to some Munchkin, was perched on its head. . . ." You might also look at the way various illustrators have pictured the Scarecrow.

Before proceeding with your sketch, consult with the costume crew about the costume planned for the character; hats and high collars will affect how your makeup, which includes hair styling, is designed. For instance, the costume designer may have decided on a straw hat instead of a pointed blue hat; show that in your character sketch. When you have completed your sketch, study the face of the actor to see how your vision of the character will translate into makeup on the actor.

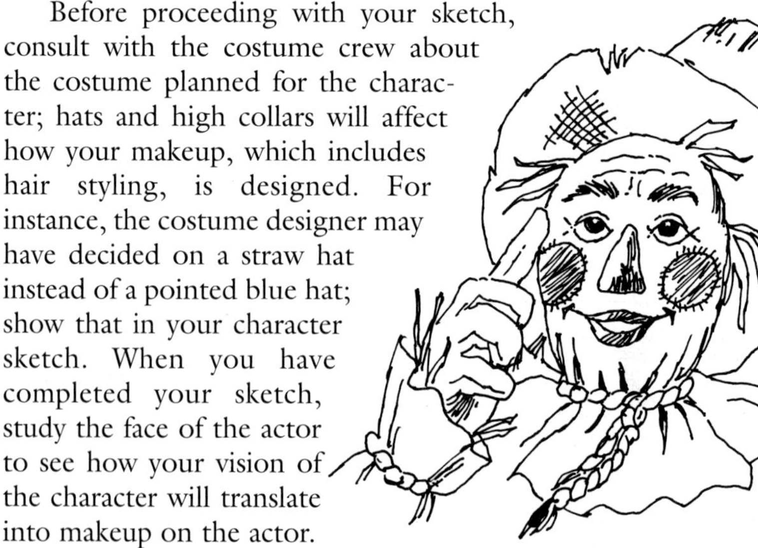

Character makeup sketch

## Makeup Plan

You can record your decisions about makeup on a makeup plan. Try it out on the actor before opening night and make any necessary modifications. Refer to the makeup plan while applying the makeup for the performance, or if the actor is doing his or her own makeup, let the actor use the plan for reference.

| **Makeup Plan**<br>Show: *The Wizard of Oz* | Character: *Scarecrow*<br>Actor: *Luis* |
|---|---|
| | *Latex cap* |

| Description | | | | |
|---|---|---|---|---|
| Forehead<br>*Light horizontal creases* | Eyes<br>*Laugh lines at corners*<br>*Eyes should twinkle* | Nose<br>*Reshape with putty—should look like tacked-on object* | Cheeks<br>*Round, rosy cheeks—should look sewn or drawn onto face* | Mouth<br>*Red lips (not scarlet) that look drawn on*<br>*Smile lines at corners* |
| Jaw/Chin<br>*Reshape with latex. Add vertical wrinkles to look like canvas stretched over round object to create head.* | Neck<br>*Vertical wrinkles to look like gathered fabric from head* | Hands<br>*White garden gloves, not especially dirty*<br>*Straw sticks out of clothes at wrists* | Hair<br>*Cover existing hair with latex cap. Top of head is covered with hat. Straw sticks out from under hat to suggest hair.* | |

| Materials | | | Notes |
|---|---|---|---|
| Foundation<br>*Light brown or golden straw color* | Highlights<br>*Wrinkles, creases, and under eyes for emphasis* | Shadows<br>*Medium brown—to emphasize wrinkles and shadows* | *General effect should be of figure put together using found objects.*<br>*Face reflects happy-go-lucky attitude of character.*<br>*Base should provide a canvas fabric look.*<br>*Use stipple to provide texture as needed.* |
| Eye Liner<br>*Dark brown on upper and lower lids* | Rouge<br>*Dark to highlight red lips* | Powder<br>*Translucent* | |

# Activities

### Elements of Production Design

**ASSESSING ELEMENTS** In your Theatre Notebook, write a review of a play, concert, movie, or TV show you have seen recently. In your review, discuss how the design elements of the production were informative, expressive, appropriate, and useable. Consider how well the production design supported the action and if one of these elements of effective production design was more evident than the others. Include sketches that illustrate what you discuss in your review.

### Set Design

**THUMBNAILS** Read a one-act play. Then develop a thumbnail sketch of the set. Present your thumbnail to your class and explain how your ideas about the set help develop the time, place, and mood or atmosphere of the story or play.

### Set Construction

**BUILD A MINIATURE FLAT** Create a miniature flat, built to a 1-inch scale (1 inch = 1 foot). Use balsa wood instead of wood, and glue instead nails, but mark where you would place the nails on the cornerblocks and keystones. Cover your flat with muslin or card-board (to simulate wood). Paint your flat, and then present it to the class, pointing out the various features, such as stiles, rails, toggles, cornerblocks, and keystones.

### Set Construction

**JOB SHADOW—CARPENTER** Arrange with a construction firm or carpentry firm to observe a carpenter at work for a day or a few hours; if possible, arrange to observe a member of a set construction crew on a theatre production in your community. Explain that you are interested in witnessing the day-to-day operations of a carpenter to see how the skills apply to set construction. Professionals are busy, but if you are polite as well as interested, they are usually willing to let you observe them at work and to answer questions about their training and background. Be sure to first get permission from your parents, teacher, and the supervisor of the business or organization where you will job shadow.

### *Joining, Bracing, and Stiffening Scenery*

**COMPARE AND CONTRAST TECHNIQUES** Working under your teacher's supervision, experiment with the methods described on pages 218–221 to join, brace, and stiffen scenery. Create a comparison and contrast chart for the methods you tried, showing the benefits and drawbacks of each. Develop criteria for your assessment, which might include strength, efficiency, and cost, as well as the potential application for permanent or temporary sets. Share your chart with your class and discuss your findings.

### *Scene Painting*

**PAINTING TECHNIQUES** Experiment with techniques such as spattering, scumbling, stippling, or marbling. Use extra flats (with permission) or large sheets of paper at home. Take notes on these techniques. Discuss what you found tricky or difficult and what you did to solve problems you encountered. Share your results with others in your class.

### *Prop Design and Construction*

**PULL/RENT/BUY/BORROW/BUILD** Use a prop list from the script of a published play to develop a pull/rent/buy/borrow/build list for the props. Check your school's current inventory for items you can pull. Brainstorm places in your school or community where you might borrow items on the list. Consider the resources you have available, and determine which props you can build. List items you will need to rent or buy and come up with a rough cost estimate for these items.

### *Prop Design and Construction*

**PROP LIST** Working individually or with a partner, think about a character from a play, book, film, or TV show. Consider the set this character might inhabit and develop a list of decorative and hand props for this set that suggest this character's traits and lifestyle. Challenge another group to guess the age, gender, nationality, personality, and interests of your character using the props list alone.

# Activities

### Lighting Design

**LIGHTING ANALYSIS** Read through the script of a favorite play or a play that you are studying in class. Note changes in location, mood, and time of day. Then make a series of sketches or collect and mount pictures that show the effect you would like to achieve with lighting. Present your analysis and sketches or pictures to others in your class, briefly summarizing the play and explaining the atmosphere you would like to convey.

### Sound Design

**FOUND SOUNDS** On your own or with a partner, travel around town with a tape recorder to make a tape of found sounds. Record sounds in public places. Find sounds that might be unique to your town or area. Keep a list of the sounds you record using the tape counter to mark where they begin and end. Then create a table of contents in which you list each sound and where it appears on the tape. Provide your tape and table of contents as a resource for future productions.

### Lighting Design

**JOB SHADOW-ELECTRICIAN** Arrange to observe an electrician at work for a day or a few hours; if possible, arrange to observe a member of a lighting crew on a theatre production or at a TV station in your community. Explain that you are interested in witnessing the day-to-day operations of an electrician to see how the skills apply to lighting for the theatre. Professionals are busy, but if you are polite as well as interested, they are usually willing to let you observe them at work and to answer questions about their training and background. Be sure to first get permission from your parents, teacher, and the supervisor of the business or organization where you will job shadow.

### Costume Design

**COSTUME PLOT AND LIST** Do a script analysis for a play, noting the specific costume requirements for two or three characters in the play. Following the script analysis, create a costume plot for these characters. From your costume plot, develop a costume list for the production. After you have determined what you can pull, compare the costs for renting or buying the remaining costume pieces.

### Costume Design

**COSTUME SKETCH** Do a sketch or color rendering of a costume you design for a character in a play. You can do the costumes for that character in one scene only or all the scenes for the play. Present your designs mounted on matte board. As an extra challenge, choose a character from a period play. You will need to research the period clothing, including shoes, hats, and so on.

### Costume Design

**FOUND COSTUMES** Choose a character from a play. Develop a costume list for that character for one scene of the play. You may also wish to make a costume sketch. Then go through your own closet to find items that you can use to create a costume for this character. You can model the costume for your class or ask an actor (who is your size) to do a brief bit from the scene wearing your "found" costume.

### Makeup Design

**MAKEUP DESIGN FROM A PHOTOGRAPH** Using a school photograph (or frontal headshot) of yourself or another student, create a character makeup design for a character in a play you know. By putting tracing paper over the photograph, you can trace the general outline of the face and add defining features required for the character.

### Makeup Design

**CHARACTER MAKEUP SKETCH** Analyze a character from a play, novel, or short story. Develop a character makeup sketch based on your analysis. Then develop a character makeup plan that will help an actor to become this character onstage. You may wish to apply the makeup on an actor and present your finished design to the class.

# Projects
preparation

PROJECT 11

## Open Dialogue with Stage Movement

**ASSIGNMENT** With a partner, improvise, rehearse, and perform an open dialogue scene.

| Project Planner | |
|---|---|
| Product | Open dialogue performance of two characters in a specific situation |
| Purpose | To improvise using an open dialogue and to demonstrate stage-sharing techniques |
| Specs | To accomplish this project, you will<br>• work creatively with a partner<br>• invent the circumstances of an open dialogue<br>• improvise dialogue specific to a character<br>• perform a scene that has a beginning, middle, and end<br>• express conflict with movement and stage positions<br>• stay open and share the stage<br>• project lines clearly |

### Creating

**CHOOSE YOUR DIALOGUE** An open dialogue is a brief scene with given lines that may be interpreted in different ways. Some of the lines you must fill in yourselves. With your partner, choose one of the open dialogues that follow.

**OPEN DIALOGUE 1**

**ACTOR A.** What's going on?

**ACTOR B.** . . .

**ACTOR A.** . . .

**ACTOR B.** Well, it didn't happen.

**ACTOR A.** . . .

**ACTOR B.** . . .

**ACTOR A.** That's a big problem.

**ACTOR B.** I know.

**ACTOR A.** . . .

**ACTOR B.** . . .

**ACTOR A.** . . .

**ACTOR B.** . . .

**OPEN DIALOGUE 2**

**ACTOR A.** I came over as soon as you called.

**ACTOR B.** I have some bad news.

**ACTOR A.** Tell me.

**ACTOR B.** . . .

**ACTOR A.** . . .

**ACTOR B.** . . .

**ACTOR A.** We've got to do something now.

**ACTOR B.** What do you suggest?

**ACTOR A.** . . .

**ACTOR B.** . . .

**ACTOR A.** . . .

**ACTOR B.** . . .

**OPEN DIALOGUE 3**

**ACTOR A.** You'd better come on in.

**ACTOR B.** Thanks.

**ACTOR A.** What do you want?

**ACTOR B.** . . .

**ACTOR A.** . . .

**ACTOR B.** But I didn't do anything wrong!

**ACTOR A.** . . .

**ACTOR B.** I'm telling you the truth.

**ACTOR A.** We'll see.

**ACTOR B.** . . .

**ACTOR A.** . . .

**ACTOR B.** . . .

**DEVELOP YOUR DIALOGUE** Now work together to invent the circumstances of your scene.

- Who are these characters? What are their ages, occupations, and relationship to each other?
- When does the action take place?
- Where does the action take place?
- What are their objectives?

- What are their obstacles?
- What strategies and actions are they taking to overcome their obstacles?
- What are the stakes of not meeting their objectives?

Improvise a scene based on the open dialogue you have selected and the circumstances you have determined. You will need to improvise lines to fill the spaces marked by ellipses (. . .).

**CREATE THE SCENE** Act out the scene. You may use simple set pieces and props if you wish. Plan where your entrance and exit will be.

Try to convey conflict both in your voice and in your movements. You don't have to resolve the conflict completely, but your scene should have a definite ending—even if it's only that your characters decide on a course of action. As you rehearse, ask yourself the following questions:

- Am I keeping my body open?
- Am I sharing the stage with my partner?
- Am I projecting my voice to fill the performance space?
- Are my movements motivated and in character?
- Do all of my lines make logical sense?

## Performing

You don't need to memorize your lines exactly, but you should rehearse often enough that you feel secure in them. Before performing, ask someone to watch the scene to see that your dialogue and actions are understandable.

Make sure that you have the props you need and that the stage is set properly before you begin. Perform your scene for the class or for another small group.

## Responding

How well you have fulfilled the Specs in the Project Planner will help assess your project. You may also ask yourself or your audience these questions to help you improve:

- Could the audience hear and understand the dialogue?
- Could the audience understand who the characters were?
- Could the audience see all gestures, expressions, and movements?
- Were the actors' movements appropriate to their characters?
- Did the actors share the stage equally?

Include responses to these questions in your Theatre Notebook.

## Adapting the Project

1. Switch places: if you played Actor A before, now play Actor B. Keep the same open dialogue but invent new characters and circumstances; improvise a whole new scene.

2. Work with another team. Write open dialogues for each other and challenge the other team to create a scene from your open dialogue.

## Building Characters

PROJECT 

**ASSIGNMENT** Develop three distinct characters and perform them in an original scene.

| | Project Planner |
|---|---|
| Product | An improvised scene with three different characterizations |
| Purpose | To be able to create distinctive characters |
| Specs | To accomplish this project, you will<br>• devise a situation that will accommodate characters of different types<br>• create three different physical and vocal characterizations<br>• improvise monologues for the three characters<br>• demonstrate vocal and physical flexibility in portraying the characters<br>• perform a series of actions that have a beginning, middle, and end<br>• demonstrate focus by staying in character and control by switching characters smoothly |

### Creating

**CHOOSE YOUR SITUATION** Choose one of the following situations or devise one of your own. It should be a situation in which several different types of people can interact with each other.

- shopping or clerking at a big sale
- placing or taking a fast food order
- getting dressed in the locker room for a big game
- answering the phones or making appointments in a very busy office
- waiting for an important audition

**DEVELOP YOUR CHARACTERS** Develop three different characters to play the same scene in three different ways or to interact with each other in one scene. One characterization may be similar to yourself, but the other two should be very unlike you—and each other. Answer the following questions differently for each of your three characters:

- What is my name?
- What is my background?
- How does my voice sound? What are my vocal characteristics?
- What are my physical characteristics? How do I move?
- What is my dominant character attribute?
- What is my objective in this scene?
- What are my obstacles?

**SHAPE YOUR SCENE** Plan a short scene for each character, or plan one scene that includes all three of your characters. If you show them in separate scenes, you might have them react to the same situation, such as a fast food clerk who can't get the orders straight. If you show them in the same scene, you don't need to skip back and forth; you can have one character speak a monologue, and then the second, followed by the third—but they should all interact somehow. Plan to give each character just under two minutes of monologue.

Now improvise movement and lines for your characters. Include an entrance and exit; make clear your objective, obstacles, actions, and outcome for each character. You will probably include one or more characters whom the audience can't see or hear. Consider carefully how your characters' reactions can help the audience imagine those other characters. You can use real props if you wish, but your performance may be smoother if you simply pantomime them.

**REHEARSE YOUR SCENE** Rehearse the scene as each different character. Imagine how other characters in the scene (speaking or nonspeaking) react differently to your three characterizations. Rehearse until you feel confident that each of your characters is fully developed and that you can maintain each character's distinctive traits throughout your scene(s).

Now plan how you will make the transition from one character to the next. You might move from a freeze to a freeze or you might turn your back on the audience and make your change at that moment. Or, you might add a costume piece, such as a hat or a scarf, and instantly become a new character. Practice these transitions until you can do them smoothly and naturally.

## Performing

Before you begin, make sure your performance area is ready and that you have all necessary props and costumes. Announce your scene and briefly explain the situation. As you perform, remain focused and in character throughout your three portrayals. At the end, you will probably want to freeze for a moment to signal that you have finished.

## Responding

How well you have fulfilled the Specs in the Project Planner will help assess your project. You may also ask yourself or your audience these questions to help you improve:

- Did the audience understand the situation?
- Could the audience distinguish three unique characters and their objectives?
- Could the audience understand the action of your scene(s)?
- Did you stay focused and in character throughout your scene(s)?
- Was there a sense of a beginning, middle, and end?

Include responses to these questions in your Theatre Notebook.

## Adapting the Project

Work with a partner to develop three sets of dialogues for six characters; that is, your three characters will actually have other characters with whom they can speak and react. Keep the basic situation the same or nearly the same for the three dialogues.

# Delivering a Monologue

PROJECT 13

**ASSIGNMENT** Perform a two- to three-minute monologue.

| Project Planner | |
|---|---|
| Product | A monologue |
| Purpose | To learn a basic audition and performance skills |
| Specs | To accomplish this project, you will<br>• choose or develop a monologue appropriate to your individual skills<br>• analyze the character and situation<br>• develop an identifiable character, including voice and movement<br>• introduce the scene as needed<br>• perform convincingly and with focus |

## Creating

**CHOOSE YOUR MONOLOGUE** Choose a monologue that works for you. You may be able to find one in various books of monologues and scenes for acting practice. You may instead develop a monologue by taking a scene from a favorite play and eliminating other characters' dialogue.

**ANALYZE YOUR SCENE** First, read the entire play for an understanding of your character and how the scene you have chosen fits into the plot. Analyze your character using the guidelines for creating specific characters (p. 136–139).

Break down your monologue into beats (p. 147). It may be helpful to annotate your script with the subtext (p. 138) of each beat.

**REHEARSE YOUR MONOLOGUE** To re-create believable emotions, plan a sequence of movements. Make sure they are specific and help you express appropriate emotions for the scene. Annotate your script with these movements as well. Use the technique of emotional memory (p. 132) or using action to generate emotions (p. 132) if you like.

**INCLUDING OTHER CHARACTERS** When performing a monologue in which you are speaking to another character, it's a good idea to visualize that character in one spot and keep him or her there. Do this by glancing at the imaginary character at appropriate times and by directing lines to him or her. Even if you move about the stage, that character's location should probably stay constant. (You might ask a friend to be a silent stand-in for this character during early rehearsals.)

If another character is supposed to be speaking during your monologue, ask yourself the following questions to determine how you can indicate what he or she is saying:

- How long should I pause to listen?
- Should I look constantly at that character, or glance at him or her occasionally?
- How should I respond with my posture and facial expressions to what that character is saying?

**THE CLIMAX** If your monologue is well constructed, there will be a climax to your speech, a moment when your character reaches a point of high emotion, makes a major point, or finally communicates what you really want to say. Decide what the climax of your speech is and how you can most effectively build to it.

Memorize your lines exactly and rehearse them until you are comfortable with your characterization and delivery. You might tape-record your rehearsal so that you can get an idea of how well your voice is expressing the thoughts and emotions you want to convey. You can also have someone videotape your rehearsal, so that you can analyze your job of acting.

## Performing

Walk into the audition space with confidence. Stop, pause, and look at the audience for a moment. Give your name, the character's name, the name of the play from which the scene was taken, and the playwright's name. Add any background or information the audience may need to understand what's going on. Then take a moment to focus yourself. Imagine the environment of the scene and what the other character has just said to you. Take a breath and begin.

## Responding

How well you have fulfilled the Specs in the Project Planner will help assess your project. You may also ask yourself or your audience these questions to help you improve:

- Did the audience understand who you were and who the other characters were?
- Could the audience see all gestures, expressions, and movements?
- Were your movements or gestures motivated by subtext and appropriate to your character?
- Did you project and use a variety of vocal inflections throughout?
- Did you communicate the climax effectively?

Include responses to these questions in your Theatre Notebook.

## Adapting the Project

1. Work with other students to perform your monologues as though in a formal audition. Place a table outside the audition space. Ask one student to sign-in actors and have them fill out audition forms. Bring resumés and be prepared to answer interview questions from the director/producer, who may be played by your teacher or by an experienced actor or director you know in your community.
2. Use your monologue to audition for an actual role in a community theatre, youth theatre, or professional theatre production, or for a scholarship or admittance to a college or university program.
3. Work with a small group to write or adapt a play into a number of monologues. There should be at least three characters represented. Such collections are most effective when the characters disagree or interpret events differently. Have each member of your group take on a character and present your collection of monologues for an audience.

P R O J E C T 

# Entrances and Exits

**ASSIGNMENT** Plan and perform a scene portraying a jury entering and exiting a jury room before and after deciding a verdict.

## Project Planner

| | |
|---|---|
| Product | Performance of a scene in a jury room |
| Purpose | To practice making entrances and exits in character and to create effective blocking |
| Specs | To accomplish this project, you will<br>• work cooperatively within a large group<br>• establish a strong stage entrance and exit, in character<br>• portray the physical, mental, and emotional attributes of your character through pantomime<br>• perform a series of actions that have a beginning, middle, and end<br>• help plan an effective blocking arrangement so that your audience can view the central action |

## Creating

**ESTABLISH CHARACTER ATTRIBUTES** Juries are made up of 12 people of varying ages, personalities, and physical types from nearly every walk of life. Work with a group of 12 actors (or fewer, if necessary). Choose the age and attributes of the character each of you will portray; concentrate on what you can show through pantomime—facial expression, gestures, posture, and walk. You may want to establish the character attributes as a group to ensure an interesting balance of types on the jury.

You can choose character attributes from lists that you compile or general attributes such as the following:

**Physical:** strong, weak, graceful, clumsy, wiry, overweight, nervous, calm, swift, slow

**Mental/Emotional:** clever, dull, attentive, preoccupied, understanding, selfish, shy, outgoing, pompous, paranoid

Decide upon at least one physical and one mental/emotional attribute for each character as well as the age of each. It may help to make a chart showing the ages and attributes of all the characters.

Next, work on fleshing out your character's attributes. Practice walking through doorways, sitting, and so on, while exhibiting your character's attributes.

**PLAN YOUR PERFORMANCE SPACE** Your scene will take place in the jury room, which is next to the courtroom. You will need a table and at least one chair for each juror. Plan where the entrance will be and perhaps some props, such as a coffee maker.

**PLAN YOUR SCENE** Your performance will be in two parts: (1) coming in after the closing arguments to debate the guilt or innocence of the defendant, and (2) going out to the courtroom after you have reached your verdict. As an ensemble, you will need to decide the following:

- What was the nature of the trial—a minor traffic accident? a grisly murder?
- What is the overall mood of the jury?
- Do they expect a quick decision or a long, drawn-out argument?
- In what order do the jurors enter?
- Where does each juror sit?

For your exits you will need to decide similar questions:

- Was your deliberation easy or difficult?
- Is your verdict guilty or not guilty?
- Is everyone satisfied with the verdict?
- In what order do the jurors exit?

**ESTABLISH YOUR CHARACTER** What does your character do once he or she is in the room? Do you walk right to a chair and sit down? Do you go to a window and look out? Do you and two or three other jury members stand by the coffee maker and chat? This is where you can bring out your character's attributes. Remember, you don't have to go with the prevailing mood or opinion. The ensemble's decisions about blocking the whole scene must be based on individual characters and their attributes and on the performance space.

**PLAN YOUR INTERACTIONS** Work with at least one other juror to plan an interaction for your entrance and another for your exit. For example, Juror 3 might be distraught at having to vote guilty for a sympathetic defendant while Juror 8 might offer consolation.

**REHEARSE THE SCENE** Run through the scene several times. You can experiment with your character, trying different moods and different movements or gestures, but you need to stick to the general plan of blocking. After everyone is finally seated at the table, arrange for someone to give a signal for all characters to freeze in position. If you can, arrange for a classmate to black out the lights at this point. When the lights come up again, it is after you have reached your decision: plan on a different freeze to begin this part of the scene. At an arranged signal, start to exit. Don't forget to work in your interactions with your fellow jurors.

## Performing

After you have rehearsed the scene enough so that everyone is comfortable with his or her characterization, perform the scene for the class. If you can't use a blackout, plan in advance how you will make the transition from the before freeze to the after freeze. Be sure the audience understands that there is a time lapse involved.

## Responding

How well you have fulfilled the Specs in the Project Planner will help assess your project. You can also ask yourself, your ensemble, or your audience these questions to help you improve:

- Could the audience see all gestures, expressions, and movements?
- Did the actors' movements and gestures establish believable characters?
- Could the audience tell from the interactions how some of these characters felt about each other?
- Could the audience tell from the group performance the nature of what happened before the scene began and during the time lapse?
- Did all the actors work together as an effective ensemble?

Include responses to these questions in your Theatre Notebook.

## Adapting the Project

1. Repeat the same two-part scene, but add improvised dialogue. Every bit of dialogue should reflect individual character as well as the group's decision about the nature of the trial and the deliberation.
2. Work with a smaller group to show entrances and exits in different settings, such as a fancy restaurant, the bleachers at a homecoming game, or a surprise birthday party. Follow the same procedures regarding individual character attributes and interactions.

# Creating Stage Pictures



**ASSIGNMENT** With a group, create a series of stage pictures that tell a story.

## Project Planner

| | |
|---|---|
| **Product** | Stage pictures that create a narrative |
| **Purpose** | To practice creating stage pictures |
| **Specs** | To accomplish this project, you will<br>• work cooperatively within a group<br>• choose a story or narrative poem<br>• analyze the story for main actions<br>• plan pictures or tableaus that show each main action<br>• develop smooth transitions from one picture to the next<br>• present an effective narration<br>• develop skill in ensemble work |

## Creating

**PREPARE THE SCRIPT** Choose a story or narrative poem that has a number of strong, clear actions that would lend themselves to dynamic stage pictures. If you choose a poem, you may be able to use it as is for your narration. If you choose a story, you will need to write a narration or choose sentences from the story to piece together a narration, but wait until you have analyzed the actions.

**ANALYZE THE ACTIONS** Who are the main characters? What main actions are they involved in throughout? You should be able to identify at least five main actions for an effective project. If your ensemble contains more actors than you have main characters, you can still put those people to good use.

As a group, determine the theme of the story. Brainstorm ideas and images that you can use to tell your story effectively.

**PLAN YOUR PICTURES** There are several ways that you can determine which pictures to stage and how to stage them. One member of your ensemble might act as director and make these decisions. One or more members might sketch compositions of people that illustrate the actions you have chosen, which the ensemble could then copy. Or, you might all experiment together with body arrangements and stage pictures.

Keep in mind the principles of effective stage composition, such as focus, levels, and planes (pp. 177–181).

**COMPLETE THE PICTURES** You can use simple props or costume pieces if you wish, but you might find it more convenient to pantomime everything. Consider how you can use your bodies to create animals or inanimate objects, such as a car, a doorway, a tree, a city skyline, or a mountain. You can also use your bodies to create abstract or symbolic shapes, such as fear or puzzlement. These pictures should all be freezes, however, with no movement.

**DEVELOP THE NARRATION** If your narration needs to be written, do it now. For the narration, consider where the narrator will be during the performance—offstage or visible onstage? You might consider using more than one narrator or having having actors who are forming the pictures perform the narration.

**REHEARSE YOUR STORY** When you are taking part in a tableau (p. 105), memorize exactly your position as well as the positions of the actors near you so that you can recreate this picture within seconds. As you rehearse as an ensemble, plan how you will enter and exit the performing area and how you will make transitions between pictures. You might do them in blackouts, but if you do them in view of the audience, they should be carefully rehearsed.

## Performing

Before performing, check props, set pieces, and costumes (if any). Introduce the name of the work and its author and explain whatever background is necessary. Then take your place as an ensemble and begin your performance. Concentrate on holding your body position and facial expression as long as necessary to avoid breaking the freeze and spoiling the focus of the scene.

## Responding

How well you have fulfilled the Specs in the Project Planner will help assess your project. You may also ask yourself or your audience these questions to help you improve:

- Was the story told clearly through narration and stage pictures?
- Did the narrator or narrators project sufficiently?
- Which were the most effective stage pictures and which were the least effective? Why?
- How well did the ensemble work together?
- Were transitions smooth and unobtrusive?

Include responses to these questions in your Theatre Notebook.

## Adapting the Project

1. Have someone document your work with photographs. Mount them in an album along with the printed narration to create a story told in words and pictures.
2. Repeat the project with a narrative you have written yourselves based on stories in the news today.
3. Experiment telling a different story using two people only. Have two actors share the narration, but keep it as narration—don't turn it into dialogue.

# Developing a Director's Promptbook

PROJECT 

**ASSIGNMENT** Prepare a director's promptbook.

| Project Planner | |
|---|---|
| Product | A director's promptbook |
| Purpose | To learn how a director analyzes a script and prepares a promptbook |
| Specs | To accomplish this project, you will<br>• choose a one-act play<br>• write a detailed script analysis of the play<br>• develop a style and production concept<br>• visualize technical elements of the production<br>• draw a ground plan for the production<br>• write blocking for at least two pages of the script |

## Creating

**CHOOSE YOUR PLAY** Decide on a one-act play that is appealing to you as a director. If you are using this script to prepare for an actual production, you will need to get final approval from your teacher and may need to pay royalties.

**DEVELOP YOUR PROMPTBOOK** You will need a three-ring binder and six dividers for different sections of the promptbook. Label them *Script Analysis, Character Analysis, Genre/Style, Ground Plan, Technical Requirements*, and *Blocking*.

**SECTION 1: SCRIPT ANALYSIS** First read through the entire play. Then go back and reread it as you analyze the script (p. 166–173).

The following outline may help you in your analysis:

**I. Theme**

A. What is the central theme?
B. What are the secondary themes, if any?
C. How does the title relate to the theme?
D. Summarize the idea of the play in one sentence.

**II. Characters**

A. Who is the protagonist?
B. Who is the antagonist?
C. Who are the secondary characters?

**III. Plot Analysis**

A. What is the exposition?
B. What is the inciting incident?
C. What are the sources of conflict during the rising action?
D. When does the climax occur?
E. What events make up the falling action?
F. What is the dènouement?

**SECTION 2: CHARACTER ANALYSIS** Analyze each major character in the play by writing answers to the following questions:

- What is the character's background and status quo?
- How might you describe the character's body and voice?
- What are the physical and mental/emotional attributes of the character?
- What are the character's major objectives?
- What are the character's major obstacles?
- What strategies does the character use to overcome these obstacles?
- What are the character's major actions in the plot?
- What is the character's relationship to other characters?
- How does the character use language?

**SECTION 3: GENRE/STYLE** What kind of play is this? comedy? farce? tragedy? drama? What style is it? If it is a modern realistic play there may be little to add, but you still have some choice in *how* realistic you want to make your sets, costumes, and other production elements.

Does the play itself suggest a certain kind of style? If so, consider what you can do to fulfill it. You can, of course, bring your own sense of style to the play. To develop a visual and emotional sense of the play, explore your sensory response to the play by asking yourself the following questions:

- What images and colors do I see?
- What is the quality of the light?
- What sounds do I hear?
- What smells might be present?
- How does the play make me feel?

What images and associations come to your mind? For example, a mystery might evoke an image of long shadows cast onstage. The shadows provoke an emotional response. You might feel the possibility of danger, see the power of the light and darkness, and hear danger in the silence.

Write at least one paragraph each on the genre of the play and on the style of the production you envision. Then develop your production concept (p. 54).

**SECTION 4: GROUND PLAN** First decide what type of performance space you will use—proscenium, thrust, or arena (pp. 58–59). Some play scripts contain ground plans, but many directors prefer to design their own (p. 176). As you plan, be sure to account for the requirements of the script; for example, one door to the kitchen and one to the hall, a window that can be opened. Include the furniture that you must have before adding decorative touches. If possible, include a couple of levels to give yourself more choices for composition and variety. At the very least, include a number of acting areas so that you can use the whole stage effectively.

Draw a finished ground plan to scale and include it in your promptbook. You can also copy this ground plan to use in the section on blocking.

**SECTION 5: TECHNICAL REQUIREMENTS** On a scene-by-scene basis, describe the lighting and sound requirements for your production. Make a list of the major or most difficult props needed. Also note some of the special costume needs. The designers or crew heads would be responsible for the complete lists, but as director, you need to know what some of the problems or challenges might be before beginning work on a production.

**SECTION 6: BLOCKING** You will need to prepare the script so that you can put it in the binder and make room for your notes and ground plan (p. 183). Block two or more pages of the script, using blocking symbols (p. 183) or shorthand that you have devised. It will be safest to do a rough blocking on extra copies of the script pages before you prepare your final copy. A promptbook doesn't necessarily need to be neat, but it does need to be readable.

## Presenting

Present your promptbook to the class. You may either do a formal presentation or discuss it in a small group.

## Responding

How well you have fulfilled the Specs in the Project Planner will help assess your project. You may also ask yourself or your classmates these questions to help you improve:

- Is the promptbook well organized and in the correct format?
- Is the script analysis detailed enough to guide the production concept?
- Are the production elements of the play taken into consideration?
- Is the ground plan drawn to scale?
- Is the blocking workable and responsive to the physical and emotional content of the scene?

Include responses to these questions in your Theatre Notebook.

## Adapting the Project

1. Continue working on the same play. Block an entire scene or the whole play. If possible, engage some of your classmates to walk through the blocking you have devised so that you can see what it looks like in three dimensions.
2. Research earlier productions of the play you have chosen. Add a section to your promptbook to include such things as the time period during which the play happens, the ground plan of a professional production, pictures of the professional actors who have appeared in the play, costume designs from other productions, and reviews or critical analysis of the play.

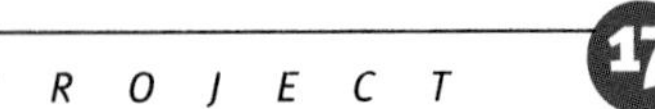

# PROJECT 17 Producing a Play

**ASSIGNMENT** Prepare a financial proposal for a production of a play on a given budget.

| Project Planner | |
|---|---|
| Product | A presentation of the financial planning for a production |
| Purpose | To understand the process of producing a show |
| Specs | To accomplish this project, you will<br>• interview a producer or staff member of a community or professional theatre company<br>• choose a play or musical as an example<br>• analyze the play in terms of technical needs and costs<br>• put together a complete budget for a production<br>• use a clear and understandable format to present your information |

## Creating

**IMAGINE YOUR CIRCUMSTANCES** For the purpose of this project, you are the producer for a small professional theatre company with a

250-seat theatre in your community or area. It's a nonprofit company, so your goal is to break even on your productions. You have a budget of $50,000.

**RESEARCH YOUR NEEDS** First make a list of all the expenses you can imagine would be involved in a professional production. To compile your list, you can research published or documented production costs for a number of professional productions. You may also check on costs for previous productions done at your school, a local college or university, or an area community theatre.

**INTERVIEW A PRO** Call or write to a producer or production staff member at a professional theatre to set up an interview over the phone. Include the following questions:

- How do you finance your shows?
- What is your average budget per show?
- How do you forecast income and expenses?
- What percentage of a play's budget do you allocate for staff salaries, actors' salaries, utilities, space rental, equipment rental, costumes and sets, rights and royalties, insurance, ticket and box office expenses, and promotion?
- What unexpected expenses have you encountered in the past?

Your interviewee may not be willing to give you all this information, but anything you learn can be helpful. (Many professional theatres have a community or educational outreach division, which can be very helpful in providing information.)

**CHOOSE YOUR PRODUCTION** Choose and read a play or musical that you would like to produce. It will be easier if you choose a play with a small cast and just one set, but some musicals can be done with limited means. Analyze the script to determine how many and what kind of sets would need to be built, how many actors would be needed, sound system or musical requirements, and special effects needed.

Remember that you are limited to shows that can be done in your 250-seat theatre. This is not a particularly large theatre, but there are many that are smaller. Assume that you have a good collection of flats, basic lighting and sound equipment, and so on.

As you choose a play or musical, consider your audience. Is the show you have chosen the sort that would draw a good audience in your community? Before going on, review your choice of plays with your teacher.

**CALCULATE AND FILL IN YOUR BUDGET** Once you have decided on a show to produce, contact the publisher or copyright holder to find out what the royalties will be (p. 185).

Based on the information you gathered in your interviews and contacts, determine an overall production budget with a bottom-line cost and bottom-line income. Standard sources of income are ticket sales, program advertising, and sponsors or donors, but you might be able to come up with some further creative ideas—such as souvenir T-shirts. Using percentages based on professional budget allocations and using the information you have received from your contacts, fill in individual line items in your budget. (Remember that you have a maximum of $50,000 at your disposal; that doesn't mean you have to spend it all.)

**WRITE A PROPOSAL** As a producer, you may have to convince a theatre's board of directors or a potential sponsor that the play or musical is worth producing. Write a proposal that includes why you think the show is a good choice to produce, a general production schedule, your planned budget, and your potential sources of income.

List the assumptions on which you are basing your forecasts. For example, if your theatre company has had an average attendance of 200 people per performance, you can use this number to forecast your ticket sales.

## Presenting

You may make copies or overhead transparencies of your forms for your presentation. Arrange in advance for any audio-visual equipment you might need. You may also want to include pictures or reviews from past productions of the show you chose.

Make sure your materials are ready and your equipment is working properly. Present your proposal to the class as if they were your theatre's board of directors. After your formal presentation, answer any questions they may have. If a question is asked that you don't know the answer to, make a note to find out.

## Responding

How well you have fulfilled the Specs in the Project Planner will help assess your project. You may also ask yourself or your classmates these questions to help you improve:

- Does the budget cover all needful elements of a production?
- Are the presentation materials clear and understandable?
- Are the mathematical calculations correct?
- Did you make your audience want to produce the show?

Include responses to these questions in your Theatre Notebook.

## Adapting the Project

1. Work as a producer for your school's next production, or work with your teacher to fulfill some of the tasks of a producer. You will be doing essentially the same things as in this project, but in a real-life situation.
2. Use what you have learned to write a grant proposal for a student production. First contact an area corporation or your state's fine arts agency to find out what they require in a formal grant proposal. Obtain copies of whatever forms and paperwork are needed. Then follow their requirements to the letter.

# Designing a Set

PROJECT 18

**ASSIGNMENT** Design a set for a specific play.

| Project Planner | |
|---|---|
| **Product** | A set design for a play |
| **Purpose** | To practice design skills |
| **Specs** | To accomplish this project, you will<br>• choose a play for which you would like to design a set<br>• analyze the technical and dramatic needs for one setting<br>• draw a ground plan and a front elevation<br>• specify details of furniture, fabrics, and colors<br>• work within a chosen style |

## Creating

**CHOOSE YOUR PLAY** Choose a play that is appealing to you as a designer. If it's a one-act play, it will probably have only one setting; if it's a full-length play, it may have multiple settings. Choose one.

**ANALYZE YOUR PERFORMANCE SPACE** Plan to design a set for your school's main performance space. You will need a scale drawing of that space; if you don't already have one, do that first. As you survey the performance space, note sight lines and distances to the rear of the house, as well as how the stage looks from different angles.

Whether your stage is a proscenium, thrust, or arena will, of course, have a great influence on your design.

**ANALYZE YOUR PLAY** First read the entire play. Then go back and reread it as you analyze the script. Even if you're designing one set for a multiset show, it must fit in with other sets in other scenes. Some playscripts contain ground plans, but they were developed with specific theatres in mind. You need to design for *your* theatre.

What does the playwright have to say about the technical requirements of the set? What kind of room or outdoor setting is it supposed to represent? How many doors and windows are specified? What is each of these supposed to lead to or overlook? What major pieces of furniture, colors, or design elements are specified? Sometimes you can fulfill these exactly; at other times you can only use them as suggestions or impressions.

Next think about the dramatic requirements of the set. Who lives here? How should that character's personality influence the setting? If someone feels isolated and alone, for example, you might design an area of the set to emphasize that isolation. If a large family gathers at a dinner table, you will have to include a table large enough to seat them all. Make notes on all these requirements before you start your design.

**CHOOSE A STYLE** Style is usually decided by an entire production team, but for this project you can choose your own. Most shows are realistic, but even then you have a range of choices about how much detail you will show. The style you choose may influence your lines, textures, colors, number and placement of set props, lighting—even whether the walls of the set are solid or merely suggested.

**DESIGN YOUR SET** You may start with a ground plan and front elevation (pp. 208–209) and use it to develop sketches and renderings (pp. 206–207), or work in reverse order. Allow yourself to discard plenty of rough sketches before making your final choices and drawing a finished plan and elevation. Label your design plans as necessary. Color the rendering and elevation with water colors or marking pens to show the colors and textures of the set.

You may also wish to include paint and wallpaper samples, magazine pictures of furniture, or sketches of architectural details. Designers often furnish such items so that set construction crews have a clear idea of what is wanted.

## Presenting

Present your set design to the class. You may either do a formal presentation or discuss it in a small group. You may need to describe the play to your classmates if they are not familiar with it.

## Responding

How well you have fulfilled the Specs in the Project Planner will help assess your project. You can also ask yourself or your classmates these questions to help you improve:

- Are the ground plan and front elevation rendered neatly and completely?
- Do they provide sufficient information for set construction?
- Does the design give the audience information about the play or the characters?
- Is the design workable and responsive to the technical and dramatic needs of the scene?
- Do the design elements represent a style that is appropriate to the play?

Include responses to these questions in your Theatre Notebook.

## Adapting the Project

1. Build a three-dimensional scale model of your set design, using cardboard, matte board, or foamcore (p. 115). Color it with watercolors, marking pens, or tempera paints. Add set pieces constructed of the same materials or purchase dollhouse model furniture at a hobby shop (you can reuse these pieces) and paint them to match your design. Use thin, nonpatterned fabric for curtains (avoid curtain fabric; it's too large in scale).
2. Draw up a prop plot for a full-length, multiscene play. Read and analyze the play. Create a chart that shows which props you need to pull, rent, buy, borrow, or build. Draw sketches for props you need to build. Make a scale drawing of one and construct it.
3. Work with a set designer to design a lighting plot for at least two different scenes using the same set. If you can, design for day and night scenes or for two scenes that have different moods and dramatic requirements. Draw your lighting plots on copies of your classmate's set designs. Create an instrument schedule based on your plot.
4. Draw up a sound plot for a full-length, multiscene play. Read and analyze the play. Create a chart of recorded, created, and found sounds you need to prepare for the show. Locate, create, or record at least five of the sounds in each category. Splice them together onto a tape and present each sound to the class, explaining its importance to the play.
5. Design costumes for two main characters in at least two scenes of a full-length, multiscene play. Begin with costume lists and sketches, then create complete costume renderings in pen and ink and a chosen color medium. Include fabric swatches for each part of the costumes.
6. Read and analyze a favorite play. Create character makeup sketches for two characters in the show who require character makeup. Enlist two classmates to participate as the actors. Do makeup plans for each (p. 239). Then do the makeup on the actors and present the actors in makeup to the class.

PROJECT 

# Reupholstering a Set Prop

**ASSIGNMENT** Reupholster a piece of stage furniture.

## Project Planner

| | |
|---|---|
| Product | A reupholstered set prop |
| Purpose | To adapt furniture for use in a play |
| Specs | To accomplish this project, you will<br>• determine the style and color needs of a production<br>• remove the original fabric from an upholstered chair or sofa<br>• repair the framework as needed<br>• cover the piece with heavyweight muslin or canvas<br>• cover the piece with new fabric |

## Creating

**STRIP THE FURNITURE** Work with an upholstered chair or sofa that needs refurbishing. (See your teacher.) First, remove the existing fabric carefully, so that it can be used as a template for cutting the new fabric. To do so, rip the seams by cutting through the stitches or cut carefully through the fabric along the seams. Use a seam ripper if you have one available. Spread the old upholstery out flat. (If you plan to show before-and-after images, take a photograph or make a sketch of the item before removing the old fabric.)

**REPAIR THE FRAMEWORK** Examine and repair the existing padding, springs, and webbing. Replace damaged padding with new padding of an identical or similar type. Do the same for damaged webbing. Be sure that no springs are loose to poke through the upholstery. If the piece includes any decorative wood, sand and refinish or paint the wood.

**CHOOSE THE FABRIC** If this is simply a practice or project piece, any heavy upholstery fabric will do. If this piece is to be used in a production, check first with the set designer to be sure the style, color, and fabric are appropriate. Remember that fabric can be painted using special painting techniques to look richer or more worn.

**CUT THE PATTERN** Use the old upholstery as a template to cut an undercover of heavyweight muslin or light canvas. Be sure to cut off or fold under any seam allowance left on the old fabric, and to add new seam allowances to the new fabric. (You may find it helpful to make a template from brown paper before marking and cutting any fabric.) Staple the muslin or canvas in place with a staple gun. Now use the same pattern to mark and cut the new upholstery fabric. If the new fabric has any pattern, you will need to plan carefully how to match that pattern, so that stripes run in the same direction or large figures are centered. Then cover the muslin with the new fabric. Pull it tight, turning seam allowances under, and tack, nail, or staple it in place. Because this is stage furniture, you can leave some staples exposed as long as they cannot be seen by the audience. Otherwise, cover the staples by gluing a decorative border in the style of the chair or by using decorative upholstery tacks. Be sure that no staples or nailheads can snag actors' clothing.

## Presenting

Take photograph of your finished product if you like, or draw a sketch. Display your work for your classmates. Display as well your before-and-after photographs or sketches.

## Responding

How well you have fulfilled the Specs in the Project Planner will help assess your project. You may also ask yourself or your classmates these questions to help you improve:

- Is the finished piece fully and smoothly padded?
- Is the upholstery firmly and completely attached?
- If there is a pattern, does it match exactly?
- Does the style and color of the finished piece fit the needs of the production?

Include responses to these questions in your Theatre Notebook.

## Adapting the Project

1. Pad and upholster an original set prop. Build a footstool, chair, covered bench, or sofa following instructions from your teacher or a basic carpentry manual. Then add padding, heavyweight muslin, and fabric to create an entirely original set prop.
2. Make pillows or curtains to match or accent your newly upholstered furniture. If these are to be used in a production, check first with the set designer to be sure your style, color, and fabric are appropriate

PROJECT 20

# Grid Transfer

**ASSIGNMENT** Use a grid to enlarge a design.

## Project Planner

| | |
|---|---|
| Product | An enlargement of an existing image |
| Purpose | To practice using the grid method of enlargement |
| Specs | To accomplish this project, you will<br>• choose an appropriate image<br>• select and prepare the surface for your design<br>• develop a grid<br>• enlarge the image as you transfer it to your surface<br>• paint or finish the image as needed |

## Creating

**CHOOSE AN IMAGE** Look at a number of images before choosing one that might be appropriate for a drop or backcloth. Images that you might consider include landscapes, forests, city skylines, and so on. If you were creating a drop for an actual production, you would need to work from the designer's specifications or from an original painting that the designer or you create.

**SELECT AND PREPARE YOUR SURFACE** The expense of a theatrical drop ($750–$900) and the paint required to cover it ($200–$300) would only be justified in the case of an actual production. To complete this project, you might instead transfer your design onto a large piece of canvas, poster board, butcher paper, or even a white bedsheet. Paint the surface of your material with a background color if you like, but make it a light tone so you can see what you will draw on it.

**DEVELOP YOUR GRID** First determine whether you can use the whole of the original image or whether you need to crop it to fit. The height-to-width ratio of the original must be exactly the same as that of the surface you have chosen. That means that the original can be divided into exactly the same number of squares down and across as your surface. If this doesn't work, mask the sides or the bottom of the image until it does.

Now draw a grid of squares on top of the image or a copy of the image that you're going to enlarge. Assign numbers to the horizontal lines on the grid and letters to the vertical lines.

**TRANSFER AND ENLARGE THE IMAGE** You can work either with your surface spread on the floor or fastened to a wall. Use a soft pencil to draw an enlargement of the grid on your surface. Remember that the grid on your surface must have the same number of squares down and across as the grid on the image. Number and letter the lines.

Work one square at a time. Draw freehand what you see in square 1-A. You can use a ruler or just judge by eye where lines of the image should intersect the grid lines. It's best to create bold outlines first, and then go back to fill in details. Step back from time to time to judge the overall effect.

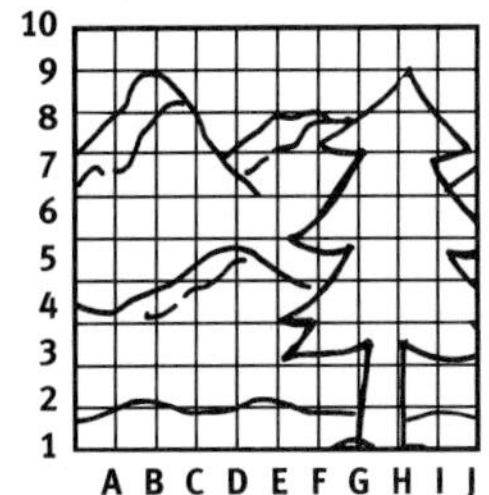


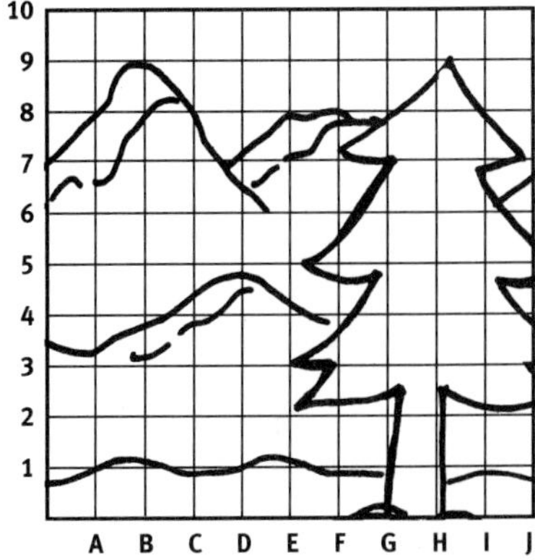


Grid-transfer technique

**FINISH YOUR SURFACE** When you have transferred and enlarged the entire image, go over the bold outlines with charcoal or chalk to smooth curves and clean up lines that don't quite match. Next, add the finishing details.

Now paint your surface with whatever medium you choose, imitating the color scheme of the original image if you like. Depending on the original and on the effect you are trying to create, you may want to tone down or heighten the color scheme a bit.

## Presenting

If the surface you have created is sufficiently large, you might hang it in your classroom and use it as a backdrop for a performance for your fellow students. If not, you might simply exhibit it—with the original image, if you like—in your classroom.

## Responding

How well you have fulfilled the Specs in the Project Planner will help assess your project. You can also ask yourself and your classmates these questions to help you improve:

- Is the image appropriate for a drop or backcloth?
- Are the dimensions accurate in relation to the original image?
- Is the image clear and visible from a distance?

Include responses to these questions in your Theatre Notebook.

## Adapting the Project

Use the grid method to transfer and enlarge a design onto plywood or particle board for a free-standing set piece, such as a tree. Using a band saw under the supervision of your teacher, cut out the outline and nail a jack to the back to brace it (p. 220). Paint the front appropriately.

# Performance

theatre—art in action

## Acting


273 Working with the Script
278 Acting Styles
282 The Rehearsal Process
291 The Performance
294 Activities
296 **Historical Profile:** Kabuki

## Directing & Producing


307 Desire and Dedication
308 A Young Director's Journal
324 Activities
326 **Historical Profile:** Chekhov

## Technical Theatre


335 Shifting Scenery
337 Organizing Props
339 Hanging, Focusing, and Running Lights
345 Setting Up Sound
346 Completing Costumes
349 Applying Makeup
352 Final Rehearsals
353 Tech Rehearsal
355 Dress Rehearsal
357 Run of the Show
360 Postproduction
362 Activities


## Projects


366 21: Duet Performance
369 22: Characterization Using Animal Traits
371 23: Commedia dell'arte Performance
374 24: Stage Composition and Emphasis
377 25: Dealing with a Difficult Actor
379 26: Directing a One-Act Play
382 27: Creating a Gobo
384 28: Making a Show Tape
387 29: Analyzing Scene Changes
390 30: Old-Age Makeup

# Acting performance

Rehearsals are where a play starts to come alive. Beginning with a careful analysis of the script, actors build an understanding of their characters, gradually becoming fluent in the words and actions with which they will express these people onstage. Rehearsals are also the ensemble portion of the creative process: director, actors, and crews coordinate their efforts so that everyone supports and complements each other. The result is a successful performance on opening night.

## THE LANGUAGE OF THEATRE

**cue line** final line that signals an actor to begin the next speech

**fourth wall** an imaginary wall between the audience and the actors in a representational play

**off book** rehearsing without a script after lines are memorized; as opposed to **on book,** rehearsing with a script

**presentational style** theatrical style in which the actors acknowledge the presence of the audience

**read-through** a complete reading of a play aloud by the assembled cast, usually at the first rehearsal

**representational style** theatrical style in which the actors do not acknowledge the presence of the audience, but try to duplicate life

**scenario** a standard plot outline

**spike** to mark the floor of a rehearsal space with tape that indicates significant parts of a ground plan

**stage business** movements employing props, costumes, and makeup; used to strengthen the personality of a character

# Working with the Script

One of the most exciting experiences for an actor is being cast for a show. If the script was available before your audition you may have already read it at least once. The director may have suggested you look carefully at a particular role for the callbacks, or you may have read for several roles at the callback. Now you know which role you will play. The fun—and the work—has just begun.

That work begins with the script. The script isn't just a series of lines to be memorized; it's one of your most important resources as an actor, and it's the final authority and basis for all character choices you make. If you approach it creatively from a variety of angles, the script can help you build your characterization and deepen your experience of the play.

Script analysis should begin immediately, even before formal rehearsals start, and it will continue throughout the rehearsal process. The following is a sequential approach you can take to the process of script analysis. Because a large part of your script analysis involves studying your character's objectives and obstacles, you may wish to review the information on motivation and behavior (p. 134).

## Preliminary Analysis

Once you have the script, read it all the way through—without stopping, if possible. Now read the entire play again, this time aloud to yourself. Reading aloud lets you hear your character speak and may spark insights into both the play and your character that you can't get by reading silently. As you read, note your impressions in your Theatre Notebook.

When you have finished your second reading, review the questions posed here to formalize your responses for this preliminary analysis. Begin by answering factual questions from your perspective as a reader.

- What happens in the play?
- When and where does the action of the play occur?
- What are the period manners and customs of the play?
- What are my character's dominant attributes and attitudes?
- What images come to mind when I think of my character?

By way of example, imagine that you are cast as the legendary Sherlock Holmes in an adaptation of Sir Arthur Conan Doyle's story, "The Final Problem." In this story, Holmes faces his arch foe, the criminal mastermind Professor Moriarty. Here is an example of how you might answer these questions:

***The Final Problem*, adaptation of a story by Sir Arthur Conan Doyle**

**What happens in the play?**
*Sherlock Holmes asks his old friend Dr. Watson to help him escape from the criminal mastermind Professor Moriarty, who is trying to kill Holmes because Holmes has arranged for his arrest. Moriarty eludes the police and follows Holmes and Watson throughout Europe. Holmes finally confronts Moriarty atop a mountain waterfall. Holmes succeeds in ridding the world of Moriarty but apparently gets himself killed in the process.*

**When and where does the action of the play occur?**
*In 1891 in the London home of Dr. Watson; later, on a train; and finally, in the Swiss Alps*

**What are the period manners and customs of the play?**
*Formal upper-class British; very polite and distant*

**What are my character's dominant attributes and attitudes?**
*Extremely intelligent, perceptive, and analytical. Concise in his choice of words. Conceited, sarcastic, and frank. Cares about ridding society of Moriarty, mostly as a cherry on top of his brilliant career.*

**What images come to mind when I think of my character?**
*Typical image of checkered deer-stalker cap, high-collared caped coat, pipe, and magnifying glass. Uptight English gentleman with his nose in the air, sniffing, or looking down his nose at others. A prowling, aloof cat.*

Now move on to ask yourself more internal questions, answering as your character would:

- What thoughts, feelings, and images come to mind as I go through the action of the story?
- What is my overall objective?
- What obstacles stand in the way of achieving this objective?
- What actions do I take to overcome these obstacles?
- What are the stakes?
- What is the outcome of my actions?

Again, here is an example of how you might answer these questions, as your character, Sherlock Holmes:

**What thoughts, feelings, and images come to mind as I go through the action of the story?**
*I feel drained and nervous as I tell Watson about Moriarty trying to kill me. The room is dark, except for the reading lamp. Later on the train, I feel satisfied that we have eluded Moriarty and amused that I fooled Watson with my disguise as an old Italian priest. I see landscapes and cities as we travel through Europe to Switzerland. I feel nervous, but not fearful. I am*

*annoyed when I hear that Moriarty slipped through the grasp of the London police. I hear roaring and see the blackness of the rocks and whiteness of the mist at the waterfall where I meet Moriarty.*

***What is my overall objective?***
*I must rid society of the world's greatest criminal, Moriarty, proving that my intelligence used for good can overcome his intelligence used for evil.*

***What obstacles stand in the way of achieving this objective?***

- *The evil Professor Moriarty and his criminal mind. He is my equal, brilliant and resourceful. He has a personal vendetta against me and is aided by his extensive criminal network.*
- *Myself and my fears: fear of failure and humiliation, fear of death, fear for my friend's life.*
- *The environment—it always contains the potential for harm, especially with Moriarty around.*

***What actions do I take to overcome these obstacles?***

- *With Dr. Watson's assistance, I sneak out of London, and then travel through Europe, using my observation skills to stay one step ahead of Moriarty.*
- *I reassure myself—and Watson—that if Moriarty finds me I will not let him escape, even if it causes my death. I repeatedly state that eliminating Moriarty would be my crowning achievement.*
- *I keep a constant lookout for dangers that Moriarty could arrange in my environment.*

***What are the stakes?***
*Capture the elusive Moriarty and end my career at its peak, or die by his hand, leaving him to survive and continue his criminal career.*

***What is the outcome of my actions?***
*I succeed in ridding the world of Moriarity and maintain my self-respect, but apparently die in so doing.*

By applying an approach such as this to guide your analysis, you will greatly increase your knowledge of your character and the play.

Wearing Sherlock Holmes's trademark Ulster coat and deer-stalker cap, Basil Rathbone (left) played the detective in a long series of films based on the Sherlock Holmes stories by Sir Arthur Conan Doyle. Nigel Bruce (right) was a particularly bumbling Doctor Watson.

## Character Analysis

One of the great creative challenges—and pleasures—in acting is building your character. In developing your characterization, you will make a variety of decisions (pp. 136–139); these decisions must all be grounded in your script. Carefully analyze the script to determine how the dialogue and actions of your character and other characters reveal aspects of your character. You might employ the following technique in doing this analysis, including it in your Theatre Notebook: Draw three columns on a page, heading the first, "What the Playwright Says About Me"; the second, "What I Say About Myself"; and the third, "What Other Characters Say About Me." (If you are portraying a historic character, you might add a fourth column, "Facts about my character.") Fill in the appropriate information about your character in each column.

A sample of this approach is included here, again using the character of Holmes in the adaptation *The Final Problem.* Only a portion of the chart is completed. Any chart you complete for your character will be full of information gleaned from the script.

| *What the Playwright Says About Me* | *What I Say About Myself* | *What Other Characters Say About Me* |
|---|---|---|
| *English detective of the 1880s and 1890s* | *I have been using myself up rather too freely.* | *You look even paler and thinner than usual.* |
| *well-educated gentleman* | *. . . I have been a little pressed of late.* | *It is not in your nature to take an aimless holiday.* |
| *intellectually brilliant* | | |
| *unemotional* | *I am by no means a nervous man.* | *You have less frontal development than I should have expected.* |
| *tall, thin, athletic* | *Danger is part of my trade.* | *. . . the best and the wisest man I have ever known.* |

## Scene-by-Scene Analysis

The essence of theatre is in the action that drives the stories. Interpreting a character in the playwright's story onstage in a way that will hold the attention of the audience is the basic job of the actor. To understand the story your script tells, you must analyze the play by breaking it down into its working parts, into scenes, or even beats (p. 147).

Begin by asking yourself the questions that determine your status quo in a play (p. 136). These same questions can be applied on a scene-by-scene basis. Then ask yourself the following questions, which address the subtext of your dialogue and actions (p. 138) and any transformations your character may undergo in the scene. You might write your responses to these questions in the margins of your script, or include them in your Theatre Notebook.

**SUBTEXT**

- What am I implying by my dialogue and actions?
- How does this subtext differ from my spoken words?
- How does my background influence my thoughts, words, and actions?
- How does my subtext influence my actions and emotional responses to other characters' words and actions?
- How does my subtext help the audience understand the meaning of the play?

**TRANSFORMATION**

- Do I change during the scene? If so, how?
- How do I react to this change?
- Does my overall objective change? If so, how?

If you were performing in *The Diary of Anne Frank* by Frances Goodrich and Albert Hackett, what background research might aid you in developing your understanding of the play?

## The Background of the Play

Another dimension of the script that you should explore in your analysis is the literary background and historical context of the play. If your director doesn't discuss the background of the play with you, or if you want more information, do some homework on your own. You can begin by answering questions such as these, which you may want to include—along with other notes from your research—in your Theatre Notebook:

- Why did the dramatist write the play?
- What is the theme of the play?
- What is the genre (p. 164) and style (p. 174) of the play?
- What was daily life like during the time period of the play? What did people eat? What music did they listen to? What was their clothing like?
- What cultural, political, social, and scientific events were happening at the time?
- What was occurring in the rest of the world?
- What do pictures or paintings of people from that time and place reveal?

# Acting Styles

Theatrical style may be classified into two broad types, each reflecting a particular kind of relationship between the actors and the audience. In the **presentational style,** actors look at the audience and speak to them directly. They may share things with the audience that other characters aren't supposed to know (as the Stage Manager does in Thornton Wilder's *Our Town*). In the **representational style,** actors are supposed to be living real lives that the audience is observing. The actors don't acknowledge the presence of the audience. The representational style employs the concept of the **fourth wall,** an imaginary wall between the actors and the audience; through this "wall" the audience witnesses the action of the play.

The mugging of this masked actor in a scene from Geoff Hoyle's commedia dell'arte performance, *The Feast of Fools,* shows the physical comedy typical of farce.

Another defining characteristic of theatrical style is the degree of exaggeration employed by the actors. Today actors in most plays try to give the impression of complete realism. Earlier in theatre history (and in some productions today), actors exaggerated their vocal inflections, eye movements, facial expressions, and physical gestures. At its most extreme, this kind of acting resulted in a declamatory or oratorical style, with broad, conventional gestures and movements to represent emotions (such as anger and love) and actions (such as to threaten or search), and a vocal style designed not only to emphasize important words and ideas but to wring the emotional potential from a speech.

Yet another factor that impacts on theatrical style is genre (p. 164). Following are some of the principal theatrical genres, with their specific characteristics as they apply to acting styles.

## Farce

One of the most characteristic types of farce (p. 164) is the **commedia dell'arte,** a professional form of theatrical improvisation that developed in Italy in the 1500s. Commedia dell'arte farces are based on standard plot outlines, or **scenarios,** featuring established, or **stock,** comic characters such as elderly husbands and young wives, gullible masters and tricky servants, young lovers and overprotective fathers. Commedia performers are often masked and exhibit energetic, sometimes acrobatic, physical activity, which constitutes much of the humor in farce.

## EXERCISE Physical Comedy

In one classic physical comedy routine—memorably done by the Marx Brothers in their film *Duck Soup*—two actors pretend to be the mirror image of the other. Work in groups of three on this routine. Two of you can perform while the third observes and provides feedback on how well you succeed in creating the illusion of a mirror. Alternate until each of you has had a chance to perform and observe.

## Comedy of Manners

Balancing satire and flattery, the **comedy of manners** deals with the vices and follies of the upper class. Plots feature social competition of witty characters whose depth comes from intelligence, not emotion. Characters speak rapidly and with exaggerated vocal variety. Unlike the physical comedy of farce, the humor lies in the quick and witty exchange of dialogue. Characters in a comedy of manners are generally graceful and constrained in their movements, which largely consist of curtsies, bows, and so on. Hand and facial gestures are especially important, as is the use of the complex language of fans.

Oscar Wilde's comedy of manners, *The Importance of Being Earnest,* is an amusing look at courtship among the upper crust of 1890s England.

## Shakespearean Tragedy

Many of Shakespeare's plays are tragedies (p. 165). Tragic characters generally have more grace and majesty than comic characters. They move, think, and act more deliberately and slowly. Their pace and rhythm are steady and consistent. Tragic characters deal seriously with love, faith, virtue, ambition, mortality, and other basic human issues.

The most salient feature of Shakespeare's writing is its rich complexity. To perform his plays, you must thoroughly understand what the characters are saying. Study the footnotes. Research unfamiliar words or phrases. To better grasp the meaning of particular speeches, paraphrase them in modern English. Don't be intimidated by the unrhymed verse characteristic of Shakespeare's dialogue. Particularly at first, read it as though it were prose, without pausing at the end of a line unless directed to by punctuation. Even later, when you introduce his poetic rhythms into your delivery, avoid doing so in a heavy-handed way.

*Othello* is one of Shakespeare's great tragedies of ill-fated love. It revolves around issues of virtue, faith, ambition, betrayal, and jealousy.

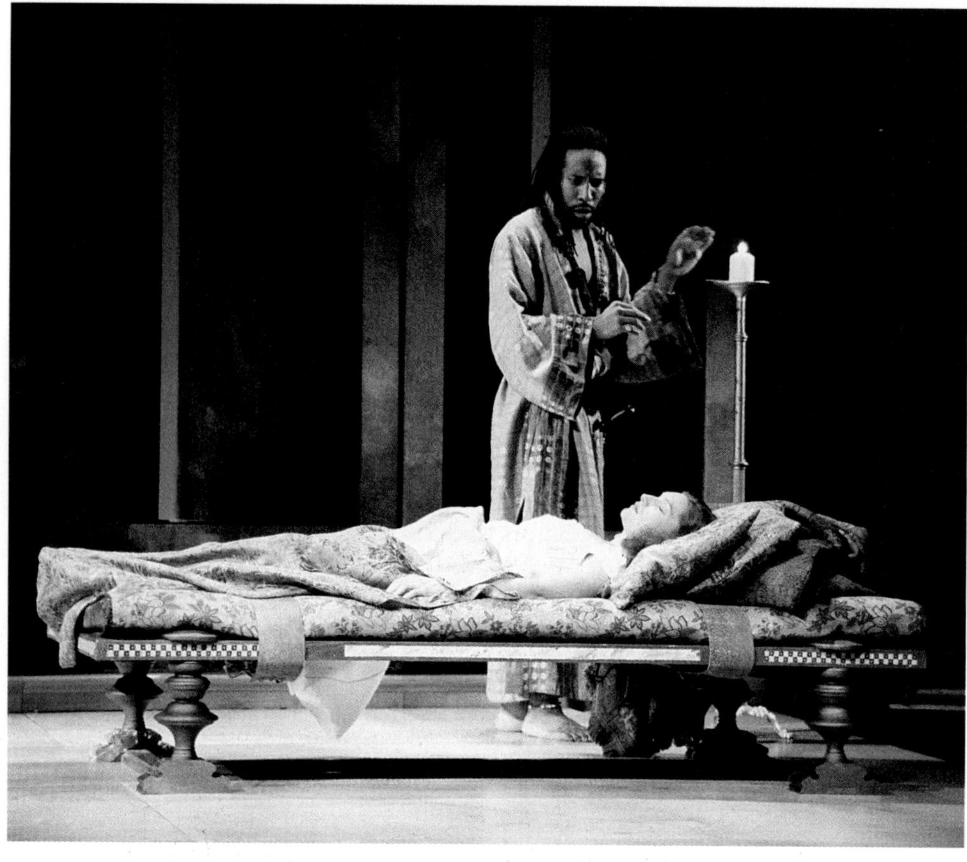

### EXERCISE Paraphrasing Shakespeare

Paraphrase this famous speech by the character Macbeth from Shakespeare's play of the same name:

> Tomorrow, and tomorrow, and tomorrow
> Creeps in this petty pace from day to day
> To the last syllable of recorded time,
> And all our yesterdays have lighted fools
> The way to dusty death. Out, out brief candle!
> Life's but a walking shadow, a poor player
> That struts and frets his hour upon the stage
> And then is heard no more. It is a tale
> Told by an idiot, full of sound and fury,
> Signifying nothing.

Now read the lines again and discuss how paraphrasing enhanced your understanding of the meaning of the words.

## Realistic Drama

During most of the 1800s, the Romantic movement influenced drama, poetry, painting, music, and the other arts. **Romanticism** in drama emphasized heroism and sentiment, extraordinary characters and melodramatic plots. Actors used large, overly dramatic, and symbolic gestures and postures. In the second half of the century, a counter movement, known as **realism,** began to develop. Romantic dramatists had depicted the remote and exotic; in contrast, realists sought to create the appearance of ordinary reality in theatrical works. In the extreme, naturalistic form of this style, props and sets are very detailed and elaborate in an attempt to actually re-create the environment of the play. Actors attempt to become their characters. Barely modified physical contact between characters may be used for stage fights or love scenes. Most directors and playwrights, however, choose a more representational version of realism. Since a play is performed on a stage in front of an audience, it's difficult to present every minute detail of real life. Set designers, therefore, try to convey an illusion or impression of the environment of the play. Actors are aware they are performing. They may use their own thoughts and experiences to evoke emotions and carry out the actions of their characters onstage.

Many of Tennessee Williams's plays, such as *Cat on a Hot Tin Roof*, portray the American South of the 1930s–1960s. Actors often speak with regional accents, and the sets are dressed to accurately represent that culture.

### EXERCISE Romance and Realism

Work with a partner to improvise two scenes, both based on the same situation with the same basic characters. Do one scene in a Romantic acting style and the other in a realistic style. Present the Romantic style seriously; if not, it might become farce. Discuss the effect of the different styles with your audience. Why do you think most plays use realism?

# The Rehearsal Process

School productions usually rehearse for six to eight weeks—and longer for musicals. (The four-week rehearsal period typical of professional companies is possible because the actors can spend an entire work day rehearsing.) Progress depends on all cast members carrying out their responsibilities on time and with their best effort. The production schedule (which includes rehearsals) is typically put together by the director and given to cast and crews.

## Rehearsal Etiquette

Time allotted for rehearsals is precious and should not be wasted in waiting for someone to arrive or in settling petty disputes caused by rude behavior. By following the guidelines below, you can help ensure that time is used wisely and that everyone involved is treated with respect.

- Be on time.
- Clear any potential schedule conflicts with the director at the beginning of the rehearsal process so that adjustments can be made to the schedule.
- Make sure your parents or guardians know your rehearsal schedule. Let them know when there might be a late night.
- If you have a question about whether or not you are required at a certain rehearsal, ask!
- Work outside of rehearsal, researching, analyzing, and developing your character. Memorize your lines on time. Come prepared for your scenes.
- Take the initiative to find rehearsal props and clothing that will prepare you for moving around in your costume.
- Be an attentive audience member while others are performing.
- Be courteous, responsible, and pleasant.

## EXERCISE Rehearsal Etiquette

With other students, discuss and compare rehearsal etiquette with the standards or rules of other classes, sports activities, musical ensembles, or similar group activities. How does each violation of etiquette affect individuals and the rehearsal as a whole? Discuss how you think directors, actors, and tech crews should deal with breaches of etiquette. Formalize these suggestions if you like as a policy or list of suggestions for rehearsal troubleshooting.

## Read-Through

Some directors prefer to begin rehearsals by doing improvisations. Others begin by going over the background of the play and their vision for this production. Many directors begin the rehearsal process with a formal **read-through** in which the entire cast sits down together and reads aloud their parts from the beginning to the end of the play. During the read-through, listen closely to everyone's lines and contemplate your overall impression of the play with the various voices and interpretations of others. How does it differ from your personal first-time reading of the play?

## Marking a Script

Your initial impressions will change as rehearsals progress and you deepen your understanding of the script, your character, the play, and its background. To prepare for rehearsals, you should clearly mark your script, indicating all of your lines. If your script is one you have purchased, the best method is to use a highlighter; with a rented script, use only pencil. For the highlighter method, use two different colored highlighters. Use one color to indicate your speaking lines by marking your character's name. Use the second to mark your cue lines. A **cue line** is the final line of another character's speech that signals the time for your character's next speech.

If you were to mark your script for your role as Holmes in the first scene of *The Final Problem,* it might look like this:

*(The room has one table and three chairs. There is a window in the center of one wall. It has interior shutters. Watson is reading at the table, on which sits a lit reading lamp. Holmes enters without knocking. He looks pale and nervous. Watson looks at him in surprise and then concern.)*

**HOLMES.** Yes, I have been using myself up rather too freely. I have been a little pressed of late. Have you any objection to my closing your shutters? *(He edges his way around the wall, and, slamming the shutters together, he bolts them decisively.)*

**WATSON.** You are afraid of something?

**HOLMES.** Well, I am.

**WATSON.** Of what?

**HOLMES.** Of air guns.

## Taking Direction

Developing a positive working relationship with your director can make your experience in the show much more rewarding. Good communication and a positive attitude will help immensely. Bring a pencil and your script to every rehearsal. Take notes while the director is talking about the play. If you are not clear about what the director wants or what a particular comment means, ask for clarification as soon as you can. If you have a problem or complaint, speak privately with the director before or after rehearsal. Check with the director before making any changes (like a haircut) to your personal appearance. Remember to be patient; a director has many responsibilities, and sometimes you may have to wait.

Don't give direction to other actors. It's not your job. If you have a suggestion, discuss it privately with the director.

One of the most rewarding aspects of acting is exploration and expansion of your capabilities, so don't be afraid to make a mistake, look foolish, or try something totally new.

### Director's Terminology

Like other disciplines, theatre is filled with jargon and terminology. Understanding what a director is saying to you is vital, so you should learn the meaning of some of the common director's terms and turns-of-phrase, such as these below, and note them in your Theatre Notebook.

| If the Director says . . . | It means . . . |
|---|---|
| • You are topping the line. | You are delivering a line with more volume than the actor delivering the cue line. |
| • Pick up your cues. | Take less time to speak a line after being given a cue line. |
| • You are dropping lines. | You are losing projection at the ends of sentences or speeches. |
| • Open up. | Turn more toward the audience. |
| • You are stepping on laughs. | You are not allowing enough time for audience laughter to subside before delivering lines. |

## Blocking Rehearsals

One of the first tasks of rehearsals is to block the play (p. 182). The director has usually done preliminary blocking, but it's during **blocking rehearsals** that these plans are physically worked out onstage. Note in your scripts all blocking and direction that affects you. In addition to the abbreviations for the stage areas (p. 62), you can use blocking symbols (p. 183) to write blocking notes.

Blocking notes for Sherlock Holmes's movements in the selection from *The Final Problem* might look like this:

*(The room has one table and three chairs. There is a window in the center of one wall. It has interior shutters. Watson is reading at the table, on which sits a lit reading lamp. Holmes enters without knocking. He looks pale and nervous. Watson looks at him in surprise and then concern.)*

← *Ent RC through door, X UR, stay along wall*

**Holmes.** Yes, I have been using myself up rather too freely. I have been a little pressed of late. Have you any objection to my closing your shutters? *(He edges his way around the wall, and, slamming the shutters together, he bolts them decisively.)*

← *edge 2 window UC, close shutters, circle 2 LC, stand left of table*

**Watson.** You are afraid of something?

**Holmes.** Well, I am.

**Watson.** Of what?

**Holmes.** Of air guns.

## Crowd Scenes

When you are in a scene with many people, there are certain actions you can do to make the scene more believable and to help maintain the focus (p. 144). Listen and react to what the main characters are saying, especially to specific words or sentences that affect you. If your reaction is talking to your neighbor, make sure what you say relates to the action.

If you are part of a crowd in the background and not involved in the major action, pantomime your conversations. Don't upstage characters who have focus by making big gestures or attracting too much attention in any other way.

As a crowd member, you may not have a character name; make one up. Create a background for yourself. Determine why you are in the crowd and what you want. Decide how you feel about the other characters in the scene, especially the main characters. Remain involved in the scene by listening and reacting as your character.

### EXERCISE In the Crowd

In small groups, improvise a two-minute scene with one or two major characters who engage in conversation while a small crowd listens and discusses among themselves in the background. Follow the guidelines to maintain the focus of the scene. Be sure to establish the topic of your crowd's discussion, which should relate to the situation. Have an audience critique your success.

## Memorization

Most directors prefer that you do not begin rehearsals with your lines already memorized. The concern is that you may develop a pattern or rhythm that differs from the director's idea or you may sound emotionally flat because you learned your lines in a block without fully understanding their meaning. Therefore, typically during the first two weeks of rehearsals, actors rehearse **on book;** that is, they read their lines from the script. During this period you will be memorizing your lines. Only after you have memorized your lines, and can go **off book,** or rehearse without a script, will you be able to speak and move with sufficient freedom to fully realize your character.

Once the rehearsal process is underway, there will be memorization deadlines. This means you almost never have to memorize all your lines at once, but in increments as the rehearsal schedule dictates.

### Memorization Techniques

Actors usually develop a unique memorization method for themselves. You might try to memorize your lines and blocking movements together. It often helps to have someone read lines opposite you. Another strategy is to tape-record your cues and lines and then listen and practice with the tape.

Using an offstage reader is an especially useful technique that will help you memorize your lines with your blocking. From offstage, have another actor (or the stage manager) read each line of your dialogue. You then repeat it, while doing your blocking onstage for that line. You may ask the offstage reader to combine some lines and break up longer patches of dialogue and monologues into beats to make this process faster and smoother.

## Rehearsal Spaces

Many theatres have rehearsal spaces where actors and directors work out preliminary blocking and character development before moving into the performance space. The stage manager or assistant director may tape the outline of the ground plan or significant spots on the ground plan onto the floor in this rehearsal space. This is known as **spiking** the set; the tape marks are called **spikes.** The spike tape is usually white or glow-in-the-dark so actors can see it even under dim lighting. Set pieces similar to those that will be used in the play are often arranged into a makeshift set so actors can get used to working around real furniture.

At some point, actors move onto the actual set. There, scenes are played again and again until the words of the script become fully fleshed-out theatre in action.

The director and actors for *Goodbye Stranger* by Carrie Luft work out blocking in a designated rehearsal space.

The director and the director's staff set up office in the auditorium, with promptbooks and recording equipment.

Although actors may be off book, they continue to refer to the script throughout the rehearsal process, often in consultation with the director, who knows the script inside and out.

## Working Rehearsals

After memorizing your lines, a second phase of rehearsals and character-building begins. Throughout this stage, you should continue to employ the script-analysis techniques mentioned earlier (p. 273) as well as the guidelines for creating specific characters (pp. 136–139). In **working rehearsals** you will be working through every scene to develop motivation for the blocking that has been established, to increase your insight into your character's behavior and relationships, and to pinpoint your character's objectives, all of which are vital to internal character development. It will be helpful to review motivation (p. 134) and subtext (pp. 138–139 and p. 227).

External factors will also contribute to building your character. Externals are tangible objects or sensory stimuli that affect your characterization from the outside in. They may affect how you move, how you carry yourself, and how you physically react to other characters and your environment. This, in turn, may affect some of your character decisions, may create new obstacles, or may become part of your character's plan to overcome obstacles.

### Costumes

Costumes can have a significant affect on an actor's movement; for example, for women unaccustomed to wearing long skirts or men unaccustomed to formal wear. Unusual clothing items, such as capes, bustles, or hats, may influence your posture and gestures. Shoes, too, have a big impact on how you move onstage. Practice rehearsing while wearing clothing as similar to your costume as possible. You may make some different choices for your character.

Molière's plays, such as *The Miser,* require actors to wear period costumes: women wear layers of bustling fabric and men may wear high-heeled shoes and ruffles. Elaborate wigs are common in these plays as well—for both men and women.

### Makeup

Think about your makeup early in the rehearsal process. You may be able to utilize your makeup to create a defining gesture, such as a man who fools with his mustache when he lies or a woman who bats her very long eyelashes when she's flirting. Like costumes, some makeup may require getting used to, especially wigs and facial hair pieces.

## Stage Business

Some of your time onstage may be occupied by **stage business,** specific movements, often employing props, costumes, and makeup, that strengthen the personality of the character. Inventing ways for your character to use stage business can contribute new dimensions to your character. For instance, a man who normally carries an umbrella may use it as a sword if provoked into a fight. Work on your stage business in rehearsals and make each piece of business as creative as possible. Allow your business to become an extension of your own body to express your character's personality.

### EXERCISE Prop Business

Experiment with communicating personality with a prop from your theatre stock or an item in your classroom. Practice expressing different emotions or character traits by, for instance, bowing with a fan, walking with a cane, tipping your hat, fiddling with a ring, opening a letter, or using a handkerchief. Work with another actor to express characters through stage business. Then, do a brief improvisation involving both your characters using the stage business you have developed.

### EXERCISE Stage Business in Situations

As a class write a variety of people on one set of cards (for example, "nurse"), a variety of attributes on another set of cards (for example, "shy"), and a variety of situations on a third set of cards (for example, "you just won the lottery"). With a partner, draw one card from each pile. Create stage business for your chosen character in your chosen situation that expresses your chosen attribute for that character. Improvise a solo scene based on your choices. Have your partner critique your scene. Then do the same for your partner.

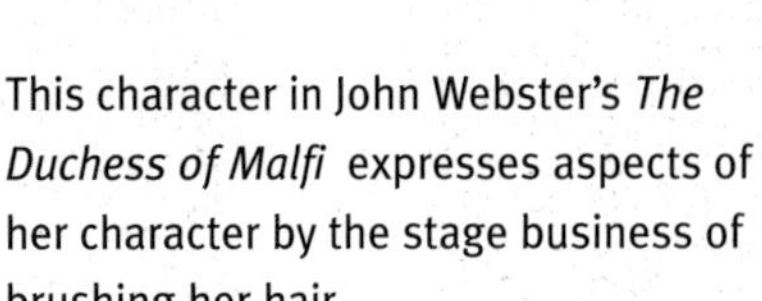

This character in John Webster's *The Duchess of Malfi* expresses aspects of her character by the stage business of brushing her hair.

## Polishing Rehearsals

Dress rehearsals are necessary to ensure that everything is running perfectly. What could go wrong in this scene from the farce *An Italian Straw Hat* by Eugène Labiche that a dress rehearsal might correct?

During the last few weeks of rehearsals, the actors have polished their movements on stage, delivery of lines, and interpretations of their characters. Up to this point, the director has stopped scenes when necessary and corrected blocking and line delivery. Now, unless there are major problems, these **polishing rehearsals** proceed without interruption. This is also the period during which technical elements of the production (scenery, props, lighting, sound, costumes, and makeup) are integrated.

## Dress Rehearsals

The **dress rehearsal** occurs a day or two before the scheduled opening night performance. Complete with all technical elements, the play will be run from beginning to end. It's just like opening night but without the audience. You should try to make your performance as polished and prepared as possible while dealing with the stress and chaos around you. Dress rehearsals are for the express purpose of finding out where any remaining weaknesses are and then taking measures to correct them.

# The Performance

Finally, it's opening night. Most actors feel nervous as well as excited. The key is to stay focused on preparing for the performance. Warm up as usual to prepare your body and your voice. Before the audience arrives, you might walk across the set in character. You will probably have a rush of adrenaline—use it to give you energy.



## Backstage

Arrive early to warm up, get into your costume and apply your makeup, and make sure your props are in place and your costume pieces are ready for any costume changes. Use the time to move emotionally from the "real world" to the world of the play.

Before and during the performance don't interfere with the work of the backstage crews; they may be moving large set pieces or furniture around and need space. They also need to be able to communicate with each other about technical cues.

Once the performance is underway, keep dressing rooms quiet. Stereos, visitors, and loud voices are unnecessary distractions. You need this time to concentrate. While waiting in the wings, pay attention to what is happening onstage so that you won't miss your entrance cues. The stage manager is prepared to answer any questions about cues and is the person you should approach for any emergencies.

Don't interact with the audience before or during the show unless it's part of the script or the director's concept. Your challenge during the show is to create the illusion of someone other than yourself; don't destroy that illusion before the show even begins.

After each performance, make sure you hang up your costumes, put away all your props, and tidy up your makeup area.

### Performance Checklist

Create a personal performance checklist to avoid becoming complacent as you become more comfortable with the show. The reminders you include can be both general ("Don't swallow ends of sentences—ever!" or "Keep up energy level after intermission") and specific ("Most important scene in show—act II, scene i" or "Don't forget props—watch in pocket, act I, scene iii"). You might want to attach your performance checklist to your script and post a copy of it in your dressing room next to your makeup area.

## Onstage

Really listen to other characters onstage—and respond with motivated words and actions.

Be careful not to change the speed of your performance by slowing down or rushing. Remember that your job is to tell the story of the play. If something goes wrong onstage, fix it while staying focused and in character. If you need to improvise, do so. Finally, don't despair; even if you make a mistake, the show will go on.

Acting means constant performance, constant work. Onstage, perform your character in each moment of the play. Say each line as if you were saying it for the first time. Before making an entrance, imagine where you are coming from, what you were just doing, who you were just speaking with, and why you entered.

The actors in Marivaux's *Changes of Heart* take their final bows.

## Curtain Call

This is the opportunity for the entire company to be recognized for the work they have done. The director will stage and rehearse the curtain call at one of the final dress rehearsals. Actors should take their bows quickly, gracefully, and with a smile. Generally, actors do not applaud onstage unless the production is a musical and the conductor is introduced.

It takes many people to create a finished performance. Actors get their thank-yous from the audience. Share the appreciation with the whole cast. Thank your director and crew members either in person or in writing.

# Activities

### *Working with the Script*

**CHARACTER BIOGRAPHY** Choose a one-act play featuring a character that interests you. Beginning with the information provided by your analysis of the script, create a brief biography for this character. When you have exhausted the script, you may invent facts about the character that are not specifically given by the playwright in order to complete your biography. Your invented details, however, should be consistent with the character as developed by the playwright. Include this character biography in your Theatre Notebook.

### *Working with the Script*

**RESEARCHING BACKGROUND** Select a period of history that interests you. With help from your teacher or a librarian, choose a play depicting that period. When you have selected a play, research the playwright, critical commentary, and the performance history. You might include this research in your Theatre Notebook.

### *Acting Styles*

**FORMAL SITUATIONS** Observe the movements and actions of people who work in formal situations, such as school administrators, clergy, diplomats, royalty, and military, political, or social leaders. Watch for repeated postures and gestures. Listen to how they speak and observe their facial expressions. Make notes or draw sketches of your observations. Apply some of these external characteristics to a character in a comedy of manners or a different play with a formal character. Perform a scene as that character for your class.

### *Acting Styles*

**TRAGIC HERO/HEROINE** Learn a monologue of a tragic hero or heroine from a Shakespearean play. Be sure that you thoroughly grasp the meaning of the lines before you begin working on your delivery of the verse. Use clues provided in the script to realize your character physically. Present your monologue to a partner who can offer you constructive feedback.

***The Rehearsal Process***

**INCORPORATING STAGE BUSINESS** Read a play and determine how you might incorporate stage business for a character. Try out your stage business and see how it works. Present a short scene in which you demonstrate stage business for your character.

***The Rehearsal Process***

**WHAT-IF CHARACTER BUILDING** To work on building your character outside of rehearsals, imagine how your character would behave in a variety of hypothetical situations. For example, what if your character were going on a blind date or delivering a political speech—how would your character act? Choose a character from a play and analyze that character. Then ask yourself a variety of "what-if" questions. Act out the reactions you imagine for your character. You might explain in your Theatre Notebook how this activity helped you understand the character.

***The Rehearsal Process***

**HOT SEAT** Read a play and analyze your character, as well as the background of the play. Ask members of your class, or a small group, to fire questions at you regarding your character. You must answer each question from your "hot seat" in character. These questions can range from concrete ("What is your favorite food?") to more conceptual and introspective ("What do you think life is all about?"). You should be familiar enough with the script and your character to improvise answers; some of your answers will come directly from the script; for others, you will need your

***The Performance***

**GROUP WARM-UPS** A useful energy-builder for a performance is a group warm-up. Research group warm-up exercises and, particularly, preperformance exercises. Collect the best—those that will get the creative spirit flowing. You might interview actors or directors to tap into favorite group exercises they have done on performance night. Try them in class and discuss their effectiveness. Then revise your collection and prepare a file, together with necessary illustrations, to have onhand for your school performances.

## Historical Profile

# Kabuki

There are three main traditional types of theatre in Japan. **Noh** (nō) is serious and abstract, with most of the actors wearing stylized character masks. **Bunraku** (bu̇n rä´kü) is a puppet theatre, with puppets so large that it takes three supposedly invisible operators to move each one. **Kabuki** (kə bü´kē) is a popular theatre form that in some ways resembles the American musical. Noh, Bunraku, and Kabuki share many elements of costume, music, dance, and set design; the differences are largely matters of degree. In fact, plays written for one of these theatrical forms are often borrowed and adapted by one or both of the other forms.

Kabuki theatre came into existence around 1600 when a female dancer named Okuni (ô kü nē) created performances combining traditional Buddhist dances with more popular contemporary forms. Soon theatre troupes had formed to imitate these new dances. In the mid-1600s, when women of the Japanese theatre were officially barred from the stage because of their supposed immorality, male actors took all the roles, beginning the Kabuki tradition of female impersonation. This and other conventions of Kabuki drama and stagecraft have remained largely unchanged to the present. Many of the plays that are performed in modern Kabuki theatre have been around for hundreds of years.

## The Theatre Space

The Kabuki stage is a raised wooden platform at one end of an auditorium. Rectangular wooden sections may be laid on top of the stage to amplify the sound of the foot-stomping that is so much a part of Kabuki dance. One of the most characteristic features is the **hanamichi** (ho no mē chē), or "flower path"—a raised passageway that extends from downstage right through the audience to a curtained doorway in the back of the auditorium. It's used for spectacular entrances and exits and as a kind of secondary stage. Often an actor using the hanamichi will pause at a point one-third of the total distance from the stage to pose, speak, or dance.

Curtains are used, but not in the conventional Western sense, to signal beginnings and endings of scenes. Entrances and exits that do not involve the hanamichi are made through a curtained doorway at stage right. The curtain is patterned in broad vertical stripes of orange, green, and black, and is drawn from the side rather than raised and lowered. Another kind of curtain in pale blue may be suspended over the stage and, at some point, is released from above to reveal a new and impressive scene behind this curtain. Stage sets may be elaborate, relatively realistic, and changed several times during a show.

Generally a chorus (p. 67) sits on an angled platform at the right of the stage, and an orchestra sits on a platform at the rear of the stage. Depending upon the nature of the play there may be variety to this arrangement. The chorus of 12 to 18 singers takes over narration and even dialogue at points of heightened emotion. Chorus members all dress alike and have large fans that they use while singing. The musicians, dressed like the chorus, play a three-stringed instrument called a **samisen** (sam′i sen), drums, and flute. In addition, two wooden blocks are struck together or against the stage floor to accentuate entrances, exits, pantomime fights, or certain poses struck by the actors.

## Costumes and Makeup

The basic costume is the **kimono** (kə mō′nō), a floor-length robe with long, flowing sleeves. Kimonos are worn by both male and female characters. They may be of brilliant colors and luxurious fabrics with elaborate embroidery. A male character might instead wear a vest or a hip-length robe with trousers cut very full and so long that they fold under the feet and trail four to six feet behind. All characters may carry

Kabuki costumes can weigh as much as 50 pounds; stage attendants assist the actors in keeping them properly arranged onstage.

folding fans, which are used for a variety of conventional, sometimes symbolic, gestures.

Makeup is not realistic; the face is painted white with bold lines, principally red or blue. The designs and the colors have symbolic meaning: for example, red lines represent virtue or strength and blue represents evil (see the actor on p. 296). Wigs, usually black, may be elaborately dressed into a tremendous variety of styles, according to a character's age, sex, and social class.

## Acting Styles

Kabuki is a highly stylized form of storytelling in which the audience is always completely aware that they are in a theatre watching a play. All the visual elements—costumes, makeup, settings, patterns of movement, and vocal delivery—contribute to this awareness. In addition, the actors frequently address the audience directly in presentational style, sometimes even drawing attention to the fact that they are actors. Both male and female roles are traditionally played by men. Actors tend to specialize, not only as males or females, but as certain types—such as comic characters or villains. Speeches are always delivered in a markedly rhythmic fashion timed to musical accompaniment. A single speech might be shared by a number of actors speaking in turn. Speeches may be taken up by the chorus to allow the actor to dance or to engage in elaborate pantomime. Movement is also stylized. An entrance or exit might be made in a series of athletic leaps. Fights or violent actions are shown not in physical contact but in symbolic movements that might even be done in slow motion.

There are no set props or hand props onstage at the beginning of a play; these are brought in and placed for the actor or handed to the actor as needed. The people who do this are a stage manager and stage assistants, who are dressed completely in black with black netting over their faces. They are thus considered to be "invisible," a theatrical convention readily accepted by the experienced audience.

## Try It Out

It will be difficult for you to imitate Kabuki theatre without actually having seen it, but you can incorporate some Kabuki elements into the following scene from a Kabuki comedy written in 1910. Lengthy stage directions by the English adaptors attempt to suggest something of the acting style and stage conventions that were a part of the Japanese original. You can use a chorus or a single narrator to recite the chorus's lines.

from

# The Zen Substitute

*by* **Okamuka Shiko**

Lord Ukyo (ůk yō), wanting to slip away for the evening to see his girlfriend Hanako (ho no kō) has told his wife, Lady Tamanoi (to mo nō ē), a rather desperate lie. Because he's been having nightmares, he says he needs to spend the night in meditation, as prescribed by Zen, a sect of Buddhism that stresses silent and solitary contemplation. His wife gives her grudging consent. Lord Ukyo absolutely forbids her to disturb him while he's meditating, but knowing that she will check up on him, he plans a little deception: his servant Tarokaja (to rō ko jo) will cover for him.

**LORD UKYO.** *(lets out a boisterous laugh)* Ho ho! I fooled her, I fooled her, didn't I. She's clever that one, but after all only a woman! Ha ha! Now where's that Taro.[1] *(With a flourish of trouser ends[2] he turns and calls off right.)* Heh, Taro! Tarooooooooooo! *(Without waiting for any response, and bubbling with good spirits, he swiftly strides stage left.)*

**TAROKAJA.** *(skittering on in a great rush)* Yes, my Lord.

**LORD UKYO.** *(in midstride)*. It's you, Taro?

**TAROKAJA.** Yes, my Lord.

**LORD UKYO.** You're here?

**TAROKAJA.** Yes, sir.

**LORD UKYO.** You're really here.

**TAROKAJA.** *(with a little bow.)* Before you, sir.

**LORD UKYO.** Well what do you know. *(Turns to him with face beaming.)* You're fast today, Taro.

1. Though a lord, Ukyo is a comic character. He's thoroughly dominated by his wife, but he enjoys dominating his servant. How might you hint at both sides of his nature in this brief scene?
2. See the costume description on page 297.

3. Conventional stage blocking doesn't apply here. The men should probably play their scene down center without moving about much.

4. **shrew** bad-tempered wife

5. **zazen** (zä zen) literally, "sitting zen," meaning Zen contemplation while seated

6. How might Tarokaja deliver this line?

7. **Nirvana** (nir vä´nə) in Buddhism, the ultimate desired state of being, sometimes described as the absence of all desire, the state of nothingness

8. What might Tarokaja's hesitation suggest?

9. This dance-pantomime is meant to be very funny, a comic *tour de force* for the actor playing Tarokaja. How might Tarokaja express the chorus's ideas and images in gesture and action?

10. If you're using music to accompany the chorus's singing or chanting, how might the nature of the music change for this part?

**TAROKAJA.** And you, my Lord, seem happy today.

**LORD UKYO.** With good reason, Taro. With good reason. Ho ho! What do you think. *(Moves in close to* TAROKAJA. *Confidentially.)*[3] I got the night off! The whole night, and I'm going to see Hanako!

**TAROKAJA.** Oh, that's wonderful, sir! *(He begins to laugh, then quickly catches himself.)* How did you manage that, sir?

**LORD UKYO.** Well, you know the dear shrew.[4] (TAROKAJA *nods.)* She'd never just give me the night off. So I gave her this cock-and-bull story about nightmares and how I had to do *zazen* [5] all night to cleanse my soul.

**TAROKAJA.** Ohh, that was clever, sir! [6]

**LORD UKYO.** Yes, wasn't it! I thought so, too. Now, Taro, there's just one thing I want you to do for me.

**TAROKAJA.** *(bows respectfully)*. Yes, my Lord.

**LORD UKYO.** I forbade her, absolutely, to come meddling around while I'm in Nirvana.[7] But you know the kind of old busybody she is. *(One conspirator to another.)* Sure enough, in the middle of the night, she'll come sneaking through the bushes to spy on me. And if she doesn't see someone in meditation she'll be fit to be tied. Now I know it may be a bit uncomfortable, Taro, but it's only till morning. How about you taking my place and being religious tonight?

**TAROKAJA.** *(swallows hard and bows very respectfully)*. Of course, anything for my Lord. But please sir, not this.

**LORD UKYO.** Ehhh? *(Commandingly.)* What's this?

**TAROKAJA.** Sir! It's your wife's . . . terrible temper.[8]

*(Music.* TAROKAJA *bows low to* LORD UKYO, *then moves down stage and faces the audience. As the* CHORUS *sings, he mimics* LADY TAMANOI *in dance-pantomime.*[9] *His movements are half-feminine, half-loutish. Off-stage drums punctuate the samisen melody).*[10]

**FULL CHORUS.** The dear thing loves you so,

When you're at home

Her face is wreathed in smiles.

*(Kneeling before an imaginary mirror,* TAROKAJA *coyly adjusts the hang of his kimono. He pats powder on his beaming face.)*

Her chubby cheeks glow

And burst with joy

Like eternally smiling Otafuku.

*(Rising,* TAROKAJA *puffs out his cheeks, mocking the looks of Otafuku* (o to fü kü), *the overweight Goddess of Happiness. Angry and amused at the same time,* LORD UKYO *reprimands* TAROKAJA *by tapping him smartly on the forehead with his fan.* TAROKAJA *is undaunted, but he at least makes an attempt to hide his mirth, as he turns away and continues his dance.)*

But when she's angry,

She's a raving demon.

And when she hates

She's a witch!

A fiend!

A devil!

Like a gargoyle perched on a rain spout![11]

If she ever finds out

About a trick like this!

This Taro's as good as dead!

(TAROKAJA *cowers, then beats himself wildly on the head with both hands. Finally he sinks in a heap to the floor as if dead. His act finished, he bows.)*

So excuse me just this once, he said.

He begged.

He bowed.

He implored.

**LORD UKYO.** *(He has had enough nonsense. He tucks the fan under the collar of his kimono and steps forward threateningly).*

So! You're afraid of her but not of me! Eh Taro? That mistake will cost you your head!

*(He rears back, stamps, and grasps the hilt of his sword. Legs wide apart, arms akimbo, he poses for a moment without moving.)*

**TAROKAJA.** *(throws up his hands to ward off the blow).*

No, no, no, my Lord! Wait!

*(There is good reason for* TAROKAJA *to be afraid, for in feudal Japan it was a Samurai's*[12] *prerogative to kill on the spot any commoner who opposed his will.)*

I was wrong. My Lordship is the frightening one. I shall do whatever you say.

11. What different movements or positions might Tarokaja use to demonstrate a demon, witch, fiend, devil, and gargoyle?

12. **Samurai** (sam´ü rī) a member of the warrior aristocracy

*(He bows low, but almost immediately pops up again, as he realizes he is presenting an inviting target for his master's sword.)*

**LORD UKYO.** *(without moving).* You're sure of that, Taro?

**TAROKAJA.** Yes, my Lord!

**LORD UKYO.** Truthfully?

**TAROKAJA.** Yes, yes, my Lord.

**LORD UKYO.** *(turns his head slightly to hide a smile he can't completely suppress).* Positively?

**TAROKAJA.** *(frantic, he bows again and again).* Yes sir! Yes sir!

**LORD UKYO.** *(with a hearty laugh he drops his pose and crosses center).* Then I won't kill you today. It was only a joke, Taro.

**TAROKAJA.** It was a bad joke, sir.

**LORD UKYO.** Sometimes you need a good frightening. Now here. Sit.

*(A* STAGE ASSISTANT *has brought a black lacquered cask about two feet high to just left of center stage.* LORD UKYO *motions for* TAROKAJA *to sit, and* TAROKAJA *does so.*[13] *The* STAGE ASSISTANT *hands* LORD UKYO *a folded silk robe.)* On with the robe. *(*LORD UKYO *and the* STAGE ASSISTANT *drape the robe of golden silk over* TAROKAJA'S *head. The* STAGE ASSISTANT *kneels behind the cask, where he remains unobtrusively throughout most of the remainder of the play.)*

13. As a matter of convention, the stage assistant is absolutely expressionless, and neither actor acknowledges his presence in any way.

**CHORUS LEADER.** A brilliant colored robe,

Hides the seated form.

*(*LORD UKYO *circles* TAROKAJA. *He examines the robe from all angles, carefully adjusting a fold here, a drape there. He returns center stage, and stands back a few paces, the better to survey his handiwork.)*[14]

14. How might Lord Ukyo wring some comedy out of this arrangement of the exact drape of the robe?

**LORD UKYO.** Perfect. From the front, the side, the back, you'd never know it wasn't me.

**TAROKAJA.** *(he pops his head out).* I think Zen meditation is just a fancy way of saying torture, my Lord. I can tell it already.

**LORD UKYO.** Be brave! It's only one night. *(Glances fearfully off in the direction of his wife, then tiptoes up to* TAROKAJA. *Confidentially.)* Remember. If she shows up keep the robe on and you'll be all right.

**TAROKAJA.** Yes sir.

**LORD UKYO.** And whatever you do, God help you, don't open your mouth.

**TAROKAJA.** Yes sir.

**LORD UKYO.** *(glowing with anticipation).* Well then. I'm off.

**TAROKAJA.** Hurry back, sir. Please, sir!

**"Perfect.**

From the **front,**

the **side,**

the **back,**

you'd never know

it wasn't

**me."**

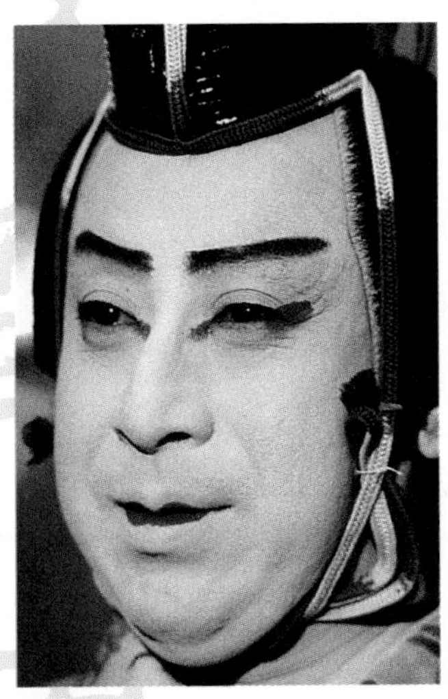

**LORD UKYO.** Goodbye! *(He turns and starts to go off.)*

**TAROKAJA.** Goodbye!

**LORD UKYO.** Goodbye!

**TAROKAJA.** Goodbye!

**BOTH.** *(their alternate goodbyes rhythmically increase in speed until they are speaking as rapidly as possible and finally in unison).* Goodbye, goodbye, goodbye, goodbye, goodbye, goodbye, goodbye!

15. See the explanation of hanamichi on page 297.

16. **Kobai** (kō bo ē)

17. How might Lord Ukyo handle this doubletake?

18. This on-again, off-again business with the robe can be funny as well, particularly if Lord Ukyo exactly repeats a bit of stage business.

19. If these goodbyes are carefully rehearsed so that they are exactly the same as before, they will be funnier.

20. The sighing lover has always been the stuff of comedy, particularly when he is otherwise a strong or powerful person. How might you show the contrast between the domineering lord and the love-sick boyfriend?

21. How should the nature of this music differ from what has been used before?

**TAROKAJA.** Just a moment, sir! *(LORD UKYO stops downstage right, before the hanamichi.*[15] *TAROKAJA rises and crosses to his master. The robe falls to his shoulders.)* Excuse me, sir, I know it's a bother, but . . . when you get to Lady Hanako's, would you please say hello to her for me? To Kobai,[16] her maid?

**LORD UKYO.** Hehhh? You mean you and Kobai? While I was . . . *(TAROKAJA nods happily. LORD UKYO bursts out in delighted laughter.)* Ha ha ha!

**TAROKAJA.** *(rhythmically repeating the laughter).* Ha ha ha!

**LORD UKYO.** *(pokes TAROKAJA playfully in the chest with his closed fan).* Ho ho ho!

**TAROKAJA.** Then you will say hello for me, sir?

**LORD UKYO.** Of course, I . . . *(Suddenly catches himself.)*[17] Here now, what kind of Zen meditation is this? Are you trying to walk to Nirvana? *(He stamps his foot in mock anger and shoos TAROKAJA back to the cask.)* Sit, sit, sit, sit! And meditate! *(He carefully scrutinizes the covered form as the STAGE ASSISTANT adjusts the folds of the robe on all sides.)*[18] Now, not a word. I'm off.

**TAROKAJA.** *(peeping out sadly).* I'll be waiting, sir. Hurry back, please.

**LORD UKYO.** *(happy as a lark, he moves right toward the hanamichi).* Goodbye.

**TAROKAJA.** Goodbye.

**LORD UKYO.** Goodbye.

**BOTH.** *(same rhythmic speaking as before).* Goodbye, goodbye, goodbye, goodbye, goodbye, goodbye![19]

*(Just as he is about to step onto the hanamichi, LORD UKYO stops and casts one last glance at the forlorn huddled figure center stage. Free at last, he sighs; a fatuous grin covers his round face.*[20] *As the CHORUS sings, he moves with simpering dance steps onto the hanamichi.)*

**FULL CHORUS.** Into the night,[21]

Into the mists,

"Goodbye, goodbye!"

Heedless of eyes,

Heedless of gossip,

Away, away!

Wet by dew,

And the warmth of love,

He dreams, he dreams.

*(*LORD UKYO *pauses for a moment on the hanamichi. He smiles a love-sick smile and bashfully lowers his eyes. Then he charges into action: he straightens up, stamps loudly on the floor, whirls the long kimono sleeve around his right arm with a great flourish*[22] *and points off down the hanamichi with trembling fan.)*

**LORD UKYO** *(half elf, half devil)*[23] Whee! I'm off at last! Going, going, going, going, gone! *(He races delightedly down the hanamichi*[24] *and whisks out of sight.)*[25]

22. Kabuki actors make much use of their costumes in this way. Look for other places in this scene where costumes can be used effectively.
23. How might you suggest these qualities?
24. Lord Ukyo's exit might be accompanied by the clacking of wooden blocks. See page 297.
25. Tarokaja probably can't resist peeking out one last time at his departing master.

## Extension

Though it shares such conventions as stylized makeup and the use of invisible stage assistants with other types of Asian theatre, Kabuki's highly specialized elements don't show up in much of Western theatre, except in plays that deliberately make use of Kabuki as Kabuki. For example, in recent years American theatre companies have done Kabuki versions of the Greek tragedy *Medea* (shown here) and Shakespeare's *Macbeth.*

1. Stage a fight sequence in which the two combatants don't actually touch each other, but perform stylized movements in slow motion.
2. Experiment with using an invisible stage assistant as you stage a realistic one-act play. Discuss the effect this stage convention has in a theatre for which it was not originally intended.

# Directing & Producing

The director and producer work feverishly through rehearsals to ensure a successful and satisfying performance experience for everyone involved in the production. Enter the stage manager, who also plays a starring role in this task, and the publicity staff, who draw in the audience to make the experience complete.

## THE LANGUAGE OF THEATRE

**cast by type** to cast a show by choosing actors who fit a particular character type

**color-blind casting** casting without regard to race or ethnicity of the characters or actors

**dinner theatre** theatre presented to an audience that is dining at tables around the performance space; usually dinner is included in the price of the theatre ticket

**director's notes** comments by the director on the performance of each actor and on the production in general, usually given before or after rehearsals

**nontraditional casting** casting that ignores the general conventions of casting by type

**pacing** the tempo of a performance as it progresses

**preblocking** blocking on paper a director does before blocking rehearsals begin

**strike** to take down the set

**understudy** someone who learns a role for the purpose of performing in the absence of the actor cast in that role

## Desire and Dedication

Perhaps the most alluring aspect of theatre is that anyone can do it. Granted, some will do it better than others. Talent, experience, and funding go a long way toward creating a top-notch production. The fact remains, however, that if you can draw together a group of people to perform a story for an audience, you have created theatre. Yet, to create truly successful theatre, you have to desire the magic that happens in theatre and be dedicated to making it happen. Talent can be developed, experience gained, and funding acquired, but desire and dedication are still all important. These are qualities a director must have in abundance and be able to instill and sustain in actors and crew from conception through performance.

The following pages present a first-person account by a fictional novice director, a 17-year-old high school girl named Holly Sung, who has all the desire and dedication required for creating theatre. Holly has had experience in directing classmates in short performances in her theatre class and as assistant director to her drama teacher, Ms. Tate, on Howard Ashman and Alan Menken's *Little Shop of Horrors.* She also has had experience as an actor; playing many roles in her theatre class and portraying Rizzo in her school's production of Jim Jacobs and Warren Casey's *Grease.* In addition, she has explored the technical side of theatre: she painted the drop used for last year's production of Rodgers and Hammerstein's *Oklahoma!* and was prop master for Westley M. Pederson's *Take Five.*

Over the past year, however, she has come to a realization that she enjoys directing more than anything else. She admires the directing style of Ms. Tate and has given serious thought to becoming a director herself. What she wants more than anything is the opportunity to direct an entire play on her own. In the spring of her junior year, she gets what she has been waiting for—the chance to direct (and co-produce) her own independent show.

As you read from her journal, jot down notes in your own Theatre Notebook. You will find helpful information on establishing as a theatre company, working with a production team, arranging for a performance space, planning rehearsals, conducting auditions, communicating with actors, and handling the business of theatre. You will come away not only with greater insight about what it's like to be a novice director—and producer—but also with a vivid sense of the ensemble effort required to pull off any successful theatrical endeavor. You will also understand the value of mentors, those who guide and teach you. If you decide to direct or produce your own show, don't be afraid to ask for help from mentors, parents, and other community members; chances are, others will be drawn in by your desire and dedication and will be happy to oblige.

# A Young Director's Journal

*April 15: I've been waiting tables at Joy Chen's China Palace for a year to save up enough so I can produce and direct a play. Now I think it's finally going to happen! Last week my friend Nate said he would help me raise the rest of the money we need: I have $500, and we figure it'll take about $1,000 to do a play with all the technical elements, plus rental of a space and publicity. We'll have to try everything. Nate will work on it; he was business manager on two shows at school.*

### *Our Theatre Company*

*April 18: We decided to call ourselves "Magpie Theatre Company." Magpies are clever birds that learn quickly. They're always picking up things—like ideas—which is what resourceful theatre people do. A magpie has a black body with a really long, green iridescent tail and white stripes on its wings—very dramatic. It'll be perfect for our logo. Now I just have to find the right play.*

### *A Play Is Chosen*

*May 2: After two weeks of reading plays, I finally decided on Neil Simon's Star-Spangled Girl, one of his early comedies. It's a simple one-set show with a three-person cast: Andy and Norman are hippie roommates in San Francisco in the 1960s. They run a protest newspaper. Sophie, an all-American girl type, moves in down the hall. Norman falls for Sophie, Sophie falls for Andy, and eventually, Andy falls for Sophie. I'm sure I can get actors of about the right age to play the parts, and the royalties shouldn't be too bad since it's not running on Broadway. Tickets will be easy to sell for a comedy—especially one by Neil Simon (everybody knows The Odd Couple).*

*I think we'll do pretty well with this play. People are still intrigued with the 1960s, and that whole battle of the younger generation rebelling against the establishment is as relevant as ever. Besides, it's a love triangle, which always makes for a good story,*

***Business Arrangements***

*May 5: Nate and I talked Joy into doing the show as dinner theatre on the thrust stage in the banquet room of her restaurant. The other spaces we checked out were either too expensive or not big enough. We're going to need the space for seven weeks of rehearsals and three performances. We'll give Joy $100 for the use of the banquet room plus 50 percent of the profits for supplying the food for our patrons. The remainder will be split among the production team, cast, and crews.*

***Our Production Team***

*May 14: We finally rounded up all members of the production team: My friend Darth will be technical director. He aced the tech strand of our theatre course. He'll do most of the set construction and props himself. Tyler, another tech student, will do lighting. My brother Lin's friend, José, has a lot of recording gear in his basement, and Lin talked him into doing sound. A very talented girl, Sara, will do the set design, and her sister Paola will do costumes and makeup. Nate's sister Julia will take care of publicity, and Nate's going to handle the business manager and box office manager jobs himself. My best friend, Naomi, is going to be house manager. She'll round up some of our other friends to serve as ushers. Another friend, Jared, volunteered to be stage manager. He's been stage manager on two school productions.*

*We're expecting the scripts tomorrow. Jared will make sure everyone on the production team gets one right away. In the meantime, I'm doing my homework on Star-Spangled Girl.*

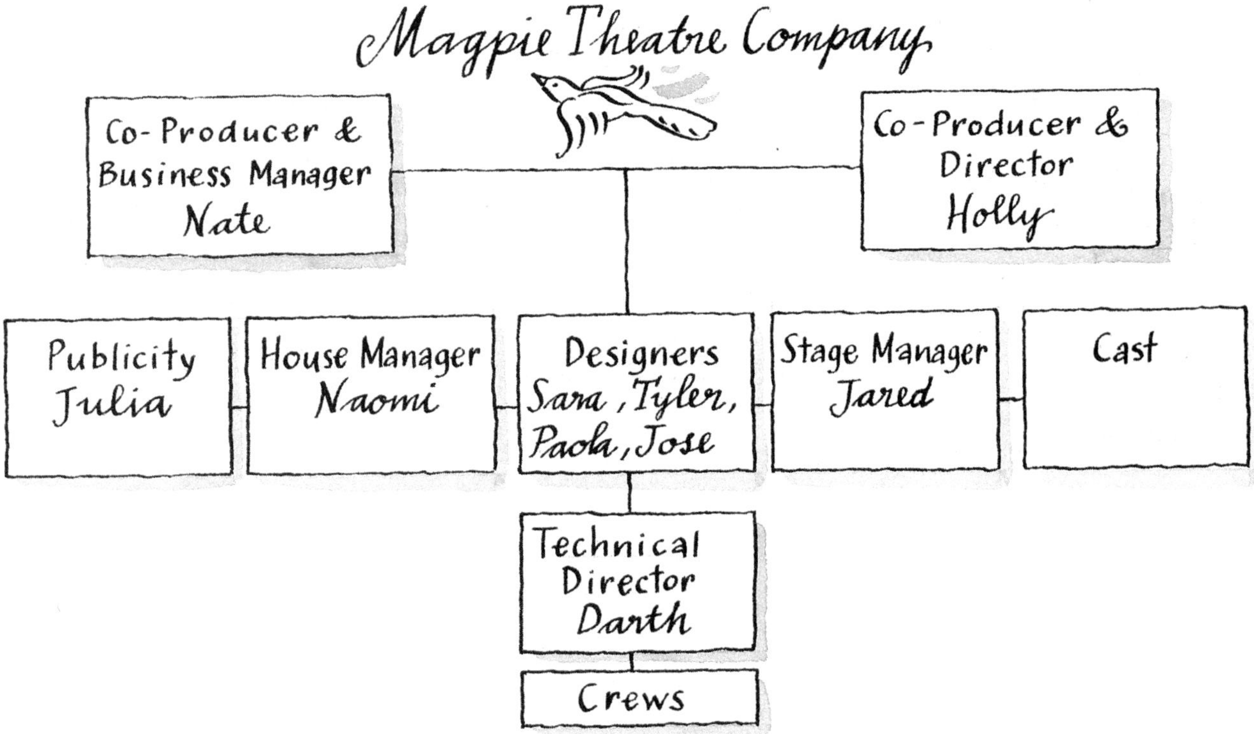

Magpie Theatre Company

Co-Producer & Business Manager Nate

Co-Producer & Director Holly

Publicity Julia

House Manager Naomi

Designers Sara, Tyler, Paola, Jose

Stage Manager Jared

Cast

Technical Director Darth

Crews

***Getting Started on Publicity***

*May 15: Yesterday I showed Julia my sketches for the logo. She took a graphic design class and did the programs last year for Oklahoma! She'll work up a more finished sketch from the one here and then do the final version of a graphics program so it looks professional. She'll include the logo on all of our publicity materials—the production program, flyers, and ad, as well as the audition posters and ads, which she and Jared will take care of this week. She's also going to design the tickets and is tracking down someone to do the publicity photos, which we'll send with our news releases.*

***My Ground Plan***

*May 18: I've started my director's promptbook and completed my analysis of the script. Nate and I looked over the performance space yesterday. I figured out where the furniture will go so I can do some interesting blocking.*

*This is a brief sketch of my ground plan. We decided to put Andy's and Norman's beds up on the landing instead of having their bedrooms offstage like it calls for in the script; it adds more tension to their relationship with Sophie and gives me levels to work with.*

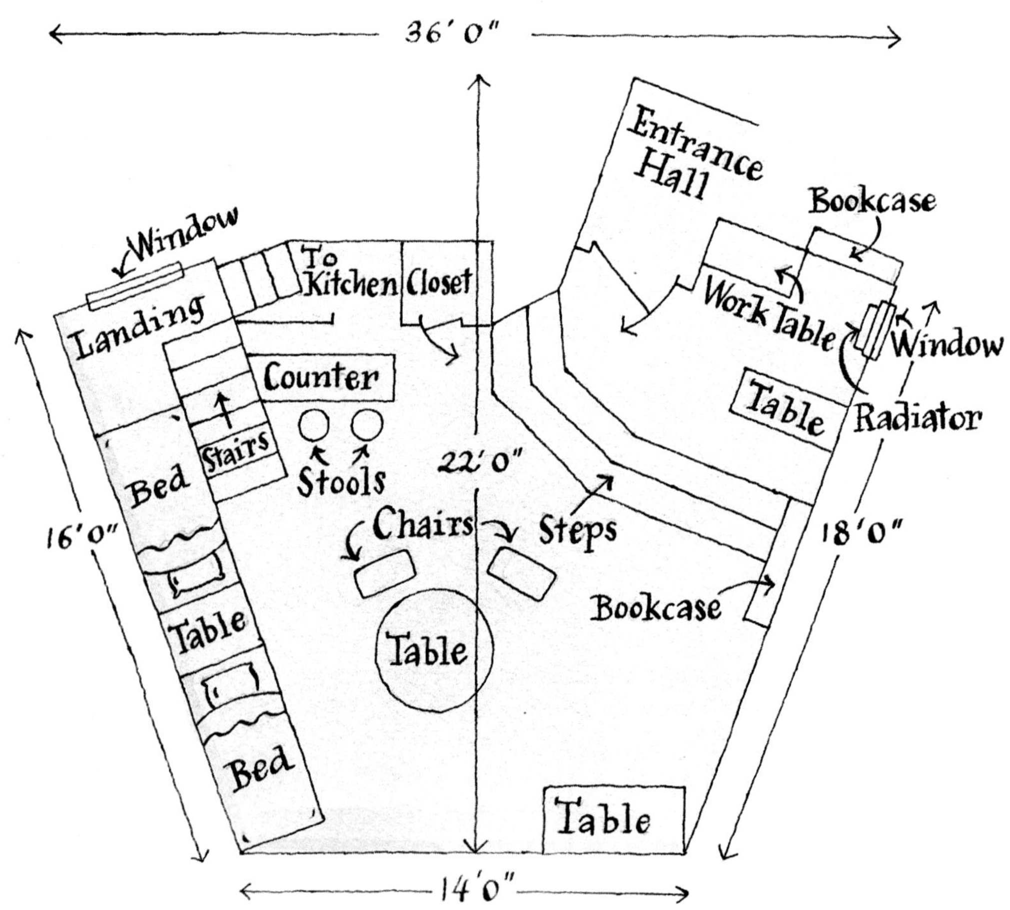

### *Our First Production Meeting*

*June 5: Staff members have had their scripts for over two weeks. I'm interested to hear their ideas. The first production meeting is scheduled for tonight here at my house. This is the agenda:*

1. *Production concept: me*
2. *Budget: me and Nate*
3. *Overall design concepts: Sara (set design) Darth (tech director, set construction and props). Tyler (lighting), José (sound), Paola (costumes and makeup)*
4. *Publicity: Julia*
5. *Technical considerations of mounting the show: Darth*
6. *Production schedule: determine in meeting*
7. *Rehearsal schedule: me and Jared*
8. *Dates and times of production meetings: determine in meeting*

*June 6: The meeting went pretty well. I shared what I believe is the theme of the play, the playwright's message: Nothing is constant except love and change. Times change and people change and through it all people continue to fall in and out of love. A secondary theme might be that love conquers all. It conquers Andy and Sophie because they fall in love and conquer their own prejudices about each other. It also conquers society's traditional views of male and female sex roles.*

*Then I explained my production concept: to reflect the profound social changes happening in the country during the 1960s—especially how relationships between the sexes began to change. I see this being shown through contrasts between liberal, hippie-culture images and ideas and the more conservative middle-class images and ideas of that time.*

*Since this play takes place in San Francisco, home of the 1960s peace-loving flower children and antigovernment radicals, I really want to recreate the look of a hippie pad where Andy and Norman live and work, putting out their protest newspaper, which attacks everything the government does. I see strings of beads serving as one of the doors, tie-dyed curtains, Indian-print bedspreads, posters of the Beatles and Bob Dylan all over the walls, and maybe a lava lamp. All this needs to be contrasted with the more middle-class decorating scheme of the period (lots of green, orange, and brown), showing up in things like crocheted pillows, dishes, a clock—all hand-me-downs from Andy's and Norman's families.*

*The actors' clothing and hairstyles should also reflect the clash of revolutionary flower children and the traditional middle class. By the end of the play, in fact, Sophie has gone from a pony-tailed, red, white, and blue girl-next-door to more of a let-her-hair-down flower child; the jarring contrast of styles in the set and costumes reflects the struggle of her transformation.*

*The music should reinforce the mood of freedom and change, as it did at that time. We can also do some cool things with lighting to add to that mood.*

*Then we moved on to the budget. Nate explained that we have $1,000 max. Script and royalties cost about $300. Joy is only charging us $100 for rental of her banquet room, plus 50 percent of the profits, (which is pretty reasonable since she's providing the food for the dinner theatre). That means we have a balance of $600 for everything else. Nate handed out a copy of everyone's budgets. He used part of the $600 to establish a line of credit at the hardware store. He asked everybody to give him original invoices and receipts—and keep copies of both themselves.*

*Sara then showed us her rendering for the set, which she based on my ground plan; she'll modify her set design to match the production concept. We're all going to scrounge around for furniture and props in attics and garages; then we'll hit the thrift stores for what we can't find free. We'll have to build a platform for the landing and maybe borrow some stair units from school. I'm going to call up our drama teacher, Ms. Tate, and see if she can loan us the stair units. José said his mom might let us borrow the spare twin beds they haven't used since his sisters went to college. I reminded everyone that we have to write up lender's agreements for everything we borrow. Julia handed out copies of her sketches for the logo, which everybody loved, and copies of her rough designs for the program and newspaper ad. She'll also do a flyer that we can post around town.*

MAGPIE THEATRE CO.

Magpie Theatre Company

*presents*

Neil Simon's

*Star-Spangled Girl*

*directed by*

*Holly Sung*

**Thursday, July 31 and Friday, August 1, 8:00 PM**

**Saturday, August 2, 2:00 PM matinee**

Used by special arrangement with the Dramatist's Play Service, Inc.

**Magpie Theatre Company**

*presents*

**Neil Simon's**

***Star-Spangled Girl***

*directed by Holly Sung*

**Thursday, July 31 and Friday, August 1, 8:00 PM**
**Saturday, August 2, 2:00 PM matinee**

Dinner Theatre
in the Banquet Room of
Joy Chen's China Palace
2105 W. Broadway

Tickets (includes dinner):

| | |
|---|---|
| Adults | $10.00 |
| Students | $7.50 |
| Seniors | $5.00 |

Dinner: choice of two appetizers, three entrees, beverage

*Darth thinks he can get some lumber from his dad to build the kitchen bar we need. We'll have to find some bar stools, but he isn't worried about that. He's worried about getting set construction done: Joy has a big wedding party scheduled in the banquet room two weeks after our rehearsals start, and we can't have any set pieces there until after that. We all talked about it and if we plan carefully, we can work around that problem. I'm pretty sure that we can start on the set in our garage and my uncle will probably let us use his truck to haul the set pieces to the stage on the day after the wedding party. We'll check on that.*

*In the meantime, Jared will mark the ground plan in tape on the stage and we'll use whatever furniture is in the banquet room as rehearsal set props until we can get our set in there.*

*Eventually, we came up with a production and rehearsal schedule that will work around everyone's summer jobs. We have our assignments, and we'll have our next production team meeting in about two weeks to look at final design plans. After that, we'll meet every week on Mondays an hour before rehearsal begins.*

*Jared has a quick way of developing the rehearsal schedule. Here's how he does it:*

1. *Find your opening night on a calendar.*
2. *Go backward six weeks.*
3. *Schedule four to five two- or three-hour rehearsals per week.*
4. *Add some extra, optional rehearsals just before dress rehearsals.*
5. *Note that rehearsals for the last two weeks before opening will probably run closer to three or four hours each.*

## Rehearsal and Production Schedule — Magpie Theatre Company

**Show:** *Star-Spangled Girl*

| | SUN | MON | TUE | WED | THU | FRI | SAT |
|---|---|---|---|---|---|---|---|
| | June 1 | 2 | 3 | 4 | 5<br>1st Production Meeting (Holly's house) 7–9 pm | 6 | 7 |
| | 8<br>Auditions | 9 | 10 | 11 | 12 | 13<br>Callbacks | 14 |
| **WEEK 1**<br>1st News Release | 15 | 16<br>1st Read-Through (Holly's house) 7–9 pm | 17<br>2nd Read-Through (Holly's house) 7–9 pm | 18<br>Block Act I, scene i Walk-Through Blocking 7–9 pm | 19<br>Block Act I, scene ii Walk-Through Blocking 7–9 pm | 20 | 21 |
| **WEEK 2** | 22 | 23<br>Block Act II, scene i Walk-Through Blocking 7–9 pm Prod mtg. 6 pm | 24<br>Block Act II, scene ii Walk-Through Blocking 7–9 pm | 25<br>Block Act III, Walk-Through Blocking 7–9 pm | 26<br>Working Rehearsal Act I with props 7–9 pm | 27 | 28 |
| **WEEK 3** | 29 | 30<br>Working Rehearsal Act I with props 7–10 pm Prod mtg. 6 pm | July 1<br>Working Rehearsal Act II with props 7–9 pm | 2<br>Working Rehearsal Act II with props 7–9 pm | 3<br>Working Rehearsal Act III with props 7–9 pm | 4 | 5<br>(Wedding party) |
| **WEEK 4**<br>Off book<br>2nd News Release | 6<br>Tech Work noon–5 pm | 7<br>Working Rehearsal Act III with props 7–9 pm Prod mtg. 6 pm | 8<br>Run-Through Act I Articulation (off book) 7–9 pm | 9<br>Run-Through Act II Articulation (off book) 7–9 pm | 10<br>Run-Through Act III Articulation (off book) 7–9 pm | 11 | 12<br>Tech Work 10 am–noon |
| **WEEK 5**<br>Start working with set | 13<br>Tech Work noon–5 pm | 14<br>Polishing Rehearsals Act I 7–9 pm Prod mtg. 6 pm | 15<br>Polishing Rehearsals Act II 7–9 pm Photos 5–6 pm | 16<br>Polishing Rehearsals Act III Opera-style (two scenes) 7–10 pm | 17<br>Pacing Act I 7–9 pm | 18 | 19<br>Tech Work 10 am–noon |
| **WEEK 6**<br>3rd News Release | 20<br>Tech Work noon–5 pm | 21<br>Tech Run: Hang Lights (cast & crew) 6–10 pm Prod mtg. 5 pm | 22<br>Dry Tech (crew only) 6–10 pm | 23<br>Tech Run: Dress Parade (cast & crew) 6–10 pm | 24<br>Tech Run: (cast & crew) 7–10 pm | 25 | 26<br>Tech Work 10 am–noon |
| **WEEK 7** | 27<br>Tech Work noon–5 pm Optional Run-Through 5 pm | 28<br>Dress Rehearsal Block Curtain Call 7–10 pm | 29<br>Dress Rehearsal 7–10 pm | 30<br>Dress Rehearsal 7–10 pm | 31<br>Opening Night 8 pm 7 pm call | August 1<br>2nd Performance 8 pm 7 pm call | 2<br>Matinee 2 pm 1 pm call Cast Party Strike |

## Getting Ready for Auditions

*June 7: Auditions are tomorrow. I've helped Ms. Tate as an assistant director with auditions at school, and Jared has done them too, so I think we're ready.*

*We made scripts available at the area libraries three weeks ago when we put up the audition posters. Julia has been running an ad for the auditions each week in the paper since then. The posters and the ad explained what type of audition we're holding. If it's a dance audition, the actors have to know it, so they will wear appropriate clothing. If it's a prepared audition, you need to present monologue guidelines in advance, which we did. For cold reading auditions, you're supposed to prepare two to three character scenes for the actors to read. These aren't cold reading auditions, but I did this anyway in preparation for callbacks, when I'll want them to read from the script. The audition poster and ad also notified actors that we would be holding a preaudition discussion, which we held last week, to talk about the play. A couple of the actors had some really interesting insights into the play and the characters.*

*When the actors arrive tomorrow Jared will give them an audition form to complete. If there's a big turnout, he'll take a Polaroid of each actor so we won't have any problem identifying them later when we're casting the show.*

*We're going to try to make the audition as comfortable for the actors as possible. As an actor, I know that the way I present myself at auditions sets the tone for the rest of the production.*

*Ms. Tate arranged for us to use the stage at the high school for the auditions. Everyone will feel comfortable there since that's where we hold auditions for school productions. We organized the audition process to give every actor 15 minutes. That's time to do two monologues and time to let me ask questions about each person's experience, schedule, and so on. I give myself five minutes between each actor to read resumes and get prepared. I have to remember to ask the actors to introduce themselves so I know that I have the right audition form before they begin.*

*Once the actors are finished, Jared will direct them to where we have copies of the rehearsal schedule and the actor's contracts. (We're going to have the actors sign the contract like the one Ms. Tate has us sign for productions at school.) If an actor consistently breaks the conditions of the contract, he or she is dismissed from the cast. The contract includes a commitment to maintain a positive attitude; comply with safety rules; memorize the script by the date specified in the schedule; do character analysis homework assigned by the director, show up on time and ready to work for rehearsals; communicate concerns to the director or stage manager (instead of to the cast or crew); and keep clear of drugs and alcohol. To be cast, the actors need to return a signed contract at callbacks.*

When Ms. Tate does school auditions, she likes to give a week between the first auditions and the callbacks. This allows the actors time to reflect whether they really want the part and whether they expect any conflicts with the rehearsal schedule. We can only give them five days because we have to have the show cast at the end of this week.

At callbacks, I'll be looking for who can best portray the roles. I'll keep my callback list to a manageable number of actors—only those I would seriously consider casting. A director should beware of casting by type. An actor may look the part, but if he or she can't act, you're in trouble. The script calls for Sophie to be a beautiful blond who is also an Olympic swimmer, but we plan to do color-blind casting; the race and ethnicity of the characters doesn't matter to our production concept. We'll cast the most talented. We'll also need to cast some understudies; if any member of the cast has to drop out or is absent from a rehearsal, his or her understudy can step in and do the part.

During callbacks, I'll ask the actors to perform the cold readings from the script that I've prepared. An actor may be wonderful, but have a terrible time initially reading from the script. I plan to give the actors a chance to practice the scene before I watch them perform. I'll mix and match partners and try actors in various roles to find their strengths and capabilities. I also plan to use improvisation situations from the script; I've learned in theatre classes at school that freeing actors from the script often gives you a clearer impression of their talent.

In my final selection, I'll use this checklist:

- Does the actor physically and mentally fit my image of the character?
- Does the cast fit together and is there variety in the way the actors look and sound?
- Does the actor work well with others and is he or she reliable?
- Does the actor have the time to commit to the project?

June 13, midnight: Auditions went smoothly and I have a great cast! I remembered to thank all actors who auditioned. It was a tough choice; there's lots of talent out there. Lin will play Norman. He's my brother, but he's also a great actor with impeccable comic timing. A new, very talented African American girl named Elise Chambers will play Sophie. Marcos Velasquez will play Andy. They were really fabulous together and have all signed their contracts. Elsie doesn't exactly fit Neil Simon's original description; but she fits my concept of the character just fine. I'm sure Neil Simon never saw Norman as Asian American or Andy as Hispanic either. I think the mixed-race relationships will give this play a relevant contemporary force.

### Read-Throughs

*June 16: Our first read-through of the play is tonight at my house. All actors and the production team will be here. I'll introduce everyone, talk about my concepts, and discuss the schedule. Then the actors will read the play aloud.*

*We'll probably talk about the script for a while after we finish reading. I want everyone to know why we're doing this play. It's not just to make money or get some experience. I want to show the beginnings of change in men's and women's roles in our society. Also, by using nontraditional casting, I want to challenge our community—get them to open up their minds to accept multiracial relationships more than I suspect they do. And, of course, I want to entertain the audience. It is a very funny play.*

*June 16, midnight: We just had our first read-through. I'm convinced that the casting is perfect.*

### Blocking Rehearsals

*June 18: I've completed all my written preblocking—and just in time. Tonight is our first blocking rehearsal. I divided each scene into beats and blocked each beat and the transitions between them. First, I'll walk the actors through my blocking for tonight's scenes, while they write their own blocking in their scripts. Then, we'll walk through the entire scene.*

*June 20: There are some challenging scenes to block in this play. I had to rethink and research my blocking for the kissing scene and the karate scene. Stage kissing can be kind of complicated:*

- *Have the two actors stand facing each other with the woman slightly upstage of the man. Both actors' bodies should be slightly open to the audience. If the giver of the kiss is a man, he should put his upstage arm on or around the woman's upstage shoulder.*
- *Next, he should lean toward her as he shifts so that his body is more closed, and bring his downstage arm up around her waist.*
- *At the same time she should shift her body so it is more open and bring her upstage arm around his waist and her downstage arm up around his downstage shoulder, cupping the back of his head with her hand. Or, she can bring it to his waist.*
- *He now tilts his head downstage, and she tilts hers upstage. (This prevents nose-bumping). As he pulls her to him, he closes his body off further so that he blocks the full action from the audience. He kisses her on her face next to her mouth.*
- *Now, if the giver of the kiss is a woman, the body positions are the same, but she reaches up first with her upstage hand and cups her upstage hand around the man's neck and head. The movements then follow as before. This time, though, the woman has both hands around the man's head.*

### *Tech Update*

*June 24: All the tech crews are on schedule. José is having a blast mixing music from the 1960s. Darth has found some good carpenters, including his dad. Mom has been shopping at secondhand stores to help Sara and Paola find 1960s props and clothes. We begin working rehearsals, with props, in a few days. We'll work on motivation and building characters.*

### *Working Rehearsals*

*June 26: The actors and I have been discussing basic motivation questions. Before going into each scene, they ask themselves these questions, as their characters: What is my objective in this scene? What are my obstacles? What strategies am I using to overcome my obstacles? What are the stakes?*

*July 1: We're well into the working rehearsals, which will include improv. Experimenting—in character—is what this is all about. Improvising the "return of the canned goods" scene worked really well for Sophie (Elise). It helped her to understand the possibilities in her monologue, how she could break it down into workable beats with specific actions.*

*July 2: We've discovered some very touching moments onstage, like when Andy is attempting to pat Sophie's hair dry with her towel in act II, scene i. The actions define and shape their relationship. This is why I love directing.*

### *Coaching Actors*

*July 3: Ms. Tate sat in on a few rehearsals. In general, she thinks I'm doing a great job. She shared with me some of her tips on working with actors. Number one is to communicate. You should explain in your first rehearsals how you see your role as director and how you see their roles as actors. If you ever have problems, don't hesitate to talk one-on-one to resolve them. We talked about how you have to develop effective ways of communicating with each individual actor since each is unique.*



*She also pointed out that beginning actors need more coaching than experienced actors. I guess I'm lucky to be working with somewhat experienced actors (they've all been in several school productions), but I've directed beginning actors in class, so I know what she means.*

*You have to work in close collaboration with your actors. Tell them that you expect them to do their homework in developing their characters and to be "thinking actors" on stage. Encourage them to explore and experiment and if you think they have developed a better approach than yours, use theirs. It's all part of being respectful of the actors. There's nothing worse than an egotistical, bullying director.*

*Ms. Tate also suggested that I might use more specific observations or comments to explain what I mean when I'm talking to the actors. Instead of saying, "Be more like a tomato," I should say something like, "When you move, imagine that your torso is much rounder and heavier and that your legs are shorter. Take smaller steps." I'll remember this when we go into our run-through rehearsals in a few days. My director's notes—my comments on the performance of each actor and the production in general—will have to be very clear. I'll be giving them at the end of the run-through, and I'll want the actors to be able to write them down—the more specific, the better.*

July 7: Julia sent off our second press release (with our publicity photos). She's working on an online ad to put on our school's Internet homepage and one to run with the events that are posted on the local cable-access channels.

I'd like to try to help everybody loosen up. Tonight, I think I'll have them read each other's lines. Tomorrow, every actor must pretend to slip on a banana peel at least once per scene—just for laughs. We can't be afraid of the physical side of this comedy.

### Off Book!

July 8: Off book and into run-throughs! Naomi sat in and served as prompter. She said she can do it for a few nights while we're making the transition from on book to off book, which will help us a lot. Prompting is a tough job because you have to be ready to give a line at any moment. Naomi has all the ushers lined up and is briefing them on the arrangement of the seating and on answers to questions the audience might ask, like the location of restrooms and information about our theatre company.

### Marcos Misses Rehearsal

July 10: Marcos didn't show up for rehearsal tonight and we were all really worried and then angry when we didn't hear from him. Jared called his house, but no one was home. We had his understudy do his role.

July 11: I found out that Marcos stepped on a nail in his brother's shop and had to go to the emergency room. He said that he asked his sister to call us, but she didn't. He called this morning and apologized for not notifying us. He'll be limping for a week or so.

### Polishing Rehearsals

July 14: We're into polishing rehearsals—working on stage business and other details. I'm giving the actors my notes at the beginning of the next rehearsal instead of at the end of the night. They seem to be sharper and take better notes. It also gives me some time between rehearsals to come up with solutions to problems I've noticed. I always try to include something positive in my notes about what they've done.

July 16: Last week we worked on articulation and projection and added some new warm-ups to our pre- and post-rehearsal routines. José gave us a mix of 1960s tunes for our warm-ups to get us in the mood of the period.

July 17: Oh, this was so great: Last night I had the actors pretend they were doing opera. They sang their lines and used big operatic gestures. Lin said that it really helped him to portray Norman, who is supposed to be an over-the-top kind of guy. Tonight we'll work on pacing.

### Working on Pacing

July 18: Pacing is slow at the end of the beginning of the play. You don't want the tempo to drag, especially in the first act, and especially in comedy. Everything in comedy must be timed just so. The actors have to respond to each other right on cue and keep up their energy. Last night we did the first act in double-time. The actors spoke, gestured, and moved at twice their normal speed. Whenever anyone dropped the pace, we started again. Then we repeated the act at the tempo it was supposed to be.

### The Bracing Problem

July 19: The landing where the beds are positioned is still a bit unsteady. The other night, Lin and Darth got into an argument about whether it was safe. I had to talk to them both (privately, away from the rest of the cast and crew). It's critical that we fix the problem now or I'll have to reblock, which would be a shame since the elevation gives us a variety in levels. Darth and his crew are coming in tomorrow again and work on it. If we have to, we'll pull the beds down to the lower level. Sara thinks she made a mistake designing it that way, but I reminded her that she and Darth and I all looked at the elevations together and we all thought it would work, and it may yet.

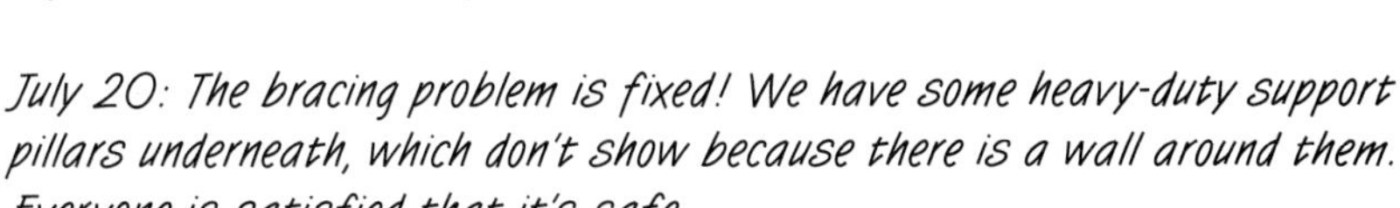

July 20: The bracing problem is fixed! We have some heavy-duty support pillars underneath, which don't show because there is a wall around them. Everyone is satisfied that it's safe.

### Ticket Sales

July 21: Nate reported that ticket sales are picking up rapidly for both nights and the matinee. We're passing the word to friends, neighbors, and local businesses.

### Technical Rehearsals

July 22: We had our first technical rehearsal last night,and it went well. Tech rehearsals are hard for the actors sometimes because they have to keep stopping so that the stage crew can check and arrange all the technical elements of the production; but everyone was very cooperative, and things went pretty well. There are a few dark spots in some scenes, but Tyler is working on that. Norman (Lin) pulled off some strings of beads from the kitchen door when he was flailing his arms around trying to do a crazy entrance. We should have those problems solved by tomorrow night. The dressed and lit set really helped the actors feel the atmosphere of the 1960s.

### *Dress Rehearsals*

*July 28: It's our first night of dress rehearsals. Jared is doing a great job of handling things backstage. He really knows what he's doing, calling the rehearsals and the show. I'm feeling good and so are the actors. They all have their costume changes timed just right, and no one is tripping on their bellbottoms anymore.*

### *Opening Night!*

*July 31, 6:00 P.M.: Here it is: opening night! I can't believe I'm done with my part of the production. The show is now in the hands of everybody else. I've written little positive notes to each person. I'm a nervous wreck, but I'll never let anyone know it—except Naomi. Your best friend can always tell. I'm going to try to stay out of everyone's way backstage. Jared will make sure the actors are warmed up. When cast and crew are ready for places, then I'll get them together for a pep talk, compliment the stage crew, and wish everyone a good show.*

*July 31, 11:30 P.M.: This was absolutely the best night of my life! Everybody worked so hard. The audience positively howled their way through the show and gave a standing ovation! I had such a good time watching the show from out in the audience. I took a few notes, but overall I'm really pleased. Nate said he thinks we made our money back on tonight's performance alone! I can't wait for tomorrow's performance.*

*August 2: We had our cast party after the 2:00 matinee. Jared arranged for Joy to have this incredible buffet set up for us. I had a great time talking and laughing with everyone. I made a point to thank every one of the cast and crew personally. They were all great to work with.*

*Nate caught up with me to show me the final breakdown of the budget. He was really proud that we stayed under $1,000. He's paying off the credit tomorrow, and once all the other bills are settled, we'll send off the checks to Joy and the cast and crew. I've attached his budget here for reference.*

**Magpie Theatre Co.**
**Production Budget for *Star-Spangled Girl***

**Income**

| Item | | | Estimated | Actual |
|---|---|---|---|---|
| Adult | 104 @ | $10.00 | $1,000.00 | $1,040.00 |
| Student | 47 @ | $7.50 | $250.00 | $352.50 |
| Senior | 93 @ | $7.50 | $250.00 | $465.00 |
| Advertising in Programs | | | $100.00 | $110.00 |
| **Total** | | | **$1,600.00** | **$1,967.50** |

**Expenses**

| Item | Budget | Actual |
|---|---|---|
| Royalty | $250.00 | $180.00 |
| Scripts | $50.00 | $52.50 |
| Set | $200.00 | $169.42 |
| Props | $50.00 | $21.00 |
| Lighting/Sound | $50.00 | $21.00 |
| Costumes | $50.00 | $53.36 |
| Makeup | $25.00 | $24.44 |
| Publicity | $115.00 | $120.00 |
| Tickets | $10.00 | $5.00 |
| Programs | $25.00 | $26.65 |
| Performance Space Rental | $150.00 | $100.00 |
| Miscellaneous | $25.00 | $59.00 |
| **Total** | **$1,000.00** | **$832.36** |

| | |
|---|---|
| **Profit (or loss)** | **$1,135.14** |
| **Profit Share** (50% profits to Joy) | **$567.57** |
| **Profit Share** (remainder to production team, cast, and crews) | **$567.57** |

### *Striking the Set*

*After the party everybody pitched in to strike the set. I never thought ripping apart a set could be so much fun! We made sure everything borrowed was set aside for return, which we'll do tomorrow. Darth's dad said he'd save the lumber from this set in his garage in case we decide to do another show anytime soon. He's so nice! I'll send a thank-you note to him and all the other people who helped us. Jared made several checks of the set to see that the crews put everything away and that the stage was clean.*

*Just as we were leaving, Joy came up to me and told me how pleased she was at the success of the show and the success of the dinner theatre idea. She says we can do the same thing next summer if we want. I guess the Magpie Theatre Company had better start picking up a few new ideas if we want to top this year's performance!*

# Activities

*A Young Director's Journal*

**CHOOSING A PLAY** Working with several other students, imagine that you have decided to start a theatre company. Draw up a list of five plays that could be produced by a small amateur theatre company in your community with only $1,000 in funding. Assess the pros and cons of each play, examining such issues as the size of the cast required, the number and type of sets, royalties to be paid (p. 185), probable audience appeal, and so on. Together, write your evaluation in a report. If you like, vote on which play you would most like to produce.

*A Young Director's Journal*

**COMMUNITY RESOURCES** Together with a small group, assess the community resources that your group could draw upon in support of a local theatre company. Identify possible theatre spaces, family and friends with special skills who might volunteer, local media resources, the availability of arts funding from government or private sources, and so on. When you have concluded your research, you might want to write a report and include it in your Theatre Notebook.

*A Young Director's Journal*

**THEATRE COMPANY LOGO** Come up with a name for a theatre company that expresses what you want to accomplish in the theatre or that expresses an idea about theatre. Then design a logo for your company. Experiment with your design at different scales to make sure that it would be effective both large (on a T-shirt or banner) and small (for letterhead or business cards). You might want to include your design in your Theatre Notebook.

*A Young Director's Journal*

**REHEARSAL SCHEDULE** Select a play. After reading it and assessing the time it would take to rehearse each scene, draw up a rehearsal schedule. If you have a job, work your schedule around your job hours. Prepare your schedule as an electronic document in a word-processing, spread-sheet, or calendar program. Now imagine that a situation arises in which you can't hold rehearsals for several days during the third week of your schedule. Adjust your schedule so that you are still prepared to open on time.

*A Young Director's Journal*

**THEATRE PROMOTION** With a partner, choose a play that interests you and then work out a publicity campaign that you might use to promote a production of this play. Establish a realistic budget for your campaign; identify the most cost-effective promotional methods; create a news release for your production (p. 546); and design a program, an advertising flyer, and a newspaper ad.

### A Young Director's Journal

**MOCK AUDITION** Work with a small group to hold a mock audition for a play. Follow the guidelines suggested by Ms. Tate, including making scripts available in advance, presiding over a pre-audition discussion of the play, and drafting an actor's contract. Are there other issues that arose during your mock audition that you could share with the class? Write a response to this activity in your Theatre Notebook for possible future reference.

### A Young Director's Journal

**CASTING A PLAY** Investigate and evaluate the different approaches that can be taken in casting a play. Read articles on casting, interview directors and actors, and read plays with an eye for the demands of casting. When might casting by type be important? What are the some of the pitfalls of casting by type? What are the advantages and disadvantages of the nontraditional casting approach? You might want to write the results of your research in your Theatre Notebook.

### A Young Director's Journal

**BLOCKING REHEARSAL** Select an act in a play and work out the blocking movements on a ground plan you devise. Then ask several actors to work through your blocking. Which parts of the blocking were more difficult than others? Why? How might you better prepare for the next blocking rehearsal? Is there anything your actors could do before rehearsal that would help? Write any suggestions about this process in your Theatre Notebook.

### A Young Director's Journal

**COACHING ACTORS** Direct one or two actors in a scene you have chosen. (Be sure that you and the actors have read and analyzed the play first.) After you have coached the actors through the scene, invite them to offer constructive feedback on your methods. Take notes. What are your most effective directorial approaches? What do they feel you need to work on? Include your notes and your responses to this experience in your Theatre Notebook.

HISTORICAL PROFILE

# Chekhov

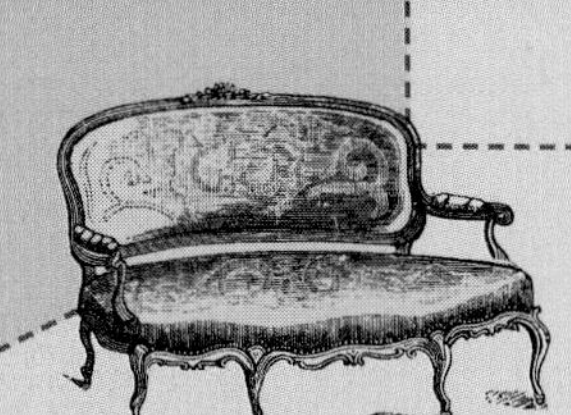

The father of modern Russian drama, Anton Chekhov (chek´ ôf) had trouble convincing his producers that his plays were meant to be funny. Born in 1860 in a Russian seaport town, Chekhov had a painful childhood, which nevertheless provided inspiration for his later writings. His father was a struggling grocer who had been born a serf, and the family teetered on the edge of poverty. After briefly attending a local primary school, Chekhov entered the town high school, where he remained for 10 years. He received a good education that enabled him, during his last 3 years there, to support himself by coaching younger boys.

By this time his father, having gone bankrupt, had moved the rest of the family to Moscow to make a fresh start. In 1879 Chekhov joined his family there, where he enrolled in medical school; he graduated as a doctor in 1884. While in medical school,

Chekhov supported himself and much of his family by freelance journalism and humorous stories. Although much of his later writing focuses on human misery and despair, humor always remains an important element. Becoming a full-time writer, Chekhov soon became very well known, producing a large number of sketches and short stories that made him popular with the "lowbrow" public. He was less successful with the critics, who took him to task for holding no firm political and social views and for refusing to pass judgment even on his most despicable characters.

During the late 1880s, Chekhov also began experimenting as a playwright, ranging from the tragedy *Ivanov* (1887), which ends with the suicide of the main character, to a number of hilarious one-act farces. His first important play was *The Seagull,* a flop when first produced in 1896, but successful in its 1898 revival by the Moscow Art Theatre. The play helped establish Chekhov as a dramatist. Already ill with the tuberculosis that would eventually kill him, Chekhov moved to Yalta, a resort on the Black Sea. In 1901 he married Olga Knipper, a young actress who had appeared in his plays. Since she continued her acting career in Moscow, and Chekhov spent his winters in Yalta or on the French Riviera, they lived apart during most of the winter months.

Chekhov continued to write for the Moscow Art Theatre. *Uncle Vanya* (1899), *The Three Sisters* (1901), and *The Cherry Orchard* (1904) were his last—and best—works. They are all poignant studies of the Russian landowning class in decline. But Chekhov was not completely satisfied with the way his plays were produced, repeatedly insisting that they were comedies rather than tragedies, despite the fact that his characters frequently complain about the boredom and lack of meaning in their lives. Chekhov died in 1904, at a health resort in Germany. His influence on modern fiction and drama has been immense—even though he wrote comparatively few major plays. His works continue to be read, performed, and enjoyed around the world.

## Romanticism and Realism

During most of the 1800s, the cultural movement known as Romanticism was a dominant influence on drama, poetry, painting, music, and the other arts. Romanticism in drama produced an emphasis on heroic and sentimental gestures and melodramatic stories set in exotic, far-off lands or distant times. Stage settings were elaborate, involving painted perspectives and such stage machinery as trapdoors, treadmills, flying rigs, and smoke and fire effects.

By the 1880s, many writers—including Chekhov—had started writing in a new style that came to be called realism. Realist playwrights focused on ordinary, contemporary people living more or less everyday lives. Chekhov himself contributed to this sense of realism by developing a dramatic style that is both elusive and

This production of Chekhov's tragedy *Ivanov* uses a box set.

deceptively simple. Conversations seem to go nowhere in particular; thoughts and actions may not be concluded; what is left unsaid may be more important than what is said.

Realistic theatre featured the **box set,** a two- or three-walled set representing the interior of a room, with authentic props that could be handled. This emphasis on realism gave rise to the convention of the "fourth wall" (p. 278); that is, actors were supposed to be living their lives in real rooms, with the audience spying on them through an invisible fourth wall. Actors were never supposed to acknowledge this invisible wall or the audience.

Costumes were contemporary. For the women that meant dresses with long, full skirts worn over corsets with one or more petticoats and usually with high necks and long sleeves, except for formal evening wear. For the men it meant suits cut in a style close to our modern style, but with longer coats and differently shaped lapels. In public, men always wore white shirts with high, stiff collars and neckties. Movements were much more relaxed than in Molière's plays (p. 195), although like actors in Molière's plays, the costumes as well as the manners of the day demanded that women and men could never relax so far as to slouch.

## The Moscow Art Theatre

The movement toward realism reached its peak in 1898 with the founding of the Moscow Art Theatre. One of its co-founders, Konstantin Stanislavski (stan i slav′skē), not only insisted on the new realistic acting techniques for his cast members but went on to develop his ideas about acting in three books on what became known as the **Stanislavski method**. Rejecting the use of overemphasized, declamatory vocal techniques and standardized gestures and poses, he claimed that acting must be based on inner "artistic truth." Stanislavsky's methods spread to other countries and have had particular influence in the United States.

Despite Stanislavski's reputation as an innovator of acting style, his productions were still never quite natural and nondeclamatory enough for Chekhov. He felt that the productions given his plays were too heavy and serious, overemphasizing the characters' dissatisfactions and failures. Chekhov wanted to stress the comic elements by having actors perform with the lightest possible touch.

This scene from a production of Chekhov's *The Three Sisters* suggests the prevailing mood of frustration that animates his plays.

## Try It Out

Bear in mind the lightness of touch Chekhov wanted in his plays as you direct the following scene from *Uncle Vanya*. Each of the characters confesses to a grand passion—and, to each of them, the situation is serious. How can you help the audience understand that their situations are nowhere near tragic, and were written to be viewed with amusement?

*from*

# Uncle Vanya

*adapted by* **David Mamet**

Retired Professor Serebryakov (sėr ə´brē k ôf) and his young wife, Yelena (yə lā´nə), return to the country estate left by his deceased first wife. The first wife's brother —called Uncle Vanya (van´yə)—falls in love with Yelena. A neighbor, Doctor Mikhail Lvovich Astrov (mē kīl´lə vōv´ich as´trôf), is also attracted to her, unaware that the Professor's daughter, Sonya (sōn´yə), loves him. In this scene Vanya, Sonya, and Yelena wait for the Professor to make an announcement.

**VANYA.** The Herr Professor has been so good as to express this: that he wishes that we should gather in this drawing room, at one o'clock this afternoon *(checks his watch)*[1], that being in one quarter hour. At which time he has some *"thing"* which he wishes to share with the world.

**YELENA.** Some business matter, probably.

**VANYA.** But what business? He has none anymore. He writes garbage, he grumbles, he envies the world, and that's his life.

**SONYA.** . . . *Uncle!*

**VANYA.** Alright. Alright. You're right. *Ecco*[2], *how* she walks, this woman. Eh? Morbid with laziness.[3] A panorama of inaction. *Bella.*[4]

**YELENA.** Must you *prate* all day? Must you go on always? I'm *dying* of boredom. *Is* there nothing to do?

**SONYA.** There's no lack of things to do. If you wished to *do* them.

**YELENA.** *Tell* me one.

**SONYA.** Teach. Treat the sick. Care for the Estate.

1. Vanya's watch should be a pocket watch with a fob. What business is involved in checking the time?

2. ***Ecco*** (ek´kō) behold. [Italian]

3. What kind of walk might Yelena use to prompt Vanya's comment that she is "morbid with laziness"?

4. **Bella** (bel´lə) beautiful. [Italian] Educated Russians might be proud of their mastery of other languages. How might Vanya pronounce these words to give them emphasis?

**YELENA.** . . . mmm . . . hmm . . .[5]

**SONYA.** Much to do. *(Pause.)* When you and Papa weren't here, Uncle and I would go to the market and sell flour.

**YELENA.** I wouldn't know how. And, besides, it doesn't interest me. In ideological novels people jump up and declare they're going to Teach, or treat the sick. But how should I do that? Just, suddenly . . . just . . .

**SONYA.** If you *did* it, you'd be *drawn* to it. Oh, yes, my darling. *(They embrace. SONYA laughs.)* You're bored. You don't know what to do. There's no end to it. I know. It's so contagious. Uncle *Vanya* has it, now. And *he* does nothing. And follows you like a cloud on a leash. I put my *own* work down and come over to chat. I've grown so lazy. And our *doctor,* Mikhail Lvovich, who came once a month, if that, is here every day. And turns his back both on his forests and his *medicine.* And lives under your spell.[6]

**YELENA.** . . . my spell?

**SONYA.** You *Sorcerer!*

**VANYA.** Oh, but why are you languishing? My Dear? My Splendor? Awaken and pulse with life. You, when the blood of *mermaids* courses in your veins . . . wake to your mermaid life! Rise to the heights and plunge into the frothy brine. Love with a water spirit waits you. In your guise as Naiad[7] of Perfection. So our Herr Professor, so that *all* of us throw up our heads and say, "Who is that nymph?"[8]

**YELENA.** Oh, will you shut up?

**VANYA.** . . . did I . . . ?

**YELENA.** This cruel . . . cruel . . .

**VANYA.** Forgive me. My Joy. Forgive me. I apologize. Forgive me. Peace.

**YELENA.** An Angel of Patience would become short with you.

**VANYA.** . . . as a peace offering . . .

**YELENA.** . . . *admit* it.

**VANYA.** . . . as an offering of peace, I'm going to present you with a bouquet of roses, which flowers I have had the foresight to've obtained this morning. Autumn roses. Sad roses. For you. *(Exits.)*[9]

**SONYA.** . . . sad autumn roses . . .

5. How enthusiastic is Yelena about these suggested activities? Why?

6. In what tone of voice should Sonya deliver these accusations?

7. ***Naiad*** (nī´ad) a water nymph

8. To the audience, Vanya may be a comic fool, but to Vanya his situation is deadly serious. What movements should the actor use? What facial expressions and tone of voice?

9. How quickly or slowly should Vanya exit? Why did you make this choice?

10. How might Vanya's exit change the dynamic between the two women?

11. How and where should Sonya move to have this secret conversation?

12. What might Sonya be doing at this moment to cause Yelena to comfort her with these words?

13. If a mirror is important to Sonya's speeches about being plain, you can specify one in the props list. But is it important?

14. **him** Doctor Astrov

15. In the light of Yelena's following soliloquy, what is her subtext here? How much of it should she reveal to the audience?

16. Why doesn't Sonya answer aloud?

17. What causes Sonya to have second thoughts about Yelena's plan?

**YELENA.** Already September. How are we to live through one more winter here? Where is the doctor?[10]

**SONYA.** Uncle Vanya's room. He's writing something. I'm glad Uncle's gone. I have to talk with you.[11]

**YELENA.** About what?

**SONYA.** About what. *(Pause.)* About what . . . ?

**YELENA.** . . . there . . . there . . .[12]

**SONYA.** I'm plain.

**YELENA.** You have beautiful hair.

**SONYA.** No! No! The homely woman's told, "Oh, what beautiful hair."[13] I've loved him[14] for six years. I love him more than I love my own mother. I hear him every moment and I feel his hand. I look at the door and I think, "At any moment . . ." I keep coming to you about him, he's here, he looks right through me; I have no hope and I *know* it. Oh, God, give me strength. All night I pray. I can't *stop* myself from going up to him. I look in his eyes. I confessed yesterday to Uncle Vanya. All the servants know I love him. Everybody knows. *(Pause.)*

**YELENA.** What does *he* think?

**SONYA.** He doesn't notice me.

**YELENA.** Aha. You know, he's a strange man. Do you know what? If . . . let me approach him. I'll be discreet. A most gentle hint. What do you think?[15] Really, how long are you to live in uncertainty? *(Pause.)* Yes? (SONYA *nods.*) Good. The question: he loves you, or doesn't, and can that be hard to know? Now, don't you be embarrassed, my girl. Don't you worry. I'll be very gentle, and I'll find the answer. I'll probe him, and he will never know. Yes. Or no. And if it's no, then let him stop coming here. Yes? *(Pause.* SONYA *nods.)*[16] I think so. Yes. Alright. Well, then, "Well begun is nearly done." We'll put the question. He was going to show me some maps. Tell him that I want him.

I'm *dying* of boredom.

**IS there nothing to do?**

**SONYA.** You'll tell me the truth?

**YELENA.** I will, because I think the *truth,* no matter how bad, is never so bad as an uncertainty. I promise you.

**SONYA.** You wish to see his maps.

**YELENA.** That's right.

**SONYA.** But in uncertainty, at least . . .

**YELENA.** . . . yes?

**SONYA.** . . . is hope.[17]

**YELENA.** Excuse me . . . ?

**SONYA.** No. *(Pause.)* You're right. *(Exits.)* [18]

**YELENA.** *Lord.* Lord. What is worse than knowing someone's secret and standing by powerless? Clearly the man cares nothing for her. But why shouldn't he take her? Granted, she isn't beautiful. For a country doctor his age, a kind, pure, intelligent girl—what's wrong with her for a wife. Nothing. Not a thing. Poor child. *(Pause.)* Live in a Grey World like this, and you hear nothing but the *banal* all day. What everyone eats, drinks, *thinks* . . . And then this man appears. A captivating man, a handsome man . . . like a bright-colored moon rose from the trees. To *yield* to such a man . . .[19] *(Pause.)* Vanya said, "Mermaid's blood runs in your veins. For once in your life indulge yourself." Well. *Should* I not do that? For once in my life . . . ? As the man said, once in my life, and fly away from all these sleepy countenances, these dull faces, this sameness, this death-in-life, why shouldn't I? Great coward that I am, when the man comes here *every day* and I know every day the reason that he comes? Oh, God, I'm stained already, and I should fall on my knees to Sonya and beg for forgiveness.[20]

18. With how much hesitation or determination should Sonya exit?

19. How might Yelena suggest her turbulent emotions through her movements?

20. Is Yelena feeling true shame and remorse? If so, how might she show it? If not, how might she show it?

## Extension

Chekhov's realistic dialogue, unspoken subtexts, and amusingly eccentric characters have had a great effect on modern dramatic writing.

1. Describe a situation in a comedy you have seen in which a character feels great frustration over not being able to get what he or she wants. What makes it funny?
2. Write and perform a monologue in which you talk about something you want and your frustration at not getting it. Keep it light: your character may be feeling unhappy, but the audience should be amused.

# Technical Theatre

performance

**The countdown to performance has begun. The stage crew completes construction, assembles equipment and supplies, prepares checklists, and rehearses technical operations. The stage manager helps coordinate these efforts, and as opening night approaches, supervises the operations of the stage crew and all other backstage activities. On opening night, everything and everyone come together to run the show.**

## THE LANGUAGE OF THEATRE

**boom** or **boomerang** an aluminum tripod with a cross bar at the top on which lights are hung; also called a **lighting tree**

**call** to notify cast and crew of cues, rehearsal times, and the rise and fall of the curtain

**cyclorama** or **cyc** a background drop or curtain, hung on a U-shaped batten around the three sides of the stage; serves to mask the backstage area during shifting of scenery

**dry tech** a technical rehearsal without actors present

**fly** to be raised or lowered on lines in the fly space

**gobo** a thin metal template with a pattern punched out; attached to a lighting instrument to create patterned or textured lighting effects

**grip** a member of the stage crew who shifts scenery

**paper tech** a meeting of the stage crew and the stage manager to run through cues on paper and create a master cue sheet

**rigging** the way in which mobile scenery and lights are mounted and controlled

**wagon** a flat or platform rigged with wheels

# Shifting Scenery

Whether your production is a one-act or full-length play, you will need to manage quick and unobtrusive scene changes. Loud, slow, and conspicuous scene changes destroy the play's continuity and annoy the audience; a general rule of thumb is that no shift should take longer than 60 seconds. If the set for the play involves multiple or complex scene changes, you will need to rig it for shifting. **Rigging** is the way in which mobile scenery and lights are mounted and controlled. Scenery can be rigged to **fly,** or be raised or lowered on lines in the fly space (p. 216). The lines (heavyweight rope or wire) are attached to a **grid** or **gridiron,** a steel framework above the stage. A counterweight rigging system (p. 216) is often used to fly scenery.

Scenery can also be rolled on- and offstage. Flats or platforms rigged with wheels are called **wagons** or **trucks.** Wheel casters with rubber tires on the wagons help ensure quiet scene changes. Swivel casters with brakes allow you to move scenery in any direction and then lock it in place until you are ready to move it again. Wagons are generally employed for shifting heavy set pieces or large, joined units. Sometimes, entire sets are built on a large wagon that is pivoted onto the stage from the wings. These are known as **jackknife sets.**

Some theatres change scenery by means of a revolving stage, which consists of a central circular platform that is turned mechanically. A revolving stage can be divided to present as many as three distinct sets. Theatres with elevator stages can shift scenery by lowering sections of the stage floor into the basement while other sections are in place above.

A background drop or curtain, called a **cyclorama** or **cyc,** masks the backstage area during shifting of scenery. It hangs on a U-shaped batten around the three sides of the stage. It's typically a continuous curtain or drop, but may have breaks to accommodate shifting of scenery. The cyclorama may be a black curtain or a neutral drop. A drop cyc may be painted as the sky or as a general locale, such as a forest.

If you have designed a single set to include more than one setting, the scene changes might be as minor as shifting a few flats and changing the lighting. Most often, your set will fall somewhere in the middle. You will probably need to shift flats, carry scenery, and perhaps roll one or more heavy objects on- or offstage.

In professional theatre, shifting scenery is normally done by union workers. In community and school theatre, the set construction crew often becomes the shifting crew during rehearsals and performance. Members of the stage crew who shift scenery are known as **grips.**

## Shifting Flats

Although flats are generally lightweight, they can be cumbersome to carry unless you balance them correctly. To **run,** or carry, a flat from one place to another, follow the steps below.

### RUNNING A FLAT

1. Stand behind the flat and position it vertically so that the edge of one stile is pointed in the direction in which you need to run the flat. Move to that end.
2. Spreading your arms vertically, grip the stile with one hand at a position above your head. With the other hand grip the stile at waist height.
3. Use your lower hand to lift the forward corner of the flat slightly off the floor and your upper hand to balance the flat. Then drag it lightly across the floor.
4. Maintain a moderate speed so that air pressure around the moving flat can help you balance it.

### TECH TIPS: RUNNING FLATS

- Don't run a flat by grabbing both stiles and lifting the entire flat off the ground; the flat will trap moving air and act as a sail, which can throw you off balance.
- If the flat is especially wide or tall, ask a crew member to help balance the flat and push it from the rear.

## Storing Flats

The most efficient way to store flats between scenes or after a show is to stack them upright against a wall. Stack finished flats face-to-face to protect the painted surfaces. Check for protruding hardware that could puncture other flats. Make sure your flats are stacked by the order in which you will need them; having the right flat handy can save you precious time during a scene change. An alternative to stacking flats against a wall is to store them in a **flat dock.** This storage method allows you to access flats as you would books off a shelf.

At times you will need to stack flats on top of each other. In those cases you may need to **float** your flat to the ground, and then lift it into place.

### FLOATING A FLAT

1. Check that the floor area is clear of obstructions and big enough to accommodate the flat.
2. Place your foot firmly against the bottom rail of the flat.
3. Gently tip the flat away from you and let it float to the floor.
4. Make sure the frames of the stacked flats rest on each other and not on unsupported fabric.

Props for Athol Fugard's *The Road to Mecca* are a vital part of the production. How many set, decorative, and hand props can you identify in this set?

## Organizing Props

Props can be an essential part of a production. They help establish time, place, and identity, and they often move the action of a play forward. To fulfill their function, however, props must be available when and where they are needed.

To keep track of set and decorative props use your prop plot (p. 227) to make a separate list of these props for each scene. Annotate your list by indicating the exact onstage location for each prop. You can also draw a property map, laid over the ground plan, that shows exactly where each prop belongs. Your list and map should also indicate where each prop will be stored between scenes.

### Hand Props

Using the prop plot, make a detailed list of props handled by the actors in each scene. The hand prop list should include notes regarding the intended onstage location of each prop, including information about where to place the prop at the beginning of the scene and where to pick it up at the end of the scene. If an actor will carry a prop on- or offstage, the list should indicate that detail as well.

## The Prop Table

Like the prop crew, actors who carry props on- or offstage must return each prop to its assigned location. To make offstage placement simple and convenient, you will probably want to set up a prop table. Make sure props are returned to the same part of the prop table each time they are used. If an actor has an unusually quick entrance and exit, station a member of the prop crew offstage to take the prop and put it in its proper place. The prop crew must make sure that the props are on the right side of the stage where they will be carried on by the actors.

During rehearsals, you should practice setting props quickly in the proper locations. Once you have your movements down, coordinate scene changes with the shifting crew. Try mapping out alternative shifting and prop crew movements on paper so that each crew can ultimately make one sweep of the stage.

### MAKING A PROP TABLE

1. Cover a large table with butcher paper. Tape it down.
2. Set the props on the table, organized according to scene or character use.
3. Draw an outline around each prop. Write a label identifying the prop that belongs in that space.
4. In the space, write the act and scene in which the prop will be used.

Prop table for *Life with Father* by Howard Lindsay and Russel Crouse

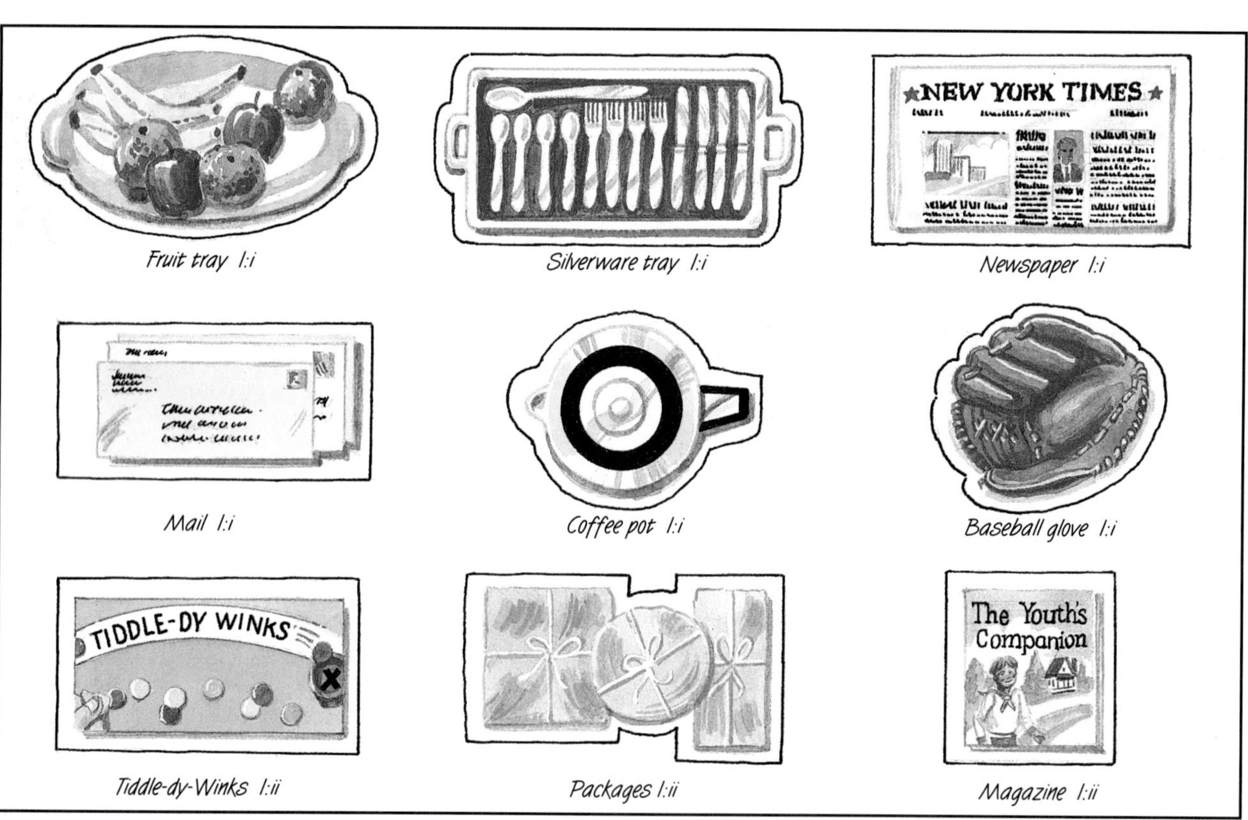

# Hanging, Focusing, and Running Lights

The lighting designer has determined how the lighting should look and where the instruments should be hung; the lighting crew makes the design a reality. The hanging and focusing of lights must be done during nonrehearsal hours because it demands exclusive use of the stage and auditorium and often the backstage area as well. In many proscenium stages, lights are hung on battens suspended from the grid in the fly space and on battens hanging in the house. In thrust and arena stages, the lights are hung on a grid of battens above the stage and house.

Another place where lights may be hung is on a **lighting tree.** Also called a **boom** or **boomerang,** a lighting tree is an aluminum tripod with a cross bar at the top. The tripod is usually nine feet tall; lights are clamped along the aluminum upright and the cross bar. Lighting trees allow shows to be brought into smaller, nontraditional theatre spaces that are not equipped with batten systems. They also provide a way to bring more lighting to the front or side of a traditional stage.

Lighting for this scene from Molière's *School for Wives* illuminates the set and actors from various positions in the theatre space.

## Hanging Lights

When you hang the lights, you will be working from the designer's lighting plot and the instrument schedule (p. 231). The lighting crew should be organized into a working team with duties assigned to each person on the crew. Make sure you plan together how you will counterweight, or balance, the batten before you start hanging lights. An unstable batten is a safety risk; it's a good idea to assign at least one crew member the task of counterweighting the batten as the instruments and cables are mounted.

When you hang the instruments, take special care not to overload a dimmer; as a general rule, don't load more than 1500 watts on each dimmer. This should be accounted for on your lighting plot and instrument schedule, but sometimes you need to change the circuits during the actual hanging. Correct your plot and schedule to reflect any changes.

**RIGGING A LIGHTING BATTEN**

1. Assemble your equipment: electrical cable (including extension cables, p. 85); Crescent wrenches; safety chains or cords; and cotton cord, duct tape, or gaffer's tape.
2. Lower the batten to a comfortable working height. (Call "Heads!" to warn everyone that a batten is coming down.) If you are using a ladder or lift, make sure it's the appropriate height. Check the lighting plot to find out the type of lighting instrument required and the rough position of the instrument.
3. Begin with lights farthest from the **drop end,** the end where the cables will drop to the floor and run to the circuits.
4. Position each light on the batten and tighten the clamp by hand.
5. Check the position again against the lighting plot; if it's accurate, tighten the clamp securely with your wrench.
6. Add a safety chain or cord to prevent the instrument from falling if the clamp should come undone. A **safety cord** is a two-foot length of wire rope with a loop at one end and a snap clip at the other.
7. Secure the cable to the batten at two- or three-foot intervals using cotton cord, duct tape, or gaffer's tape. Leave enough slack between the batten and the instrument so that it can be moved easily during angling and focusing. Make sure that the cable doesn't touch any part of the instrument that will get hot and that it doesn't hang below the bottom of the instrument where it can get caught or get in the path of the light beam.
8. If any of the instruments operate together and need to be plugged into the same dimmer circuit, connect the two instruments with a short cable and a twofer (p. 85).
9. Pull out the shutters on the ellipsoidal reflector spotlights so you can see when the instruments are on.

10. Secure cables together at the drop end and let them drop loosely.
11. Adjust the counterweights to make sure the batten is balanced.
12. Run the cables to the dimmer circuits.
13. Test each instrument. If one doesn't operate, adjust the connections or check the lamp.
14. Raise the batten to operating height.
15. Tape loose cables to the floor with duct tape or gaffer's tape.

**TECH TIPS: HANGING LIGHTS**

- Mark on the **yoke,** or handle, of each the instrument type and the wattage before you begin hanging the lights to ensure that you have the right instruments and lamps.
- Wear cotton garden gloves to protect your hands from hot instruments.
- On a piece of tape, mark the ends of each instrument cable with the number of the instrument and its circuit. When all the cables are grouped together at the drop end, you will know where each is to go.
- Attach your Crescent wrench to a phone cord on a dog clip attached to your belt loop to prevent it from falling while you are working.
- Coil five or six feet of extra cable around the far end of the batten in case you need to make changes to the rigging.
- To prevent a faulty instrument from short-circuiting a dimmer, first test your instruments using nondimmer circuits.

Gel and gel frame

## Installing Gels

Gels are thin pieces of colored plastic that fit into a frame on the end of a spotlight. Gels change the color of light that falls onstage. They can be used singly to create a colored spot, or combined with other gels to create special lighting effects. To prepare a gel, use scissors or a matte knife and straight edge to cut the gel to size. If you are using a matte knife, be sure to cut on a cutting board to protect the surface under the gel. Use a white grease pencil to write the manufacturer name and number on the gel (or whatever name your school uses for the color). Then insert the gel into a gel frame. You can attach gel frames to the lights as you angle and focus them.

At this point, you can also insert any gobos you may be using. A **gobo** is a thin metal template with a pattern punched out. It can be attached to ellipsoidal reflector spotlights in a frame to project a patterned or textured light.

Lighting on this set for *Shimada* by Jill Shearer dramatically conveys different times of day and moods, primarily through the use of color.

This actor, portraying Peter Pan in Elizabeth Egloff's *Peter and Wendy,* an adaptation of J. M. Barrie's *Peter Pan,* is strikingly illuminated by a combination of side and front lighting.

## Angling and Focusing Lights

You need at least three people to angle and focus lights. One person must occupy the control board to view lighting effects and turn lights on and off. Another crew member or two must remain onstage to help pinpoint the places where light and shadows fall. The other crew members take positions at the lights that require angling and focusing.

To ensure lighting for each acting area, the crew members onstage should walk through parts of important scenes. Any time that they can see only one bright light, they should report that they are in a **dead zone.** Additional lights should be focused on that spot. Any time they find three or more bright lights in view, they should report a potential **hot spot,** so the crew can angle some light away. The goal is to avoid having dead zones and hot spots. Remember, you will be focusing lights to illuminate actors, especially at the level of their heads. Avoid angling and focusing lights to illuminate the stage floor.

Hood or top hat

**Hoods,** or **top hats,** can be attached to instruments to reduce the spill of light from an instrument. **Barn doors** can be added to shape the beam of light so that it shines into a prescribed space.

Each time lights are adjusted in one area, they will change the lighting in all other areas, too; therefore, every time you make an adjustment, you must recheck all the areas you checked before. It may not seem possible, but eventually, you will find a combination that works everywhere onstage.

## Running the Lights

Lighting systems in different theatres vary in complexity and flexibility. In some systems, each dimmer is hardwired to a specific light or set of lights. In others, a **patch bay** or **panel** makes it possible to group lights together by acting or lighting areas (p. 229). One setup may seem more logical to you than the other, but both require concentration and close attention to the lighting cue sheet.

Barn door

### Lighting Cue Sheet

Once you have hung the lights, experiment with intensity, movement, color, and lighting angles. When you find the arrangement you want, record it on your lighting cue sheet.

If your school has a computerized lighting board, input the cues into electronic storage. If you are working with a manual lighting board, record the data on paper using a lighting cue sheet. Number each cue and include a description of the cue, the page of the script on which it is found, and the action you will need to take. Practice responding to the cues by having a crew member state each cue while you make the appropriate lighting changes.

**Lighting Cue Sheet**

| Show: *Life with Father* | | | | | Crew: *Cory* | | | |
|---|---|---|---|---|---|---|---|---|
| | | | | | Begin | | End | |
| Cue No. | Script Page | Dimmer | Stage Area | Count | Cue | Level | Cue | Level |
| *1* | *2* | *2, 3* | *G, H* | *8* | *Curtain* | *1* | *Good morning, ma'am* | *8* |
| *2* | *6* | *5* | *1* | *5* | *Good morning, Mother* | *0* | *Good morning, Clarence* | *6* |
| *3* | *12* | *5* | *1* | *3* | *Good morning, boys* | *6* | *Good morning, Vinnie* | *8* |
| *4* | *15* | *2* | *G* | *3* | *devil of a row* | *0* | *Clare, I do hope* | *5* |

## Setting Up Sound

After preparing the appropriate sounds for your production, you must transmit them in a way that is effective for the audience and convenient for you during the production. For a production to run smoothly, sound must travel from the stage to the audience and to the sound booth where it can be monitored. In most cases, sound travels to the audience via actors' voices and speakers.

In some cases, schools amplify the actors onstage. If this is the case with your school, you will need to hang or rig microphones onstage but out of sight as part of your set up. Connecting one of those microphones to a speaker in the sound booth will enable the sound crew to hear the cues without straining. Headsets with battery-operated transmitters may also be used to connect the sound crew as well as other members of the stage crew. A backstage monitoring system allows the stage crew and cast members who are not onstage to keep track of what is happening. Some theatres use audio only and others use audio and video. If your theatre uses a monitoring system, this is the time to set up that system.

You will also need to set up amplifiers or speakers out of sight near the stage in such a way that sound effects will be audible to the actors and audience members alike. Run cable for microphones and amplifiers in the same manner that you would run cable for lights. Test the sound coming from each location to make sure your connections are working and your volume is appropriate. Then make a cue sheet and practice your cues.

### Sound Cue Sheet

Record on your sound cue sheet the cue, the script page on which it occurs, the equipment number, the sound level, and whether the cue should fade in or start at a given level. Here is one way to organize a sound cue sheet.

**Sound Cue Sheet**

| Show: *Life with Father* | | | Crew: *Naveed* | | | |
|---|---|---|---|---|---|---|
| Script Page | Sound | Cue Line | Ends | Level | Deck | Counter No. |
| *6* | *Door chimes/ whistle* | *Sit down, boys.* | *That's the doorbell.* | *6* | *1* | *005* |
| *12* | *Door slam* | *We'll put you in jail. (count 3)* | | *8* | *N/A* | *Backstage* |
| *12* | *Crash of dishes* | *Maid's scream* | *What is it?* | *9* | *1* | *009* |
| *16* | *Door chimes* | *He gets used to the idea.* | *Yes, it's Cousin Cora.* | *6* | *1* | *014* |
| *20* | *Door slam* | *Contributing to that . . .* | | *8* | *N/A* | *Backstage* |

# Completing Costumes

When a costume can't be pulled or borrowed or is too expensive to rent or buy, the costume crew must build the costumes, which generally involves sewing them from patterns.

## Patterns

**Commercial patterns** are available at any fabric store and can often be adapted for your needs. They come in one size or cover a range of sizes. Take the actor's measurement card (p. 237) and your costume sketch (p. 239) with you when you buy the pattern and fabric.

Most commercial patterns are too modern for period productions, but some can be adjusted to suit the production. Wedding patterns often employ extravagant styles that work well for period costumes. Some patterns for period costumes are available in libraries or through companies specializing in vintage patterns.

Establish a library of easy-to-sew multisize patterns that can be quickly sewn and adapted for different periods. Suggested patterns include those for a vest, draw-string or elastic-waist pants (with optional pockets), an elastic-waist A-line skirt (adjustable for length), a cape, a unisex peasant blouse, and a tunic. Costumes sewn from these simple patterns can be embellished with period decoration to suit a range of needs. A velveteen vest with gold braid and a leather vest with fringe can both be cut from the same pattern. Depending on the fabric, trim, and clasp, a cape pattern can yield a costume piece for a Roman centurion or an English gentlewoman of the 1700s.

All costumes should be completed at least halfway through the rehearsal period so actors will have an opportunity to work onstage wearing them. Most schedules allow for two fittings (p. 237).

## Dyeing

If you are color-coding costumes to show relationships among characters or need to change the color of an existing stock costume, you may need to dye garments. **Union dyes** are the commercial dyes such as RIT and Tintex that are available in supermarkets and fabric stores.

These dyes are suitable for dyeing fabrics made of natural fibers and rayon, but will only dye these fabrics to a light or medium shade. For deep shades, use a **unified aniline dye** (for most fabrics) or a **disperse dye** (for synthetic fabrics), available from theatrical supply houses.

Before dying large amounts of fabric, dye a scrap piece and test it under the stage lights. Costumes that need to be dyed the same color should be dyed together; dye intensity is hard to control from batch to batch. To keep the color of dyed and painted costumes from fading, always wash them in cold water or have them dry cleaned.

Amazing decorative and special effects can be accomplished in costuming, as shown here in *Juan Darien* by Julie Taymor and Elliot Goldenthall. Taymor was also director and designer of the costumes and set.

## Decorations and Special Effects

Costumes often require treatments that decorate, texturize, or age them. Most **decorations** consist of lace, trim, or appliqué materials that are sewn or glued in place with a hot-glue gun. Some decorations are painted on with indelible markers or fabric paint. You can stencil a border onto a dress or stamp patterns with shapes cut from hard foam or sponge material dipped in paint. You can achieve **texturizing** with spray paints or a spray gun filled with dye. Selective use of bleach on a sponge can also add texture by removing or muting color. (Bleach will weaken the fibers of many fabrics, so use it sparingly.) To **age** a costume, distress the elbows, knees, collars, cuffs, and hems with sandpaper or a wire brush. Stretch knits out of shape by wetting them and pulling on them in the places where they are likely to stretch with use, such as cuffs and knees.

When you iron a garment that you have painted or texturized, use a pressing cloth (a white cotton cloth) between the iron and the garment. This will keep your iron clean and prevent it from sticking to—and perhaps burning—your masterpiece.

## Dressing List

When you have finished acquiring or building all the costumes, you can develop a **dressing list** for each character. The dressing list itemizes everything the actor wears during each scene of the play. A copy of the dressing list should be posted in the actor's dressing room for reference when changing between scenes and to serve as a preperformance costume checklist.

| **Dressing List** | | |
|---|---|---|
| Show: *Life with Father* | | Character: *Mr. Day*<br>Actor: *Drew* |
| Act & Scene | Costume Description | |
| *I: i* | *3-piece black suit; white shirt w/detachable collar; red and gray rep tie with gold tie-pin; gold pocketwatch with chain and fob; black tie shoes; black socks; black derby; white gloves; walking stick* | |
| *I: ii* | *Same* | |
| *II: i* | *Black cutaway coat; gray and black striped trousers; white shirt; gray four-in-hand tie with pearl tie-pin; silk hat; white gloves; silver pocketwatch with chain and fob; black tie shoes; black socks; walking stick* | |

The well-dressed family in Howard Lindsay and Russel Crouse's *Life with Father* requires careful attention to costume details.

# Applying Makeup

Because most actors apply their own makeup for performances, you may need to coach the actors on how to reshape their faces according to your makeup plans (p. 239).

## Reshaping

Reshaping of the face generally involves the jaw line, nose, and cheeks. An understanding of the facial anatomy and bone structure is helpful to accomplish the best effects.

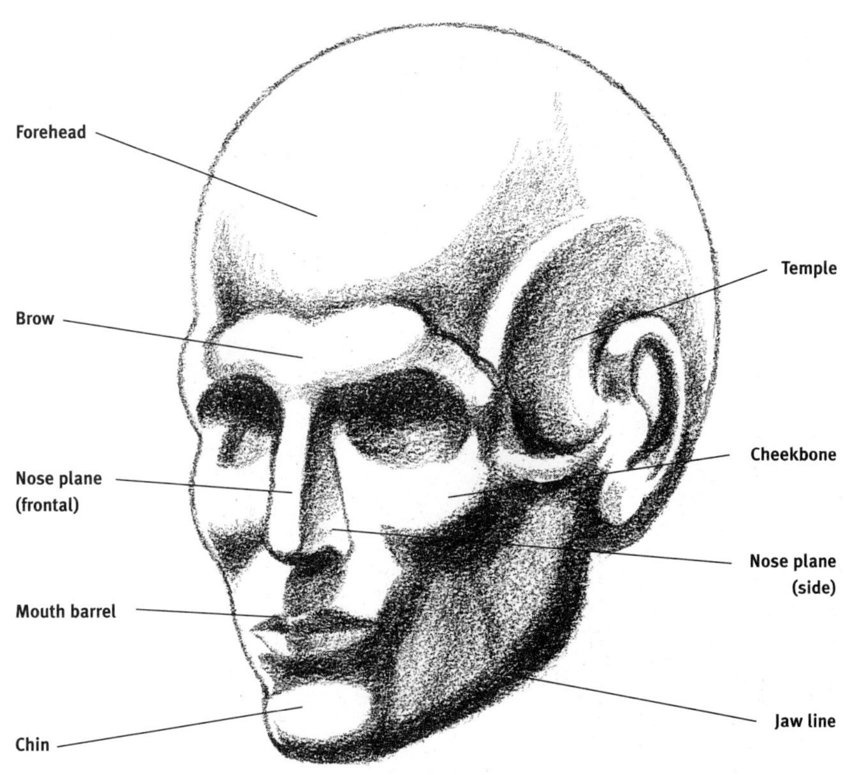

## Blending

When you reshape the face with makeup, you will be blending between colors and between highlights and shadows. **Blending** means diminishing the intensity of a makeup color from strongest to lightest and is probably the most important technique you will learn in makeup application. Blend by patting with your fingertips from the darkest point outward until the makeup fades into the base color. Strive for a smooth gradual transition. Patting removes makeup you don't need instead of smearing it and spreading it around.

White foundation is traditional for actors in Kabuki theatre (p. 296), who wear highly stylized makeup.

## Foundation

All makeup application begins with foundation (p. 95). For light-skinned actors, foundation can add color to the face so it doesn't wash out under lights. For dark-skinned actors, foundation lightly applied evens out skin tone and provides a uniform surface for additional makeup. Colored foundations can also be used to create a skin tone that may help an actor establish an ethnic identity.

Whatever color you are using, make sure it's blended into the hairline so there isn't an abrupt shift from the skin tone to the foundation color.

## Highlights and Shadows

Generally, you create the illusion of narrow, deep, or sunken features by using dark colors. Create wide, full, prominent features by using lighter tones. Blend darker and lighter colors gradually into the foundation. For example, you can create the illusion of a low forehead by applying a dark foundation to the skin near the hairline. You can make the forehead seem higher by applying a lighter shade at the hairline. Similarly, you can apply darker foundation at the sides of the nose to make it seem narrower, or lighter foundation at the sides to make it seem wider. Many makeup artists—and even ordinary people—apply darker tones of rouge or foundation under the cheekbone to sink the cheek and lighter tones on the cheekbone to highlight the bone; this creates the illusion of higher, sculpted cheekbones and a thinner face. You can make a face seem fuller by using light tones under the cheekbone to highlight the cheek itself. If you apply more shadow to the inside corners of the eyelids, the eyes will seem closely set. If you apply it to the outside corner of the lids, the eyes will seem farther apart.

## Accents

Certain features, such as eyes and lips can be accented simply by tracing their outlines. To accent the eyes, use eyeliner or an eyebrow pencil and draw a line along the upper lid, close to the eyelashes. Then do the same for the bottom lid. To make eyes appear large, apply a thin line on the upper and lower lid about one third of the way out from the tear ducts. To make the eyes appear small, use heavy liner around the entire eye. To accent the eyelashes, curl them using an eyelash curler, and then apply black mascara to the top and bottom lashes.

Lip liner can be used to accent or enhance the shape of the lips. Outline lips in lip liner several shades darker than the lipstick you will use. For fuller lips, **overdraw,** or outline beyond the natural line of the lip. Be conservative when overdrawing the lip or you will create a caricature rather than a character.

The "bee-stung" lips of silent film star Clara Bow typify a fashionable look of the 1920s.

# Final Rehearsals

During rehearsals, the stage manager may perform a variety of duties to aid the director (p. 187). During the final rehearsals and performance, however, the stage manager's role in the technical aspects of the production becomes increasingly prominent. By troubleshooting, giving notes, and **calling,** or notifying, cast and crew of their cues, the stage manager is instrumental in holding the production together.

## Final Rehearsals: Stage Manager

If you have rehearsed the play elsewhere, one of your biggest landmarks as a stage manager will be the day rehearsals are moved from the rehearsal space to the stage. If you have measured and organized the rehearsal space, the transition to the stage should be relatively easy. Still, you will need to make adjustments in placing set pieces and props. With the stage crew, spike (p. 286) the placement of anything onstage that is moveable, such as set pieces, lights, or speakers, as soon as they are positioned. If a change is made, remember to change the spikes as well. As long as the spikes are clearly set, the crews will be able to set furniture and props as they should be.

Once the environment onstage is completed, work with the crew to set the prop table and costume rack in a convenient place offstage. Also set aside a spot for quick costume changes, if needed. Use glow tape to mark areas of safe passage, and make sure work lights (generally scoops) are in place backstage and in prop storage areas.

# Tech Rehearsal

A production may have one or more **technical rehearsals,** or **tech runs,** scheduled, usually within the last two weeks before opening night. The purpose of tech runs is to coordinate, practice, and perfect the technical operations of the production. Many directors schedule a **dry tech,** one without actors present, to iron out any glitches. They then combine further tech rehearsals with dress rehearsals.

## Tech Rehearsal: Stage Manager

Begin by encouraging each of the crews to meet for a pretech conference prior to the full tech rehearsal for the show. This is called a **paper tech.** The paper tech gives crews an opportunity to go over each cue in the show on paper without actually performing the cues.

## Master Cue Sheet

At the paper tech, you should create a **master cue sheet** in which you record all light and sound cues as well as scenery shifts, prop information, and costume changes.

Establish a code system of letters and numbers; for example, you might use L for lights, S for sound, P for props, C for costumes, and F for flying or shifting curtains and scenery. You could then number each cue sequentially in each category.

At the tech rehearsal, update the master cue sheet to reflect any changes. Then update your promptbook, which you will use to call the show.

**Master Cue Sheet**

Show: *Life with Father* | Stage Manager: *Carmen*

| Cue No. | Script Page | Cue Line | Action |
|---|---|---|---|
| *F1* | *2* | *[curtain]* | *Curtain rises* |
| *L1* | *2* | *[curtain]* | *Lights on areas G, H; level 8* |
| *L2* | *6* | *Good morning, Mother* | *Lights on area I; level 6* |
| *S1* | *6* | *Sit down, boys* | *Door chimes; level 6* |
| | | | |

To make the tech runs as efficient as possible, develop a schedule and try to stick to it. Establish call times for the cast and crew, depending on when they are needed in the show. Ask them to sign in when they arrive and to be on hand in case they are needed to run a scene. Build in extra breaks, which you can use if you run overtime. Do run-throughs or work particular scenes if you finish ahead of schedule. If you run into a technical glitch, ask the actors to hold their positions until it can be corrected. At the end of a tech rehearsal, give notes, or comments, to the stage crew.

## Tech Rehearsal: Scenery and Props

Every movement of the shifting and prop crews must be choreographed to create seamless scene changes. Stay on the routes you worked out in earlier rehearsals. If people get in your way, stand still until they pass; dodging them may take you into the established path of another grip or prop person. When you have a break, take notes on what is working and what isn't. If any item poses a danger, report it to the stage manager immediately; otherwise, wait until the end of the tech run to address problems that come to light.

## Tech Rehearsal: Lighting and Sound

If you have the time before the full tech rehearsal, run your own lighting tech rehearsals by having a crew member or the stage manager run through cues. Respond to each cue with the appropriate lighting change. Be prepared for changes to the lighting cue sheet during tech rehearsals; adjustments to the timing and intensities are common.

Running sound cues prior to tech is crucial to avoid glitches and unnecessary delays. Preset your volume for microphones, music, and sound effects. Practice responding to onstage cues and calls from the stage manager. During the tech run, discuss moments in the play that might be disrupted by audience response, such as laughter, and make the necessary adjustments.

This actor is in full makeup for Dale Wasserman's *Man of La Mancha.*

## Tech Rehearsal: Costumes and Makeup

If possible, try to schedule a **dress parade** on the same day as the tech rehearsal just before it is scheduled to start. In a dress parade, the actors try on each of their costumes and walk under the lights. This gives you an opportunity to look critically at the costumes under the lights and note any necessary last-minute changes. After individual actors have shown their costumes, the entire company assembles onstage for a similar preview.

Actors should be in full makeup for the dress parade and tech rehearsal. With actors in makeup, the lighting designer can adjust lighting as necessary with a clearer impression of how it will look during the actual show.

Scheduling the dress parade for the same day as the tech rehearsal serves several functions. The actors will be in costume and on hand as needed during the tech run. It will also provide the costume crew with extra time to make any last-minute costume fixes before dress rehearsal.

# Dress Rehearsal

The dress rehearsal is as close to opening night as possible. Cast and crew should behave accordingly. No one should be wandering around. Everyone should be attentive to the action onstage and their own specific duties.

## Dress Rehearsal: Stage Manager

During the dress rehearsal and performances, the stage manager is in charge backstage. The director will stop the show if and when necessary, but the stage manager is the one to call the cues. Following is a list of the stage manager's duties during the dress rehearsal and performances:

- Post a call sheet with assigned arrival times for cast and crew.
- Monitor the sign-in sheet to ensure that people are arriving as they should; call those who are missing.
- Receive reports from crew members after they have completed their checks; make a final check of the stage.
- Provide 30-minute, 15-minute, and 5-minute calls to cast and crew.
- Gather cast and crew for a final meeting prior to curtain for director's final words.
- Call places for cast and crew. (The "places" call is a notification to get ready for the curtain to rise and the performance to begin.)
- Maintain backstage order.
- Control emergencies: make sure a fire extinguisher and first aid kit are backstage.
- Call the show.
- After the performance, make sure all areas are clean, the set is ready for the next performance, and all equipment is locked up; report to director that the theatre is ready to close for the night.

Work with the director to coordinate the curtain call; make sure everyone is acknowledged, including the producer and the producer's staff, which includes the front-of-house staff.

The stage manager may take responsibility for planning a party on closing night or the night after. If possible, include a video of the show as part of the party, so everyone in the play can finally see the entire performance.

## Dress Rehearsal: Scenery and Props

Most issues relative to shifting scenery should have been worked out in the technical rehearsal, but props will need to be checked before every performance. Together with the costume crew, determine which hand props will be handled by the costume crew and which will be handled by the prop crew.

Unusual costumes are a highlight of *Le Bourgeois Avant Garde, A Comedy After Molière* by Charles Ludlam.

## Dress Rehearsal: Lighting and Sound

Dress rehearsal is the final run-through for the show. Problems running lighting and sound cues should have been ironed out by now; this is the final opportunity to make sure cues are correct. Everything necessary to run lights and sound should be in place before the dress rehearsal starts. Make note of any problems and correct them immediately after the dress rehearsal is completed.

## Dress Rehearsal: Costumes and Makeup

To treat dress rehearsal as much like an actual show as possible, makeup and costume crews should coordinate their call times and post this information for the actors. Lists of costumes, accessories, and makeup should be posted for each actor, and any costumes or costume pieces needed for quick changes should be placed in their designated areas. Crew members must be on hand to help actors apply makeup or get into costumes.

After the rehearsal, the makeup crew should make sure that cotton swabs, mineral oil, and antiseptic cleanser are available for removing makeup. The makeup area should be cleaned up and makeup should be put back in the appropriate location for the next performance. Costume crew members should gather and account for all costumes and hang them where they belong.

# Run of the Show

The tech rehearsal may establish the high-water mark for anxiety and excitement, but opening night is a close runner-up. During the **run of the show,** or series of performances, the show may change based on feedback from the director, who often sits in the audience during the performances, the producer, and even the audience.

## Run of the Show: Stage Manager

You can avoid much of opening-night chaos by planning. First, establish a call time for cast and crews. Many theatres ask actors to arrive an hour and a half before show time. Crews sometimes arrive a half hour later than actors.

Hold each crew responsible for making sure everything is in place. Crew heads should report problems and difficulties so you can help find solutions quickly. Also request that they notify you when they are ready for the curtain to rise. Enforce backstage etiquette by insisting that actors and crew members provide each other with privacy, quiet, and personal space.

The deputy stage manager for Andrew Lloyd Webber and Tim Rice's *The Phantom of the Opera* gives 350 cues during each performance.

Confer with the house manager and other **front-of-house** staff to determine when the house will open and when you will start the show. Give the actors and crew a five-minute warning and a one-minute warning, and then tell them exactly when the house is open. That means life backstage must be silent. Provide notice before the curtain goes up. Call places one minute before curtain, and cue the first actors to appear onstage.

Make every effort to raise the curtain at the very minute curtain time was advertised. If the audience is still filing into the auditorium, the house manager should let you know when everyone is in. Audiences hate to be kept waiting more than five minutes after a show is supposed to start.

During the show, take notes to remember any problems that occur. Carry a flashlight for signaling, but use it sparingly; that little circle of light can be seen very far away.

At the end of a night's performance, after curtain calls and costume changes, gather the actors and crew so the director can give notes. Add any of your own that the director didn't touch upon, and slant your comments toward the positive. Compliment people for what they did well, and offer suggestions for improving things that didn't work. Then ask the cast and crew for notes of their own.

### Run of the Show: Scenery and Props

If the run of the show is especially long or if the scenery receives extensive handling, it may be necessary to perform repairs between shows. Check the joining and bracing hardware for scenery before and after each performance. Props often have to be revitalized since many are built for short-term use. Make sure props are in good condition well before show time; last-minute repairs and replacements make everyone nervous and invite trouble.

### Run of the Show: Lighting and Sound

Before each performance, check each dimmer and lighting instrument to make sure it's functional. Make sure lights are focused, gels are intact, and your cue sheet is in place.

For extra security, keep on hand one spare lamp of each type you use during the show. Then, if something breaks or burns out, you will be able to make repairs. You should also have a supply of fuses, keys to the system's circuit breaker panel, and copies of the lighting plot to help you locate trouble spots.

If you or someone else sees smoke or fire at any point, immediately cut off power to the circuit involved and investigate the source of the trouble. Be prepared to turn on the house lights and stop the show if the smoke or fire poses a danger to the cast, crew, or audience.

Before each performance, check your show tapes to make sure they are cued up properly. Check cables, connectors, and volume controls to avoid unpleasant surprises. If possible, keep on hand a duplicate of each show tape, so that a broken tape doesn't stop the show. At the very least, have a backup plan and share it with the cast and crews.

Before the production comes to a close, set a night aside to record the show. If video cameras are available, you may also want to videotape the entire production so that the entire cast and crew can evaluate it.

## Run of the Show: Costumes and Makeup

Members of the costume crew should be present for every performance to iron fabric, make minor repairs, and help with costume changes as required. Someone on the costume crew should be responsible for checking the costumes at the end of each show to determine which items need to be laundered or cleaned before the next curtain. Throughout the run of the show all costumes should be accounted for after each performance. The makeup crew should be available to help actors apply makeup and fix hair or wigs. Makeup should be inventoried regularly to make sure that none is running low.

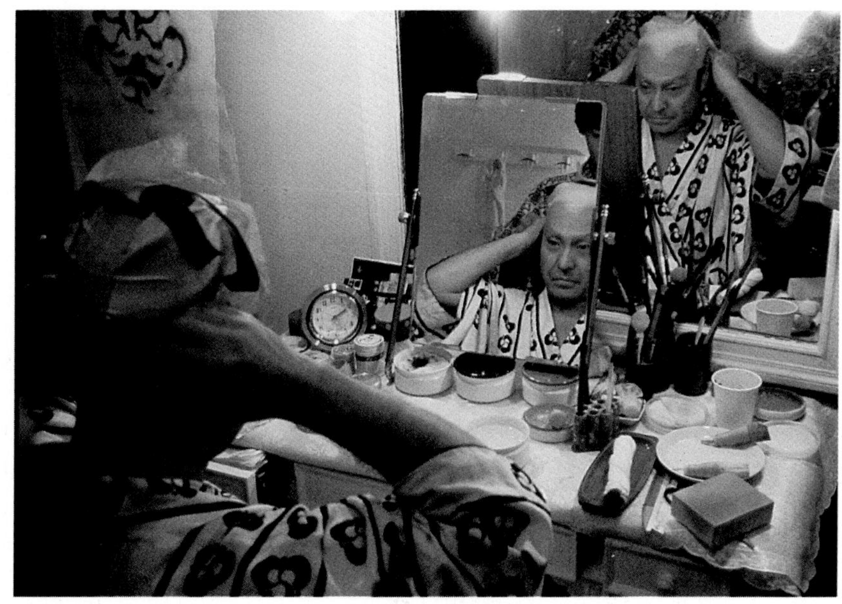

For a Kabuki actor, getting into costume and makeup is a formalized ritual. This actor's final makeup is on page 350.

# Postproduction

The last night of a show generates a mixed bag of emotions. It's important to remember that your last performance is still the first performance for the audience. Be on guard not to lose focus as you think about the end of the run and the cast party.

## Postproduction: Stage Manager

When the curtain closes on the final performance, it's time to strike the set (p. 323). Different theatres have various procedures for the strike. Some require actors and crew members to be present, and others only want the crew members present. Some theatres strike the set the night of the last performance, while others strike the next day. Follow the procedure for your theatre and inform all those who are required to be present of the date and time.

An efficient way to strike a set is to have each crew responsible for its own equipment. They should inventory and store any items that can be used again. The rest should be discarded appropriately. Make sure you are organized before going into the strike. Check with each crew to see what they might need, and make sure you have plenty of containers for trash. The following list outlines the stage manager's duties during the strike:

- In coordination with the set construction (shifting) and prop crews, account for and store all scenery, props, and rigging equipment.
- In coordination with the lighting and sound crews, account for and store all equipment.
- In coordination with the costume crew, account for and hang up all costumes.
- In coordination with the makeup crew (or actors), account for and store all makeup, including wigs and other hair pieces, that belong to the theatre.
- Supervise cleaning of the entire theatre—stage, backstage, and house.
- Check in scores and scripts and make sure the rented scripts are completely erased.
- Consult with crews to ensure that assignments have been made for returning rented and borrowed equipment.

## Postproduction: Scenery and Props

Some set pieces may need to be dismantled during the strike, and lumber and hardware may need to be stored. Be careful to clean up spare nails and staples.

Store flats and props backstage in their designated areas. Check in props you pulled from stock and add any new props built for the show on your inventory.

## Postproduction: Lighting and Sound

Store lighting and cords in their designated spots. If any of your lights were borrowed or rented, make sure they are in working order and are returned promptly. You may want to file your lighting plot and cue sheet for future reference by other production crews.

When the show closes, return microphones, cords, speakers, and amplifiers to their proper places. Anything that was borrowed or rented should be returned in good working order. Make a table of contents of your sound-effects tapes and file those with the tapes for use in any future productions.

## Postproduction: Costumes and Makeup

The costume crew must return pulled, rented, and borrowed items and determine which new items can go into the theatre's permanent stock. New items should be added to the inventory.

The makeup crew should inventory the remaining makeup, store what is still useable, and discard any that is not. Additional makeup should be added to the theatre's inventory.

# Activities

### *Shifting Scenery*

**RUNNING AND FLOATING** With permission from your teacher, work with another student to practice running and floating flats of various sizes on- and offstage. When you carry them onstage, set them up using your theatre's standard bracing method. When you carry them offstage, place them or store them as you would during a production. Discuss any problems you encountered and propose solutions.

### *Organizing Props*

**PROP TABLE** Prepare a prop plot for a play. Using the plot, prepare a prop table that would fit in the wings of your theatre and still allow room for backstage traffic. You can use household items as substitutes for props that are difficult to find (but make your labels reflect the prop as specified in the play). You might find it helpful to draw a plan on paper first. Present your prop table to the class. Lead a discussion for other practical methods of handling props during a performance.

### *Hanging, Focusing, and Running*

**RIG A BATTEN** Work together with a small group of students (under your teacher's supervision) to rig a lighting batten according to an existing lighting plot (p. 230) for your school theatre, or work up a simple plot for at least one batten. Follow the guidelines for marking each instrument and testing the lights. Then brainstorm how you could make the task run smoother. Record suggestions or tips in your Theatre Notebook.

### *Hanging, Focusing, and Running Lights*

**EXPERIMENT WITH COLORED LIGHT** Gather together gels of various colors. Focus two lighting instruments on a white flat. Insert different gel colors into each of the instruments and note how the colors mix together on the flat. Try it with a partner standing in the light. Which colors seem to mix into natural light combinations? Which colors did not work well together? How do colors and shadows change when your partner stands in the light? Describe the effects of your experiments in your Theatre Notebook, using color diagrams for clarity.

### Setting Up Sound

**SOUND CUES PRACTICE** Choose one scene in a play, noting in the script where music and sound effects are required and how long each lasts (the count). Use a watch with a second hand to help you determine the count for each sound. Prepare a sound cue sheet for the scene. Enlist the help of actors to read the scene while you record them on cassette tape. Play the tape and practice responding to your cues by "pushing" imaginary play, pause, and stop buttons as you would on your theatre sound system. Make any necessary adjustments to your cue sheet, and then run through your cues until you are satisfied you know them well.

### Completing Costumes

**SUPPLEMENT YOUR PATTERN STOCK** Take a trip to the fabric store and look through pattern books for inexpensive, adaptable patterns to supplement your theatre department's pattern stock. If your department doesn't have a pattern collection, make a list of suggested patterns to create a collection and present it to your teacher. Give a rationale for each pattern that includes an explanation of how each pattern might be adapted for period plays, for various genres, and for actors of various sizes, as well as the cost of the pattern, the approximate cost of material to sew the garment, the level of sewing expertise required to sew it, and the approximate time it would take to build the garment using the pattern.

### Completing Costumes

**JOB SHADOW—TAILOR** Arrange to observe a professional tailor at work for a day or a few hours. Explain that you are interested in witnessing the day-to-day operations of a tailor to see how the skills of a tailor are similar to those used by a costumer. (If possible, job shadow a costumer at a theatre.) Professionals are busy, but if you are polite as well as interested, they are usually willing to let you observe them at work and to answer questions about their training and background. Be sure to first get permission from your parents, teacher, and the supervisor of the business or organization where you will job shadow.

# Activities

### Completing Costumes

**SPECIAL EFFECTS** Try dyeing, texturizing, or aging a costume. If you are currently involved in a production, talk to the costume designer about any costume pieces that might require any of these treatments. If you don't have access to any costume pieces, work with a spare piece of fabric, such as muslin or canvas, or on an old shirt of your own. If you have an old sweater or a pair of blue jeans, try aging techniques. Show your results to others in your class.

### Applying Makeup

**RESHAPE YOUR FACE** Work with a partner to change the shape of each other's face to look like a face you find in a magazine. Study the general structure of the head first. Apply the principles of using highlight and shadow to alter your forehead, nose, cheeks, eyes, and lips. Accent where appropriate using accenting techniques. Pay careful attention to blending. When you are finished, you might take photographs of your reshaped faces and include them in your Theatre Notebook next to the magazine pictures.

### Final Rehearsals

**FROM REHEARSAL SPACE TO STAGE** With a small group, brainstorm the steps involved in moving a production from a rehearsal space to the actual stage. If you have never been involved in a production that moved from one space to another, imagine what this might entail based on what you know of the rehearsal process. Develop a series of checklists that the stage manager and stage crew might use to ensure a smooth transition. Discuss these with the class and revise as necessary.

### Tech Rehearsal

**MOCK DRESS PARADE** To better see the value of a dress parade, stage a mock one. Work with a small group: at least two students working lights, three wearing costumes and full makeup, and two acting as director and costume designer. Vary the lighting and the costumes to see the way certain costume colors and fabrics appear under certain colors, angles, and intensities of light. After a critique by the director and designers, make adjustments to the lighting, costumes, or makeup.

### *Dress Rehearsal*

**QUICK COSTUME CHANGES** Work with a partner to simulate the rapid costume changes often required for a performance, which you must perfect during a dress rehearsal. Assemble five costume changes for each of you—some simple, some complex. Work in your theatre's dressing rooms and wings (for simple changes) or in a space simulating those areas. Establish a time limit for each change, varying from very brief (2 to 5 minutes) to longer (10 to 15 minutes), allowing time to touch up your makeup (you should be in full makeup as in a real dress rehearsal). Time yourselves. Be efficient and quiet. As in a dress rehearsal, note any problems you had and make suggestions for addressing potential crises such as lost shoes and popped buttons.

### *Run of the Show*

**FRONT-OF-HOUSE STAFF** Work with a large group of students to establish and practice protocol for taking tickets, handing out programs, and seating the audience. Establish a set of procedures for standard operations as well as troubleshooting (dealing with latecomers and disruptive audience members). You might also craft standard greetings and precise answers to common questions, such as directions to the restrooms, drinking fountains, greenroom, and box office. You should be prepared for questions about the play and performers (you can decide on a particular play to use for your simulation). Then do an improvisation of an opening night with one student acting as house manager, one as box office manager, several as ushers, and the rest as the audience.

### *Postproduction*

**STRIKE CHECKLIST** Devise a checklist that a stage manager could use during strike. One way to organize your checklist is to divide it into categories that correspond to the stage crews. Add a general category for miscellaneous details that might otherwise be forgotten. Try to keep your checklist as simple and straightforward as possible and useable for any production. If possible, try it out for a production. Revise your checklist as necessary. Include it in your Theatre Notebook for possible future use.

# Projects

# performance

PROJECT 21

## Duet Performance

**ASSIGNMENT** With a partner, prepare and perform a brief dramatic scene.

| Project Planner | |
|---|---|
| **Product** | A performance of an 5–10 minute dramatic scene |
| **Purpose** | To develop skills in creating a character |
| **Specs** | To accomplish this project, you will<br>• work closely with a partner to create a duet scene<br>• choose an 8–12 minute scene appropriate to both of your abilities<br>• analyze the script for each character, as well as the action and pacing<br>• rehearse, using rehearsal skills, including improvisation<br>• communicate your character's emotions through movement, gesture, and voice<br>• perform the scene for an audience |

## Creating

**CHOOSE YOUR SCENE** With your partner, choose a two-character scene from a published play. The scene should be at least 5 minutes long but no more than 10 minutes. The characters in the scene should be appropriate and within your age range (2 or 3 years younger or 10 years older). Look for a scene that is challenging but not beyond what you are prepared for. It should have a definite beginning, middle, and end. You may want to clear your choice with your teacher before beginning work on it.

**ANALYZE THE SCENE** First read the entire play from which you chose the scene. Picture the action as you read. Working with your partner, discuss these questions:

- What is the plot of the play?
- How does the scene you have chosen fit into the plot?
- Who are your characters?
- What is the setting (time and place) of the play? of the scene?
- What is the theme of the play?
- What are your characters' objectives in the play? in the scene?
- What are your characters' obstacles in the play? in the scene?
- What actions do your characters take to achieve their objectives in this scene?
- What are the stakes?
- What is the outcome of each of your character's actions in this scene?
- How do your characters change during the course of the play?

**BLOCKING REHEARSALS** Together with your partner, read your scene aloud. As you read, consider what your characters actually say to each other, how they act and react, and the nature of their subtexts (p. 138). At this point, you may want to improvise to explore the characters and their relationship.

Start walking through your scene. First agree on a simple ground plan (p. 176) and place the needed furniture within it. Then block the major actions, such as entrances and exits. As you continue to work, break down the scene into beats (p. 147). Identify each beat by finding the beginning, middle, and end. You can rehearse each beat individually before putting them back together for a seamless whole.

Determine the rising action (p. 170), climax (p. 171), and falling action (p. 171) of the scene. Pace the action to build toward the climax.

Work individually on memorizing your lines. When you are ready to go off book, arrange for a classmate to prompt you until you have your lines.

**POLISHING REHEARSALS** Refine and polish your scene, adding or removing actions or gestures to make the scene work better. Decide on what costuming and props you will use for your performance. Perfect any stage business you develop for the scene. Experiment with vocal inflection.

You might perform a preview for other class members. Discuss with your audience what they enjoyed about your performance and what they felt needed improvement. In your final rehearsals, use their criticisms and incorporate the changes you feel will strengthen your performance.

**DRESS REHEARSAL** Perform a complete dress rehearsal. You may also choose to have an audience for this performance for a final round of critiquing. It would be best if you could perform in the space where your final performance will be.

## Performing

Before beginning, make sure that your set, props, and costumes are ready. Warm up or go through your preparation ritual. Introduce the scene to your audience briefly. Include the title of the play and the author's name. Then perform, keeping these points in mind:

- Keep your actions direct and motivated.
- Stay focused and listen to the other character.
- Project and articulate.
- Build the scene to its climax.

## Responding

How well you have fulfilled the Specs in the Project Planner will help assess your performance. You may also ask yourself, your partner, or your audience these questions to help you improve:

- Could the audience see all the action, gestures, and facial expressions critical to the scene?
- Did all actions, movement, and gestures appear natural, motivated, and in character?
- Did you project and use vocal variety?
- Did you stay in character?
- Did the dialogue sound as if it were being spoken for the first time?
- Were the costumes and props appropriate?
- Did you and the audience connect emotionally through the performance?

Include responses to these questions in your Theatre Notebook.

## Adapting the Project

1. Perform a longer, more complex scene with three or four characters. Follow the same procedure outlined in this project.
2. Participate in a round-table discussion with other actors who have completed this project. Describe problems you and your partner encountered while working on your scene and how you overcame them. You might also include how you incorporated the changes suggested after your preview performance.
3. Plan a duet acting festival at your school. If possible, ask professionals from the theatre community or other community members to act as evaluators.
4. Use the project format to rehearse scenes from a production that is currently in rehearsal at school.

# Characterization Using Animal Traits

**ASSIGNMENT** Perform a character incorporating traits observed in an animal.

## Project Planner

| | |
|---|---|
| **Product** | A brief monologue or scene |
| **Purpose** | To refine characterization skills |
| **Specs** | To accomplish this project, you will<br>• choose a monologue or a scene from a play<br>• analyze the character for animal characteristics<br>• observe the real animal and record your observations<br>• incorporate observed animal behavior into the character in the monologue or scene<br>• perform the monologue or scene for an audience |

## Creating

**CHOOSE A MONOLOGUE OR SCENE** Conceiving a character with animal traits can help provide insight into the characterization process. For example, you may have heard a person described as "sly as a fox" or "wise as an owl." In Ben Jonson's play *Volpone* the character names Volpone and Mosca actually mean "fox" and "fly," providing clues to their personalities.

First choose a brief monologue or scene. Read the entire play before doing your character analysis. Pay attention to what the playwright and other characters say about the character you are analyzing as well as what your character says about himself or herself. In most instances, you won't find a description as direct as "sly as a fox," so you will have to look for suggestions of animal behavior in what your character says and does.

**OBSERVE THE ANIMAL** If possible, observe the real animal in its environment (which might be a zoo, a park, a home, or a farm). If that's not possible, you might observe the animal on film. Take notes on its behavior, including the following:

- the pace and rhythm of its movements
- how it holds its head and opens its mouth

- how it uses its senses of taste, smell, touch, sight, and hearing
- the way it uses its muscles to walk, eat, yawn, sit, and sleep
- repeated actions

**DEVELOP YOUR CHARACTER** To play your chosen animal you may physicalize any number of its traits from the way it holds its head to the way it eats. Experiment with what you can do with your body to imitate your animal's movements. Now incorporate these movements into the character in your scene. If you wish, incorporate some of the noises the animal makes into your vocal interpretation.

You will have to judge how far you want to go; it may be that one small, suggestive movement will do the job, or you may want to include several traits. In general, however, your actions should be clear and specific enough so that the audience will know what animal your character suggests. The result will not be realistic, but the stylized movements should add something to the audience's understanding of your character.

## Performing

Try to rehearse at least once in the space in which you will be performing. Introduce your scene as usual, but don't explain to the audience what animal your character suggests. Perform your scene.

## Responding

How well you have fulfilled the Specs in the Project Planner will help assess your project. You may also ask yourself or your audience these questions to help you improve:

- Could the audience see all your gestures, expressions, and movements?
- Were your actions specific enough for the audience to understand your activities?
- Could the audience understand what animal your character suggested?
- Did the animal behavior reveal something important about the character you were portraying?

Include responses to these questions in your Theatre Notebook.

## Adapting the Project

1. Use the animal traits you observed and practiced to help flesh out a character you are playing in a production.
2. Analyze a full-length play in terms of what animal behaviors might be exhibited by each character and what the behavior would reveal about each character's personality.

# Commedia dell'Arte Performance

**ASSIGNMENT** With an ensemble, improvise a commedia dell'arte performance based on a given scenario, or plot outline.

## Project Planner

| | |
|---|---|
| **Product** | An improvised performance |
| **Purpose** | To refine improvisation and ensemble skills |
| **Specs** | To accomplish this project, you will<br>• form an ensemble and assign parts<br>• study together the given scenario<br>• develop a ground plan for the performance<br>• improvise dialogue, movement, and gestures<br>• rehearse and polish the performance<br>• perform for an audience |

Pantalone

## Creating

**CAST YOUR PERFORMANCE** Commedia dell'arte (p. 278) made use of stock characters, basic human types whose names and personalities were the same from play to play. Form an ensemble of two males and two females and decide who will play each of the following stock commedia characters:

**Pantalone** (pän tä lōn´ā) a pompous, middle-aged man

**Flaminia** (flə min´ē ə) his daughter, a proper young woman, but with a mind of her own

**Orazio** (ôr äts´ē ō) Flaminia's ardent lover—unknown to Pantalone

**Franceschina** (frän ches kēn´ə) Pantalone's bright and sassy maid-servant

**STUDY THE SCENARIO** Commedia dell'arte had no written scripts. Interpreting standard scenarios, actors improvised their dialogue and stage business (p. 289). As you study this plot outline below, think about dialogue, movements, and gestures you could use to bring your character to life.

Flaminia wonders why she hasn't heard from Orazio today. Her father has forbidden her to see any men and plans

Orazio

to arrange her marriage; but she is determined to wed the man of her own choosing. Pantalone tells Flaminia that he hopes to complete the marriage arrangements in a day or two. Meanwhile she is not to go outdoors or let herself be seen at any window. Franceschina gives Flaminia a love letter from Orazio, which she has smuggled into the house. Delighted, Flaminia reads it and gives Franceschina a letter of her own to carry to Orazio.

Pantalone stops Franceschina as she is leaving the house and asks what she is carrying, but she convinces him that Flaminia's letter is nothing. He tells her to be especially watchful while he is out and not to let any men near the house. She readily agrees.

Franceschina meets Orazio in a prearranged place to give him Flaminia's letter. She tells him about the marriage arrangements underway, and Orazio vows to put a stop to them somehow. Together they plot how Orazio will sneak into the house to see Flaminia. Pantalone sees Orazio and tells him that, as neighbors, his family will be invited to Flaminia's wedding. Upset, Orazio almost blurts out the truth, but holds his tongue. Orazio renews his vow to marry Flaminia himself.

Francheschina

**REHEARSE THE PERFORMANCE** Since most of the scenes given involve two people, you can rehearse them that way to start. Improvise appropriate dialogue and stage business. Try to make your dialogue witty and your movements big and broad. This is farce, so have fun with physical humor. If you don't like the effect of a line or movement, go back and try something else. Get suggestions and feedback from your fellow performers about how you can improve a speech or a stage business. Remember your best lines and stage business and incorporate them into the final performance.

As you rehearse, be sure to consider the motivation of your characters and the subtext of their words and actions. This is important for any character development; but in comedy the contrast between what is said and the subtext of those words revealed in action can be very funny.

Commedia dell'arte performers wore distinctive traditional costumes and masks (as indicated by the illustrations). Plan what costume pieces you might devise to give your performance an authentic sense of style.

Continue rehearsing until you are comfortable with the whole piece. Commedia dell'arte actors did not re-create every performance anew; they memorized long stretches of dialogue or elaborate business that worked particularly well and used them again and again. Some of your speeches may be set by the time you come to perform them.

## Performing

Perform your scenario for your classmates or another audience. Since your performance should still be improvisational, it's vital that you stay focused. Listen to the other characters and respond to them. Keep up the energy level during the entire performance.

## Responding

How well you have fulfilled the Specs in the Project Planner will help assess your project. You may also ask yourself, your ensemble, or your audience these questions to help you improve:

- Did the audience understand who these characters were and what they were doing?
- Did the audience understand the underlying motivation and subtext for each character?
- Did all actions, movements, and gestures appear natural, motivated, and in character?
- Did all ensemble members project and use vocal variety?
- Did the audience laugh?

Include responses to these questions in your Theatre Notebook.

## Adapting the Project

1. Continue the scenario in several more scenes. You will probably want to include a meeting between Flaminia and Orazio, their discovery by Pantalone, their fooling Pantalone into believing that what he saw was not actually a lovers' meeting, and so on. How can you develop the situation so that it gets increasingly complex yet ends with the lovers getting together?
2. There were many more stock characters in commedia dell'arte. Here are two that you can add to those you have already developed to work up multi-character scenes that are more complex in structure:

   **Dottore** (dot tor´e) a middle-aged man who uses big words and convoluted language

   **Arlecchino** (ar lek ken´o) or **Harlequin** a servant constantly in and out of trouble

**Arlecchino or Harlequin**

P R O J E C T 

# Stage Composition and Emphasis

**ASSIGNMENT** Create a series of tableaux with various composition emphases.

## Project Planner

| | |
|---|---|
| **Product** | Eight different tableaux with various composition emphases |
| **Purpose** | To refine stage composition skills |
| **Specs** | To accomplish this project, you will<br>• plan eight stage compositions based on a situation<br>• direct a small ensemble to create these compositions<br>• create balanced stage compositions<br>• demonstrate the ability to draw focus<br>• use direct emphasis, duoemphasis, secondary emphasis, and diversified emphasis<br>• present the tableaux to an audience |

## Creating

**CHOOSE YOUR SETTING** Choose a setting that will involve a number of people in a variety of activities. Avoid static situations in which most people would be sitting most of the time. Instead choose a setting in which people are coming and going and moving around doing a variety of things. Here are some suggestions:

- a high school prom
- the scene of an accident
- lunchtime in a park or city plaza
- evening in a homeless shelter
- a bus stop
- an auto shop
- a protest rally

**DEVELOP A SCENARIO** Briefly describe a series of 8 to 10 events that might occur in your chosen setting. This will be your scenario (p. 371), or plot outline. For the purpose of this project, each event will constitute one scene within your scenario.

**PLAN YOUR STAGE COMPOSITION** Choose a performance space and draw a ground plan of your set. If possible, include a platform or set of stairs for more variety in levels. Enlist the help of 6 or 8 actors, taking note of their heights, which will help as you plan your composition. You may wish to make character assignments, so you can plan your composition with character relationships in mind. Now draw sketches for your scenes. You can use blocking symbols or your own shorthand.

All your stage compositions should be balanced, with a different kind of emphasis in each picture. (You don't need to use your entire ensemble in every picture.) Use diagonals, triangles, and other basics of stage composition to create these standard forms of emphasis (p. 180):

- direct emphasis
- duoemphasis
- secondary emphasis
- diversified emphasis

Remember that visual symmetry has its place onstage, but the more interesting stage pictures are usually asymmetrical. Try not to concentrate too much activity in one area of the stage. Your goal should be a balanced and interesting composition using the whole stage and with a clear and purposeful focus.

**REHEARSE YOUR ENSEMBLE** Explain your ground plan and your general scenario to your actors. Then position the actors to form the compositions you have planned. Explain the focus for each scene and the reason for the focus. You may experiment with props, lighting, sound, and costumes to help achieve focus in some scenes.

Rehearse all eight compositions. The stage composition itself should support any attitude and emotion you want to convey; the expressions and gestures of your actors should do the rest. Remember, the actors play a major role in creating focus. Rehearse also the transitions from picture to picture (p. 147), so that the actors can make them as quickly and smoothly as possible. You may ask them to make the transitions in or out of character if you have assigned any general characters for the scene.

## Performing

You should be responsible for seeing that all costumes and props are assembled and that the stage is ready for performance. Introduce your scenes to your audience in as few words as possible. The compositions and actors' expressions should tell the story. Then have your ensemble perform as rehearsed. Be sure to thank them afterward for their work.

## Responding

How well you have fulfilled the Specs in the Project Planner will help assess your project. You may also ask yourself, your ensemble, or your audience these questions to help you improve:

- Were you able to explain your ideas to your actors effectively?
- Did your ensemble work well together?
- Did you use a variety of methods to achieve a variety of focuses?
- Was the audience able to determine the focus in each picture?
- Were all stage pictures balanced?
- Did the audience get a sense of the scenario from the pictures alone?

Include responses to these questions in your Theatre Notebook.

## Adapting the Project

1. Use your scenario and the series of tableaux you have created as the basis for a short play. The story should have a beginning, middle, and end, and it should run three to five minutes. You may write dialogue or have your actors improvise. This time they should actually perform the actions implied by the static stage pictures.
2. Have at least three directors complete this project using the same scenario. Compare the way different directors achieve approximately the same effects using different means.

# Dealing with a Difficult Actor

**ASSIGNMENT** Role-play solutions or ways to handle personnel problems.

## Project Planner

| | |
|---|---|
| **Product** | Role-playing of a director facing problems with actors |
| **Purpose** | To assess problems you may face as a director and to practice communication techniques |
| **Specs** | To accomplish this project, you will<br>• work with a small group of actors<br>• as a group, read and analyze a case study<br>• assign actors parts in role-playing<br>• role-play the situation before an audience or other small group<br>• lead a discussion analyzing the outcome |

## Creating

**STUDY THE SITUATION** Form a small ensemble of three actors with yourself as director. Together, read the following case study, which describes the situation of a director dealing with a difficult actor.

> It's your first directing project. The main character in your play is a challenging role requiring a strong actor. At the audition, your best choice is Actor A, who has a reputation for being an outstanding performer, but also for causing problems during rehearsals. Before casting, you talk to this actor to clarify expectations.
>
> Actor A agrees to meet all your conditions and claims to be committed to this project. You cast Actor A in the main role. You have your actors sign a contract for rehearsals and performances (p. 315). Your contract specifies a "three strikes and you're out" rule. A strike is tardiness to rehearsal, unexcused absence from rehearsal, or displaying a detrimental attitude during rehearsal. All actors agree to the rules and sign their contracts.
>
> At the third rehearsal, Actor A is one-half hour late and merely states it was unavoidable. You note a first strike. During the second week of rehearsals, Actor A simply doesn't show up one day. Actor B (who was your second choice for the main

role) claims Actor A can never be trusted. Actor C tries to justify or make excuses for Actor A. You note a second strike.

During the third week of rehearsal, Actor A is late again. After 30 minutes, you ask the stage manager to fill in. Actors B and C get into an argument over Actor A's talent and sense of commitment. Their argument gets personal and rather heated. Then Actor A walks in.

**PREPARE TO ROLE-PLAY** Decide which actors will play Actors A, B, and C. Together, create specifics for the case study, such as names for Actors A, B, and C, which play you are rehearsing, whether you are onstage or in a rehearsal room, and so on. The more specifically you can envision the case study, the more realistic your role-playing will be. Explain the situation to your audience.

## Performing

Improvise dialogue, movement, and gestures as you—the director—put an end to the argument between Actors B and C and deal with Actor A's lateness and violation of the acting contract. Consider your directorial options:

- You can fire Actor A, but your other choices weren't nearly as good. If you cast Actor B, you will have to find somebody else to take that role.
- You can keep Actor A in the role and add a makeup rehearsal or two, but you will have to justify your leniency with the rest of the cast.
- You can cancel the production.

Perhaps you can think of other options. Remember, your main objective should be to put on the best play under the given circumstances.

**LEAD THE DISCUSSION** Now lead your ensemble and the audience in a discussion of what has taken place.

- What are the major problems in this situation?
- Is there anything that might have been done earlier to avoid this final confrontation?
- How well did you—as director—handle the situation? Did you keep the respect of the rest of the cast?

## Responding

How well you have fulfilled the Specs in the Project Planner will help assess your project. You may also ask yourself, your ensemble, or your audience these questions to help you improve:

- How effectively did the ensemble analyze the problems of the case study?
- Did each actor sincerely and realistically role-play his or her character?
- Did the role play reach a satisfactory conclusion?
- Did the group have an effective discussion after the performance?

- Did this project lead to greater awareness of the challenges facing both directors and actors in such situations?

Include responses to these questions in your Theatre Notebook.

## Adapting the Project

Create different case studies to focus on different problems. Problems may be as simple or as complex as communication between director and staff or crises during a performance. Here are some examples:

- The director and technical director disagree about the production concept.
- An actor is injured during a performance.
- An actor is having difficulty memorizing lines.
- The director miscasts a role and must decide whether or not to recast the role.

# Directing a One-Act Play

PROJECT 26

**ASSIGNMENT** Direct a one-act play.

| Project Planner | |
|---|---|
| **Product** | A performance of a one-act play |
| **Purpose** | To refine directing skills |
| **Specs** | To accomplish this project, you will<br>• choose and analyze a one-act play<br>• develop a production concept<br>• design a ground plan<br>• conduct auditions and cast the play<br>• develop a rehearsal schedule<br>• direct rehearsals of the play<br>• oversee technical elements of the production<br>• perform the play for an audience |

## Creating

**CHOOSE YOUR PLAY** Select a one-act play that you would like to direct. The play should have at least two characters, but one with three or four will provide a more interesting challenge. Consider if you have the potential actors to cast the show. Consider any special needs you have for sets, props, or costumes, even for a bare-bones theatre class production. Discuss your choice of play with your teacher, and discuss whether you must obtain rights from the publisher (p. 185).

**ANALYZE YOUR PLAY** Read the play several times and analyze it in terms of characters, structure, and technical requirements (p. 166). Keep your notes in your Theatre Notebook.

Analyze your theatre space. You may need to perform the play in your classroom, but if possible, perform it on the main stage in your school. Develop a production concept; make sure you consider the style of the play (p. 174). Draw a ground plan (p. 176). The set you outline should meet the following objectives:

- It fulfills the technical requirements (number of doors and windows, type of furniture, and so on).
- It provides enough acting areas for you to achieve variety in blocking and stage composition.
- It makes good use of the available theatre space.
- It is artistically interesting.

**CREATE A DIRECTOR'S PROMPTBOOK** Prepare a promptbook (p. 183). Block the show in your promptbook using blocking symbols or your own shorthand (p. 183). Remember to work in pencil so that you can make changes and corrections. Keep a daily log of your work in your promptbook or your Theatre Notebook. Note any problems and how you are dealing with them, discoveries you make during rehearsals, and your communications with actors and technicians.

**CAST YOUR PLAY** Before your auditions you should have a thorough understanding of the personalities and actions of all the characters in your play, but try to keep an open mind about their appearances. Hold auditions and cast your show (p. 315). Distribute copies of the script and rehearsal schedule (p. 314).

**REHEARSE YOUR PLAY** Following your rehearsal schedule exactly, rehearse the show as you direct the actors in their blocking, characterizations, gestures, and vocal interpretations. A two- to three-week rehearsal schedule should be enough for most one-act plays. Be sure to include memorization deadlines in your schedule.

If possible, have your teacher attend one rehearsal each week to assess your work and perhaps give you some advice. The last two rehearsals should be dress rehearsals in which you run the complete show without interruptions or directorial input until after the rehearsal.

**PROVIDE FOR TECHNICAL ELEMENTS** Most plays can be staged without scenery and with folding chairs and boxes for set props. Such bare-bones productions usually have no costumes except for necessary hats and coats and perhaps long skirts for period plays. You may have your actors pantomime all hand props or you may provide simple substitutes. You can ask your actors to help you assemble these costumes and props, but you should be the one who makes certain that the actors have everything they need. During the performance you can assign responsibility for assembling set pieces, props, and costumes to one or more actors.

## Performing

Your play should stand on its own without an introduction on your part, but you may find it necessary to explain to the audience some things that they need to imagine about the set, costumes, or props. During the performance, your responsibility as director is to watch the show closely. Enjoy the work of your actors. Whether or not you take notes is up to you; if there is to be a second performance, you may want to schedule an extra rehearsal to fix any problems.

After the performance, be sure to thank the actors for their work and congratulate them on a job well done.

## Responding

How well you have fulfilled the Specs in the Project Planner will help assess your project. You may also ask yourself, your actors, and your audience these questions to help you improve:

- Did you complete all your necessary preparatory work before the rehearsal period?
- Did you make competent use of rehearsal time?
- Did you communicate effectively with your actors?
- Did you handle any problems successfully?
- Did the actual performance go smoothly?
- Did the play display good directing skills in such things as effective blocking, balanced and interesting stage compositions, appropriate design, and understandable character development?
- Did the play communicate the playwright's message to the audience?

Include responses to these questions in your Theatre Notebook.

## Adapting the Project

Do a full-scale production of your play, complete with sets, props, lighting, sound, costumes, and makeup. One-act plays are seldom done on their own; your play might be performed as part of a festival of one-act plays. You will need to develop a budget for the show and work with technical people on set design and construction, lighting, and so on.

PROJECT 

# Creating a Gobo

**ASSIGNMENT** Create a design and construct a gobo for a specific lighting instrument.

## Project Planner

| | |
|---|---|
| **Product** | A metal gobo cut from an original design |
| **Purpose** | To develop lighting design and workshop skills |
| **Specs** | To accomplish this project, you will<br>• measure the pattern slot or color frame of a chosen lighting instrument<br>• design a pattern to create a specific effect<br>• cut the pattern out of aluminum or steel<br>• demonstrate the gobo in use |

## Creating

**MEASURE YOUR LIGHTING INSTRUMENT** Choose the lighting instrument for which you will be creating your gobo. The usual instrument is an ellipsoidal reflector spotlight. You may want to ask your teacher's help in choosing this instrument. If the instrument has a built-in pattern slot, measure it carefully. If you need to use a color frame instead, measure that.

**DESIGN YOUR PATTERN** Because a gobo projects a pattern, it can be used to add texture to light or to suggest certain kinds of shadows or certain shapes of light. For example, an irregular cutout might be used to project clouds on a sky drop or cutouts of specific patterns might be used to project leafy shade on the stage floor or the shadows of prison bars on a prisoner's face.

Choose the kind of pattern you will design. It will probably help if you design a pattern to fit a specific lighting effect or a specific scene in a play. Remember that light will shine through the areas you cut out. If you want to project prison bars, for example, you would cut out not the bars but the spaces between them.

Draw your design on paper first. Keep in mind the location of the instrument and the distance the projection must travel, or it might become larger than you intend; even small holes can project large areas of light over the distance of the throw.

**CONSTRUCT YOUR GOBO** Transfer your pattern onto a sheet of metal. Heavyweight disposable aluminum roasting pans and pie plates will work, but the aluminum won't hold up to extended use if the pattern is too detailed. Intricately designed gobos should be cut from offset printing sheets (such as those used in printing newspapers) or stainless steel. Aluminum cookware can be cut with scissors or a utility knife, and offset printing sheets can be cut with scissors, chisels, or a Dremel tool. For a sheet of stainless steel, you may need to drill holes through first, and then cut with a coping saw.

Rough edges won't effect the operation of the gobo, but you may want to touch up burrs and slivers with a file to prevent cutting yourself.

## Presenting

Install and test your gobo before presenting it. Depending on the effect you want to create, you may need to experiment with sharpness of focus. Show your gobo lighting effect to your teacher and classmates, and explain its intended use for a particular effect in a play.

## Responding

How well you have fulfilled the Specs in the Project Planner will help assess your project. You may also ask yourself or your classmates these questions to help you improve:

- Does the gobo create an effective pattern—an interesting texture or distinctive shadows?
- Does it help create a specific lighting effect or contribute to mood lighting for a scene?

Include responses to these questions in your Theatre Notebook.

## Adapting the Project

1. Use the gobo in combination with various gels or other gobo patterns to create different visual effects.
2. Design and create a series of gobos that will create a shadow setting, such as a city skyline, mountains, or a forest.

PROJECT 

# Making a Show Tape

**ASSIGNMENT** Make a show tape for a one-act play or a scene from a play.

| Project Planner | |
|---|---|
| **Product** | A show tape including sound effects and background music |
| **Purpose** | To refine sound design and recording skills |
| **Specs** | To accomplish this project, you will<br>• choose and analyze a script to determine what sound effects are needed<br>• decide which sound effects should be created live and which should be edited from recorded sound effects, audiotapes, or CDs<br>• decide how each live sound effect should be created<br>• locate and choose the needed sounds on tapes or CDs<br>• record and edit the chosen sound effects or music onto a new show tape<br>• create a cue sheet<br>• enlist the aid of actors to read the script<br>• perform the live and recorded sounds during a reading of the script |

## Creating

**ANALYZE YOUR SCENE** Choose a one-act play or a scene from a full-length play. Look for a scene with an interesting variety of sound requirements to provide a challenge and to showcase your efforts. Analyze the scene carefully and create a sound plot in which you list every sound effect needed and where it occurs. Most of the time the playwright will include such sounds in stage directions. Sometimes, though, you may need to infer sound effects from a close reading of the script. For example, if a character says, "Somebody just drove up," you might decide you need the sound effects of a car coming to a stop and car doors opening and closing.

Decide whether you want to include music for mood or background or to lead into and out of the scene. Ordinarily you would work with the director on artistic choices regarding music, but for this project you can make the choice yourself.

**DESIGN THE SOUNDS** Now you need to determine how you will make the sound effects you need. For such frequently needed sounds as a doorbell, most theatres already have a board rigged electronically with a doorbell, but if not, you may need to mount a doorbell on a board with a push button. Ringing telephones can be handled in the same way, but it's much more satisfying if the audience perceives that the ringing is actually coming from the telephone onstage.

There are traditional ways of creating many common sounds, such as using a crash box. A crash box is a high-sided wooden or metal box with a metal weight on the bottom and a lid that is firmly attached. When old china plates or pieces of glass are placed inside the box, the crashing sounds and shattering glass sounds are simulated when the box is shaken or dropped. Crash boxes are available from theatre supply sources.

You also need to make decisions about the quality of the sounds. For example, a squeaking door might sound homey, ominous, or merely irritating. You may have to experiment with different ways of creating a sound in order to get the quality you want.

When recording sounds such as a foghorn, a church bell, a gunshot, an explosion, or thunder, be sure to allow sufficient time for the "echo," or reverberation, of the sound to die out naturally; otherwise, the effect sounds unnatural or artificial.

If you are going to include music, be sure that the music is appropriate to the mood of the scene and to the time period of the play. Generally, background music should not include vocals, but there may be times when you want to use vocal music to help establish a time period. For example, the Andrews Sisters singing "Boogie Woogie Bugle Boy of Company B" immediately puts an audience in mind of World War II.

Make sure you check copyright issues surrounding the use of recorded sounds (on tapes, CDs, radio, TV, and so on.) You may need to get permission from the copyright holder if you plan to use your show tape outside the classroom.

**RECORD THE SHOW TAPE** Don't try to use the original recordings during a performance because it's almost impossible to start and stop them exactly as you need. Instead, rerecord each of the sounds onto a master show tape. As you record the sounds, edit them to begin and end exactly as you need and monitor them for relative volume. Splice in a piece of white leader or cue tape between sounds (p. 87). You can annotate this leader tape with a code so that you know what sound is coming up.

If you need to have a sound—such as rainfall—running continuously during a scene, you will need to make a tape loop (p. 88) and run it on equipment that is dedicated to that sound only during the length of the scene.

**DO A TRIAL RUN** Recorded effects must be played through speakers, but they must also give the impression of coming from a specific place. This sometimes means you cannot play the sounds through the main theatre speakers. For example, you want the audience to think that the sound of rain is coming from outside the windows of the set, not that they themselves are sitting in the rain. If necessary, place extra speakers in the wings or behind the set.

Sit in the house while your show tape is being played so that you can determine relative volume levels. Since the sound effects are meant to be part of the world of the play, they should be as loud in relation to the actor's voices as they would be in real life.

**MAKE A CUE SHEET** Now develop a cue sheet that lists each sound, where it occurs in the script, the source, and other necessary information (p. 345). You will need this so that you or the sound operator can work the show smoothly and without mishaps.

**REHEARSE THE SOUNDS AND CUES** The timing of sound effects is essential. Enlist some actors to read the script aloud while you rehearse playing or creating the sound effects for the scene. Follow the script and refer frequently to your cue sheet so that all the sounds come in where they are supposed to. Rehearse until you can work the scene without error.

## Presenting

Perform your sounds for an audience. While the actors read the scene aloud, supply the sound effects you have planned, including music, if any.

## Responding

How well you have fulfilled the Specs in the Project Planner will help assess your project. You may also ask yourself or your audience these questions to help you improve:

- Were the sound effects appropriate and realistic?
- Did the sounds come in at the right times and for the right lengths of time?
- Were the volumes appropriate throughout?
- Did the sounds seem to be coming from the right places?
- If music was used, was it appropriate to the mood of the scene? Did it add useful information?

Include responses to these questions in your Theatre Notebook.

## Adapting the Project

Use the process outlined here to make a show tape for a full-length play. If the sound plot is complex, you might share the work with a partner.

# Analyzing Scene Changes

**ASSIGNMENT** Analyze the scene changes needed for a full-length, multiset play.

## Project Planner

| | |
|---|---|
| **Product** | Annotated ground plans with lists of crew duties |
| **Purpose** | To refine the skill to solve logistics problems |
| **Specs** | To accomplish this project, you will<br>• work cooperatively within a small group<br>• analyze the technical capabilities of your theatre space<br>• analyze a play for needed set changes<br>• design a series of sets or work with existing designs from previous shows<br>• plan the movement of each set piece for each change<br>• plan the duties of each crew member for each change<br>• annotate a series of ground plans |

## Creating

**ANALYZE YOUR THEATRE SPACE** First be sure that you are totally familiar with the technical capabilities of your theatre space. If a scale drawing that shows overall dimensions is not already available, prepare one, making sure you measure exactly. Now consider the possibilities. A theatre with a fly space (p. 216) and equipment can do things a theatre without such equipment can't do. A theatre with ample backstage area allows for easy multiple scene changes; a theatre with limited backstage area provides challenges.

**ANALYZE YOUR PLAY** Choose a play with multiple sets. Musicals are often very complex, but even a straight play can be challenging—especially if its multiple sets are supposed to be realistic. If you can, work with a set of ground plans and elevations that have already been proved workable in a previous production. Ground plans are sometimes provided in acting editions of plays, but you will almost surely have to adapt them to fit your theatre space. If no such plans are available for the play you want to work on, create your own.

If you create your own ground plans, be sure that each plan meets the technical requirements of the scene; that is, the number of doors and windows required, stairs, platforms, and major set props.

**PLAN THE CHANGES** Now study the ground plans for scenes one and two. Think about how the first configuration of flats, platforms, and so on must be changed or rearranged to become the second configuration. Your goal here is to create a change that is as quick and smooth as possible. It may be that a few simple changes in design will save a large amount of physical work. Ask yourself these questions:

- Can a platform or stair unit be masked (p. 208) or adapted instead of being moved?
- Can walls be changed by using various stage curtains instead of running flats?
- Can the entire set be built on a wagon and moved as a unit?
- Can large pieces of furniture fit easily through the doors or other available spaces?
- Can any set be simplified by eliminating or combining some set pieces or set props?

Do the same for scenes two and three, three and four, and so on through the entire show.

Part of your plan must include where and how sets and set pieces are stored when they are not onstage. For instance, if you decide to use three wagons for your sets, you must have enough backstage room to move them easily past each other. Plan exactly which wagon gets moved first and to where, identifying where each wagon is at all times. Do the same for large pieces of furniture. Draw these positions on your ground plans so that every set change can follow the same pattern and there are no surprises for the set crew, the actors, or other backstage personnel.

**DO A MENTAL RUN-THROUGH** In your mind, go through the entire set change for every scene throughout the show. Be sure that you have based the logistics for each change on information from all previous scenes. That is, if you have moved a sofa to the right wing after act I, scene ii, you can't bring it on from off left for act II, scene iv.

**PLAN YOUR CREW DUTIES** After you are reasonably sure that your set changes will run smoothly, staff them. For example, decide how many crew members will be needed to move a particular wagon. Decide how many crew members will be needed to do the other things that must be done *while* a particular wagon is being moved. You can, of course, give each crew member multiple duties during each scene change, but that will stretch out the length of the scene change, and no audience likes to sit in the dark waiting for lengthy, elaborate scene changes. A good rule of thumb is to give each crew member one pass through the set—doing however many things can be done—for each change.

Write all duties down for Crew Member A, Crew Member B, and so on. Include in your lists where each crew member should wait offstage to start the change efficiently.

## Presenting

You may want to present all your materials by walking your classmates and your teacher through all your set changes, using your ground plans and crew lists as visuals. To make your presentation easier, copy your ground plan and crew lists onto acetate. Then use an overhead projector to project this onto a screen. You might then mount your originals in a scrapbook or on a bulletin board backstage to serve as a reference guide for others.

## Responding

How well you have fulfilled the Specs in the Project Planner will help assess your project. You may also ask yourself or your classmates these questions to help you improve:

- Are the ground plans sufficient for the technical needs of the play?
- Do the ground plans take into account the technical capabilities of the theatre space?
- Are the logistics carefully worked out for the moving and positioning of each set piece?
- Do the crew assignments seem reasonable for the number of people you can expect to be available?
- Do the plans seem as though they would yield quick, smooth scene changes?

Include responses to these questions in your Theatre Notebook.

## Adapting the Project

1. This project can be adapted for any complexity of a multiset show. If you have designed for a play with three scene changes, try one with more, perhaps a musical.
2. Follow this project format to plan for multiple costume changes or prop changes.

PROJECT 30

# Old-Age Makeup

**ASSIGNMENT** Create old-age makeup for a specific actor playing a specific part.

## Project Planner

| | |
|---|---|
| **Product** | Old-age makeup on an actor |
| **Purpose** | To practice makeup design and application |
| **Specs** | To accomplish this project, you will<br>• work with an actor to choose a part<br>• read the play and analyze the character<br>• analyze the actor's face and physical characteristics<br>• plan the makeup products and their application for an old-age effect<br>• apply makeup to the actor |

## Creating

**CHOOSE YOUR ACTOR AND CHARACTER** Work with an actor to consider a number of elderly characters in various plays. Together, choose a character that is consistent with the actor's physical characteristics but that is more the age of the actor's grandparent.

**ANALYZE THE CHARACTER** Read the entire play. Discuss the character with the actor. Together, do a standard character analysis, including personality, motivations, and so on, but also include such physical things as general health, long-range occupation, time spent outdoors, and physical infirmities, all of which may effect the aging of the face.

**ANALYZE THE ACTOR** You can do some of your planning from photographs of the actor, but it will be better if the actor is willing to sit while you study him or her intensely for several minutes. Look at bone structure; the shape of the eyes, nose, and mouth; the arch and fullness of the eyebrows; the tautness or looseness of the skin.

This would be a good time to choose a makeup foundation that matches the actor's skin tones. Be sure that you work under stage lights or makeup lights to do this. Then choose shadow and highlight colors. You will probably not want to use the color that you have chosen to match your partner's skin tones; try going a shade or two lighter, or more sallow, or more ruddy, depending on the physical condition of the character. Choose the other colors of makeup from the same color range.

**PLAN THE MAKEUP** Fill out a makeup plan (p. 239). You can get a blank form from your teacher. Use the blank face to sketch in shadows, lines, highlights, and so on. Remember that every older person does not have a face crisscrossed with age lines. If you have collected photographs of facial types in your Theatre Notebook or if you have created a Makeup Scrapbook (p. 123), now is a good time to review them. Look for a picture of a person of the same physical type as your partner to see how that person has aged.

If you are going to apply any special effects, such as a skin blemish or a moustache, sketch them in on the makeup-plan face and write notes about how you plan to achieve them. If you are going to use a product to gray or whiten the hair, note that as well.

**APPLY THE MAKEUP** Be sure that your partner's clothes are sufficiently protected before you begin. Apply the makeup you have planned to your partner's face. Work in the makeup area of your theatre or before a well-lit mirror so that you will have good, strong lighting.

Most actors apply their own makeup for a performance. As you work, point out to your partner what you are doing with shadowed areas, lines and highlights, and rouge. Give the actor the opportunity to study just how heavy the lines are to start with and how much you blend them out. This way she or he will be more able to apply the makeup for a performance.

In creating old-age makeup, remember that not every face ages in the same way. The steps below reflect typical effects of aging, in which a person's face grows leaner; however some elderly people's faces grow fuller, and if you were creating such a character, you would have to adapt your age makeup accordingly.

As usual, begin by applying the foundation you have chosen to your actor's face (p. 95).

To create the highlights and shadows that form wrinkles, use a narrow brush and apply a line of shadow along the crease of the wrinkle. On the upper side of the line only, blend upward into the foundation. Using another brush, apply highlight above that blended line and below the sharper, lower side of the line. Blend both highlights into the foundation.

The following steps are illustrated in the completed old-age makeup on page 393:

**Step 1** The bone structure of people's faces becomes more prominent as they age. Use highlights and shadows to accentuate your actor's bone structure. Create highlights on the brow bone below the eyebrow, on the cheekbone, and down the bridge of the nose. Create shadows in upper area of the eye socket, under the cheekbones, on the sides of the nose, and in the hollows of the temples.

**Step 2** Aging skin sags and wrinkles around the mouth. Have your actor smile. Use highlights and shadows along the line of the large

crease that runs from the base of the nose to the corner of the mouth. Do the same to create downward creases at the corners of the mouth.

**Step 3** The skin also wrinkles and droops around the eyes. Have your actor squint and then relax. Use highlights and shadows to create crows' feet around the eye. Create the drooping fold of skin above the eye by applying highlights and shadows along a diagonal line running from beneath the eyebrow at a spot close to the inside of the eye, down along the rim of the bone bordering the eye socket to the outside of the eye. Create bags under the eyes using highlights and shadows along the lower edge of the eye socket.

**Step 4** Wrinkles also appear on the forehead. Have your actor raise his or her eyebrows, forming wrinkles in the forehead. Use highlights and shadows to accentuate these wrinkles.

**Step 5** As people age, their lips become thinner and lose color. Using a reddish-brown or purplish rouge, color an area within your actor's actual lip line. Use highlights and shadows to create tiny vertical wrinkles above the upper lip.

**Step 6** The skin of the neck sags and wrinkles. Use highlights and shadows to accentuate these features.

Aging people's hair and eyebrows tend to grow gray in streaks, not in patches. Use a hair-coloring liquid or spray to gray your actor's hair, making sure to comb the color into the hair. Brush white makeup into your actor's eyebrows to gray them.

To create the effect of a bald head or a receding hairline, you may wish to use a latex **skull cap,** which covers the head like a hairless wig. You can affix crepe hair to the skull cap.

After you have powdered your partner and completed whatever details you have planned, study the effect together in a distant mirror to approximate the audience viewpoint. Make any adjustments you feel necessary.

## Presenting

If possible, present your work to your classmates onstage under stage lights. If your partner wears a costume piece and adopts a physical posture to suggest his or her character, the effect will be heightened. Take one or more photographs to document your work and to add to your Theatre Notebook.

## Responding

How well you have fulfilled the Specs in the Project Planner will help assess your project. You may also ask yourself, your partner, and your classmates these questions to help you improve:

- Is the makeup appropriate for the character?
- Does the makeup enhance the actor's own physical characteristics?
- Does the overall effect seem natural and not like makeup?

Include responses to these questions in your Theatre Notebook.

## Adapting the Project

1. Follow the project format to plan and apply old-age makeup for an actual production.
2. Prepare three makeup plans for one character at young, middle, and old age. Use an actor as a model for this plan and then apply the makeup, taking a photograph of each. Present each completed makeup to the class. Later, display your "stages of life" makeup photographs for closer inspection.

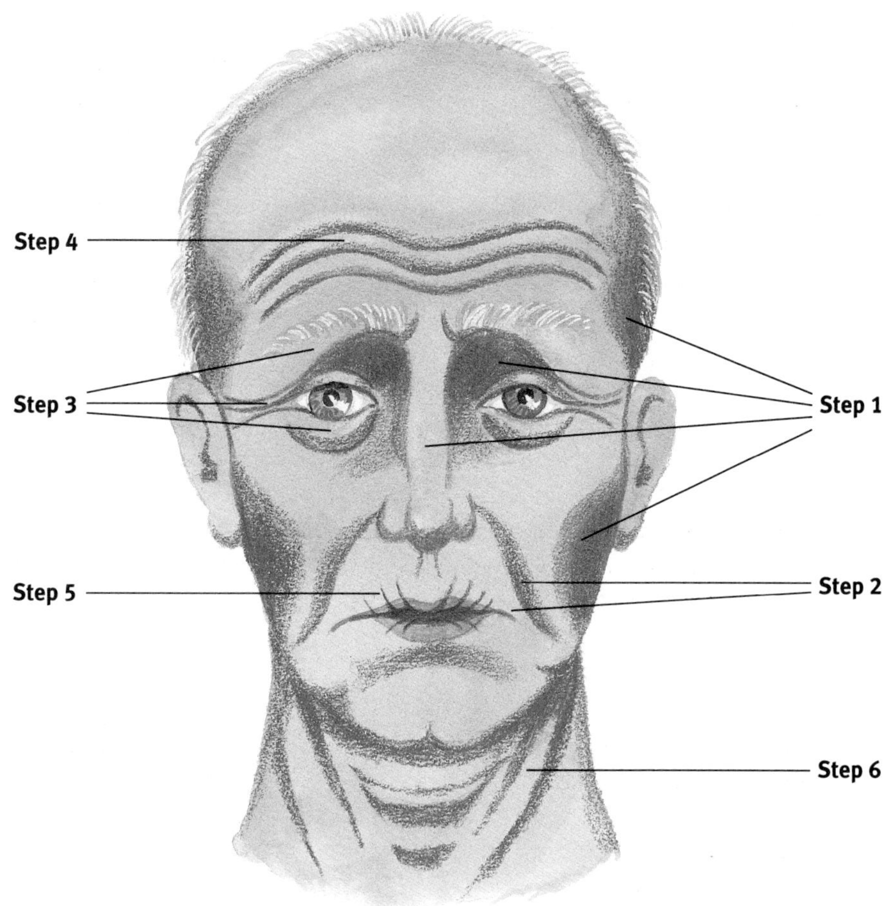

# Specialization

## Acting

397 Reader's Theatre
399 Movement Specialties
410 Voice Specialties
412 Masks
415 Musical Theatre
418 Film and TV
420 Multimedia and Performance Art
422 Activities
426 **Historical Profile:** Beckett


## Directing & Producing

437 Reader's Theatre
440 Musical Theatre
446 Film and TV
453 Multimedia and Performance Art
454 Activities
456 **Historical Profile:** Wilson


## Technical Theatre

465 Scenery Techniques
470 Prop Techniques
478 Lighting Techniques
483 Sound Techniques
485 Costume Techniques
491 Makeup Techniques
496 Activities


## Projects


500 31: Using an Accent
503 32: Performing a Song
506 33: Staging a Fight
509 34: Acting On-Camera
512 35: Directing a Reader's Theatre Piece
515 36: Developing a Musical
518 37: Three-Dimensional Scenery
520 38: Projecting a Background
523 39: Creating Jewelry
525 40: Making a Mask

# Acting specialization

The show closes. The challenge of crafting your performance as an actor is, for the moment, behind you. Where do you go from here? There are many acting specialties that can offer you fascinating new challenges, including Reader's Theatre; movement specialties, such as mime and stage combat; voice specialties, such as dialects and accents; mask work; musical theatre; acting in film and TV; and multimedia and performance art.

## THE LANGUAGE OF THEATRE

**choreographer** an artist who designs (choreographs) dances for the stage

**mime** an art form based on pantomime using conventionalized gestures to express ideas rather than represent actions; a performer of mime

**multimedia** theatrical performances incorporating a variety of artistic and technological media

**musical theatre** a type of entertainment containing music, songs, and usually, dance

**principal** an actor who has a major role in a musical show

**production number** a large-scale performance within a musical show, usually combining both song and dance

**Reader's Theatre** a performance created by reading a script based on a literary work

**screenplay** the script for a film

**stage combat** physical conflict onstage, both armed and unarmed

# Reader's Theatre

In Reader's Theatre, two or more actors create a performance by reading a script based on a literary work. Many types of literature are used as the basis for a Reader's Theatre script, including plays, fiction, poetry, letters, diaries, journals, and biographies. Scripts may be adapted from a short work of literature or from an excerpt of a longer work. Follow the guidelines in Writing & Theatre (p. 558).

ACTING

## Acting in Reader's Theatre

Acting in a Reader's Theatre performance has several basic characteristics in common with acting in a play: script analysis (p. 273) and character development are required; vocal interpretation is critical; and the ability to work creatively and flexibly as part of an ensemble is important.

While Reader's Theatre can be performed in a variety of ways, there are certain conventions. Generally, actors perform seated on chairs or stools arranged in a way that suggests the characters' relationships to one another. If there is a narrator, he or she will probably be positioned to the side. Most often the entire cast will remain onstage throughout the performance, although sometimes a director may want an actor to enter or exit or change places to reflect a change in character relationships.

### Auditions

In many cases, a Reader's Theatre production is organized by a group of people interested in presenting a literary work, and there are typically no auditions. Occasionally, there may be formal auditions as for a play. Other times there may be informal auditions in which the director has actors read parts of the script individually or works with small groups of actors, rotating readers in certain parts. In any case, you should know the story and the characters' relationships well, so you might want to read the literary work on which the script is based.

### The Rehearsal Process

Rehearsals for a Reader's Theatre performance are basically a series of read-throughs (p. 283). During your initial reading of a Reader's Theatre script, become familiar with the basic elements of plot, character, setting, and theme. Then reread, analyzing the characters and their interactions. Rehearsal schedules will vary with the length of the script: a script about the length of a one-act play might involve 20 to 25 hours of rehearsals. You may have your part memorized by the time of the first performance, but you should continue to read or pretend to read from your script for the performance.

### Movement

Your director may incorporate some limited blocking for your Reader's Theatre performance, but in general, you will stay in a seated position, full-front or one-quarter. You may use some gestures, but they should be those that you can do with a script in your hand and of a type your character would normally do while seated.

### Voice

As an actor in a Reader's Theatre ensemble, you will express your character primarily through what you say and how you say it. Understand thoroughly what you are saying and use vocal inflection creatively—not only to convey the meaning of your words to the audience but to keep them interested and entertained. Since you will be reading from a script, take special care to project out rather than down at your script.

### Focus

In general, you will focus front but speak and react—with facial expressions and limited gestures—as though you are interacting face to face with the other actors. If you don't have a part in a particular scene, listen but don't react, and do nothing to detract from the focus of the scene; even shifting in your chair can be distracting. You shouldn't make eye contact with the audience unless your director requests you to do so. If you are playing a narrator, however, you should make eye-contact with the audience whenever it's possible to look up from the script, directing one or two lines to a different audience member each time.

## EXERCISE Dramatic Monologue

Working with another student, select a dramatic monologue, a poem in which the speaker addresses someone whose replies are not part of the poem. (Some famous dramatic monologues are Robert Browning's "My Last Duchess," Alfred, Lord Tennyson's "Ulysses," and Ezra Pound's "The River-Merchant's Wife.") Work together on character analysis and development. Perform a reading of the poem, with your partner as your audience, and then switch roles. Critique each other's performance.

## Movement Specialties

There are three basic types of movement onstage: movement from place to place, gestures, and stage business (p. 141). Actors use these basic types of movement to craft expressive action onstage. Actors develop the style and repertoire of their movements by drawing on a variety of sources.

The actor's most basic source is careful observation of other people in everyday activities (p. 129). In performing the realistic drama that remains the dominant form of contemporary theatre, observation is probably the most valuable resource for actors in developing movement. Actors also study styles of movement in various theatre traditions—such as commedia dell'arte (p. 278) and Kabuki (p. 296)—and adapt some of their conventions of movement.

Another important source from which actors derive inspiration for movement onstage is their experience of movement as interpreted by other arts and forms of entertainment. Allowing other arts to influence your work as an actor will help make your performance more creative and interesting. Both visual and nontheatre performing arts can provide inspiration for expressing your character through movement. You can enrich your repertoire of stage movement by examining postures and gestures in paintings and sculptures; observing circus performers, dancers, and puppets; watching athletes in action; and listening to music, which can suggest emotion, rhythm, and pacing. Attention to movement in all of these cultural activities can broaden your sense of artistic style and provide new choices for you as an actor.

Circus performers, such as these in the world-famous Cirque du Soleil, are a rich source for movement techniques and specialties, such as clowning and acrobatics.

## Styles of Movement

Movement styles fall into two general categories—realistic and stylized. Literal realistic movement is the imitation of the natural actions people perform every day: talking on the phone, eating a meal, walking up stairs, and so on. Sometimes ordinary actions are endowed with an added significance by making them bigger and broader in scope. This enlarged, stylized movement is still realistic and easily recognizable, but more overtly dramatic. An actor employing this stylized movement makes every gesture as if it were very important.

Stylized movement may also be used to create certain effects. For example, mechanistic, synchronized movements by a group of actors might suggest the tedium of factory work. The quick, fluttery movements of the gossiping women in Meredith Wilson's musical *The Music Man* as they sing "Pick-a-Little, Talk-a-Little" imparts the fitting impression of a flock of hens.

These two productions illustrate the contrast between realistic and stylized movement. In the scene from Arthur Miller's *Broken Glass* (right), the movement is dramatic but essentially realistic; in the scene from Molière's *The School for Wives* (below), movement is stylized for comic effect.

Another form of stylization is symbolic movement, in which a conventional gesture is made to stand for something else, such as an emotion or a more complex physical activity. A symbolic gesture is stripped of most of the detail of realistic action and retains only a few of the larger or crucial elements of movement. For example, thrusting out your chest may symbolize aggression or dominance, and looking at your wrist as if checking the time on a wristwatch may symbolize impatience.

The style of a production determines the style of the actors' movement. Realistic drama would generally require literal realistic movement. A melodrama or farce might call for enlarged realistic or other stylized movement. Symbolic movement might be employed in specialized situations, such as in a dream sequence or in mime.

## EXERCISE The Wave

Experiment with a simple gesture—a wave of your hand that says hello or goodbye. Your wave may vary depending on whom you are waving to—a close friend, an acquaintance, a small child. Invent four very different waves that might be performed by four different characters. Use a variety of movement styles. Determine not only who your character is but to whom your character is waving. Then experiment with other types of waves—the wave that means "No!" or "Over here" or "Go away" or "Yeah, whatever you say." How does the basic movement change depending on your character, what you are saying with your wave, whom you are waving to, and the movement style you employ?

## EXERCISE Movement Styles

Using a literal realistic style, perform a common activity, such as writing with a pen or hitting a baseball. Repeat and enlarge the movement. Now, stylize the movement with a flourish or exaggerated slowness or speed. Finally, transform the movement into a symbolic gesture, stripped down to its essence. Perform these variations in movement for the class. See if they can categorize each movement correctly.

## EXERCISE Symbolic Gestures

Brainstorm with a partner to come up with a variety of symbolic gestures, such as holding your fist in the air to symbolize unity and power. Then pantomime a short scene in which you use these symbolic gestures to communicate ideas. How does the use of symbolic gestures affect the overall style of the scene? Perform your scene for an audience, and then ask them how the symbolic gestures affected their understanding of the scene.

This scene from the famous French film by Marcel Carné, *Children of Paradise,* shows actor Jean-Louis Barrault in the role of the famous mime Jean-Baptiste Gaspard Deburau.

A mime's face must be very flexible and expressive. Makeup helps to accentuate facial expressions and stylize the features.

## Mime

The modern tradition of **mime,** based on the technique of pantomime (p. 28), is an abstract art form employing exaggerated, conventionalized gestures to express ideas rather than to represent actions. The formal art of mime emerged in the early 1800s, when Jean-Baptiste Gaspard Deburau began the process of refining the commedia dell'arte (p. 278) slapstick style of pantomime. Some credit him with the creation of the Pierrot character, the wistful lover.

Today's most famous mime, Marcel Marceau, was inspired by the great silent film comedians Charlie Chaplin and Buster Keaton. He developed a character called Bip, who has a personality similar to Pierrot's. Because of Marceau, the art of mime has become more popular. Marceau has stated that he feels mime has become popular because it has no language barriers and because it's so simple that it can be performed anywhere.

Mimes never use words (though some employ sounds). They generally wear **whiteface** makeup (white foundation with accentuated eyes and mouth) and eccentric clothing and work on a bare stage with few props. Even if you don't ever perform mime, its lessons can prove valuable tools. Using your body and gestures to communicate without words is an excellent discipline. Because mime often involves the creation of an original story, an actor who performs it develops a strong sense of narrative. In addition, since mime is typically a solo performance, an actor who does mime becomes more confident and independent.

For the following mime exercises, wear comfortable clothes that you can move in easily. Clear sufficient space to work in. Remember that these exercises must all be performed without words.

## EXERCISE The Mime Walk

Mime includes a number of symbolic movements that represent specific actions. The mime walk is the most basic of these conventionalized movements. To perform the mime walk, first make sure you are relaxed and standing in a balanced posture.

With your weight on your left leg, lift your right knee and your right heel so that your right foot is resting only on the ball of the foot (fig. 1). Shift your weight to your right leg and straighten it, pressing your right heel flat to the floor. At the same time, slide your left foot backwards, keeping it flat to the floor and your left leg straight (fig. 2). Next, lift your left knee (fig. 3) and bring your left foot even with your right foot. Set the ball of your left foot on the floor (fig. 4). Now, shift your weight to your left, pressing your left heel flat to the floor and sliding your right foot backwards, keeping it flat to the floor and your right leg straight (fig. 5). Repeat the process. Make your movements as fluid as possible. When you get your feet moving smoothly, begin swinging your arms as if walking. Your right arm moves forward and back in time with your left leg; your left arm moves in time with your right leg.

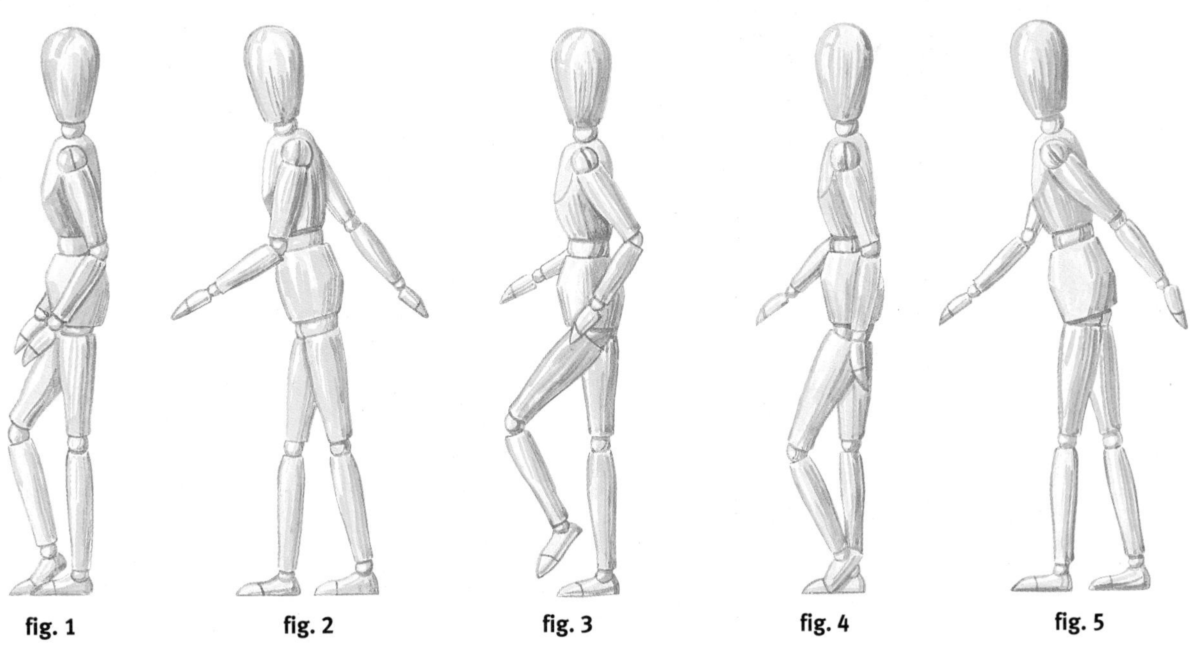

fig. 1 fig. 2 fig. 3 fig. 4 fig. 5

## Stage Combat

Stage combat includes all types of physical conflict onstage, armed and unarmed, from a simple slap to a swashbuckling swordfight. To perform stage combat, which demands precision and control, you must be in excellent physical condition. You must have command and awareness of your body at all times. Well-done stage combat will arouse a sense of danger in an audience and keep them on the edge of their seats; but the danger must only be an illusion. You must never actually be in physical danger while performing stage combat; therefore, you must be well trained and well rehearsed. Because of the potential for injury, it's advisable that you work with a **fight director,** a directing specialist who choreographs both armed and unarmed fight scenes and stunts onstage.

Armed combats onstage, like this one from a production of Shakespeare's *Hamlet* (above), are choreographed by a fight director. Using a mat, a fight director works with an actor (right) in a children's theatre company.

## Stage Combat Guidelines

Approach stage combat with respect and serious attention. Study the guidelines below and perform the exercises that follow under the supervision of your teacher.

- For stage combat rehearsals use a well-lit space with plenty of room. The area should be completely cleared of furniture, props, and scenery. Actors not involved in the action should also stay out of the combat area.
- Work on a surface that is neither slippery, nor extremely hard. An unpolished wood floor is good. Using floor mats while learning and practicing is helpful.
- Wear comfortable clothes that you can move in and nonslippery shoes. Don't wear jewelry, big belt buckles, or any clothing item with sharp edges. If you wear glasses, they should be strapped on. Athletic goggles or safety glasses should be worn over contacts.
- Warm up before choreographing, rehearsing, or performing stage combat.
- Think before you move and don't look at your feet; you must be aware of who is moving around you at all times.
- Communicate with your entire body; remember, appearance is everything.
- Keep in mind that in every stage combat move, the combat victim, or receiver, must be the one in control of the situation.
- Practice diligently to master the techniques. Don't perform until your combat moves are natural and confident; therefore, allow abundant rehearsal time.
- If you feel a stunt or movement is dangerous, don't do it. If at any time during the exercises you feel pain or hurt anywhere, ask for help immediately!

## Falls

Falling techniques should be learned by every actor, since falls are required in various onstage situations. Dramatic scenes sometimes call for fainting. Comic scenes occasionally require tripping and falling.

### EXERCISE Sitting Fall

Sitting on the floor with your legs out in front of you, fall back to the floor on your right side. As you fall, lift your right arm above your head. When your body lands on the floor, slap the floor with your right forearm and the fleshy part of your palm to cushion the impact. Try the same exercise on your left side. Repeat the movements until you are familiar and comfortable with them.

## EXERCISE Squatting Fall

Try the sitting fall from a squatting position. For this fall you will roll backwards during the fall, stretching out one of your arms as you fall. When you land on your side, cushion the impact as you did before, by slapping the floor with your forearm and palm. Repeat these movements until you feel confident you can do them well.

## EXERCISE Standing Fall

Don't try this fall until you are completely comfortable with the sitting and squatting falls. Stand with your knees slightly bent. From this position, the shock of the impact must be absorbed by your upper leg. Begin by falling back and to the left. As you begin to fall, move your left foot backward about 12 inches. Your weight should be centered on the outside of your left foot (fig. 1). As you fall, shift your weight upward along the outside of your left leg to your thigh. When your torso lands, follow through as you would for a sitting or squatting fall, cushioning your upper body with your outstretched forearm and palm (fig. 2). Your head should be cushioned by your shoulder and biceps as you land (fig. 3). Try falling to your right. Again, repeat the movements of the standing fall until you can do them easily and correctly.

fig. 1

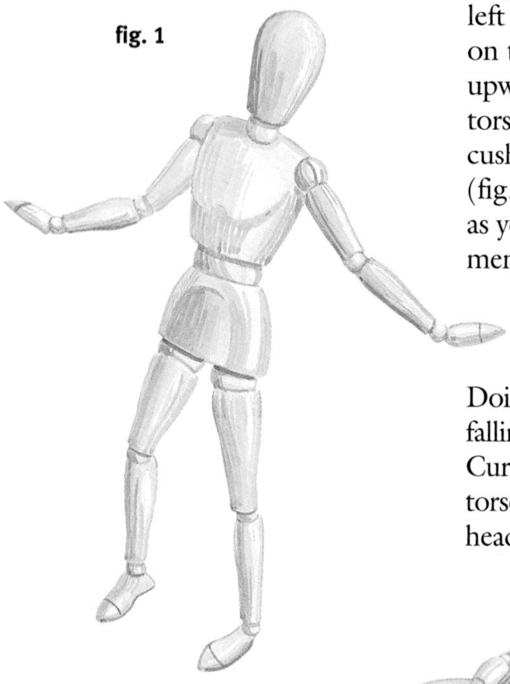

## EXERCISE Forward Standing Fall

Doing a forward standing fall is similar to the standing fall. If you are falling to the right, place your weight on the outside of your right foot. Curl down the outside of your right leg and the right side of your torso. As you fall, lift your right arm and hand up near your head. Your head should be cushioned by your shoulder and biceps as you land. Again, repeat the movements of the forward standing fall until you can do them easily and correctly.

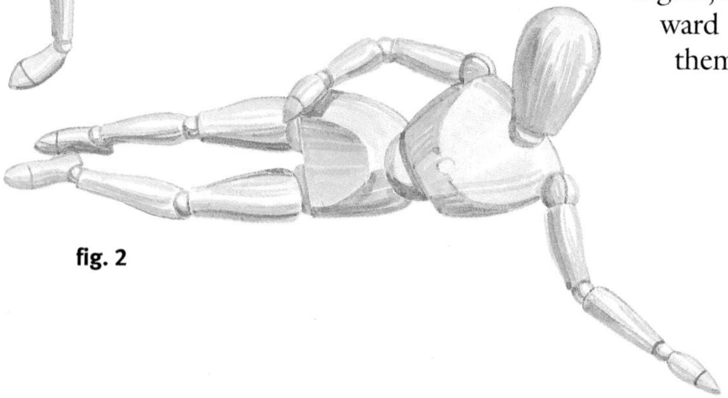

fig. 2

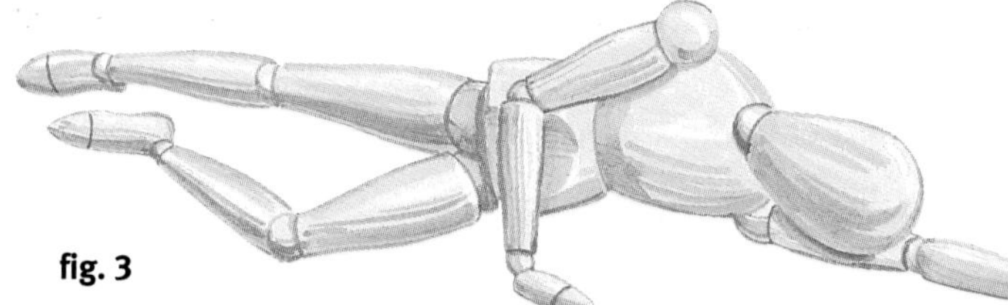

fig. 3

## Kicks

The most important detail about kicks is that they must be pulled before contact; that is, the giver of the kick must pull back, halting the momentum of the kick, before the foot reaches its target, the receiver. The second most important detail is the receiver's reaction; the timing for the reaction to a kick is critical to make it look believable. The giver should give an audible signal prior to giving the kick, such as a click of the tongue, a sharp exhalation, or a concealed finger snap.

Practice kicking against an upright exercise mat (if one is available) so that you will learn to pull your kick before contact. When you can consistently control your movement, practice with another actor—in slow motion at first. During rehearsals, both the giver and receiver should count aloud together while timing the kick and the reaction to make sure they are in sync. When performing, the counting must be inaudible and the movements should be done in real time.

### EXERCISE Kicks from Behind

If you are the giver, kicking the standing receiver's legs or rear end, give the kick with the top of your foot (your toes should be pointed), with the side of your foot, or with the instep of your foot. If you are kicking the receiver in the small of the back, use the top of your foot or the flat sole of your foot. Be careful to avoid the kidneys, located at the sides of the lower back.

### EXERCISE Kicks from the Front

If you are the giver, all of your kicks from the front will be pulled, but will also be defended by the receiver's hands. A kick to the receiver's shins must be given with the instep of your foot; a kick to the stomach, with the top and side of your foot or knee; a kick to the head, with the top or side of your foot or knee. The receiver should catch or block the kicks with his or her hands.

## Chokes

When performing a choking move in stage combat, never touch the larynx or any front part of another actor's throat. The source of the speaking voice, the larynx is one of an actor's most precious possessions. It's also a fragile instrument, easily damaged; therefore, you and your combat partner must be extremely careful and learn the choke moves perfectly before attempting to perform them. Again, first work in slow motion with well-timed movements to help ensure your mutual safety and effective technique.

### EXERCISE Open Choke

If you are the giver and the receiver is facing the audience, you must keep your hands in sight. Put your hands on either side of the receiver's neck and overlap your thumbs in front of the throat, higher than the larynx. Your hands can be tense holding the side of the receiver's neck. You can also help bear some of the receiver's weight at the back part of his or her neck. If you are the receiver, hold onto the arms or wrists of the giver so you can bear some of the weight of the attack and control the action.

### EXERCISE Closed Choke

If you are the giver and the audience can't actually see your hands, place them at the base of the receiver's neck with your thumbs resting on the receiver's collarbones. The receiver should hold onto your arms for support. When the receiver is "overcome," the receiver's arms and body should go limp. You should then "drop" the body and the receiver should fall, using appropriate falling techniques.

## Slaps

The stage slap may be used onstage as a response to a rude comment or unwanted advance. In addition, developing facility at stage slaps will help you with other stage combat techniques, such as fist fights. As with kicks, the receiver's reaction is critical to making the slap look believable.

### EXERCISE Simple Slap

Stand facing your partner at distance of about one inch farther than the length of your extended arm. One of you should be in the full front position, the other in the full back position. If you are the giver, raise your arm; the receiver should drop both arms in front of his or her body. Take an open palm swing at the receiver's face, missing by an inch. As your hand passes the receiver's face, the receiver should slap his or her hands together for a sound effect and jerk his or her head to the side as if hit. Your hand should follow through, finishing the motion.

### EXERCISE Complex Slap

Follow the directions for the simple slap up to the point where your hand approaches the receiver's face. The receiver should position his or her hand near the face, palm facing your palm. When your hand passes the receiver's face, your hand will slap the receiver's hand. The receiver should snap his or her head to react and drop the slapped hand or put it up to his or her face to touch the "injury."

## Fistfights

Fistfights demand the same careful analysis of distance and timing as slaps. A safe punch to the face requires a distance of at least two inches between the giver's and the receiver's face. As in the stage slaps, the most important thing is the receiver's reaction to the blow and the volume and timing of the sound effect.

### EXERCISE Face Punch

If you are the giver, as your fist passes the receiver's face, his or her head should snap back as if receiving the impact. You should make the set-up (creating a fist and winding up for the swing) larger than life and clearly visible to the audience. At the moment your fist would connect with the receiver's face, the receiver should use his or her upstage hand to slap his or her chest or leg to make the sound effect of the punch landing. You should follow through on the swing and action of the striking arm. These actions help further the illusion. During the first few rehearsals, you and the receiver should make your movements in slow motion. Practice your coordinated actions until all the movements look and sound realistic.

*Blade to the Heat* by Oliver Mayer is a play in which stage combat is used extensively to depict boxing.

### EXERCISE Body Blows

A blow to the body is different than one to the face because there is no follow-through motion for the striking fist. If you are the giver, you should pull the punch just before contact. The receiver must double over in reaction. To protect your hand, learn how and when to stop the momentum of the fist. You should practice first against an exercise mat or other solid, but soft, surface. When first practicing with the receiver, both of you should move in slow motion to coordinate your actions; don't perform at normal speed until you are completely at ease with the movements.

## Voice Specialties

Each person's way of speaking is distinctive and contributes to expressing his or her personality. Altering your articulation, pronunciation, inflection, and projection can contribute to creating a unique-sounding character. Some actors have more vocal flexibility than others. Actors known for their vocal variety and flexibility include Mandy Patinkin, Meryl Streep, Robin Williams, John Leguizamo, and Tracey Ullman.

Two actors who specialize in creating a wide range of character voices are John Leguizamo and Tracey Ullman. Leguizamo (above) appears as two of his different characters from his one-man show *Freak*. Ullman (right) is shown in three of the multiple characters she creates in *Tracey Takes On*.

### Dialect and Accent

You can often tell where a person is from by their speech. The regions of the United States each leave a distinctive mark on the speech of a person raised there. Similarly, the ways in which English is spoken by people from the various regions of England, Scotland, Wales, Ireland, Canada, Australia, the West Indies, and elsewhere, display different grammatical structures, vocabulary, idiomatic expressions, and pronunciation. The term **dialect** is applied to all of the language features peculiar to the speech of a particular region. The term **accent** refers specifically to the sound qualities of the speech of a region.

In his play *Riders to the Sea,* Irish playwright John Millington Synge renders the speech of the peasants of the West of Ireland, which shows dialectical features:

**MAURYA.** *(a little defiantly)* I'm after seeing him this day, and he riding and galloping.

The use of *after* to indicate the past tense of the verb *see* is characteristic of Irish dialect, as is the deletion of the auxiliary verb *was* with the participles *riding* and *galloping.* In using dialect, playwrights often attempt to render grammatical features, vocabulary, and idiomatic expressions; they less often attempt to express accents systematically. Early in his play *Pygmalion,* George Bernard Shaw attempts to do this by phonetically rendering a lower-class London flower-girl's Cockney accent:

**THE FLOWER GIRL.** *(picking up her scattered flowers and replacing them in the basket)* Theres menners f' yer! Te-oo banches o voylets trod into the mad.

Shaw almost immediately gives up this effort, observing that his attempt to represent her accent would not be understood outside London. Playwrights writing in dialect may write out words phonetically as Shaw attempted or explain how to pronounce certain key words. In general, however, the sound qualities of a character's speech are left to the actor's research and interpretation.

Books on dialects and accents are available, but it's usually best to learn by listening to a native speaker in person or on audiotapes or other recordings. To mimic an accent, first listen to the accent, trying to develop an ear for sound substitutions (such as the long *i* for the long *a* in the Cockney accent), variations in pronunciation, and the melody and inflection patterns of speech.

When performing, it's not necessary for you to make all the sound substitutions of an accent. In fact, you may sound like a caricature if you do. What is important is to get the style or flavor of the sound and then perform it consistently.

Most directors don't want an accent during auditions. During the first few rehearsals, even if you have a good ear, don't consciously use an accent. Develop it on your own time. Practice with your everyday speech when talking with friends and family. Privately, experiment with your lines using your accent. Later in the rehearsal process when you have a better understanding of your character, you can make strategic accent choices.

### EXERCISE Dialect Readings

Read dialect passages aloud from plays such as George Bernard Shaw's *Pygmalion* or *Major Barbara* or John Millington Synge's *Riders to the Sea* or *Playboy of the Western World.*

Masks and costume work together in *Naomi's Road* by Betty Quan.

## Masks

Masks have been part of the theatre experience since the earliest days. The pair of smiling and frowning masks is a symbol of the **thespian,** or actor, a term rooted in the belief that Thespis, an ancient Greek poet, was the originator of the role of the actor. Greek masks accentuated facial features and expressed basic emotions (p. 67), as do masks used in the theatre traditions of China and Japan. Masks worn by the commedia dell'arte characters (p. 278) expressed a specific character and were an integral part of the stock character costume. (Traditionally, only young lover characters did not wear masks.) Masks can thus be used to convey basic emotions and express specific characters.

Depending on the style of the mask, the presence created by the masked actor may be mysterious, commanding, sorrowful, or outrageously funny. Depending on how they are constructed, masks can change under different lighting or when tilted at different angles to provide a range of expression rivaling the human face.

A masked actor *presents* a character through the use of the mask; as such, if you use masks you will likely be performing in a presentational style. Realistic Elizabethan and Renaissance period plays, however, may feature actors wearing masks at a costume ball or dance party. Such masked balls do not make use of the power of the mask except to exploit its use for disguise, mystery, or flirtation.

Masks have been used in a wide range of productions for various purposes. They have been used with particular effect in farce because they lend themselves to the creation of exaggerated and physical characters and in tragedy because they can be very expressive of high emotion. Masks may be used to distinguish roles in a play: a chorus may wear identical masks; major characters may wear certain masks to highlight or indicate their importance. Masks are often used symbolically—a masked actor's face is hidden, which may symbolize detachment; a nondetailed, or neutral, mask may symbolize anonymity or conformity; the conceptual or unfathomable aspects of individuality may be represented by an abstract mask.

Masks can also be used effectively to present an ethnic identity in a play that calls for such distinctions. Jean Genet's *The Blacks* featured black actors wearing white masks to present—in a concrete way—issues of power and race relations. Masks can serve equally well to create characters in such a way that casting can be race- and gender-blind. If you find yourself vying for a role in a masked production, you could be cast for any part because the mask itself is a dominant part of the character; the race or gender of the actor may not matter.

This masked character performs in Cirque du Soleil skits.

## Exploring Masks

The power and magic of masks can be experienced with simple or complex masks, **half masks** (covering the top half of the face) or **full masks** (covering the entire face). Often, just trying on a mask and taking a look in the mirror will provide instant inspiration for a character. (The word *person* comes from *persona,* the Latin word for an actor's mask.)

Far from limiting you as an actor, masks can inspire you to be more conscious of your body and voice in the creation of a character. Keep these points in mind while working with masks:

- Study a mask before you put it on; each has a personality and mood. Imagine who the mask might be if it were a character. Then put it on and see how the character emerges as you add voice and movement.
- Think of the mask as a character rather than a costume or prop. Don't fidget with it; let it lead you.
- Continue to make facial expressions under your mask, which will help you to animate the mask.
- Particularly with full masks, work on articulation and projection, which can be difficult because nose and mouth holes are not usually very large. (You might want to limit your use of full masks to pantomime or work that does not involve much speech.)
- Stay open to the audience when wearing a mask; try not to let them see any part of your face under the mask.

## EXERCISE Experimenting with Masks

If you have masks available to you in your theatre stock, experiment with them. You will need a mirror; seeing the mask on your face is necessary to help you find a character in the mask. If you can work with a half-mask, play with your lower face and your neck to see how it affects the mask and inspires various characters. If you can work with a full mask, experiment with body movement to animate the mask. For added complexity, incorporate changes in lighting to see the effects on the masks.

Director/designer Julie Taymor and composer Elliot Goldenthall use puppets, masks, pantomime, and song in *Juan Darien*, adapted from a story by Horacio Quinoga.

## EXERCISE Masked Improvisation

For this exercise use masks from your stock or make simple masks. Even masks you make in a few minutes can be effective: use construction paper or cardboard; color them if you wish and secure them around your head with a section of rubber band attached to each side of the mask. With a partner, perform an improvisation of your choosing using masks. How is the performance affected? How are your vision and voice affected by the mask? Ask your audience to comment on the effect of the masks.

Geoff Hoyle wrote *Feast of Fools*, in which he performs as various masked characters.

# Musical Theatre

Musical theatre is a type of entertainment containing music, songs, and, usually, dance. While various types of musical theatre, such as opera and operetta, had long been popular in Europe, the modern musical comedy is a characteristically American theatrical form. In the 1920s and 1930s, American composers such as Jerome Kern, George Gershwin, and Irving Berlin wrote popular songs that were incorporated into light comedy plots or musical reviews with choruses of dancers. In 1927, Kern's *Showboat* indicated a new direction in musical theatre by touching on more serious subject matter and by closely weaving songs and dances into the action. It was not until 1943, however, when Richard Rodgers and Oscar Hammerstein II created *Oklahoma!* that a musical play fully integrated a story with dialogue, songs, and dance. Musical theatre was changed forever.

Musicals are typically more elaborately staged than other plays. They have orchestral music, songs, and big dance numbers. They are usually very visually exciting with complex sets, costumes, and sometimes special effects. Because of this complexity, there are more people involved in the production of a musical than are required by other plays.

## Acting in Musicals

In addition to working with a director, actors may also work with a music director and a choreographer. As an actor in a musical, you may be a **principal,** an actor who has one of the major roles, or a member of the chorus. You must be able to work with a large cast, sing parts in an ensemble, and handle a large number of scene and costume changes.

### Dance

In the original production of *Oklahoma!* Agnes De Mille served as the **choreographer,** the artist who designs dances for the stage. De Mille worked with the writers and directors to create dance numbers that enhanced the story and tapped into the psychological world of the characters. Through dance, a new dimension of characterization opened up.

In a musical, there are solo dance numbers and ensemble dance numbers. Sometimes, there is a separate ballet sequence. The whole cast is usually involved in a **production number,** a large-scale performance within a musical show, usually combining both song and dance. Musical theatre choreography may use techniques and steps from modern dance, jazz, tap, and street dance.

Whether you are a principal or a member of the chorus, you should learn to communicate and build your character through dance.

Dance numbers enliven the musicals *Bye, Bye, Birdie* (right) by Michael Stewart, Charles Strouse, and Lee Adams, and *Singin' in the Rain* (below), adapted from the 1952 MGM movie co-directed by choreographer/actors Gene Kelly and Stanley Donen.

Julie Andrews, as Eliza Doolittle, sings of her simple aspirations in Alan Jay Lerner and Frederick Loewe's musical *My Fair Lady,* based on George Bernard Shaw's play, *Pygmalion* (right); an ensemble number heightens a climactic scene in Alan Boublil and Claude-Michel Schönberg's *Les Misérables,* based on the novel by Victor Hugo (below).

## Song

In musicals, songs are used to heighten the emotion and dramatic climax of scenes. Solos may replace monologues; a duet may be central to a love-scene. Group numbers may serve the function of choruses in Greek drama (p. 68) or Kabuki (p. 296).

For an actor in a musical the ability to bring a character to life through song is critical. Learning to express emotion and to project a distinct character through your interpretation of a song is what distinguishes you as an actor who sings. The music director or a singing teacher can help you develop your vocal range and projection and sing on pitch and with emotion. He or she can also help you interpret a song with a unique perspective and approach.

# Film and TV

In performing for a film or TV camera, you use many of the same skills as acting onstage, but there are some distinct differences.

Onstage, your voice must project great distances with expressiveness, subtlety, and clarity. Conveying the nuances of the words depends on your vocal skill, which includes pacing of dialogue. In film and TV, your vocal inflection is important, but microphones address issues of projection, and film editors and directors ensure the overall pacing of dialogue.

An actor onstage must be seen at all times. On film and TV, you may turn your back or hide under a bed and the audience (filmgoers and TV viewers) may still be able to see you through the camera's lens. You may, moreover, be seen very close by the camera, so your acting needs to be realistic. Facial expressions that are appropriate for the stage may be too large, or "stagey," for film and TV.

The ability for the camera to move in very close also means that actors must play roles close to their own ages on film and TV, whereas makeup and distance may allow an actor to play roles in a wider age range onstage.

## Emotion and Concentration

Performing for the camera requires just as much emotional commitment and energy—and perhaps even more honesty—as performing onstage. When you are talking to someone, he or she can see if you are being honest or sincere by the expression and focus of your eyes. Communicating with the camera requires this same degree of directness as well as strong concentration skills and attention to consistency; the camera can pick up a flicker of wandering attention or a momentary lapse in character revealed in the face.

## Film and TV Terminology

To be fully prepared for film and TV work, you should be familiar with basic film terminology.

A **screenplay,** the script for a film, is divided into scenes, just as a play is; however, in a screenplay, a **scene** usually consists of the continuous action that can be recorded in one place with one camera setup. A **setup** is each new camera position or change in the composition of the scene in the camera frame. The **frame** is the rectangular-shaped area of the film onto which is recorded what is seen by the camera in a minute portion of each shot. A **shot,** or **take,** is the actual recording on film or videotape of a scene. Shots are planned in advance of the actual filming. One scene in a film or TV program may include several different shots from different angles.

The most commonly used shots are an **extreme close-up,** in which a part of your face or a small object may fill the frame; a **close-up,** in which your face and shoulders fill the frame; a **medium shot,** which includes part of your body; a **two shot,** a medium shot that includes two people; and a **long shot,** which includes your whole body and a good part of the foreground or background.

Never look directly at the camera unless directed to do so. In a close-up, focus slightly to one side or the other of the camera lens.

These scenes from Ted Sod's film *Crocodile Tears* show a close-up (left), a two shot (center), and a long shot (above).

## Structure and Time

Perhaps the most jarring difference between performing onstage and on-camera is the difference in time, specifically the sequence of scenes in the performance. Onstage, you generally rehearse and perform the action of the play in the same order in which it's written. One action builds upon another leading to the climax of the play. In film and TV, scenes are shot in the order that is most convenient for the director and production crew. Sometimes this means performing the most climactic scene of the film on the first day of shooting. You must be prepared for the scenes to be shot each day, no matter where they fall in the sequence of the script.

### Continuity

An important skill that you need as an on-camera actor is to remember and repeat your movements exactly. You must be able to match your gestures and action on a long or medium shot to a close-up or different angle shot of the same scene. You must also remember how you ended a scene if there is another scene that continues the action. You will need to start where you left off. This logical coherence from scene to scene is called **continuity.** Usually, a crew person on the set is designated to watch for this, but you should be aware and responsible for yourself.

## Multimedia and Performance Art

From its beginnings, theatre has been a hybrid art form, incorporating dance, song, ritual, storytelling, and other art forms in performances. Throughout the history of theatre, specialists in the other arts and in technology have contributed their creativity and expertise: architects designed theatre spaces and constructed stage machinery; painters designed scenery and costumes; composers created music to accompany performances.

In the 20th century, the development of technological media, such as film, television, video, and computers, has had a profound influence on theatre. In the 1920s directors such as Erwin Piscator and Vsevolod Meyerhold incorporated screen projections into theatrical performances. The Federal Theatre Project of the 1930s combined documentary film with theatre in its series *Living Newspapers.*

Since the 1960s there has been widespread experimentation with incorporating a variety of artistic and technological media into

Multimedia artist Laurie Anderson emphasizes a point in one of her performance pieces (below); actor Lily Tomlin incorporated multimedia elements in her show *The Search for Signs of Intelligent Life in the Universe* (right), in which she portrays myriad characters.

theatrical performances. This **multimedia** approach to theatre can include dance, music, sculpture, painting, film, video, puppets, animation, recorded sound, laser technology, and computers. Today, some theatre groups are experimenting with presenting performances on the Internet.

Both traditional theatre and avant-garde theatre have been presented in multimedia performances. One form of contemporary avant-garde theatre that has made extensive use of multimedia is **performance art.** Appearing in the 1970s, performance art grew out of unstructured theatrical "happenings" of the preceding decade, which featured a spontaneous mix of theatre games, song, dance, and other elements that might be performed anywhere, from a church to a public park. Like happenings, performance art doesn't employ traditional theatrical conventions and often takes place in nontheatre performance spaces. The emphasis in performance art isn't on plot and characterization, but on making a statement (frequently a controversial one) and on self-expression.

A video camera is used in this production of Samuel Beckett's *Ghost Trio* (above); director Robert Wilson is well known for his use of multimedia, as in this scene from *the CIVIL WarS: a tree is best measured when it is down* (right).

# Activities

### Reader's Theatre

**READ A SCENE** Working with two other actors, choose a scene from a play to do as a Reader's Theatre performance. If you can't find a scene that is long enough, you may adapt it by recombining portions of the script for your performance. Follow the guidelines in Writing & Theatre (p. 558). Analyze the script and characters together, recording your comments in your Theatre Notebook. Before performing, practice reading with articulation, projection, and inflection, and focusing front when you are not reading. Use a narrator to explain the play and how the scene fits into the plot.

### Reader's Theatre

**READ A DUET** Write or adapt a Reader's Theatre piece with a partner that highlights the relationship between two people. Consider a series of letters or phone calls, or a dialogue during a long walk, a lunch, or an interview. When you perform your piece, you may sit side by side or engage in limited blocking that can be accomplished with scripts in hand. Present your piece to the class. Summarize their comments about your performance in your Theatre Notebook.

### Movement Specialties

**DRAMATIC DANCE** Attend a dance performance or watch one on TV or in a movie. In your Theatre Notebook, sketch and write about movements you observed that you could apply to your craft as an actor. If you are working on a production, experiment with applying any appropriate movements into your performance (after consultation with your director). Or, choose one or two movements and explore how they might be used to enhance a type of character, such as a prim woman or a folksy grandfather.

*Movement Specialties*

**MIMING A SEQUENCE OF EMOTIONS** Select several emotions—for example, love, jealousy, and remorse—and devise a simple narrative in which a character successively experiences each of these emotions. Create a mime performance based on this narrative and present it to a small group of students. See if they can identity each of the emotions in turn. In your Theatre Notebook write about the challenges of expressing emotions via silent, stylized movements.

*Movement Specialties*

**THE LONELY ROAD** In *The Rime of the Ancient Mariner,* Samuel Taylor Coleridge describes a terrified traveler: "Like one, that on a lonesome road/Doth walk in fear and dread,/ And having once turned round walks on,/And no more turns his head;/Because he knows, a frightful fiend/Doth close behind him tread." Mime this situation, adapting the mime walk to suggest the movements of someone who is very frightened. Adapt the mime walk to express other emotions, such as joy, sorrow, and frustration. Use stylized facial expressions that convey these emotions as well.

*Movement Specialties*

**SLOW-MOTION FIGHT** Work with a partner to perform a short scene in which you get into an argument and end up fighting. Decide what you will disagree upon. Then script the piece, which should be no more than 10 lines. Choose three stage combat moves—such as a fall, a kick, and a choke—to use in your fight. Carefully choreograph and rehearse your movements. Present your scene to the class, doing the entire scene in slow motion to prevent injury.

*Movement Specialties*

**MARTIAL ARTS EXPERT** Mime this situation, developing a humorous character: You are a pompous expert at martial arts. You bow arrogantly to your invisible opponent and assume a stance. Go through a range of defensive and offensive movements – slash the air with your arms and legs, turn and spin. Suddenly you feel you are going to sneeze. You struggle to maintain your concentration as the tickle in your nose grows stronger. Finally, you can no longer contain it and you sneeze explosively. Your opponent knocks you to the floor. You rise to your feet with wounded dignity and bow to the victor.

# Activities

*Voice Specialties*

**JOB SHADOW-RADIO ANNOUNCER** Arrange with an area radio station to observe an announcer at work for a day or a few hours. Explain that you are interested in witnessing the day-to-day operations of a radio announcer to see how skill in vocal inflection is applied on the job. Professionals are busy, but if you are polite as well as interested, they are usually willing to let you observe them at work and to answer questions about their training and background. Be sure to first get permission from your parents, teacher, and the supervisor of the business or organization where you will job shadow.

*Voice Specialties*

**UNDERSTANDING DIALECT** Listen to recordings or read aloud to yourself passages from the following novels that feature dialect: *Cold Sassy Tree* by Olive Ann Burns, *The House of the Seven Gables* by Nathaniel Hawthorne, *The Grapes of Wrath* by John Steinbeck, *Moby Dick* by Herman Melville, *The Joy Luck Club* by Amy Tan, *The House of the Spirits* by Isabel Allende, or *The Color Purple* by Alice Walker. In your Theatre Notebook write about how the dialect enhances your understanding of the characters and their environment.

*Masks*

**MASKED MONOLOGUE** Read a Greek play while envisioning the actors using masks. Write your comments about the play in your Theatre Notebook as you read; you might also include sketches of how you envision the characters in their masks. Then choose a monologue from the play. Using simple materials, create a mask (or use one from your theatre stock) and present the monologue to the class. If you like, do some research and make your mask similar to those used in ancient Greece.

*MUSICAL THEATRE*

**CREATING A DANCE NUMBER** Working with a group of students, select a song you like and then devise a dance number based on it. First imagine a story into which your dance number might naturally fit, the setting for the number, and the principals who perform it. Then get some help from a dance teacher in working out the choreography. Or, borrow dance steps you see in musicals on TV or film and adapt them for your number. What kind of acting skills can be applied in the dancing?

*FILM AND TV*

**STAGE AND FILM ACTING** In a small group discussion, respond to the following statement by actor Kim Stanley: "No matter what you do in film, it is after all, bits and pieces for the director, and that's marvelous for the director, but it doesn't allow the actor to learn to mold a part. In films, it's the director who is the artist. An actor has much more chance to create on stage." Based on what you know about acting onstage and on film, do you agree or disagree with this statement?

*FILM AND TV*

**MAINTAINING CONTINUITY** Working with several other students, locate a scene from a screenplay that interests you. (Libraries and bookstores offer published screenplays.) Cast the scene and do a series of takes on videotape, using different kinds of shots. Watch the videotape to see whether you have maintained continuity throughout the different takes.

*MULTIMEDIA AND PERFORMANCE ART*

**PERFORMANCE PIECE** Choose an issue about which you feel strongly—such as racism, animal rights, censorship, capital punishment—and create a 5- to 10-minute multimedia performance piece expressing your views. You might include slide projections, videotape, recorded sound, lighting effects, computer technology, and so on.

**Historical Profile**

# Beckett

In 1953 modern theatre was changed by *Waiting for Godot,* a play about nothing that was written in French by an Irishman. Born in 1906 in a suburb of Dublin, Ireland, Samuel Beckett came from a Protestant background and studied Romance languages at Trinity College in Dublin. After teaching for a time, he moved to Paris, the first step in a period of restless travel throughout England, France, Germany, and Italy. In 1937 Beckett decided to settle in Paris. As a citizen of Ireland, a country that was neutral in World War II, he was able to stay in Paris even after the city was occupied by the Germans. He joined an underground resistance group in 1941. When Beckett heard that members of his group had been arrested by the Nazis, he went into hiding in the French countryside, returning to Paris in 1945.

After World War II Beckett entered a period of intense creativity. Before the war he had written some essays, short stories, and a novel, *Murphy.* From 1946 to 1947 Beckett produced more short stories, the novels *Molloy* and *Malone Dies,* and two plays. Many of these works remained unpublished until the success of his play *Waiting for Godot* made Beckett famous. Originally written in French, *En attendant Godot* opened at the small Théâtre de Babylone in Paris in 1953. It came to be seen as the first example of a new type of drama—soon called "absurdist" (see below).

The premise that life is hopeless is evident in the desertlike setting of this production of Beckett's *Waiting for Godot.*

He almost always wrote his plays first in French, later translating them into English. This process forced him to concentrate on the meaning of his words, rather than any superficial eloquence. Beckett's later works became shorter and shorter and more concentrated. For example, *Come and Go* contains only 121 words spoken by three characters, and his *Acts Without Words* is just that. Beckett was awarded the Nobel Prize for Literature in 1969. He died in 1989 in Paris. Among the major writers of the 20th century, Beckett stands out for the simplicity and purity of his approach to literature and for his insights into basic human experience. His works are also major experiments in modern theatrical form.

## Theatre of the Absurd

In his 1942 essay *The Myth of Sisyphus,* French writer Albert Camus defined the human condition as essentially absurd, or meaningless. In the 1950s a number of dramatists, including Beckett, Eugène Ionesco, Fernando Arrabal, and Edward Albee, created works representing the universe as unknowable and humankind's existence as hopeless and seemingly without purpose. The characters in these works are bewildered, troubled, and endlessly threatened by inner turmoil or external, unexplained forces. They seem to be out of sync with the universe.

The influential critic Martin Esslin was the first to label these theatrical works as *absurdist* and began to speak of the **theatre of the absurd** as a movement; none of these playwrights described his own work as absurd, nor were they consciously working to create an artistic movement. Yet, although each playwright developed an individual style and tone, the eventual outcome of their plays is largely the same: no matter how frantically a character tries to improve his or

This scene from a production of Beckett's *Happy Days* shows Winnie's ludicrous, desperate situation.

her fortunes, nothing will change the human condition. Ludicrous, even farcical, character behavior and strange, twisted dialogue create humor, but there remains a fundamental seriousness and internal disquiet.

Theatre of the absurd often contains combinations of these established performance devices:

- theatrical effects like those used by jugglers, acrobats, bullfighters, and mimes
- clowning and fooling
- scenes of madness and crazed behavior
- disjointed language full of clichés, puns, repetitions, nonsequiturs (words that do not relate to what was previously said), and nonsense
- elements of dream and fantasy

In the theatre of the absurd these devices were harnessed together to serve a new philosophy of existence—one in which a nonsequitur might seem a right and logical response.

## Beckett's Contributions to the Absurd

Beckett's writings, simultaneously comic and pessimistic, force readers and audiences to question the basic assumptions of their lives. In *Waiting for Godot,* two characters wait for an individual named Godot (god′ō) who never comes; by the end of the play it seems that the characters must go on like this forever. *Endgame* dramatizes the breakdown of the relationship between a master, Hamm, and his servant, Clov. Nothing substantial happens, and it's this absence of anything important that is the point. Like other comedy, Beckett uses physical humor. In *Happy Days* a woman named Winnie sinks deeper and deeper into a pile of dirt onstage as she rattles on about the trivialities of life. Even as she nears her death and is about to be swallowed up by the ground, she persists in pretending furiously that life will continue normally. Beckett's theatre is no different from other theatre that you might attend—but the world that his theatre creates could almost be that of another planet.

## Try It Out

Although the world that the characters inhabit in *Waiting for Godot* is a weird, abstract one, the characters don't think of themselves as weird or abstract. Your challenge as you act out the following scene will be to ground these characters in reality. Elsewhere in the play they complain that they are hungry or that their feet hurt. Though the audience may see them as stuck in eternity, Vladimir and Estragon are concerned with what is happening to them *right now.* As you work on this scene, you may wish to consider the following:

- Are there elements of humor in this scene? How can you emphasize them?
- How can you make the repetitious language and word play sound like real conversation?
- There is a fair amount of activity in *Waiting for Godot*—in the form of stage business with hats, boots, vegetables, and other props—but there are also long periods of inactivity. Is this scene one of activity or inactivity? What can you do during periods of inactivity to retain the visual attention of your audience?

*from*

# Waiting for Godot

***Waiting for Godot*** concerns two tramplike characters, Vladimir and Estragon, who wait in an empty space with a solitary tree. They wait for someone named Godot, but who—or what—is Godot is never made clear. While they wait, Vladimir and Estragon philosophize, joke, play games, perform vaudeville routines, and discuss whether their existence has any meaning.

1. Imagine what might have happened immediately before, to cause Vladimir's exasperation.

2. Does he mean this literally?

3. One meaning of *sententious* is "in a heavily moralizing way." How might you deliver this line?

**VLADIMIR.** You're a hard man to get on with, Gogo.[1]

**ESTRAGON.** It'd be better if we parted.

**VLADIMIR.** You always say that and you always come crawling back.

**ESTRAGON.** The best thing would be to kill me, like the other.

**VLADIMIR.** What other? *(Pause.)* What other?

**ESTRAGON** Like billions of others.[2]

**VLADIMIR** *(sententious).*[3] To every man his little cross. *(He sighs.)* Till he dies. *(Afterthought.)* And is forgotten.

**ESTRAGON.** In the meantime let us try and converse calmly, since we are incapable of keeping silent.

**VLADIMIR.** You're right, we're inexhaustible.

**ESTRAGON.** It's so we won't think.

**VLADIMIR.** We have that excuse.

**ESTRAGON.** It's so we won't hear.

**VLADIMIR.** We have our reasons.

**ESTRAGON.** All the dead voices.[4]

**VLADIMIR.** They make a noise like wings.

**ESTRAGON.** Like leaves.

**VLADIMIR.** Like sand.

**ESTRAGON.** Like leaves.

*Silence.*

**VLADIMIR.** They all speak at once.

**ESTRAGON.** Each one to itself.

*Silence.*

**VLADIMIR.** Rather they whisper.

**ESTRAGON.** They rustle.

**VLADIMIR.** They murmur.

**ESTRAGON.** They rustle.[5]

*Silence.*

**VLADIMIR.** What do they say?

**ESTRAGON.** They talk about their lives.

**VLADIMIR.** To have lived is not enough for them.

**ESTRAGON.** They have to talk about it.[6]

**VLADIMIR.** To be dead is not enough for them.

**ESTRAGON.** It is not sufficient.

*Silence.*

**VLADIMIR.** They make a noise like feathers.

**ESTRAGON.** Like leaves.

**VLADIMIR.** Like ashes.

**ESTRAGON.** Like leaves.[7]

*Long silence.*

**VLADIMIR.** Say something!

**ESTRAGON.** I'm trying.

*Long silence.*

**VLADIMIR** *(in anguish)*. Say anything at all!

**ESTRAGON.** What do we do now?

4. In these lines, how might you suggest wings, leaves, and sand?

5. What's going on here? Should these repetitions be stated in a detached, abstract style or in a realistic, immediate style?

6. A lot of this play consists of talking about talking. Do you think Estragon is being sympathetic or impatient here? How might you show it?

7. Are these images complimentary or contradictory? Are the men building on each other's speeches or denying them?

**VLADIMIR.** Wait for Godot.

8. They have been waiting a long time already. Experiment with saying these three lines in various ways to suggest resignation, exasperation, anxiety, or boredom before you decide on a final interpretation.

**ESTRAGON.** Ah![8]

*Silence.*

**VLADIMIR.** This is awful!

**ESTRAGON.** Sing something.

**VLADIMIR.** No no! *(He reflects.)* We could start all over again perhaps.

**ESTRAGON.** That should be easy.

**VLADIMIR.** It's the start that's difficult.

**ESTRAGON.** You can start from anything.

**VLADIMIR.** Yes, but you have to decide.

**ESTRAGON.** True.

*Silence.*

9. To what does this refer?

**VLADIMIR.** Help me![9]

**ESTRAGON.** I'm trying.

*Silence.*

**VLADIMIR.** When you seek you hear.

**ESTRAGON.** You do.

**VLADIMIR.** That prevents you from finding.

**ESTRAGON.** It does.

**VLADIMIR.** That prevents you from thinking.

**ESTRAGON.** You think all the same.

**VLADIMIR.** No no, impossible.

**ESTRAGON.** That's the idea, let's contradict each other.

10. Does Vladimir's "impossible" mean that he is beginning a game of contradicting each other or denying that they can play such a game? How might Estragon react?

**VLADIMIR.** Impossible.[10]

**ESTRAGON.** You think so?

**VLADIMIR.** We're in no danger of ever thinking any more.

**ESTRAGON.** Then what are we complaining about?

11. Estragon is making yet another attempt to start a game, to give some direction to their conversation. How does Vladimir respond? What happens to this attempt?

**VLADIMIR.** Thinking is not the worst.

**ESTRAGON.** Perhaps not. But at least there's that.

**VLADIMIR.** That what?

**ESTRAGON.** That's the idea, let's ask each other questions.[11]

**VLADIMIR.** What do you mean, at least there's that?

**ESTRAGON.** That much less misery.

**VLADIMIR.** True.

**ESTRAGON.** Well? If we gave thanks for our mercies?

**VLADIMIR.** What is terrible is to *have* thought.

**ESTRAGON.** But did that ever happen to us?[12]

**VLADIMIR.** Where are all these corpses from?[13]

**ESTRAGON.** These skeletons.

**VLADIMIR.** Tell me that.

**ESTRAGON.** True.

**VLADIMIR.** We must have thought a little.

**ESTRAGON.** At the very beginning.

**VLADIMIR.** A charnel-house! A charnel-house![14]

**ESTRAGON.** You don't have to look.

**VLADIMIR.** You can't help looking.

**ESTRAGON.** True.

**VLADIMIR.** Try as one may.

**ESTRAGON.** I beg your pardon?

**VLADIMIR.** Try as one may.

**ESTRAGON.** We should turn resolutely towards Nature.[15]

**VLADIMIR.** We've tried that.

**ESTRAGON.** True.

**VLADIMIR.** Oh it's not the worst, I know.

**ESTRAGON.** What?

**VLADIMIR.** To have thought.

**ESTRAGON.** Obviously.

**VLADIMIR.** But we could have done without it.

**ESTRAGON.** Que voulez-vous?[16]

**VLADIMIR.** I beg your pardon?

**ESTRAGON.** Que voulez-vous.

**VLADIMIR.** Ah! que voulez-vous. Exactly.

12. Is this funny? Why? How?

13. There are no corpses onstage. What are the men imagining?

14. **charnel-house** a place where corpses or bones are deposited

15. In spite of the fact that the context suggests that Estragon and Vladimir have repeated their thoughts and actions many times, each thought should seem new and original—even a brainstorm—at the moment.

16. **Que voulez-vous** (kə vü la´ vü) "What do you expect?" or "It can't be helped." [French]

*Silence.*

17. **canter** an easy gallop; run; scamper. Estragon may be talking about the session of word play they have just come through. If so, where does this session begin? Where does it end?

**ESTRAGON.** That wasn't such a bad little canter.[17]

**VLADIMIR.** Yes, but now we'll have to find something else.

**ESTRAGON.** Let me see.

*He takes off his hat, concentrates.*

18. Notice this and the preceding stage direction. How might these bits of stage business be handled?

**VLADIMIR.** Let me see. *(He takes off his hat, concentrates.*[18] *Long silence.)* Ah!

*They put on their hats, relax.*

**ESTRAGON.** Well?

**VLADIMIR.** What was I saying, we could go on from there.

**ESTRAGON.** What were you saying when?

**VLADIMIR.** At the very beginning.

**ESTRAGON.** The very beginning of WHAT?

**VLADIMIR.** This evening . . . I was saying . . . I was saying . . .

19. What does Estragon mean? Should he speak with irony or irritation?

**ESTRAGON.** I'm not a historian.[19]

**VLADIMIR.** Wait . . . we embraced . . . we were happy . . . happy . . . what do we do now that we're happy . . . go on waiting . . . waiting . . . let me think . . . it's coming . . . go on waiting . . . now that we're happy . . . let me see . . . ah! The tree![20]

20. Vladimir seems to be mentally replaying the events of the evening so as to remember what he was saying. How might this speech be phrased? How might Vladimir also replay his movements?

**ESTRAGON.** The tree?

**VLADIMIR.** Do you not remember?

**ESTRAGON.** I'm tired.

**VLADIMIR.** Look at it.

*They look at the tree.*

**ESTRAGON.** I see nothing.

**"That's the idea, let's contradict each other."**

**VLADIMIR.** But yesterday evening it was all black and bare. And now it's covered with leaves.[21]

**ESTRAGON.** Leaves?

**VLADIMIR.** In a single night.

**ESTRAGON.** It must be the Spring.

**VLADIMIR.** But in a single night!

**ESTRAGON.** I tell you we weren't here yesterday. Another of your nightmares.[22]

**VLADIMIR.** And where were we yesterday evening according to you?

**ESTRAGON.** How would I know? In another compartment. There's no lack of void.

**VLADIMIR** *(sure of himself)*. Good. We weren't here yesterday evening. Now what did we do yesterday evening?

**ESTRAGON.** Do?

**VLADIMIR.** Try and remember.

**ESTRAGON.** Do . . . I suppose we blathered.

**VLADIMIR** *(controlling himself)*. About what?

**ESTRAGON.** Oh . . . this and that I suppose, nothing in particular. *(With assurance.)* Yes, now I remember, yesterday evening we spent blathering about nothing in particular. That's been going on now for half a century.[23]

21. The setting is the same for both acts I and II: "A country road. A tree." No matter how many leaves the set designer puts on or omits from the tree, Vladimir and Estragon must still take their lines literally.

22. There are enough of these disagreements in the scene to provide variety for interpretation, emotional expression, and movement. How you build and pace these conflicts and resolutions is important to the overall effectiveness of the scene.

23. Which seems more important—the satisfaction that Estragon does manage to remember or the bleakness of what he remembers?

## Extension

The devices mentioned on page 428 are not specific to the theatre of the absurd; they are longstanding theatrical devices that continue to entertain audiences today, as in the performances of the Montreal-based Cirque du Soleil (shown here).

1. Describe theatrical effects, such as juggling, acrobatics, or mime that you have seen in theatrical works, movies, or television in which the primary purpose was to tell a story. How do these effects supplement or heighten the storytelling?
2. Find examples of disjointed language in other plays or in other media. Read them out loud by yourself or with a partner. Consider how much meaning is transmitted by what is not said directly.

# Directing & Producing

specialization

**Directing and producing skills are essential to theatre. These skills can be applied to Reader's Theatre and musical theatre as well as to other performance media such as film and television. Directors and producers are also becoming increasingly involved in multimedia and performance art, where financial, organizational, and aesthetic abilities are valued as much as they are in more conventional theatre.**

## THE LANGUAGE OF THEATRE

**book** the script for a musical
**final cut** the finished film or videotape
**fine cut** the second draft of a film or videotape
**footage** a length of exposed film
**location** a real setting where a production may be filmed or videotaped, rather than on a soundstage or backlot; off the studio lot
**lot** the site of a film or TV studio
**lyricist** the person who writes the words for the music in a musical
**music director** shapes the musical character of a show
**option** the offer of an opportunity to buy the rights to produce a show during a particular time frame
**rough cut** the first draft of a film or videotape
**rushes** or **dailies** unedited film or videotaped footage
**soundstage** the area of a studio building in which a film or TV program is shot
**storyboard** a series of individual sketches showing a sequence of possible shots for scenes in a script
**teleplay** a TV script

# Reader's Theatre

Reader's Theatre (p. 397) affords a director the opportunity to concentrate on presenting the idea of a story without the necessity of coordinating extensive movement to support the idea and move the story along. As such, the choice and interpretation of a script for a Reader's Theatre production take on an enhanced importance.

## Choosing the Script

A Reader's Theatre script may be adapted from a short work of literature or from an excerpt of a longer work. The work may be drawn from plays, fiction, poetry, letters, diaries, journals, and biographies. Generally, you can adapt any work of literature that interests you; however, directors have found that literary works that meet the following criteria lend themselves best to successful Reader's Theatre productions:

- emotional appeal
- a limited number of characters
- vivid characters, at least some of whom are likeable
- picturesque, animated, and unusual language
- plenty of dialogue
- dialogue that serves to distinguish characters through unique phrasing

As a director, you may choose to employ a narrator that speaks directly to the audience during the production. Even if the dialogue is lively and distinctive, a narrator may be necessary to help the audience follow the story and keep track of the characters. The narrator sets the time and place, describes details not contained in dialogue, and may comment on the action. You may choose to create a single narrator, divide the role of narrator among several actors, or give every actor a passage of narration.

## Scripting the Story

You should perform a standard analysis (p. 166) of the literary work from which you will script your story. Then select the portion you feel best represents the story and adapt it according to the guidelines presented in Writing & Theatre (p. 558).

## Casting

While skill at reading aloud is helpful in a Reader's Theatre production, it's not the most important performance skill. Your actors must also be excellent interpreters, flexible ensemble members, and enthusiastic fans of the script.

Auditions for Reader's Theatre will be more informal than those for other plays. You may ask actors to read parts individually, or you may have small groups of actors read from the script and then periodically rotate readers in certain parts. As with other casting procedures, make your adapted script available in advance of auditions if possible. During auditions discuss with actors their understanding of the story and the characters they might play. Explore each character's particular choice of words and phrasing. Ask questions relating to characters' motivation and behavior (p. 134). Speculate on the subtext of characters' words and movements (p. 138). Find out how well the actors can take direction by asking them to employ variety in vocal inflection as they read. Encourage them to display their range of expression (p. 34).

## The Rehearsal Process

Once you have chosen an ensemble, you can begin the rehearsal process. Like any rehearsal process, this one should begin with vocal and movement warm-ups to help the cast relax and focus on their work.

After warm-ups, position your actors as they will be in performance and begin read-throughs; rehearsals will essentially be a series of read-throughs. Words are of primary importance in this form of theatre; therefore, articulation and projection will need special attention. If you use music stands to hold scripts be careful to keep them low enough so they don't block actors' faces or interfere with projection. Actors usually have no need to be off book, but over the standard two-week rehearsal period for a Reader's Theatre production, they should become familiar enough with the script to look up periodically. Encourage your actors to listen as well as read, to experience the events in the piece, and to communicate that experience in the way they say their lines. As in other types of theatre, your rehearsals should include characterization work that will animate the actors as they say their lines. Polishing rehearsals will likely focus on perfecting the expressive interpretation of the story, primarily through voice, but also through limited movement.

## Movement

Standard placement of actors in Reader's Theatre is on chairs or stools, arranged in a configuration that supports the characters' relationships to one another. For that reason, you will probably want to place the narrator off to the side. You might want to position a leading character in the middle, with opposing forces on opposite sides. You may use levels or planes in your seating arrangements to express relationships among characters. Because every story is different, you will need to experiment with the arrangement that suits your story best.

Most directors find it easier to keep the entire cast onstage and in their assigned positions throughout the performance, but you may want to make exceptions to this convention by allowing some movement. If a character dies, for example, you may want that actor to leave the stage; if, on the other hand, a surprise character appears, you may want the actor to enter from offstage. Perhaps you will want to show how one character assumes power over another by having the actors switch places on stage. Or, you may wish to have two characters who are engaged in a long dialogue come forward in a shared position (p. 143) and read to each other as in a duet. Gestures are also possible, even if actors are holding a script in one hand. Facial expressions are used when delivering lines and reacting to lines. When you do employ movement, make sure it is carefully planned, not spontaneous. In general, keep stage movements and gestures to a minimum to avoid stealing focus from the story itself.

## Focus

Convention in Reader's Theatre holds that actors focus front but react as if they were face to face with other actors. This is so that an actor can play a scene with another actor seated several seats away. If, however, actors are next to each other and are playing a scene together or if they move down front to play a scene, they will face each other. Actors not active in a scene seemingly do not exist during that scene and will merely follow along in the script until they "enter" again.

Focus front doesn't mean that the actors should make eye-contact with the audience—at least when playing a character. An actor as narrator, however, should make eye contact with the audience whenever it's possible to look up from the script, directing one or two lines to a different audience member each time.

## Technical Elements

Aside from seating, Reader's Theatre typically has no set. Lighting should be sufficient to see the actors and may be used to set a mood, but should not be distracting. Music, too, may be used to create a certain ambience but should not interfere with the dialogue; sound effects should be used sparingly. Ask your actors to dress in simple clothing that expresses the mood of the story; clothing should not draw focus from the reading or to any particular actor, including the narrator. White shirts and black pants or skirts, for example, are common dress for actors in Reader's Theatre. Straight makeup (p. 95) may also be worn but should be subdued.

Timothy Dalton and Whoopi Goldberg participate in a Reader's Theatre presentation of A. R. Gurney's *Love Letters*. Note the similar clothing, a common costuming decision for Reader's Theatre.

One of the longest running musicals on Broadway is *The King and I* by Richard Rodgers and Oscar Hammerstein II. The set and costumes, simulating the palace of the King of Siam (Thailand) in the mid-1800s, make this a particularly lavish and expensive musical to produce.

# Musical Theatre

The importance and popularity of musicals in theatre are undisputed (p. 415). As a genre combining story with song and dance, musicals pose a special challenge to directors and producers. The cast of musicals is usually very large, and the ensemble effort is heightened by the use of choruses. Directors of musicals must therefore be skilled at working with large groups in stage composition and movement.

The challenge of musicals extends to managing the technical elements of the production. Because musical sets are often lavish and complex, making the production concept a reality requires elaborate plans and extremely close coordination with the design team.

## The Directing Team

In school, community, and professional theatre, the enterprise of directing a musical is usually a team effort involving the director, a music director, and a choreographer (p. 415). Producers, especially in professional theatre, are also integral to creating successful musical theatre. Everybody works together on the production concept, but each has distinct responsibilities for the production.

## The Music Director

The **music director** shapes the musical tone of the show. In addition to working with the producer to obtain the musical rights for the show and renting musical scores, the music director's duties include working with the chorus and principal actors/singers to develop the tone of the musical numbers. Because important moments of the show take place through music, the music director influences the tone of the entire show. The music director is sometimes responsible for choosing the instrumentation for the music, which must be appropriate for the style of the musical. This may be one piano or synthesizer, a small ensemble of instruments, or a full-scale orchestra, depending on the budget and the production concept. For shows that do not have a conductor, the music director conducts the musicians and the singers from the orchestra pit during the performance.

## The Choreographer

The choreographer, as coordinator of the dance elements of a production, is another associate of the director (p. 415). The choreographer often works with the director on blocking so that musical and nonmusical portions of a show flow together well.

## The Producer

Producing a musical is often a risky venture because of the great expense involved. A high school musical can cost from 2 to 15 thousand dollars—a sizeable chunk of any high school theatre budget. In professional theatre, a musical can cost from 4 to 10 million dollars to produce. Producers in the professional theatre often join forces with each other and with other professionals—theatre managers, accountants, lawyers—to raise and manage the money to mount a show.

Producers of musicals must be especially skilled at forecasting and managing productions with special requirements. Compared to most nonmusical plays, musicals require larger performance spaces, involve more elaborate sets and costumes, and have larger casts, crews, and production staff. All these factors mean producers have more to lose financially if a musical is not successful.

The music director for this high school production conducts the musical ensemble from the orchestra pit.

## Choosing a Musical

You already know that the choice of which play to produce may be made by a director, by one or more individuals acting as producer, or by the director and producer together. The same is true of musicals. The choice of a show in the professional theatre is typically made by a producer because of the tremendous financial responsibility of producing a musical at that level. Before money can be invested, however, a producer needs to find a musical to produce, one with the potential to be a hit. Playwrights often enlist the services of a **theatrical agent.** Agents promote and sell the work of theatrical talent such as playwrights and actors. When an agent receives new work from a playwright, the agent contacts producers to offer an **option** on the work, that is, to offer an opportunity to buy the rights to produce it during a particular time frame. If a producer picks up (agrees to buy) the option, he or she then negotiates the fee and the length of the option.

When producers of professional musicals make choices about which musicals to option, they may be responding to trends in the market for particular types of musicals. In recent years, a popular trend has been producing revivals of hit shows in the American musical theatre of the 1920s to the 1960s, including *Carousel* by Richard Rodgers and Oscar Hammerstein II and *Hello Dolly!* by Michael Stewart and Jerry Herman. *Hello Dolly!* is a musical remake of Thornton Wilder's play, *The Matchmaker.* Many musicals are adaptations of plays. If the play was successful, it's likely the musical will be too.

*The Happy End* by Bertolt Brecht, with music by Kurt Weill, is set in 1920s Chicago. It pits gangsters against the Salvation Army, making it a forerunner of *Guys and Dolls* by Frank Loesser, Jo Swerling, and Abe Burrows, which, though set in New York City, utilizes the same situation.

Producers also watch for new musicals being produced in college, university, and regional theatres, where musicals are produced on a somewhat smaller scale, allowing the theatres to take creative risks—creative risks that may result in a hit show. A producer may pick up an option to turn the show into an even greater hit on **Broadway,** the famous theatre district of New York City.

Your first impulse—as director or producer—might be to plunge into your favorite show. It's a good impulse, and one you should explore; you should feel passionate about the musical you choose. On the other hand, you need to consider your resources before you commit to a particular show.

## Budget

Whether you are a producer or director, in the professional theatre or in educational theatre, your choice of a musical will depend in great part on your budget. Plan your production scaled to the amount of cash you have available. Use a budget worksheet that includes entries for estimating costs in every area of production, which may include royalties, salaries for actors and crews, rental of theatre space, and materials and supplies.

## Performance Space

Musicals need a large space for song and dance numbers and considerable wing and fly space to accommodate large casts and elaborate sets. Arena and thrust stages are therefore not particularly well suited for musical productions.

## Cast and Crew

Once you have a budget, consider the cast available to you. Although many productions ask actors to double up on some roles, you must have a strong principal (p. 415) who can sing and several supporting actors who can dedicate themselves to one role each. If the show you want to do includes complex dance steps, you must be able to engage a choreographer—and dancers who are skilled enough to learn the steps.

You will need a larger stage crew for a musical than you would for most other plays. Think about whether the crew available to you is sufficient for the task, in both numbers and skill of handling what may be a range of particularly complex technical design and production elements.

## Audience

Finally, consider your audience. A high school production must appeal to a wide range of people, including senior citizens, parents, teachers, classmates, and small children. Some themes you find compelling or appealing may not be suitable for portions of your intended audience.

## Production Concept

As a director, once you have found a play that meets your production criteria, you can begin to develop an artistic vision for the show—your production concept (p. 54). Begin by performing a standard script analysis of the production you have chosen (p. 166).

Read as much as possible about the original production. Learn what you can about the **composer,** the person who writes the music for a musical; the **lyricist,** the person who writes the words for the music; and writer of the **book,** as the script for the musical is called. Study recent and past reviews of the musical. View videotapes and listen to recordings of the show if they are available. While doing so, make notes to answer the following questions:

- What are your favorite parts of the musical?
- What are your favorite songs?
- What are your favorite dances?
- What parts seem boring or silly to you?
- What parts present production problems?
- Do you agree or disagree with critics regarding the musical?

Use these questions to guide you, your music director, and your choreographer in developing your production concept. As soon as possible, meet with the rest of the production team (p. 54).

*Sunday in the Park with George* by James Lapine and Stephen Sondheim is based on a painting by Georges Seurat. Seurat's painting style, pointillism, was composed of small dots. Sondheim's music features a musical equivalent to pointillism through the use of staccato (short and sharp) notes. The musical's heroine is named Dot.

*South Pacific,* adapted by Joshua Logan from James Michener's stories of the South Pacific, features music by Richard Rodgers and lyrics by Oscar Hammerstein II. Logan directed the original stage and film versions.

## Planning the Production

Once you have gathered a production team and developed a vision for the musical, you can draw up plans and schedules for the entire production. First, count the number of scene changes in the musical. Then use what you have learned about production planning to determine the sets, lighting effects, and actors you will need in each scene.

With the help of the music director, conductor, and choreographer, draw up a full schedule for the entire rehearsal period. As you would for other rehearsal schedules (p. 187), include times and dates for the various stages of the rehearsal process (p. 282), but add time to each stage for singing and choreography. Because musicals often include solos, duets, and crowd scenes, you may be able to schedule more than one rehearsal at a time. For example, you may be working on blocking one scene for a duet while the music director might be training a soloist, and the choreographer might be working on rehearsing dance steps with the chorus. If possible, allow 10 to 12 weeks of rehearsal time to produce a musical.

### Musical Rehearsal Schedule

The following is a sample rehearsal schedule for a musical:

**WEEK 1**
Introduce show and concept to cast.
Provide background information.
Discuss technical elements and music.
Director establishes production policies.

**WEEKS 2–7**
Music director rehearses songs with principals and chorus.
Choreographer works with dancers.
Director blocks and refines scenes.

**WEEK 8**
Do run-throughs: quarters of show.

**WEEK 9**
Do run-throughs: halves of show.

**WEEKS 10–11**
Do run-throughs: complete show.
Hold tech rehearsals without cast.
Hold dress parade.
Add orchestra to rehearsals.

**WEEK 12**
Hold complete tech rehearsals.
Hold dress rehearsals.
Run a preview performance of the show.

# Film and TV

Film and TV productions have much in common with live theatre productions. For example, they all begin with a story or script. All require the support of a producer and the guiding hand of a director. All are expressed through the efforts of actors and crew members, and all are intended to please an audience. The major difference lies in the extent of the use of technology.

Film and TV are dependent upon technology to a greater degree than live theatre. The technology involved in directing a film or TV production requires personnel who understand this technology and its potential; many directors have hands-on experience running a camera. A director and producer's understanding of the technology used in film and TV becomes particularly relevant in genres that require extensive use of technology, such as science fiction.

Luc Besson's film *The Fifth Element* is a big-budget science fiction comedy featuring a range of special effects and futuristic sets.

## Film

Film requires the collaboration of hundreds of professionals. You can get a good impression of the size of a film production team by watching the credits. The **credits**, which usually appear at the end of a film or TV program, list all the people involved in the production. Producers and directors are integral to this collaboration and work very closely together throughout a production. As in live theatre, the producer and the director are sometimes the same person; in fact, there are many actors who also direct and produce the films in which they star.

In film production, executive producers for a film company often supervise the work of a single producer, who takes responsibility for a particular film. The film producer manages all the business and financial issues surrounding the film. The executive producers and the producer may work together to choose a director, screenwriters, and other major contributors for that film. The director handles the artistic issues with input from the producer on those issues that might affect the financial success of the production.

## Stages of Film Production

Film production may be broken down into four different, but often overlapping, stages: development, preproduction, production, and postproduction.

### Development

Development is largely the job of the producer, who must hire or approve the screenwriters for the film and then find reliable financing. With input from the producers, the director develops a plan for hiring screenwriters, cast, and crew. He or she also develops the production schedule that will take the film through its production stages.

The producer often works with the director to put together an informational package attractive to investors. The package includes a working script (one which will provide the basis for the film, but which may change), a description of key artists (director, actors, designers), a budget, and a rough shooting schedule. If investors feel that the combination of story and artists will attract a large enough audience to support advertising and production costs, they agree to invest money in exchange for a percentage of profits.

### Preproduction

Once financing is secured, the producers, director, and other key contributors take on preproduction tasks to prepare for shooting the film. First, the director hires the production team. He or she relies on the production manager to refine the shooting schedule and develop a budget for the film. Next, the producers, director, and casting director interview and audition actors. If time permits, the director might hold preproduction rehearsals to prepare the actors for the production of the film. The director may work with the screenwriter and an artist to develop a **storyboard,** a series of individual sketches showing the sequence of possible shots for scenes in the script. From there, the **shooting script** is developed, in which each individual shot is specified by number and type of shot (p. 555).

## Production

During production, the film gets underway. The director becomes immersed in shooting the film, working with the cast and crews on a soundstage, a backlot, or on location. A **soundstage** is a building on the studio **lot,** or site of a film (or TV) studio, in which a film (or TV program) may be shot. A **backlot** is an outdoor soundstage in which open-air scenes can be constructed and filmed. Many films today are made on **location,** a real setting rather than a setting on a soundstage or backlot. This location may be the actual geographic spot specified in the script or one that closely resembles it.

Shooting on a film is nonsequential: scenes are filmed in an order that does not necessarily follow the script, but rather is most convenient for getting all the shots (p. 419) required for a specific location or a specific setup (p. 418) at that location. Film production teams film most or all of the scenes related to a particular setting and then move to another location to film the scenes that take place there.

As crews adjust equipment for the setup, the director consults with the actors about blocking and pacing of the scene and other factors affecting how he or she would like the scene to unfold. The film crew often produces several takes (p. 418) of each scene. The director may call for several camera angles and photographic techniques to achieve special effects, or the crew members or actors may require several tries to get things right. A special piece of equipment known as a **video assist,** which is attached to the camera, allows the director to see the framing (p. 418) of the scene as it is shot.

Actor George Clooney discusses a scene between takes on the set of Steven Soderbergh's *Out of Sight.*

When the director is satisfied with a take, he or she sends it to the film lab to be printed. The crew keeps the negatives of the rejected takes, in case they are needed later. Then everyone moves on to another scene.

The role of the producer during the production and postproduction stages varies with each individual producer. During production, most producers want to stay close to the shooting but don't want to get in the way of the work or make people nervous by their presence. For these reasons, a producer may stay away from the set during the actual shooting of scenes, but he or she might want to view the rushes. Problems that might come up during production that require the producer's attention include cutting scenes, revising the shooting schedule, or going over budget.

During the production process the producer begins the marketing plan for the film, including supervision of the **trailer,** a preview to be shown as coming attractions in movie theatres across the country, and coordinating print publicity for newspapers, magazines, and billboards. The trailer needs to be ready to show about six months before the film is released. The print publicity is released a month or so before the film opens.

The **slate** (pictured here) offers an easy way for film and TV editors to synchronize images and sound. It also provides reference information about the date, the production, the scene, and the take number: Actors Robert DeNiro and Liza Minnelli perform the sixth take of scene ii during filming of Martin Scorcese's *New York, New York.*

## Postproduction

At the end of the day, the director meets with the production manager and the cinematographer to plan the next day's shooting. The **cinematographer** is the person who designs the way each shot should be lit and filmed to meet the vision of the director and producer. The cast members study the next day's script (which may change on a daily basis), and the crews pack up equipment and prepare for the next day's shoot.

After a day's shooting, the film editor makes a work print of the best takes from that day's shoot. A **work print** is a print used for cutting and editing; this saves the original negative of the film so it's not marred during corrections. The film editor also synchronizes the film images with the sound. The assistant editor makes a written record of every shot, so nothing gets lost. Then the director and editor **screen,** or view, the unedited film footage known as **rushes** or **dailies** made from the editor's print. **Footage** is a length of exposed film. The director and editor discuss which shots to use and the way in which they should be arranged.

After all the film has been assembled in this way, the editor cuts and splices the film to create a **rough cut,** or first draft, of the film. The editor shows the rough cut to the director, who makes further suggestions about ways to add, drop, and rearrange the footage. The editor uses those suggestions to make a fine cut of the film, including music and sound effects; the **fine cut** is a sort of second draft.

Investors, friends, or colleagues invited to screen the fine cut may help to shape the **final cut,** or final draft, of the film.

In the postproduction stage, the producer might want to view the rough cut and have input concerning footage for the fine cut. Working collaboratively with the editor and the director, the producer is involved with editing the final cut of the film.

Based on the progress of the editing process, the producer decides if the release date for the film should be changed. Prior to release, films are frequently shown in sneak previews at selected theatres throughout the country, and the producer will attend these with others involved in the film. Based on audience reaction, the producer and director will make necessary changes before the film is released nationally.

Once a film is released, the producer and director are finished. The performances of cast and crew have been captured, manipulated, and preserved to be shown again and again to audiences around the world.

Robert Altman's film *The Player* is a murder mystery revolving around a Hollywood film producer.

## TV

Like film, TV often is shot and recorded in advance and shown later. Most TV programs are **taped,** or filmed, on videotape, which is a less expensive medium than the film used for making movies. In many other ways, however, the TV production process is much like the process of making a film.

A television producer usually begins the process by obtaining a script or hiring writers to write the script. At the same time, the producer chooses a director and the production crew. The producer and the director also cast the actors who will appear in the show.

After writers complete a TV script, or **teleplay,** for a show, the director reviews it and sends it to an artist to make storyboards (p. 448). As the script is refined, the director holds script readings and perhaps a **dry run** of the show, a run-through without tech crews. Then come dress rehearsals, which are much like the technical rehearsals for live theatre. Sometimes, directors tape the dress rehearsal so they have a backup tape for the show.

While a television program is being taped, the technical director monitors visuals and sound. Three cameras tape the action, and the technical director responds to commands by the director to show the scene from the angle of camera one, two, or three. The technical director also initiates special visual effects requested by the director such as a **dissolve,** in which a picture is faded in while a previous picture is faded out; a **superimposition,** in which one picture is brought on top of another; a **wipe,** in which a shot succeeds a previous shot by wiping it off the screen; and a **matte,** in which a false background (such as a world map) replaces the background in a scene. The technical director also inputs sounds produced by the audio engineer.

Some television programs, such as the news, are broadcast live as they are taped. Many television programs allow a studio audience to watch the taping process, but in most cases, they broadcast the tape later, to minimize the opportunity for serious mishaps to occur.

Once a show is taped, the video editor reviews the shoot with the director. The video editor then cuts and splices tape to preserve the best scenes and to maintain the pacing and timing. Because television programs must fit into a tightly controlled schedule, the timing must be extremely precise. Television actors must be especially conscious of continuity (p. 419) to be able to recreate their exact position so that the action flows smoothly from take to take. The director and producer review the fine cuts and release the final cut of the tape to be shown on TV.

## TV Genres

If you are interested in directing and producing for TV, there are a variety of genres in which to try your skills, including news programs, commercials, soap operas, documentaries, situation comedies, dramas, and talk shows, to name a few. Situation comedies and dramas have the most in common with genres of live theatre.

**Situation comedies,** called sitcoms, are recurring programs that explore comic situations with the same basic cast of characters. Most situation comedies run thirty minutes in length. These programs combine vaudeville skits with theatrical comedy of manners to offer a conflict, climax, and resolution, all within a single episode. The characters in a popular situation comedy, like their counterparts in a soap opera, might become a small part of the daily lives of the program viewers. Producers of popular situation comedies sometimes feature one of the characters in a related show, called a **spin-off.**

Dramas are serious fictional programs with realistic characters and settings, such as doctors in a hospital, a family in a home, or police officers in a big city. These programs explore social problems, family crises, or serious illnesses, and like situation comedies, they usually provide conflict, climax, and resolution in a single episode. Some programs recur each week with the same cast of characters, while others are one-time performances. Many dramas last about an hour. A longer, more in-depth drama might find a slot as a **miniseries.** Lasting from 4 to 16 hours and usually shown in 2-hour segments, a miniseries can gain the scope of a full-length novel.

Soap operas traditionally focus on sensational problems suffered by glamorous, well-to-do characters. Night-time soap operas, such as *Melrose Place* (below) have become increasingly popular. The challenge in producing and directing these programs is to hook an audience on the characters and their lives.

*Einstein on the Beach,* a collaboration between multimedia writer/director Robert Wilson and composer Phillip Glass, is a five-hour play exploring the physics genius Albert Einstein.

## Multimedia and Performance Arts

When talking about performance art and the use of multimedia (p. 420), the lines between producer, director, and actor and those between live theatre and film begin to blur. A performance art piece is often conceived, directed, scripted, acted, and produced by a single individual. Performance art frequently combines live performance with other media such as film, television, and computer. Performance art and multimedia on the Internet are growing genres that use the technology of the Internet to reach a mass audience in a way that live performance art is unable to do.

Craig Lucas's *God's Heart* employs a large-screen TV. Characters interact with the character on the TV screen. As a director, what types of challenges might a multimedia situation like this present?

# Activities

### *Reader's Theatre*

**VISUALIZING READER'S THEATRE** Read several short stories and visualize how you might stage a Reader's Theatre production of each. In your Theatre Notebook, take notes and make sketches about which portions would be good to adapt, what type of narration would be effective, how you might incorporate simple blocking, and how you might use simple sound effects and lighting.

### *Reader's Theatre*

**ADAPTING SCRIPTS** Read several short pieces of literature and evaluate them to see if they meet the criteria for adaptation to a Reader's Theatre script (p. 558). Then use the guidelines included in Writing & Theatre to adapt one of the pieces that meets the criteria. Include your evaluations and your adapted script in your Theatre Notebook. If you like, follow through and direct your own Reader's Theatre production.

### *Musical Theatre*

**OPTIONING UNFAMILIAR MUSICALS** Watch on video several musicals with which you are unfamiliar. Imagine you are a producer considering these musicals to option for production. Explain in your Theatre Notebook whether you would produce any in your community and give the reasons for your decisions.

### *Musical Theatre*

**PRODUCTION CONCEPT FOR A MUSICAL** Choose a musical to direct and then establish a production concept using the guidelines in this chapter (p. 444). Plan a production schedule (p. 445) for the musical. Present your choice, your production concept, and your rehearsal schedule to the class or a small group. Listen to their feedback and add their constructive comments to your Theatre Notebook along with your concept and schedule.

*Film and TV*

**PLAYS INTO FILM** Work with a partner to brainstorm plays that have been made into movies. Read one of two of these plays and watch the movies on video. Compare and contrast the way the different elements of the story—plot, character, setting, and theme—are treated in each medium. Why do you think the film producers and directors made the choices they did in adapting the story for film? Discuss your analysis and write your conclusions in your Theatre Notebook.

*Film and TV*

**JOB SHADOW—TV DIRECTOR OR PRODUCER** Arrange with an area TV station to observe a director or producer at work for a day or a few hours. Explain that you are interested in witnessing the day-to-day operations of a TV director or producer. Professionals are busy, but if you are polite as well as interested, they are usually willing to let you observe them at work and to answer questions about their training and background. Be sure to first get permission from your parents, teacher, and the supervisor of the business or organization where you will job shadow.

*Multimedia and Performance Art*

**DIRECT A MULTIMEDIA PERFORMANCE** On your own, with a partner, or with a small group, stage a multimedia performance. You can present a scene from a play, write a poem, or create a piece of performance art. Incorporate videotape of previously recorded broadcasts from TV or from video that you have created, sound and lighting effects, computers, original artwork, and anything else that will create an interesting performance. Present your piece to your class. Be sure to rehearse your piece first to iron out any technical problems. You might write about what you learned during this experience in your Theatre Notebook.

## Historical Profile

# Wilson

August Wilson was born in 1945 in Pittsburgh, Pennsylvania. He was raised with three older sisters and two younger brothers in a two-room, cold-water apartment. His father, Frederick August Kittel, who was white, did not live with the family; his African American mother, Daisy Wilson, raised her six children herself, relying on welfare until she was able to find work cleaning. Disgusted with the racism he encountered at the various schools he attended and feeling the need to further his creativity, interests, and learning abilities, Wilson dropped out of the ninth grade at age 15 and began educating himself at the local library. He enlisted in the U.S. Army in 1962 and received an honorable discharge the following year.

A turning point in Wilson's life came in 1965 when he bought a typewriter and began writing poetry. His early work was influenced by the Welsh poet Dylan Thomas and by the Black Power movement of the late 1960s. In 1968 he became co-founder, script writer, and director of Black Horizons on the Hill, a black activist theatre company in Pittsburgh. These early plays were not commercial successes, but they did lay the groundwork for his more important work to come. In 1978 Wilson moved to St. Paul, Minnesota, where he continued writing plays that were notable for the truth with which they presented black speech and life.

His first success was *Ma Rainey's Black Bottom,* about the famed blues singer Ma Rainey and set at a recording session in 1927 in Chicago. This won him the New York Drama Critics Circle award for best play of 1984–85. His next play, *Fences,* about a disillusioned former baseball player in the 1950s, won not only the Drama Critics Circle award but also the Tony Award and the 1987 Pulitzer Prize for drama. *Joe Turner's Come and Gone,* set in a Pittsburgh boarding house in 1911, and concerning an ex-convict's efforts to find his wife, solidified Wilson's position as one of the most significant writers of the day. His next major success, *The Piano Lesson,* set during the Great Depression of the 1930s, concerns the conflict between a brother and sister over selling a treasured heirloom. It earned Wilson his second Pulitzer Prize in 1990 and was adapted for television in 1995. *Two Trains Running* and *Seven Guitars* continued Wilson's commitment to portraying African Americans realistically and sensitively and to "raise consciousness through theatre."

The success of Lorraine Hansberry's *A Raisin in the Sun* marked a new era in African American theatre. After her early death, some of Hansberry's unpublished writings were collected in *To Be Young, Gifted, and Black,* here dramatized for the stage.

## African American Theatre

Theatre by or about African Americans was very limited throughout much of U.S. history. During the 1800s blacks were portrayed on stage largely as fools, clowns, or incompetents; even the occasional black character that was conceived with a degree of nobility, as in dramatizations of Harriet Beecher Stowe's novel, *Uncle Tom's Cabin,* was still a stereotype. The first play by an African American playwright to appear on a Broadway stage was Garland Anderson's *Appearances* in 1925.

Because of the number of emerging black writers and artists who congregated in New York's Harlem area during the mid-1920s, the period became known as the Harlem Renaissance. One of the most important of these writers was Langston Hughes. Though primarily a poet, he wrote dozens of plays, including *Little Ham, Simply Heavenly,* and *Tambourines to Glory.* His contemporaries Arna Bontemps and Countee Cullen collaborated on the musical *St. Louis Woman.* A watershed in African American theatre was reached in 1959 when Lorraine Hansberry's *A Raisin in the Sun* became a great popular success and was later made into a movie.

The 1960s saw a rise in writing on black themes, especially by such playwrights as Amiri Baraka (Le Roi Jones) and Ed Bullins. Many of these works were angry and confrontational. Lonne Elder III won a number of awards for *Ceremonies in Dark Old Men,* which was later adapted for television.

The first black playwright to win the Pulitzer Prize for drama was Charles Gordone, in 1970, for *No Place to Be Somebody.* Since that time African American playwrights have found increasing acceptance. Notable among these was Ntozake Shange, whose Tony Award-winning study of the oppression of black women, *for colored girls who have considered suicide/when the rainbow is enuf* (1976), demonstrated that African American themes had become mainstream.

Ntozake's Shange's play *for colored girls who have considered suicide/when the rainbow is enuf* combines poetry, music, dance, and drama.

## Wilson's Theatrical Style

One of the most important features in Wilson's plays is storytelling: the characters tell each other stories—sometimes at great length—about their lives and histories and about the histories of family, friends, and acquaintances. His characters do so, according to Wilson, not just to pass the time or entertain themselves, but as a way of "creating and preserving themselves."

Wilson's use of language is distinctive: it includes a variety of verbal structures typical of African American language:

- **signifying** engaging in a humorous insult match
- **sounding** getting on someone's case
- **rapping** using street language to create poetry
- **sweet talking** trying to win someone over
- **marking** mimicking the words of others
- **loud talking** speaking to a second person words intended to be overheard by a third person.

Music is also inherent in Wilson's plays, as it is in the storytelling of the African griot (p. 44). He calls blues "the wellspring of my art," and in all of his major plays, characters sing, dance, play musical instruments, or beat out elaborate rhythms. Several of his plays, in fact, take their titles or their themes from traditional blues songs.

Wilson thinks that African Americans have "the most dramatic story of all mankind to tell." Feeling that his generation of blacks knew very little about the past of their parents, Wilson set out to change the situation by creating a series of 10 plays, each set in a different decade of the 20th century, tracing hopes and dreams, successes and failures, from one generation to the next. Although Wilson deals with historical black themes, many are universal themes, which make his complex dramatic works not merely African American theatre but universal theatre.

## Try It Out

Although Floyd has many more lines in the following scene than Vera, she has an equally important job: to listen attentively and to keep the focus of the scene where it is supposed to be. As a director, your challenges will be to establish that focus, to pace the scene, and to orchestrate the many beats (p. 147) that occur even within a few words.

*from*

# Seven Guitars

**F**loyd Barton and Vera Dotson are lovers in 1948 Pittsburgh. However, when Floyd goes to Chicago to record his song "That's All Right," he takes another woman with him because Vera refuses to go. Floyd is in jail on a false arrest for vagrancy when his recording is released and becomes a hit. Now, months later, the record company wants Floyd to return to Chicago for another recording session. This time when he asks Vera to go with him, she agrees.

1. After you have read the scene, determine how Floyd might call for Vera.

2. Is Vera speaking with puzzlement, annoyance, or relief?

3. **Muddy Waters** popular performer of traditional blues, whose harsh vocal style carried great emotional intensity.

4. With what tone of voice might Vera say this?

5. Why does Floyd start referring to himself in the third person? What tone of voice might he use for this announcement?

(FLOYD *has a guitar case and a dress box with him. He calls for* VERA *to come to the window.)*

**FLOYD.** Hey . . . Vera! . . . Vera![1]

(VERA *comes to the window.* FLOYD *holds the guitar up triumphantly.)*

**VERA** *(from window).* Floyd, where you been? You been gone for two days. Ain't nobody seen you.[2]

(VERA *enters.* FLOYD *picks up the guitar to show her.)*

**FLOYD.** Look at this! Look at this! That's the same kind of guitar as Muddy Waters[3] got. Same color and everything . . .

**VERA.** Floyd, that's brand-new.[4]

**FLOYD.** Wait till you hear how it sound. We ain't gonna talk about how nice it look till after you hear how it sound. To do that you got to come to the Blue Goose . . . the number-one blues club in Pittsburgh . . . where the one and only Floyd "Schoolboy" Barton is appearing this Sunday[5] . . . one night only . . . Mother's Day . . . courtesy of Savoy Records. Come one, come all, to hear him perform his hit record "That's All Right" along with his new songs and future hits. That ain't all.

Wait till you see this here.

*(He takes a dress from the box.)*

Size nine. That's your size.[6]

**VERA.** Floyd, it's beautiful. I don't believe it. I ain't never had nothing like this.[7]

**FLOYD.** If you gonna be with Floyd Barton, you got to go down to the Blue Goose looking nice.

**VERA.** Floyd, where you been? Where you get all this from?[8]

**FLOYD.** You know better than to ask me where I get anything from.[9] I took a chance. Lots of times in life you taking a chance. Some people say that's all life is. Say, "I'm gonna take a chance on this . . . and I'm gonna take a chance on that . . . and I'm gonna take a chance on the other." And then sometime you be taking your last chance. If you taking your last chance then you done used up your life. I say I'm just getting started and I didn't want to take no chance of not getting back up to Chicago. So yeah, I took a chance.[10] I went out there to pay the gravestone man the rest of the money. He had the gravestone already made up. It's gray marble. It say "Maude

6. How might Floyd display this dress?

7. What might Vera do with the dress? How long might she continue to do it? At what point during the scene might she put the dress back in the box?

8. Why is Vera suddenly suspicious?

9. Floyd has robbed a loan office with two accomplices, one of whom was shot and killed by police. That guilty secret forms a large part of his subtext in this scene. The audience won't learn of this until a later scene, but Floyd needs to signal to the audience somehow that all is not on the level.

10. How can Floyd show that he changes topics here?

"Try me one more time and I'll never JUMP BACK on you in life."

11. Floyd's mother, who died three months ago.

12. How might Floyd deliver this line?

13. This is another change of topic. What is Floyd's mood now?

14. What's the significance of Vera's name on the ticket?

15. This was a considerable amount of money for a phone call in 1948. How might Floyd announce this expenditure?

16. Vera has her own secret, one that she will reveal at the end of this scene. How might this subtext affect the way she listens to Floyd's speech?

17. Analyze the following speech to see how many beats it contains. Where does Floyd's mood change? Where and how might he move?

18. That is, by going with me, she told me that my success was possible.

19. What might Vera be doing during this long speech? How might she show that she is listening and reacting to every word?

20. What might Floyd do vocally or physically to emphasize this boxing simile?

21. Pacing is important in this speech. Where does it build to a climax? How many climaxes does it build to?

Avery Barton."[11] Got two roses. One on each side. It looked so pretty. He say he have it on the grave by Mother's Day. We gonna go out there and see it.[12] I left out of there and went down to the Greyhound bus station. Look here . . .[13]

*(He pulls some tickets out of his pocket.)*

What that say? "Pittsburgh to Chicago." I told the man to write your name on it . . . he said they didn't do that. I took a pencil and wrote it on there myself.[14]

*(He shows her the ticket.)*

Then I made a long-distance phone call . . . cost me three dollars and ten cents.[15] I called Mr. Wilber H. Gardner, president of Savoy Records, and told him I would be there on the tenth of June. Then I called the Delaware Towers Hotel on State Street and told them to get ready their best room for Miss Vera Dotson . . . soon to be Mrs. Floyd Barton. That is . . . if she say yeah.

**VERA.** I want to say yeah, but what am I saying yeah to?[16] Another heartache? Another time for you to walk out the door with another woman?

**FLOYD.** You was there too, Vera.[17] You had a hand in whatever it was. Maybe all the times we don't know the effect of what we do. But we cause what happens to us. Sometimes even in little ways we can't see. I went up to Chicago with Pearl Brown cause she was willing to believe that I could take her someplace she wanted to go. That I could give her things that she wanted to have. She told me by that . . . it was possible.[18] Even sometimes when you question yourself . . . when you wonder can you really make the music work for you . . . can you find a way to get it out into the world so it can burst in the air and have it mean something to somebody.[19] She didn't know if I could do that. If I could have a hit record. But she was willing to believe it. Maybe it was selfish of her. Maybe she believed for all the wrong reasons. But that gave me a chance to try. So yeah . . . I took it. It wasn't easy. I was scared. But when them red lights came on in that recording studio it was like a bell ringing in the boxing match,[20] and I did it! I reached down inside me and I pulled out whatever was there. I did like my mama told me. I did my best. And I figured nobody could fault me for that. Then when they didn't release the record, Pearl Brown left. She thought she had believed wrong. I don't fault her for that. But I never lost the belief in myself.[21]

Then when they released the record I realized I didn't have nothing but a hit record. I come back to you[22] figuring you couldn't say no to a man who got a hit record. But you did. And that made me see that you wanted more than Pearl Brown. I'm here saying I can give it to you. Try me one more time and I'll never jump back on you in life.

**VERA.** I got to thinking and I went down to the Greyhound bus station too.[23]

*(She hands him a ticket.)*[24]

Here. See that? What that say? It say, "One way . . . Chicago to Pittsburgh." It's good for one year from date of purchase. I'm gonna put that in my shoe. When we get to Chicago I'm gonna walk around on it.[25] I hope I never have to use it.

**FLOYD.** Well, that's all right.[26]

(FLOYD *and* VERA *embrace with a renewed spirit of commitment.)*[27]

22. His speech now focuses again on Vera. How might Floyd focus on her physically as well?

23. How might Vera respond here?

24. Where has Vera kept her ticket until now?

25. What is the significance of Vera's second ticket?

26. Remember that "That's All Right" is the name of Floyd's hit record. If he is quoting himself, how might he deliver this line?

27. Consider carefully how to stage this embrace. Does Floyd move to Vera, Vera to Floyd, or do they both move? Who moves first? In what stage area do they meet? How do they embrace—tentatively, because they've been apart a long while, or with passion? Do they kiss? If so, how might their bodies be positioned? their arms? their heads? This is the end of the scene. Should the lights dim out slowly or black out quickly?

## Extension

Musicals are a specialized dramatic form, but many plays use music effectively in the form of songs that characters perform or background music to establish time and place or to set a mood.

1. Locate a film or TV comedy or drama that is not a musical but that contains music in some form. Choose a scene and explain the effect that the music creates—to set a mood, to heighten emotion, to express character, or merely to entertain.
2. Choose a one-act play or a scene from a longer play and plan background music to be played at the beginning or end or with some significant action.

In the comic western film *Cat Ballou*, narrators Nat King Cole and Stubby Kaye delivered periodic exposition in musical form.

# Technical Theatre

## Specialization

**You have learned about and experimented with many of the basic and essential approaches and skills in technical design, construction, and production. You can now build upon those stagecraft basics as you further explore a range of techniques in all areas of technical theatre.**

### THE LANGUAGE OF THEATRE

**ambient light** existing surrounding light that may interfere with a projected image

**hot spot** an intense circle of light created when a projector lens is seen through the screen

**keystoning** the distortion that occurs when an image is projected at an angle onto a screen or other projection surface

**life mask** a mask made by taking an impression of a person's face

**profile** a scenic element cut from a large sheet of plywood and attached to a flat using keystones

**swag** a hanging curve of fabric between two points

**synthesizer** an electronic device used to create artificial sounds

**three-dimensional scenery** stock units such as platforms and stair units, as well as objects such as buildings, trees, rocks, and other sculptural forms

**track** a path along which information is recorded electronically

**voice-over** a recording of a voice that plays over other sounds

# Scenery Techniques

Set design is an area that is constantly evolving. The trend continues toward abstract and symbolic sets that strike a mood rather than sets that merely recreate reality. New materials, tools, and techniques make possible sets that would have been impractical or impossible half a century ago. Metal, plastics, and materials such as fiberglass and foam are increasingly used in set and prop construction. Cost and safety concerns in working with many of these materials have, however, limited their use to theatres with bigger budgets and better facilities than most high schools have available. Still, amazing sets can be created with traditional materials.

## Three-Dimensional Scenery

Many set designs call for **three-dimensional scenery,** which includes stock units such as platforms and stair units, as well as objects such as buildings, trees, rocks, and other sculptural forms. Three-dimensional scenery is often an interactive part of the set; actors may move around, inside, or on top of a piece of three-dimensional scenery. You should consider the following when designing and constructing three-dimensional scenery:

- How will the scenery be used? Will actors interact with it? If so, how much?
- How does this piece need to be designed to mesh with the style of the play as determined by the set designer and the director?
- What materials should be used? What materials can be substituted for these materials, if necessary?
- How will the scenery be rigged, if necessary (p. 335)?
- How will lighting affect the various dimensions of the scenery?

### CONSTRUCTING THREE-DIMENSIONAL SCENERY

For most three-dimensional scenery, the following technique is used:

1. Construct a wooden frame in the shape of the object.
2. Wrap the frame in chicken wire. Secure the chicken wire to the wooden frame with staples.
3. Cover the chicken wire with either papier mâché (p. 470) or muslin or canvas dipped in a papier mâché mixture.
4. Trim and cover any remaining loose pieces of wire that might snag or cut.
5. Paint the object in realistic or nonrealistic style, depending on the specified design.

### TECH TIPS: THREE-DIMENSIONAL SCENERY

- Use screws rather than nails to make your wood frame. Many of your boards will be attached at angles, making it difficult to flush the nail heads; you can countersink the screws (screw them in so that the heads are below the wood surface).
- Use twist ties to secure loose sections of chicken wire together.
- If you are using muslin or canvas, or if the object will be handled extensively, include a layer of padding (cotton, wool, or synthetic batting) between the chicken wire and the covering; otherwise, the outlines of the chicken wire will show through
- Don't forget to apply the appropriate preliminary coats (p. 222) before painting if you are using muslin or canvas.

For Patrick Meyer's *K-2,* which takes place on a ledge in the Himalayan mountains, designer Ming Cho Lee created a set that is realistic but at the same time is symbolic of isolation and the harshness of nature. Plastic foam over a wooden framework form the set, which features an avalanche of artificial snow during one part of the performance.

The set for this production of Shakespeare's *Pericles* includes a large three-dimensional head suspended over the stage. Try to answer the questions posed on page 465 for designing and constructing three-dimensional scenery in relation to this piece of scenery.

## Trees

One common item of three-dimensional scenery is a tree. To construct a stage tree, use the basic technique for creating three-dimensional scenery described (p. 465). Your wooden frame can be constructed using 1 x 2 stock lumber to build a vertical frame that follows the angles of the tree and attaching horizontal sections of the trunk and branches cut out of plywood to the frame. Your frame will need a base to provide support if your tree is to be free-standing.

Using one of several different methods, you can create foliage trees and plants. You can cut leaves from felt or painted paper and attach them to the tree or plant using glue or staples. Another method is to stretch a length of cheesecloth between two chairs and paint it with a green gloss paint, or autumn colors if you need autumn leaves. When the paint is dry, cut leaves from the cheesecloth. This method results in leaves that are somewhat shiny and translucent. The cutting and gluing of leaves in these two methods is a time-consuming process. Another option for making tree foliage—and one that takes less time—is to paint the leaves on a large piece of canvas or netting; the leaves can be painted individually, with a stencil, or as a more abstract grouping represented more by color modeling and less by line and specific leaf forms. Cut out the leaf shapes around the edge of the cloth only and make holes in the cloth itself to suggest breaks in the foliage. Then suspend the cloth from a batten or pipe to hang just in front of the tree trunk and branches. This works very well if you have a large number of trees as in a forest, orchard, or garden. This method can be adapted for a presentational or realistic set.

If a specific type of tree is required for the set, consult a book on trees for the correct appearance of the bark and leaves of the tree you are creating. If your set is realistic, be sure that you are representing trees that would actually grow in the geographic region in which the play is set.

If you would rather not build trees, talk to the owner of a local garden center to see if you can borrow trees and other plants to use on your set. If you do this, fill out a written lending agreement with the garden center.

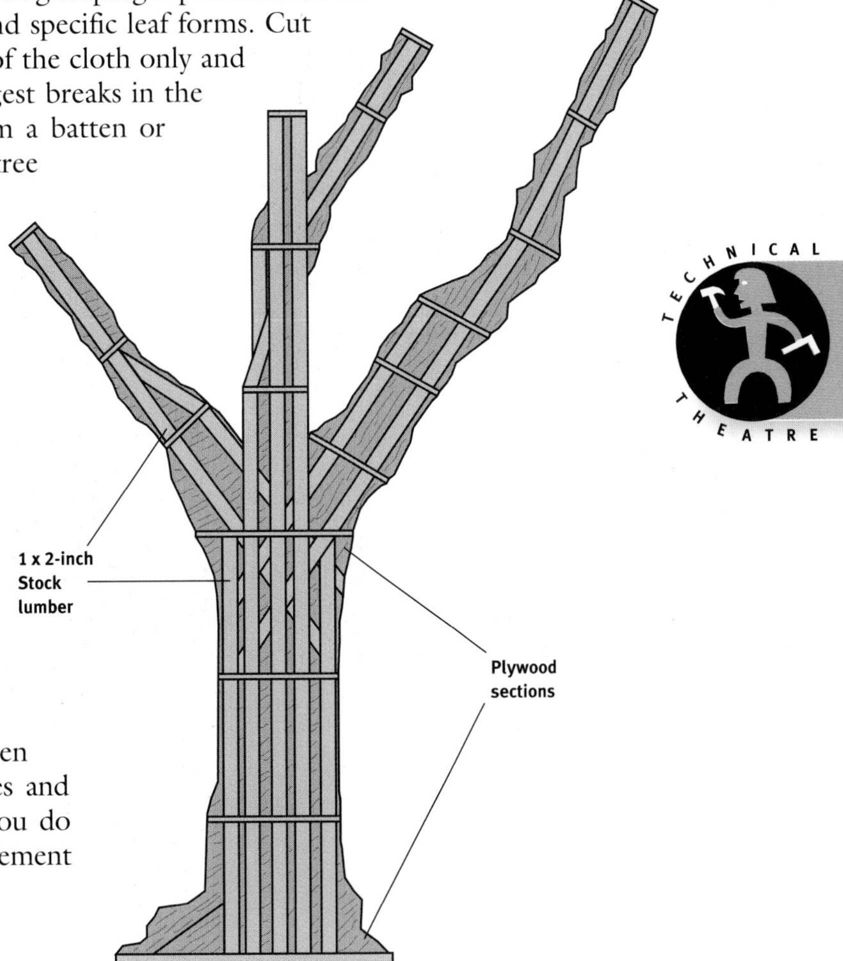


TECHNICAL THEATRE

## Rocks

Stage rocks should look like large, heavy pieces of stone, but they should also be easy to maneuver around the stage. One way to build a stage rock that is easy to shift is to build it on a wagon (p. 335). On the platform, construct a frame using pieces of ¾-inch plywood; attach pieces that extend beyond the edges of the platform of the frame so your rock isn't rectangular at its base. How the rock is to be used in the production will determine the size of the platform and the shape of the frame. If actors are to sit, stand, or walk on it, there might be some flat surfaces incorporated into the design. Once the frame is built, it is covered as described in the basic process of constructing three-dimensional scenery (p. 465).

Another method for constructing rocks—and other sculptural objects—is to make use of a series of plywood plates as a frame. Think of the object in sectional views; that is, slice it through in a number of places as you would a loaf of bread. For each of these sections, cut a plywood plate that roughly matches the outline of the object at that point. This series of plywood plates then becomes the frame for a three-dimensional object. Use 1 x 2 stock lumber to join this framework together. Notching the plywood plates to the depth of your 1 x 2 stock pieces will give you a smooth surface to cover with chicken wire. The shape is given dimension and covered using the standard technique for covering three-dimensional scenery (p. 465).

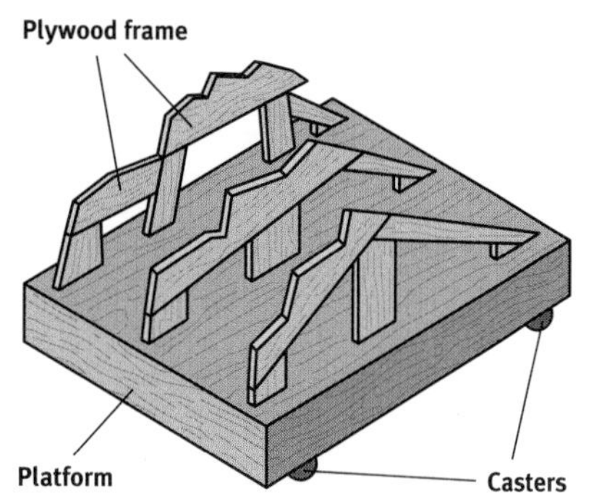


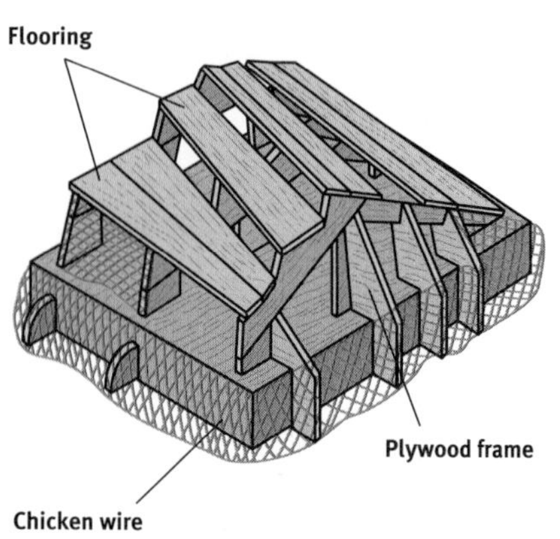


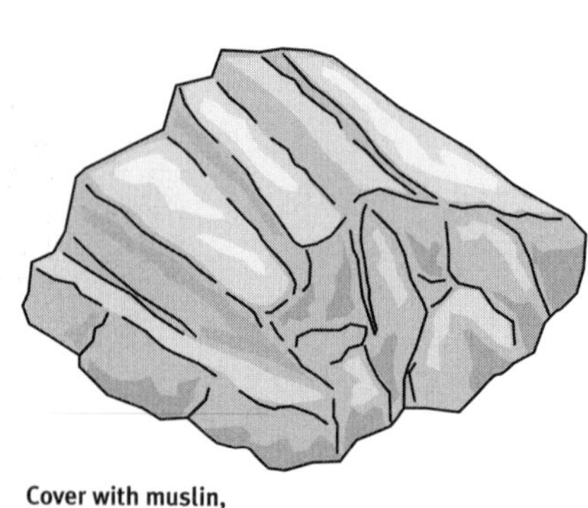

Cover with muslin, papier-mâché, or canvas

**Wagon rock**

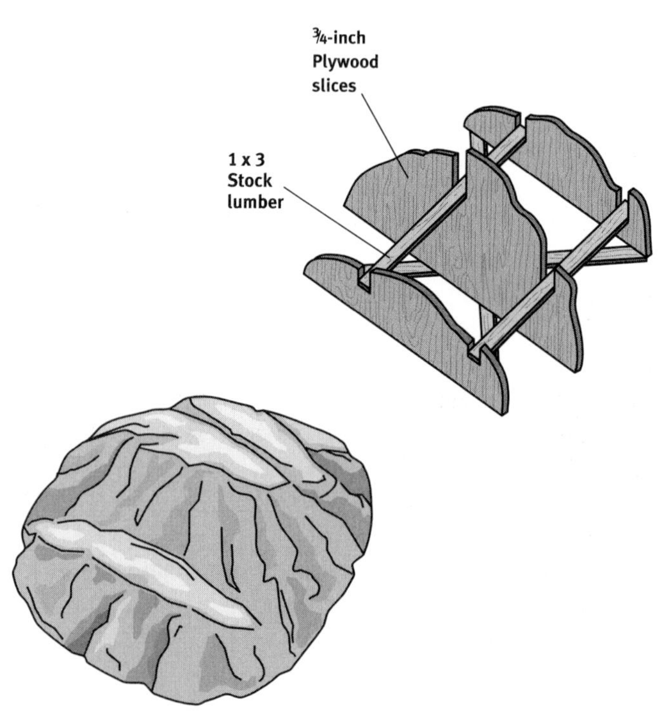


**Plywood-frame rock**

## Profiles

Although a flat has three dimensions (height, width, and depth), it's not considered three-dimensional because its depth is so narrow that it seems two-dimensional, or flat (hence, the name). A **profile** is a scenic element cut from a large sheet of plywood and attached to a flat using keystones (p. 210). The function of a flat can be extended through the use of these profiles. The scenic element of the profile continues onto the flat itself and adds dimensionality to a set constructed from flats. For example, you can extend a forest scene painted on a flat by cutting out the shape of one half of a tree, attaching it to the flat, and painting the other half of the tree on the flat itself. By combining profiles, you can create even more interesting settings.

To construct profiles, draw the scenic element on ¼-inch plywood and cut the shape out of the plywood using a sabre saw (p. 78). Then attach the plywood to the appropriate side of the flat using keystones. Paint the profile and flat to blend together in one scene.

Profiles can also be freestanding, that is, not attached to flats. As with other kinds of two-dimensional scenery, you will need to brace the scenery to the stage (p. 220).

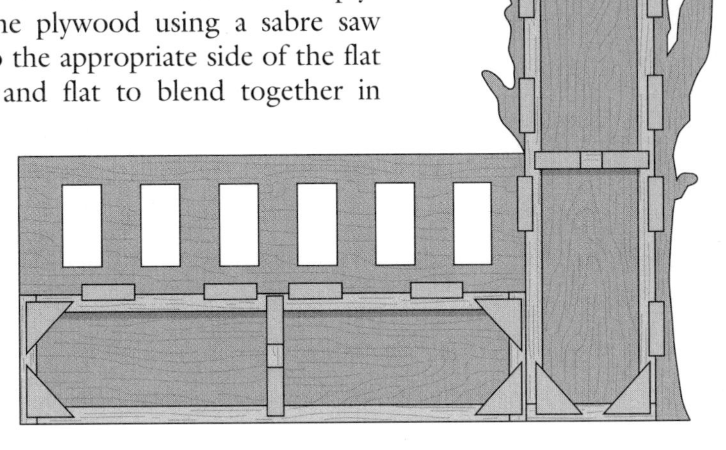

Rear view of tree profile (above) and front view of the same profile (below)

# Prop Techniques

The ever-expanding range of craft materials and techniques to create special effects increases the creative possibilities for prop construction; however, some materials have been in use for generations and are still proving themselves useful and flexible.

## Papier-Mâché

A time-tested and popular technique for creating all kinds of props—set, hand, or decorative—is **papier mâché** (pā′pər mə shā′). This inexpensive technique requires wire to make a form, newspaper torn into strips, and a paste-like mixture to coat the newspaper and serve as a binding agent. This is the technique commonly used in the process of constructing three-dimensional scenery (p. 465).

Several recipes are in use for papier mâché paste. One popular recipe is to mix wheat paste or flour with water until it's the consistency of a thick soup. While this is effective, the flour mixture can sour quickly. In addition, papier mâché items made with this mixture should be stored carefully in sealed plastic containers because they attract rodents and other pests. Powdered wallpaper paste or white glue thinned with water both work well and don't have the drawbacks of the flour-and-water paste.

When working with papier mâché, always use torn strips of newspaper rather than strips cut with a scissors or paper cutter. The torn edges blend better than those that are cut, and the tears follow the grain of the paper, providing a smoother surface.

*Little Shop of Horrors* by Howard Ashman and Alan Menken features a human-munching plant that grows during the play, requiring several versions of the plant in different sizes. Although this production uses a cloth and fake-fur puppet, you can use papier mâché to create the different-sized versions of the blood-thirsty plant.

**USING PAPIER MÂCHÉ**

The basic process for papier mâché is as follows:

1. Make a chicken wire form of the object you want, such as a log for a fireplace.
2. Soak each strip of the torn newspaper in the paste mixture. Using your first and second fingers as a squeegee, remove the excess paste. Then apply the newspaper strip over the chicken-wire form of your object. Cover the form completely with a layer of newspaper.
3. Apply three to six layers. If you are applying more than three layers, allow for drying time after the first three are applied. If you are using flour and water, allow each layer to dry before applying the next.
4. Once the papier mâché has dried, you can paint it to look like the object you are replicating. You may wish to lightly sand the surface to even out bumps.

Many craft stores sell a papier mâché product that is a prepared mixture of finely shredded paper and wheat paste. Adding water creates a substance that can be used for sculpture or as a finish coat over rough objects.

## Curtains and Drapes

Curtains are typically hung on windows in kitchens and bedrooms; they are often lightweight and semitransparent. They usually cover the length of the window down to the sill but may be a foot or two longer. Draperies, or drapes, are longer and heavier than curtains and are often lined or are thick enough to prevent light from passing through. Living and dining rooms and other formal rooms usually feature drapes.

### Curtain and Drape Fabrics

Fabrics used for curtains and drapes should have a soft, nonreflective surface, be available in many colors, and be flame-retardant. Don't attempt to flameproof material yourself. It's difficult to do successfully, and often, the color will darken in an uneven pattern. Fabric for curtains is relatively inexpensive. Fabric for drapes, however, can be very expensive, but there are inexpensive fabrics that look fine and even luxurious from the perspective of the audience.

Commando cloth, also known as duvetyn, is a cotton fabric resembling felt. It has a variety of scenic uses. The heavyweight variety is appropriate for stage drapes masking backstage areas. The lightweight variety is suitable for set drapes and is a good alternative to velour. Velour is a fine drapery material. It's rich and lustrous and absorbs light well. Narrow-wale or no-wale corduroy makes an excellent substitute for velvet in drapes. Netting, chiffon, and lightweight muslin may be used for sheers, the lightweight fabric that hangs between heavier drapes or curtains.

This set for Molière's *The Miser* displays swagged drapes that reinforce the symmetry and elegance of the entire design.

## Hanging Curtains and Drapes

Curtains and drapes are generally constructed to hang from a rod that rests in hooks on either side of or along the top of a window. A curtain may be hung by passing the rod through a wide seam at the top of the curtain or by fabric ties attached to the curtain and tied over the rod in a decorative fashion. Drapes typically hang on a rod by means of rings or are fitted with drapery hooks that hook over a narrow flat rod.

When constructing drapes for a set, you may want to swag the drapes to give them a more attractive appearance or to recreate a period style. A **swag** is a hanging curve of fabric between two points. There can be one or more swags in a drape. Creating these swags isn't difficult if you measure the distance between the swags rather than try to do it by eye.

### SWAGGING DRAPES

1. After you hang the drapes, decide how you want them positioned along the rod, either closed all the way or partially opened.
2. Measure the distance from the rod down to the point where you want the lowest swag to hang.

3. Divide that measurement by the number of swags you want in each drape.
4. Starting at the top of the drape, mark the position where each swag will start with a straight pin.
5. Carefully gather the fabric at each point so the fabric folds over itself.
6. Tie or staple each swag to the set.
7. Arrange the swags so they appear to fall into a natural scalloped pattern.

## Bookcases

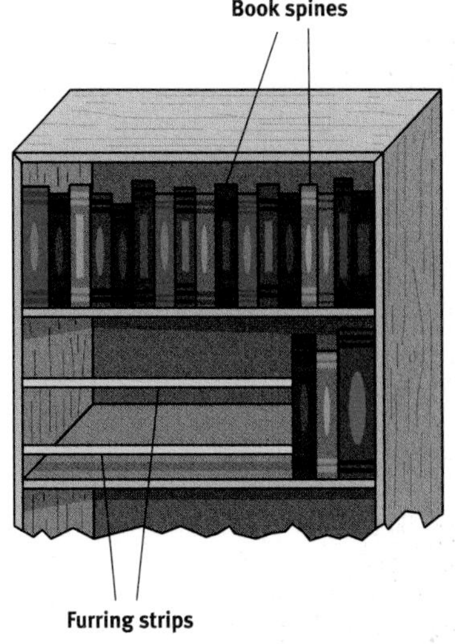


Many plays call for a set featuring one or more bookcases filled with books, especially if a scene is set in a library. Shelves filled with actual books would be difficult because they would be too heavy to move; luckily, there are several ways to simulate books so the bookcases look real to the audience and are easy to shift.

For all techniques, you will need to collect old hardcover books at rummage, garage, or library sales. Using a utility knife, cut the spines—the edge of the book that shows on the shelf—off of the books. If you are using an actual set of bookshelves on the set, you will need to run two furring strips (thin strips of wood) along the bottom and about a third of the way from the top of each shelf. Decide how you want to arrange the "books" on the shelf and then use a hot glue gun to attach the spines to the furring strips.

If you are using a bookshelf that is a nice piece of furniture and you would rather not nail furring strips into it, you can cut a piece of plywood about eight inches high and the length of the shelf or shelves that will hold the books. Glue the spines to one side of the plywood and attach two triangle braces near each end of the other side. Then stand this up on the shelf with the spines facing the audience.

If you are not using an actual bookshelf, you can create the illusion of a bookshelf unit. Cut a sheet of three-quarter inch plywood to the necessary dimensions. Draw lines on the plywood to represent each shelf, and then paint the entire shelving unit, adding any interesting furniture details that the design suggests. Position the spines from the books on the shelves and use hot glue to attach them to the plywood. The whole unit can then be attached to a flat or left freestanding and supported with stage braces.

## Stage Food

Stage food poses particular problems for the prop crew. The prop master should study the play carefully to determine whether scenes requiring food can be served by using inedible food instead of edible food, which causes most of the problems.

## Edible Stage Food

Edible stage food is required in scenes where the actors need to eat it. Hygiene in handling edible stage food is important: hands and utensils need to be kept clean. Keep packets of moist towelettes or antibacterial hand soap backstage; wash utensils in soap and hot water after every use.

A primary concern is to keep edible stage food fresh. Storing food properly or replenishing it for each performance will keep most nonperishable food fresh (and safe from pests). Ready access to refrigeration is necessary for perishable food; a cooler backstage may serve this purpose during performances. For hot foods, cooking facilities or a microwave may be required. Edible stage food should be warm but never hot. If the script calls for steaming food, a concealed lump of dry ice can provide the look of steam.

Not all stage foods need to be what the audience thinks they are. Squares of white bread can be dusted with cocoa powder to simulate brownies. Toasted and sliced white bread will look like french fries to the audience. Scoops of mashed potatoes can look like ice cream, and adding food coloring can create different flavors. Bread and mashed potatoes can be prepared backstage and are cheaper than the real foods. Cranberry juice can be used for wine (don't use grape juice; the stains on costumes will never come out); apple juice can stand in for beer. Colored glasses can hide liquid, preventing the audience from seeing how much or what is actually in the glass. Avoid using chewy and crumbly foods, such as crackers, because the crumbs get into beards and moustaches and such dry food can cause dry mouth, making it hard for actors to deliver their lines. Milk should never be used because it coats the throat and inhibits vocalizing.

Any spilled food should be cleaned up immediately if it could cause someone to slip; otherwise, it should be taken care of as soon as possible—between scenes or after the rehearsal or performance.

## Inedible Food

If no one is going to eat the stage food, of course, it doesn't have to be real; it only has to look real to the audience. Inedible stage food can be made with chicken wire and papier mâché or from a block of urethane foam. Whichever method works best for your play, always start with a picture of the food or with the food itself for a model. If you are using papier mâché, create a form in the shape of the food using the chicken wire. Then cover the form with papier mâché.

If you are using urethane foam, start with a block that is slightly larger than the item you will be creating. Use a wood rasp or a sculpting tool of your choice to shape the foam. When you are finished, cover the object with a thin coat of spackling compound. When the first coat dries, add a second thin coat. When this is dry, sand the object to achieve the desired surface texture.

When the papier mâché or urethane base is ready, paint the object to look as much like the original food as possible. Remember that most foods are not a single color. Think about the various colors and shades of an oven-roasted turkey or a loaf of bread. Painting food props requires highlighting, shadowing, and blending of colors to achieve a realistic look.

This set for George Bernard Shaw's *Misalliance* features a conservatory setting with a number of plants. How would you handle the challenge of providing plants for this set?

## Plants

There are various ways to create plants to decorate a set. If the play is a fantasy and the set calls for unusual plants and flowers, you might need to build them using a technique such as papier mâché. If the set is realistic, you will want the plants and flowers to look as real as possible. Silk flowers and plants have solved many problems of realism on a set. Unlike their plastic counterparts, silk plants and flowers don't reflect the stage lights. They are also more fluid than rigid plastic plants and will sway in a breeze or rustle when an actor walks quickly past. Silk plants and flowers are also durable and can be used repeatedly.

Smoke and fire are staged on the set of this production of J. B. Priestley's *An Inspector Calls.* Ian MacNeil designed the set, which features a building that unfolds onstage to show a realistic interior.

## Smoke

Stage smoke can be produced with a smoke machine or a dry-ice kettle. Smoke machines use a liquid, sometimes called "smoke juice." This liquid is fed into a heated chamber. The liquid vaporizes in this chamber and is released as a dense cloud of white smoke. The formula for smoke juice varies, depending on how long the smoke needs to linger in the air. Theatres usually use the formula that dissipates quickly.

Smoke machines shoot a dense cloud of smoke from one location; in many instances the desired effect is for the smoke to cover the stage. To achieve this effect, smoke machines come with an adapter to which you can attach duct work to run to different parts of the stage. Common flexible dryer ducting, available at most home-supply stores, is an inexpensive solution to the problem. This duct work is usually silver colored, so you will want to spray it black to avoid any reflection from stage lights.

Dry-ice kettles consist of a sealed plastic box with heating elements at the bottom and a metal basket that can be raised or lowered. The bottom half of the plastic box is filled with water and heated almost to boiling. The dry ice is placed in the basket and lowered into the hot water. When the dry ice hits the hot water, it sublimes—changes to a dense, white vapor—and is forced out of a nozzle at the front of the kettle. Since dry ice smoke is dense, it will stay close to the stage floor. Store dry ice in a polystyrene cooler that is *not* airtight. Dry ice is carbon dioxide ($CO_2$), and the buildup in an airtight cooler could blow the top off. It will keep for two to four days in the polystyrene cooler.

## Fire

Common sense and fire codes should prevent you from even considering open flame anywhere in the theatre; however, there are effective ways to simulate fire onstage.

Fire in a fireplace can be effectively simulated using flame-shaped pieces of silk painted in fire colors. When building the actual fireplace, put two rows of holes about an inch apart in the bottom of the firebox. In between these rows, glue the flame-shaped pieces of silk, as if they were flames coming from the logs in the fireplace. A fan running at a low speed underneath the silk will provide the necessary movement for your fire. Be careful of the placement of the fan; you don't want the silk to catch in it. Electric blazing logs are another effective alternative to real fire, especially when viewed from a distance. Finally, red and orange holiday lights hidden in logs will give the effect of hot embers.

If you want to suggest a fire outside the boundaries of the set, but still somewhat visible—outside a window, through a doorway in another room—a flickering red light will do the trick. A fan running in front of the light will enhance the flickering effect. For a more irregular flicker—one that is more like a real fire—cut odd-shaped holes in a piece of cardboard, and wave this in between the red light source and the projection surface.

Theatrical supply companies sell battery-operated candles that waver and flicker just as real candles do. Budget considerations may require you to rent these candles rather than buy them.

## Paintings

Many times a set will require paintings that hang on a wall. If the paintings are nonspecific pieces of art, the set decorator, with the help of the set designer, might find items to hang. If the painting required is a piece of fine art, specific or not, you will probably be able to locate an inexpensive reproduction in a museum, an art store, or a framing shop. Give yourself plenty of time; the item may need to be specially-ordered. If the painting is a portrait of a character in the play, use a poster-sized enlargement of a photo portrait of the actor who is playing the character. The photo can be doctored to look like a painted portrait by adding brushstrokes using thinned paint. Remember, illusion is all that is necessary, and from the distance of the audience, the portrait will look real.

# Lighting Techniques

Projections of still or moving images can complement, accent, or at times, even substitute for other visual elements on a stage. A **projection** is an image or patterned light cast onto a screen or other surface. Projections provide some of the most dramatic and accessible lighting techniques for large and small theatres. Lighting designers can choose between lensless or lens projection systems.

## Lensless Projectors

Lensless projectors work in much the same way as putting your hands in front of a light to make shadow pictures on a wall. If you want to project a silhouette, use opaque objects such as an outline of an image cut from heavy paper or wood. If you want to project a colored image, use a transparent colored object such as a color slide or a transparency. A transparency can be made by painting an image on a piece of glass or transparent acetate with transparent acetate inks.

### Image Sharpness

Two factors determine the sharpness of your image when using lensless projectors. One is the size of the light source. A smaller filament (one resulting in a more pointed, narrow beam of light) will result in a sharper image. To get a sharp, large-scale image, use a 500-, 750-, or 1,000-watt bulb, 120-volt tungsten-halogen lamp, like the kind used in an ellipsoidal reflector spotlight.

The other factor affecting image sharpness is the distance between the image you want to project and the surface onto which it is projected. The closer the image is to the projection surface, the sharper the projection. The closer the image is to the light source, the less sharp the image. Ideally, the image should be equidistant between the light source and the projection surface.

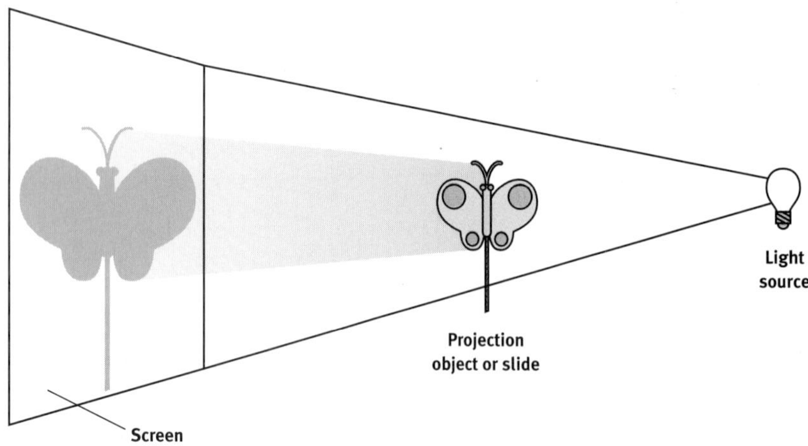


A fresnel spotlight can be used as a makeshift lensless projector by using the gel frame to hold the transparency or slide. It won't project large, sharp images, but it will work for projecting softer images onto small areas of the stage or projection surface. Similarly, an ellipsoidal reflector spotlight functions as a lensless projector when you use a gobo (p. 342) to project a pattern of light.

## Lens Projectors

A lens projector uses a lens to control the size and focus of the image projected. New-model lens projectors will give you the most high-tech image-making and will be safe to use. They can be expensive, but their price will be more than justified in the effects you can achieve.

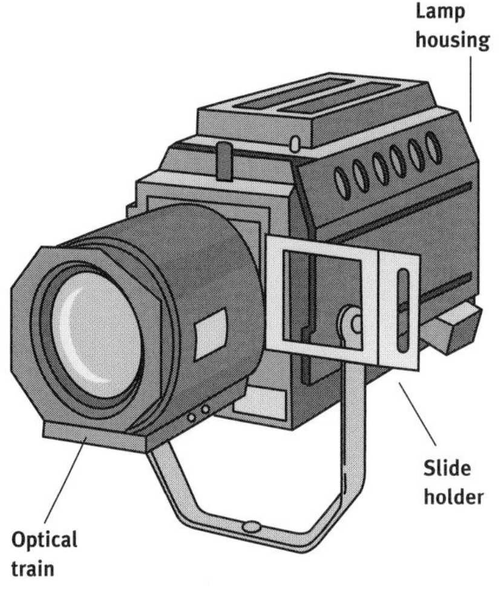


### Scenic Projector

A scenic projector is a high-wattage instrument used for projecting large slides or moving images. It's composed of three parts: a lamp housing, an optical train, and a slide holder. The lamp housing holds a 1,000- to 2,000-watt incandescent lamp and, frequently, a blower. Since the blower is usually noisy, the projector needs to be placed in a location that will mask the noise. The **optical train** holds the lamp, various lenses and filters, and the slide itself, when the slide holder is inserted. The slide holder holds glass slides onto which images have been painted or photographic transparencies sandwiched between two glass slides.

### Slide Projector

Use a slide projector, preferably a carousel type, for 35mm transparent slides. Choose the 80-slide rather than the 140-slide tray. The 80-slide tray has a wider space for each slide, and this keeps the slides from sticking in the carousel. Put slides in plastic mounts, available from a photography store, rather than pasteboard ones; the slicker and heavier mounting makes it easier to feed them into the carousel. Use the highest-wattage lamp allowed for the projector model. Place the projector as close to the projection surface as possible and limit the projected width of the image to no more than six to eight feet.

The geometric shapes, reflecting stage surface, golden light, and projections that form the scenery for this production of *Cymbeline* evoke a fantastical, fairy tale atmosphere for this late play of Shakespeare's.

Using a front-screen projection for this image from *Evita!* isn't problematic because the actors are not in front of the screen.

## Projection Screens

You can project images onto a projection screen from a projector sitting somewhere in front of the screen—**front-screen projection,** or from a projector positioned behind the screen—**rear-screen projection.** Your choice of front-screen or rear-screen projection will determine the appropriate projection screen.

### Front-Screen Projection

White, highly reflective commercial screens are designed to reflect light. An inexpensive alternative to a commercial screen is to cover a smooth surface, such as muslin or Masonite, with white paint. You can project images onto a white cyclorama (p. 335) as well.

Unless you are continuously projecting an image or a color wash during a production, you won't want to distract the audience with a large white screen in the middle of a stage. One alternative is to use parts of the set itself as screens. Obviously this will have some impact on the paint used on the set, or at least those parts that will be used for projections, and the set designer will have to take that into account in the set design.

One of the drawbacks of front-screen projection is that the onstage actors may cast shadows on the screen. You can eliminate this problem by using rear-screen projection.

### Rear-Screen Projection

The challenge of a rear-screen projection approach is the **hot spot,** an intense circle of light created when a projector lens is seen through the screen. To avoid hot spots, either position the projector at an angle to the screen, outside the audience's sight lines or use a screen material that eliminates it.

If you position the projector outside the audience's sight lines, you can use translucent materials such as scenic muslin and other fabrics of similar weight and weave that transmit light. For a crisper image, prime the muslin with a solution of starch and water—one cup of starch per gallon of hot water. If the muslin is to blend in with the scenery you can paint it with dye. Do not use paint on the muslin since paint is not transparent. A couple of options to muslin screens include white plastic shower curtains and white plastic drop cloths sold in paint stores.

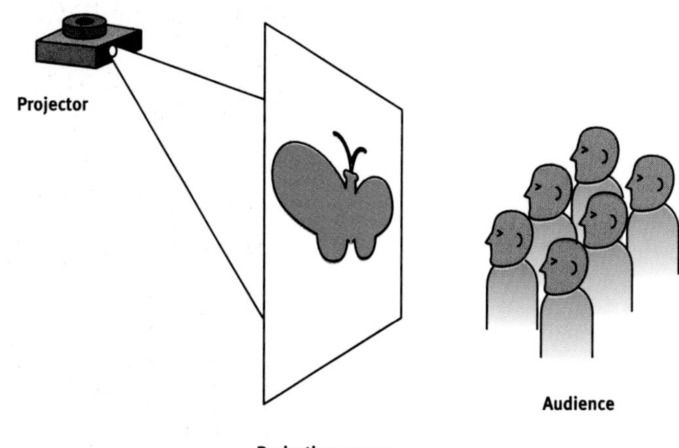


## Image Interference

In both front- or rear-screen projection, eliminate **ambient light,** or existing surrounding light, as much as possible and position the screen so that actors don't block the screen from the audience's view. Hanging the screen so that its bottom edge is five to seven feet above the stage floor will help with these types of image interference. Rear-screen projection is less affected by ambient light than front-screen projection so try to use that technique whenever possible.

## Keystoning

When designing projections and projection systems, be conscious of the distortion that occurs when an image is projected at an angle onto a screen or other projection surface. This commonly happens when you angle a projector for rear-screen projections to avoid hot spots and when you project an image from a spotlight on a overhead batten. The distortion is called **keystoning** because it resembles the shape of a traditional triangular keystone (p. 210). To compensate for keystoning, you can either angle the screen so the projection axis is perpendicular to the screen surface or design the image so that it's distorted at an angle equal and opposite to the angle at which the projection strikes the screen.

## Slide Preparation

Scenic projectors use both painted slides and photographic transparencies. Remember to sandwich both kinds of slides between sheets of projection-grade glass available at photography stores. The glass prevents the slides from crinkling or melting and it also keeps the slide vertical. Use transparent inks on glass slides; opaque ink absorbs heat and it may cause the glass to crack.

This setting for Richard Wagner's opera *Tristan and Isolde* is the deck of a ship. Josef Svoboda's set design features a cyclorama onto which are projected simple, suggestive images, such as the clouds and sky shown here.

In *Das Rheingold,* part of Wagner's *Ring Cycle,* Svoboda uses a lighted series of concentric rings to present the impression of the rainbow bridge leading to Valhalla (the halls of honor in Norwegian mythology). The lit cube at the center is Valhalla.

In another production of *Das Rheingold* designed by Svoboda, the rainbow bridge is conveyed by a rainbow of light projected onto a staircase. The rainbow is reflected in mirrors. The stairs can fold flat into a platform, which is supported by a hydraulic column that can make the platform rotate, tilt, rise, and fall in various combinations.

## Sound Techniques

The possibilities for manipulating sound through computerized sound production present options for sound dimensions in theatre rivaling those used in film and TV. One area of theatre that has taken advantage of new sound technologies is multimedia, including performance art (p. 420). Read the script excerpt below, thinking as you read about the layers of sound in the scene.

***Diary of the Chair: A Performance Art Piece***

**CAST:** a WAITER or WAITRESS, a WOMAN, a MAN, a DOG

**SETTING:** *A small café table and two chairs, suggesting a French café, are downstage center. Upstage left of center, the* WAITER *or* WAITRESS *stands behind a table and polishes silverware, dropping and picking up the pieces so that they clink together. The "diary entries" are prerecorded, with French cabaret music in the background. Each diary entry signifies a scene in the performance; the actions of the scenes have no apparent relation to the diary entries except that they take place in a café. The music increases in volume between each diary entry, and the lights are dimmed and brought up again. The narrator speaks slowly, with a bad French accent.*

**SCENE 1:** *The lights come up, revealing a* WOMAN *seated at the table. As the first diary entry is heard, she busies herself by rummaging through her purse and applying makeup: eyeshadow, powder, and lipstick. She then fishes a camera from her purse and begins taking flash pictures of the audience. While she is doing this, a small motorized rubber head, mounted on wheels and controlled with a remote, enters from stage right, crosses in front of the* WOMAN *(who ignores it), circles around the table, and disappears stage left.*

7 May
I am a chair. It is a table.
I am a chair. It is a table.

I am a small black wrought-iron chair. I have four legs. I have a fan-tailed back. On the back of my back is painted in white letters, Café du Monde.

It is a square black wrought-iron table with a glass top. It has four legs. After five o'clock it wears a white tablecloth. Before that it is nude.

We work at the same café. Café du Monde.

I am a chair so most of my friends are other chairs. I did not notice the table for a long time. Now I have. Now my dreams are full of tables.

*Lights dim; music swells.*

## Layering and Mixing Sounds

Consider the opportunities for sound in the performance art scene. The script mentions the sounds of clinking silverware and French cabaret music that fades and swells with the voice-over. A **voice-over** is a recording of a voice that plays over other sounds. The voice-over itself is another layer of sound that is used in the scene. What other sounds can be added to enhance this setting? What sounds are suggested by the café?

The sounds you might use here are not constant. Rather, they come in and out at various points in the action. Since they are not scripted, it's up to the sound designer to decide where they will occur. Adding sound to a scene such as this requires layering sounds. You would likely record each type of sound on a separate track. A **track** is a path along which information is recorded electronically; typically, a track is one of a series of parallel paths. Individual tracks can be manipulated to adjust volume and other sound characteristics. Tracks can then be mixed together through a mixer (p. 86) to achieve a variety of dramatic effects. Although you can manipulate the sound characteristics of a track on a reel-to-reel system, you need a computerized system to manipulate the sequence of the tracks. For example, if you recorded the silverware and the sound of a truck horn as it passed by the café at the same point on a reel-to-reel tape but on different tracks, you could manipulate the sound characteristics of each track individually, but you couldn't change their sequential relationship to each other; you can't move the sounds, only record over them. In a computerized system the sequence of tracks can be changed, providing more options for mixing.

## Synthesizers

On a computerized sound system, the hardware typically has a built-in synthesizer. A **synthesizer** is an electronic device used to synthesize, or artificially create, sounds. With the appropriate synthesizer software, you can invent sounds within the computer system or create realistic sounds without having to depend on recorded and found sounds (p. 232).

A built-in synthesizer will also allow you to compose music. Special software programs and separate synthesizer units can be added to your system for more control and flexibility. You can compose short pieces of music to underlie scenes or parts of scenes or compose entire symphonies, all of which can be manipulated track by track along with other sounds to create your show tape.

# Costume Techniques

Specialized costume techniques involve some of the same products as those used for prop construction. As with props, the range of materials makes constructing costumes an exciting and creative challenge.

## Armor

Painted cardboard, papier mâché, and wood are still common materials for making shields and swords, but various other materials may be used for the armor and helmets. One of these is a thermoplastic substance called Hexolite. When heated with hot water, you can shape, mold, fold, tuck, and stretch it. Hexolite forms may lose shape under hot lights or if the actor becomes overheated. Another possibility is industrial-weight sized felt (with a high percentage of wool fiber), which must be cut, soaked in white glue (two parts) and water (one part), pinned to a mold, and dried (possibly for several days). Following the molding and drying processes, you can easily paint each of these materials and then detail them with decorative trim or other materials that simulate the rivets of armor.

Armor varies considerably over the course of its use in history and from country to country, so be certain to research the design you need. Medieval plays often require a type of armor called chain mail, which is generally covered by a tunic emblazoned with a symbol. Although you can rent chain mail, you can also make it by using heavy-yarn, open-weave or knitted fabrics. Dye the fabric dark gray or black, and then dry-brush the surface with silver. If the weave is very open, add a black lining.

For this production, Shakespeare's *Antony and Cleopatra* is set in the Elizabethan period, requiring that armor of that period be reproduced.

## Headpieces

Period hats and headpieces can be constructed in a number of ways. Buckram, a fabric sized with glue, is frequently used in millinery (hat) construction. When the glue is dampened, buckram becomes soft and pliable and can be configured into many different shapes. When the glue dries, the fabric stiffens again, and the hat or headpiece can be decorated. Felt hats with broad brims and deep crowns can be reconfigured into hats of various styles. Steaming a felt hat will make it soft and pliable. Then, using a hat mold, the original hat can be reshaped into a new hat. When dry, the felt retains the new shape and is ready to be decorated.

You can use existing hats or headbands as the base on which to build a costume headpiece. For example, you can make a replica of the headpiece shown below by cutting out the half-moon shape from strong cardboard or buckram, cutting out the head opening and gluing a plastic headband to the rim of it. Using a hot-glue gun, you can then decorate the headpiece with gold sequins. You can attach a fabric veil to the back of the headpiece.

## Jewelry and Ornaments

Keep a collection of junk jewelry in your costume workshop, separated according to size and use. Remember to check the light reflectivity of brooches, necklaces, bracelets and other pieces of jewelry; light reflecting from jewelry may distract the audience. Either soap or wax the pieces to reduce glare.

You can also make jewelry and ornaments such as buckles, clasps, crowns, and brooches from papier-mâché, plaster of Paris, or sized felt and incorporate glass beads, bits of metal, or fake gemstones into the objects as you are making them. Foam rubber, which takes dye, paint, or metallics, can be carved or cut into bold decorative shapes for lightweight jewelry or accessories. A serrated knife works best.

For pendant chains, visit your local hardware store where you may find small brass or chrome chains, which can be cut to the desired length, or lightweight, large-link chains such as those used for hanging plants or lamps; the large-link chains can be painted to match the pendant.

## Footwear

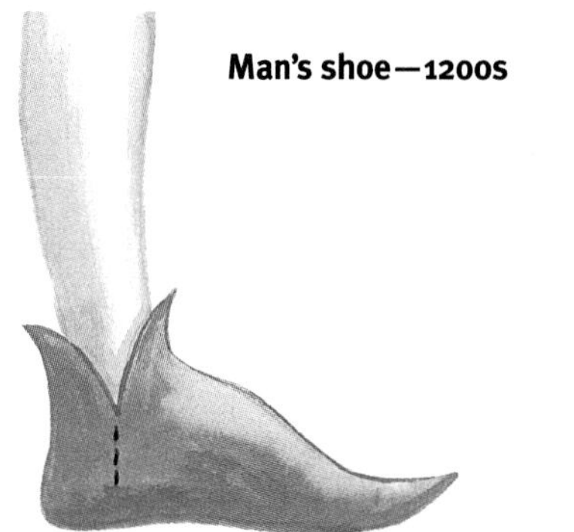

**Man's shoe—1200s**

Shoes that actors wear often determine their stature and movement. For both men and women, heel height is critical. Only in a play set after 1900, for example, would women appropriately wear high heels; for plays set during earlier periods, women should wear medium- or low-heels or slippers.

If a period shoe is required, the actor can wear a contemporary shoe or slipper covered with brocade or velveteen and decorated with bows, buckles, ties, or jewelry. Inexpensive bedroom slippers can be recut and reshaped on top, covered by gluing on fabric, or dyed and trimmed to match a costume. Or, the soles only can be used as a shoe base on which to build a shoe. Simply cut off the existing top and add another with a hot-glue gun. This method can also be used to make sandals or medieval slippers with curved toes. For boots, make a boot top of leather, heavy vinyl, or industrial-weight felt, cut and sewn to leave one opening in the top and one where the sole would be. Attach an elastic band to the bottom and slip it over an actor's existing boot; this solves the problem of finding boots of a certain type in a particular size.

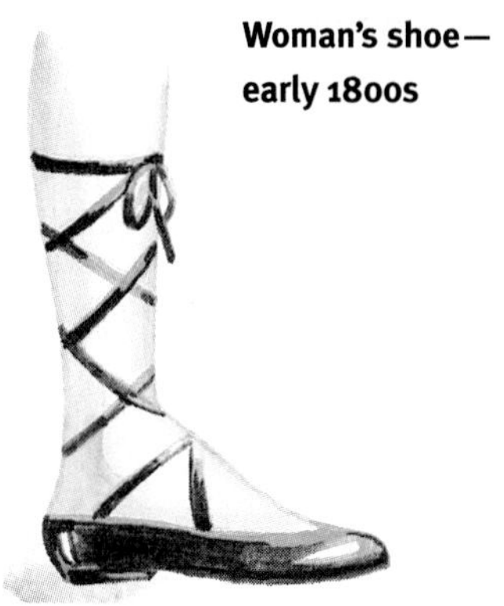

**Woman's shoe—early 1800s**

## Draped Costumes

The tunic (also known as a *chiton*) is a basic costume piece for plays set in the ancient world and is relatively easy to assemble. A tunic is usually made from muslin or broadcloth in white or earthtones. It takes about 2 ½ to 3 yards of fabric to make each tunic, depending on the actor and the length of the tunic desired. While some sewing is involved, draping is an important technique in building these costumes.

### MAKING A TUNIC

1. Calculate the total yardage needed for the tunic by measuring the actor from shoulder to mid-calf (or farther down for a longer tunic), doubling that measurement (for front and back), and adding 3 inches for the hem. Use that figure to cut the length of fabric needed.
2. Fold the fabric in half with the inside facing out to the length you have figured, and cut from selvage to selvage. The **selvage** is the finished edge of the fabric.
3. Keep the insides facing out and put the two pieces of fabric together. Calculate the armhole opening by measuring the actor from shoulder to ribcage. Starting from the bottom, pin the two pieces of fabric together, leaving the armhole measurement open. Do this on each side.
4. Measure the circumference of the actor's head, add 3 to 10 inches (depending on how loose you want the neck to drape), and divide by 2. As you pin the shoulder, leave an opening in the middle the size of this head measurement.
5. Sew from the bottom to the armhole and from the shoulder to the head opening on each side. Sew a 3-inch hem at the bottom. Turn the edge of the neck under ¼ inch on each side and sew that.
6. Turn it rightside out, and you have a basic tunic.

Check a costume history book for accurate decoration such as trim at the hem, sleeves, or neck and a rope or cord for the belt (also called a *girdle).* Once the basic tunic is completed, you can drape a toga over this. Togas usually hang from the left shoulder and under the right arm and are draped and folded in elaborate fashion.

Director–designer Julie Taymor created both the inventive costumes and the masks for this adaptation of an old folk tale, *King Stag*.

## Masks

Masks can be constructed from a variety of materials using several different techniques. One popular method is to create a life mask using plaster bandages, available in art and hobby stores. A **life mask** is made by taking an impression of a person's face.

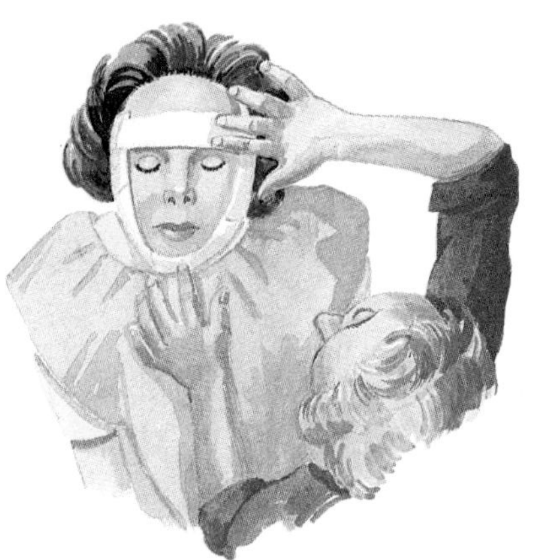

fig. 1

fig. 2

## MAKING A LIFE MASK

1. Cut plaster bandages into strips 1 inch wide and 6 to 8 inches long. Assemble the bandages, a bowl of water, petroleum jelly, a pair of scissors, a blow dryer, a large plastic trash bag, cellophane tape or plastic bandages, face soap, and paper towels. The trash bag will act as a smock for your model, so cut head and arm holes.
2. After putting on the smock, your model should sit with his or her head tilted back. Secure the hair back from the forehead with bobbie pins, a headband, or a shower cap. Apply a thin layer of petroleum jelly to the model's face and chin. Be sure to coat any facial hair, including eyebrows and eyelashes, with the jelly. The petroleum jelly acts as a release agent for the mask and keeps the hair from sticking to the plaster.
3. Apply the bandages one at a time. Dip each one in the water and use your first two fingers to squeegee out any excess water. Create an even layer to cover the entire area of the face that will become the mask (fig.1). If you intend to cover the eyes with the plaster bandages, first put cellophane tape or a plastic bandage over each eye. Make sure to leave breathing holes for the nose (fig. 2).
4. After the first layer has been applied, add one or two additional layers for a total of two or three layers. When all the layers are applied, use the blow dryer until the plaster bandages are dry to the touch. This might take 15 or 20 minutes. Be sure to tell your model not to worry if the plaster begins to feel warm. Plaster warms as it dries.
5. To remove the mask, carefully work your fingers around the edges. It helps if the model wrinkles his or her forehead and nose during the removal process. Once the mask is removed the model should immediately clean up with soap and water. If the inside of the mask is still damp to the touch, use the blow dryer to dry it.
6. Once the mask is completely dry, you can use a scissors to shape it and add holes for the eyes and mouth, if necessary. Put a small hole in each temple of the mask to attach ties. If the mask is to be handheld, attach a dowel rod with glue or another plaster bandage in the location specified by the costume designer. The mask is now ready to be decorated according to the costume design.

A neutral life mask can serve as a base for other masks if a layer of aluminum foil is laid over its structure first. Coat the aluminum foil with petroleum jelly and apply plaster bandages or build up the mask with papier mâché. Crumpled newspaper applied with masking tape can be used to build up a mask into larger and more unusual dimensions. Layers of papier mâché would then be added to this structure.

# Makeup Techniques

As it has been for centuries, makeup is an extremely useful tool for altering appearances to suggest character and to excite the imagination of theatregoers. In addition, actors and makeup artists alike enjoy painting the canvas of the human face, applying substances to sculpt new features, and fashioning hair pieces that are often the crowning touch for a costume.

## Three-Dimensional Makeup

One of the standard techniques you need to know for stage makeup is how to work with various substances applied to the face to create three-dimensional makeup. For several of these techniques you will need **spirit gum,** a substance that provides a sticky surface on your skin, and a **stipple sponge,** a course spongelike block that is patted onto makeup to create texture.

### Nose Putty

Using **nose putty,** a soft pliable substance, you can alter the shape of a nose, chin, or forehead.

In *Roxanne,* a film adaptation of Edmond Rostand's *Cyrano de Bergerac,* actor Steve Martin had to wear a false nose. The Cyrano character's nose is a major part of his personality and the plot of the play. Martin also wrote the screenplay.

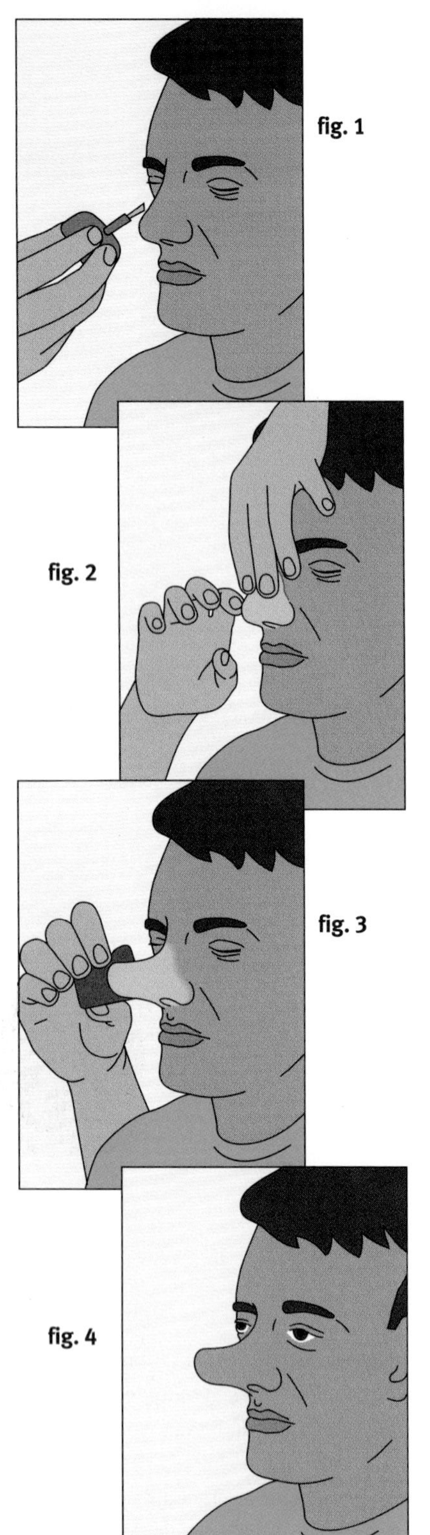


**APPLYING NOSE PUTTY**

1. Clean the application area so that it's free from makeup and grease.
2. Apply cleansing cream to your hands to prevent the putty from sticking.
3. Soften the putty by kneading it. If necessary, you can first coat the area with spirit gum (fig. 1). Allow the spirit gum to dry until it's tacky. Then press it onto the area and shape it (fig. 2). Blend the edges smoothly with the skin.
4. Pat the putty with a stipple sponge to give the skin texture (fig. 3).
5. Apply makeup to match the actor's natural skin tone, powder, and finally, the stage foundation color and any highlights or shadow colors (fig. 4).

To remove the putty, pull or scrape it off, using all-purpose makeup remover if necessary.

### Derma Wax

Derma wax is similar to but softer than nose putty. It's applied in the same manner as nose putty, but it requires the use of spirit gum. You can increase the adhesion by pressing a cotton ball into the spirit gum when it's tacky. After the gum dries, pull the ball off. Some of the cotton fibers will be left behind. Work a bit of the derma wax into these fibers. Then add the rest of the wax and build it into the shape you want.

To remove makeup made with derma wax, pull off the structure and remove the residue with makeup remover. If this isn't effective enough, use both spirit-gum remover and makeup remover.

## Wrinkles

Latex is particularly effective for creating wrinkles. Liquid latex comes either clear or flesh-colored. To make wrinkles using liquid latex, pull the skin tight and paint on clear latex with a sponge or your fingers. Then stipple the latex to add texture. When the stretched skin is released, wrinkles automatically form. Additional coats deepen the wrinkles. If you want extremely deep wrinkles, apply torn (not cut) tissue or paper towel to the stretched skin with either spirit gum or latex. Then cover with latex.

When you pull off latex applied directly to the skin, hair will come with it. To avoid this, shave the hair before applying the latex. As an alternative to shaving, you can cover the area with soap, spirit gum, wax, or preformed plastic film before applying the latex. This will prevent the latex from adhering directly to the hair on your skin. If the actor feels any burning, itching, or irritation, stop the latex application. Since each manufacturer uses a different formula, try other brands until you find one that doesn't irritate. Remember, too, that latex designed for forming in molds should *never* be applied directly to the skin.

## Stage Blood

You can buy stage blood in most costume shops and from theatrical suppliers, but it's easy and inexpensive to make.

### MAKING STAGE BLOOD

1. Pour a 16-ounce bottle of white corn syrup into a bowl or a bottle that holds more than 16 ounces.
2. Add 1 tablespoon of red food coloring (not red dye) and ¼ cup clear liquid laundry detergent to the syrup. The liquid detergent prevents the stage blood from drying out during the show and makes it easier to clean costumes with blood on them.
3. To achieve true blood color, add two or three drops of blue food coloring, one drop at a time until you achieve the shade of red you want. Store this in a jar, and shake it well before using.

Stage blood can be inserted into a **blood pack,** which consists of a sealed plastic bag taped to the part of the actor's body that will be bleeding. A projecting tack attached to an actor's finger by an adhesive bandage (Band-Aid) can be used to puncture the bag at the right moment.

The cast of Carlo Gozzi's *Love for Three Oranges* displays a wide range of theatrical makeup effects.

## Beards and Moustaches

To make a false beard or moustache, you can use crepe hair, animal hair, or human hair. Crepe hair is the least expensive and the most commonly used. It's available in a variety of colors packaged in long, braided strands. When the strands are unbraided, they tend to be curly. You can straighten crepe hair by dampening the unbraided hair and either stretching it across the arms or back of a chair or pressing it with an iron. Don't let the iron get too hot or the crepe hair might melt.

Captain Hook in J. M. Barrie's *Peter Pan* typically wears a long black wig and fiendish moustache.

Carelessly made beards and moustaches will look exactly like what they are—fake. To make a false beard or moustache as realistic as possible, study the way the actor's facial hair grows. Facial hair doesn't all grow in the same direction. Try to apply the fake hair in those same directions in which the real hair grows. Beards and moustaches also consist of hairs of different colors. For added realism, blend various colors of crepe hair together in a beard or moustache. Note that the hair is usually lighter nearer the skin. After determining the blend of colors you will use, cut the crepe hair to double the length of your final product. Apply spirit gum to a small area on the face and allow it to dry until tacky. Press a small amount of crepe hair onto the spirit gum, and repeat the process until the beard or moustache is fully applied. Then trim to the desired shape.

A reusable beard can save time in makeup if an actor has to apply it for repeated performances. Build the beard on a latex base and apply it to the face with spirit gum.

The stage adaptation of the Disney movie based on the folk tale *Beauty and the Beast* presents the makeup and costume designer with the challenge of creating a kind-hearted beast with a horrifying appearance. Wigs and facial and body hair are major components in the creation of the Beast.

The wig worn by Elsa Lanchester in James Whale's 1935 classic film *The Bride of Frankenstein* has become an icon. Here Elsa fixes her makeup between takes on the set.

TECHNICAL THEATRE

## Wigs

Basic wigs are much easier to buy than they are to make. With the right theatrical catalogue in hand, you will find that wigs are not too expensive, especially considering the hours a costumer might put into making one for a character. Many wig and costume companies also post their catalogues on the Internet, so you might check there to compare prices.

# Activities

### *Scenery Techniques*

**DESIGNING THREE-DIMENSIONAL SCENERY** Use a setting from a favorite folk tale that might be adapted for the stage. Choose a story that takes place outdoors and design a rock or a tree for the setting. Consider all the major points for designing three-dimensional scenery for a specific play (p. 465). Then create sketches and design plans that show the framework required for building three-dimensional scenery (p. 465). Specify the covering you will use and the colors it should be painted. Keep this information in your Theatre Notebook and present it to others in your class. Ask for feedback on the effectiveness of your design and instructions.

### *Scenery Techniques*

**BUILD A PROFILE** Using the methods and diagrams in this chapter (p. 469), design and build a profile for a set in a specific scene in a specific play. You will need to ask your teacher if there are any existing flats you can use; otherwise, build a new flat onto which you can attach your profile. You should work under your teacher's supervision when you cut the profile if you have never worked with a power saw. Present your finished profile to your teacher and classmates and include their feedback, along with your designs and perhaps a photo of your product, in your Theatre Notebook.

### *Prop Techniques*

**BUILD A PAPIER MÂCHÉ OBJECT** Using the technique of papier-mâché, create a set, decorative, or hand prop that could be used for a variety of plays, such as a statue, a bowl of fruit, or a small pyramid of three logs for a fireplace. Present your object to the class and, if you like, donate it to your school's theatre department. If you use flour-and-water paste, provide an adequate and air-tight storage container for your article.

### PROP TECHNIQUES

**CHOOSING FABRICS** Read a play and do a design analysis. Study one scene carefully and create thumbnail sketches for furniture and draperies in that scene, with notes about color and fabric textures or styles you think would be appropriate. For a period play, you may first wish to do research on furniture and draperies of that time. Visit a fabric store and choose fabrics for the furniture and draperies. First choose expensive fabrics for furniture and drapes and then look for less-expensive alternatives. Get swatches of each fabric. Mount these on a board with your sketches and present what you have found to others in the class.

### PROP TECHNIQUES

**PORTRAIT PAINTING** Using the technique described in this chapter (p. 477), create a fake portrait of a specific character in a play to hang on a set for a scene in the play. You may use a photo of yourself or another person to enlarge and paint, but make sure whoever you choose fits the character portrayed in the portrait. Build or find a frame that fits the period style of the play.

### PROP TECHNIQUES

**FAKE FEAST** Work with a partner or a small group to stage a feast. You may use all inedible food or a combination of edible and inedible food. Follow all the hygiene guidelines outlined in the chapter (p. 474). See if you can invent practical and effective inedible foods. Test the effectiveness of your design before an audience by viewing the stage from various perspectives to simulate different theatre spaces. Lead a discussion about other possibilities for food props and include the best ones in your Theatre Notebook.

# Activities

*Lighting Techniques*

**SILHOUETTE PROJECTIONS** Read a play set in the late 1700s and early 1800s, a period during which there was a craze for making silhouettes. Create a series of silhouettes of characters in the play that could be projected on a screen using a lensless projector. Show your projections to the class, describing the play and each of the characters.

*Lighting Techniques*

**PROJECTED CAPTIONS** Create slides for projections of the act titles for a specific play or of captions for actions in a scene from a specific play. The letters should reflect the period or style of the play. Add small graphics, pictures, or symbols if appropriate, for interest. Make sure you consider keystoning (p. 481) when you create your designs. Present your finished projections to the class together with information about how and why they would be used in the play.

*Sound Techniques*

**MIXING SOUND** Write or find a scene from a play or performance piece and analyze the sound needs for the scene. Prepare a show tape that demonstrates layering of at least four or five sounds. If you have access to a computerized sound system, do your mixing on that; otherwise, record your tracks on a multitrack reel-to-reel system. Play your show tape to the class. If possible, arrange for actors to perform the scene as you play your tape.

### *Costume Techniques*

**LIFE MASKS** Working with a partner, create a life mask, using the techniques discussed in this chapter (p. 490). Then make multiple copies of the mask using the original as a model (p. 490). Paint them a neutral white, so that they can be used by a group of actors forming a chorus in a play. Donate some or all of your masks to your theatre department to use as neutral masks or to decorate for specific productions.

### *Costume Techniques*

**MAKING JEWELRY** Make a gold-filigree choker necklace using a two-inch wide piece of lace. Cut a piece of lace long enough to fit around the neck as a choker would. Treat the lace with white flexible glue to stiffen it. When it has dried, spray the lace with gold paint. Decorate with fake pearls or rhinestones, and attach a hook and eye at the back. Create variations on this by using different materials, such as velvet, or leather. Model your chokers for the class.

### *Makeup Techniques*

**FALSE FACE** Create a false nose, beard, or moustache (or a combination of these) using the materials and techniques described in this chapter (pp. 491–494) and apply them to yourself or a partner. You might first look through photographs in various sources to find reference images. Take before and after photographs. Include these in a presentation of your makeup to the class, and then add the photos to your Theatre Notebook.

### *Makeup Techniques*

**BLOOD PACK** Prepare stage blood and a blood pack. Stage a scene from a play or write a short scene in which you can demonstrate the use of the blood and the blood pack. Rehearse your scene several times to get the logistics worked out. Bring an extra change of clothing and wash the clothing stained with the stage blood on the same day.

# Projects

## specialization

PROJECT 

## Using an Accent

**ASSIGNMENT** Perform a monologue using an accent.

### Project Planner

| | |
|---|---|
| Product | **A performance of a monologue using an accent** |
| Purpose | **To learn to use an accent** |
| Specs | **To accomplish this project, you will**<br>• **learn to hear variations in speech sounds**<br>• **choose a monologue in which a character displays an accent**<br>• **learn an accent appropriate to that character**<br>• **develop the character and rehearse the monologue**<br>• **perform the monologue for an audience**<br>• **demonstrate consistent use of the accent in performance** |

## Creating

**CHOOSE A MONOLOGUE** Everyone speaks with an accent. (In one science fiction story, an alien reveals himself by possessing no accent.) The speech of everyone from a particular region displays certain common features, including grammatical patterns, idioms, vocabulary, and pronunciation. You may recall that these features are referred to collectively as the dialect of that region and that the term *accent* refers specifically to the sound qualities of the speech of a region (p. 410). People from a certain place tend to sound like one another. Even after moving to a new region, people often retain traces of their original accent. Likewise, people who grow up speaking one language and then learn another often have traces of their original language in their speech—the so-called "foreign accent." By listening closely, you can learn to identify and mimic the accent of a particular region, which may help you to better create a character from that region.

Choose a play featuring characters who speak with an accent that interests you. Although you might choose a play where the speech of the characters also displays dialectical features, this project focuses on learning an accent. If you choose a play that is written in dialect, you will still probably need to add an accent to fully and accurately convey the language features. Dialect can be expressed in a script by word choice, phrasing, and sentence structure; it's less likely that a playwright will attempt to render accent, since this is awkward to do in a text.

To concentrate on accent alone, choose a play that is set in a region that features a distinctive accent and apply the accent to your chosen character's speech. Challenge yourself; if you live in Boston or the Carolinas, do not choose a character from a play set there. Prepare a monologue (p. 146) from a scene in your play that presents ample opportunity to demonstrate your character's accent.

**LEARN THE ACCENT** If possible, arrange to talk with a person who is a native speaker of the accent of your character. You might ask this person to read your monologue aloud so you can listen and tape record the characteristics of the accent. As an alternative, find a recording of someone speaking in that accent. You should be able to find one at a library or a bookstore; you might even find a recorded version of the play you have chosen. A movie in which the characters speak with your chosen accent may also be helpful. You can also learn an accent from books on the subject, but it's most effective to hear the accent as it is spoken. While listening to spoken accent, pay attention to the following:

- the articulation and pronunciation of vowels and consonants
- patterns of pitch
- phrasing (speed, pauses, omissions of sounds)
- vocal quality (such as guttural or nasal sounds)

Practice your accent aloud, not only with lines from your chosen scene, but also with other material—or even in conversation—so that you become thoroughly familiar with this accent.

**DEVELOP YOUR CHARACTER** As you practice your accent, develop your character as you would any other. Pay special attention to your character's background and education and length of residency in the area where the accent was acquired. You may decide, for example, that you don't want to use a heavy accent but only a trace because your character has been away from home for a number of years. Consider also motivations and subtext. Is your character proud of the way he or she talks or ashamed of it? Is your character even trying to hide an accent?

A person's speech is part of his or her personality. As you rehearse your character, do so always in that character's accent. You may find it makes a difference in the creative choices you make in interpretation.

**GET FEEDBACK** As you rehearse, use a tape recorder to record your voice and interpretation. Listen to it critically and compare the way you sound with that of your model. Keep in mind that you are not trying to mimic all the qualities of another individual's voice. Your goal is to be able to reproduce the vocal characteristics of an accent. As you rehearse, make whatever adjustments to your accent you feel are necessary. Toward the end of your rehearsal process, ask someone to listen to you or to your latest tape and provide feedback. If possible, your listener should be a native speaker of your accent or someone very familiar with it.

## Performing

When you feel sufficiently rehearsed, do a dress rehearsal in the performance space with whatever props, costumes, and makeup you have chosen to use.

Perform your speech or monologue for your classmates or for a small group. Keep in mind that your accent should seem natural to your character and be consistent. In concentrating on getting your accent right, don't forget to project and to use a variety of inflections during your performance.

## Responding

How well you have fulfilled the Specs in the Project Planner will help assess your project. You may also ask yourself or your audience these questions to help you improve:

- Was your accent appropriate to the character?
- Did it remain consistent throughout your performance?
- Did it sound natural and authentic?
- Was your character convincing?
- Did you project and use a variety of inflections?

## Adapting the Project

1. Follow the steps outlined to learn an accent for a character you are portraying in a full-length play.
2. Apply the accent you have learned to other materials; for example, you might try using an accent to read the *Declaration of Independence,* Lincoln's *Gettysburg Address,* or a literary selection, such as a poem.
3. If you have chosen a character whose speech shows dialectical features, use these to create another scene for your character or for a new character of your devising. You can either improvise the dialogue and then write it down,

or you can write the entire scene first and then act it with one or more of your classmates.

4. Incorporate multimedia into a performance that focuses on accents and dialect. Working with several other students, each of you can learn a distinctive accent that you apply to the same character's speech from a specific play. Project an image of the region associated with the accent or dialect on a screen behind the actor as you take turns performing the speech. Discuss with your audience how an accent affects their understanding of a character. Experiment with other ways to present the correlation between region, character, and voice through the use of multimedia.

## Performing a Song

PROJECT 

**ASSIGNMENT** Perform a song from a musical.

### Project Planner

| | |
|---|---|
| Product | A solo performance of a song |
| Purpose | To use acting skills to interpret a song |
| Specs | To accomplish this project, you will<br>• choose a song appropriate to your vocal range<br>• analyze the scene in which the song appears<br>• analyze the lyrics of the song<br>• develop a unique and identifiable character<br>• develop appropriate movement and gestures<br>• demonstrate vocal projection<br>• communicate emotion through your voice |

### Creating

**CHOOSE YOUR SONG** Choose a song from a musical. The song should be a solo appropriate to your vocal range. Even if you don't have a trained voice, you can still perform a song effectively—think of the songs of Professor Harold Hill in Meredith Wilson's *The Music Man,* which are usually done in a style that is half singing and half speaking in rhythm.

**ANALYZE YOUR SCENE AND YOUR CHARACTER** Read the entire script of the musical from which your song comes. Identify your character and how he or she functions in the musical. Do a character analysis, as you would for any character work, determining your character's objectives, obstacles, and actions for the scene.

If possible, work with another actor who will play the scene with you to lead up to your solo. Unlike songs you might hear on the radio, songs in musicals are expressly character-driven. They are the emotional outpourings of a specific character in a specific situation, and the more your audience knows about your character and your situation, the better they will be able to understand and assess your performance. Theoretically, characters in musicals break into song when their emotions become too heightened to express in mere spoken words. Together, analyze the character motivations or interactions that bring about the song.

**ANALYZE YOUR SONG** Write the lyrics of your song and analyze them in the same way you would for a dialogue. What is the purpose of the song? Is the song sung to another character, or just to the audience? Where does the song begin emotionally, and where does it end? How does the song build in volume, change in pace, and conclude?

**REHEARSE YOUR SONG** Rehearse your song several times before rehearsing the scene. Have someone play and tape record the musical accompaniment for you, or arrange for that person to accompany you in rehearsals and in performance.

Always warm up your voice before you rehearse, and always rehearse on your feet to get the benefits of diaphragmatic breathing (p. 30) that is vital for projection. Once you have memorized the lyrics, add movement and gestures that reveal your character's state of mind and what is happening in the lyrics. Some songs, for example, are meant to be sung very simply, while standing or even sitting in one spot for most of the song; others call for strutting and large gestures. If you like, incorporate choreography.

**REHEARSE YOUR SCENE** If you are working with another actor, block the scene so that it leads up to your solo; show the relationship between your character and the character portrayed by the other actor. If you are not working with another actor, plan how you will set up your song for the audience. You will need to explain who your character is and what happens in the scene.

Rehearse the scene as you would any other scene. If the other character exits before your song, plan that exit. Then think carefully about how presentational your song should be: should you sing directly to the audience or to yourself, as if you were just voicing your thoughts?

If the other character remains on stage for you to sing to, block the scene so that he or she doesn't distract from your performance but can still be seen reacting to the meaning of your lyrics.

## Performing

Before your performance, warm up your voice and your body. If you are performing with a taped version of the musical accompaniment, make sure it is cued and ready to go. Introduce your scene and then perform it for your classmates or for another audience. Introduce your song by telling what musical it is from, what characters are involved, and any other information the audience needs to know to understand the scene.

## Responding

How well you have fulfilled the Specs in the Project Planner will help assess your project. You may also ask yourself or your audience these questions to help you improve:

- Was the song you chose appropriate to your vocal range?
- Could the audience see all your gestures and expressions?
- Were your gestures and expressions appropriate to your character and to the song?
- Did you project your voice to fill the performance space?
- Did your singing convey your character's emotions?

## Adapting the Project

1. Organize a cabaret or other event that features soloists doing songs from a variety of musicals. Generally, such shows do not include scenes, just the songs. You may choose to begin or end the show with a production number involving all participants.
2. Choose two contrasting songs, for instance a comic song and a love song. The songs may be from the same musical or two different musicals. Rehearse them thoroughly and be prepared to use them in musical auditions.
3. Incorporate multimedia into your performance. Do a singing duet with another artist in a recording of the song you have chosen. You will need to edit the song so that blank leader tape plays during your portion of the song (p. 87). Or, incorporate backup singers into your song and project images of them onto a screen behind you while their voices play from speakers. Multimedia can create startling effects in a musical performance; don't be afraid to experiment.

PROJECT  

# Staging a Fight

**ASSIGNMENT** With one or two partners, perform a scene with stage combat.

## Project Planner

| | |
|---|---|
| Product | A performance of a staged fight scene |
| Purpose | To develop and practice stage combat skills |
| Specs | To accomplish this project, you will<br>• work with one or two partners to choose or write a scene with a fight<br>• choreograph the scene to determine each specific movement of the fight<br>• work individually to perfect your movements<br>• rehearse each group movement until everyone has perfected timing and pacing<br>• portray a developed character<br>• communicate clear, visible stage actions<br>• perform with conviction<br>• follow all safety precautions in rehearsal and in performance |

## Creating

**CHOOSE YOUR ENSEMBLE** Choose one or two partners that you can work with comfortably. Generally, it would be desirable to work with partners who share your level of physical skill or athleticism, but a more skilled partner can often help a less skilled partner in stage combat. Being able to trust each partner is vital.

**CHOOSE YOUR SCENE** Choose a scene from a published play that contains a fight or write a scene yourselves. In either case, your scene should not involve weapons. Weapons combat requires special training. If the scene you choose involves weapons in the fight, choose another scene without weapons or adapt the scene

If you write a scene, make sure it has a central conflict that leads up to the fight and that it has a clear beginning, middle, and end. If you are performing a scene from a play, read the entire play.

**DEVELOP YOUR CHARACTERS** Do a character analysis for your character. Determine your character's objectives, obstacles, and plan of action for the scene. As a group, determine the relationships among your characters and share what you learned in your individual character analysis.

Don't neglect character development and interpretation of lines in your effort to stage a realistic fight. Part of the realism of the scene will depend on expressing who your characters are, why they are fighting, and how they feel about their opponents.

**CHOREOGRAPH YOUR FIGHT** Before beginning, review the guidelines for stage combat (p. 405). Now consider how the scene develops. How does the fight get started, and how far does it go? You must determine what type of fight is appropriate for the characters in this scene. What type of moves will they make—kicks, chokes, punches, slaps? How will they deliver the moves—as well-trained soldiers? as scrappy street fighters? as kids lashing out as friends or lovers who lose control?

Following the directions for stage combat moves (p. 405–409), plan a sequence that will convincingly convey the essence of this particular fight between these particular characters. You will probably want to start out slowly and escalate in pacing and complexity, saving the most violent moves for the last. Plan the structure of the scene—its inciting incident, rising action, climax, falling action, and dénouement (pp. 170–172). Block your entrances and the movements that lead up to the fight sequence. Determine how the end of the scene will be indicated: Will you black out the lights, or will the combatants make up and go limping off arm in arm?

**REHEARSE YOUR SCENE** Do a routine of physical warm-ups before every rehearsal. Begin by walking through your combat moves in slow motion. Note how every part of your body is positioned during each move, how you are balanced, and just how far you are from each partner. After you have memorized your sequence of moves, gradually begin to speed them up. You may have to rehearse some moves dozens of times before you achieve a realistic timing for the whole sequence.

Collaboration is key to stage combat: talk constantly with your partner(s) about how they can help you and what you can do to help them. Do not perform until all of you feel comfortable with your own moves and those of your partner(s). No one should get hurt in the rehearsal or performance.

Plan what information you need to give your audience when you introduce the fight scene.

## Performing

Before your performance, go through your physical warm-up routine. Introduce your scene. Perform convincingly for your audience. Stay focused and maintain control and awareness. It's important that you perform every move exactly as you rehearsed it.

## Responding

How well you have fulfilled the Specs in the Project Planner will help assess your project. You may also ask yourself, your partners, or your audience the following questions to help you improve:

- Was the audience able to see and understand every action?
- Was the reason for the fight presented clearly?
- Were the movements and style of the fight appropriate for the characters?
- Were the characters convincing?
- Was the fight realistic?
- Did everyone work well together?
- Did anyone get hurt?

## Adapting the Project

1. Perform the scene in mime, in slow motion, or both. You will find that combat in slow motion has its own challenges: it's easier to pull your punches, but it's harder to keep your balance.
2. Choreograph a fight sequence among a larger number of actors, such as the opening scene of Shakespeare's *Romeo and Juliet.*
3. Follow the procedures outlined here to choreograph and perform stage combat in a fully produced play.
4. Incorporate multimedia by adding layers of sound effects playing from various speakers set up around the performance area. For example, if you were staging a street fight, you might have people yelling from one speaker, sounds of rhythmic punching from another, music playing from another, and so on. This would cast the scene in a more presentational rather than realistic style. Combined with lighting effects, you can create a mood that is ominous, comical, or thought-provoking.

# Acting On-Camera

**ASSIGNMENT** With an ensemble, perform a scene from a play to be recorded on videotape.

## Project Planner

| | |
|---|---|
| Product | A taped performance of a scene from a play |
| Purpose | To learn on-camera acting techniques |
| Specs | To accomplish this project, you will<br>• work with an ensemble to choose a scene from a play<br>• work with a director to stage the scene for a camera<br>• rehearse the scene as an ensemble<br>• develop an effective on-camera characterization<br>• learn film and video terminology, as needed<br>• work with a camera operator to record the scene on videotape<br>• show the scene to an audience |

## Creating

**CHOOSE YOUR SCENE** Work with an ensemble to choose a scene to perform. There are two ways you can do this: you can find a scene that you like and then form an ensemble to perform it with you, or you can search as an ensemble for a scene that requires the number of actors you have available. Try to find a scene that will give everyone a roughly equal amount of time on-camera.

**REHEARSE YOUR SCENE** Arrange for a student director who is interested in film or TV directing to work with your ensemble. You will also need to find a camera operator who can handle a video camera with confidence and expertise.

After you have cast your scene, begin to work out the staging following your director's suggestions. The staging will resemble proscenium staging but with an even narrower focus: the single eye of the camera lens.

Before meeting for your first rehearsal, each member of your ensemble should do a standard play script analysis and character analysis of the play in which your scene appears. At your first rehearsal, share your ideas about the characters and their relationships, including individual objectives, obstacles, strategies, stakes, and the outcome of the action in the scene. Then do a read-through of the scene.

A film or TV play is filmed out of sequence, often with several cameras. If you do not have access to several cameras—as well as the equipment needed to edit together dozens of different shots—you will need to film your scene sequentially. This means that in order to include different camera angles or close-ups, the actors will need to pause—sometimes in midspeech—for each new camera setup and to maintain those positions to retain the continuity of the scene (p. 419). You will probably find it easier and more satisfying to keep such setups to a minimum or even to work with a stationary camera—one set up in a single spot on a tripod and rotated to point to different locations during the scene.

It's a good idea to use a minimum of stage scenery, so you don't have to worry about repositioning furniture in exact locations at each setup. Make plans for props, costumes, makeup, and lighting so you can address each of these as you rehearse your setups; not only will you need to maintain continuity in your positions as actors but in the technical elements as well.

As you rehearse, keep in mind the differences between acting for the stage and acting for the camera. You do not need to project your voice to the last row of the balcony and use large facial expressions because the audience will see and hear you in as close a proximity as the camera does. Nor do you need to stay open for the camera as much as you would on a proscenium stage. On the other hand, your focus becomes even more important. Keep your eyes on the focus of the scene—usually the character speaking—unless you are directed otherwise. Never glance at the camera, even for a second. You will also have to be especially conscious of the pacing of the scene. Since it's broken up for filming, you can lose momentum. Keep in mind the structure of the scene and how it builds. Work with your director to find the right pacing and rhythm for the parts of the scene.

If possible, include the camera operator in your rehearsals, especially the last few rehearsals. If the operator plans to track, or follow, any stage movements, it's essential that he or she knows exactly when and where those movements occur.

When your scene is sufficiently rehearsed, do one or two dress rehearsals. Include whatever props, costumes, makeup, and lighting effects you have planned. For the camera operator, this will serve as a technical rehearsal.

## Performing

Perform your scene while the camera operator shoots it. If you perform the scene sequentially for one camera, you will be able to view the videotape immediately. If you are using more sophisticated equipment, you will have to wait for a technician to edit the tape.

Arrange for a room and equipment (a TV monitor and VCR). Then play the scene for your classmates or another audience.

## Responding

How well you have fulfilled the Specs in the Project Planner will help assess your project. You may also ask yourself, your ensemble, or your audience these questions to help you improve:

- Was the scene appropriate for the acting ensemble?
- Was each characterization effective and believable?
- Did the scene move smoothly, and was it well paced?
- Was the focus of the scene in complete control at all times?
- Did all the actors successfully adapt their stage techniques for acting on camera?

## Adapting the Project

1. Write, perform, and shoot a commercial. You can choose a real product to promote. In this case, you will probably want to study real commercials for this product to get a sense of how the maker of this product presents its image. Or, you could shoot a commercial for an imaginary product, serious or silly.
2. Apply your on-camera acting techniques in a videotape performance delivering a news broadcast or hosting a talk show or children's show. Study the presentational style of broadcasters and TV hosts. How does the content of the show and the intended audience affect the acting style you need to use?
3. Incorporate multimedia by showing takes of your scene, shot from various angles, on multiple TV monitors of different sizes. Or, perhaps film your scene in pantomime and dub dialogue later, playing it back during your presentation from boom boxes positioned at points around the room. You might also mix live performance with videotape performance by having some actors live onstage interacting with actors on video (timing of dialogue will be critical). Be creative; experiment with technology. Remember that multimedia will automatically make your production presentational rather than realistic.

PROJECT 

# Directing a Reader's Theatre Piece

**ASSIGNMENT** Direct an ensemble in a Reader's Theatre presentation.

## Project Planner

| | |
|---|---|
| Product | **A Reader's Theatre presentation** |
| Purpose | **To explore using voice for characterization and sound effects, and using limited movement in a presentation** |
| Specs | **To accomplish this project, you will**<br>• **choose a literary work to adapt**<br>• **develop a Reader's Theatre script**<br>• **cast the show and direct the ensemble**<br>• **be creative in solving problems of narration, characterization, movement, and sound effects**<br>• **conduct rehearsals**<br>• **stage the show** |

## Creating

**CHOOSE A LITERARY WORK TO ADAPT** Almost any piece of writing might be adapted into a Reader's Theatre presentation (p. 437). Choose one you will enjoy working with, especially one for which you can imagine some creative staging effects. Note that if you present your Reader's Theatre production for any purpose other than a classroom project, you will have to get permission to adapt copyrighted material; therefore, you may wish to use material that is in the public domain, that which has no copyright restrictions; see your teacher for suggestions.

**WRITE YOUR SCRIPT** One quality of Reader's Theatre is that it can combine dialogue, narration, and description, along with bits of poetry, song lyrics, newspaper clippings, letters, and practically any other kind of writing.

Follow the guidelines for creating a Reader's Theatre script in Writing & Theatre (p. 558). These guidelines will help you choose and prepare your source material, but you may first wish to analyze it for plot and character development, parts of which may be retained in the adaptation. Make sure your final script has a clear beginning, middle, and end.

To simplify a work, you may drop minor characters; however, since your actors can play more than one role you can use a comparatively small ensemble to play a large number of characters. Work with your ensemble in mind. While some actors might take on a number of characters, you will probably want to save one or two actors to play your main characters and no others. This will save the audience some confusion in following your story. You will also want to appoint a narrator or divide the task of narration among your actors.

For this project, plan on a presentation that runs about 15–20 minutes.

**PLAN YOUR STAGING** Although the convention of Reader's Theatre holds that actors read from their scripts and don't physically interact, these conventions can be modified. The actors can hold their books or rest them on lecterns or music stands. You can keep your cast seated on stools the whole time. You can have each actor stand to play a character and then sit down. You can have actors meet each other downstage center to play a brief scene together. You can have them go through limited blocking and use limited gestures. The unbending requirement is that the actors must keep their books on hand at all times.

One Reader's Theatre convention is that actors sharing a scene don't look at each other very often but rather face full-front. If two actors have many lines together, however, you should position them near each other, so that the audience doesn't have to keep looking back and forth from one actor to the other.

Be creative in how you use your ensemble. You might have them provide sound effects or apply stylized vocalizing in which you have them experiment with pitch, tone, tempo, and other vocal qualities for various effects. Consider what you can do within the movement limitations of Reader's Theatre. You might have actors position their bodies to create scenery, such as trees or mountains, or have them employ simple symbolic gestures and movements (p. 141), many of which can be done with script in hand.

As you plan your staging, annotate your script with your blocking and other notes about interpretation and presentation.

**REHEARSE YOUR ENSEMBLE** Cast your show and assemble your actors for a first reading. If necessary, explain the conventions of Reader's Theatre to your cast and review how they will be affected by multiple roles and limited movement. Discuss strategies for distinguishing characters by using different character voices or by using different areas of the stage for different characters.

Although you will have planned most of your major blocking and effects, you can still experiment during rehearsal. Encourage your cast to suggest creative solutions and incorporate them if they are useful. Have the actors annotate their scripts in pencil with blocking and interpretation notes, which they can refer to during the performance if necessary.

Rehearse your actors entrances and exits, and how to sit during scenes in which they have no lines. Usually, actors will continue to follow in their books and direct their attention to those who are in the scene being played

Although Reader's Theatre looks much more casual than a staged play, it can incorporate some of the effects of a fully staged production. Be careful to keep these elements minimal and make sure they do not steal the focus from the reading actors. Character costumes, for example, are not very effective for Reader's Theatre, especially if actors must switch roles often. Many directors have the ensemble dress alike in simple clothes to create an ensemble look and one that does not draw undue attention to any one actor.

## Performing

Don't introduce your work to the audience. The narrators or characters should tell the audience what they need to know. Let the work tell its own story. If possible, have someone videotape the performance to document your work and that of your ensemble.

## Responding

How well you have fulfilled the Specs in the Project Planner will help assess your project. You may also ask yourself, your ensemble, or your audience these questions to help you improve.

- Did the adaptation tell a clear story with a beginning, middle, and end?
- Did the material seem suitable to a Reader's Theatre presentation?
- Did the ensemble work together well?
- Was the focus of the story maintained throughout?
- Were characters sufficiently delineated?
- Was the ensemble used to create special or unusual effects?
- Was the presentation entertaining?

## Adapting the Project

1. Since Reader's Theatre can be created from a wide variety of literary works, you can follow the procedure here to create any number of presentations. One focus might be a current news event, in which you combine newspaper and news magazine articles, interview transcripts, scripts from television news commentary, and fictional scenes of dialogue to portray someone currently in the public eye.
2. Incorporate multimedia techniques by using actors reading on multiple TV monitors onstage, showing videotape of actors reading on a screen set up onstage, or projecting images of text onto large screens for actors to read.

# Developing a Musical



**ASSIGNMENT** With a group, develop a musical based on a short story or nonmusical play.

## Project Planner

| | |
|---|---|
| Product | A musical adaptation |
| Purpose | To practice working as a team to adapt material musically |
| Specs | To accomplish this project, you will<br>• work cooperatively within an ensemble<br>• mutually identify and assign the functions of each ensemble member<br>• choose a short story or nonmusical play to adapt<br>• write a musical script, or book<br>• create at least three songs<br>• cast and rehearse the show<br>• perform the musical for an audience |

## Creating

**CHOOSE YOUR ENSEMBLE** An original musical is developed by dozens of people: book (p. 444) writer, composer, lyricist, director, producer, music director, choreographer, actors, musicians, and so on. With your ensemble, establish who is going to perform what functions. For example, you may decide that you want to write the book and the lyrics as well as act in the show. Or, you may decide that you want to write the music and lyrics but stay behind the scenes.

**CHOOSE YOUR MATERIAL** First, choose a short story you would like to adapt or a one-act play that you would like to adapt as a musical. The entire ensemble can have input on this choice, but the writing team should have the final choice because they will be more creative with a story they like. This choice will be limited, however, to the number of actors available and the physical limitations of your theatre space.

Use the scripting techniques described in Writing & Theatre (p. 536) to break the play into scenes and to develop characters, dialogue, and actions. Even an existing one-act play will need to be scripted so that the dialogue leads up to, or sets up, the songs. Note that if you present the musical for any purpose other than a classroom project, you will have to get permission to adapt copyrighted

material; therefore, you may wish to use material that is in the public domain, that which has no copyright restrictions; see your teacher for suggestions.

**PLAN THE MUSIC** With your writing team, analyze the script and note places where song and dance might enhance the action or emotion of the story. Remember that songs in musicals are the avenues through which specific characters express intense emotions. You need to analyze the character interactions that bring about each song and the kind of song (such as a love song) that would fulfill the needs of the scene. Plan to incorporate at least three songs for your show.

**CREATE THE SONGS** If you are going to use original music, the lyricist may write the lyrics first, or the composer may write the music first. (Professional writing teams do it both ways.) If you don't have anyone who can compose music, you can write new lyrics to an already existing tune. If you do this, be sure to follow the existing rhyme scheme and be sure that all stressed syllables fall exactly where the original stresses fall. You can, however, make changes to tempo or tone, for example, by turning a ballad into a comedy song. Again, you will need to abide by copyright restrictions on copyrighted music if you present the musical for any purpose other than a classroom project.

For lyric ideas, go first to the book. You may find words that say exactly what you want the song to say. Use these words in your lyrics and then expand upon them. Try to be original in your imagery; songs that simply repeat clichés become tiresome quickly. Remember that you are writing words for a specific character, so use words that character would use.

The book writer will need to adapt the book to cut any words the lyricist has taken and incorporated into the lyrics and to set up the song so that it seems a natural extension of the dialogue preceding it.

**REHEARSE THE SHOW** Cast the show, set up a rehearsal schedule, and begin rehearsals. Often in musical theatre, music rehearsals start before book rehearsals to allow extra time for learning music, lyrics, and choreography. Your music director may also serve as musical accompanist or conductor, or you can work with recorded music. If you have a choreographer, that person must work closely with both the music director to be sure that the dance fits the music and with the director to be sure that the dance enhances the mood and meaning of the scene.

While rehearsals are in progress, ensemble members responsible for the technical elements such as set, props, lighting, sound, costumes, and makeup should be at work on their jobs, keeping an eye on the rehearsal schedule to be sure that everything comes together on time. Since you are not doing a full production, you might experiment with ways that the actors can provide sound effects or change sets and costumes in view of the audience; such actor involvement can create surprising and interesting effects.

Plan to have more than one dress rehearsal and at least one tech rehearsal. A musical has many more parts than a straight play, which means many more things need to be checked and coordinated for the actual performance. Be sure to plan the blocking of your curtain call, including how and when the cast acknowledges the musicians, if there are any.

## Performing

Perform your musical for an audience. Do so without any introduction; let the story tell itself. End your performance with the curtain call. You might play recorded music from your show afterward as you discuss the performance with your audience. If possible, arrange for someone to videotape your performance to document your ensemble work.

## Responding

How well you have fulfilled the Specs in the Project Planner will help assess your project. You may also ask yourself, your ensemble, or your audience these questions to help you improve:

- Was the story told clearly?
- Were the characters developed so that the audience could care about them?
- Did the actors perform with energy and conviction?
- Did the music enhance the action and emotions of the story?
- Were the lyrics fresh and original?
- Were each of the technical elements appropriate?
- Was the musical entertaining?

## Adapting the Project

1. Go through this process to create a musical based on an original idea; that is, not based on an existing literary work.
2. Incorporate multimedia into your musical. Show slide projections of images that relate to the theme of your musical, or project song lyrics on TV monitors or large screens and invite your audience to sing along at the chorus of certain songs. Combine live and recorded music for your accompaniment. Musicals are essentially nonrealistic in that they have characters bursting into song in ways that real people do not, so the presentational style of multimedia will not seem entirely out of place. Have fun with the possibilities it offers.

PROJECT 

# Three-Dimensional Scenery

**ASSIGNMENT** Alone or with a partner, construct a three-dimensional set piece of a rock or log.

## Project Planner

| | |
|---|---|
| Product | A three-dimensional set piece |
| Purpose | To develop construction skills |
| Specs | To accomplish this project, you will<br>• create a rough sketch of the set piece<br>• make a scale drawing of the set piece, including structural members<br>• construct a wooden framework<br>• cover the frame with chicken wire and papier mâché<br>• paint the set piece<br>• display the set piece |

## Creating

**PLAN YOUR SET PIECE** Decide first whether you want to create a log or a rock. Do some rough sketches showing your piece from at least two angles, front and side. It might help for you to do some observations and sketches from nature because there are many different kinds of logs and rocks. Include color notes; you might even shade some of your sketches with colored pencils. When you are satisfied with your rough sketch, decide on the exact dimensions of the piece you will create, and then do a scale drawing. Your scale drawing should show front and side elevations (p. 209). For this project, your set piece should be small enough that one crew member could lift and move it easily.

On your scale drawing, show whatever plywood sections and lumber framework you will need. Label your scale drawing with dimensions for all the pieces.

**CONSTRUCT YOUR FRAMEWORK** From ¾-inch plywood, cut the sections shown on your scale drawing. Because logs and rocks are not exactly symmetrical, you can probably draw them freehand on the plywood once you have marked the overall measurements. If the exact shape of your section is important, however, you can enlarge it from your scale drawing using the grid transfer method (p. 268).

Next, cut your lumber—2 x 4 stock lumber for strength—to the proper lengths. Screw your framework together according to your scale drawing.

**COVER YOUR FRAMEWORK** Now cover the framework with chicken wire, cut to size and stapled into place. If you have designed a cut log, you probably don't want to cover the end section because the flat end will better resemble cut wood. If you have designed a rock, you might want to let it rest on a flat bottom; that part should not be covered with chicken wire.

Cover the chicken wire framework with papier mâché or with heavy-weight muslin or canvas dipped in a papier mâché mixture (p. 470). Use as many layers as necessary to keep the pattern of the chicken wire from showing through. As you work, you can change the basic shape somewhat by adding crumpled paper or burlap and pasting more strips on top of it. Trim any wires or rough places that might cause cuts or snags. Allow time for your set piece to dry thoroughly before doing any more work on it.

**PAINT YOUR SET PIECE** First paint the entire set piece with sizing, perhaps white latex. If you are creating a realistic rock or log, follow nature in choosing the colors to paint your set piece. If you are going to add shading, your base coat should be a medium shade. Next add the darker shading, followed with the lighter highlights. You can effectively create the look of bark by using several shades of color using the dry-brush painting technique (p. 225). Let each color dry before applying the next.

If you are creating a log, add concentric circles on each end to show the lines of tree growth. These should not be perfect circles, so you can draw them freehand. Let your project dry thoroughly.

## Presenting

Present your project by displaying it on stage, preferably under stage lights. You might also see how it looks surrounded by other scenic elements. Invite your classmates and your teacher to view your work.

## Responding

How well you have fulfilled the Specs in the Project Planner will help assess your project. You may also ask yourself, your classmates, or your teacher these questions to help you improve:

- Does the piece have an appropriate shape?
- Does the piece have appropriate coloring?
- Does your painting or sculpting suggest appropriate textures?
- Does it look real?
- Can the piece be moved easily by one person?
- Are there any wire ends or rough places to cause cuts or snags?

## Adapting the Project

1. Create a rock or a tree stump of sufficient height and sturdiness that an actor can sit, climb, or stand on it. That means that you will have to measure a chair to get an appropriate height, plan a section of appropriate diameter to serve as a seat or step, and devise a supporting framework that is strong enough to support someone's weight and sturdy enough that the piece won't move when used.
2. Create a larger set piece, such as a tree or a fountain. This doesn't have to be completely three-dimensional; you could start with a plywood profile (p. 469) and add a framework and papier mâché sculpting to the front only. Be sure to plan appropriate bracing so that the front-heavy piece won't topple over.

PROJECT 38

# Projecting a Background

**ASSIGNMENT** Alone or with a partner, create two slides for projected scenery.

### Project Planner

| | |
|---|---|
| Product | **Slide projections that create scenery for a production** |
| Purpose | **To develop skill in working with projections** |
| Specs | **To accomplish this project, you will**<br>• **choose a multiscene show for which to design light projections as scenic elements**<br>• **design light projections for two scenes**<br>• **create slides from your designs**<br>• **project the slides using front- or rear-screen projection**<br>• **demonstrate how your projected slides would blend in with or supplement other scenic elements** |

## Creating

**CHOOSE YOUR PLAY** Any scenic design will be more effective if it is not generic but created for a specific show. By yourself or with a partner, choose a play or a musical for which you would like to design scenery. The show should have multiple scenes that will allow for some variety in design.

**INVENTORY YOUR EQUIPMENT** You should know what sort of projection equipment and method you will be using before you do any actual designing—whether you will be using front-screen or rear-screen projection, a scenic projector or a slide projector, and so on (pp. 478–481). Different equipment and methods will require different height-to-width ratios for your slides and particular positioning of your equipment.

**ANALYZE THE PLAY** Analyze the scenic requirements of the play as you would for any play for which you are designing lighting (p. 228). Sometimes projected scenery may be all that is necessary for several scenes; sometimes your light projections must blend into or complement other scenic elements. If your projections will form only part of the entire setting, you do not need to design the other elements, but you should be prepared to demonstrate how all these elements will function together. You may want to do some sketches or even create a model to show what part of the scenery your projections will form.

Choose two scenes that differ from each other in scenic requirements; that is, if one scene is a park at night, the second might be a city street during the afternoon. Keeping in mind the dimensions of the final projection, as well as the height-to-width ratio required, design backgrounds for these two scenes.

**CREATE THE SLIDES** How you proceed next will depend largely on the equipment you are using (pp. 478–481). You may be using shadows; you may be painting transparent images; you may be taking slides of paintings or photo collages or even three-dimensional objects. If you are adept at computer-enhanced design, you could create your designs on-screen and photograph the printouts from which you could make slides. If you need to enlarge or reduce your original designs, use the grid transfer method (p. 268).

**TEST THE RESULTS** Set up your screen and your projection equipment and try out your finished slides. Either darken the stage or try to approximate the light levels that you imagine would be used in the production. Be sure to pay attention to the influence of ambient light (p. 481) and—if you are using rear-screen projection—possible hot spots (p. 481). Check also the sight lines from different parts of the house. If you need to adjust the position of your screen so that it's clearly visible to the entire audience, do so now. Make any changes to your slides that you feel are necessary after you have seen them enlarged through projection.

## Presenting

Demonstrate your projections for your classmates. Identify the play and explain why you have chosen to use projected scenery for these particular scenes. Describe how your light projections function with other scenic elements.

## Responding

How well you have fulfilled the Specs in the Project Planner will help assess your project. You may also ask yourself or your classmates these questions to help you improve:

- Do the scenes seem to be well chosen?
- Do your designs fulfill the design requirements of the chosen scenes?
- Do the designs further the mood of each scene?
- Are the designs well executed—are lines and colors as bright and clear as they are intended to be?
- Are the projections in focus, with little ambient light and no hot spots?
- Do the projections suggest the world of the play in an interesting and artistic way?

## Adapting the Project

1. Design projection slides for an entire multiscene show.
2. Incorporate multimedia by combining images using multiple projectors and TV monitors.

# Creating Jewelry

**ASSIGNMENT** Create a piece of stage jewelry.

## Project Planner

| | |
|---|---|
| Product | A piece of stage jewelry |
| Purpose | To develop skill in creating special costume pieces |
| Specs | To accomplish this project, you will<br>• design a piece of stage jewelry<br>• create the piece of jewelry from found or inexpensive materials<br>• decorate the piece of jewelry appropriately<br>• model your jewelry yourself or choose an actor to model it |

## Creating

**DESIGN YOUR PIECE OF JEWELRY** Decide first what kind of jewelry you want to create: it might be a crown or tiara, a large medallion or an amulet, or a fancy bracelet. Designing for a specific character in a play may lead to a more effective design; however, every costume shop will have a number of jewelry pieces of various sizes, shapes, and degrees of elegance, so if you create a generic piece of jewelry it might still be used in a production someday.

Before you begin your design, decide on a style; if you are designing for a particular play, this will depend on the play you have chosen. You might design for a Greek tragedy, a Shakespearean history play, a fairy tale kingdom, or a modern-day farce. If you are going to adapt a historical design, you will need to research the types of jewelry worn and commonly used design motifs.

Decide also on the medium you will use. Papier mâché, sized felt, foam rubber, and other media available to you differ in their rigidity and the amount of detail work you can do. Since this is stage jewelry, some amount of exaggeration may be desirable and even necessary.

**CREATE YOUR JEWELRY PIECE** If you are creating a crown or tiara, measure your own head or the head of the actor who will model the finished piece for you. If you are creating a bracelet, measure your wrist or the actor's wrist. Remember that you must increase the circumference slightly to allow the bracelet to be put on and taken off over the hand unless you are planning to include a clasp of some sort.

Sculpt, mold, or cut the piece of jewelry. How you proceed in this will depend upon the medium you have chosen.

**DECORATE THE PIECE** Paint the piece if necessary. Then decorate it with beads, fake jewels, or scraps of jewelry you have found in the costume shop junk jewelry collection. You can use white glue or a hot-glue gun for these attachments. If you have created a crown, you will need to pad the inside so that it can be worn comfortably without slipping. If you have created a tiara, you may need to attach combs so that it can be fastened securely in the hair. Add chains to medallions and such pieces so that they can be worn around the neck.

Remember that you are creating wearable jewelry, so be sure there are no sharp edges protruding that could dig into an actor's skin or snag a costume.

## Presenting

Model your finished piece of jewelry yourself or have an actor model it for your classmates—if possible onstage, under stage lights, and perhaps with some other costume pieces to suggest how the jewelry would be worn in production. Stage jewelry is not meant to be seen close-up, and a final judgment of your work should not be based on handling or examining the jewelry.

## Responding

How well you have fulfilled the Specs in the Project Planner will help assess your project. You may also ask yourself or your classmates these questions to help you improve:

- Properly viewed, does the piece of jewelry have the desired effect?
- If it's an adaptation of a period piece, does it seem appropriate to the period style?
- Does it complement a costume without calling undue attention to itself?
- Is it comfortable and easy to wear?

## Adapting the Project

1. Use a different medium to create a different piece of jewelry; that is, if you have created a medallion, next create a crown.
2. Use the same process to create a nonwearable set piece, such as a fancy picture frame or piece of statuary.

# Making a Mask

**ASSIGNMENT** Create a mask for a specific character in a play or one that can be used in a variety of theatre productions.

## Project Planner

| | |
|---|---|
| Product | A mask that suggests a character |
| Purpose | To develop skill in creating special costume pieces |
| Specs | To accomplish this project, you will<br>• create a mask using one of several techniques<br>• paint and decorate the mask to suggest a character<br>• present the mask yourself or have an actor present it |

## Creating

A variety of techniques may be used to create masks. Before creating your mask, however, decide whether you want to create a mask for a specific character in a play or one that can be used in a variety of productions. Also decide whether you want to create a full or half mask (p. 413).

**DESIGN THE MASK** If you want to create a mask for a specific character in a play, choose a play and analyze both the play and the character. Determine what character traits, if any, you want to emphasize. Keep in mind that the mask will not show any of the actor's expressions, so the expression you create on the mask should be either neutral or flexible enough to show the range of emotions the character experiences. You might decide that the mask will be worn only during certain scenes and, therefore, an intense expression of one kind would be appropriate. For example, if you were designing for Shakespeare's *King Lear,* you might design the mask to symbolize Lear's madness during the climactic scenes of the play.

If you are designing a character mask that can be used for a variety of productions, you might want to look through magazines or books with pictures from theatre productions for inspiration. Or simply let your imagination be your guide.

If you are designing a mask to be used for a particular period or theatrical style, you will need to do some research. Sophocles' *Antigone* (p. 69), for example, requires masks that are typical of young women but show the characteristics of tragedy. Masks worn by commedia dell'arte characters had a distinctive style (p. 372). Draw sketches before you begin and work from your chosen sketch.

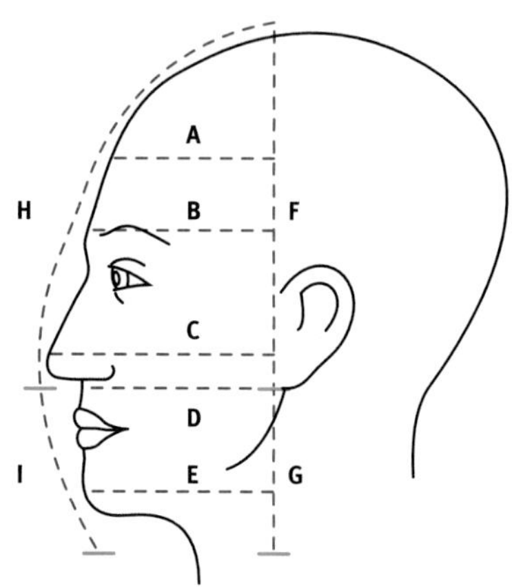

fig. 1

**Half-mask measurements:** A, B, C, D, F, and H (add 1/2 inch to A, B, C, and D for padding and air space; add 1 inch to F for padding, air space, and your hair)
**Full-mask measurements:** A, B, C, E, F + G. amd H + I (add 1/2 inch to A, B, C, and E for padding and air space; add 1 inch to F + G for padding, air space, and your hair)

fig. 2

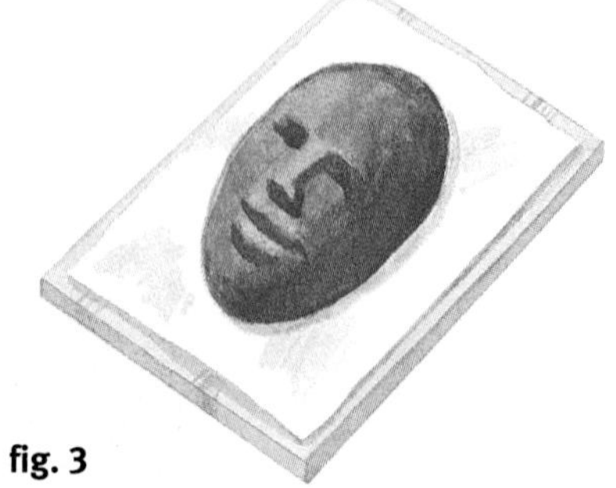
fig. 3

**MAKE YOUR MASK** One process for creating a mask is to make a life mask, using a medium such as plaster bandages (p. 489). Be sure to follow all safety precautions and to do everything you can to keep the person serving as your model comfortable during this process. You could also form a mask with the same materials on a life-sized artificial head, such as a milliner's dummy.

You can add plaster bandage sculpting or papier mâché to change the shape of the face, if desired. If you do, be sure that the mask is completely dry before decorating.

If you choose papier mâché as your medium for creating a mask, apply it to an existing mask or artificial head. (Never use papier mâché on a human face: it will traumatize the skin.) If you use an existing mask, you might need to put something inside the mask to keep it firm while you are working on it. After your mask is thoroughly dry, cut holes for the eyes and mouth, if that is part of your design.

A challenging alternative is to mold a face (human or animal) in clay and apply mask-making material over the clay. Follow the steps below:

1. Think about the bone structure of the head and the facial features; refer to your sketch. How will you need to sculpt these to create the face you have designed?
2. Measure the dimensions of your head (fig. 1) to make sure the finished mask will fit; this is especially important if you are making a half-mask because the nose must end where your nose ends or it will cover your mouth.
3. Prepare your clay by softening it with your hands. Use red clay, available at most art supply stores. The clay is usually purchased in 20 pound blocks; you will need about 10 pounds, so you might want to share the purchase with another student. When it is pliable, lay the clay on wax paper on a steady flat surface and form it into a half egg shape as shown (fig. 2). Your work area should be a place where you will not have to move the clay model if you have to leave it and come back to it.
4. Rough out the basic features of your mask face (fig. 3). Then begin your modeling. Use a damp (not wet) sponge to smooth areas as you model; continue to measure as you work so you maintain the correct head dimensions. If you must leave your work at any time, cover the clay so no air gets to it; otherwise, it will dry and crack and your work will be ruined.
5. When you have the face you want, run a sponge over its surface so that it is damp but not too wet; don't let it dry out in any area (fig. 4).
6. Apply petroleum jelly all over the mask, working it into every crevice of the face.
7. You can apply plaster bandages or papier mâché over your mask. Or, you can use strips of white sheets coated with a mixture of acrylic gel medium and modeling paste (both available at art supply stores) to create a flexible, durable, and smooth surface that can be easily painted. Cut strips of white sheets in various widths (from 1/2 inch to 2 inches) and lengths (from 1 inch to 5 inches).

8. Dip the strips of sheets into your mixture, removing any excess. Apply them to the surface of the petroleum-jelly coated clay face in several smooth layers (fig. 5).
9. Let your mask dry to the point where you can easily peel it away from the clay. Remove any remaining petroleum jelly or clay from the mask with a damp paper towel. Salvage the clay that is still damp and wrap it securely in a plastic bag so that no air will get to it; that way it won't dry out and you can use it again.
10. Trim any excess material from the edges of your mask (fig.6). If you like, you can sand the mask lightly with low-grade sandpaper to even out its surface and remove any scratching burrs at the edges.

fig. 4

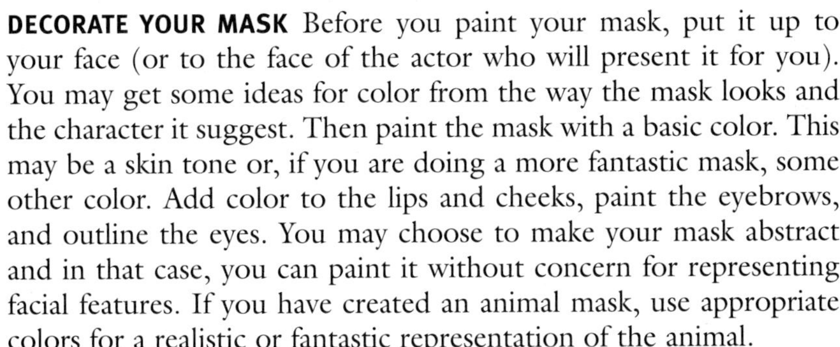
fig. 5

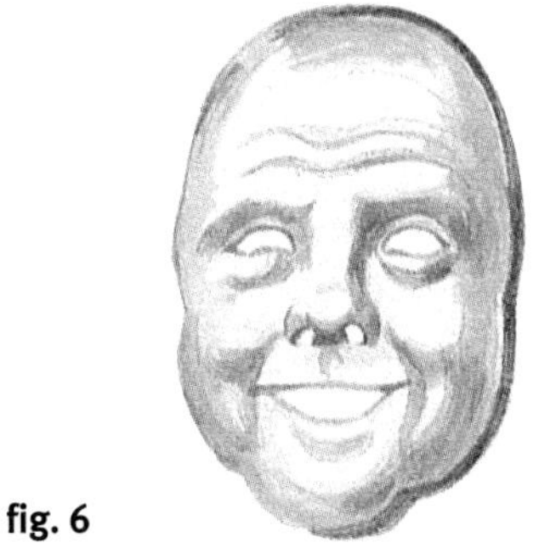
fig. 6

**DECORATE YOUR MASK** Before you paint your mask, put it up to your face (or to the face of the actor who will present it for you). You may get some ideas for color from the way the mask looks and the character it suggest. Then paint the mask with a basic color. This may be a skin tone or, if you are doing a more fantastic mask, some other color. Add color to the lips and cheeks, paint the eyebrows, and outline the eyes. You may choose to make your mask abstract and in that case, you can paint it without concern for representing facial features. If you have created an animal mask, use appropriate colors for a realistic or fantastic representation of the animal.

For a human face, you might add a beard or eyebrows of crepe hair. Glue hair on with white glue instead of the spirit gum you would use on skin, or use a hot-glue gun. You can even attach a whole wig to the mask, as the Greeks did. For animal marks, you may add hair, horns, or other features, such as whiskers or fangs.

Line the inside of the mask with fabric or some cushion material to make wearing it more comfortable. If the mask is to be worn attached to the head, punch holes in the edges to attach elastic or ribbon ties to go around the head just above the ears. If the mask is to be handheld, mount it to a stick of an appropriate length.

## Presenting

Present your mask yourself or have an actor wear it—preferably onstage under stage lights and with some costume pieces to suggest the character you have depicted in the mask. Present the mask in a number of different positions and under different lighting conditions; masks can seem to undergo surprising changes of expression under various conditions. Invite your classmates to critique your work and try on your mask.

## Responding

How well you have fulfilled the Specs in the Project Planner will help assess your project. You may also ask yourself or your classmates these questions to help you improve:

- If the mask was intended to suggest a specific character or animal, does it succeed?
- Is it interesting to watch from different positions?
- Is it well executed—are the molding, painting, and decorating carefully done?
- Is it comfortable and wearable for a period of time?
- Does the wearer have sufficient vision?
- Can the wearer project his or her voice reasonably well?

## Adapting the Project

1. Design masks for all the major characters in a play or for all the chorus members in a play.
2. Follow the same procedures to create a mask that is fantastic or appropriate to a carnival scene.
3. Create a whole head that could be used as a severed head in a play.
4. Incorporate various high-tech lighting effects, such as gobos (p. 342) and colored lights. Combine these with music to create an interesting piece of performance art with your mask.

# Resources

## Writing & Theatre

530 Analyzing Drama
534 Writing a Play
540 Writing a Review
544 Promoting a Show
551 Writing a Screenplay
558 Adapting Reader's Theatre
562 Writing a Research Paper
566 Activities

## Careers & Theatre

570 The Producer
571 The Director
572 The Stage Manager
573 The Actor
574 The Set Designer
575 The Lighting Designer
576 The Costume Designer
577 The Choreographer
578 The Playwright
579 The Critic

580 Glossary

593 Acknowledgments

597 Index

# Writing & Theatre resources

**Many different kinds of writing are associated with theatre, including plays, critical theory, reviews, publicity, Reader's Theatre, and research. The following articles offer guidelines and models for you to follow in your own theatre writing.**

## Analyzing Drama

To do an analysis means to separate something complex into its parts and to describe these different elements. You have already been introduced to different methods of script analysis as done by actors, directors, and stage designers as they prepare for a performance. These methods do not exhaust the possibilities; there are other ways of analyzing drama.

### Aristotle's *Poetics*

The first and most influential analysis of drama is included in the *Poetics,* a brief book by Aristotle (ar ə stot′l), a celebrated Greek philosopher and scientist who lived from 384 to 322 B.C. In the *Poetics,* the earliest literary criticism in Western culture, Aristotle also makes references to epic and lyric poetry, but the surviving portions concentrate primarily on tragic drama. He approaches his literary criticism in a scientific way, classifying specific types of literature and then investigating the essential characteristics of tragedy.

#### The Purpose of Tragedy

Before discussing the elements of tragic drama, he examines the purpose of watching a tragedy. Why would an audience be fascinated by the depiction of events that would horrify and repel them outside of a theatre? Aristotle locates the source of this pleasure is the delight that human beings experience in imitation. Aristotle then defines tragedy as an "imitation of life." Although he was defining tragedy,

Aristotle's famous definition has been applied to all drama and to art in general. An audience can therefore take pleasure in Sophocles's *Oedipus the King* (a play in which the hero puts out his eyes) because the play is only an imitation of a dreadful action.

According to Aristotle, the purpose of viewing the terrible events depicted in a tragedy is to arouse and dispel certain emotions. By giving the perspective of art to the events it portrays, a play can heighten a viewer's awareness and senses. Powerful plays such as tragedies can bring about a **catharsis,** an emotional purification or relief. Or, as Aristotle puts it, " . . . through pity and fear [tragedies succeed in] effecting the proper purgation of these emotions." He explains that watching a play in which a great figure is brought low arouses intense emotions such as pity and fear in the spectators. When that character is defeated (usually as the result of a combination of the will of the gods and the character's own free will—subject to **hubris,** or reckless pride, in the case of Oedipus), the audience experiences both relief *and* pleasure. They feel, as the old saying expresses it, "There but for fortune, go I," and depart determined to be better people. The audience's experience of pleasure from a combination of distress and relief is the product of a playwright's artistry—the ability to observe and record events, conversation, and movement to create an imitation of life.

## The Elements of Drama

Using the tragic dramas of Sophocles (p. 66) as his basic models, Aristotle identifies six elements of tragedy—and by extension, of all drama. The first three—plot, character, and thought—deal with the subject matter of tragic drama. For Aristotle plot is the most important element, "the soul of a tragedy." By plot, he means the arrangement of the incidents. He goes on to explain that a plot's basic structure consists of a single complete action—one that has a beginning, a middle, and an end. The parts of the plot, Aristotle reasons, should be joined together so well that if any one of them is displaced or removed, the whole will be disjointed and disturbed. Aristotle also observes that the plot should be unified; by this he means that the single action should occupy no more than a day. He notes that the works of Sophocles (whose *Oedipus the King* Aristotle regarded as structurally almost the perfect play) had a single setting.

During the Renaissance, dramatic theorists derived the so-called **"unities"** of action, time, and place from their interpretation of translations of the *Poetics;* these became iron-clad rules for the neoclassical dramatists of the 1600s, particularly in France. English dramatists, such as Shakespeare, ignored these "rules," preferring a less-structured drama in which a play's action could occur in many places over a long period of time.

Aristotle subordinates his second element, character, to plot. Aristotle says that characterization should stress morality; that it should be appropriate; that it should be true to life; and that it should be consistent. The hero of a tragedy should be above "the common level," not just socially but ethically as well. As examples of inappropriate characterization he offers noble language and diction in a peasant or cleverness in an unscrupulous person.

The third element Aristotle treats is thought, the main idea or abstract concept that characters make concrete in the action of the drama. Aristotle associates thought with oratory, saying that thought is found "where something is proved to be or not to be, or a general maxim is enunciated." An example of this element of thought in tragic drama is the statement by the chorus at the end of *Oedipus the King:* "Count no man happy till he dies, free of pain at last."

The last three of Aristotle's elements—diction, song, and spectacle—deal with language and performance. **Diction,** the fourth element, is language, "the expression of meaning in words." When a dramatist is choosing words with which to create a tragedy, Aristotle feels that these words should be clear without being commonplace. The fifth element is song or music. In Aristotle's time a singing and dancing chorus was an integral part of drama, as was the accompaniment of flute playing.

The last element is **spectacle,** the technical stagecraft used in presenting a drama. For Aristotle, spectacle is the least important element: "The spectacle has, indeed, an emotional attraction of its own, but of all the parts, it is the least artistic, and connected least with the art of poetry. . . . The production of spectacular effects depends more on the art of the stage machinist than on that of the poet." Of course, playwrights since Aristotle's time have employed a different mix of these elements than he saw in the works of Sophocles. For example, in musicals, song and spectacle are often much more important than Aristotle's other four elements.

## The Natyasastra

Aristotle's *Poetics* defined the classical rules of drama in European literature. An equivalent role is served for the classical Sanskrit drama of ancient India by the *Natyasastra* (The Science of Dramaturgy) ascribed to the semilegendary sage Bharata. Unlike the restricted focus of the *Poetics,* the *Natyasastra* is an encyclopedic work, laying down rules in a broad range of artistic areas, including playwriting, dance, music, makeup, costume, acting, and theatre architecture. There are, however, a number of close parallels between the analysis of drama in the *Poetics* and in the *Natyasastra.* For example, both works define drama as imitation; both also insist on the need for unity of action and of time.

A significant difference between Greek and Indian drama is in the classification of plays. In Indian drama plays are not divided into comedies and tragedies; instead, they are categorized according to a classification based on the dominant mood, or **rasa,** each play expresses. There are nine rasas: erotic, comic, pathetic, furious, heroic, terrible, hateful, marvelous, and peaceful. Another important distinction is that tragedy was not permitted in classical Indian drama. As one historian observes, "Happy endings are unavoidable; faithful love must always triumph, virtue must always be rewarded, if only to balance reality." In Indian theatre, the imitation of defeat and death in this world does not serve the therapeutic purpose that it does in Greek tragedy.

## Zeami on *Noh* Drama

The critical writing of Zeami Motokiyo, the greatest master of Japanese *Noh* drama, presents a very different approach to the analysis of drama than those of the *Poetics* or the *Natyasastra.* An important literary theorist, Zeami identifies the basic aesthetic element of Noh drama as **yugen**—a Japanese term that has been defined as "mystery"—and discusses at length how yugen is attained. Beauty, gentleness, tranquility, and elegant costumes all contribute to creating this element. When an actor conveys yugen, the audience is aware of experiencing something eternal, something beyond what is merely represented. Zeami describes the perfect expression of yugen as "silence beyond the form," and uses the image of snow piling up in a silver bowl as a metaphor for the stillness he associates with yugen.

Zeami's analysis of drama reflects the influence of Zen Buddhism, a spiritual tradition that stresses the unreality of the material world. Unlike Aristotle, Zeami does not locate the pleasure of an audience in watching action, but in the experience of "no action." He observes that the highest points of pleasure that an audience experiences in watching a *Noh* drama are often not in the dialogue, dancing, singing, and pantomiming performed by the actors; instead, they occur in the moments of "no action" between actions: "When we examine why such moments without action are enjoyable, we find that it is due to the underlying spiritual strength of the actor which unremittingly holds the attention. He does not relax the tension when the dancing or singing comes to an end or at intervals between the dialogue and the different types of miming, but maintains an unwavering inner strength. This feeling of inner strength will faintly reveal itself and bring enjoyment."

# Writing a Play

Aristotle rated drama higher than history because drama expressed the universal; history, the particular. Playwrights do seek to express some essential truth about human beings or the human condition. To achieve that goal, a playwright needs three things—a vision to communicate, a mastery of the craft of playwriting, and a facility with the playwright's basic tools of plot, character, and language.

## Vision, Craft, and Tools

A playwright's vision grows out of intuitions, thoughts, convictions, assumptions, perceptions, and emotional sensitivities. These attributes affect selection of plot, characters, and language. This vision is also fed by reacting to the work of other playwrights; if you intend to write plays, you should see and read as many plays as possible.

The craft of playwriting involves mastering the three phases of writing: invention—discovering an idea; planning—finding a plot and suitable characters to move that plot; and expression—writing appropriate dialogue and action that reveals your characters and theme. Mastering this craft also demands that a playwright be willing to rewrite many times.

A playwright's major tools are plot, character, and language. A novelist uses the same tools, but a finished novel is a complete work; a play is not complete until it is performed. A play script is a blueprint for the director, the actors, and the stage crew. In a real sense, a play is a work in progress. During rehearsals of a new play in its first production, a playwright may revise the play in order to allow more time for an actor to make an entrance, or to make a line more emphatic, or to increase suspense.

## Invention

The sources of ideas for plays are as different as the playwrights themselves. The origin of Eugene O'Neill's great trilogy *Mourning Becomes Electra* can be traced to the spring of 1926, when he made the following notation in his diary: "Modern psychological drama using one of the old legend plots of Greek tragedy for its basic theme." Arthur Miller's play *The Crucible,* set during the Salem witch trials of the 1690s, was a response to Senator Joseph McCarthy's anticommunist witch hunt in the early 1950s. Tennessee Williams's memory play *The Glass Menagerie* is autobiographical. Your Theatre Notebook might contain the following types of script ideas:

- sketches of unusual people
- provocative lines from overheard conversations
- topics about which you have strong feelings or opinions

- folk tales or fairy tales that could be retold or updated
- events in history
- current newspaper or magazine stories
- incidents from your own life

If you have strong feelings about crime, for example, you might be drawn to a newspaper story about a young girl accused of a terrible murder. You might ask yourself a series of "What if—" questions that might generate a number of ideas for a play:

- What if she really didn't do it?
- If she did do it, why did she?
- What if this was just one in a series of murders?
- What if she had not been caught? What kind of adult would she become?

## Planning

Most scripts grow out of two elements: the **through line**—the major action of the play—and the conflict. In a mystery story, for example, a detective's effort to solve the crime is the through line; the conflict is the struggle between the detective's efforts to solve the crime and the criminal's efforts to escape detection. In L. Frank Baum's *The Wizard of Oz,* the through line is Dorothy's journey to the Wizard who will enable her to get back to Kansas; the conflict is provided by the Wicked Witch.

There are four general types of **dramatic conflict.** The main character in a play can be in conflict (1) with another person; (2) with him- or herself; (3) with society; (4) with the forces of nature or fate. Conflict can be physical, but onstage it is usually more interesting if it is personal, moral, or social.

The action of most plays is organized into major divisions called **acts,** which are subdivided into **scenes.** Each scene deals with a significant crisis or confrontation. The scene is the basic structural element of a play. Before you begin to write, outline the scenes to be included. One method of outlining is to write the central action of each scene on a 3 x 5 card. Spread the cards out on the floor or pin them to a board. Look for scenes you can cut or put in a different order. Once your arrangement satisfies you, write a first draft.

### Grabbing the Audience

Begin your play with a hook. A **hook** is something in the script—an action, a line of dialogue, a piece of stage business, an actor's reaction—that grabs the audience's interest. For example, if a man is to be fired, don't begin by showing this man acting incompetently. Instead, as a hook, you might start with the boss saying, "We've decided to let you go." Then quickly provide exposition (p. 169), material that establishes the situation, introduces the characters, and provides any necessary background information on events that occurred before the opening of the play.

## Structuring the Action

The movement of a well-crafted plot begins with an inciting incident (p. 170), the catalyst for the play's action. The inciting incident may take the form of an idea or action on the part of the main character, or it may occur through some external force imposed upon a character. The rising action (p. 170) of a play consists of a series of complications and discoveries that create conflict. The rising action makes up the middle portion of the play. Each of the scenes that make up the rising action also needs a hook, plus an ending that makes the audience want to keep watching. Scenes are separated and linked by **transitions,** verbal or visual connections or bridges. For example, if scene iv shows someone going to bed and turning out lights, scene v might begin with an alarm clock ringing or the sun rising.

The climax (p. 171) is the turning point in the plot when everything comes to an emotional crest. The falling action (p. 171) is the series of events following the climax. The ending or dénouement (p. 172) is the resolution of the conflicts that made up the rising action. If it's plausible and inevitable, an ending can be happy or unhappy.

## Creating Characters

Characters advance the action of a play. The basic action of your play, the through line, already dictates a certain cast of characters. The action of *The Wizard of Oz,* for example, requires at least Dorothy, the Wizard, and the Wicked Witch.

**KINDS OF CHARACTERS** Your chief characters will be the protagonist (p. 172), the central character, and the antagonist (p. 172), the character with whom the protagonist struggles in the dramatic conflict. These characters are usually the most complex and, thus, the most fully developed.

Characters other than the protagonist and antagonist are known as secondary characters (p. 172). One of these might be a **foil,** a character whose personality and (sometimes) physical appearance contrast with and thus accentuate those of the protagonist. Dialogue between the foil and the protagonist enables you to convey realistically a protagonist's thoughts or plans. Some minor characters, such as a bellboy or a maid, may be **functionaries;** that is, what they do is more important than who they are like. You must decide the degree to which each character should be distinctive.

As you begin to shape your principal characters, you will need to develop each one's background, what has happened to him or her in the past, and status quo, or present circumstances. Some questions to help you in developing the background and status quo of your characters appear on pages 136–137. Some of these questions address the motivation and behavior (p. 134) of a character, which are a reflection of a character's strategies to overcome obstacles to achieve particular objectives, or goals. As you develop the words and actions of each character, consider the character's overall motivation in each scene. Also consider how you might reveal the subtext (p. 138) of the character's words and actions, what is implied but not spoken.

## Expression

Theatre language is not the same as everyday conversation. Because it both shapes the action and expresses each character's thoughts, attitudes, and intentions, theatre language must be selective and controlled. Furthermore, in an actor's gestures or pauses theatre language can even be nonverbal.

In Shakespeare's time almost all theatre language was rhythmic, poetic, and relied heavily on elaborate imagery. By the 1800s, most playwrights had abandoned poetry for prose, particularly prose that revealed a character's class and education. Today, film and TV writers continue to write realistic dialogue. Your own personality as well as requirements of your plot and characters will affect your style.

### Writing Dialogue

Although the language you use will be as much a reflection of the characters in your play as your style, there are some truisms about writing dialogue.

**FITTING DIALOGUE TO CHARACTER** As you develop the background and status quo of your characters, you should already begin to think about the manner in which each one speaks. An excited teenager, for example, might speak in fragments; a middle-aged trial lawyer, in long and complex sentences. Don't give lines filled with sophisticated or mythological allusions to an uneducated character—unless you are aiming for a comic effect. Look in your Theatre Notebook or search your memory for authentic words or habits of speech that make a character really come alive for your audience.

**UNDERSTANDING TIME AND PLACE** Fit the dialogue to the historical period and geography. If your play is set in the 1920s, don't use slang expressions from a later period. If your play is set in England, don't use words or expressions typical of Americans.

**CONTROLLING THE PACING** Have an ear for the pacing of a scene. Some scenes need to move quickly; others can move at a more leisurely pace. Short speeches or interrupted lines tend to quicken a scene; lengthy speeches slow it down.

**WRITING IN A STRAIGHT LINE** Avoid "byways." The expression "by the way" is usually the prelude to a digression, a drifting away from the main point of the scene. If the digression is important, introduce it earlier or later; otherwise, you will lose your flow—and possibly your audience.

**STEPPING ON LAUGHS** Space funny lines appropriately. Beginning comic writers often "kill" the laugh from one line by following it too quickly with another funny line. Give your audience time to laugh and to recover from laughing.

**BEING ECONOMICAL** Don't fall in love with every word. The biggest danger in scriptwriting is overwriting—writing too much dialogue. As you draft, "hear" your script. Then rewrite, eliminating words, phrases, and sentences that aren't necessary.

If your actions are arranged in a provocative form, if your characters are distinctively characterized, if your actors create dramatic tension, if the stage crew has reinforced that tension through appropriate effects—the audience should identify emotionally with the characters and understand the meaning of your play.

## Formatting a Play

Plays vary in format, but there are some constants. As you read plays, pay attention to similarities and differences in the way playwrights format their plays regarding the elements described below.

### Characters and Dialogue

Before a play begins, the entire cast of characters is presented. This may take the form of a list of names only or may be supplemented with brief information about the characters, such as their ages, physical types, important attributes, and relationships to each other.

In the body of the play, when a character speaks, the character's name is given, usually in capital letters (or small capital letters), and is followed by a period or colon. The dialogue follows on the same line.

### Act and Scene Designations

Each act and scene is identified and numbered before it begins, often centered and in capital letters. Most plays number acts and scenes using Roman numerals. Usually the scene designation is followed by a description of the setting. A playwright may go into detail about how the set should be arranged or may only indicate furnishings necessary for the action of the scene. This description may be set up as a stage direction.

### Stage Directions

Throughout a play, a playwright includes **stage directions,** which are indications to the director and actors about a variety of aspects of the play—generally, information on characters, how the play should proceed, how it should look, and commentary about intended moods or effects. More specifically, stage directions might include the following:

- descriptions of the setting or set, including lighting and sound effects
- descriptions of a character, including physical type, costume, vocal tone, and attitude
- notes on gestures or facial expressions
- stage movements (including entrances, exits, and other blocking)
- focus of vocal delivery (that is, to whom a line is delivered)

In a stage play, the stage directions appear in italics and in parentheses. Stage directions that explain entrances and exits and effects related to the set, such as dimming of lights, are often centered and appear on separate lines between the dialogue. Stage directions relating to specific characters, particularly delivery of lines or movements, are set in parentheses following the character's name. In the format of most plays, the character's name is typically set in capital letters (or small capital letters) in the stage directions whenever it appears.

## Prologue and Epilogue

Some plays include a prologue. A **prologue** is a type of introduction. It may be a monologue by a major character or a commentary by a chorus. The prologue hints at or provokes audience interest in the events and themes of the play that will follow. An epilogue is a concluding speech and therefore follows the final action of a play. As such, an **epilogue** may review the play's action and highlight important events and themes. The epilogue may also include information about what happens to characters after the action of the play ends. Popular in the 1600s and 1700s, prologues and epilogues disappeared in the mid-1800s and are rarely used in later plays.

# Writing a Review

There are two basic approaches to analyzing theatre—theoretical writing and reviewing. Theorists such as Aristotle or Zeami consider the general nature and purpose of theatre; reviewers offer opinions and assessments of specific productions. This article provides approaches and guidelines for writing theatre reviews.

A good theatre review does not merely summarize the plot of the play. A good review does several things. It provides the reader with any necessary—or interesting—background for understanding the play and its production: information about the playwright, the historical or cultural context of the play, previous important productions, media hype surrounding the play, and so on. It describes important details of the production—such as acting, direction, and staging—and how these factors contribute to the play's total impact. Additionally, a good review offers the reader an overall assessment of the performance experience from the insightful perspective of a seasoned theatregoer; therefore, reading plays and experiencing performances of all types is vital to gain the ability to give readers a sound and dependable review.

## Collecting Data

Before attending a performance, become familiar with the play. If it's a published play, read it. If it's a new play by a well-known dramatist, read his or her earlier work, looking for common themes. If it's a new play by a new playwright, read any feature stories about or interviews with the playwright, the director, or the actors.

### Note-taking

Take notes during the performance, or, since it's less distracting, between acts. Some critics simply write on the program; others carry a notebook—and more than one pen or pencil. The notes you take should include factual description—of actors' performances, the scenery, the costumes or lighting, the direction—as well as your personal and analytical response. Reviews combine both types of information.

## Responding to a Production

Following are four approaches to responding to a performance. The first is a personal response; the other three are analytical or critical responses. You will probably want to combine elements from more than one of these approaches in developing your own reviewing strategy.

## Personal Response

Reviewers are audience members first and critics second. Your first reactions will be personal responses to questions such as these:

- **Is the play interesting?** Does it capture your interest and hold it? What most interests you—the plot? characters? theme? dialogue? production (sets, props, lighting, sound, costumes, and makeup)?
- **Is the play convincing?** Do you accept what you see? Even if the play is not realistic, are you willing to make what the critic Samuel Taylor Coleridge called a "willing suspension of disbelief"? That is, you know you are watching a play, not reality, but you agree to be convinced by what you see.
- **Is the play moving?** Do you feel something or respond to something? Do you laugh? cry? sympathize with the characters or their situation? feel the suspense or mystery?
- **Is the play stimulating?** Does it give you something to think about? Does it give you new ideas? make a point you hadn't considered? give a new insight into some part of life?

Once you respond to these four questions, you are ready to shift from reacting personally to thinking critically as you analyze why the play worked or did not work for you. Although readers may be interested in your personal responses, they generally expect—and respect—a more objective critical approach. The next three approaches provide different methods of analyzing a play. Once again, you may want to combine elements from each of them in developing your own critical strategies.

## The Playwright's Purpose

Considering the following three questions is a simple but useful approach in analyzing a play:

- What is the playwright trying to do?
- How well has he or she done it?
- Is it worth doing?

## Dramatic Elements

Another way to analyze what you saw, heard, and understood is to consider the basic elements of a production. Notes on each element will provide details to support your opinions.

- **Plot** Does the exposition provide sufficient background information? Are the events of the play causally linked? If not, is the lack of causality an important element in the plot? What conflict does the plot reveal? Does the plot move to a climax? Is the ending inevitable?
- **Character** Who are the major and minor characters? What are their relationships? Which roles are particularly well-acted—and how?

- **Setting** Where does the action of the play occur? Are there multiple settings? What impact does the setting have on plot? character? theme?
- **Theme** What insights into human beings or the human condition has the playwright given you?
- **Style** What is the overall style of the play? Is it light or serious? realistic or fantastic?
- **Language** Is the playwright's language realistic or poetic? Is the dialogue appropriate to the characters? to the situation?
- **Production** Do the scenery, lighting, sound, costumes, and makeup reinforce the impact of the other elements of the play? Do they overwhelm them?
- **Music/Dance** (if relevant) Do music and/or dance advance the plot, reveal character, convey meaning?

### The Play's Effect

Asking yourself the following questions is a way of extending your analysis of the play:

- **What does this performance do for me?** Does it tell me something about being a human being, about people's motivations, behavior, fears, desires, relationships?
- **What does this performance do for the community?** Does it enable me to recognize social injustice or political corruption, or to encourage me to think about how to solve such problems?
- **What does this performance do for the theatre?** Does the performance provide playwrights and directors with new ways to write or stage drama?
- **What does this performance do simply as entertainment?** Does the experience satisfy those in the audience basically looking for diversion?

## Writing the Review

When you have collected your data, and applied whatever approach (or approaches) you have decided to take in responding to the performance, it's time to write the review.

### Being Fair

Before writing, try to separate your own feelings from your assessment of the play; for example, don't blame the playwright or the performers if they presented tragedy and you were in the mood for comedy. Second, distinguish responsibilities: don't blame the actors for the words they say; don't blame the playwright for inappropriate costumes or confusing scenery. Third, don't demand that all shows be alike; that is, don't expect one company's production of Shakespeare's *Macbeth* to be the same as that of another company. Finally, compare the quality of work to that of other productions you have seen. The more shows you see, the more valid your comparisons will be.

Some professional reviewers are famous (or notorious) for the harshness of their reviews. They delight in calling attention to the defects, to the lack of perfection in a performance. You may find the style of such reviews amusing, but the director, actors, and general public rarely find this approach helpful. Before simply announcing that a production is bad, try to answer questions such as these: What is it that the people who created it are trying to say to me? What are they doing for me? What are they showing me? Try to be as open to what you have experienced and as objective and accurate in your description of it as possible. If you still think that the play is bad, carefully detail why it is bad.

## Structuring a Review

A good review conveys the background, description of the production, and overall assessment of the performance experience through the careful presentation of facts and opinions supported by details and examples. Below is one way to structure a review.

**FIRST PARAGRAPH** A journalistic reviewer is both a journalist and a reviewer. As a journalist, remember that the **lead,** or opening, of the review should include answers to the five W's, journalism's five essential questions: Who? (the playwright, director, actors), What? (the play), Where? (the name of the theatre), When? (performance dates or times), and Why? (general assessment of the play's purpose and/or worth).

Newspaper reviews often convey this information in a box adjoining the review; sometimes it begins, or heads, the review. If so, you might instead begin your review by giving your opinion of one element of the performance.

**SECOND PARAGRAPH** If the play is new, briefly summarize the action and touch on the major themes of the play; if the author is well known, you might compare the plot or themes of the present play to those in the author's previous works.

**SUCCEEDING PARAGRAPHS** Discuss the acting, always identifying the character being portrayed and that character's purpose in the play. Examine any technical aspects of the production, especially as they reinforce or further the production's effectiveness. Comment on the stage direction or, if it is a musical play, the choreography. In the final paragraph, state or restate your general opinion.

# Promoting a Show

Theatre promotion refers to any activities that encourage potential audience members' support and attendance; in practice, this usually means publicity from various forms of advertising. In educational theatre, the business manager usually handles publicity. In professional theatre companies, this is done by public relations directors, sometimes called **publicists,** whose working assumption is simple—the more exposure, the more ticket sales. The goal therefore is to bring the company's name and productions to the public's attention.

## Steps to Effective Promotion

Effective promotion makes potential audience members aware of who you are and what you are doing. Whether announcing an upcoming season, advertising a specific show, or writing a story on a member of the company, there are many ways to get the news out to a potential audience.

### Step 1: Create Contact Lists

Identify all local media sources—newspapers, radio and TV stations, and business and organization newsletters. For each source, create a list containing the following information:

- source name
- deadline date for media materials
- key contact person
- mailing address
- phone number
- fax number
- e-mail address
- website address

Develop a personal relationship with the key person in each medium or organization. A good way to store your source information is in a file of 5 x 7 index cards or in a computer database.

### Step 2: Choose Methods

In promotion, only two things limit you—your budget and your creativity. The following are a few of the many possible ways of promoting a show:

- a media kit containing news releases, feature stories, and photographs
- advertisements
- radio/TV interviews
- posters and flyers

- newsletters
- website pages
- promotional booths
- announcement marquees
- street/hall banners
- sneak previews
- promotional items—T-shirts, mugs, key chains, buttons, baseball caps

### Step 3: Establish a Budget

Once you have a budget, decide what kind of promotions—paid advertising, posters, flyers, show banners, promotional items, and so on—will work best for you.

### Step 4: Make Timelines

With the director, producer, and technical staff, develop a year-long calendar that lists performance dates and such promotional activities as interviews and photo shoots (sessions in which photographs are taken of the cast). Since production people need to know when interviews and photo shoots are scheduled, and what their role in promotion is to be, create a specific timeline for each production. State the date and time of the following activities:

- media kit finished
- auditions, interviews, and photo shoots scheduled
- promotional items ordered
- promotional booth staffed
- announcement marquee put up
- tickets ordered
- posters and flyers developed and distributed
- program sent to printer
- sneak previews scheduled

### Step 5: Create a Look

Develop a distinctive logo (that is, a trademark or symbol) for your organization. Use it on stationery, media kits, and promotional materials.

### Step 6: Develop a Media Kit

A media kit consists of two elements: a fact sheet about your organization and a news release or feature story (which may include photographs). A theatre fact sheet, written in outline form, should contain the following information:

- name of organization
- publicity contact
- mailing address

- phone number
- fax number
- e-mail address
- website address
- key people in the organization, with brief biographies of each
- purpose of the organization
- board members or booster club sponsors
- theatre season, including dates of productions and fundraising events
- helpful background information (such as awards the group has received, successful past productions, and so on)

A **news release** prepared for the media is a short, factual description of an event. A **feature story,** on the other hand, instructs, entertains, or interprets, adding depth and color to news. Its tone should be informative and friendly; its first sentence, or lead, must grab a reader's interest. Feature stories often profile key people associated with an event—actors, director, designers.

Photographs appeal to both readers/viewers and to media people. Newspapers prefer black and white photos; TV and magazines prefer color. Newspapers prefer glossy prints, sizes 5 x 7 or 8 x 10; TV reproduction requires matte or dull-surfaced photos that won't reflect studio lights. Poster-size photos are best, but 8 x 10s will do; check station requirements.

Prepare for your photo shoots. Before the photographer arrives, plan your subject matter. Pictures with emotional appeal rank first in any readership survey. Detailed close-ups reproduce best. Choose the background carefully. Avoid signs over a subject's head and bold-patterned, busy backgrounds. Have the subject(s) doing/looking at something. Limit the number of people in the picture, and pose them close together to avoid expanses of dead space. To avoid harsh shadows, place your subjects at least six feet from a wall.

In submitting a photograph, accompany it with a caption clearly identifying the people and the activity pictured. (For individuals in groups, use locating phrases such as "from the left," "in the front row," and so on.) Put the caption on plain paper and include your-name, address, and affiliation. Tape the caption sheet to the back of the photograph and, if the picture is small enough, fold the caption sheet up over the picture face to protect it. Make sure all copy is visible. Never write on the photograph itself.

## Step 7: Create a Newsletter or Website

A newsletter or website can serve as an ongoing source of current news and information to keep theatre supporters and the media up-to-date about your theatre's activities. Newsletters and websites should include specialized news not available from other sources. Check with your post office for bulk mailing rates and restrictions if you plan to mail newsletters. You can also distribute newsletters to area businesses by hand, but check with the business owners first before delivering of copies.

If you create a website, make sure it's doesn't require a highly sophisticated computer system for viewing; make it accessible from a range of computer systems. You can provide a variety of interesting pieces of information on a website, such as links to other websites about the playwright, and photos and commentary from the production team, actors, and stage crew.

## Step 8: Prepare for Sales

You may have your tickets printed by a professional printing firm (check the yellow pages for information on ticket printers in your area). Or, you may have facilities in your own school for printing tickets. Order your tickets at least two months in advance of your performance and begin distribution at least one month prior.

The following information should be included on your tickets:

- name of the school or theatre group
- name of the play and playwright
- day, date, and time of the performance
- name of the theatre where the performance will be held
- price
- number of the ticket
- seat numbers (for reserved seating)

If you have reserved seating, you will need a seating chart on which you indicate which seats are sold. This is necessary if you intend to sell tickets at the door; you don't want to sell a seat that is already sold.

You should also determine the following when designing and ordering your tickets:

- How many ticket price levels do you need? Will you have separate ticket prices for students, adults, children, and senior citizens?
- Do you want the ticket stubs to tear off, or will you have patrons turn in their whole tickets?
- How many tickets should you order at each price level for each performance date? These numbers will be estimates. If your tickets are complicated, you would be wise to over-estimate; otherwise, if you can print more without much delay, you may make closer estimates.

## Step 9: Develop the Play Program

Some programs simply state the play's title, author, dates of production, publisher's copyright information, and the names of the director, cast, and technical crew. Others are more elaborate, featuring pictures of the show, as well as biographies and head shots of the actors, director, and designers.

The following is one approach (suggested order of items for each page is top to bottom):

- **Cover:** title of the play, playwright, director, illustration, name of school or theatre group, dates and times of performances
- **Interior, left-hand page:** name of play and playwright, cast listing of each character and the actor portraying each character (in order of appearance), setting of each act/scene, intermission information, copyright information identifying the play script publisher
- **Interior, right-hand page:** titles and names of the production team (p. 54) and stage crew (p. 74), acknowledgments to people and organizations who helped in the production
- **Back page:** notice of upcoming theatrical events

The arrangement of items on each page should make logical sense, and the color, type, and illustrations should not interfere with the readability of the program contents. Use no more than three type styles (fonts) to avoid a cluttered, overdone look. Don't use all capital letters; they can be difficult to read. Instead, vary your type sizes according to the importance of information and make use of bold and italic to further distinguish kinds of copy. For readability, keep your type flush left (aligned on the left margin of the page) for long blocks of copy, and use leader lines (dotted) between characters and the names of actors and between titles and the names of team/crew members.

### Step 10: Host a Media Night

In the professional theatre, opening night is usually referred to as "press night." Send a personalized letter to each of your contact people in the media, along with two complimentary tickets for the opening night of the production. Individual letters to school board members inviting them to your show can generate good will. Personalize the letter with the director's signature.

### Step 11: Thank the Media

After your production, send a personal note to each of your media contact people thanking them for covering your event. This not only shows your appreciation but may assure further publicity.

## Writing for the Media

Before you write either a news release or a feature story, have the following clearly in mind: your objective, audience, format, approach, and a detailed outline.

In publicity material, word choice is critical. For maximum effectiveness, aim for an average of 100–130 syllables per 100 words. In all promotional writing, follow these suggestions.

- Use present tense verbs.
- Use active not passive verbs: *performs* not *is being performed.*
- Use short, simple words: *used* not *employed.*
- Change nouns made from verbs into verbs: *present* not *presentation.*
- Use emotive words: *gripping, thrilling, heart-warming, magical.*
- Use synonyms for the word *said: stated, added, explained,* and so on.
- Use specific, concrete words and terms.
- Avoid technical words, or define them immediately.
- Avoid clichés.

For an adult audience, aim for an average sentence length of 17–20 words; for children, 10 words or less. Vary the lengths of sentences. Include only one idea per sentence, and use few compound or complex sentences. Vary the sentence beginnings, and end with a forceful word. Minimize the number of prepositional phrases. When you revise, check for unclear pronoun references, misplaced modifiers, or passive voice.

Reduce the impression of density by limiting paragraphs to three or four lines. Express only one idea per paragraph. Use transitional words and phrases, such as *also, however,* and *for example.* Use subheadings to break up paragraphs.

### Writing a News Release

Both print and broadcast journalists expect the lead (p. 543) or first sentence to contain answers to the five W's: Who? What? When? Where? Why?

*Example:*

> The Starbright Theatre (Who) moves its production of Euripedes' *Medea* (What) this coming weekend (When) to the Municipal Theatre (Where) in response to an overwhelming demand for tickets (Why).

Feel free to arrange the order of the W's, and note that you may not always be able to explain Why.

The structure of a news story is usually represented as an inverted pyramid in which information moves from the significant to the disposable. Since editors often need to cut stories, get your most important information high in the body of your copy.

To make your news releases effective, follow these additional guidelines:

- Limit releases to one or two pages.
- Cover only one topic per release.
- Use direct quotes from named individuals to add interest and credibility.
- Avoid negatives.
- Relate the material to the medium's readers or viewers.
- Avoid *we* in favor of *you*.
- Support all facts and figures.
- Don't use all capital letters for words and don't underline.
- Above all, study the medium to learn its editorial style. For example, some newspapers have their own style manuals; ask for a copy.

Type and double-space all material on standard 8 ½ x 11 paper. Use one side only. Limit the characters to 62 per line. As with all publicity material, include a fact sheet on your organization. It's a good idea to also include your name and organization on the news release, in the upper left-hand corner. Put the release date—for example, "For Immediate Release" or "For (date) Release"—in the upper right-hand corner. Begin your story one-third of the way down the first page. If the release is longer than one page, write "More" at the bottom of the page and circle the word. Indicate the end by typing three number signs (###), centered below the last line of copy and circled.

## Editing Your Copy

Don't mail anything until you have corrected the grammar, punctuation, and spelling; checked facts, such as titles, dates, and figures; rewritten awkward sentences; reread the copy to be sure the thoughts and facts follow logically; and had someone else read for typing errors.

# Writing a Screenplay

Film and TV are big business, hard to break into. To do so, a writer needs a strong command of the format and complexities of screenplays, an agent to help generate interest in the screenplay and above all, persistence. To begin on a smaller scale, do what Mira Nair, Rachel Talalay, Steven Spielberg, Spike Lee, and numerous others did: make short films with inexpensive equipment, such as an 8mm movie camera or even a camcorder.

## Developing the Screenplay

The steps by which a screenplay is written are essentially the same as those for writing a play (p. 534). Like the playwright, the screenwriter needs vision, craft, and tools. A screenwriter must have a vision that drives the script. A screenwriter must master the three phases of writing: invention—discovering an idea; planning—finding a plot and suitable characters to move that plot; and expression—writing appropriate dialogue and action that reveals your characters and theme. And like a playwright, a screenwriter must develop a facility and finesse at using the tools of plot, character, and language.

## Formatting the Screenplay

One of the distinctive differences in writing for the screen rather than the stage is the formatting of the script. In a stage play the playwright includes stage directions (p. 538), usually italicized and in parentheses. Screenplays contain directions too, but they are presented differently from those in a play; other differences between play scripts and screenplay formats include how characters are introduced and how scenes are designated. Producers and others who review screenplays expect them to follow a standard format; many will not even consider reading a screenplay that doesn't follow the standards outlined below.

### General Guidelines

- Set the left margin 15–20 spaces from the left side of the page.
- Number each page in the upper right hand corner except for the first page, which is unnumbered.
- Begin with the film's title centered, in capital letters and in quotation marks at line 6. At line 10 place the words "Fade In," in capital letters, at the left margin, and followed by a colon. Put the first scene heading (p. 552) on line 12 at the left margin.
- Begin scene descriptions 2 lines below the scene heading.
- Characters names should appear in capital letters the first time they are introduced in the script.

- Center, in capital letters, the name of a character speaking a line.
- Center instructions to the actor in parentheses below the name of his or her character.
- Indent character dialogue on both right and left margins.
- Place indications of scene endings, such as "Fade to" or "Cut to," 2 lines below the end of the scene, in capital letters, at the right margin, and followed by a colon.
- Triple-space between scene endings and new scene headings.
- End the script with the words "Fade out," in capital letters, at the right margin, and followed by a period.

## Setting the Scene

Screenplays typically contain far more scene changes than plays. A new scene is indicated by a scene heading. The **scene heading** (sometimes called a **slug line**) contains information about the setting of the scene, whether it's indoors—indicated by "Int," in capital letters, at the left margin, and followed by a period; or outdoors—indicated by "Ext," in capital letter, at the left margin, and followed by a period. The scene heading is followed by a brief and simple description, in capital letters, of where and when the scene takes place.

*Examples:*

INT. OVAL OFFICE—NIGHT
EXT. BARNYARD—DAY

When you write a screenplay, it's not necessary to number the scenes as in a play. Once the screenplay is in production, there will likely be revisions to your script and scenes may be numbered and renumbered.

## Describing a Character

When a character is introduced, you should briefly describe his or her characteristics. This description can be a short characterizing phrase, such as "a sly con-artist" or "a naive tourist." It can also provide more specific details of physical characteristics and demeanor, but it should always leave room for the director's interpretation. Character descriptions are often included in the initial scene description.

*Examples:*

KYOKO, a stylish woman in her mid-thirties with a cynical outlook on life
HAROLD, a poor Saxon, haggard and bent from toiling in the king's copper mines

## Describing the Action

Although the same basic tools and creative processes are used in writing a play and a screenplay, there are significant differences. In theatre the action generally takes place onstage and the audience's spatial relationship to the stage is fixed. In film and TV the audience views the action through the camera's eye and the camera can be placed in virtually any spatial relationship to the action. This visual flexibility enables filmmakers to tell much of the story through visual imagery. Thus, a two-hour screenplay usually contains far less dialogue than a two-hour play. Furthermore, in writing a screenplay you must use words not only to convey dialogue but also to convey all action—entrances and exits as well as gestures and movement. A character's actions should propel the story along or reveal something about his or her motivations (p. 134). Descriptions of action should begin at the left margin and indicate who or what is performing the action.

*Example:*

> EXT. HOTEL ENTRANCE—DAY
> A limousine pulls up, the driver gets out, and helps
> THORNE a miserly old business tycoon, out of the car.
> Thorne straightens his tie and dusts off his coat sleeve.
> An elaborately uniformed doorman holds the hotel door
> open as Thorne strides purposefully into the building.

## Interruptions and Continuations

Within a scene, show the continuation of the scene across page breaks by writing "Continued" at the bottom right-hand margin, in capitals letters and parentheses. At the top left-hand margin of the following page, write "Continued" again, in capital letters followed by a colon, but not in parentheses.

When dialogue is interrupted by stage directions or a page break, write "More" at the bottom of the page, centered, capitalized, and in parentheses. On the next page, write the character's name again (centered and in capital letters as usual) and follow it with the word "Continued" in parentheses.

## Indicating Sound Effects

Sound effects can be anything from a phone ringing, to rain hitting a tin roof, to a violent automobile crash, to mood music. The sound should appear in capital letters preceded by the abbreviation "fx" (for the word *effects),* also in capital letters, and followed by a period.

*Examples:*

> FX BOMB TICKING.
> FX HEAVENLY CHORUS SINGING TRIUMPHANTLY.

## The Finished Product

When you have finished writing, the format of your screenplay should look something like the following example:

"The Test"

FADE IN:

INT. CLASSROOM—DAY

The students are hunched over their desks, frantically scribbling on their test sheets. The TEACHER is reading through some term papers at his desk. He checks his wristwatch and looks around the room, then returns to his work. The classroom is silent except for the faint, rhythmic drumming of a pencil on a desktop. GREG, a student, glances around anxiously seeking the source of the drumming. He frowns as he identifies the "drummer," a girl slouched back in the desk behind him and to the right. He glances warily at the teacher, leans toward the girl, and whispers urgently.

GREG
(annoyed)
Will you knock it off. Some of us
actually want to pass this class.

The teacher clears his throat meaningfully.

CUT TO:

EXT. SCHOOLYARD—DAY

The schoolyard is deserted and silent. FX SCHOOLBELL RINGS. Dozens of students emerge from the school doors and head off in a variety of directions. Greg storms out of the school clutching a pink detention slip in his hand and stomps off toward home.

FADE OUT.

## Other Script Formats

Once you've pitched your screenplay and made a deal with a studio, the script is turned over to the director who reads and analyzes it. Working with the cinematographer, the director breaks the screenplay down into individual shots and creates a storyboard (p. 449), a series of simple sketches indicating the way each shot will appear on the screen. Using the storyboard as a guide, the script is then reformatted into a shooting script (p. 449), which numbers each shot and identifies the type of shot to be used. In addition to close-ups, two-shots, and long shots (p. 449), other types of shots include medium shot (MS), medium close-up (MCU), and point-of-view shot (POV). The following is an excerpt from a shooting script:

39. **LS:** *Carl, sitting alone in the library reading a book. He is seated at a table near an open window. His papers are strewn on the table in front of him. A sudden gust of wind blows his papers off the table.*

40. **MCU:** *Carl glances at the open window and frowns.*

41. **MS:** *He puts the book down on the table and gets up.*

42. **ECU:** *The book has a very distinctive, brightly colored cover.*

43. **LS:** *Carl is chasing his papers across the room as Ted, the librarian, strolls by with a book cart. He sees Carl's book on the table and pauses to retrieve it. Placing the book on the cart, he continues on his way.*

44. **MS:** *Carl dives after a page and bumps his head on a table leg. He grimaces in pain.*

45. **LS:** *Carl has retrieved most of his papers and is grabbing for the last one but another gust blows the page out of his grasp. The page settles on a nearby table where Jill is hunched over some papers writing fervently. She does not notice Carl's wandering paper landing on her table.*

46. **MS:** *Carl leans over and quietly takes the page. Without looking up, Jill shoots out a hand and slaps the page back down on the table.*

**JILL** *(still writing):* Do your own homework, buddy.
**CARL** *(quietly):* No, it's okay. This is my paper.

47. **MCU:** *Jill stops working and directs a cold stare at Carl.*

48. **MCU:** *Carl gestures at the open window.*

**CARL:** No, really. The wind blew my papers and one of them landed over here.

49. **MS:** *Jill sneers at Carl's explanation.*

**JILL:** Oh sure, happens all the time. . . (returning to her work) Get lost, creep.
**CARL** (raising his voice): It's true.
**JILL:** You'd better think up a better story to tell your teacher.
**CARL** (leaning forward): That's what happened.

50. **LS:** *Ted approaches and intervenes.*

**TED** *(to Carl):* There are people trying to study here. If you cannot conduct yourself appropriately then you will be asked to leave.
**CARL:** But . . .
**TED** *(cutting him off):* I'm not interested in any excuses. Just return to your seat and mind your own business.

51. **MS:** *Carl scowls at Jill and shuffles up to the open window. He reaches up and pulls on the window sash. It won't move. Carl puts his papers down and grips the window with both hands. He pulls as hard as he can. The window gives suddenly and closes with a loud crash.*

**TED** *(out of shot):* I'm not going to warn you again. Be quiet.

*Carl winces slightly at the sound of Ted's voice.*

52. **LS:** *Carl picks up his papers and carefully tiptoes back to his table.*

53. **MS:** *Carl is about to sit down when he realizes that his book is no longer there. Mystified, he looks around.*

54. **MCU:** *Jill sits at her table reading Carl's book.*

55. **LS:** *Carl's gaze falls upon Jill. He recognizes the brightly colored cover of the book she is reading. He throws his papers down on his table and strides angrily toward Jill.*

56. **MS:** *Carl steps up to Jill's table and clears his throat. She ignores him. He leans in and taps on the table with his finger.*

**JILL** *(still reading):* What is your problem?
**CARL:** That's my book.
**JILL** *(still reading):* Okay, whatever.
**CARL:** I need it to finish my homework.

*She looks up from the book and smiles at him.*

**JILL** *(gesturing to the far side of the room):* Could you please stand over there for about twenty minutes?

*She returns her attention to the book.*

57. **MCU:** *Carl seethes with anger and frustration. In desperation, he makes a grab for the book.*

58. **ECU:** *A man's hand shoots out and grabs Carl's wrist before he touches the book.*

59. **LS:** *Ted is holding Carl's wrist.*

**TED:** Okay, mister. I've had enough of your shenanigans. Let's go.

*He leads Carl away toward the exit.*

**CARL:** But . . . my paper, my book. . . .
**JILL** *(holding up her pen):* Hey, isn't this your pen? *(she picks up her purse)* Oh, and don't forget your purse.

## Tips for Writing Effective Screenplays

- **Keep it moving.** It's boring to watch two people talking to each other in one room unless you make both the room and the dialogue unusual.
- **Keep it fresh.** If your script idea has been done to death, don't do it—or at least use a fresh approach to the situation.
- **Keep it relevant.** Get rid of unnecessary scenes, dialogue, and descriptions.
- **Keep scenes brief.** Extremely long scenes slow the film's pace and can put audiences off.
- **Keep it clear.** Follow traditional structure—a beginning, middle, and end. Avoid flashbacks; they are far too overused. Once you are an experienced screenwriter you will know when to depart from the rules.
- **Keep informed.** Read as many professionally written scripts as possible and study their structure. Read books on scriptwriting.

Finally, recognize that film and TV are collaborative media and are filled with frustrations for writers. Producers, directors, and actors will ask you to tinker with your script or may make dramatic changes on their own. The finished product may bear little resemblance to your original script. Still, screenwriters keep writing because the media of film and TV are very exciting and the rewards can be tremendous.

# Adapting Reader's Theatre

In Reader's Theatre, two or more actors create a performance by reading a script based on a literary work. Many types of literature can be used as the basis of a Reader's Theatre script, including plays, fiction, poetry, letters, diaries, journals, and biographies. Entire brief works or excerpts can be used.

## Finding a Source

Any literary work can be adapted for Reader's Theatre, but you will make your task easier if you choose one with a limited number of characters and a good mixture of narration, description, and dialogue. The qualities that will make a work of literature successful as Reader's Theatre are basically the same ones that make it compelling to an individual reader: an interesting plot and characters, a theme with broad emotional appeal, and vivid, picturesque language. In addition, you may also want to choose a work that includes a number of likeable characters and has dialogue that serves to sharply distinguish characters.

If you choose to adapt a longer work, such as a novel or biography, you will only be able to present excerpts. It's not practical to do an entire novel as Reader's Theatre. Even a brief one would take hours to perform in its entirety. Decide which scenes best convey the work's essential character.

A practical note: If you present your Reader's Theatre production for any purpose other than a classroom project, you will have to get permission to use copyrighted works of literature; therefore you may wish to use material in the public domain (that is, not covered by copyright). See your teacher for clarification on copyright issues and suggestions for material.

## Adapting the Work

Your initial reading of the work you have chosen to adapt will acquaint you with its basic elements of plot, character, setting, theme, style, and language. Now reread, analyzing in detail the structure of the plot, the nature of the characters and their interactions, the description of the setting, the development of the theme, the overall style of the work, and the texture of the language.

### Narration and Description

Decide what narration and description you should retain. Note lines that have to be kept if the audience is to understand the work.

Add narrator lines to bridge gaps, to show time lapses, or to summarize action. If such lines appear in the narration sections of the work, use them; if not, write them.

You can either use a single actor to deliver the narrative and descriptive passages in your source or you can divide these passages among several characters. If the source contains lengthy narration and description, it might help maintain audience attention if you distribute these sections among several actors. Write an introduction for your narrator (or narrators) that identifies the characters, gives needed information about preceding events, and establishes the setting. If the work is told in first person, that character should narrate the introduction.

### Characters

To avoid audience confusion, eliminate minor characters and give any of their critical lines to the major characters. In a Reader's Theatre production, actors often take more than one role, including that of a narrator. If actors are sharing narration, it's important that they clearly distinguish the voices they employ in delivering narration from those they use as characters.

### Stage Directions

When only a limited amount of revision is being done to the source work, a Reader's Theatre script can be created by simply annotating the margins of the existing text with stage directions (p. 538). If you are revising more extensively, you will need to create a new script. You can use either a stage play (p. 538) or screenplay format (p. 551).

## Two Sample Scripts

Below are two sample Reader's Theatre scripts based on well-known American short stories. The first is Nathaniel Hawthorne's "Dr. Heidegger's Experiment," which concerns an old scientist who possesses water from the legendary Fountain of Youth. He invites three elderly friends to sample the water, with astonishing results. The second is Bret Harte's "The Outcasts of Poker Flat," in which a group of undesirables expelled from a mining camp are snowbound in the mountains. In the first script there is a single narrator; in the second the narration is divided among the various actors.

### from "Dr. Heidegger's Experiment"
*by Nathaniel Hawthorne*

CHARACTERS

**NARRATOR**

**DR. HEIDEGGER**

**WIDOW WYCHERLY**

**COLONEL KILLIGREW**

**MR. GASCOIGNE**

**MR. MEDBOURNE**

**WYCHERLY, KILLGREW, GASCOIGNE, MEDBOURNE** *(gleeful)*. We are young! We are young!

**NARRATOR.** All shouted mirthfully and leaped about the room. The Widow Wycherly tripped up to the doctor's chair, with mischievous merriment in her face.

**WYCHERLY** *(coyly)*. Doctor, you dear old soul, get up and dance with me!

**HEIDEGGER** *(coldly)*. Pray excuse me. I am old and rheumatic, and my dancing days were over long ago. *(He gestures toward the others.)* But any of these high-spirited gentlemen will be glad of so pretty a partner.

**KILLIGREW** *(commanding, to* WYCHERLY*)*. Dance with me, Clara!

**GASCOIGNE** *(competitive, to* KILLIGREW*)*. No, no, I will be her partner!

**MEDBOURNE** *(pleading, to* WYCHERLY*)*. You promised me your hand, fifty years ago!

**NARRATOR.** They all gathered around her, each attempting to embrace her. Blushing, panting, struggling, chiding, laughing, her warm breath fanning each of their faces by turns, Widow Wycherly strove to disengage herself, yet still remained in their triple embrace.

**WYCHERLY** *(breathless, laughing, to* KILLIGREW, GASCOIGNE, *and* MEDBOURNE IN *turn)*. Colonel, please . . . Mr. Gascoigne, behave . . . Mr. Medbourne, release me . . .

**NARRATOR.** Never was there a livelier picture of youthful rivalry, with bewitching beauty for the prize. *(The lights grow dimmer.)* Yet, owing to the duskiness of his chamber, and the antique dresses they still wore, Dr. Heidegger became aware of a strange phenomenon.

**HEIDEGGER** *(with horrified fascination)*. My tall mirror still reflects the figures of three, old gray, withered grandsires, ridiculously contending for the skinny ugliness of a shriveled grandam.

## from "The Outcasts of Poker Flat"
## *by Bret Harte*

### CHARACTERS

**NARRATOR 1 (JOHN OAKHURST)**
**NARRATOR 2 (THE DUCHESS)**
**NARRATOR 3 (UNCLE BILLY)**
**NARRATOR 4 (MOTHER SHIPTON)**
**NARRATOR 5 (TOM SIMSON)**
**NARRATOR 6 (PINEY WOODS)**

**NARRATOR 1.** Mr. Oakhurst was a light sleeper. Toward morning he awoke benumbed and cold.

**NARRATOR 2.** As he stirred the dying fire, the wind, which was now blowing strongly, brought to his cheek that which caused the blood to leave it—

**ALL** *(Drawn out and overlapping; not simultaneously).* Snow . . . sno-ow . . . sno-o-ow!

**NARRATOR 2.** He started to his feet with the intention of awakening the sleepers, for there was no time to lose.

**NARRATOR 5.** But turning to where Uncle Billy had been lying—

**JOHN OAKHURST.** He's gone!

**NARRATOR 4.** A suspicion leaped to his brain, and a curse to his lips.

**NARRATOR 3.** He ran to the spot where the mules had been tethered—

**JOHN OAKHURST.** The mules! That old thief has taken the mules!

**NARRATOR 6.** The tracks were already rapidly disappearing in the snow.

**NARRATOR 1.** The momentary excitement brought Mr. Oakhurst back to the fire with his usual calm. He did not waken the sleepers.

**NARRATOR 5.** Tom, the Innocent, slumbered peacefully, with a smile on his good-humored, freckled face.

**NARRATOR 6.** And Piney slept beside her frailer sisters as sweetly as though attended by angels.

**NARRATOR 1.** And Mr. Oakhurst, drawing his blanket over his shoulders, stroked his mustaches and waited for the dawn.

**NARRATOR 2.** It came slowly—

**NARRATOR 4.** In a whirling mist of snowflakes—

**NARRATOR 6.** That dazzled and confused the eye.

**NARRATOR 3.** What could be seen of the landscape appeared magically changed.

**NARRATOR 5.** He looked over the valley, and summed up the present and future in two words—

**JOHN OAKHURST** *(grimly).* Snowed in!

# Writing A Research Paper

Another way of writing about theatre is doing a research paper. You will sometimes be assigned a research paper as part of a theatre course. Your assignment might be an expository essay comparing and contrasting the styles of two playwrights; a persuasive essay taking a position on an issue in contemporary theatre practice; or perhaps a descriptive essay imagining a theatre performance during a historical period.

When you are assigned a topic for a research paper, it's important that you identify clearly what you are being asked to do. The following are directives that you will frequently encounter in an assignment for a research paper:

- **analyze** identify the components of something complex
- **compare/contrast** point out similarities and differences
- **defend** write in favor of an opinion
- **discuss** consider all sides of a question
- **describe** give a picture or account of something
- **define** identify the essential nature of something
- **explain** make something understandable
- **imagine** form an idea or an image

## Choosing a Topic

Sometimes you will be allowed to choose your own topic for a research paper. If so, be sure it interests you; your writing will convey that interest to your audience. You might begin by identifying an area of research that interests you and then focusing on a topic:

- If you are interested in acting, you might describe the way different actors have portrayed a famous character, such as Antigone or Hamlet.
- If you are interested in directing, you might defend nontraditional casting.
- If you are interested in producing, you might explain the economics of organizing a theatre festival.
- If you are interested in technical theatre, you might discuss how the set, props, and lighting, as described by Henrik Ibsen in his stage directions for *The Wild Duck,* contribute to the theme of the play.
- If you are interested in theatre history, you might define theatre of the absurd.

## Prewriting

In doing any paper, it's often the planning, rather than the actual writing that takes the most effort. Prewriting includes identifying your purpose and audience, developing your topic and thesis, and gathering and organizing your research.

### Purpose and Audience

The general purpose of writing is to inform or persuade a reader; the specific purpose is to present a clear point of view about a topic, one that leads to a conclusion, and possibly some desired action. If your paper is an assignment in your theatre course, your audience is your teacher (and possibly your fellow students) and your specific purpose is to fulfill the assignment. If you are writing an article for your local newspaper urging the establishment or support of a community theatre, your audience is your fellow citizens and your specific purpose is to encourage them to be theatregoers.

### Developing Your Thesis

Once you have a topic, consider the limits of time (to research and write) and space (the length of your paper). If necessary, limit your topic. For example, a topic such as Shakespeare's *The Tempest* is certainly too broad; however, the stage history of *The Tempest* would be more manageable. As you research, you may have to further limit the topic, depending on what you find. For example, you might further limit the stage history of *The Tempest* to the interpretations of the role of Caliban. You may also find you need or want to expand the topic.

### Thesis Statement

Your thesis statement informs the reader of your topic and identifies the approach you are going to take. For example, if you were writing about interpretations of the role of Caliban, your thesis statement might read as follows: "In the recent past, interpretations of the role of Caliban in Shakespeare's *The Tempest* have strongly reflected contemporary attitudes about imperialism and racism." If you are writing on an assigned topic, the assignment itself will supply much of the wording of your thesis statement.

### Gathering Information

Before researching using such conventional sources as print and electronic media—microfilm, cassette tapes, videotapes, CD-ROMS, the Internet—consider more personal methods of research: reflections on your own past experiences and personal knowledge; interviews with other people who have special knowledge about your topic; a survey questionnaire, conducted either by telephone or mail.

Take careful notes during your research period, paraphrasing (or restating) what you have read, seen, and heard. Identify the source of a note with the name and date of the publication or other media.

For direct quotations, use quotation marks and cite the person and source quoted. For personal interview quotations, cite the place and date of the interview.

### Organizing Your Notes

If your notes are on separate cards or pieces of paper, and if the subject of each note is identified, you can manually sort them into a logical sequence that will argue, or present, your position coherently and convincingly. If your notes are in your computer, cut and paste them into a cohesive, logical sequence of ideas.

## Writing the Paper

Write your first draft quickly, getting your ideas down before you lose them. Don't worry about grammar, spelling, and correctness at this stage. Just put your notes into rough sentence and paragraph form.

The main purpose of your first paragraph is to present your thesis statement. If your teacher is your audience, you can assume background knowledge on your topic; for a general audience, however, you may need to provide more information as context for your thesis statement.

In the succeeding paragraphs, present the substance of your explanation or argument. Generally, each main point you wish to make will be presented in a separate paragraph headed by a topic sentence.

The concluding paragraph ordinarily restates the thesis statement with certain amplifications, or it can summarize or make a final comment. It should not, however, merely repeat the introduction.

## Revising and Proofreading

Read your first draft aloud, being careful to both see and hear each word. Examine the organization and development of your paper, asking yourself the following questions: Is the thesis statement clearly stated? Is the evidence you offer in support of your thesis statement presented effectively? Does each paragraph have a clear topic sentence? Does your concluding paragraph refocus the reader's attention on the central points you are making? Finally, proofread your paper, correcting any errors in grammar, punctuation, and spelling.

## Peer Editing

When you have reached the stage of revising your research paper, a helpful strategy to employ is peer editing. Several different approaches may be taken to peer editing. The simplest way is to work with another student as an editing partner. Exchange your papers and read each other's work. It's a good idea to review your partner's work twice. The first time read for content, checking to see that the writing is clearly organized and well-expressed. The second time make sure that your partner has used correct grammar, usage, spelling, and mechanics. Write detailed comments to help your partner's revision. These comments should clearly focus on specific things you observe in your partner's writing. Your criticism should be helpful and positive, not sarcastic or rude. Before you return your comments to your partner, read them over to make sure they are clear, specific, and constructive. When you get back your paper from your partner, read over his or her comments carefully, asking for clarification if you are unsure what is meant. Assess your partner's comments on your work, deciding which you want to incorporate into your paper.

Another method of peer editing is to work with other students in an editing group, with each member reading each paper for one specific area of content or form, such as effective transitions or incomplete sentences.

## Titling and Bibliography

Once the paper is finished, add a title page. The best titles are simple and brief and express clearly what your essay is about. Along with the title include your name, the date, and, if your teacher has assigned the paper, the name of the course and the teacher. At the end of the paper include a bibliography, a list of all the sources of information you have used in researching your paper. Make sure to use the correct bibliographic format for each type of source (magazine, book, play, website).

# Activities

### Analyzing Drama

**ANALYSIS OF *THE TEMPEST*** In his plays Shakespeare almost never observes the so-called "unities" of time, place, and action that Renaissance critics derived from Aristotle. One exception is *The Tempest*, in which the action takes place during a single day on an island. Read this play and analyze it in terms of Aristotle's six elements (p. 531). Ask yourself: Is the plot of *The Tempest* a single, complete action? Are there parts that could be eliminated without affecting the integrity of the whole? Does the characterization stress morality? Is it appropriate? consistent? What principal thought does Shakespeare express in *The Tempest?* What use of song and spectacle is made? Include this analysis in your Theatre Notebook.

### Analyzing Drama

**DETERMINING THE SPINE** Before his first rehearsal of Tennessee William's play *A Streetcar Named Desire*, director Elia Kazan determined the spine, or essential motivation, of each character. For Blanche, the central character, it was "to find protection"; for Stanley, Blanche's brother-in-law, "to keep things his way." Choose a play and determine the spine of the central characters. Express each character's spine in a short phrase. Include these in your Theatre Notebook.

### Writing a Play

**FOUND DIALOGUE** In streets, restaurants, shops, and other public places, everyone sometimes hears scraps of conversation that would make wonderful dialogue in a play. In your Theatre Notebook write down funny, sad, illuminating things you hear people say. Working with other students, write these phrases on the chalkboard or on separate pieces of paper that can be taped up around the room. Imagine a situation and characters for which the phrases might be appropriate lines of dialogue. Build up a scene, improvising the remaining dialogue.

### Writing a Play

**STAGE DIRECTIONS** Some places carry a special feeling—good or bad—about them. Sit in a place you especially like—or hate—and note details about it. Then imagine the place as the setting for a one-act play. Write the opening stage direction for your play, describing the place as vividly as you can and suggesting in your description the special feeling the place holds for you.

### Writing a Review

**RATING THE REVIEWERS** Three different reviewers might reach three quite different conclusions about the worth of a performance. Find reviews by three different reviewers of a film you particularly liked or disliked. Read each review, then assess all three, answering questions such as the following: Which reviewer came closest to expressing your opinion? Did any of the reviewers prompt you to change your opinion? Did any of the reviewers reveal bias? Include these assessments in your Theatre Notebook.

### Writing a Review

**A PERFECT PRODUCTION** Pick your favorite play and then imagine your ideal production—the perfect director, cast, design team, performance space, and so on. Don't worry about whether the members of your dream team are alive or dead, or whether they lived at the same time. If you want Orson Welles to direct James Dean and Mira Sorvino in a production of *As You Like It* designed by Maurice Sendak, that's fine. When you have shaped this perfect production in your head, write a review detailing an imaginary performance and providing reasons why this production is so perfect. Include this review in your Theatre Notebook.

# Activities

*Promoting a Show*

**FEATURE STORY** Use your school or community newspaper to arouse interest in a current production through a profile of someone associated with it. Write a feature story of 500–750 words about the director, one of the principal actors, or a member of the design team. Deal with your subject's life both inside and outside the theatre and enliven the feature with direct quotes. Include this feature story in your Theatre Notebook.

*Promoting a Show*

**PROMOTIONAL GIMMICKS** Working with other students, brainstorm ideas for nonprint items—T-shirts, baseball caps, mugs, totebags—to promote either a show you are currently involved with or one that you would like to do. Create design ideas, including images and slogans, for the promotional ideas you propose. Save these ideas in your Theatre Notebook.

*Writing a Screenplay*

**SCRIPTING A COMMERCIAL** Create the script for a 30- or a 60-second commercial. Decide the product, the customer, and the basic situation. List the characters in the commercial and develop a short character sketch (name, gender, age, occupation, role in the commercial). If you like, use a storyboard approach (p. 436) with drawings, stick figures, cutouts, tracings, or photographs. Sequence the images to create your running order. Include the script in your Theatre Notebook.

*Writing a Screenplay*

**CONFLICT CHART** Drawing on a variety of sources—including family lore, gossip, newspapers, magazines, television, the Internet—make brief notes of conflict situations that you might use as ideas for screenplays. You might record your information on a chart with three columns, headed Conflict, Time/Place, and Participants. For example, under Conflict you might write, "votes for women;" under Time/Place, "early 1900s, United States;" and under Participants, "suffragists and conservatives." Save your conflict chart in your Theatre Notebook.

### *Adapting Reader's Theatre*

**SHORT SHORT ADAPTATIONS** Working with other students, choose several short short stories, each no more than two or three pages in length. Aim for variety. For example, one story might be a humorous anecdote that is nearly all dialogue; another might be an atmospheric tale that is mostly narration. Create Reader's Theatre scripts based on each of the stories and then perform them as a group.

### *Adapting Reader's Theatre*

**LITERARY COLLAGE** Create a Reader's Theatre script by assembling a number of short pieces. The tone of your collage could be poignant (for example, letters left at the Vietnam Memorial) or silly (for example, excerpts from stories about aliens from supermarket tabloids). When you have assembled your collage, write narration to introduce, bridge, and conclude your pieces. Include your collage in your Theatre Notebook.

### *Writing a Research Paper*

**DEVELOPING A THESIS STATEMENT** Select an area of theatre that interests you, such as acting, directing, technical theatre, or theatre history. Then develop three topics for research within this area. From these three, choose the topic that would be the most manageable to research. Finally, create a thesis statement based on this topic. Include the three topics and the thesis statement for each in your Theatre Notebook.

### *Writing a Research Paper*

**PERSONAL RESEARCH** Identify a topic for which personal research—interviews or a survey—would be an appropriate method. For example, if you were trying to measure how much support there was in your area for the establishment of a community theatre, you might conduct a phone survey. When you have identified your topic, create an interview script or questionnaire form to get the required information. Include the script or survey in your Theatre Notebook.

# Careers & Theatre resources

**Theatre—as well as film and TV—offers myriad opportunities for you to apply the skills you have learned to a wide range of jobs, both in theatre and beyond in the world of work. Read on to hear the personal accounts of a number of people who have made notable careers for themselves in theatre.**

## The Producer

Every theatrical venture begins with the producer, the person who puts together the package: financing, management, publicity, and artistic teams. Elizabeth Ireland McCann has been one of the most important producers in the United States for more than 20 years.

McCann has earned more than 60 Tony nominations. The Tony, named for Antoinette Perry, is Broadway's equivalent of the film industry's Oscar. McCann has produced dozens of Broadway hits, including Bernard Pomerance's *The Elephant Man,* Peter Shaffer's *Amadeus,* D. L. Coburn's *The Gin Game,* Tennessee Williams's *Orpheus Descending,* Todd James Smeltzer's *Mass Appeal,* and Edmond Rostand's *Cyrano de Bergerac.*

McCann, the daughter of a New York City subway motorman, attended Manhattanville College in the late 1950s. A chance remark from one of her teachers, urging her not waste her life as a telephone operator, led her to try for a career in the theatre. She began as a box office attendant and then a producer's secretary, then became a theatre management apprentice working for Hal Prince, Maurice Evans, and Saint Subber.

At age 32, convinced she was going nowhere in the theatre, she chose to study law. After graduating from Fordham Law School three years later, she decided her future did lie in the theatre after all. Hired as managing director for the Nederlander Organization, a top producer and presenter of Broadway plays, she produced *Sherlock Holmes,* Simon Gray's *Otherwise Engaged,* and *My Fat Friend.*

In 1976 Elizabeth McCann formed her own producing management firm, McCann and Nugent, and in 1984 she decided she preferred a solo operation. Her successes include 20 Tony Awards, as well as several New York Drama Critics, Drama Desk, Drama League, and Outer Critics Circle Awards.

In a 1990 *TheaterWeek* interview, McCann declared that timing is a central consideration in determining whether a play will be successful. "Besides the right timing and the right play, casting is the most essential ingredient," she added. "It's not going to happen often, but the goal is to be the producer of a play in which the actor's chemistry combined with the material breaks through to the heart of the writer."

The producer usually is not involved with the artistic direction of the production; however, because the producer hires—and, if necessary, fires—the artistic personnel, he or she puts a personal stamp on the finished production.

## The Director

Since the director of a play is responsible for its interpretation, many directors are tempted to make all the choices for the actors. That is not the case with Tony Award-winning director Lloyd Richards, who explained in an *American Theatre* interview, "My desire is to lead the actor to discover what I want him to discover so that he feels it is his own. He has to perform it, so it should come out of him rather than out of something I said." Apparently this preference goes back to Richards's own days as an actor, when he didn't appreciate directors who gave him line readings.

Richards has served as dean of the prestigious Yale School of Drama, director of the Yale Repertory Theatre, artistic director of the National Playwrights Conference of the Eugene O'Neill Theatre Center, president of Theatre Communications Group, and the first representative from a not-for-profit professional (regional) theatre to the National Council for the Arts. His collaboration with playwright August Wilson (p. 456) began in 1982, and over the years the two have won an impressive array of awards, including Tonys for *Fences*, for which Wilson also won a Pulitzer Prize.

Richards was born in Toronto and grew up in Detroit. His father, a Jamaican-born carpenter, died when Richards was nine, and his mother, who became blind when Richards was in his teens, raised five children alone during the Depression. Richards was a prelaw student at Wayne State University until World War II interrupted his studies. After serving in the army he returned to college, but soon acting in college productions replaced his interest in the legal profession. While still in Detroit he hosted a radio jazz show called "The Good Will Hour."

By the 1950s he had moved to New York City, where he worked in radio, Off Broadway and on Broadway in *Freight*. (Off Broadway refers to the small, often experimental, theatres located outside Broadway, the principal New York theatre district.) The turning point came in 1959, when he directed his first Broadway production, Lorraine Hansberry's New York Drama Critics Circle Award-winning *A Raisin in the Sun*. After that he never returned to acting.

The entire Richards family is involved in show business. Richards is married to actor Barbara Davenport. One son, Scott, is a composer, and the other, Thomas, is a protégé of director Jerzy Grotowski.

Richards's belief in the potential of America's regional theatre is evident in his desire to share the work he does with regional theatres all over the country. He explains that when he first began as artistic director of the National Playwrights Conference he received about 300 scripts a year. Now the figure is 1,300 to 1,800 submissions annually, and Richards detects better writing even in the scripts he cannot accept for production. He attributes this improvement largely to the growth of the regional theatre.

## The Stage Manager

Sarahjane Allison, who is the theatre manager and executive stage manager for the Interact Theatre at Cuesta College in San Luis Obispo, California, is a strong believer in education. She says it's the base from which theatre can grow, adding, "It doesn't matter if you want to work in a tech, acting, or directing job; for any job in theatre you need a strong base to grow from." She also encourages people interested in theatre to take any class they can, to try every different job. "You have to know a little bit about everything when you work in a company."

Allison herself has a bachelor of arts degree from Western Washington University, where her major was theatre, with an emphasis in technical and stage management. Her collegiate production experience includes acting as props supervisor at Essex Community College, scene technician at the Porthouse Summer Theatre, lighting technician at the Harford Opera Theatre in Baltimore, Maryland, lighting designer for the Bellingham Theatre Guild, and stage manager at the regionals of the American College Theatre Festival and for Full Circle Tour, a university group that toured high schools and community colleges in the state of Washington. Her collegiate career certainly bears out her belief in the value of having experience in as many areas of theatre as possible.

Beginning her professional career as a lighting technician with the Vancouver Symphony, Allison went on to work as stage manager for Prince George's Civic Opera Company and then for the Great American Melodrama and Vaudeville in Bakersfield, California. She spent several years touring with Ringling Brothers and Barnum and

Bailey Circus, first as lighting director and sound technician, then as assistant performance director, and finally as performance director of the Blue Unit of the circus. When asked what the most difficult aspect of the job was, Allison answered that communication was the most difficult part because there were 18 different languages spoken in the company. She explained, "Rehearsal would be in English, and then a Chinese interpreter would translate for the Chinese, a Russian interpreter for the Russians, a Spanish interpreter for the Spaniards, and so on. With all the different languages, it was almost impossible to communicate with each other."

Now, Allison manages the Interact Theatre and acts as executive stage manager to the professional company in residence and the three student companies that share the performance space. She is especially helpful and encouraging to the fledgling student stage managers and finds great satisfaction in seeing them learn and succeed.

## The Actor

Anyone with experience in the theatre knows that every member of a theatre company makes a valuable contribution to the production. For most audience members, however, the actors *are* the show. This places a heavy responsibility on the actor, who must give the best performance possible each time he or she steps on the stage. To ensure a superior level of performance, actor Michael Jeter says he never stops rehearsing.

Jeter, born in 1952 in Lawrenceburg, Tennessee, was one of six children. He attended the University of Memphis, first as a premedical major and then as an acting major. Following graduation he moved to New York City and almost immediately was cast in the 1978 Circle in the Square revival of George S. Kaufman and Moss Hart's *Once in a Lifetime*. Next he appeared in the Public Theatre's production of Mikhail Bulgakov's *The Master and Margarita*. He won a *Theatre World* Award the following year for his work as Straw in David Berry's Vietnam-era play *G. R. Point*.

Jeter followed that part with a variety of roles in Elizabeth Swado's *Alice in Concert,* a musical version of *Alice in Wonderland* that starred Meryl Streep. Next he played an Irish American police officer in *El Bravo,* a reworking of the Robin Hood legend. He worked with famed choreographer Tommy Tune when he took over a part in Caryl Churchill's *Cloud 9*. Later he took over for another actor, Jason Williams, in the Circle in the Square's production of *Greater Tuna*. Since there are only two actors in the show, Michael Jeter played eleven roles and remarked that every time he left the stage he changed clothes!

For the role of Arnold, a mentally retarded adult in Tom Griffin's *The Boys Next Door,* Jeter prepared by spending time in a group home for the mentally retarded. He found it a "joyful experience." The same year, in Jim Geoghan's *Only Kidding!,* the critic Howard Kissel called him "brilliant" as a nervous wreck of a writer.

One of his more recent Broadway appearances was as Kringelein in Luther Davis's *Grand Hotel,* in which he was again directed by Tommy Tune. Edith Oliver, stage critic for *The New Yorker,* called him a "dandy eccentric dancer," and *TheaterWeek* reviewer Ken Mandelbaum said Jeter had "walked off" with the show. Jeter won a Tony Award for that role, and in his acceptance speech, alluding to his personal struggles, he asked anyone watching the awards program who felt hopeless to see Jeter as living proof that life can change and that dreams do come true.

Michael Jeter is familiar to millions of television viewers for his Emmy Award-winning role of Herman Stiles in the TV sitcom *Evening Shade.* His character was the favorite of many, but Jeter remained the true ensemble player, working always for the good of the show.

## The Set Designer

Adrianne Lobel, a set designer whose work ranges from operas and Broadway musicals to Hollywood films and music videos, approaches each project by sketching, sketching, and sketching until something interesting shows up.

Because her parents wrote and illustrated children's books and led rather isolated lives, Lobel decided very early that she wanted to work in a field that involved other people. She went to Art and Design High School in New York City, where she learned to letter and "things like that." At the same time, she was taking evening classes at the Brooklyn Museum School. She was quite serious about painting and wanted to be an Impressionist. But she also felt she should be doing something more collaborative.

After high school, Lobel attended Marlboro College in Vermont for a year. Marlboro had a small theatre department, and Lobel worked in the basement, building sets and making costumes for the productions. The summer after her first year there, she received a scholarship to work as a costume assistant at a summer stock theatre in the Berkshire Mountains. She took responsibility for the props and scenery because no one else seemed interested. Impressed with Lobel's talents, the wardrobe manager suggested she study at the Lester Polakov Studio in New York City.

While at the Polakov Studio, Lobel took a mask-making class with Fred Nihda and a set model-making class from Paul Zalon. She worked for awhile as Zalon's assistant, but wanted to be a designer. She applied to Yale School of Drama and was accepted, but chose to go first to California, where she worked in film rather than theatre.

After two and a half years, Lobel felt ready to attend Yale, where she studied with Tony Award-winning designer Ming Cho Lee. At Yale she met future Broadway director Peter Sellars, with whom she worked on eight productions, including George Gershwin's *My One and Only* and Mozart's opera *The Magic Flute.*

Some of Adrianne Lobel's other credits include such films as Tony Bill's *Five Corners* and Deborah Reinisch's *Ask Me Again,* as well as music videos. She designed the sets for Michael Jackson's music video "Bad," Herbie Hancock's "Hard Rock," and Janet Jackson's "Let's Wait Awhile." When Ronn Smith interviewed Lobel for his book *American Set Design 2,* Lobel described her designs as having a strong logic, adding, "I also think my work is very clean and modern . . . my sets require very good, neat, solid construction."

## The Lighting Designer

In the New York theatre, today's lighting designers are predominantly women, and premier among them is Tharon Musser, who has designed the lighting for more than 100 Broadway shows. She has three Tony Awards and is responsible for establishing lighting design as a category in the Tonys. In 1970, when Musser was asked to buy an ad in the Tony Awards ceremony program, she protested that lighting designers weren't even being recognized by the Tonys. Chuck Bowden, then producer of the ceremonies, called her a few days later to report not only that there would be a lighting design category in the awards, but also that she had been nominated for her work on Betty Comden and Adolph Green's *Applause.*

In the early 1900s the purpose of stage lighting was visibility, and it was considered part of the set designer's job. There was no "painting with lights." The lighting crew hung the lighting instruments and moved them around, often in response to a star's request.

Although lighting may not be the first thing an audience appreciates about a play, it plays a major role in many shows, such as Michael Bennett's *A Chorus Line* and *Dreamgirls*—two shows for which Musser won Tonys. Early in her career she felt she was being typecast as a designer for serious plays, but she managed to make a transition to musicals with *Shinbone Alley.* Other musicals—*Mame, Applause, A Little Night Music,* and *Hallelujah Baby!*—followed.

In an interview with *TheatreWeek* writer Simi Horwitz, Musser commented that the big difference between designing a straight play and a musical is the quantity of lights required for a musical. Lighting plays an important role in the musical, tipping off the audience to the big numbers.

Musser was an early supporter of the computerized lighting board, which can provide valued smoothness and consistency. To those who would find a computerized system too mechanical,

Musser points out that use of the board frees the designer from concerns about a lighting crew member who decides to change things or who forgets a cue.

Throughout her English and philosophy studies at Berea College in Kentucky, Musser did sets and lighting for college productions. Later, at Yale University she decided to specialize in lighting, even though she studied set and costume design as well.

Color is the key ingredient in Musser's designs. She studies the play first. Then, after conferring with the set and costume designers and the director, she decides on the colors that best evoke the desired mood. She explains, "The end result has to look like the creation of one set of eyes, not three. [Lighting design] is a collaborative art."

## The Costume Designer

Until the 1940s, costume design was often seen as an extension of set design and was under the set designer's jurisdiction. According to Tony Award-winning costume designer Patricia Zipprodt, if the set designer was too busy, "the producer might even send his wife or girlfriend out to shop for costumes." In fact, the Scenic Artists Guild did not offer separate costume design examinations for membership until the late 1940s.

Zipprodt, who teaches in the Master of Fine Arts program at Brandeis University in addition to her Broadway design career, was at Wellesley College when the separate costume design examination was finally offered. By the 1950s she had moved to New York City, worked at a variety of jobs, and, while viewing a ballet performance, discovered what she really wanted to do. The ballet was a production of George Balanchine's *La Valse,* with costumes by Karinska. Zipprodt later told *TheaterWeek* writer Simi Horwitz, "I had never seen costumes like those. There was just something extraordinary about the layers of silk and net and beads. And the way the light hit those beads. . . . I knew, as I stared, that that's what I wanted to do for the rest of my life—just design costumes."

Zipprodt grew up in the suburbs of Chicago and intended to be an artist. She feels it's unfortunate that people with ambitions to design costumes don't have a solid background in art, particularly in drawing and design. When she was designing costumes for the Broadway production of James Clavell's *Shogun,* she researched arts books and films depicting Japanese society of the 1600s and 1700s. She wanted not only to provide the historical authenticity required but also to interpret that history in her costume designs.

After deciding she wanted a career in costume design, Zipprodt enrolled at the Fashion Institute of Technology in New York City. After a few semesters of training, she got jobs with apparel companies and later with fashion designers in a variety of entry-level positions. Next, she applied for membership in the Scenic Artists Guild, and she passed the exam the first time. She worked as an assistant to such famous designers as William and Jean Eckhart, Irene Sharaf, and the design group Motley. Now she herself is famous, having designed the costumes for such Broadway hits as Joseph Stein's *Fiddler on the Roof,* James Presson Allen's *Cabaret,* Neil Simon's *Sweet Charity,* and a recent production of Tennessee Williams's *Cat on a Hot Tin Roof.*

## The Choreographer

In 1991 Tommy Tune won his seventh and eighth Tony Awards. He was named Best Director of a Musical and Best Choreographer for *The Will Rogers Follies.* Because he was on tour as Albert in Michael Stewart's *Bye Bye Birdie,* he had to accept the awards via satellite.

This practice of taking Broadway shows on the road so that people all over the country can see first-rate casts is one to which Tune feels strongly committed. In fact, when asked why there had been no Tune-directed or -choreographed show on Broadway between George Gershwin's *My One and Only* in 1983 and *Grand Hotel* in 1990, Tune pointed out that he had been on the road with *My One and Only* for most of that time. He told *TheatreWeek* writer Ken Mandelbaum that he felt a moral responsibility to stay with the show on tour because the role had been created for him.

Describing himself as "a guy who puts on shows," Tune traces his involvement in performing and directing back to the "patio revues" he organized at the age of five in his Houston, Texas, neighborhood. He continued staging shows through elementary school, high school, and summer stock. By 1974 he had won his first Tony Award, for Best Supporting Actor in a musical (Cy Coleman and Dorothy Fields's *Seesaw*). In all, Tune has won Tonys in four categories: Best Supporting Actor in a Musical, Best Actor in a Musical, Best Choreographer, and Best Director of a Musical.

According to actor Karen Akers, who played Raffaella in Tune's production of *Grand Hotel* and who published a journal of her experiences when the company was workshopping (that is, continuing to work on a play that's already in production), Tommy Tune worked closely with his associates and was always willing to. She noted that he is positive in addressing the company, commenting on the good work at the end of a rehearsal. Walter Willson, who played Gustafsson in the same show and who wrote an article about life backstage, mentioned the sense of "company" present in a Tune show. From the yoga breathing exercises at the beginning of each rehearsal day to the hand-holding "circle" formed at half-hour to curtain, the performers connect their energies.

As for his choreography, it has always been imaginative and energetic. He seems eager to take an adventurous leap both mentally and physically in designing the steps of his dances. His own elegant line as he dances and his exuberance is passed along in the choreography to those who do his shows.

Tommy Tune's early work with the late Michael Bennett, famed choreographer of *A Chorus Line,* has left him with lasting admiration for Bennett's work, but Tune is his own person—making his mark on the development of choreography in the American musical.

## The Playwright

British playwright Alan Ayckbourn is known for his witty, brilliant farces. Having written more plays than Noël Coward and as many as Shakespeare, already Ayckbourn would have a place in theatre history based on sheer numbers alone. Popular as well as successful, his work has been translated into 24 languages and performed around the world.

Ayckbourn was born in London to a symphony violinist father and a novelist mother. In school he wrote poetry and joined the drama club, where he was encouraged by a teacher who loved the theatre. After leaving school he worked as a stage manager and eventually as an actor. According to Ayckbourn, he began to take an interest in writing and directing when he realized that his acting ability was only average.

Ayckbourn's ongoing association with England's Stephen Joseph Theatre in the Round began in the 1960s while he was still a drama producer for the British Broadcasting Corporation. By 1970 he had taken over as full-time artistic director at the theatre and began to expand the seasonal theatre into an almost year-round operation. All the while he has adhered to the basic tenets laid down by founder Stephen Joseph: new work, a company structure, and playing in the round (arena staging).

Ayckbourn has never felt obliged to rebel against the tradition of the carefully plotted "well-made play." He says he has a tidy mind and likes symmetry, feeling that if a play's structure is right, it can sustain an evening's entertainment. He reminds people that the term *playwright* suggests the act of crafting a play.

Ayckbourn's love for puzzles and games is evident in the way he plays with shape and form in *The Norman Conquests.* This ambitious production is a group of three plays, all set in the same cottage on the same weekend with the same cast of three couples. The trilogy can be seen in any order and each stands on its own, although it's even more enjoyable to see all three within a short period. The twist is the way Ayckbourn has interwoven the three plays. Events occurring in one play are referred to in another, and audiences enjoy the thrill of recognition as they discover what was happening in another room at the same time.

Ayckbourn says his plays' chief objective is laughter, explaining, "There is nothing I want to say that can't be said through laughter.

. . . I find laughter arising from understanding and recognition between the audience and the stage characters is the most rewarding." For the past few years critics have found a serious thread running through Ayckbourn's recent plays, but in all cases the serious content continues to be conveyed in a lighthearted farcical manner, answering some questions while raising others.

## The Critic

Brendan Gill, a longtime theatre critic for *The New Yorker* magazine, once explained two principles he followed: There is often little to be said about a very bad piece of work except that it is to be avoided, and there is often little to be said about a very good piece of work except that it is to be embraced. He once "avoided" *Dear Oscar* by dismissing it in a brief paragraph, calling it "a sad wisp of a musical which closed after five performances at the Playhouse. It succeeded in making Wilde the prince of bores—a remarkable feat, though unworthy of celebration." And he "embraced" Brian Friel's *Lovers* by observing, "His plays, like his short stories, are modest, gentle, and winning; they take us by the hand instead of by the throat . . ." That wit, that turn of phrase, is a hallmark of Gill's style.

Gill was born in Hartford, Connecticut, and attended school there. In school he not only wrote stories and poems for the literary magazine, he also drew the illustrations, took the copy to the printer, corrected galley proofs, and, in general, assumed responsibility. As a student at Yale University, he wrote for the university literary magazine and was elected editor in his junior year. Around that time he began sending poems and stories to *The New Yorker,* which promptly rejected them.

At Yale, Gill met the Nobel Prize-winning novelist Sinclair Lewis, and upon graduation Gill was asked to be the famous author's secretary. Instead, Gill, who graduated *magna cum laude* and was elected to Phi Beta Kappa, decided to marry and begin his literary career. After several weeks of flooding *The New Yorker* with carefully revised poems and having them rejected, Gill dashed off a short piece describing a fictional meeting between Sinclair Lewis and a Dr. McGrady, and the magazine accepted it. That success was followed by another story and then several others. Within a year he had moved on to writing "Reporter at Large" pieces. Soon he was invited to New York City and offered a job in *The New Yorker's* "Talk of the Town" department. Later, he wrote movie reviews. In 1967, Gill became the drama editor.

Although he says he received little mail, in his book *Here at The New Yorker* he does tell of an occasional exchange of ideas with playwrights such as Edward Albee. In summing up his professional career, Gill explained, "I started at the place where I most wanted to be—*The New Yorker* magazine—and with much pleasure . . . I have remained there ever since."

# Glossary

**PRONUNCIATION KEY**

| | | | | | | | | | |
|---|---|---|---|---|---|---|---|---|---|
| a | bat | ėr | her | oi | soil | ch | change | ə | a in along |
| ā | cage | i | hit | ou | scout | ng | song | | e in shaken |
| ä | star | ī | nice | u | up | sh | shell | | i in stencil |
| â | dare | o | cot | u̇ | put | th | think | | o in lemon |
| e | bet | ō | old | ü | tube | TH | there | | u in bus |
| ē | even | ô | ornate | | | zh | pleasure | | |

## A

**accent** the specific sound qualities of the speech of a region

**act curtain** a curtain made of lighter fabric used between scenes of a play, often decorated to reflect the mood or theme of a play

**act** the major division of a play

**acting areas** spaces onstage defined by the blocking patterns of actors in a scene

**ad lib** See **improvise.**

**age** to make a costume or other item look old

**ambient light** existing surrounding light that may interfere with a projected image

**amplifier** an electronic device that provides a power supply to speakers and other audio equipment

**antagonist** a person, situation, or the protagonist's own inner conflict that is in opposition to the protagonist's goals

**apron** the acting area of the stage that extends beyond the proscenium arch

**arena stage** a performance space in which the audience sits all around the stage; sometimes called **in-the-round**

**articulation** the clear and precise pronunciation of words

**articulators** the parts of the body that create consonant sounds

**artistic director** the person who hires the director, designers, and cast. In some theatre companies, these duties are handled by a production committee.

**aside** a statement by an actor spoken half to him- or herself and half to the audience

**assistant director** the person who assists the director by organizing the rehearsal process, coordinating rehearsal schedules, working with individual actors, and taking the director's notes

**audition** an interview-like opportunity in which actors are able to demonstrate their talents, meet the person hiring the cast, and leave impressions of themselves

**auditorium** the area of a theatre where the audience sits

**auditors** the individuals who conduct the auditions, usually the director and assistant director

## B

**back wall** a wall separating the stage house from the backstage area. Doors in the back wall allow large pieces of scenery to be brought onstage.

**backing** flats, draperies, or drops placed on the offstage side of openings in the set, such as windows and doors, to block the backstage area from the audience's view

**backlot** an outdoor soundstage at a film picture studio in which open-air scenes can be constructed and filmed

**backstage** all areas of a stage other than the acting area that are out of sight of the audience

**backstitch** a sewing stitch formed by taking one

forward stitch and then beginning a short stitch from the back of it

**balcony** upper floor in an auditorium that projects out over the main floor and provides additional seating for the audience

**ballad opera** a burlesque form of Italian opera, originating in England in the 1700s, that combined spoken dialogue and songs set to popular tunes

**barn door** an accessory for a Fresnel spotlight that controls the light beam with movable flippers

**base coat** a preliminary coat of paint upon which effects are painted

**basting** a sewing stitch made by long, widely-spaced running stitches, used for temporarily holding hems and seams

**batten** a wood or metal pipe from which stage lights, drops, and scenery are hung

**beat** a smaller section of a scene, divided where a shift in emotion or topic occurs

**bevel cut** See **miter cut.**

**blank verse** unrhymed poetry in which each line has five accented syllables; the verse pattern in which Shakespeare wrote many of his plays

**blending** to diminish the intensity of a makeup color from strongest to lightest

**blocking** coordination of actors' movements onstage

**blocking rehearsals** a phase of rehearsals in which the director and actors work through blocking

**blood pack** for use with stage blood, a sealed plastic bag that is taped to the part of an actor's body that will bleed

**book** the script for a musical

**boom** or **boomerang** an aluminum tripod with a cross bar at the top on which lights are hung; also called a **lighting tree**

**box office** where ticket sales are handled, usually located in the lobby of a theatre

**box set** a feature of realistic theatre, a two- or three- walled set representing the interior of a room

**brace** to anchor scenery to the stage so it doesn't wobble

**Broadway** New York City's principal theatre district

**build** to make a costume or a set piece

**Bunraku** (bün rä´kü) traditional Japanese puppet theatre

**business manager** the person who handles fund-raising, publicity, programs, ticket sales, bill payments, and other business details of running a theatre

**butt joint** a wood joint in which two square-cut boards are joined end-to-face, end-to-edge, edge-to-edge, or end-to-end and fastened with nails or glue and screws

## C

**call** to notify cast and crew of cues, rehearsal times, and the rise and fall of the curtain

**callback** an invitation to an actor to return for a second audition

**call board** a bulletin board for posting rehearsal times, performance changes, and special notices

**cast** (verb) to be chosen to play a specific role in a play; (noun) the group of actors who take the roles in a play

**cast by type** to cast a show by choosing actors who fit a particular character type

**catharsis** an emotional purification or relief

**center** the center of the acting area; centerstage

**character makeup** makeup used to create a specific character in a play. See **straight makeup.**

**choreographer** an artist who designs (choreographs) dances for the stage

**chorus** a group of actors reciting dialogue or singing in unison, often accompanied by synchronized movement. In Greek theatre the chorus functioned as a commentary on and accompaniment to the action of a play.

**cinematographer** the person who designs the way each shot in a film should be lit and filmed

**climax** the turning point in a plot when conflict comes to an emotional crest; the point at which the rising action becomes the falling action

**close-up** a film shot in which an actor's face and shoulders fill the frame

**cold reading** auditioning with a script that you have not had the opportunity to read before the audition

**color-blind casting** casting without regard to race or ethnicity of the characters or actors

**comedy** a light and amusing play that typically has a happy ending

**comedy of manners** a genre of plays popular in England beginning in the late 1600s characterized by ribald wit and fashionable characters and dealing with the vices and follies of the upper classes

**commedia dell'arte** (kō mā ′dē ə del är′tā) a professional form of theatrical improvisation developed in Italy in the 1500s. These farces feature standard plot outlines and stock characters.

**commercial pattern** pattern for making clothes, available in any fabric store

**composer** the person who writes the music for a musical

**constructivism** an antirealist artistic movement developed in Russia shortly before World War I in which stage designs were clearly artificial

**continuity** in film or TV production, the coherence from shot to shot in the same scene

**corral** a courtyard theatre that was a typical performance space in Spain in the 1600s

**cornerblock** a triangular piece of plywood that bridges a corner joint in flat construction, providing extra bracing and support

**costume** any clothing an actor wears onstage for a performance

**costume designer** the person who designs costumes to build or chooses costumes to rent, borrow, or buy for a production

**costume list** breakdown of every character in a play and all of his or her costumes and accessories

**costume plot** a list, by acts and scenes of a play, of each character in a particular scene itemizing each costume piece a character wears for each appearance

**costume shop** a space where costumes can be built, maintained, and stored

**counterweight system** a system of ropes, steel cables, pulleys, and weights used to raise and lower battens on which are hung lights, scenery, or drops

**created sound** self-created sounds or music played live

**credits** a list, usually at the end of a film or TV program, of all the people involved in the production

**cross cut** a basic saw cut in which the wood is cut across the grain

**cross** to move from one place onstage to another

**cue** a signal for something to happen

**cue line** a final line that signals an actor to begin the next speech

**cue tape** on a show tape, a piece of nonrecording leader tape inserted between segments of tape with recorded sound

**cyclorama** or **cyc** a background drop or curtain, hung on a U-shaped batten around the three sides of the stage; serves to mask the backstage area during scenery shifts

# D

**dead zone** an area of a stage lighted by only one bright light

**deck** the top of a platform

**decorations** lace, trim, or appliqué materials applied to costumes

**decorative props** items on a set, such as curtains, pictures, linens, knickknacks, and magazines, that offer clues about the lifestyles of characters in a play

**dénouement** (dā nü maN′) the final resolution of the conflict in a plot

**design team** those who design and coordinate a production's set, props, lighting, sound, costumes, and makeup

**diagonal** a stage composition of two actors who are not on the same plane or in a shared position

**dialect** language features peculiar to the speech of a particular region

**diaphragmatic breathing** a breathing technique useful to actors that increases air capacity and improves breath control

**diction** language, or meaning expressed in words; one of the six elements of tragedy set forth by Aristotle

**dimmer** an electrical device that controls the brightness of lights

**dinner theatre** theatre presented to an audience that is dining at tables around the performance space. Usually dinner is included in the price of the theatre ticket

**director** the person who oversees the entire process of staging a production

**direct emphasis** a stage picture in which the focus is on one actor

**director's notes** comments by the director on the performance of each actor and on the production in general, usually given before or after rehearsals

**disperse dye** a dye for synthetic fabrics that results in a deep shade of color

**dissolve** in film and TV, the visual effect achieved when one picture is faded in while a previous picture is faded out

**dithyramb** in the theatre of Ancient Greece, a hymn sung and danced by a chorus of 50 men to the Greek god Dionysius at annual Dionysian festivals

**diversified emphasis** a stage picture in which there is a frequent change of focus

**domestic tragedy** a form of British theatre popular in the early 1700s that showed the destruction of a good person who yields to temptation. See **sentimental comedy.**

**downstage** the stage area toward the audience

**drama** a play, film, or TV program dealing with a serious subject matter, but that does not necessarily have a disastrous ending

**dramatic conflict** refers to the conflict in which the main character in a play engages; one of two elements out of which most scripts grow. There are four types of dramatic conflict: 1) person against person; 2) person against self; 3) person against society; 4) person against nature or fate.

**dramatic unities** See **unities.**

**dramaturg** a special consultant who provides specific, in-depth knowledge and literary resources to a director, producer, or entire theatre company

**dress** to add decorative props to a set

**dress parade** an onstage wardrobe check under stage lighting and with actors in makeup, providing the director and costume designer with an opportunity to address any last-minute changes

**dress rehearsals** the final phase of rehearsals before an opening night performance, run with all technical elements in place and without interruption

**dressing list** an itemized list of everything an actor wears during each scene of a play

**dressing rooms** areas where actors put on makeup and change into and store costumes

**drop end** the end of a lighting batten where the cables drop to the floor

**drop** or **backdrop** a large canvas or muslin curtain that hangs at the back of the stage setting

**dry brush** a painting technique in which a brush is dipped in paint, scraped nearly dry, and then streaked across a surface; often used to create wood-grain effects

**dry run** a run-through of a TV program without tech crews

**dry tech** a technical rehearsal without actors present

**duoemphasis** a stage picture in which there are two equal focuses

**dutchman** a strip of fabric covering the crack between two flats to enhance the illusion that a series of joined flats comprise a wall

## E

**emotional memory** the technique of calling upon your own memories of emotions to understand a character's emotions

**epic theatre** a theatrical movement of the 1920s and 1930s characterized by the use of such artificial devices as cartoons, posters, and film sequences in order to distance the audience from theatrical illusion and allow them to focus on the play's message

**epilogue** a concluding speech to a play that follows the action of the play

**equalizer** an electronic device that balances the blended sounds from a mixer

**exposition** the beginning part of a plot that provides important background information

**expressionism** an artistic movement that developed in Europe, especially Germany, around the time of World War I; expressionism presents a subjective view of reality that is often fragmented, exaggerated, or distorted.

**extreme close-up** a film shot in which a part of an actor's face or a small object fills the frame

## F

**falling action** the series of events following the climax of a plot

**farce** comedy with exaggerated characterizations, abundant physical or visual humor, and often an improbable plot

**feature story** a news story that adds depth and

color to an event as it instructs, entertains, or interprets the event, typically in a tone that is informative and friendly

**fight director** a directing specialist who choreographs both armed and unarmed fight scenes and stunts onstage

**fill light** one of two lights focused on a lighting area that fills in shadows created by the key light

**final cut** the finished film or videotape

**fine cut** the second draft of a film or videotape

**fire curtain** metal or fireproof fabric across the front of a stage that prevents fire from spreading

**fitting** a costume session in which an actor tries on a costume and the designer and costume crew assess any necessary alterations

**flat** a set piece consisting of a lightweight frame covered with canvas, muslin, or wood

**flat dock** a storage device for flats in which the flats are stored vertically and accessed like books from a bookshelf

**float a flat** to lower a flat to the ground by positioning one foot along the bottom rail and letting the flat fall gently

**fly space** the area above a stage where lights, drops, and scenery may be flown, or suspended on wire ropes

**fly** to be raised or lowered on lines in the fly space

**focus** the intended point of interest onstage

**foil** a character whose personality and physical appearance contrast with those of the protagonist

**footage** a length of exposed film

**found sounds** sounds found in different environments such as zoos, construction sites, and playgrounds

**foundation** makeup applied to the entire face to provide a base of uniform color

**fourth wall** an imaginary wall between the audience and the actors in a representational play

**frame** the rectangular-shaped area of film onto which is recorded what is seen by the camera in a minute portion of each shot

**front elevation** a scale drawing showing the front view of the set as if it were flattened out onto a single plane

**front-of-house staff** members of a production who are involved with nonstage-related concerns such as ticket sales, seating, concessions, auditorium maintenance, and opening and closing the theatre

**front-screen projection** a method of projection in which the slide projector is situated somewhere in front of the projection screen

**full mask** a mask that covers the entire face

**functionaries** minor characters whose actions are more important than who they are

## G

**gel** a thin piece of colored plastic, available in a wide array of colors, that can be cut and fitted to a light to color the beam directed onto the stage

**genre** classification by type; a distinct classification of literature

**gesture** an expressive movement of the body or limbs

**gobo** a thin metal template with a pattern punched out attached to a lighting instrument to create patterned or textured lighting effects

**grand drape** front curtain on a stage, usually made of luxurious fabric in deep colors

**green room** the lounge area where actors may wait while not onstage or greet members of the audience after a performance

**grid** or **gridiron** a steel framework above a stage to which lines are attached to fly scenery

**griot** (grē´ō) West African oral historian

**grip** a member of the stage crew who shifts scenery

**ground plan** a top-view drawing of the floor plan of a set, usually in scale

## H

**half mask** a mask that covers the top half of the face

**hanamichi** (ho no mē chē) in Kabuki theatre, a raised passageway that extends from downstage right through the audience to the back of the auditorium

**hand props** items that are handled or carried by an actor in a play, including such things as books, letters, and fans

**hang** to attach and position a stage light on a batten

**hood** an accessory for a Fresnel spotlight that fits

into the color-frame slot and reduces the spill of light to a circular pattern; also called a **top hat**

**hook** an element in a script that grabs the audience's interest

**hot spot** an area of a stage lighted by more than three bright lights; an intense circle of light created when a projector lens is seen through the screen

**house** the auditorium, or the area where the audience sits

**housing** the metal structure that encloses a lighting system

**hubris** (hyü´bris) reckless pride; in some Greek tragedies, hubris is the main character's tragic flaw and contributes to the character's downfall.

## I

**improvise** to speak or to act without a script

**inciting incident** the event that sets in motion the action of a plot

**inflection** variety in speech reflecting changing thoughts and emotions

**instrument schedule** a chart listing all the technical information about lighting instruments used in a production

## J

**jack** an anchoring option using triangular-frame units attached to a flat and weighted

**jackknife set** a set that is built on a large wagon and pivoted onto the stage from the wings

**joists** parallel boards that run perpendicular to two end boards and serve as support for a platform

## K

**Kabuki** (kə bü´kē) one of traditional forms of Japanese theatre, originating in the 1600s, that combines stylized acting, elaborate costumes, and musical accompaniment

**key light** the brighter of two lights focused on a lighting area

**keystone** a small piece of plywood that bridges a toggle joint in flat construction, providing extra bracing and support

**keystoning** the distortion that occurs when an image is projected at an angle onto a screen or other projection surface

**kimono** (kə mō´ nō) a floor-length robe with long, flowing sleeves

## L

**lamp** the source of light in a lighting instrument

**lap joint** or **overlap joint** a wood joint in which the face of one board is attached to the face of another and fastened with nails or glue and screws

**lashing** a method of temporarily joining flats in which rope is laced through specialized hardware and tied off

**lead** the opening paragraph of a news article that includes answers to the questions who?, what?, where?, when?, and why?

**leading center** the part of a character's body that leads in movements and reflects the nature of the character

**left** the left side of the stage from the perspective of an actor facing the audience

**lens** the part of a lighting instrument that shapes the light from the lamp

**level** the height of an actor's head onstage

**life mask** a mask made by taking an impression of a person's face

**light booth** or **sound booth** a booth at the top of the balcony that houses the technician who controls the lights, music, or sound effects

**lighting** any illumination of the set and actors during a performance

**lighting areas** areas on the stage floor, 8 to 12 feet in diameter, where light beams strike

**lighting designer** the person who develops a lighting concept and design for a production. The lighting designer oversees installation and operation of lighting for the production.

**lighting key** a simple plan showing angles and colors for each lighting area

**lighting plot** a plan, usually drawn to scale, showing the placement of lighting instruments

**lighting tree** See **boom.**

**lobby** the area of a theatre where the audience gathers before and after performances and during breaks

**location** a real setting where a production may be filmed or videotaped, rather than on a soundstage or backlot; off the studio lot

**long shot** a film shot that includes an actor's entire body and part of the foreground or background

**lot** the site of a film or TV studio

**lyricist** the person who writes the words for the music in a musical

## M

**makeup** cosmetics and hairstyling that an actor uses to emphasize facial features or to add age or other special qualities called for by a character

**makeup designer** the person who determines what kind of makeup each actor will wear, designs specialty makeup for actors, and supervises the makeup artists and makeup crew

**makeup plan** a form on which you can record your makeup design decisions

**makeup room** in some theatres, a room separate from the dressing rooms that is devoted to makeup

**mask** (verb) to use backing, such as flats, draperies, or drops, to hide backstage areas from the view of the audience; (noun) an artificial covering for all or part of the face

**masque** an expensive, lavish spectacle, popular in the English court of the early 1600s, that combined a huge cast, gorgeous costumes, beautiful scenery, music, and elaborate stagecraft

**master cue sheet** a list of all lighting and sound cues, scenery shifts, prop use, and costume changes

**master gesture** a characteristic gesture

**matte** in film and TV, a visual effect achieved when a false background or another background replaces the original background of a scene

**medium shot** a film shot in which the face, shoulders, and part of an actor's body fill the frame

**melodrama** a dramatic form popular in the 1800s, characterized by cliff-hanging plots, heart-tugging emotional appeals, the celebration of virtue, and a strongly moralistic tone

**mezzanine** the balcony closest to the main floor

**mime** an art form based on pantomime using conventionalized gestures to express ideas rather than to represent actions; a performer of mime

**miniseries** a TV program, often based on a popular book or social event, that runs from 4 to 16 hours and is usually shown in 2-hour installments

**miracle play** one of the principal types of medieval European drama; a miracle play told the lives of saints and martyrs.

**miter cut** a basic saw cut in which the wood is cut at an angle

**miter joint** a wood joint in which two boards cut at an angle are joined using glue and corrugated fasteners or glue and nails or screws; a kind of butt joint

**mixer** an electronic device that mixes and blends sounds from several different sources

**monologue** a story, speech, or scene performed by one actor alone

**morality play** one of the principal types of medieval European drama; a morality play presented personified virtues and vices in dramas depicting the moral struggle of the soul.

**motivation** a character's reason for doing or saying things

**multimedia** theatrical performances incorporating a variety of artistic and technological media

**music director** the person who shapes the musical tone of a show

**musical theatre** a type of entertainment containing music, songs, and usually dance

**mystery play** one of the principal types of medieval European drama that depicted episodes from the Bible.

## N

**naturalism** a literary movement with views based on contemporary scientific theory and the belief that everything in life is determined by heredity and environment

**neoclassicism** a theatrical movement based on the theories of the Greek philosopher Aristotle and the Roman poet Horace, influential throughout Europe in the 1600s. Neoclassical theory set down rules for playwriting including the division of plays into five acts; the dramatic unities of time, place, and action; and purity of genre.

**news release** a short factual description of an event

**Noh** (nō) one of the traditional forms of Japanese theatre. In Noh drama masked male actors employ highly stylized dance and poetry to tell stories of ghosts, doomed love, and revenge.

**nontraditional casting** casting that ignores the general conventions of casting by type

**nose putty** a soft, pliable substance used to alter the shape of the nose, chin, or forehead

## O

**objective** a character's goal or intention

**obstacle** something that stands between a character and his or her ability to meet an objective or achieve a goal

**off book** rehearsing without a script after lines are memorized

**on book** rehearsing with a script

**open** to keep your face and the front of your body visible to the audience as much as possible

**optical train** the part of a scenic projector that holds the lamp, various lenses, and a slide

**option** the offer of an opportunity to buy the rights to produce a show during a particular time frame

**orchestra** the seats in an auditorium that are nearest the stage; in Greek theatre, a semicircular stone pavement with an altar in the center; a group of musicians who play during a performance

**orchestra pit** the area immediately in front of the stage where the **orchestra** sits. The orchestra pit may extend underneath the stage floor.

**outcome** result of an action taken by a character or characters to overcome an obstacle and achieve an objective

**overdraw** to outline the lips beyond the natural line to make them appear fuller

**overlap joint** See **lap joint.**

## P

**pacing** the tempo of a performance as it progresses

**paint shop** in some theatres, a separate room where scenery is painted after it is built

**pantomime** to act without words through facial expression and gesture

**paper tech** a meeting of the stage crew and the stage manager to run through cues on paper and create a master cue sheet

**papier mâché** (pā′pər mə shā′) a technique for building props and set pieces using torn strips of newspaper and a pastelike mixture of wheat paste or flour and water molded onto a wire frame

**patch bay** an interconnecting device for a lighting system that makes it possible to group lights together on circuits devoted to specific acting or lighting areas. Also called a **patch panel.**

**Peking Opera** a tradition established by acting companies in the Chinese capital in the 1800s, characterized by an emphasis on the actors' performances, minimal sets and props, elaborate costumes, and stylized movements and songs

**performance art** a nontraditional theatrical genre that incorporates a variety of art forms, including music, dance, and multimedia, and may be performed in traditional and nontraditional spaces

**phrasing** how you divide your speeches into smaller parts, with pauses added to create emphasis and a rhythmic pattern of sounds and silences

**Pit** in the Globe Theatre, the open area in front of the galleries (or covered seating), which provided standing room for people who couldn't afford gallery seats

**pitch** how high or low your voice is

**plane** the depth of an actor's position onstage

**platform** a set piece with a solid top and braced legs, built to support the weight of actors, furniture, and props

**plot** the structure of a play, including the exposition, inciting incident, rising action, climax, falling action, and dénouement

**polishing rehearsals** a phase of rehearsals in which actors polish movements, line delivery, and characterizations and in which technical elements of the production are integrated. These rehearsals proceed without interruption, unless there are major problems.

**posture** your customary way of holding your body

**preblocking** blocking on paper that a director does before blocking rehearsals begin

**presentational style** theatrical style in which the actors acknowledge the presence of the audience

**prime coat** a preliminary coat of paint that serves as a uniform base for successive layers of paint

**principal** an actor who has a major role in a musical

**producer** the person who oversees the business details of a theatrical production

**production concept** how the play should look and feel

**production model** a scale model of a set and all its set pieces

**production number** a large-scale performance within a musical, usually combining both song and dance

**production team** the director, producer, and their staffs, and the designers who work together to design and coordinate the production

**profile** a scenic element cut from a large sheet of plywood and attached to a flat using keystones

**project** to make your voice fill the performing space; to cast an image or patterned light onto a screen or other surface

**projection** an image or patterned light cast onto a screen or other surface

**prologue** an introduction to a play. A prologue may be in the form of a monologue by a major character or a commentary by a chorus.

**promptbook** a notebook containing the pages of a script pasted onto larger sheets of blank paper to allow space for notes

**prompter** the person who provides lines for actors when they forget them

**prop master** the person responsible for design and construction or acquisition of props. The prop master manages the prop crew.

**prop plot** a list of props needed for each scene in a play

**prop shop** in some theatres, a separate space where props are constructed or stored

**prop table** place where all items carried onstage by the actors are located

**property** or **prop** anything that an actor handles onstage as well as furniture and other items used to enhance the set

**proscenium arch** the frame around a proscenium stage

**proscenium stage** a performance space in which the audience views the action as if through a picture frame

**proskenion** (prō skē´nē on) in Greek theatre, a framework located in front of the skene that supported a wide, shallow stage

**protagonist** the main character of a play and the character with which the audience identifies most strongly

**publicist** a public relations director whose job it is to advertise a show and encourage potential audience members to support and attend a production

**pull** to use an item from stock

**pull/rent/buy/borrow/build list** a means of organizing costume acquisition by identifying the actor, character, and costume pieces required and how to acquire each

## Q

**quality** whether your voice is shrill, nasal, raspy, breathy, booming, and so on

## R

**rails** the two shorter, horizontal top and bottom pieces of a flat frame

**raked** performance space in which the stage floor is slanted upward toward the back of the stage

**rasa** in Indian drama, a classification of plays according to a dominant mood, such as comic, pathetic, or heroic

**read-through** a complete reading of a play aloud by the assembled cast, usually at the first rehearsal

**Reader's Theatre** a performance created by reading a script based on a literary work

**realism** a style of writing in which the author tries to represent life situations as they really are

**rear-screen projection** a method of projection in which the slide projector is situated behind the projection screen

**recorded sounds** recorded music and sound effects available on tape and CD

**reflector** the part of a lighting instrument that reflects the light from the lamp

**rendering** a finished representation of a set or costume, produced with colored pencil, paint, pastel, marking pens, or computer graphics

**representational style** theatrical style in which the actors do not acknowledge the presence of the audience, but try to duplicate life

**resonance** a quality caused by vibration that enriches vocal tone

**resonators** the parts of the body that create vowel sounds

**Restoration comedy** See **comedy of manners.**

**rigging** the way in which mobile scenery and lights are mounted and controlled

**right** the right side of the stage from the perspective of an actor facing the audience

**rip cut** a basic saw cut in which the wood is cut with the grain

**rising action** the middle part of a plot, consisting of complications and discoveries that create conflict

**role** a part in a play

**Romanticism** a literary movement that, in drama, emphasized heroism and sentiment, featuring extraordinary characters and melodramatic plots

**rough cut** the first draft of a film or videotape

**royalty** a fee paid for producing a written work

**run a flat** to carry a flat from one place to another

**run of the show** the series of performances from opening to closing

**running stitch** a sewing stitch made by pulling the needle in and out of the fabric in a straight line

**rushes** or **dailies** unedited film or videotape footage

## S

**safety cord** a two-foot length of wire with a loop at one end and a snap clip at the other used to prevent lighting instruments from falling from a batten or lighting tree

**saint play** See **miracle play.**

**samisen** (sam´ i sen) a three-stringed instrument used in Kabuki theatre

**scale** at a fixed ratio to the full size

**scenario** a standard plot outline

**scene heading** a heading appearing in the left margin of a screenplay that contains information about the setting of a scene; also called a **slug line.**

**scene** the basic structural element of a play; each scene deals with a significant crisis or confrontation. In filmmaking, a scene is a segment of continuous action that can be recorded in one place with one camera.

**scene shop** the place where scenery and props are built; the stage crew's center of operations

**scenery** onstage decoration to help establish the time and place of a play

**screen** to project or view film footage

**screenplay** the script for a film

**scrim** a drop made from sharkstooth scrim or theatrical gauze and dyed or lightly painted, which are transparent when lit from behind

**script** the text of a play

**scull cap** a latex cap that covers the head like a hairless wig; used to create the effect of a bald head, or with the addition of crepe hair, a receding hairline

**scumbling** the wet blending of several hues of paint in patterns created with curved or straight brush strokes

**seam** a line of stitches joining two or more pieces of fabric

**seam allowance** the distance between the edge of the fabric and the seam. Standard seam allowance is ⅝ inches wide.

**secondary characters** characters in a play other than the **protagonist** or **antagonist**

**secondary emphasis** a stage picture in which one focus is subordinante to another focus

**sectional** design plan showing a vertical or horizontal slice of a set

**selvage** the finished edge of a piece of fabric

**sense memory** memories of sights, sounds, smells, tastes, and textures; used to help define a character in a certain situation

**sentimental comedy** a form of British comedy popular in the early 1700s that emphasized triumphant virtue rather than laughter. See **domestic tragedy.**

**set** the onstage physical space and its structures in which the actors perform

**set designer** the person who develops the concept for and designs a set

**set props** furniture, appliances, lamps, and rugs that help establish a play's era and the socioeconomic status of the characters

**setting the time** place and social situation in which the action of a literary work takes place

**setup** in filmmaking, a new camera position or a change in the composition of a scene in a camera frame

**shared position** a position onstage in which one actor mirrors another actor's body position

**shifting crew** the crew responsible for changing the set from scene to scene

**shooting script** a script in which each individual shot is specified by number and type of shot

**shot** the actual recording of a scene on film or videotape. Also called a **take.**

**show tape** a tape of distinct sound segments played at particular points in a performance

**sight lines** lines indicating visibility of onstage and backstage areas from various points in the house

**situation comedies** or **sitcoms** recurring TV programs, usually weekly, that explore comic situations with the same basic cast of characters

**size** to apply a preliminary coat of paint or a glue mixture to fabric to shrink and tighten the fabric on the frame

**skene** (skē´nē) in Greek theatre, a permanent building at the back of the orchestra

**slate** in film and TV production, a record-keeping device that provides reference information about the production, date, scene, and take number, allowing film editors to synchronize images and sound

**slipstitch** a small, loose sewing stitch looped from the outside of the fabric, under the folded edge, and up; used for hems

**slug line** See **scene heading.**

**soliloquy** See **monologue.**

**sound** the audio portion of a theatrical production, including music, sound effects, and the amplification of the performers' voices

**sound booth** See **light booth.**

**sound designer** the person who determines the kinds of sound needed for a production. The sound designer supervises the sound crew in recording sounds and providing live sounds, setting up sound equipment, and sound playback during a show.

**soundstage** the area of a studio building in which a film or TV program is shot

**spattering** a method for applying paint to scenery in which drops of paint are flung onto a painted surface using quick jerks of a paint brush. Spattering requires a minimum of two colors of paint that are different from the base coat.

**speaker** converts the signal received from the amplifier from electrical to mechanical energy, which can be heard

**spectacle** the technical stagecraft used in presenting a drama; according to Aristotle, the least important of the six elements of tragedy

**spike** (verb) to mark the floor of a rehearsal space with tape to indicate significant parts of a ground plan; (noun) a tape mark on a set that indicates the position of a set piece or a boundary of the set

**spin-off** a TV program that features a character from another popular TV program

**spirit gum** a sticky substance applied to the skin for adhesion of three-dimensional makeup, such as noses, chins, and beards

**splicing** the act of cutting and joining pieces of magnetic recording tape

**stage** (noun) the area of a theatre where the actors perform; (verb) to bring to life onstage

**stage business** movements employing props, costumes, or makeup; used to strengthen the personality of the character

**stage combat** physical conflict onstage, both armed and unarmed

**stage crew** the group of people working on set construction, props, lighting, sound, costumes, and makeup

**stage directions** indications to the director and actors about various aspects of a play, including information on characters, how a play should proceed, how a play should look, and the mood or effects of a play

**stage door** a private theatre entrance for actors and other theatre personnel

**stage house** the area in a theatre that includes the stage and the fly space above the stage

**stage manager** the director's technical liaison backstage during rehearsals and performance

**stage manager's booth** place from which the stage manager calls the show

**stakes** the consequences of an outcome

**Stanislavski method** an introspective method of acting developed by Russian director Konstantin Stanislavski (1863–1938) that requires actors to look inside themselves to find the motivation they need to portray a character accurately

**status quo** a character's present circumstances

**stiffening batten** a piece of lumber attached across the backs of two or three adjacent flats to prevent them from shifting

**stiles** the long vertical side pieces of a flat frame

**stipple sponge** a coarse, spongelike block patted onto makeup to create a textured surface

**stippling** a method of applying paint in dots or short strokes using a sea sponge, wadded up rag, or featherduster

**stock characters** established characters, such as young lovers, neighborhood busybodies, sneaky villains, and overprotective fathers, that are immediately recognizable by an audience

**stock unit** standard set piece that can be adapted and used for various purposes

**storyboard** a series of individual sketches showing a sequence of possible shots for scenes in the script

**straight makeup** stage makeup that enhances your natural features and intensifies your coloring. See **character makeup.**

**strike** to take down the set

**Study** in the Globe Theatre, a curtained recess at the back of the stage

**Sturm und Drang** literally "Storm and Stress," a German Romantic movement of the late 1700s that rejected the tight structure of neoclassicism and embraced the less constrictive dramatic form of William Shakespeare

**subtext** information that is implied but not stated by a character; thoughts or actions of a character that do not express the same meaning as the character's spoken words

**superimposition** in film and TV, a visual effect achieved when one picture is brought on top of another

**swag** a hanging curve of fabric between two points

**symbol** a concrete image used to represent an abstract concept or idea

**synthesizer** an electronic device used to create artificial sounds

## T

**tableau** a silent and motionless depiction of a scene, often from a picture

**tape** to record on videotape

**tape loop** a piece of magnetic recording tape with the ends joined together so that the sound recorded on it repeats. Tape loops are used for sounds that must continue for an extended period, such as rainfall or crickets.

**Tarras** (terrace) a balcony above the stage in the Globe Theatre that served as another acting area

**tech rehearsal** or **tech run** a rehearsal dedicated to coordinating, practicing, and perfecting the technical operations of a production

**teleplay** a TV script

**tempo** how fast or slow you speak

**texturize** to alter the appearance of a fabric by such means as paint, dyes, and bleach.

**theatre of alienation** See **epic theatre.**

**theatre of cruelty** a form of theatre employing nonverbal communication, developed by the French avant-garde playwright, actor, and director Atonin Artaud in the 1920s and 1930s

**theatre of the absurd** a theatrical movement beginning in the 1950s in which playwrights created works representing the universe as unknowable and humankind's existence as meaningless

**theatrical agent** a professional who promotes and sells the work of playwrights and actors

**theme** the underlying meaning of a literary work

**thespian** an actor

**three-dimensional scenery** stock units such as platforms and stair units, as well as objects such as buildings, trees, rocks, and other sculptural forms

**through line** the major action of a play and one of two elements out of which most scripts grow

**throw** the distance light can be cast from a lighting instrument

**thrust stage** a combination of the proscenium and the arena stages, with the audience sitting on two or three sides of the acting area

**thumbnail sketches** preliminary sketches or rough drawings

**Tiring House** in the Globe Theatre, a permanent structure on the stage that served as a background for all scenes

**toenail** a way to join two boards in which a nail is driven at a 60° angle from the first board into the second

**toggles** the horizontal center pieces of a flat frame

**top hat** See **hood.**

**track** a path along which information is recorded electronically

**tragedy** a form of drama in which the main character suffers disaster

**trailer** a film preview to be shown as coming attractions in movie theatres

**transition** movement, gesture, or words that acts as a bridge between beats in a monologue; verbal or visual connection that separates and links scenes

**triangle** a stage composition utilizing diagonals on each leg

**truck** See **wagon.**

**two shot** a medium film shot that includes two actors

## U

**understudy** someone who learns a role for the purpose of performing in the absence of the actor cast in that role

**unified aniline dye** a dye for most fabrics that results in a deep shade of color

**union dyes** commercial dyes available in supermarkets and fabric stores

**unities** single action, time, and place that lend structure to drama; derived from Renaissance interpretations of Aristotle's *Poetics.*

**upstage** (noun) the stage area away from the audience; (verb) to stand upstage of another actor on a proscenium stage, forcing the downstage actor to turn away from the audience to communicate with the upstage actor; to steal the focus of a scene

## V

**video assist** a piece of equipment attached to a film camera that allows the director to see the framing of a scene as it is shot

**voice-over** a recording of a voice that plays over other sounds

**volume** how loud or soft your voice is

## W

**wagon** a flat or platform rigged with wheels

**well-made plays** (European theatre in the late 1800s) plays that featured formulaic, often melodramatic, studies of middle-class domestic life; (recent theatre) plays with a traditional plot structure.

**whiteface** makeup generally worn by mimes, consisting of white foundation on the face with accentuated eyes and mouth

**wings** the left and right sides of a stage immediately outside the **scenery,** unseen by the audience

**wipe** in film and TV, a visual effect achieved when one shot succeeds a previous shot by wiping it off the screen

**work print** a print of a film used for cutting and editing

**working rehearsals** a phase of rehearsals during which actors work on exploring and building explore characterization, often through improvisation

## Y

**yoke** the handle of a lighting instrument

**yugen** (yü gen) the basic aesthetic element of Japanese Noh drama, defined as "mystery"

# Text Acknowledgments

**48** Niane, D. T. From *Sundiata, an Epic of Old Mali* by D. T. Niane translated by G. D. Pickett. Reprinted by permission of Addison Wesley Longman Ltd. **69** Sophocles. From *Antigone* from *Three Theban Plays* by Sophocles, translated by Robert Fagles, Translation copyright ©1982 by Robert Fagles. Used by permission of Viking Penguin, a division of Penguin Books USA Inc. **158** *The Complete Works of Shakespeare,* edited by David Bevington, 4th ed. (Scott, Foresman, 1992). **176** Miller, Arthur. Ground plan (drawing) for *Death of a Salesman* by Arthur Miller. Copyright ©1949 by Jo Mielziner. Copyright © Renewed 1976, Jo Mielziner. Reprinted by permission of Dramatists Play Service, Inc. **196** Wilbur, Richard. Excerpt from Act II, scene iv in *Tratuffe* by Molière, copyright ©1963, 1962, 1961 and renewed 1991, 1990, 1989 by Richard Wilbur, reprinted by permission of Harcourt Brace & Company. CAUTION: Professionals and amateurs are hereby warned that these translations, being fully protected under the copyright laws of the United States of America, the British Empire, including the Dominion of Canada, and all other countries which are signatories to the Universal Copyright Convention and the International Copyright Union, is subject to royalty. All rights, including professional, amateur, motion picture, recitation, lecturing, public reading, radio broadcasting, and television, are strictly reserved. Particular emphasis is laid on the question of readings, permission for which must be secured from the author's agent in writing. Inquiries on professional rights (except for amateur rights) should be addressed to Mr. Gilbert Parker, Curtis Brown, Ltd., 10 Astor Place, New York, New York 10003; inquiries on translation rights should be addressed to Harcourt Brace & Company, Publishers, Orlando, FL 32887. The amateur acting rights of *Tartuffe* are controlled exclusively by the Dramatists Play Service, Inc., 440 Park Avenue South, New York, New York. No amateur performance of the play may be given without obtaining in advance the written permission of the Dramatists Play Service, Inc., and paying the requisite fee. **280** Ridley, M. R. Facsimile of text of *Macbeth,* New Temple Shakespeare, edited by M. R. Ridley (1935). Reprinted by permission of J. M. Dent & Sons Ltd. Publishers, London. **299** Shiko, Okamoka. From *The Zen Substitue* by Okamoka Shiko, English adaptation by John R. Brandon and Tamako Niwa. Copyright ©1966 by Samuel French, Inc. Reprinted by permission. CAUTION: Professionals and amateurs are hereby warned *The Zen Substitute* being fully protected under the copyright laws of the United States of America, the British Commonwealth countries including Canada, and the other countries of the Copyright Union, is subject to a royalty. All rights, including professional, amateur, motion picture, recitation, public reading, radio, television and cable broadcasting, and the rights of translation into foreign languages, are strictly reserved. Any inquiry regarding the availability of performance rights, or the purchase of individual copies of the authorized acting edition, must be directed to Samuel French Inc., 45 West 25th Street, NY, NY 10010 with other locations in Hollywood and Toronto, Canada. **330** Mamet, David. From *Uncle Vanya* by Anton Chekhov, adapted by David Mamet. Copyright ©1988, 1989 by David Mamet. Used by permission of Grove/Atlantic, Inc. **430** Beckett, Samuel. From *Waiting For Godot* by Samuel Beckett. Copyright ©1954 by Grove Press, Inc.; copyright renewed ©1982 by Samuel Beckett. Used by permission of Grove/Atlantic, Inc. **460** Wilson, August. From *Seven Guitars* by August Wilson. Copyright ©1996 by August Wilson. Used by permission of Dutton Signet, a division of Penguin Books USA Inc. **483** *Diary of the Chair: A Performance Art Piece* by Mary Hawley and Matthew Evans.

# Illustration Acknowledgments

All illustrations not credited are the property of NTC/Contemporary Publishing Group, Inc. Illustrations are by Mitch Lopata, Jim Buckley, and Maj-Britt Hagsted.

## Cover

*Changes of Heart* by Pierre Carlet de Chamblain de Marivaux, directed by Steven Wadsworth, actor John Michael Higgins, McCarter Theatre. Photo by T. Charles Erickson/Theatre Pix.

## Front Matter

**i** T. Charles Erickson/Theatre Pix. **viii** (cl) T. Charles Erickson/Theatre Pix. **x** (tl) Jeff Ellis. **xii** (tl) T. Charles Erickson/Theatre Pix; (bl) The Granger Collection. **xiv** (tl) T. Charles Erickson/Theatre Pix. **xx** Jeff Ellis; Northlight Theatre playbill by Tom Peth.

## Outline of Theatre History

**1**(tl) The Granger Collection; (bl) Stock Montage, Inc; (tr) Jason Laure; (br) The Granger Collection. **2** (tl) The Granger Collection; (bl) Statuette of Comic Actor, Henry Lillie Pierce Fund, Museum of Fine Arts, Boston; (c) The Granger Collection; (tr) Scala/Art Resource; (br) Brent Nicastro. **3** (tl) Figurine, The Nelson-Atkins Museum of Art, Kansas City, Missouri (Purchase: Nelson Trust); (bl) The Granger Collection; (c) Giraudon/Art Resource, NY; (tr) Otto Muller Verlag KG; (br) The Granger Collection. **4** (tl) From *The Second Book of Architecture* (1545); (cl) Scala/Art Resource, NY; (bl) The Granger Collection; (tr) The Granger Collection; (cr) The Granger Collection. **5** (tl) Photo Fest; (bl) The Library, Chatsworth, Bakewell, Derbyshire; (c) Giraudon/Art Resource, NY; (tr) Mary Evans Picture Library; (br) Chris Bennion/Theatre Pix. **6** (tl) Corbis-Bettmann; (bl) Tate Gallery, London/Art Resource, NY; (c) The Granger Collection; (tr) Mary Evans Picture Library; (br) T. Charles Erickson/Theatre Pix. **7** (tl) T. Charles Erickson/Theatre Pix; (bl) The Granger Collection; (c) Photo Fest; (tr) The Granger Collection; (br) Sovfoto/Eastfoto. **8** (tl) T. Charles Erickson/Theatre Pix; (bl) Mary Evans Picture Library; (c) Foto Marburg/Art Resource, NY; (tr) The Granger Collection; (br) Culver Pictures. **9** (l) Chris Bennion/Theatre Pix; (tc) Chris Bennion/Theatre Pix; (bc) The Granger Collection; (tr) Mary Evans Picture Library; (br) The Granger Collection. **10** (tl) Sovfoto/Eastfoto; (bl) From *Le Decor de Theatre* by Denis Bablet © 1965 by Centre National de la Recherche Scientifique; (tr) Martha Swope/Time Inc; (c) The Granger Collection; (br) The Granger Collection. **11** (bl) Corbis-Bettmann; (ct) T. Charles Erickson/Theatre Pix; (c) T. Charles Erickson/Theatre Pix; (tr) Culver Pictures; (br) Photo Fest. **12** (tl) T. Charles Erickson/Theatre Pix; (bl) Museum of the City of New York; (c) Photo Fest; (tr) Museum of the City of New York; (br) T. Charles Erickson/Theatre Pix. **13** (tl) Photo Fest; (bl) Photo Fest; (c) Zoe Dominic; (tr) Michael Brosilow/Theatre Pix; (br) Chris Bennion/Theatre Pix. **14** (tl) Martha Swope/Time Inc; (cl) Chris Bennion/Theatre Pix; (bl) Chris Bennion/Theatre Pix; (tr) Courtesy Mark Taper Forum; (br) T. Charles Erickson/Theatre Pix. **15** (tl) Chris Bennion/Theatre Pix; (cl) Terry O'Neill/Sygma; (bl) Peter Cunningham; (tr) T. Charles Erickson/Theatre Pix; (br) Joan Marcus.

## Section 1

**16** T. Charles Erickson/Theatre Pix. **18** Michael Brosilow/Theatre Pix. **28** Chris Bennion/Theatre Pix. **31** (both) Michael Brosilow/Theatre Pix. **36** Michael Brosilow/Theatre Pix. **38** Tom Raymond. **44** The Granger Collection. **45** The Granger Collection. **46** Joan Marcus. **47** (t) Jason Laure; (b) Tom Raymond. **50** Michael Brosilow/Theatre Pix. **53** The Kobal Collection. **54** T. Charles Erickson/Theatre Pix. **55** Chris Bennion/Theatre Pix. **56** (l) George De Sota/London Features International; (tr) Gary Conner/Photo Edit; (tl) Super Stock; (cl) Tony Freeman/Photo Edit; (bl) Frank Siteman/Photo Edit; (r) Jonathan Nourok/Photo Edit. **58** (t) The Granger Collection; (b) T. Charles Erickson/ Theatr Pix. **59** Chris Bennion/Theatre Pix. **63** Itinerant actors, and a platform stage, frontispiece by William Faithome for the English translation of Paul Scarron's *Roman Comique* (1651), published in 1676. **66** The Granger Collection. **67** The Granger Collection. **68** The Granger Collection. **72** Erich Lessing/Art Resource, NY. **74** Michael Brosilow/Theatre Pix. **76** (all) Michael Brosilow/Theatre Pix. **81** Michael Brosilow/Theatre Pix. **82** (all) Michael Brosilow/Theatre Pix. **89** Michael Brosilow/Theatre Pix. **90** (tl) Jeff Ellis; (cl) Michael Brosilow/Theatre Pix; (bl) Michael Brosilow, Theatre Pix. **96** Michael Brosilow/Theatre Pix. **97** (all) Michael Brosilow/Theatre Pix.

## Section 2

**126** Jeff Ellis. **128** Michael Brosilow/Theatre Pix. **130** (top to bottom) David Young-Wolff/Photo Edit; Michael Newman/Photo Edit; Bob Daemmrich/ Stock Boston; David Young-Wolff/Photo Edit; Tony Freeman/Photo Edit. **131** Jonathan Novrok/Photo Edit. **135** Art Resource, NY. **137** Motion Picture & Television Archive. **143** (bl) Carol Rosegg; (tr) T. Charles Erickson/Theatre Pix. **147** Michael Brosilow/Theatre Pix. **149** Jeff Ellis. **154** The Granger Collection. **155** Rex Features. **156** The Granger Collection. **157** The Granger Collection. **161** Martha Swope/ Time, Inc. **162** Michael Brosilow/Theatre Pix. **164** (t) Photo Fest; (b) Joan Marcus. **165** (t) T. Charles Erickson/Theatre Pix; (b) Inge Morath/Magnum Photos, Inc. **168** T. Charles Erickson/Theatre Pix. **170** (all) T. Charles Erickson/Theatre Pix. **171** T. Charles Erickson/Theatre Pix. **173** T. Charles Erickson/Theatre Pix. **174** (all) Chris Bennion/Theatre Pix. **175** Photo Fest. **177** T. Charles Erickson/Theatre Pix. **179** T. Charles Erickson/Theatre Pix. **180** T. Charles Erickson/Theatre Pix. **181** (t) Chris Bennion/ Theatre Pix; (b) Martha Swope/Time Inc. **185** Jeff Ellis. **186** Kimberly Barnes Terzis, Creative Graphic Arts, Inc. **192** Giraudon/Art Resource, NY. **193** The Granger Collection. **194** Chris Bennion/Theatre Pix. **199** Dawn Murray/The Court Theatre. **201** John Springer/Corbis. **202** Michael Brosilow/Theatre Pix. **204** (t) Michael Brosilow/Theatre Pix; (b) T. Charles Erickson/Theatre Pix. **205** (t) T. Charles Erickson/Theatre Pix; (b) Jennifer W. Lester. **209** Michael Brosilow/Theatre Pix. **214** (all) Jeff Ellis. **216** Jeff Ellis. **217** Jeff Ellis. **222** Chris Bennion/Theatre Pix. **224** (t) and (b) Jodie Tucci. **225** T. Charles Erickson/Theatre Pix. **226** (all) Michael Brosilow/Theatre Pix. **227** Jeff Ellis. **228** T. Charles Erickson/Theatre Pix. **229** Chris Bennion/Theatre Pix. **233** Joan Marcus. **234** (all) Viktë Jankus-Moss. **236** Jeff Ellis. **237** Chris Bennion/Theatre Pix. **238** A. De Wildenberg/Gamma-Liaison.

## Section 3

**270** T. Charles Erickson/Theatre Pix. **272** Michael Brosilow/Theatre Pix. **275** Photo Fest. **277** Joan Marcus. **278** Chris Bennion/Theatre Pix. **279** T. Charles Erickson/Theatre Pix. **280** T. Charles Erickson/Theatre Pix. **281** T. Charles Erickson/Theatre Pix. **287** (all) Michael Brosilow/Theatre Pix. **288** Chris Bennion/Theatre Pix. **289** T. Charles Erickson/Theatre Pix. **290** T. Charles Erickson/Theatre Pix. **292** T. Charles Erickson/Theatre Pix. **296** P. Perrin/Sygma. **298** Kaku Kurita/Gamma-Liaison. **303** A. De Wildenberg/Gamma-Liaison. **305** Joan Marcus. **306** Michael Brosilow/Theatre Pix. **326** The Granger Collection.

**328** T. Charles Erickson/Theatre Pix. **329** Chris Bennion/Theatre Pix. **331** T. Charles Erickson/Theatre Pix. **334** Michael Brosilow/Theatre Pix. **337** T. Charles Erickson/Theatre Pix. **339** T. Charles Erickson/Theatre Pix. **341** Jeff Ellis. **342** (all) T. Charles Erickson/Theatre Pix. **343** T. Charles Erickson/Theatre Pix. **347** Joan Marcus. **348** Photo Fest. **350** A. De Wildenberg/Gamma-Liaison. **351** Photo Fest. **352** Jeff Ellis. **354** Carol Rosegg. **356** T. Charles Erickson/Theatre Pix. **357** Clive Barda, London. **359** A. De Wildenberg/Gamma-Liaison. **361** Jeff Ellis.

## Section 4

**394** T. Charles Erickson/Theatre Pix. **396** Michael Brosilow/Theatre Pix. **399** Elterman/Sipa Press. **400** (t) T. Charles Erickson/Theatre Pix. (b) Jennifer W. Lester. **402** (l) Vic Bider/Photo Edit; (r) The Kobal Collection. **404** (l) Richard Feldman; (r) Chris Bennion/Theatre Pix. **409** Michael Daniel. **410** (tl) Sara Krulwich/NYT Pictures; (bl) Sara Krulwich/NYT Pictures; (tc) Photo Fest; (cl) The Kobal Collection; (r) Jim Britt, HBO/The Kobal Collection. **412** Chris Bennion/Theatre Pix. **413** Albert/Sipa Press. **414** (l) Richard Feldman; (r) Chris Bennion/Theatre Pix. **416** (t) The Kobal Collection; (b) Chris Bennion/Theatre Pix. **417** (l) Joan Marcus; (t) Photo Fest. **419** (all) Chris Bennion/Theatre Pix. **420** (l) Tannenbawn/Sygma; (r) Photo Fest. **421** (all) Richard Feldman. **426** The Granger Collection. **427** Chris Bennion/Theatre Pix. **428** Chris Bennion/Theatre Pix. **432** T. Charles Erickson/Theatre Pix. **435** Thomas Leon/Photo Fest. **436** Michael Brosilow/Theatre Pix. **439** Barry King/Gamma-Liaison. **440** Joan Marcus. **441** Jeff Ellis. **442** T. Charles Erickson/Theatre Pix. **444** Chris Bennion/Theatre Pix. **445** Chris Bennion/Theatre Pix. **446** (t) Columbia, Tristar/Photo Fest; (b) Digital Domain/Photo Fest. **448** Photo Fest. **449** Charlie Varley Pix/Sipa Press. **450** Photo Fest. **451** Chris Bennion/Theatre Pix. **452** Larry Watson, Fox/The Kobal Collection. **453** (all) T. Charles Erickson/Theatre Pix. **456** Susan Wilson. **457** Chris Bennion/Theatre Pix. **458** Chris Bennion/Theatre Pix. **462** Joan Marcus. **463** Photo Fest. **464** Michael Brosilow/Theatre Pix. **466** (t) Martha Swope/Time Inc; (b) Jennifer W. Lester. **470** Chris Bennion/Theatre Pix. **472** T. Charles Erickson/Theatre Pix. **475** T. Charles Erickson/Theatre Pix. **476** Joan Marcus. **478** T. Charles Erickson/Theatre Pix. **479** T. Charles Erickson/Theatre Pix. **480** Martha Swope/Time Inc. **482** (all) Josef Svoboda/Jarka M. Burian. **485** T. Charles Erickson/Theatre Pix. **487** Michael Brosilow/Theatre Pix. **489** Richard M. Feldman. **491** Columbia Pictures/Photo Fest. **493** T. Charles Erickson/Theatre Pix. **494** Chris Bennion/Theatre Pix. **495** (l) Joan Marcus; (c) The Kobal Collection.

# Index

## A


Abbey Theatre, 10
Absurdist, 427
Accents (makeup), 351
Accents (vocal), 138, 410–411, 500–503
Act curtain, 60
Acting
  auditions in, 146–149
  as career choice, 571–572
  characterization in, 129–133, 136–139
  developing self-awareness in, 19
  ensemble ethic in, 20
  in film and TV, 418–419, 509–511
  improvisation in, 36–37
  masks in, 67, 412–414
  mime in, 402–403
  motivation and behavior in, 134–135
  movement in, 20–27, 140–145, 399–401
  multimedia, 420–421
  in musical theatre, 415–417, 503–505
  pantomime in, 28–29
  in performance, 291–293
  in Reader's Theatre, 397–398
  rehearsal process in, 282–290
  stage business in, 289
  stage combat in, 404–409
  storytelling in, 38–39
  voice in, 30–35, 138, 410–411, 500–503
  working with the script in, 273–277
Acting areas, 229
Acting notes, xxiii
Acting styles, 278
  in comedy of manners, 279
  in farce, 278
  in Greek theatre, 67–68
  in Kabuki, 298
  in Molière's theatre, 195
  in realistic drama, 281, 329
  in Romantic drama, 281
  in Shakespearean theatre, 157, 279–280
Action
  describing, in a screenplay, 553
  falling, 171–172
  rising, 170
  structuring, in a play script, 536
Action-generated emotion in characterization process, 132–133
Actor-manager, 51
Acts, 535
  designations for, in a play script, 538
*Acts Without Words* (Beckett), 427
Adams, Lee, 416
Advertising, 185, 310, 313, 544. *See also* Publicity.
Aeschylus, 2
African American theatre, 13, 14, 457–458, 571
Aging of costumes, 347
Albee, Edward, 13, 427, 579
*All About Eve,* 53
Allison, Sarahjane, 572–573
Altman, Robert, 450
Ambient light, 464, 481, 521
America, theatre in, 6
Amplifiers, 86, 87
Anderson, Garland, 457
Anderson, Laurie, 420
Andrews, Julie, 417
Antagonist, 172, 536
*Antigone* (Sophocles), 55, 67, 69–72
Antoine, André, 8, 203
*Antony and Cleopatra* (Shakespeare), 485
Appia, Adolphe, 203
Appropriate design, 205
Apron, 50, 60
Arena stage, 50, 59
  areas in, 62
  composition for, 181
Aristophanes, 2
Aristotle, 2, 530–532, 534, 540, 584
Arlecchino, 373
Armor, 485
Arrabal, Fernando, 427
Artaud, Antonin, 11, 14
Articulation, 18, 32
Articulators, 18, 32
Artistic director, 53
Ashman, Howard, 307, 470
Assistant director, 52, 187, 307, 315
Audience
  as an element of theatre, 56
  grabbing, in a play script, 535–536
  for musical theatre, 443
  for research paper, 563
Audiotape
  editing, 87
  splicing, 87
Auditions
  callbacks in, 149
  definition of, 146
  etiquette in, 148
  monologues in, 146–148, 249–251
  preparing for, 146, 315–316
  for Reader's Theatre, 397, 437–438
  reading from script in, 148
Auditorium, 59
Auditors, 146
Ayckbourn, Alan, 578–579


## B


Backdrop, *See* Drop.
Background in creating specific characters, 136–137
Backing, 208
Backlot, 448
Backstage, 60, 291

Backstitch, 92
Back wall, 60
Balconies, 59
Ballad opera, 6
Baraka, Amiri (Le Roi Jones), 458
Barrie, J. M., 343, 494
Barn doors, 83, 344
Basting stitches, 92
Batten, 74, 84, 216, 339
  rigging a, 340–341
Batten-clamp drop, 217
Baum, L. Frank, 233, 238
Beards, 494
Beats, 128, 147, 276, 318
*Beauty and the Beast,* 494
*Beaux' Strategem, The* (Farquhar), 143
Beckett, Samuel, 12, 426–435
  *Acts Without Words,* 427
  *Come and Go,* 427
  *Endgame,* 429
  *Ghost Trio,* 421
  *Happy Days,* 429
  *Malone Dies,* 427
  *Molloy,* 427
  *Murphy,* 427
  *Waiting for Godot,* 426–427, 429, 430–435
Behavior and motivation, 134–135, 138, 288, 318
Behn, Aphra, 5
Belasco, David, 9, 203
Berlin, Irving, 415
Bernhardt, Sarah, 8, 9
Besson, Luc, 446
Bevel cuts, 79
Blackfriars Theatre, 154
Black Horizons on the Hill, 457
Black Power movement, 457
*Blacks, The* (Genet), 413
*Blade to the Heat* (Mayer), 409
Blank verse, 4, 157, 579
Blending, 95, 349
Blocking, 162, 182
  entrances and exits, 252–254
  interactive onstage movement, 182
  rehearsals for, 284–285, 287, 314, 317–318
  symbols, 183
Blood pack, 493
*Blood Wedding* (Lorca), 174
Body blows, 409
Body positions, 140, 177–178
Bond, Edward, 13
Bontemps, Arna, 458
Book (for musical theatre), 436, 444, 516
Bookcase, 473
Boom, 334, 339
Boomerang, 334, 339
*Born Yesterday* (Kanin), 174
Boublil, Alan, 417
Box office, 59
  manager, 309
Box set, 328
Bow, Clara, 351
Brace, 77, 202
Bracing scenery, 220, 321
Branagh, Kenneth, 15
Breathing, diaphragmatic, 30–31
Brecht, Bertolt, 11, 15, 222, 442
Brickwork, 225
*Bride of Frankenstein* (Whale), 495
Broadway, 440, 443
  musicals on, 12
*Broken Glass,* (Miller), 400
Brook, Peter, 11, 14
Browning, Robert, 398
Büchner, Georg, 7
Buckram, 486
Budget, 311, 312, 323
  for musical theatre, 443
Build (costumes), 234
Bullins, Ed, III, 458
Bunraku, 296
*Buried Child* (Shepard), 204
Business manager, 53, 309
Business of play, 185–186
Butt joint, 80
*Bye, Bye, Birdie* (Stewart, Strouse, and Adams), 416

## C

Calderón de la Barca, Pedro, 5
Call, 334, 352, 353, 355, 357
Callbacks, 149, 273, 316
Call board, 60
Campesino, Teatro, 14
Camus, Albert, 427
*Candide* (Voltaire), 181
Career choices
  actor, 573–574
  choreographer, 577–578
  costume designer, 576–577
  critic, 579
  director, 571–572
  lighting designer, 575–576
  playwright, 578–579
  producer, 570–571
  set designer, 574–575
  stage manager, 572–573
Carné, Marcel, 402
*Carousel* (Rodgers & Hammerstein), 442
Cast, 146
  for musical theatre, 443
  for Reader's Theatre, 397, 437–438
Cast party, 322, 355
Casting by type, 306, 316
Catharsis, 531
*Cat on a Hot Tin Roof* (Williams), 281
*Caucasian Chalk Circle, The* (Brecht), 222
Centerstage, 62, 178
*Ceremonies in Dark Old Men* (Elder), 458

*Changes of Heart,* (Marivaux), 292
Chaplin, Charlie, 402
Character analysis, 172, 276
  antagonist, 172
  protagonist, 172
  secondary characters, 172
Character makeup sketches, 238
Character summary, 167
Characterization, 129, 172, 247–249
  action-generated emotion in, 132–133
  emotional memory in, 132
  experience in, 130–131
  external factors, 288
  imagination in, 133
  motivation and behavior, 134
  observation in, 129–130
  sense memory in, 131
  stage business, 289
  subtext, 128, 138–139, 277
  using animal traits, 369–370
Characters, 531–532, 541
  costumes for, 288
  creating (for playwrights), 536–537
  creating specific, 136–139
  describing (for screenwriters), 551
  and dialogue (for playwrights), 538
  fitting dialogue to (for playwrights), 537
  improvising, 37
  kinds of (for playwrights), 536–537
  makeup for, 288
  movement by, 137
  voices of, 137–138
Chase, 182
Checklist (for actors), 291
Chekhov, Anton, 9, 180, 326–329
  *Cherry Orchard The,* 9, 327
  *Ivanov,* 327
  *Seagull, The,* 173, 327
  *Three Sisters, The,* 9, 180, 327
  *Uncle Vanya,* 9, 327, 329–332
*Cherry Orchard, The* (Chekhov), 9, 327
*Children of Paradise* (Carné), 402
China, Peking Opera in, 7
Chinese theatre, 3
Chokes, 407–408
Choreographers, 396, 415
  as career choice, 577–578
  in musical theatre, 415, 441, 443
Chorus. *See* Greek drama.
Choruses, 417
Churchill, Caryl, 15, 573
Cinema, arrival of, 9
Cinematographer, 450
Circuit breaker, 89
Circuit number, 231
Cirque du Soleil, 399, 413
CIVIL WarS: a tree is best measured when it is down, 421
Climax, 171, 536
Clinch plate, 211
Clooney, George, 448
Clock method in designating stage areas, 62
Close-up, 419
Cold readings, 128, 148, 316
Color-blind casting, 306, 316
*Come and Go (*Beckett), 427
Comedy, 164
Comedy of manners, 5, 279
Commando cloth, 471
Commedia dell'arte, 4, 278, 371–373, 399
  stock characters in, 278, 371–373
Commercial patterns, 346
Compass method in designating stage areas, 62
Composer, 444
Conflict, 536
  with stage movement, 244–247
Congreve, William, 5
Constructivism, 10, 580
Contact lists, 544
Continuations, in a screenplay, 552
Continuity in film and TV acting, 419
Cookies, 83. *See* Gobo.
Copyright, 232, 385, 558. *See also* Permissions.
Coquelin, 8
Corneille, 5
Cornerblock, 210, 211
Cosmetics, 94
Costume designer, 75
  as career choice, 574–575
  script analysis for, 234
Costume list, 235
Costume plot, 235
Costume shop, 60, 90
Costumes, 75, 485–488
  aging, 347
  armor, 485
  completing, 346–348
  crew for, 90
  decorations for, 347–348
  design and production of, 203, 234–237
  draped, 488
  dressing list, 348
  in dress rehearsal, 356
  dyeing, 346
  equipment and supplies for, 91
  fittings, 237
  footwear, 487
  in Greek drama, 68
  headpieces, 486
  inventory, 361
  jewelry and ornaments, 487
  management, 235–237
  in Kabuki theatre, 297–298
  list of, 235
  masks, 489–490, 525–528
  measurement cards for, 237
  in Molière's theatre, 194–195
  patterns for, 346
  in postproduction, 361
  production calendar for, 237

pull/rent/buy/borrow/build list for, 235
for run of the show, 359
safety tips for, 97
sewing, 92–93
in Shakespearean theatre, 156–157
special effects for, 347
texturizing, 347
in tech rehearsal, 354
in working rehearsals, 288
Counterweight system, 216, 217
Craig, Gordon, 10, 203
Crouse, Russel, 338, 348
Credits, 446
Crepe hair, 94
Critic as career choice, 579
*Crocodile Tears* (Sod), 419
Cross cuts, 79
Crossing, 128, 141
in maintaining focus, 144
Crowd scenes, 285
Cue, 74
Cue line, 272, 283
Cue sheet
lighting, 344
master, 353
sound, 345
Cue tape, 86, 87
Cullen, Countee, 458
Curtain call, 293, 355
Curtains and drapes, 227, 471–473
hanging, 472–473
Cutting and joining wood, 80
Cyclorama or cyc, 334, 335
*Cymbeline* (Shakespeare), 479
*Cyrano de Bergerac* (Rostand), 8, 491, 570

## D

Dailies, 436, 450
Dalton, Timothy, 439
Dance, 1, 542
in musical theatre, 415
Dario Fo, 4
Data, collecting for a review, 540
Dead zone, 343
*Death of a Salesman,* 165, 176
de Bergerac, Cyrano, 192
Deburau, Jean-Baptiste Gaspard, 402
Deck, 214
Decorations, 347
Decorative props, 226
De Mille, Agnes, 415
DeNiro, Robert, 449
Dénouement, 162, 172, 536
Derma wax, 94, 492
Design
appropriate, 205
costume, 203
director's role in, 176–177
expressive, 204
informative, 204
lighting, 203
makeup, 203, 238–239
set, 203, 206–209
sound, 203, 232–233
usable, 205
Design team, 54, 203
Development in film, 447
de Vega, Lope, 5
Diagonals, 180
Dialect, 410–411
Dialogue, writing, 537–538
and characters, 537, 538
controlling pacing, 537
digressions, 537–538
fitting to historical period and geography, 537
overwriting, 538
stepping on laughs, 538
Diaphragm, 30
Diaphragmatic breathing, importance for projection, 34
*Diary of Anne Frank, The,* (Goodrich and Hackett), 277
Diction, 532
Dimmer, 84, 231
circuit, 340, 341
Dinner theatre, 306, 309
Dionysus, 2, 66
Diphthong, 33
Direct emphasis, 178
Directing, 50–63
one-act play, 379–381
Directing and producing notes, xxiv
Direction, taking, 284
Director
assistant, 52, 187, 305, 307
and blocking, 182
as career choice, 569–570
in choosing a play, 163
coaching actors, 319–320
design role of, 176–177
emergence of, 51
and genre, 164–165
journal of young, 308–323
notes of, 306, 319, 358
promptbook of, 183–184, 257–260
qualities of good, 307
resolving conflicts, 320, 321, 377–379
role of, 51–53
skills of, 52
staff of, 52
and stage composition, 177–181
and style, 174–175
terminology, 284
working with, 284
and working with script, 166–173
Disperse dye, 346
Dissolve, 451
Dithyramb, 2

Diversified emphasis, 178
*Doll's House, A* (Ibsen), 205
Domestic tragedy, 6
Dominant stage positions, 143
*Don Juan* (Molière), 225
Dogon, 1, 47
Donen, Stanley, 416
Door flat, constructing, 213
Doors, 213
Dottore, 373
Downstage, 50, 62, 63, 178
Doyle, Arthur Conan, 273–275
Drama, 165, 452
  analyzing, 530–533
  elements of, 531–532
  realistic, 280–281
Dramatic conflict, 535
Dramatic elements, 541–542
Dramatic unities. *See* Unities.
Dramaturg, 173
Draped costume technique, 488
*Dream Play, A* (Strindberg), 237
Dress parade, 354
Dress rehearsals, 290, 322, 355–356
  costumes in, 356
  curtain call in, 293
  lighting in, 356
  makeup in, 356
  props in, 356
  scenery in, 356
  sound in, 356
  stage manager in, 355
Dressing a set, 202, 226
Dressing list, 348
Dressing rooms, 60
  during performance, 291
Drop end, 340
Drop, 74, 79, 216–217
  grid transfer of image onto, 268–269
  hanging batten-clamp, 217
  hanging tie-supported, 216
Dry brush, 225
Dry ice kettles, 476
Dry run, 451
Dry tech, 334, 353
*Duchess of Malfi, The* (Webster), 289
Duoemphasis, 178
Duet, 366–368
Dutchman, 202, 219
Duvetyn, 471

## E

Egloff, Elizabeth, 343
*Einstein on the Beach* (Wilson and Glass), 453
Elder, Lonne, 458
*Electra* (Sophocles), 67
Electrical signals, 87
Electrical supplies, 83
Electricity
  extension cables in, 85
  safety tips for working with, 89
Elevation, front, 202, 209
Elizabeth I (Queen of England), 4, 154–155
Ellipsoidal reflector floodlight, 83
Ellipsoidal reflector spotlight (ERS), 83, 342, 478
Emotion, using action to generate, 132–133
Emotional memory in characterization process, 132
*Endgame* (Becket), 429
English drama, 4. *See also* Shakespeare.
  rise of, 4
Ensemble ethic, 20
Entering, 141
  through doorways, 141
Epic Theatre, 11
Epilogue, 539
Equalizers, 86, 87
Esslin, Martin, 12, 427
Etherege, George, 5
Ethics, ensemble, 20
Etiquette
  audition, 148
  rehearsal, 282
Euripides, 2
Evans, Maurice, 568
*Evita!*, 480
Exiting through doorways, 141
Experience in characterization process, 130–131
Exposition, 162, 169
Expression, 34–35
Expressionism, 10
Expressive design, 204
Expressive gestures, 45
Extension cables, 85
  making, 85
Extreme close-up, 419
Eye contact in maintaining focus, 144
Eyeliner, 94, 351

## F

Fagles, Robert, 69
Falling action, 171–172, 536
Falling techniques, 405–406
Farce, 162, 164, 278
Farquhar, George, 143
Fashion Institute of Technology, 574
Fathingale, 156–157
*Feast of Fools, The* (Hoyle), 278, 414
Feature story, 546
Federal Theatre Project, 420
*Fences* (Wilson), 457
Ferber, Edna, 11
*Fifth Element, The* (Besson), 446
Fight director, 396, 404
Fill light, 229
Film, 446–450
  acting in, 418–419

structure and time in, 419
terminology for, 418–419
Final cut, 436, 450
"Final Problem, The," (Doyle), 273
Final rehearsals, 352
Financial management skills, 53
Fine cut, 436, 450
Fire, 477
Fire curtain, 60
Fistfights, 409
Fitting equipment, 91
Flaminia, 371–372
Flat dock, 336
Flats, 74, 79, 210–212
adding profiles,
constructing, 210–211
covering, 212
door, 213
floating, 336
joining, 218–219
lashing, 218
painting,
running, 336
shifting, 336
storing, 336
Float a flat, 336
Fly, 334, 335
Fly space, 60, 216
Focus, 128, 144, 177, 178
in Reader's Theatre, 398, 439
Focus area, 231
Foil, 536
Followspot, 83
Footage, 436, 450
Footwear, 487
*for colored girls who have considered suicide/when the rainbow is enuf* (Shange), 458
Foundation, 94, 350
Fourth wall, 272, 278, 328
Frame, 418–419
Francischina, 371–372
*Freak*, 410
French neoclassical theatre, 5
Fresnel spotlight, 83, 478
Front elevation, 202, 209
Front-of-house staff, 355, 358
Front-screen projection, 480
Fugard, Athol, 181, 337
Full masks, 413
Functionaries, 536
*A Funny Thing Happened on the Way to the Forum* (Shevelove and Gelbert), 164

## G

*Game of Love and Chance, The* (Marivaux), 228
Garrick, David, 6
Gay, John, 6
Gelbart, Larry, 164
Gel frames, 83, 84, 231
Gels, 83
color, 231
installing, 342
Genet, Jean, 413
Genre, 161, 257–259, 278
comedy, 164
drama, 165
farce, 164
tragedy, 165
George II (Duke of Saxe Meiningen), 51
German Romantic drama, 7
Gershwin, George, 415
Gestures, 18, 141
master, 137
symbolic, 401
Gewel. *See* Griot.
*Ghost Trio* (Beckett), 421
Gibson, William, 131
Gill, Brendan, 579
Glaspell, Susan, 11
Glass, Phillip, 453
*Glass Menagerie, The* (Williams), 166–172
Globe Theatre, 154, 155–156
Gobo, 83, 334, 342, 382–383
*God's Heart* (Lucas), 453
Goldberg, Whoopi, 439
Goldenthall, Elliot, 347, 414
Goldoni, Carlo, 6
Goldsmith, Oliver, 7
*Goodbye Stranger* (Luft), 287
Goodrich, Frances, 277
Gordone, Charles, 458
Gorky, Maxim, 9
Gozzi, Carlo, 6, 493
Grand drape, 60
Greek drama, 2
chorus in, 2, 67–68
conventions of, 67–68
costumes in, 68
origin of, 2
style of costumes in, 68
theatre space in, 67
Green room, 60
Gregory, Lady, 10
Grid, 335
Gridiron, 335
Grid transfer, 268–269
Griot
art of, 47
role of, 45–47
Grips, 334, 335
Grotowski, Jerzy, 11, 570
Grounding plug, 89
Groundlings, 156
Ground plan, 162, 176, 202, 208, 259, 310, 312, 313
Gurney, A. R., 439
*Guys and Dolls* (Loesser), 442

## H


Hackett, Albert, 277
Hairstyling, 95
Haley, Alex, 47
Half masks, 413
Hallam, William, 6
*Hamlet* (Shakespeare), 155, 205, 404
Hammerstein, Oscar, 12, 415, 440, 442, 445
Hanamichi, 297
Hand props, 141, 226, 337
Hand stitches, 92
Hang lights, 84, 339–341
Hansberry, Lorraine, 13, 457, 458
*Happy Days* (Beckett), 429
*Happy End, The* (Brecht), 442
Harlem Renaissance, 458
Harlequin, 373
Hawks, Howard, 201
Headpieces, 486
Hellman, Lillian, 11
*Hello Dolly!* (Herman), 442
Hexolite, 485
Highlights, 351
Hildegard of Bingen, 3
*His Girl Friday* (Hawks), 201
Hispanic American Theatre, 14
Historical profiles
  Anton Chekhov, 326–333
  August Wilson, 456–463
  Kabuki, 296–305
  Molière, 192–193
  Samuel Beckett, 426–435
  Sophocles, 66–68
  Storytelling Tradition, The, 44–49
  William Shakespeare, 154–155
Holmes, Sherlock, 273–276
Homer, 1, 2, 45
Hood, 344
Hook, 535, 536
Hot spot, 343, 464, 481
House, 50, 59
Hoyle, Geoff, 278, 414
Housing, of lighting instruments, 84
Hroswitha, 3
Hubris, 531
Hughes, Langston, 458
Hugo, Victor, 417


## I


Ibsen, Henrik, 8, 9, 205
*Iliad* (Homer), 1, 45
*Illusions* (Molière), 177
Image interference, 481
*Imaginary Invalid, The* (Molière), 193
Imagination in characterization process, 133
*Importance of Being Earnest, The* (Wilde), 184, 279
Improvisation, 36–37
  of characters, 37
  with masks, 414
  with open dialogue, 244–247
  of sketches, 36–37
  with stage movement, 244–247
  and tableau, 105–107
Improvise, 18
Inciting incident, 162, 170, 536
Inflection, 18, 34–35
Informative design, 204
*An Inspector Calls* (Priestley), 477
Instrument number, 231
Instrument schedule, 229, 231
Interactive onstage movement, 182
Interruptions, in a screenplay, 552
In-the-round stage, 59
Ionesco, Eugène, 427
*Italian Straw Hat, An* (Labiche), 290
*Ivanov* (Chekhov), 327, 328


## J


Jacknife sets, 335
Jacks, 202, 220
Jaly. *See* Griot.
Japan
  Bunraku in, 296
  Kabuki theatre in, 4, 296–298, 350, 399
  Noh drama in, 3, 296
Jeter, Michael, 573–574
Jewelry, 486–487, 523–524
*Joe Turner's Come and Gone* (Wilson), 457
Joists, 214
*Joy Luck Club, The,* 204
*Juan Darien* (Taymor), 15, 347, 414


## K


Kabuki theatre, 4, 296–305, 399
  acting styles in, 298
  costume and makeup in, 238, 297–298, 238, 350, 359
  theatre space in, 297
Kanin, Garson, 174
Keaton, Buster, 402
Keller, Helen, 131
Kelly, Gene, 416
Kern, Jerome, 415
Key light, 229
Keystone, 210, 211
Keystone Cops, 175
Keystoning, 464, 481
Kicks, 407
Kimono, 297
*King and I, The* (Rodgers and Hammerstein), 440
King's Men, 154
*King Stag,* 489
Kinte, Kunta, 47
Kittel, Frederick August, 456

Kiyotsugu, Kanami, 3
*K-2* (Meyer), 466
Knipper, Olga, 326
Kushner, Tony, 15

## L

Labiche, Eugène, 290
Lanchester, Elsa, 495
Language, 542
Lapine, James, 444
Lap joint, 80
Lashing, 218
Latex, liquid, 94, 492
Laughing comedy, 7
Layering and mixing sound, 484
*Le Bourgeois Avant Garde, A Comedy After Molière* (Ludlam), 356
Leading center, 137
Left of stage, 62
Leguizamo, John, 410
Lensless projectors, 478
Lens projectors, 478–479
*Les Misérables* (Boubil and Schönberg), 417
Levels, 162, 179
Life mask, 464
  making, 489–490
*Life with Father* (Lindsay and Crouse), 338, 348
Light booth, 59
Lighting, 75
  angling and focusing, 343–344
  basics in, 84–85
  control equipment for, 83
  creating a gobo, 382–383
  crew for, 82–89
  cue sheet for, 344
  design in, 203, 228–231
  in dress rehearsal, 356
  hanging, 339–341
  image interference in, 481
  installing gels, 342
  instrument schedule, 229, 231
  keystoning in, 481
  lensless projectors in, 478
  lens projectors in, 478–479
  in postproduction, 361
  projections, 480, 520–522
  projection screens in, 480–481
  in Reader's Theater, 439
  rigging a batten, 340–341
  running, 344
  for run of the show, 358–359
  slide preparation in, 481
  in tech rehearsal, 354
Lighting areas, 229
Lighting designer, 75
  as career choice, 573–574
  script analysis for, 228
Lighting equipment, 83
Lighting instruments, 83
Lighting key, 22
Lighting plot, 229, 230
Lighting supplies, 83
Lighting tree, 334, 339
Lillo, George, 6
Lindsay, Howard, 336, 348
*Lion King, The,* 15, 46
Literary background and historical context of play in script analysis, 277
Literature, reading. *See* Reader's Theatre.
*Little Ham, Simply Heavenly* (Hughes), 458
*Little Shop of Horrors* (Ashman and Menken), 307, 470
*Living Newspapers,* 420
Lobby, 59
Lobel, Adrianne, 574–575
Location, 436, 449
Loesser, Frank, 442
Long shot, 419
*Look Back in Anger* (Osborne), 207–209, 229, 230, 231
Lorca, Federico García, 174
Lord Chamberlain's Men, 154
Lot, 436, 449
Loud talking, 459
Louis XIV, 193
*Love for Three Oranges* (Gozzi), 493
*Love Letters,* (Gurney), 439
*Love-Sick Doctor, The* (Molière), 193
Lucas, Craig, 453
Ludlam, Charles, 356
Luft, Carrie, 287
Lyricist, 436, 444, 515–516
Lyrics, 516

## M

*Macbeth* (Shakespeare), 155
Machine sewing, 93
*Mahabharata,* 1, 2
Makeup, 75, 203
  accents, 35
  applying, 95–96, 349–351
  basics in, 95–96
  beards, 493
  blending, 95, 349
  brushes for, 94
  character sketches for, 238
  crew for, 90
  design in, 203, 238–239
  in dress rehearsal, 356
  equipment and supplies, 94
  foundation, 350
  highlights, 351
  inventory, 361
  in Kabuki, 238, 297–298
  for mime, 402
  moustaches, 494
  old-age, 390–393
  plan for, 239

in postproduction, 361
for run of the show, 359
safety tips, 97
scrapbook, 123–125
shadows, 351
skull cap, 392
stage blood, 495
in tech rehearsal, 354
three-dimensional, 491–495
wigs, 495
in working rehearsals, 238
wrinkles, 492
Makeup artists, 90
Makeup designer, 75, 90
script analysis for, 238–239
Makeup kit, 96
Makeup room, 60
Making and shaping sounds, 32
Male/female connectors, 83, 84
*Malone Dies* (Beckett), 427
Mamet, David, 229
*Man of La Mancha* (Wasserman), 354
*Ma Rainey's Black Bottom* (Wilson), 457
Marbling, 224
Marceau, Marcel, 402
Marivaux, Pierre Carlet de Chamblain de, 228, 292
Marking, 459
Marlowe, Christopher, 4
Martin, Steve, 491
Marx, Groucho, 137
Mask(s), 412–414
making, 525–528
making a life mask, 489–490
in Greek drama, 67, 68
in set design, 208
Masques, 5
Master cue sheet, 353
Master gesture, 128, 137
*Master Harold and the Boys* (Fugard), 181
*Matchmaker, The* (Wilder), 442
Matte, 451
Mayer, Oliver, 409
McCann, Elizabeth Ireland, 570–571
Media, writing for, 548
Media kit, 545
Media night, 547
Medieval drama
origin of, 3
types of, 3
Medium shot, 419
Meiningen Troupe, 8, 51
Melodrama, 7, 401
Memorization, 286
techniques in, 286
Memory
emotional, 132
sense, 131
Menken, Alan, 307, 470
Meyer, Patrick, 466
Meyerhold, V. E. (Vsevolod), 10, 420
Mezzanine, 59
Middle class audience, 6
*Midsummer Night's Dream, A* (Shakespeare), 155, 158–161
Miller, Arthur, 12, 165, 176, 400
Mime, 402–403
Mime walk, 403
Minnelli, Liza, 449
Ming Cho Lee, 466, 573
Miniseries, 452
Miracle plays, 3
*Miracle Worker, The* (Gibson), 131
*Misalliance* (Shaw), 475
*Miser, The* (Molière), 288, 472
Miter cuts, 79
Miter joint, 80
Mixer, 86, 87
Models, 209, 115–117
Molière, 4, 5, 175, 177, 191–201, 225, 238, 288, 339, 400
*Don Juan,* 225
*Illusions,* 177
*Imaginary Invalid, The,* 191
*Love-Sick Doctor, The,* 191
*Misanthrope, The,* 238
*Miser, The,* 288, 472
*School for Wives, The,* 194, 339, 400
*Tartuffe,* 196–201
Molière's theatre
acting styles in, 195
costumes in, 194–195
theatre space in, 193
*Molloy* (Beckett), 427
Monologues, 146–148
analyzing your, 147
choosing, 147
delivering, 249–251
performing your, 147–148
Morality plays, 3
Moscow Art Theatre, 9, 326, 329
Motivation and behavior, 134–135, 138
Motokiyo, Zeami, 3
on *Noh* drama, 533, 540
Moustaches, 494
Movement
basics for the stage, 140–145
blocking, 181–182
character, 137
physical warm-ups, 20–27
posture, 20
in Reader's Theatre, 398, 438–439
right or left, 141
Movement specialties, 399–401
Multimedia, 396, 420–421, 453
*Murphy* (Beckett), 427
Music, 532, 542
in Reader's Theater, 439
*Music Man, The* (Wilson), 131, 400
Musical theatre, 396, 415–417, 440–450

acting in, 415
audience for, 443
on Broadway, 12, 443
budget for, 443
cast and crew for, 443
choosing show for, 442–443
choreographer in, 414, 441
developing, 515–517
music director in, 441
performance space for, 443
planning production for, 445
producer in, 441
production concept for, 444
song in, 417, 503–505
stages of film production, 447–450
Music director, 417, 436
in musical theatre, 440, 441
Musser, Tharon, 575–576
*My Fair Lady* (Lerner and Loewe), 417
*Myth of Sisyphus, The* (Camus), 427
Mystery plays, 3

## N

*Naomi's Road* (Quan), 412
Narrator in Reader's Theatre, 437
National Storytelling Festival, 38, 47
*Natyasastra,* 2, 532–533
naturalism, 8, 9
Nemirovich-Danchenko, Vladimir, 9
Neoclassical theatre, French, 5
Newsletter, creating, 546
News release, 545–546
writing, 548–549
*New York, New York* (Scorcese), 449
Niane, D. T., 45–46, 48
Nihda, Fred, 572
*Noh* drama, 3, 296
Zeami Motokiyo on, 533
Nontraditional casting, 306, 316, 317
*No Place to Be Somebody* (Gordone), 458
Nose putty, 94, 491–492
applying, 492

## O

Objective, 134
Observation in characterization process, 129–130
Obstacle, 134
O'Casey, Sean, 10
*Odd Couple, The* (Simon), 164, 308
*Odyssey* (Homer), 1, 45, 134–135, 138–139
*Oedipus at Colonus* (Sophocles), 67
*Oedipus the King* (Sophocles), 67
Off book, 272, 286, 287, 320, 397
*Oklahoma!,* (Rodgers and Hammerstein), 415
Okuni, 296
*Oleanna* (Mamet), 229
Olivier, Laurence, 11
On book, 272, 286
O'Neill, Eugene, 11
Opening, 128
to audience, 141–142
Open dialogue, 244–247
Opera
ballad, 6
Peking, 7
Optical train, 479
Option, 436, 442
Oral tradition of a culture, 45
Orazio, 371–372
Orchestra, 59, 67
Orchestra pit, 59
Ornaments as costume technique, 486–487
Osborne, John, 13, 207, 229, 230, 231
Osiris, 1
*Othello,* 155, 280
*Our Town* (Wilder), 28, 29, 278
Outcome, 134
*Out of Sight* (Soderbergh), 449
Overdraw, 351
Overlap joint, 80
Overwriting, 538

## P

Pacing, 306, 321, 537
Paint shop, 60
Painting, scenery, 222–225
supplies for, 78
techniques in, 224–225
tools for, 77
Paintings, 477
Pantalone, 371–372
Pantomine, 18, 28–29, 103–104, 402
in crowd scenes, 285
Paper tech, 334, 353
Papier mâché, 485, 487
making and using, 470–471
Patch bay or panel, 344
Patinkin, Mandy, 410
Peking Opera, 7
Performance
backstage, 291
checklist (for actors), 291
onstage, 292
Performance art, 420–421, 421, 453, 483
Performance space, 56–63. *See also* Theatre spaces.
for musical theatre, 443
stage areas in, 62–63
terminology in, 59–60
types of stages, 58–59
*Pericles* (Shakespeare), 466
Permissions, 185
*Peter and Wendy* (Egloff), 343
*Peter Pan* (Barrie), 494
*Phantom of the Opera, The* (Rice and Webber), 357

Phrasing, 35
Physical warm-ups, 20–27
*Piano Lesson The* (Wilson), 457
Piscator, Erwin, 11, 420
Pit, 155
Pitch, 34
Planes, 162, 180
Planning production for musical theatre, 445
Plants, 475
Platforms, 74, 79, 214–215
  connecting, 220
Plautus, 2
Play
  background of, 277
  business of, 185–186
  choosing, 163
  elements of, 167–168
  writing, 534–539
Play program, 186, 547
Play script, 36, 534
  ideas, 534–535
Play's effect, 542
Playback equipment, 86
Playgoing log, xxi
*Player, The* (Altman), 448
Playwright, 538
  as career choice, 578–579
  purpose of, 541
  understanding intent of, 166
  vision, craft, and tools of, 534
Plot
  analyzing, 169–172
  climax, 171, 536
  conflict, 536
  costume, 235, 265
  dénouement, 172, 536
  falling action, 171, 536
  inciting incident, 170, 536
  lighting, 230, 265
  rising action, 170, 536
  sound, 265
  structure, 169
  well-crafted, 536
Plot summary, 167
*Poetics* (Aristotle), 530–532
Poise, 144–145
Polishing rehearsals, 290, 314, 320–321
Porter, Jimmy, 13
Postproduction, 360–361
  costumes and makeup in, 361
  in film, 449–450
  lighting and sound in, 361
  scenery and props in, 361
  stage manager in, 360
Posture, 20, 144–145
Preblocking, 306, 317–318
Preliminary analysis of script, 273–275
Preproduction in film, 447–448
Presentational style, 272, 278
Priestley, J. B., 477
Principal, 396, 415
Producer, 51
  as career choice, 570–571
  in musical theatre, 441
  and budget, 260–263, 311, 312, 323
  and permissions, 185
  and programs, 186
  and writing proposal, 262
  and promotion, 185
  skills of, 53
  staff of, 53
Production, 50–63, 311, 542
  concept, 50, 54, 55
  in film, 448–449
  for musical theatre, 444
  and rehearsal schedule, 313, 314
  responding to, 540–542
Production design, elements of, 204–205
Production meeting, 54, 311–313
Production model, 209
Production number, 396, 415
Production team
  members of, 309
  function of, 54–55
Profiles, 464, 469
Programs, 186, 547
Project, 18
Projection (voice), 34
Projection (lighting), 480, 520–522
Projection screens, 480–481
Prologue, 539
Promoting a show, 544–550
Promotion, 185
Promptbook, director's, 183–184, 257–260, 287
Promptbook, stage manager's, 187, 353
Prompter, 52, 320
Prop master, 75
Prop plot, 227
Prop shop, 60
Prop table, 60, 338
  script analysis for, 226
Property, 74
*Proposals* (Simon), 143
Props, 74, 75
  bookcases, 474
  construction of, 227
  crew for, 76–81
  curtains and drapes, 471–473
  decorative, 226
  design and construction, 203, 226–227
  in dress rehearsal, 356
  fire, 477
  hand, 226, 337
  inventory, 361
  list of, 227
  organizing, 337–338
  paintings, 477
  papier mâché, 470–471
  plants, 475

in postproduction, 361
reupholstering, 266–267
for run of the show, 358
set, 226
smoke, 476
stage food, 473–475
in tech rehearsal, 354
Proscenium arch, 60
Proscenium stage, 50, 58, 178
areas in, 60–62
building a model of, 115–117
keeping open, 141
Proskenion, 67
Protagonist, 172, 536
Publicists, 544
Public relations, 185
Puccini, Giacomo, 9
Pull, 202, 227
Pull/rent/buy/borrow/build list, 235
*Pygmalion* (Shaw), 411, 417


## Q


Quality, 35
Quan, Betty, 412


## R


Rails, 202, 210, 211
*Raisin in the Sun, A* (Hansberry), 457, 458
Raked, 63
*Ramayana*, 1, 2
Rapping, 459
Rasa, 532–533
Reader's Theatre, 396, 557–560
acting in, 397–398
adapting work in, 557–558
auditions in, 397
casting in, 437–439
characters in, 559
choosing script for, 437
directing, 437–439, 512–514
finding source, 558
focus in, 398, 439
movement in, 398, 438–439
narration and description in, 558–559
rehearsals in, 397, 438
scripts in, 437, 559–561
stage directions in, 559
technical elements in, 439
voice in, 398
Read-throughs, 272, 283, 317, 438
Realism, 174, 280–281, 327–328
Realistic drama, 401
movement in, 399
Realistic movement, 400
Rear-screen projection, 481
Recording equipment, 86
Reel-to-reel tape recorders, 88
Rehearsals
blocking, 284–285, 314, 317–318
character-building in, 288
crowd scenes in, 285
definition of, 272
dress, 290, 314, 322, 355–356
duties of stage manager during, 187
duties of stage manager prior to, 187
etiquette in, 282
final, 352
first read-through in, 283
memorization in, 286
polishing, 290, 314, 320–321
in Reader's Theatre, 397, 438
schedule, 314
setting props during, 338
spaces for, 286
stage business in, 289
taking direction in, 284
technical, 321, 353–354
working, 288–289
Renaissance theatre
set design in, 4
stage design in, 63
Rendering, 206, 234
Representational style, 272, 278
Research paper, writing, 562–565
Reshaping of face, 349
Resonance, 18, 32
Resonators, 18, 32
Restoration drama, 5
Reupholstering, 266–267
Review, writing, 540–543
*Das Rheingold* (Wagner), 482
Rhythm, 26–27
Rice, Tim, 357
*Richard III* (Shakespeare), 6
Richards, Lloyd, 571–572
*Riders to the Sea* (Synge), 410
Rigging, 334, 335
Right of stage, 62
Rip cuts, 79
Rising action, 170
Ritual, 1
*Road to Mecca, The* (Fugard), 337
Rocks, 468
Rodgers, Richard, 12, 415, 440, 442, 445
Role, 146
Roman theatre, 2
Romantic drama, German, 7
Romanticism, 280, 327–328
*Romeo and Juliet* (Shakespeare), 155, 165
Rostand, Edmond, 8, 192, 491
Rough cut, 436, 450
*Roxanne,* 8, 491
Royalty, 162, 185
Running flats, 336
Running stitches, 92
Run of the show, 357–359
costumes and makeup in, 359
lighting and sound in, 358–359

scenery and props in, 358
stage manager in, 357–358
Rushes, 436, 450

## S

Safety cord, 340
St. Vincent Millay, Edna, 11
Saint plays, 3
*St. Louis Woman* (Bontemps and Cullen), 458
Samisen, 297
Sanskrit drama, 2
Sardou, Victorien, 8
Saw cuts and joints, 79–80
Scenarios, 278, 371–372
Scale, 115, 206
Scene, designations for, 538
Scene-by-scene analysis, 276–277
Scene heading, 552
Scene painting
base coat, 223
preliminary coats, 222
prime coat, 222
sizing, 222
techniques, 223–225
Scene shop, 60, 76
inventory of, 118–120
safety tips, 81
Scenery, 50, 60
bracing, 220, 321
in dress rehearsal, 356
in postproduction, 361
profiles, 469
projections, 480, 520–522
rocks, 468
for run of the show, 358
shifting, 335–336, 387–389
stiffening, 221
in tech rehearsal, 354
three-dimensional, 465–466, 518–520
trees, 467
Scenes, 418, 535
setting in a screenplay, 551
Scenic projector, 479
Scheherazade, 45
Schönberg, Claude-Michel, 417
*School for Wives, The* (Molière), 194
Scorcese, Martin, 449
Screen, 450
Screenplay, 396, 418
writing, 551–556
Scrim drops, 216
Script, 36
Script, choosing, for Reader's Theatre, 437
Script analysis, 166
background of play in, 277
character in, 276
for costume designers, 234
for directors, 166–173, 257–258
for lighting designers, 228
for makeup designers, 238
preliminary (for actors), 273–275
for prop masters, 226
scene-by-scene, 276–277
for set designers, 206, 263–265
for sound designers, 232
Scripting story for Reader's Theatre, 437
Scripts, 273
marking, 283
for Reader's Theatre, 437
reading from, in audition, 148
working with, 166–173, 273, 287
Scumbling, 223
*Seagull, The* (Chekhov), 173, 327
Seam allowance, 92
Seam finishes, 93
Seams, 92
double-stitched, 121
French, 122
lapped, 121
plain, 92
stretch-knit, 121
topstitched, 122
welt, 122
*Search for Signs of Intelligent Life in the Universe, The* (Wagner), 420
Second City, 36
Secondary characters, 172, 536
Secondary emphasis, 178
Sectionals, 209
Self-awareness, developing, 19
Selvage, 488
Seneca, 2
Sense memory in characterization process, 131
Senses, using, in characterization process, 129
Sentimental comedy, 6
Serlio, Sebastiano, 4
Set, 74, 75
Set construction
basics, 79–80
bracing scenery in, 220
connecting platforms in, 220
crews for, 76–81
doors, 213
drops, 216–217
equipment and supplies, 77–78
flats, 210–212
joining flats in, 218–219
painting scenery in, 222–225
platforms, 214–215
stiffening scenery in, 221
three-dimensional scenery, 465
Set design, 203, 206–209, 263–265
models in, 209
plans for, 208–209
script analysis in, 206
sketches and renderings in, 206–207
Set designer, 75
as career choice, 574–575
script analysis for, 206

Set props, 226
Setting analysis, 172, 542
Setting summary, 168
Setup, 418
Seurat, Georges, 105, 444
*Seven Guitars* (Wilson), 457, 460–463
Sewing
  basics, 92–93
  equipment, 91
  seams, 92, 120–123
Shadows, 351
Shakespeare, William, 4, 6, 15, 54, 131, 154–161, 165, 175, 179, 205, 234, 280, 404, 466, 479
  *Cymbeline,* 479
  *Hamlet,* 155, 205, 404
  *King Lear,* 234
  *Macbeth,* 155
  *Midsummer Night's Dream, A,* 155, 158–161
  *Othello,* 155, 280
  *Pericles,* 466
  *Richard III,* 6
  *Romeo and Juliet,* 155, 165
  *Tempest, The,* 54, 155
  *Twelfth Night,* 179
Shakespearean theatre
  acting styles in, 157
  costumes in, 156–157
  space in, 155–156
  tragedy in, 279–280
Shamanism, 1
Shange, Ntozake, 14, 458
Shared position, 128, 143
Shaw, George Bernard, 9, 411, 417, 475
Shearer, Jill, 342
Shepard, Sam, 14, 204
Sheridan, Richard Brinsley, 7
Shevelove, Burt, 164
Shifting crew, 75, 335
Shiko, Okamuka, 299
*Shimada* (Shearer), 342
Shooting script, 448, 555–557
Shot, 418
Shouting, 34
Show
  choosing for musical theatre, 442–443
  promoting, 544–550
Show tapes, 87
  making, 233, 384–386
*Showboat* (Kern), 415
Sight lines, 202, 209
Signifying, 459
Simon, Neil, 13, 143, 164, 308, 312, 313
*Singin' in the Rain* (Comden and Green), 416
Sitting, 141
  in maintaining focus, 144
Situation comedies, 452
Sizing, 222
Skene, 67
Sketch, improvising, 36–37
Skull cap, 392
Slaps, 408
Slate, 449
Slide preparation, 481
Slide projector, 479
Slipstitch, 92
Slug line, 552
Smoke, 476
Soap operas, 452
Soderbergh, Steven, 448
Sondheim, Stephen, 105, 164, 444
Song, 532
  in musical theatre, 417, 503–505
Sophocles, 2, 55, 66–72, 531
Sound
  basics in, 87–88
  collecting, 232
  control board for, 86
  crew for, 82
  cue sheet for, 345
  design in, 203, 232–233
  in dress rehearsal, 356
  equipment and supplies, 86
  indicating in a screenplay, 553
  layering and mixing sound, 484
  making and shaping, 32
  making show tapes, 233, 384–386
  with movement, 107–109
  in postproduction, 361
  in Reader's Theater, 439
  recording and editing, 88
  for run of the show, 358–359
  setting up, 345
  sources of, 232
  synthesizers, 484
  in tech rehearsal, 354
Sound booth, 59
Sound designer, 75
  script analysis for, 232
*Sound of Music, The* (Rodgers and Hammerstein), 29
Sounding, 459
Sounds, making and shaping, 32
Soundstage, 436, 449
*South Pacific* (Rodgers and Hammerstein), 445
Spain, golden age of, 5
Spattering, 224
Speakers, 86, 87
Spectacle, 532
Spike tape, 286
Spiking the set, 286
Spin-off, 452
Spirit gum, 94, 491
Spirit gum remover, 94
Splicing audiotape, 87
Stage, 162, 163
Stage areas, 178
  acting areas, 229
  arena, 62, 181

lighting areas, 229
proscenium, 62
thrust, 62, 181
Stage blood, 493
Stage brace, 220
Stage business, 272, 289
Stage combat, 396, 404, 506–508
guidelines, 405
Stage composition (pictures), 177–181
for arena stage, 181
arrangements for emphasis, 178, 374–376
diagonals, 180
focus and body positions in, 177
focus and stage areas, 178
levels, 179
planes, 180
stage areas in, 178
for thrust stage, 181
triangles, 180
Stage crew, 74, 75, 86
Stage directions, 538–539, 551
Stage door, 60
Stage food as prop techniques, 473–475
Stage hardware, 78
Stage house, 60
Stage kissing, 318
Stage makeup, 95
Stage manager, 50, 52
as director's assistant, 187, 309, 311, 313, 315, 322
as career choice, 572–573
in cast party, 322
in dress rehearsal, 355
duties during rehearsals, 187
duties prior to rehearsal period, 187
in final rehearsals, 352
in postproduction, 360
in run of the show, 357–359
in tech rehearsal, 353
Stage manager's booth, 60
Stage movement
body positions, 140
dominant stage positions, 143
focus, 144
opening to an audience, 141–142, 244–247
posture and poise, 144–145
sharing stage, 143, 244–247
Stages
of film production, 447–450
for musical theatre, 443
for TV production, 451–452
types of, 58–59
Stakes, 134
Standing, 141
Stanislavski, Konstantin, 9, 329
Stanislavski method, 329
*Star-Spangled Girl* (Simon), 307–323
Stationary cutting tools, 78
Status quo in creating specific characters, 136–137
Stenciling, 223
Stewart, Michael, 416
Stiffening batten, 221
Stiles, 202, 210, 211
Stipple sponge, 491
Stippling, 224
Stock characters, 278
Stock units, 79
Storage, 91, 94
Storyboard, 436, 448, 555
Storytelling, 1, 38–39, 100–102
tradition of, 44–49
Stowe, Harriet Beecher, 7
Straight makeup, 95
applying, 95–96
Streep, Meryl, 410, 573
Strike, 306
Striking the set, 323
Strindberg, August, 237
Strouse, Charles, 416
Study, 156
*Sturm und Drang* ("Storm and Stress"), 7
Style, 174–175, 257–259, 542
Stylized movement, 400–401
Subtext, 128, 138–139, 277
Sullivan, Annie, 131
*Sunday in the Park with George* (Lapine), 105, 444
*Sundiata, an Epic of Old Mali* (Niane), 48–49
Superimposition, 451
Supplementary design plans, 209
Svoboda, Joseph, 482
Swag, 464, 472
Swagging drapes, 472–473
Sweet talking, 459
Symbol, 173
Symbolic gestures, 401
Symbolic movements, 401, 403
Symbolism, 173
Synge, John Millington, 10, 411
Synthesizers, 464, 484

## T

Tableau, 105, 255, 256
Tagore, Rabindranath, 10
TAIFA, 46
Take, 418
Talking and moving in maintaining focus, 144
*Tambourines to Glory* (Hughes), 458
Tan, Amy, 204
Tape, 451
Tape loops, 88
making, 88
Tarras, 156
*Tartuffe* (Molière), 195, 196–201
Taymor, Julie, 15, 347, 414, 489
Teatro Campesino, 14
Technical elements in Reader's Theatre, 439
Technical rehearsals, 321, 353

costumes and makeup, 354
lighting and sound, 354
scenery and props, 354
stage manager, 353
Technical theatre. *See* Costumes; Lighting; Makeup; Props; Rehearsals; Scenery; Set construction; Sound.
Technical theatre notes, xxv
Tech runs, 314, 353
Teleplay, 436, 451
Television, 418–419, 446, 451–452
*Tempest, The* (Shakespeare), 155
Tempo, 35
Terence, 2
Texturizing, 347
Theatre history, outline of, 1–15
Theatre language, 537
Theatre Notebook, xx
Theatre of alienation, 11
Theatre of cruelty, 11, 14
Theatre of the absurd, 427–429
Beckett's contributions to, 429
characteristics of, 427–428
Theatre promotion, 544–550
Theatre space
analyzing, 112–114
in Greek drama, 67
in Kabuki, 297
layout and terms, 59–60
in Molière's theatre, 193
perspectives on, 110–112
in Shakespearean theatre, 155–156
Theatrical agent, 442
Theme analysis, 173
Theodora, 2
Thespian, 412
Thomas, Dylan, 457
Thompson, Stith, 44
*Thousand and One Nights The,* (Scheherazade), 45
Three-dimensional makeup, 491–495
Three-dimensional scenery, 464, 465–469, 518–520
*Three Sisters, The* (Chekhov), 180, 327
Through line, 535
Throw, 74, 84
Thrust stage, 50, 58, 156
areas in, 62
for musical theatre, 443
stage composition for, 181
Thumbnail sketches, 206
Tie-supported drop, 216
Tiring House, 156
Toenail, 80
Toggles, 202, 210, 211
Toller, Ernst, 10
Tomlin, Lily, 420
Tongue twisters, 33
Top hats, 83, 344
Track, 464, 484
*Tracy Takes On,* 410
Tragedy, 165
Greek, 67
purpose of, 530–531
Shakespearean, 157, 279–280
Trailer, 449
Transitions, 147, 536
Trees, 467
Triangles, 180, 181
*Tristan and Isolde* (Wagner), 482
Truck, 335
Tune, Tommy, 573, 574, 577–578
Tunic, making, 488
Turning, 141
TV genres, 452
*Twelfth Night* (Shakespeare), 179
Twofer, 83, 85, 340
Two-shot, 419
*Two Trains Running* (Wilson), 457

## U

Ullman, Tracey, 161, 410
*Uncle Tom's Cabin* (Stowe), 7
*Uncle Vanya* (Chekhov), 327, 329–333
Understudies, 306, 316
Unified aniline dye, 346
Union dyes, 346
Unities, 5, 531
Upstage, 50, 62, 63, 128, 178
Upstaging, 143
in maintaining focus, 144
Usable design, 205

## V

Valdez, Luis, 14
Velour, 471
Vibration, 32
Video assist, 448
Voice
character, 137–139
and consonants, 33
diaphragmatic breathing, 30–31
projection of, 34
in Reader's Theatre, 398
and vowels, 33
Voice-over, 464, 484
Voice specialties, 410–411
Voice warm-ups, 31
Voltaire, 181
Volume, 34
von Goethe, Johann Wolfgang, 7
Vowels, 33

## W


Wagner, Richard, 482
Wagon, 334, 335
*Waiting for Godot* (Beckett), 426, 427, 429, 430–435
Wasserman, Dale, 354
Wasserstein, Wendy, 15
Wattage, 231
Webber, Andrew Lloyd, 357
Website, creating, 546–547
Webster, John, 289
Well-made play, the, 8, 9, 578
Western theatre, decline of, 2
Whiteface, 402
Wigs, 495
Wilbur, Richard, 196
Wilde, Oscar, 184, 279
Wilder, Thornton, 12, 28, 278, 442
Williams, Robin, 410
Williams, Tennessee, 12, 166, 281
Wilson, August, 14, 456–463
  *Fences,* 457
  *Joe Turner's Come and Gone,* 457
  *Ma Rainey's Black Bottom,* 457
  *Piano Lesson, The,* 457
  *Seven Guitars,* 457, 460–463
  *Two Trains Running,* 457
Wilson, Meredith, 131, 400
Wilson, Robert, 421, 453
Wings, 60
Wipe, 451
*Wizard of Oz, The* (Baum), 233, 238
Wood, measuring, 79
Working rehearsals, 288–289, 314, 318
Working script, 447
Work print, 449
Wrinkles, 492
Writing
  for the media, 549–550
  a play, 534–539
  a research paper, 562–565
  a review, 540–543
  a screenplay, 551–557
Wycherley, William, 5


## Y


Yeats, William, 10
Yoke, 341


## Z


*Zen Substitute, The* (Shiko), 299–305
Zigzag stitch, 93
Zipprodt, Patricia, 576–577
Zola, Émile, 8